How American Governments Work

ALSO BY ROGER L. KEMP
AND FROM MCFARLAND

Homeland Security for the Private Sector:
A Handbook (2007)

Cities and Cars:
A Handbook of Best Practices (2007)

Homeland Security Handbook for
Citizens and Public Officials (2006)

Cities and Nature:
A Handbook for Renewal (2006)

Cities and the Arts:
A Handbook for Renewal (2004)

Community Renewal through Municipal
Investment: A Handbook for Citizens
and Public Officials (2003; paperback 2007)

Model Government Charters:
A City, County, Regional, State, and
Federal Handbook (2003; paperback 2007)

Regional Government Innovations:
A Handbook for Citizens and Public Officials (2003)

The Inner City:
A Handbook for Renewal (2001)

Main Street Renewal: A Handbook for Citizens
and Public Officials (2000; paperback 2006)

Forms of Local Government: A Handbook
on City, County and Regional Options (1999)

Local Government Election Practices:
A Handbook for Public Officials
and Citizens (1999; paperback 2006)

Managing America's Cities:
A Handbook for Local Government Productivity (1998)

Economic Development in Local Government:
A Handbook for Public Officials and Citizens (1995)

Strategic Planning for Local Government:
A Handbook for Officials and Citizens (1993)

Privatization: The Provision of Public
Services by the Private Sector (1991)

How American Governments Work

A Handbook of City, County, Regional, State, and Federal Operations

EDITED BY ROGER L. KEMP

McFarland & Company, Inc., Publishers
Jefferson, North Carolina, and London

To Jonathan and Wendy,
who will help shape the future

The present work is a reprint of the library bound edition of
How American Governments Work: A Handbook of City,
County, Regional, State, and Federal Operations, *first published in 2002 by McFarland.*

LIBRARY OF CONGRESS CATALOGUING-IN-PUBLICATION DATA

How American governments work : a handbook of city, county,
   regional, state, and federation operations / edited by Roger L.
Kemp.
      p.   cm.
   Includes bibliographical references and index.

   ISBN-13: 978-0-7864-3152-6
   (softcover : 50# alkaline paper) ∞

   1. Democracy — United States. 2. Representative government
and representation — United States. 3. Voting — United States.
4. United States — Politics and government. 5. Local
government — United States. 6. State governments — United
States. I. Kemp, Roger L.
JK1726.H69 2007
320.973 — dc21   2002003336

British Library cataloguing data are available

Cover photograph ©2007 Shutterstock

Manufactured in the United States of America

McFarland & Company, Inc., Publishers
  Box 611, Jefferson, North Carolina 28640
  www.mcfarlandpub.com

Table of Contents

Part VI. Federal Government

Part VII. Government Trends

Part VIII. The Future of Democracy

Acknowledgments

Grateful acknowledgment is made to the following organizations and publishers for granting permission to reprint the material contained in this volume:

American Society for Public Administration
Center for Voting and Democracy
Congressional Quarterly, Inc.
Government Finance Officers Association
International City/County Management Association
International Municipal Lawyers Association
Intertec Publishing Corporation
National Association of Regional Councils
National Civic League
National League of Cities
Stanford University
State of California
The Council of State Governments
The University of Georgia
U.S. Advisory Commission on Intergovernmental Relations
U.S. Government
University of Cincinnati

Preface

Here in the early years of the 21st century, the dawn of the third millennium, it is appropriate to describe the current state of the United States government, its various components, as well as the future of our democracy. This unusual democratic experience started with the Revolutionary War, when the newly arrived colonists broke with England and ultimately formed a new nation in what is now called North America. Although Spanish explorers landed before the English, their departure early in the history of America greatly diminished their influence, both culturally and politically. The original thirteen states were initially sovereign political entities, but later organized into a confederacy in 1781. This political arrangement was replaced by the current federal system of government that was adopted in 1789. With these dates in mind, the United States of America is the oldest federal system of government in the world.

Over the following two centuries, the federal government gained power and responsibility, while the states lost much of their original sovereignty given to them when the colonies were formed. Much of the shift of power to the federal government is attributable to the influence of Chief Justice John Marshall, during the first quarter of the nineteenth century, and the federal policies arising from the New Deal of the 1930s, when the problems of the nation were too much for state governments to resolve on their own. This gradual shift of power has also had an influence on lower levels of government since cities and counties are creations of the states. Each state's constitution and statutes determine the powers and responsibilities of these lower levels of government. Over the years, the number and types of regional governments have grown in significance, both for planning purposes and to deal with the many urban problems that spill over the artificial political boundaries of cities and counties.

All of these various levels of government are dependent upon the bedrock of the American democracy — our electoral systems and processes. Our elected officials have worked throughout the history of our nation to improve the various forms of government. While the structures represent government, governance has been ably provided by these elected officials representing the will of the American public. Generally, the federal government leaves election laws and practices to individual states. Both the methods of voting (e.g., by hand, machines, computers, and scanners) and types of voting systems (e.g., ward, at-large, combined, limited voting, cumulative voting, alternative voting, and proportional representation) are a matter of each state's rights. These election methods and processes are further complicated by the use of partisan and non-partisan election practices (i.e., party affiliation versus no party affiliation).

Our nation has evolved, over the past two centuries, from *Jacksonian Democracy*, under which every person wanted to personally get involved and have an active voice in all levels of government, to *Jeffersonian Democracy*, in which the common person desired to elect the uncommon person to represent him/her at City Hall, the State House, and the National Capital. This time span encompasses a steady transition from strong independent states, to a strong national government and regulated state sovereignty. This volume attempts to document our nation's current election systems and practices and the structures and processes of all levels of government — cities, counties, regions, states, and federal. Contemporary government trends, as well as the future of the American democracy, are also examined.

The headings used in this book were selected to present the above information in a logical and coherent manner, consistent with easy-to-understand categories. With this goal in mind, this book is broken down into the following eight sections: National Election Practices, City Government, County Government, Regional Government, State Government, Federal Government, Government Trends, and The Future of Democracy. The topics and types of information examined in these sections are highlighted below.

National Election Practices

Back when America's cities and towns were small and simple political jurisdic-

tions, citizens merely voted for their favorite candidate on a city- or town-wide basis. The representation of groups on local governing bodies was by happenstance and not by design. There was no need for complex electoral systems designed to produce legislative bodies that reflected the unique demographic characteristics of individual communities. Over the past century, the simple at-large election system has given way to several legal voting procedures that help achieve equitable citizen representation within a local government. The current state of voting methods, as well as the impact of court decisions, is examined in detail. The voting fiasco in the 2000 presidential election in Florida is also having a dramatic impact on both the voting practices and techniques used by individual states.

Joseph Zimmerman provides an excellent brief overview of representative democracy in America, from the issues of African-American suffrage to the Voting Rights Act of 1965, as well as its various amendments and numerous court interpretations. Lee L. Blackman and Erich R. Luschei examine recent voter rights litigation, while Olethia Davis examines the Voting Rights Act and the Supreme Court, focusing on minority vote dilution through the country. Richard L. Engstrom reviews current trends in redistricting and the impact of Supreme Court decisions on this practice, while Edward Still and Robert Richie review the many available voting rights remedies for citizens and groups of voters who feel that they have been disenfranchised. This section sets the bedrock for the discussion on the various levels of government within the American intergovernmental system.

City Government

The three basic forms of municipal government in the U.S. include the mayor-council, council-manager, and commission plans. Under the mayor-council plan, the duties of the mayor vary greatly, typically depending upon the size of the community in which the mayor serves. Generally, our nation's larger cities are most likely to have the strong mayor-council form of government. Under the council-manager plan, a separation of powers exists between the legislative and executive functions of municipal government. The commission plan, on the other hand, involves the direct election of legislators who serve as executives to lead the various functions of municipal government. This form of government, which merges legislative and executive functions, because of its obvious shortcomings, remains in only a few small communities in America. The council-manager plan is growing at a faster pace than any other form of municipal government. This is due to the separation of legislative and executive powers, as well as its non-partisan nature, since appointed administrators serve all citizens equally, regardless of their political affiliation.

The editor provides a brief historical review of the evolution of cities in America, including the early influences of our culture on our municipal structures, as well as an overview of the prevailing forms of municipal government. Charles R. Adrian examines our nation's search for the best form of local government. Tari Renner and Victor R. DeSantis highlight contemporary American municipal structures, while Michele Frisby examines the existing and desired separation of powers in our nation's many cities and towns. Lastly, William H. Hansell, Jr., documents the continued growth of professional management, as well as the municipal government structures that support this concept. Hansell concludes that the council-manager plan of municipal government is the fastest growing form of local government structure in the nation.

County Government

There are three primary forms of county government in our nation, including the commission, commission-administrator, and the council-executive plans. The commission plans allow for the direct election of administrators, who individually manage the various administrative functions of county government. Under the commission-administrator plan, the powers of the administrator may vary depending upon which design is used—council-manager (or strong executive), chief executive officer (weak executive), or county administrative assistant (supervisor/coordinator). Under the council-executive plan, the county executive is directly elected by voters and performs specific executive functions. These functions are typically designated by law, by citizens through the electoral process, or by the county's elected officials. The current trend, as in cities and towns, is towards the appointed county administrator who is trained as an expert in government administration, is typically non-partisan, and serves all citizens within any county equally.

Tanis J. Salant traces the evolution of America's county governments from the English shire of a thousand years ago to present-day county government. Salant also examines contemporary structures and issues in county government. Victor S. DeSantis discusses changes taking place in our county governments based upon a national survey of county officials throughout our country. Julianne Duvall examines a hot topic, but one that is not widely embraced. This is the subject of city-county consolidations throughout our nation. The number of such consolidations is relatively few. The most typical model of city-county cooperation is the Evolutionary Consolidation Model, which is examined in detail by Herbert H. Hughes and Charles Lee. This study reveals that it sometimes takes many years for a city and county to cooperate in the provision of services to the public. Lastly, Robert D. Thomas describes the contemporary transitions occurring within counties today.

Regional Government

There are five main forms of regional government agencies in the United States. These include the regional planning commission, council of governments, regional advisory committee, regional allocation agency, and special purpose regional agency. Regional planning commissions may encompass a single county, multiple counties, multiple municipal jurisdictions, or some combination of these government entities. Councils of government may include a number of contiguous cities, contiguous cities and the county they are located in, or contiguous cities and multiple neighboring counties. Regional advisory committees are created by states to oversee the planning function of portions of land within the state. Regional allocation agencies are typically responsible for allocating certain federal funds within selected geographic areas, typically substate in nature. Special purpose regional agencies have the authority to plan and control special developments and/or functions in selected areas of a state.

Richard Sybert discusses four models of regional government, referred to as the one-level, two-level, cooperative, and metropolitan council. Theodore Hershberg examines the regional cooperation model in detail in the next chapter. J. Eugene Grigsby III then reviews the growth of metropolitan governments, and gives a historical chronology of the influence that the federal and state governments have had on the formation of such agencies. David Miller then provides an in-depth analysis of fiscal regionalism, or the movement to-

wards the creation of regional funding mechanisms throughout the nation for a wide variety of public purposes. Allan D. Wallis emphasizes and documents the need for regional government in our advanced post-industrial economy. This chapter analyses the impact of the global economy and the critical need for regional governments.

State Government

When our nation was founded it had 13 colonies. When the Founding Fathers wrote the Constitution in 1787, these colonies became the first states in the United States. The Founding Fathers believed that more states would want to join the Union in the future, and that each state should have similar powers and structure. Even when the 50th state joined the Union, all states maintained these original characteristics. Each state's government is based on a constitution and a republican form of government, no state constitution contradicts the federal constitution, and each state has three branches of government (i.e., legislative, executive, and judicial). Over the years, for the reasons previously discussed, power has shifted from the states to the federal government. The current trend towards the devolution of responsibilities from the federal government to the states is restoring responsibility to the states.

Dag Ryen concludes that the states have reached a new accommodation with the federal government on key domestic issues, and that they enjoy growing resources, increased organizational sophistication, and added responsibilities. Edwin Meese III examines the authority, responsibility, and structure of our state governments. The next two chapters reveal the respective roles and relationships between the states and higher (federal) and lower (municipal) governments. Richard P. Nathan defines contemporary American federalism, examines the changing roles of states, and offers his observations about the future of state governments. David R. Berman, on the other hand, reveals the results of a national study scrutinizing the changing dynamics between state and city government, and the current relationship between states and cities in the intergovernmental system of government that currently exists. Lastly, Carl E. Van Horn documents what he calls the continuing power struggle that exists and continues between the federal and state governments in our intergovernmental system.

Federal Government

The United States Constitution defined, directly or indirectly, the responsibilities and structure of the federal government. According to the Constitution, any power not specifically given to the federal government is within the purview of individual states. The country has changed tremendously since 1787 when the Founding Fathers wrote the Constitution. Changing circumstances over the years have made it necessary to amend or change the Constitution and to expand the role of federal government in our intergovernmental system. The original philosophy and concepts contained in the Constitution, however, have not changed over the years even though the federal government has grown in both complexity and size. Political scholars have recognized the importance of early Supreme Court decisions, primarily during the first quarter of the 19th century, as well as federal government's policies of the New Deal, during the second quarter of the 20th century, as pivotal periods in redefining the role of the federal government in our nation. The role of the federal government continues to evolve.

Edwin Meese III provides an excellent overview of the various branches of the federal government, the numerous cabinet departments, as well as the various independent agencies that work for the executive branch out of the White House. The editor lends insight into the complexity of the federal government by highlighting its many independent organizations and government corporations; boards, commissions, and committees; and multilateral, bilateral, and quasi-official organizations and agencies. Lydia Bjornlund examines the decisions of the 106th Congress, the last meeting of this body in the 20th century. These proceedings included the impeachment hearings of President William Jefferson Clinton. Charles Wise lends insight into the decisions of the 1998–99 term of the U.S. Supreme Court, discussing the impact of this body on our nation's state and local governments. The final chapter, by John A. Ferejohn and Barry R. Weingast, examines the politics of new federalism, and the important role that the U.S. Congress plays in this process, especially when it passes unfunded mandates upon lower levels of government.

Government Trends

There is no doubt that an entire book could be written about trends in our election systems and practices, or about trends in any single level of government. In selecting those government trends to be examined, the editor arranged this section following the first six categories of this book. That is, the trends examined include national election practices, city government, county government, regional government, state government, and the federal government. The goal of this section is to focus on and examine significant trends in each of these areas of American government. All of these trends reflect present state-of-the-art issues and practices. The government trends examined in this section encompass major changes taking place in each level of our American intergovernmental system. While each chapter focuses on a single level of government, the impact that one level has on others is also discussed. The timely topic of elections administration is also examined. Together, these trends will directly influence the United States system of government in the coming decades.

Charles R. Wise provides an early look at the lessons our nation can learn from the 2000 presidential elections, specifically from the election systems and practices in Florida. The editor then examines major societal trends impacting American cities as we enter the next century. The six categories of trends examined include demographic shifts, prevalent economic factors, major environmental concerns, political considerations, technological trends, and emerging urban patterns. Donald C. Menzel provides an in-depth discussion about those issues and challenges facing America's 3,034 county governments. He examines issues ranging from leadership to economic development. William Dodge, in writing about regional government, states we are witnessing a "regional renaissance." Keon S. Chi, an expert on state government, reviews trends in each of the three levels of state government. He also examines issues relating to management and administration, emerging policies, and the future of the states. The last chapter, by Robert J. Dilger, provides insight into American federalism today.

The Future of Democracy

Most citizens typically get involved in the democratic process by casting their ballot at election time. From the standpoint of voter turnout, national elections yield the greatest turnout, local elections the smallest. Only a few citizens become directly involved in the democratic process, regardless of the level of government. When it comes to attending public meetings, some citizens may attend meetings of their city council, few attend meetings of their state legislature, and almost no one attends meetings of any kind in our nation's capital. As previously indicated, this is typical voter behavior under *Jeffersonian Democracy*, where citizens elect persons to represent their interests— regardless of the level of government. When it comes to campaign financing, few voters give any significant amount of money to their favorite candidates. Most of the monies needed to finance campaigns comes from special interest groups, or large organizations with active and ongoing lobbying efforts. Notwithstanding these shortcomings, the American democracy is healthy and has so far withstood the test of time. The chapters selected for this section represent timely and topical subjects that will have a dramatic impact on our democracy in the future.

Mark Schmitt examines the role of money, campaigns, and democracy, and concludes "the ability to raise money is often the decisive factor in whether someone runs for public office." New options are emerging that might change this reality of our political system. Celinda Lake and Jennifer Sosin discuss the role of public opinion polls, and the impact they have on candidates and issues, as well as the democratic process itself. Tracy Weston focuses on the impact that technology is having on our democratic institutions. She concludes that our nation is undergoing a major trend towards participatory democracy. Does this mean that our nation will return to the earlier days of *Jacksonian Democracy*? Marshall Kaplan, in examining the *American Dream* and our democratic system of government, concludes, "…We have lost the ability to reach public consensus on tough issues."

The main purpose of this book is to document the American system of government, at all levels, as it exists today. Because of its importance, the subject of elections administration is also examined. After all, the state of our democratic institutions depends on the quality of our elected public officials. Also, changes to our governmental structures require the vote of the people. A logical extension of this analysis must encompass an examination of the major trends taking place in our society in each of these areas, as well as a prognosis as to the future of our democratic institutions.

This volume will enable citizens, practitioners working in government, scholars, and students to gain insight into these important subjects. Most published works in this field focus only on one level of government. This is one of a few volumes, if not the only one, that examines our national election practices as well as all levels of government in the American intergovernmental system. For this reason, this volume represents an important codification of knowledge in this field.

Roger L. Kemp
Meriden, Connecticut
Summer 2002

• *Chapter 1* •

Representative Democracy

JOSEPH F. ZIMMERMAN

Democratic theory is premised upon representative law-making bodies, yet members of many of these bodies have been elected by systems that exclude or dilute the votes cast by members of certain racial and ethnic groups. Constructing an electoral system that will produce fair representation is a difficult task, and must commence with the removal of legal impediments to voting and replacement of electoral systems that discriminate against members of minority groups. The Voting Rights Act of 1965 as amended was designed to remedy discrimination in electoral systems and practices against blacks and members of four "foreign language minorities."

The Act is a permanent statute that also contains temporary, nationally suspensive provisions applicable to states and/or their political subdivisions if certain conditions (known informally as "triggers") are present. The "trigger provisions" originally were limited to six southern states and were designed to protect the voting rights of only blacks. Today, these provisions apply to many jurisdictions outside the South because of amendments enacted in 1975, which extend the Act's reach to jurisdictions where voter participation is low and the concentration of "protected" minorities high.

This chapter presents 1) a historical overview of the gradual liberalization of suffrage laws in the United States, 2) describes the Voting Rights Act's major provisions and their interpretation by the United States Supreme Court, and 3) examines the single-member district system, which has been promoted by implementation of the Act, vis-à-vis alternative electoral systems.

A historical review of suffrage requirements will help explain why Congress decided in 1965 to enact a statute guaranteeing the voting rights of blacks. When the United States Constitution was ratified in 1788, voting in states was confined to

Originally published as "Election Systems and Representative Democracy," *National Civic Review*, Vol. 84, No. 4, Fall/Winter, 1995. Published by the National Civic League Press, Denver, Colorado. Reprinted with permission of the publisher.

male property owners or taxpayers. All other persons—women, blacks (most were slaves), indentured servants and Native Americans—lacked the right to vote.

Vermont was the first state to provide for universal male suffrage for those of "quiet and peaceable behavior."[1] A year later, the new state of Kentucky allowed suffrage for men who met a two-year residency requirement.[2] New Hampshire and Georgia abolished their constitutional tax-paying requirements in 1792 and 1798, respectively.[3] In 1809, Maryland passed a statute granting manhood suffrage without property-owning or taxpaying qualifications.

In 1821, New York enfranchised all white male residents of one year who had paid taxes and served in the State Militia, and all others who had lived in the state for three years.[4] New York, however, retained property qualifications for blacks. Thereafter, the movement for full manhood suffrage made rapid progress, and by 1860 property-owning requirements had disappeared and taxpayer prerequisites were negligible.

Before white manhood suffrage became a nationwide reality, however, a reaction set in. Alarmed at the rapid increase in the number of illiterate immigrants, particularly Irish immigrants, Connecticut in 1855 and Massachusetts in 1857 amended their constitutions to require that all voters be able to read.[5]

Black Suffrage

Few blacks were enfranchised prior to the Civil War. Maine, Massachusetts, New Hampshire, Rhode Island, and Vermont had granted suffrage to blacks, and in New York a black could vote if he possessed a freehold. The original North Carolina Constitution permitted free blacks who met other requirements to vote, but it was amended in 1835 to provide that "no free Negro, free Mulatto, or free person of mixed blood, descended from Negro ancestors to the fourth generation inclusive ... shall vote for members of the Senate or House of Commons."[6]

Immediately after the Civil War, the movement to extend the franchise to blacks gathered momentum and led to two amendments to the United States Constitution. The Fourteenth Amendment, ratified in 1868, provides that a state's representation in the U.S. House of Representatives could be reduced in the proportion that the state denied the suffrage of male citizens 21 years of age or older. The Fifteenth Amendment, ratified in 1879, prohibits the United States or any state from denying suffrage on account of race, color or previous condition of servitude.

In 1870, Congress enacted a statute, based on the Fifteenth Amendment, making private or public obstruction of the right to vote in an election a misdemeanor punishable by imprisonment of one month to one year.[7] The law was amended the following year to authorize federal oversight of the election of United States Representatives in any local government with a population exceeding 20,000 "whenever ... there shall be two citizens thereof who ... shall make known in writing, to the Judge of the Circuit Court of the United States for the Circuit wherein such city or town shall be, their desire to have said registration, or said election, or both, guarded and scrutinized."[8]

The United States Supreme Court in 1875 invalidated sections of the 1870 Act that guaranteed the voting rights of white citizens and provided for punishment of persons interfering with the voting rights of whites, holding that the Fifteenth Amendment authorized Congress to protect only the voting rights of black citizens." This opinion remains in effect today. The most important remaining sections of the two statutes were repealed by Congress in 1894, thereby freeing states of direct supervision of elections by federal officials for 63 years.

With southern states in the control of whites by 1890, their state constitutions and statutes were amended to exclude most blacks from the franchise. For example, southern state legislatures revived the taxpayer qualification requiring a person to present poll tax receipts, sometimes for many years, before a person would be allowed to vote in an election; lengthened the residency requirements to debar transient blacks; and introduced the literacy test to assure the ability of voters to read or at least "understand" the constitution. To preserve the suffrage of illiterate whites, southerners invented the notorious "grandfather clause," which permitted the permanent registration of all persons who had served in the United States Army or the Confederate Army, or were descendants of veterans. The clause was declared unconstitutional by the United States Supreme Court in 1915.[10] The court in 1939 struck down state procedural obstacles to voting.

Blacks effectively were excluded from the nominating process in southern states by the "white primary," which debarred them from voting in the Democratic party's primary elections. The exclusionary device was invalidated in 1944 when the Supreme Court declared this type of primary unconstitutional, holding that a state could not cast its election laws in such a fashion as to allow a private organization, in this case a political party, to practice racial discrimination in elections.[11] Southern states, except Texas, continued to use the literacy test as a condition for voting, and several southern states had long residency requirements to disenfranchise blacks, who moved more frequently than whites. In 1949, the U.S. Supreme Court invalidated discriminatory application of voting tests.[12]

The racial gerrymander also was employed by state legislatures to reduce the voting power of black citizens. The most egregious racial gerrymander was drawn by the Alabama State Legislature for Tuskegee, home of the famous black university. In 1960, the U.S. Supreme Court struck down this gerrymander, which had produced a strangely shaped, irregular district with lines drawn around houses to exclude black voters from their preexisting right to vote in municipal elections by removing them from the city's limits.[13]

Public opinion against the treatment of blacks as second-class citizens was growing, especially after the end of World War II in 1945. Reacting to this sentiment, Congress in 1957 enacted a statute authorizing the Attorney General to initiate legal action on behalf of blacks denied the opportunity to register and vote, and established the United States Commission on Civil Rights, with authority to investigate and report on devices and procedures employed by state and local governments in a discriminatory manner against blacks.[14] The Civil Rights Act of 1960 mandated that states retain federal election records for 22 months, authorized the Attorney General to inspect such records, and enabled the District Court to order registration of blacks who were victims of a pattern of voting discrimination and appoint voting referees empowered to register voters.[15] Title I of the Civil Rights Act of 1964 forbids election officials to apply registration tests or standards to applicants different from the ones administered to persons previously registered. The Act also established a rebuttable presumption of literacy for registrants with a sixth-grade, English-speaking school education, and expedited procedures for judicial resolution of voting rights cases.[16]

In 1964, the 24th Amendment, abolishing the poll tax as a condition for voting in federal elections, was ratified. Only eight blacks had been elected to the United States House of Representatives by that date, several of them during the Reconstruction Period immediately following the Civil War. Literacy tests, however, remained in use in many states, and blacks in some areas were not permitted to register and vote for candidates for state and local government offices.

The Voting Rights Act of 1965

In reaction to the growing civil rights movement in the early 1960s and actions of many southern states preventing numerous blacks from exercising the franchise, Congress in 1965 passed the Voting Rights Act to protect blacks' Fifteenth Amendment voting rights.[17] President Lyndon B. Johnson proposed that the Act contain a ten-year sunset clause, but a five-year clause was adopted as a compromise for the preclearance and other temporary provisions in order to persuade a sufficient number of senators to vote for cloture to end a filibuster.[18] Certain provisions of the Act, as amended, apply to all states and local governments, and other provisions apply only to states and political subdivisions meeting the trigger conditions. Section 4 stipulates that the Act automatically applies to any state or political subdivision of a state if the Attorney General of the United States determines that as of November 1, 1964, a test or device had been employed to abridge the right of citizens to vote, and the Director of the United States Bureau of the Census determines that less than 50 percent of persons of voting age were registered to vote on November 1, 1964 or that less than 50 percent of persons of voting age exercised the franchise in the 1964 presidential election.[19] A "test or device" is defined as one involving literacy, morals, character, educational achievement, or knowledge of a specified subject.

Available evidence suggests that the factors incorporated as triggers deliberately were formulated to exclude Texas. Senator James B. Allen of Alabama maintained "it was first determined which states the law should be made applicable to, and then they proceeded to find the formula that would end up with those states being covered."[20] He added:

> ...by using the 50 percent voting in the election factor, that would have included the State of Texas. The President of the United States being a resident of Texas, ... it was thought inadvisable to include Texas in that formula. So they added a second circumstance, that is, that they must have a device that would hinder registration, namely the literacy test. [That] double factor ... is what took Texas out from under it, because they did not have the literacy test.[21]

The temporary provisions of the Act covered Alabama, Georgia, Louisiana, Mississippi, South Carolina, and Virginia, as well as counties in Alaska, Arizona, Hawaii, Idaho, and North Carolina. Texas was brought under the temporary provisions of the Act by the 1975 amendments.

Section 2 of the original Act is a statutory restatement of the Fifteenth Amendment's prohibition of the denial or abridgment of the right to vote based on "race, color, or previous condition of servitude."

Congress in effect imposed a federal "Dillon's Rule" on state and local governments subject to Section 5 of the Act, in that such jurisdictions may not change their electoral practices as they existed on November 1 of the year during which the prerequisite factors were met without first obtaining either the prior approval of the Attorney General, acting as an administrative surrogate of the court, or a declaratory judgment from the District Court of the District of Columbia. Actions implicating Section 5 include changing the location of a polling place, changing the existing voting system, transforming an elective office into an appointive one, annexation, and legislative redistricting, unless it is pursuant to a United States court order to correct an unconstitutional electoral system.[22] The preclearance requirement also applies to several activities of political parties, such as conduct of primary elections and selection of party officials and delegates to party conventions. Additionally, the Act directs the United States District Court to authorize appointment by the United States Civil Service Commission (now the Office of Personnel Management) of federal examiners to enforce constitutional guarantees in these state and local governments.

The Amendments

The trigger dates were expanded by the 1970 amendments to the Act to include November 1, 1968 and the 1968 presidential election; the 1975 amendments added November 1, 1972 and the 1972 presidential election.

The 1970 amendments suspended all voting tests and devices, including literacy tests, throughout the nation until August 6, 1975, and the 1975 amendments made the suspension permanent.[23] The 1970 amendments also authorize the Attorney General to seek a preliminary or permanent injunction to prevent a state or local government from enacting or administering a test or device in violation of the Act's provisions.[24]

The 1975 amendments broadened the coverage of the Act to include "language minorities," defined as "persons who are American Indian, Asian Americans, Alaskan Natives, or of Spanish heritage," and cited the Fourteenth and Fifteenth Amendments as the constitutional authority for the Act.[25] The language-minority triggers, providing for mandatory coverage of a governmental unit by the Act, are activated if in excess of five percent of the citizens of voting age in a state or political subdivision are members of one language minority group as of November 1, 1972 *and* less than 50 percent of all citizens of voting age participated in the presidential election of 1972. The triggers also are activated if in excess of five percent of the citizens of voting age in a state or political subdivision are members of one language minority group *and* the illiteracy rate of the group exceeds the national illiteracy rate. The definition of a test or device was expanded to include the use of only English election materials or ballots in a jurisdiction where a language minority constituted more than five percent of the voting-age population. In such jurisdictions, bilingual ballots and election materials must be provided if the group's literacy rate is lower than the national average.

The 1975 amendments also extended the preclearance and other temporary requirements for seven years. A total of 263,410 proposed changes were submitted to the Attorney General through 1994, who interposed an objection to 2,995.[26] The preclearance requirement currently applies to all or part of 16 states.

A jurisdiction's discriminatory intent may not always be apparent, since it may have maintained a racially neutral electoral system that was designed to or had the effect of diluting or eliminating the voting strength of a racial minority. In *White v. Regester*, the U.S. Supreme Court in 1973 held that the use of multimember districts in a state legislative reapportionment plan would violate the equal protection clause of the Fourteenth Amendment if "used invidiously to cancel out or minimize voting strength of racial groups."[27]

The viability of this broad interpretation of the Act, which protected black voters without proof of deliberate or explicit desire to discriminate on the part of the jurisdiction, was weakened by subsequent Supreme Court decisions holding that proof of discrimination in violation of the Fourteenth Amendment's equal protection clause requires the establishment of "subjective intent."[28] In 1980, the Court majority in *Mobile v. Bolden* rejected the argument that voting rights discrimination should be determined by a "results" test instead of an "intent" test, as well as what the Court labeled the theory behind the former test. The Court opined that such a theory "appears to be that every political group or at least that every such group that is in the minority has a federal constitutional right to elect candidates in proportion to its numbers.... The Equal Protection Clause does not require proportional representation as an imperative of political organization."[29]

This decision generated considerable debate, and induced Congress in 1982 to amend Section 2 of the Act to incorporate a "results" test providing that "The extent to which members of a protected class have been elected to office in the state or political subdivision is one circumstance which may be considered." Congress, however, added the proviso "that nothing in this section establishes a right to have members elected in numbers equal to their proportion in the population."[30]

The 1982 amendments also modified the preclearance provisions of the Act, directed Congress to reconsider these provisions in 1997, stipulated the provisions would expire in 2007, extended the language minority provisions until August 6, 1992, stipulated that no covered jurisdiction may provide voting materials only in English prior to August 6, 2007, and guarantees a voter in need of voting assistance because "of blindness, disability, or inability to read or write may be given assistance by a person of the voter's choice, other than the voter's employer or agent of that employer or officer or agent of the voter's union."[31]

Bail-Out Provisions

Section 4(a) of the Act contains "bail-out" provisions to end the special coverage resulting from the trigger. A state or local government subject to coverage because of the racial provisions of the 1965 Act and amendments of 1970 and 1975 may file suit for a declaratory judgment in the United States District Court for the District of Columbia and offer proof that it has not discriminated against the voting right of the protected group for ten years, or establish "that any such violations were trivial, were promptly corrected, and were not repeated."[32]

In practice, it is difficult for state and local governments covered by the original Act to use the bail-out provisions successfully. Virginia attempted to obtain such exemption, but its suit for a declaratory judgment was rejected by the United States Supreme Court in 1975.[33] Of course, even if a jurisdiction is successful in bailing out, it remains subject to litigation under the results standards of Section 2 of the Act.

Court Interpretation

The constitutionality of the Act was challenged on the grounds that Congress encroached on the powers reserved to the states by the United States Constitution (Tenth Amendment), since many of its key provisions were targeted at one region of the nation. Rejecting these arguments, the United States Supreme Court in 1966 ruled that "the sections of the Act which are properly before us are an appropriate means of carrying out Congress' constitutional responsibilities and are consonant with all other provisions of the Constitution."[34]

In 1968, the Court held in *Allen v. State Board of Elections* that it was the intent of Congress that the Act be given "the broadest possible scope" to reach "any state enactment which altered the election law of a covered state in even a minor way."[35] In 1973, the Court justified its 1968 decision by maintaining:

> Had Congress disagreed with the interpretation of § 5 in *Allen*, it had ample opportunity to amend that statute. After extensive deliberations in 1970 on bills to amend the Voting Rights Act, during which the *Allen* case was repeatedly discussed, the Act was extended for five years, without substantive modifications of § 5.[36]

Neither annexation *per se* nor at-large elections *per se* have been declared unconstitutional by the courts. The Voting Rights Act of 1965, however, added a federal dimension to annexation proceedings in several states, particularly southern states, as the U.S. Supreme Court observed in its 1971 opinion in *Perkins v. Matthews*.[37] The case involved annexation of territory by the City of Canton, Mississippi, and 1965 determination by Attorney General Nicholas B. Katzenbach that Mississippi and its political subdivisions were covered by the Act.[38] In 1969, the special three-judge District Court for the Southern District of Mississippi dissolved a temporary injunction against the holding of city elections issued by a federal judge, and dismissed a complaint on the ground that "the black voters still had a majority of not less than 600 after the expansions were effected."[39] A total of 82 black voters and 331 white voters had been added to the city by annexations in 1965, 1966 and 1968; no white voters were added to the city by the 1965 annexation.

The Supreme Court overturned the decision of the three-judge District Court:

> ...changing boundary lines by annexations which enlarge the City's number of eligible voters also constitutes the change of a "standard, practice, or procedure with respect to voting." Clearly, revision of boundary lines has an effect on voting in two ways: (1) by including certain voters within the City and leaving others outside, it determines who may vote in the municipal election and who may not; (2) it dilutes the weight of the voters to whom the franchise was limited before annexation, and "the right to suffrage can be denied by a debasement or dilution of the weight of a citizen's vote just as effectively as by wholly prohibiting the free exercise of the franchise." Moreover, § 5 was designed to cover changes having a potential for racial discrimination in voting, and such potential inheres in a change in composition of the electorate affected by an annexation.[40]

This decision resulted in a sharp decline in annexations by large southern cities, which have relatively broad state constitutional and/or statutory authority to annex territory. Subsequently, several large cities have sought the approval of the Attorney General to annex territory. Today, most southern annexations are small in terms of the size of the annexed territory and number of residents. The complexity of the issues involved with annexation are illustrated by cases involving the cities of Richmond and Petersburg, Virginia.

The first Richmond Case. The 1970 annexation of territory by Richmond increased the city's population and real property tax base by 19 percent and 23 percent, respectively, but was contested as violating the Voting Rights Act of 1965. A group of black plaintiffs objected to the annexation and contended it was designed to dilute black voting strength in a city with a council elected at-large, thereby violating their rights under the Fourteenth and Fifteenth Amendments and Section 5 of the Voting Rights Act. Ninety-seven percent of the residents of the annexed area were white. Fifty percent of Richmond's pre-annexation population of 202,359 was black in 1970. This proportion was lowered to 42 percent, as the annexation added 45,705 whites and 1,557 blacks to the city's population, increasing the totals to 143,857 whites and 105,764 blacks.

The United States District Court for the Eastern District of Virginia ruled in favor of the plaintiffs: "the Fourteenth Amendment forbids a deprivation of one's vote by reason of race — this Court interprets that to mean dilution as well."[41] Declaring that de-annexation would be impractical because the city had appropriated millions of dollars for improvements in the annexed area, the court ordered that the city be divided into two districts for purposes of new councilmanic elections.[42] According to the plan, seven council members would be elected from the district comprising most of the pre-annexation territory of the city, and two members would be elected from the annexed area and a small part of the city's pre-annexation territory.

The District Court's decision was reversed by the United States Court of Appeals for the Fourth Circuit, which held that "for perfectly valid reasons Richmond's elected representatives had sought annexation since 1966."[43] The U.S. Supreme Court denied a petition for writ of certiorari, thereby upholding the decision of the Court of Appeals.[44]

The Petersburg case. In a similar case, the Supreme Court in 1973 affirmed a decision of the District Court for the District of Columbia denying Petersburg the right to annex 14 square miles of land in Dinwiddie and Prince George's Counties, because the boundary extension would increase the proportion of white population from 45 to 54 percent in a city that elected its council members at-large, thereby discriminating against black voters by diluting their votes.[45]

The annexation ordinance, effective on December 31, 1971, was adopted unanimously in 1967 by the five-member city council. Two members, including the one who had introduced the ordinance, were black. The three-member district court found that the purpose of the annexation was to expand the city's growth and tax base, and there was no evidence that the annexation had a racial motive. The court, however, found that the city had "a long history of racial segregation and discrimination."[46]

Conceding "that an at-large system of electing city councilmen has many advantages over the ward system," the court ruled the annexation could be approved only if the city substituted ward elections for at-large elections of the council, which had expanded from five to seven members by the 1972 Virginia Legislature.[47]

The second Richmond case. Richmond in 1972 sought court approval for its 1970 annexation, since the Attorney General twice refused to give approval for the annexation. The city council was elected at-large in 1970 with voters from the annexed area in Chesterfield County participating; only one black councilman was elected. According to the three-judge District Court for the District of Columbia, "it is conceded here that Richmond conducted these elections illegally in violation of Section 5. It did not, prior to diluting by annexation the votes of the citizens residing within the old Richmond boundaries, obtain the approval of the Attorney General or a declaratory judgment from this Court that this dilution did not have the purpose and would not have the effect of abridging the right to vote on account of race or color. Richmond has held no councilmanic elections since 1970; the illegally elected City Council continues to serve at this time."[48] During the four-year period, three members of the nine-member council resigned and their replacements were co-opted by the council.

Subsequent to the annexation, the city substituted a single-member district system for the at-large system. The District Court concluded that the change in electoral system was "discriminatory in purpose and effect and thus violative of Section 5's substantive standards as well as the section's procedural command that prior approval be obtained from the Attorney General or this Court."[49]

The Supreme Court in 1975 reversed the lower court decision and made a distinction between the Petersburg and Richmond cases:

> Petersburg was correctly decided. On the facts here presented, the annexation of an area with a white majority, combined with at-large councilmanic elections and racial voting, created or enhanced the power of the white majority to exclude Negroes totally from participation in the governing of the city through membership on the city council. We agreed, however, that the consequence would be satisfactorily obviated if at-large elections were replaced by a ward system of choosing councilmen....
>
> We can not accept the position that such a single-member ward system would nevertheless have the effect of denying or abridging the right to vote because Negroes would constitute a lesser proportion of the population after the annexation than before, and given racial bloc voting, would have fewer seats on the city council.[50]

This decision constitutes a significant departure from the *Perkins* decision because the Court indicated it was no longer concerned that the pre-annexation black vote would be diluted, provided blacks were represented "fairly" in a city's governing body following annexation. New elections, held on March 1, 1977, resulted in the selection of five blacks and four whites as members of the city council.

While annexation may be viewed as an "indirect" form of racial gerrymandering, since annexation may have as its purpose and its effect the dilution of the voting rights of blacks living within the pre-annexation boundaries of the city, the Supreme Court in 1976 and 1977 was faced with the question of whether a "reverse racial gerrymander"—one that deliberately created a "safe" black district—was constitutional.

The Hasidic Jews case. Although the Voting Rights Act was designed to end voting discrimination in the southern states, the Attorney General in 1970 made a determination that New York State had maintained a test or device on November 1, 1968, as defined by Section 4(c) of the Act as amended. Moreover, the Director of the Bureau of the Census determined that Bronx, Kings (Brooklyn) and New York (Manhattan) Counties were subject to Sections 4 and 5 of the Act, since fewer than 50 percent of the residents of voting age cast a ballot in the 1968 presidential election and a literacy test had been used in the counties prior to 1970.[51] The specific reasons for applying the Act were the 1970 amendments changing the trigger date to 1968, and the fact that ballots were printed only in English. The District Court for the Southern District of New York ruled that "plaintiffs can not cast an effective vote without being able to comprehend fully the registration and election forms and the ballot itself."[52] The decision was affirmed by the United States Supreme Court.[53]

New York filed a complaint in the District Court for the District of Columbia seeking a declaratory judgment exempting the counties from coverage by the Act. With the approval of the United States Department of Justice, the court granted the judgment. Denied leave to intervene in the case, the National Association for the Advancement of Colored People (NAACP) unsuccessfully appealed the denial to the U.S. Supreme Court. However, on remand the NAACP's motion was granted.[54]

The NAACP, after reopening the declaratory judgment action, obtained an order from the District Court for the District of Columbia holding that the Act, as amended in 1970, applied to congressional and state legislative districts in Manhattan, Brooklyn and the Bronx, and the decision was affirmed by the Supreme Court.[55] These judgments necessitated a special session of the New York State Legislature, which on May 29, 1974 redrew congressional and state legislative district lines drawn in 1972.[56] Although the 1974 redistricting did not change the number of state senate and assembly districts with nonwhite voting majorities, it did increase the nonwhite majority *percentage* in two senate districts and two assembly districts, and decreased the nonwhite majority percentage in one senate district and two assembly districts.

Objections to several of the new district lines were advanced by representatives of Brooklyn's Hasidic Jews, who argued that the new assembly districts divided the Hasidic community and made it the victim of a racial gerrymander, thereby diluting the value of their votes in violation of the equal protection clause of the Fourteenth Amendment to the United States Constitution.[57] The Hasidic community, which had been able to elect one of its members to the state assembly, also challenged the assumption that only black legislators can represent the interests of blacks. In response to questioning in the District Court, Executive Director Richard S. Scolaro of the State Legislative Committee that drew the district lines stated that the United States Justice Department's insistence on a proportion of black voters of 65 percent was the "sole reason" why the Hasidic community was split between two assembly districts.[58]

On July 1, 1974, the Attorney General approved the new districts and dismissed the objections of Hasidic Jews and Irish, Italian and Polish groups on the grounds that the Voting Rights Act was designed to prohibit voting discrimination on the basis of race, not ethnic origin or religious beliefs.[59] In carrying out his duties under Section 5 of the Act, the Attorney General emphasized that it was not his function "to dictate to the State of New York specific actions, steps, or lines with respect to its own redistricting plan."[60]

The District Court dismissed the complaint of the Hasidic Jews on the grounds that the petitioners were not disenfranchised and that race could be considered in redistricting in order to correct previous racial discrimination.[61] The Court of Appeals affirmed the District Court's decision by reasoning that the redistricting did not under-represent whites, who composed 65 percent of the population, since approximately 70 percent of the state assembly and senate districts in Brooklyn would have white majorities.[62]

The Court of Appeals was convinced that it would be an impossible task for a legislature to reapportion itself if "a state must in a reapportionment draw lines so as to preserve ethnic community unity."[63]

The Supreme Court heard oral arguments in *United Jewish Organizations of Williamsburg v. Wilson* on October 6, 1976. Justice White asked Nathan Lewin, the plaintiffs' attorney, a question relative to the establishment of legislative districts with a specified percentage of blacks to help them elect members of their own race. Chief Justice Warren E. Burger interjected and inquired whether this action "would have the unfortunate effect to cut against the whole effort to achieve an integrated society?"[64] After Mr. Lewin responded in the affirmative, the Chief Justice added that "it does more than that. It pushes people to move into blocks" where others of the same race live.[65]

On March 1, 1977, the Court, by a seven-to-one vote, upheld the lower court ruling that the 1974 redistricting was constitutional, and ruled that the Act "was itself broadly remedial," and the use of racial considerations in drawing district lines often would be necessary.[66] The Court specifically opined that "neither the Fourteenth nor the Fifteenth Amendment mandates any *per se* rule against using racial factors in districting and apportionment."[67]

Many observers were disturbed by the Court's opinion because it appeared to overturn its 1960 decision in *Gomillion v. Lightfoot*, which invalidated racial gerrymandering. Justice Frankel of the District Court of the Southern District of New York, sitting by designation on the Court of Appeals for the Second Circuit, in his dissent offered penetrating insight into the nature of the case:

> The case is one where no preexisting wrong was shown of such a character as to justify, or render congruent, presumptively odious concept of racial "critical mass" as the principle of the fashioning of electoral districts. Indeed, it is a case where no official is willing to accept, let alone to claim, responsibility for the requirement of 65 [percent] or over nonwhite.[68]

The Court also was faulted for its uncritical acceptance of the 65 percent "nonwhite" majority as the magic percentage needed to ensure that the voting rights of "nonwhites" are not abridged. The Court presented state and local governments with a difficult choice between concentrating members of a protected minority into a single district until they constitute 65 percent of the population and spreading them out among two or more districts to permit them to exercise a "balance of power."

Evidence is lacking that white voters and black voters form respective homogeneous entities for voting purposes. Interestingly, many of the Puerto Rican voters in the Williamsburg district were described as "nonwhites," and the assumption apparently was made that blacks and Puerto Ricans have identical interests. Nevertheless, the decision provided a powerful incentive for the adoption of single-member districts apportioned solely on the basis of race.

The subject of racial gerrymandering remains a contentious one. The Supreme Court in *Shaw v. Reno* in 1993 remanded a case involving a North Carolina "serpentine" congressional district, which stretched 160 miles along Interstate 85, for a determination of whether the obvious racial gerrymander violated the equal protection clause of the Fourteenth Amendment. Writing for the majority, Justice Sandra Day O'Connor opined:

> Racial classifications ... reinforce the belief, held by too many for too much of our history, that individuals should be judged on the color of their skin. Racial gerrymandering, even for remedial purposes, may balkanize us into competing racial factions; it threatens to carry us further from the goal of a political system in which race no longer matters....[69]

Building upon its 1993 voting rights decision, the Supreme Court announced its 5-to-4 opinion in *Miller v. Johnson* on June 29, 1995, which invalidated the boundary lines of Georgia's 11th congressional district because race was the predominant factor in drawing them.[70] Writing for the majority, Justice Anthony Kennedy opined that race cannot be "the predominant factor motivating the legislature's decision to place a significant number of voters within a particular district." The majority announced the Court would employ "strict scrutiny" in future voting rights cases to determine whether districts were tailored narrowly to achieve a compelling state interest. The Kennedy opinion was particularly critical of the role of the United States Department of Justice and rejected the State of Georgia's argument that the plan was enacted to comply with the demands of the Department. The Department's performance, the Court concluded, "raises a serious constitutional question" and is "unsupportable."

Summary and Conclusion

The Voting Rights Act has succeeded in removing insidious barriers to voting by blacks and foreign language minorities, but has resulted in the remedial employment of the single-member district system, which constitutes a significant source of current political and legal controversy. Proportional representation, limited voting and cumulative voting can promote the election of minority candidates without encouraging segregation. The ideal system for candidate-based election in the United States is the single-transferable vote form of PR, which permits simultaneous representation of general and particular interests as candidates must build jurisdiction-wide coalitions in order to win election to office.

Merely changing electoral systems, however, will not necessarily increase dramatically the election of minorities to office. There are barriers to election other than the electoral system, many of which inhere to the advantages of incumbency. Incumbents in large jurisdictions have staff who spend part of their time promoting the re-election of their employers. In addition, elected officers attract media attention by presenting speeches and attending various public functions. They also may communicate with voters in their districts through newsletters printed and posted at government expense, and may make public service announcements which reinforce their name recognition. The most critical barrier to the effective challenge of an incumbent elected official often is lack of funds to mount a major campaign. Records filed with election officials in the various states reveal that incumbents, with few exceptions, possess a vastly superior ability to raise funds.[71]

The task for reformers today is to measure the quality of representation produced by various electoral systems and evaluate them in terms of the following criteria: effectiveness of ballots cast, maximization of voter participation, representation of competing interests, maximization of citizen access to elected decision makers, equity in interest group members' representation, and legitimacy of the legislative body.

Notes

1. *Vermont Constitution of 1791*, Chap. II, § 21.
2. *Kentucky Constitution of 1972*, Art. III, § 1.
3. *New Hampshire Constitution of 1784*, Part Second, Arts. 13 and 27 (1792) and *Georgia Constitution of 1798*, Art. IV, § 1.
4. *New York Constitution of 1821*, Art. II, § 1.
5. *Massachusetts Constitution of 1780*, Art. XX of Articles of Amendments.
6. *North Carolina Constitution of 1776*, Art. I of Amendments, § 3.
7. 16 Stat. 140 (1870).
8. 16 Stat. 433 (1871).
9. *United States v. Reese*, 92 U.S. 214 (1875).
10. *Guinn v. United States*, 238 U.S. 347 (1915).
11. *Smith v. Allwright*, 321 U.S. 649 (1944).
12. *Schell v. Davis*, 336 U.S. 933 (1949).
13. *Gomillion v. Lightfoot*, 364 U.S. 339 (1960).
14. *Civil Rights Act of 1957*, 71 Stat. 634, 42 U.S.C.A. § 1975 (1958 Supp.).
15. *Civil Rights Act of 1960*, 74 Stat. 86, 42 U.S.C.A. § 1971 (1961 Supp.).
16. *Civil Rights Act of 1964*, 78 Stat. 241, 42 U.S.C.A. § 2000a (1965 Supp.).

17. *Voting Rights Act of 1965*, 79 Stat. 437, 42 U.S.C.A. § 1973 (1966 Supp.).

18. *Voting Rights Extension: Hearings Before Subcommittee No. 5 of the Committee on the Judiciary, House of Representatives* (Washington, D.C.: United States Government Printing Office, 1969), Serial No. 3, p. 265.

19. *Voting Rights Act of 1965*, 79 Stat. 437, 42 U.S.C.A. § 19 (1966 Supp.).

20. *Extension of the Voting Rights Act of 1965: Hearings Before Sub-Committee on Constitutional Rights of the Committee of the Judiciary, United States Senate* (Washington, D.C.: United States Government Printing Office, 1975), p. 24.

21. *Ibid.*

22. See, 28 CFR § 51 (1993).

23. *Voting Rights Act Amendments of 1970*, 84 Stat. 312, 42 U.S.C.A. § 1973 (1971 Supp.) and *Voting Rights Act Amendments of 1975*, 89 Stat. 401, 42 U.S.C.A. § 1973b (1994).

24. *Voting Rights Act Amendments of 1970*, 84 Stat. 312, 28 U.S.C.A. §§ 1391–393 (1971 Supp.).

25. *Voting Rights Act Amendments of 1975*, 89 Stat. 402, 42 U.S.C.A. §§ 1973a, 1973d, and 1973i (1976 Supp.).

26. Data supplied to author by attorney David H. Hunter, Voting Section, United States Department of Justice, 17 January 1995.

27. *White v. Regester*, 412 U.S. 755 (1973).

28. *Washington v. Davis*, 426 U.S. 229 at 238–39 (1976) and *Village of Arlington Heights v. Metropolitan Housing Development Corporation*, 429 U.S. 252 at 256 (1977).

29. *City of Mobile v. Bolden*, 446 U.S. 55 at 75 (1980).

30. *Voting Rights Act Amendments of 1982*, 96 Stat. 134, 42 U.S.C.A. § 1973(b) (1994).

31. *Ibid.*, 96 Stat. 133–35, 42 U.S.C.A. §§ 1973b and 1973aa–6 (1994).

32. *Ibid.*, 96 Stat. 132, 42 U.S.C.A. § 1973c (1994).

33. *Virginia v. United States*, 386 F.Supp. 1319 (1974) and *Virginia v. United States* U.S. 901 (1975).

34. *South Carolina v. Katzenbach*, 383 U.S. 301 at 308 (1966).

35. *Allen v. State Board of Elections*, 393 U.S. 544 at 566–67 (1968).

36. *Georgia v. United States*, 411 U.S. 526 at 533 (1973).

37. *Perkins v. Matthews*, 400 U.S. 379 (1971).

38. 20 *Federal Register* 9897 (August 6, 1965).

39. *Perkins v. Matthews*, 301 F.Supp. 565 (S.D. Miss. 1969).

40. *Perkins v. Matthews*, 400 U.S. 379 at 388–89 (1971).

41. *Holt v. City of Richmond*, 334 F.Supp. 228 at 236 (1971).

42. *Ibid.*, pp. 238–40.

43. *Holt v. Richmond*, 459 F. 2d 1093 at 1099 (4th Cir., 1972).

44. *Holt v. Richmond*, 408 U.S. 931 (1972).

45. *City of Petersburg Virginia v. United States et al.*, 354 F.Supp. 1021 (1972); *City of Petersburg Virginia v. United States et al.*, 410 U.S. 962 (1973).

46. *City of Petersburg Virginia v. United States et al.*, 354 F.Supp. 1021 at 1025 (1972).

47. *Ibid.*, at 1027.

48. *City of Richmond v. United States*, 376 F.Supp. 1344 at 1351 (1974).

49. *Ibid.*, at 1352. Under the ward plan, blacks would have a majority of at least 64.0 percent in four wards and would constitute 40.9 percent of the population in a fifth ward. Whites would have a majority in four wards.

50. *City of Richmond v. United States*, 422 U.S. 358 at 370–71 (1975).

51. 35 *Federal Register*, 12354 (July 31, 1970) and 36 *Federal Register*, 5809 (March 21, 1971).

52. *Torres v. Sachs*, 381 F.Supp. 309 at 312 (1973).

53. *Torres v. Sachs*, 419 U.S. 888 (1974).

54. *NAACP v. New York*, 413 U.S. 345 (1973).

55. *New York v. United States*, 419 U.S. 888 (1974).

56. *New York Laws of 1974*, Chaps. 585–91 and 599.

57. Emanuel Perlmutter, "Hasidic Groups File Suit to Bar Redistricting as 'Gerrymander,'" *The New York Times*, 12 June, 1974, p. 28.

58. Linda Greenhouse, "Hasidic Jews are Called 'Victims of Racial Gerrymander' at Hearing on Suit," *The New York Times*, 21 June 1974, p. 19.

59. *Memorandum of Decision* (Washington, D.C.: Civil Rights Division, United States Department of Justice, 1 July 1974), unpublished.

60. *Ibid.*, p. 17.

61. *United Jewish Organizations of Wil-*

liamsburg, Incorporated v. Wilson, 377 F.Supp. 1164 at 1165–166 (1974).

62. *United Jewish Organizations of Williamsburg, Incorporated v. Wilson*, 510 F. 2d 512 at 523 (1975).

63. *Ibid.*, at 521.

64. Lesley Oelsner, "Brooklyn's Hasidim Argue Voting Rights Case Before the Supreme Court," *The New York Times*, 7 October 1976, p. 47.

65. *Ibid.*

66. *United Jewish Organizations of Williamsburg, Incorporated v. Carey*, 430 U.S. 144 at 156 and 159–60 (1977).

67. *Ibid.*, at 161.

68. *United Jewish Organizations of Williamsburg, Incorporated v. Wilson*, 510 F. 2d 512 at 526 (1975).

69. *Shaw v. Reno*, 113S.ct.2816 at 2832 (1993).

70. The Miller decision has not been published, but may be identified by its case numbers: 94–631, 94–797 and 94–929.

71. For additional details, see Joseph F. Zimmerman, "Fair Representation for Minorities and Women" in Wilma Rule and Joseph Zimmerman, eds., *United States Electoral Systems: Their Impact on Women and Minorities* (Westport, Conn.: Greenwood Press, 1992), pp. 1–11.

• *Chapter 2* •

Voter Rights Litigation

LEE L. BLACKMAN AND ERICH R. LUSCHEI[1]

In the United States, especially in the West, many cities, school districts, and other public entities use at-large election systems to elect public officials. Once viewed as a solution to problems associated with ward politics, the at-large system of electing representatives has become the object of numerous challenges in the federal courts.[2] The cases have challenged the at-large election process on the ground[s] that such elections eliminate or dilute the voting strength of minority groups.

A significant number of voting rights lawsuits are expected in the wake of the 1990 Census results. The Census figures document growth of minority populations throughout the country. There is little doubt that the Census and the subsequent redistricting of jurisdictions as a result of it, will spawn dozens of voting rights lawsuits in jurisdictions with sizable minority populations.

Voting rights lawsuits attacking at-large election systems typically involve for-midable plaintiffs' attorneys, complicated issues of fact and law, sensitive political considerations, and huge litigation expenses.

This chapter provides background information about cases involving at-large election systems. In addition, it discusses the applicable legal standards and the evidence typically offered on the fundamental issues, and presents an overview of the considerations facing elected officials and their counsel when deciding whether to avoid, defend, or settle voting rights lawsuits.[3]

Every citizen of voting age has the right to cast a vote that is equal in dignity to the votes cast by fellow voters.[4] Commonly known as "one person, one vote," this essential right was first recognized by the United States Supreme Court as a proper subject of judicial consideration in the 1962 decision of *Baker v. Carr*.[5]

Under the one person, one vote rule, if voters are divided into districts, each

---

Originally published as "Voting Rights Litigation," *Municipal Attorney*, Vol. 32, Nos. 5 and 6, September/December, 1991. Published by the International Municipal Lawyers Association, Washington, D.C. Reprinted with permission of the publisher.

district must be substantially equal in population to each other district which elects a representative.[6] For example, if a jurisdiction's governing body has five members elected from five districts and there are 500 voters, each district must contain 100 people. A system which has unequal populations in the electoral districts causes the votes in an "over-populated" district to be worth less, or be "diluted," when compared to the votes of people in "under-populated" districts. An alternative at-large system also may cause problems. Under the at-large system, all five representatives are elected by the entire population.[7]

Racial Vote Dilution as a Justiciable Claim

The one person, one vote rule only protects equality in the weight of a person's vote. It does not protect group interests, such as the interests of Democrats or Republicans, women or men, pro-choice or pro-life advocates, or the interests of any other group united by shared political, social, economic, or other concerns.

However, some groups, mainly racial and ethnic minorities, have received special federal protection against electoral systems which lead to group interest dilution. The vast majority of racial vote dilution cases have involved African Americans and, to an increasing extent, Hispanic Americans.

Racial vote dilution cases grew out of the one person, one vote rule and first became prevalent in the federal courts in the early 1970s. Racial vote dilution occurs when an election system allows a white majority to minimize or cancel out the votes of a cohesive minority group.[8] This occurs when the minority group is submerged in a larger population that votes against minority candidates. In an envi-

ronment of racially polarized voting, an at-large election system allows a group that is only marginally larger to select all of the representatives. This can prevent even a relatively large and cohesive minority group from electing any of its preferred candidates. This is racial vote dilution.

Under federal law, racial vote dilution is as violative of minority voting rights as the use of a poll tax, a literacy test, or any other device that directly impairs an individual's right to vote. The remedy preferred by the federal courts for curing racial vote dilution is use of a single-member district system in which at least one political district encompasses the geographic concentrations of minorities.[9] Such a system allows minority voters to comprise a majority of the voters in at least one district, and thus control the electoral outcome for at least one of the seats on the governing board.

Modern Standards for Claims

There are three sources for the substantive right in an electoral system free of racial vote dilution. First, Section 2 of the Voting Rights Act (42 U.S.C. § 1973) prohibits the use of any election system that denies minority voters an equal opportunity to elect candidates of their choice. Under Section 2, it does not matter whether the system was developed or maintained with the intent to harm the minority group. Rather, liability may be imposed if it is determined that, without the existing electoral system, the minority group would be expected, as a result of its own size, concentration, and cohesiveness, to elect representatives of its choice.

The other two sources of law are the equal protection clause of the Fourteenth Amendment and the Fifteenth Amendment of the United States Constitution. These constitutional provisions make unlawful any election system that was adopted or maintained for the purpose of reducing minority voting strength when such system has some adverse effect.

The Statutory Claim

Under Section 2, there are three primary elements of proof which a plaintiff must satisfy to prevail in a voting rights action. These elements are: 1) the minority group must be large in number and geographically concentrated enough to form an effective voting majority in one district; 2) the minority group must be politically cohesive; and 3) the minority group must prove that the majority group votes as a block against minority candidates.[10]

Under the first requirement for a Section 2 claim is that the minority group must be sufficiently numerous and sufficiently concentrated so that under a single-member district system at least one district could be created in which that minority group is a majority of those eligible to vote.[11]

It is a simple arithmetic fact that some groups do not have enough members to influence the outcome of any but the closest elections, no matter how cohesively they might vote or how favorable the electoral system might be to their interests. Other groups are large and cohesive, but are not residentially concentrated. That is, they may be dispersed throughout a political jurisdiction or integrated within the majority group. In either case, the lines of a single-member district simply could not be drawn in a way that would concentrate a sufficient number of the minority group's members to permit them to form a majority.

There are three principal factors that must be considered in assessing whether this first requirement for a Voting Rights Act claim has been satisfied.

First, the current number of seats on the governing body is assumed to be an appropriate number and will be used as the number of districts in the proposed single-member district plan.[12]

Second, each district must be allocated an equivalent portion of the population. If there are 10,000 people in the city with a five member governing board, then each district must contain 2,000 people. Taking these two quantitative considerations into account, the minority group in this hypothetical case must be able to comprise at least 1,001 of the people in one of the districts.[13]

Third, voting eligibility must be considered. If a minority group has a disproportionate number of noncitizens or citizens below the voting age, then a mere population majority will not be sufficient to demonstrate the group's ability to elect a candidate. In such circumstances, the group must be numerous enough and geographically concentrated enough to constitute an eligible voter majority in a district.[14]

Whether the district majority requirement can be established is usually the easiest issue in a Section 2 case. The evidence is readily accessible using the United States Census data. A demographer may be retained to evaluate census tracts as to racial, ethnic, and age composition. A demographer tries to determine whether a district may be drawn in which the minority group will have an effective voting majority, using the factors mentioned above.

If it appears that this first Section 2 requirement cannot be established, summary judgment may be obtained. If it appears that this requirement can be established, the second element of the claim must be satisfied. Thus the inquiry becomes whether or not voting in the jurisdiction is racially polarized. The components of racially polarized voting include political cohesion within the minority group and white bloc voting by the majority.[15] These components are described below.

Minority Political Cohesion

The political process is generally able to accommodate competing concerns. If a minority group does not have a distinct set of interests or is not intent on selecting certain candidates to champion those interests, its views generally are deemed to receive adequate representation within the general process of government. However, if the minority group does have distinct interests which the group attempts to advance, the group's submergence in the majority structure may deny representation or political responsiveness to the group's special interests.[16]

The standard and preferred method of proving minority political cohesion is analysis of the electoral behavior of the minority group in the jurisdiction under scrutiny. The question is whether minority voters vote as a reasonably unified group.

There are three primary means to determine how people vote: 1) voters are asked (through exit polls and other surveys), 2) prior voting behavior is assessed in precincts which are almost exclusively minority (homogeneous precinct analysis), or 3) the percentage of the voters that the minority group represents in each precinct is compared to the votes cast for each candidate in each precinct to infer overall minority voter preferences (ecological regression analysis).[17]

None of these methods provides direct evidence of the actual votes cast by minority and nonminority voters in specific elections. Indeed, it is not possible to know, as a matter of mathematical certainty, which person voted for which candidate because ballots are not designated by minority affiliation.

The method most commonly used in voting rights cases is ecological regression analysis. Under this statistical method, when the percentage of the vote received by a minority candidate increases as the percentage of minority group members in the precincts increases, an inference is drawn that the increase in the percent of support for the minority candidate has been provided by the increase in the percentage of minority voters. Statistical measures of significance are then used to identify the strength of the correlation.

The principal vice of this method is that one never knows whether the people actually voting are representative of the racial composition of the precinct. Thus, differences between racial groups in eligibility (i.e., age and citizenship), registration, and turnout undermine the strength of the model and the inference that those who actually cast ballots mirror the precinct population becomes attenuated.[18]

Homogeneous precinct analysis is similar to ecological regression analysis, except that it only examines precincts in which the minority group comprises 80% or more of the people in the precinct. The fundamental assumption of homogeneous precinct analysis is that voters in homogeneous precincts will mirror the preferences expressed by the minority group as a whole. If minority voters in homogeneous precincts are cohesive, it is inferred that the minority group is cohesive in the jurisdiction as a whole.[19]

Exit polls or telephone polls are a third inferential method for ascertaining how a minority group votes. People are asked their racial background and how they voted.[20]

Whatever method is used, a level of agreement among minority voters which would allow one to conclude that the minority group has distinctive interests expressed through voting patterns must exist. There is no quantitative threshold that serves as a bright line to determine cohesiveness, but only one case has determined that less than majority support demonstrated cohesion.[21]

Majority Bloc Voting

White bloc voting is the primary evil at which challenges to at-large election systems are aimed. If white voters are the majority of the electorate and consistently vote contrary to the manner in which minority voters vote, an at-large electoral system will allow white bloc voting to consistently prevent the minority group from electing its preferred candidates.[22]

To be legally significant, white bloc voting must rise to a level that routinely results in the defeat of candidates that the minority group prefers. The degree of white bloc voting which may be legally significant depends on a number of factors, including the relative numeric proportion of minority and white voters in the electorate, the extent of cross-over voting, and the size of the districts.[23]

Additional Factors

The original line of Supreme Court voting rights cases made a finding of intentional discrimination essential to a plaintiff's success.[24] The focus was on issues such as the motive of those who authored the plan under attack; the presence of racial appeals in elections, reflecting a societal attitude approving discrimination by those elected; the presence of voting on the basis of race, evidencing both an attitude of discrimination likely to be represented in those elected and the essential circumstance under which an at-large system could effectively be used to accomplish a racially discriminatory desire to deny

electoral opportunity to minority candidates; and the responsiveness of the jurisdiction to the specialized needs of the minority group, with nonresponsiveness demonstrating that the minority group was being treated differently by the elected leaders and was effectively unrepresented by the leaders elected by the majority.[25]

When Congress adopted the results test in amending Section 2, it stated that all of the factors which had been developed by the courts along the way remained pertinent to a Section 2 case. The Supreme Court's clarification of the results standard in *Thornburg v. Gingles*, however, made it clear that the three *Thornburg* preconditions are the heart of the results analysis, with the other factors being secondary or tertiary. At this juncture, it would seem that evidence concerning the factors not encompassed within the three essential elements of Section 2 will not be crucial to the outcome of a Section 2 case. Nevertheless, they are likely to be the subject of pretrial discovery, even if no constitutional claim is presented, and evidence on these issues may be effective in encouraging the finder of fact to be receptive to the plaintiff's case.

The Constitutional Claim

The earlier discussion identified the principal prerequisite to a constitutional case — evidence that the electoral system was adopted or is being maintained for a racially discriminatory purpose.[26] It is not necessary that the discriminatory purpose be the sole, compelling, or even leading motive in adopting or maintaining an electoral system. However, proof is required that the system was adopted or is being maintained, at least in part, because of, rather than in spite of the adverse impact on the minority's opportunity to elect candidates of their choice.[27]

The evidence supporting a constitutional intent claim is likely to cover each of the issues referred to during the above discussion of the statutory cause of action.[28] But the greatest emphasis will be on the events surrounding the original adoption of the electoral system and the latest modifications or reconsiderations of it. The inquiry will encompass the full legislative process, including pre- and post-deliberative conversations among legislators (although purely internal thoughts and unarticulated considerations may be protected from judicial scrutiny).

The history of the treatment of minorities in and by the political jurisdiction will be subject to judicial examination. This includes the establishment and accomplishment of affirmative action goals relating to government hiring and contracting. The claim that government services are provided on a less than even-handed basis is also likely to be litigated (providing an opportunity for the plaintiffs to collect documents and data for other potential uses).

No simple guide to the evidentiary prerequisites for an intentional vote dilution case is possible. Badly chosen language that sounds racially hostile by one of the authors of the system may be enough to convince a judge that the system was adopted, at least in part, to disadvantage a minority group's efforts to elect candidates. And, a finding that the authors were acting with the race-neutral political objectives to disadvantage every group (political or ethnic) which might mount an effective challenge to those presently in power is not likely to be sufficient to avoid the intentional discrimination claim.[29]

Litigate or Settle

The merits of a Section 2 case can be assessed by using estimates of minority group demographics and political cohesion. A demographer can be consulted. The demographer will have to look at census tract population data broken down by ethnicity and age. He or she will also consider citizenship rate estimates for each ethnic group in the jurisdiction. The demographer can be asked if a contiguous district can be drawn in which 50% or more of the voting age citizens are members of the minority group.

To assess voting cohesion and polarization, experienced political observers can be consulted to assess the number of minority voters who will select a candidate whose race is the same as theirs unless there is some strong reason to the contrary. The same question can be asked with respect to majority group voters. If there is no clear answer, data regarding voting patterns in precincts known to be ethnically homogeneous can be considered. Previous exit polls in the community can be considered. If essential, results of elections can be subjected to ecological regression analysis.

If the answer to the demographic question is that a minority majority district can be drawn, and the answer to the cohesion question is not clear, the electoral system is likely to face a serious challenge unless members of the minority community have been elected frequently and consistently.

Evaluating a constitutional case is enormously more subjective, mainly because it is often only through the pretrial discovery that it is determined whether there are the psychologically crucial anchors (what plaintiffs might consider to be warm if not smoking guns) which are essential to such a case. It is also hard to predict how well the witnesses will do and how well the various trial attorneys will do. Nevertheless, given the Supreme Court's establishment of significant preconditions to Section 2 cases, it is likely that a constitutional claim will be pursued even if the Section 2 claim appears weak.

The appropriateness of pursuing a compromise settlement will also be affected by one consideration which does not bear directly on the strength of the plaintiffs' case, namely the costs of defense and the possible obligation to pay the plaintiffs' attorneys' fees should they ultimately prevail (either by judgment or settlement). Voting rights cases are expert and discovery intensive. Each side can spend several hundred thousand dollars or more simply on pretrial discovery and preparation. The trial process can consume weeks, at a cost of several thousand dollars per day. The cost, of course, is no reason to settle a case that lacks merit. However, these tend to be cases in which the outcome is in doubt as long as the matter is pending.

While chances of success and cost are critical issues, decision makers in this area must deal with a number of other considerations, the most significant of which is the fact that the choice of an electoral system alone has profound political consequences, some of which are subtle. This consideration will probably determine whether, and how, settlement may be accomplished. Frequently, the lawsuit threatens to dissolve a partisan balance of power. Sometimes, it merely threatens individual incumbents.[30]

Two other aspects of these battles merit special comment. First, these cases intrude on governmental operations. Many documents must be collected and produced. Many individuals (usually those who run the government) must take time away from their work to prepare and to testify. Legislators and their closest aides will be asked, and are likely to be instructed to respond to, a broad collection of inquiries that they would rather not address. In addition, the press is likely to publicize every aspect of the case and to editorialize in favor of the outcome it thinks best.

Settlement Approaches

If there is no consensus on whether to defend or to settle, one possible alternative is to place the issue before the voters. If the voters decide to retain the at-large system, they will have done so with an understanding of the costs that will be incurred. They also will have provided the city council or board with a mandate on how to proceed. If the voters decide to eliminate the at-large system, further costs of litigation may be avoided and the council will be released from the responsibility for having made a potentially unpopular decision. Attorneys for the plaintiffs are often willing to forestall proceedings if a commitment is made to place an acceptable proposal before the voters in an expeditious manner.[31] The ballot measure approach is usually attractive to plaintiffs and their attorneys.[32]

In assessing the settlement option, there are a number of alternatives which can be considered short of shifting to a pure district system. The at-large system can be retained, but cumulative or single-shot voting permitted. Systems in which some seats are elected from multimember districts and some from single-member districts can be adopted. At-large systems may be modified to provide for district by district primaries, but at-large run-offs. District systems may be modified by the addition of a strong mayor, elected city wide. Even where the at-large system must be removed, one option which tends to preserve the political balance of power, as well as all of the incumbents' seats, is to increase the size of the council or board.[33]

The decision to settle and the choice of alternative arrangements will not involve an easy legal, let alone an easy political, judgment. Nevertheless, there are alternatives to lengthy, expensive, and unhappy litigation.

Conclusion

There is no litigation with the same mix of challenging legal issues, complicated factual questions, colorful personalities, serious social consequences, and omnipresent risk of miscalculation as is present in a voting rights case. Conducting a trial in such a case is inherently dangerous, but then so is trying to settle it. In many instances, the potential for settlement exists only for a limited period of time, generally at the onset of the proceedings. Settlement usually requires an act of political statesmanship at a time when elected leaders are inclined to be doctrinaire.

To the extent counsel can influence the outcome of the process, it is usually a matter of helping the participants find a way to do what they are already inclined to do rather than a matter of acting as the moving force in changing personal attitudes. Jurisdictions are well served when they avoid the circumstance where the 20% of the people who feel strongly about the issue are permitted to perpetuate a fight that the 80% who are in the middle would be perfectly ready to compromise. In such a circumstance, there is usually a way to settle the matter while still preserving to the principal participants an opportunity to retain or obtain the political outcome they seek.

Notes

1. Mr. Blackman is a partner (Los Angeles), and Mr. Luschei an associate (Boston), in the national law firm of McDermott, Will & Emery. Both have represented a number of governmental entities in litigation under the Voting Rights Act and the Fourteenth and Fifteenth Amendments of the United States Constitution.

2. This is true with regard to both the number of cases filed and the geographic reach of the cases. Prior to the mid–1980s, at-large system litigation was generally confined to jurisdictions in the South. During the 1985 to 1989 time frame, however, at-large systems in California were challenged in the cities of Watsonville, Salinas, Stockton, Pomona, Chula Vista, National City and San Diego. See *Romero v. City of Pomona*, 883 F.2d 1418 (9th Cir. 1989); *Gomez v. City of Watsonville*, 863 F.2d 1407 (9th Cir. 1988); *Skorepa v. City of Chula Vista*, 723 F.Supp. 1384 (S.D. Cal. 1989). Similarly, the Midwest began to see the spread of this litigation. See, e.g., *Sanchez v. Bond*, 875 F.2d 1488 (10th Cir. 1989) (Colorado); *McNeil v. Springfield Park Dist.*, 851 F.2d 937 (7th Cir. 1988) (Illinois); *Duchanage v. Sisseton Ind. School Dist.*, 804 F.2d 469 (8th Cir. 1986) (South Dakota). Regions in the South continued to see substantial litigation in this area. See, e.g., *Overton v. City of Austin*, 871 F.2d 529 (5th Cir. 1989) (Texas); *Citizens for a Better Gretna v. City of Gretna*, 834 F.2d 496 (5th Cir. 1987) (Louisiana); *Concerned Citizens of Hardee County v. Hardee County Board of Commissioners*, 906 F.2d 524 (11th Cir. 1990) (Florida).

3. This is not an exhaustive treatment of these subjects. In almost every situation, there is more to say, at least one qualifier which could be added, or at least one more alternative than those presented here. Much of the discussion also is applicable to reapportionment cases where a minority group contends that district lines are situated in a manner that dilutes minority voting strength either through dividing the group into two or more districts or packing the group into a single district when it has the electoral power to control two districts.

4. *Baker v. Carr*, 369 U.S. 186 (1962).

5. *Ibid.*

6. *Reynolds v. Sims*, 377 U.S. 533, 579 (1964). "[T]he overriding objective [of reapportionment] must be substantial equality of population among the various districts, so that the vote of any citizen is approximately equal in weight to that of any other citizen."

7. See note 1 and note 5 and accompanying text. See also, *Thornburg v. Gingles*, 478 U.S. 30 (1986).

8. *Thornburg v. Gingles*, 478 U.S. 48 (1986).

9. This is not the exclusive remedy, but generally is the remedy that the plaintiffs request in their complaint. For a discussion of common issues that arise on the remedy side of

these cases, see *McGhee v. Granville County*, 860 F.2d 110 (4th Cir. 1988). In *McGhee*, the district court adopted a cumulative voting proposal where it was apparent that African American voters were too dispersed in the community to comprise a "safe" majority in more than one of seven districts, even though the African American voting age population comprised 40% of the total. Cumulative voting would have allowed African American voters to control three of seven seats on the legislative body. The court of appeals reversed, finding that the government's proposed district plan was adequate even though it did not provide African American voters with their maximum potential voting strength.

10. The three essential elements of a Section 2 case are enumerated in the Supreme Court's most recent and most profound examination of Section 2 of the Voting Rights Act, *Thornburg v. Gingles*, 478 U.S. 30 (1986). These elements, sometimes referred to as the *Thornburg* preconditions, were derived from prior case law and the Senate Report on the 1982 amendments to the Voting Rights Act, Congress' last significant action in the voting rights arena. *Thornburg* at 49–50, stated succinctly, a bloc voting majority must usually be able to defeat candidates supported by a politically cohesive, geographically insular minority group.

11. While it is possible for a group that is less than a majority of the voters to elect its preferred candidate by securing cross-over support from other groups, and even though a plurality of voters may be able to exert strong influence in a close election, the critical consideration in a Section 2 case is the presence of an ability, on the basis of the minority group's own votes, to elect a representative but for the impact of the electoral system.

12. *Romero v. City of Pomona*, 883 F.2d 1418, 1425 n.10 (9th Cir. 1989).

13. This hypothetical assumes only one minority group. Where there are multiple minority groups, the calculus changes— there may be circumstances where a group without a population majority nevertheless does have an electoral majority.

14. *Romero, supra*, 883 F.2d at 1424. This may be a significant hurdle. If, for example, a minority group is one-third noncitizen, it must comprise 60 percent of a district's population

in order to be a majority of those eligible to vote.

15. *Thornburg* at 51–51, 56. "The purpose of inquiring into the existence of racially polarized voting is two fold: to ascertain whether minority group members constitute a politically cohesive unit and to determine whether whites vote sufficiently as a bloc usually to defeat the minority's preferred candidate."

16. However, it is not a defense to a Section 2 case that the political jurisdiction is responsive to the special needs of the minority group. Similarly, it is no defense that minority group members are appointed to local boards and commissions and are fairly represented in the ranks of government employees. Section 2 is not focused on policy, or even on policy making, but rather on the impact that the electoral system has on the opportunity of a minority group to elect candidates that are distinctively the preferred choice of the minority group.

17. See, e.g., *Thornburg*, 478 U.S. at 52–53 (recognizing homogeneous or "extreme case" analysis and ecological regression analysis as standard methods for ascertaining whether voting is racially polarized); *Romero v. City of Pomona*, 665 F.Supp. 853 (C.D. Cal. 1987), aff'd., 883 F.2d 1418 (9th Cir. 1989) (finding that results of exit polls were more reliable tha[n] results of homogeneous precinct and ecological regression analysis); *Gomez v. City of Watsonville*, 863 F.2d 1407 (9th Cir. 1988) (holding that evidence of expected preference inferred from socioeconomic and cultural factors could not outweigh actual voting results presented through undisputed ecological regression and homogeneous precinct analysis).

18. Ecological regression is not highly regarded by statisticians. However, it is well liked by lawyers and social scientists when it tends to confirm what they intuitively believe.

19. The principal vice of homogeneous precinct analysis is its assumption that members of the minority group who live in precincts which are not ethnically homogeneous vote the same way as the usually smaller number of minority group members who reside in different precincts. In addition, rates of eligibility, registration, and turnout also undermine the method.

20. Telephone polls are subject to question because the passage of time and the act ual outcome of the election tend to color the recollections of those contacted. The lack of

complete anonymity has also been raised as an issue. Exit polls are the best means to assess actual voting behavior. However, such polls (which must be conducted on the day of the election) are both expensive and limited in coverage.

21. Other means to predict voting cohesiveness have been used, including attitudinal surveys and lay or expert opinions on the existence of minority group agreement on current issues. These are not irrelevant to a voting rights case, but they are useful only to the extent they contribute to the determination of voting cohesiveness. The appearance of unity on issues which affect the minority community will not prevail over demonstrated disagreement in voting patterns. Nor will obviously disparate views within different components of a minority group defeat a claim where agreement in voting preference is expressed when it comes time to vote. *Citizens for a Better Gretna v. City of Gretna*, 834 F.2d 496, 501–02 (5th Cir. 1987) (holding that 49% support by black voters for a black candidate was enough to demonstrate that the black candidate was the preferred candidate of black voters).

22. Of course, minority candidates could still be elected from time to time in such an at-large system. But the election of such candidates will not necessarily defeat a Section 2 claim. There are, for example, minority candidates who appeal to the majority and may be selected as the preferred candidate of the majority, even though that candidate is not the preferred minority choice. Such an election will not demonstrate an absence of polarized voting or that the failure of other minority candidates to be elected is unrelated to the use of an at-large system.

23. *Thornburg*, 478 U.S. at 56–57.

24. For a discussion of the historical evolution of these standards, see generally, *City of Mobile v. Bolden*, 446 U.S. 56 (1980) and *Thornburg* at 43–46.

25. Other factors that were important included candidate slating requirements, the size of the districts, the use of run-offs in primary elections, restrictions against cumulative or single-shot voting, the use of other voting provisions or restrictions which could enhance the adverse effects on minorities of an at-large structure, the extent to which historically ended discrimination had continuing impacts

which diminished the opportunity of minority groups to be politically effective, and the strength of the race-neutral policy which was said to support use of the at-large system.

26. *Mobile v. Bolden*, 446 U.S. 55 (1980).

27. *Personnel Administrator v. Feeney*, 442 U.S. 256, 278 (1979)

28. Evidence will likely address the events leading to adoption of the system, the history of intentional discrimination in and by the jurisdiction and the state, the presence of racial appeals in elections, the presence of voting on the basis of race (minority cohesion and majority bloc voting), the responsiveness of the jurisdiction to the specialized needs of the minority group, past electoral success or failure by minority candidates, candidate slating processes, the size of the districts, the use of run-offs in primary elections, restrictions against cumulative or single-shot voting, the use of other voting provisions or restrictions which could enhance the adverse effects on minorities of an at-large system, the continuing impact of historical discrimination on the ability of minorities to participate effectively in the political process, the tenuousness of the policy underlying the electoral system, and the extent of the minority group's residential concentration or dispersion. "Any evidence which tends to demonstrate the presence of a discriminatory motive is probative on the intent issue." See, e.g., *Rodgers v. Lodge*, 458 U.S. 613 (1982); *Garza v. County of Los Angeles*, 756 F.Supp. 1298, aff'd., 918 F.2d 763 (9th Cir. 1990), *cert. denied*, 111 S.Ct. 681 (1991).

29. *Garza v. County of Los Angeles*, 756 F.Supp. 1298, aff'd., 918 F.2d 763 (9th Cir. 1990), *cert. denied*, 111 S.Ct. 681 (1991).

30. Incumbents have legitimate reason to favor incumbency. The people who elect the incumbents do so in order that they might serve, not in order that they might restructure the system in a way which deprives the electorate of the people they have chosen.

31. There is little certainty in most litigated cases. Plaintiffs' attorneys advance their time and significant costs. They all but invariably have a genuine concern about the effect of a negative outcome on the group they represent.

32. If such an approach is taken, the parties should stipulate to a conditional stay of proceedings and obtain a stay order from the

court to avoid misunderstandings that are otherwise sure to arise. Plaintiffs' attorneys are entitled to recover fees and costs if a case is settled, whether by ballot or otherwise. Pre-filing investigations are routine and plaintiffs' attorneys probably will have spent substantial time preparing the case. For this reason, a firm commitment should be obtained from the plaintiffs' attorneys concerning fees in the event that the proposal is adopted. Unless a firm figure is agreed to, and made part of the stay order to a contemporaneous contract, the city will be faced with an unnegotiated claim for fees even after the plaintiffs obtain the relief they desired without having prevailed on the merits at trial.

In addition, fees incurred by the plaintiffs' attorneys to obtain their fees are generally recoverable in themselves.

33. The range of options will depend on a number of facts, including whether the city is operated under the state's general law or a charter (in California, for example, charter cities have a broader array of options). The willingness of the elected officials to stipulate to a finding of liability may also affect the range of settlement options, because a stipulation for judgment may allow the court to order a remedy without a vote of the residents of the jurisdiction.

Chapter 3

The Voting Rights Act and the Supreme Court

Olethia Davis

Minority vote dilution continues to be a hotly debated issue 30 years after passage of the Voting Rights Act. Responsibility has fallen largely to the judiciary to determine whether unlawful vote dilution has occurred in jurisdictions covered by Sections 2 and 5 of the Act. Yet, a review of case law reveals that the Court has been inconsistent in its interpretation of Sections 2 and 5. This ambiguity has provided ammunition for opponents of voting rights and intensified the debate over federal civil rights guarantees.

In the context of voting rights, this debate centers around such issues as the appropriate evidence required to prove minority vote dilution, the types of election systems that might be challenged on the grounds of Section 2 and/or Section 5, and whether the three-pronged test devised by the Supreme Court in *Thornburg v. Gingles* is a supplement to the 1982 re-vised version of Section 2 or a reiteration of the legislative intent of the U.S. Senate.[1]

Judicial Interpretation of Section 5

Most challenges to vote dilution have been brought on grounds other than Section 5 because of its limited scope. Until 1987, the required test of retrogression — whether a change in electoral laws or structures has a dilutionary effect — and proof of intentional discrimination were difficult and in many cases impossible to prove.

In 1987, however, the U.S. Department of Justice adopted the language of the Senate report on voting rights, which indicated that the legislative intent of the amended Act was to incorporate the results standard of Section 2 into the preclearance requirement of Section 5.[2] This interpre-

Originally published as "The Supreme Court and the Voting Rights Act," *National Civic Review*, Vol. 84, No. 4, Fall/Winter, 1995. Published by the National Civic League Press, Denver, Colorado. Reprinted with permission of the publisher.

tation is based on that portion of Section 2 that mandates that a "totality of circumstances" must be met in order for jurisdictions to receive declaratory judgment as mandated by Section 2 and set forth in section 4(f)(2).[3]

The Court in several earlier rulings expanded the scope of Section 5, thus protecting the voting rights of minorities. In *Allen v. State Board of Elections*, the Court required preclearance when a jurisdiction attempted to replace elections with appointment of officials.[4] The Court's opinion shifted the focus of Section 5 challenges from vote denial — disenfranchisement — to vote dilution, and indicated that Section 5 encompassed a broad range of voting practices and procedures. The Court's holding in *Georgia v. United States* reinforced its decision in *Allen*.[5] In *Georgia*, the Court contended that "had Congress disagreed with the interpretations of Section 5 in *Allen*, it had ample opportunity to amend the statute, [therefore,] we can only conclude ... that *Allen* [was] correctly interpreted."[6] In *Hadnott v. Amos*, the Court required federal approval of a change in the declaration deadline for independent candidates.[7] In *Perkins v. Matthews*, the Court required preclearance of a change in location of polling places as well as approval of a change from single-member district to at-large elections.[8] In *City of Petersburg, Virginia v. United States*, the Court ruled that annexations that diluted minority voting strength were illegal, even in the absence of an invidious or discriminatory intent.[9] Likewise, in *City of Rome v. United States*, the Court ruled that annexations violated the Voting Rights Act.[10] In *Rome*, the Court held that the change in electoral structure "would lead to a retrogression in the position of racial minorities with respect to their *effective* [emphasis added] exercise of the [franchise]."[11]

However, in *City of Richmond, Virginia v. United States* and *Beer v. United States*, the Court began to limit the scope of its interpretation of Section 5.[12] In both of these cases, the Court rejected Section 5 voting rights claims. In contrast to its preclearance inclusion of a broad range of election procedures in *Allen* and *Georgia*, the Court placed limitations on the type of changes it considered violative of Section 5 in *Beer* and *Richmond*. In *Beer*, the Court placed weight on the retrogression test of Section 5. In *Richmond*, the Court upheld an annexation that decreased the percentage of blacks in the population of Richmond, Virginia. According to the Court, "as long as the ward system fairly represents the voting strength of the Negro community as it exists after annexation we cannot hold ... that such an annexation is nevertheless barred by Section 5."[13] Despite the Court's ruling in *Richmond*, its focus on the dilutive effect of a reapportionment plan resulted in a deviation from a strict application of the *Beer* retrogression standard to a "dilutive effect" standard.[14]

The Court's ambiguity in Section 5 litigation reached its peak in *Presley v. Etowah County Commission*.[15] According to the Court, shifts in power on local governmental bodies were not covered by the preclearance provisions of Section 5 unless such changes resulted in disenfranchisement of a protected class. The Court concluded that the Voting Rights Act covers only four types of voting changes: 1) the manner of voting, such as switching from single-member districts to at-large elections; 2) candidate qualifications; 3) voter registration; and 4) creation or abolition of an elected office.[16] Furthermore, the Court held that election changes, in order to be declared violative of Section 5, must have a direct impact on the electoral process.

In *Presley*, Justice Stevens disagreed with the Court's interpretation of Section 5. In his dissenting opinion, Stevens emphasized that *Presley* resulted in the Court's ignoring "the broad scope of Section 5 coverage" established by its ruling in *Allen*.[17] Stevens concluded that "the reallocation of decision making authority of an elective office that is taken 1) after the victory of a black candidate, and 2) after the entry of a consent decree designed to give black voters an opportunity to have representation on an elective body [should be] covered by Section 5."[18]

The 1982 Amendment of Section 2

As a result of problems encountered by individuals and organizations pursuing voting rights complaints under Section 5, the case law of the Court on vote dilution mostly involves allegations of Section 2 violations. In 1982, Congress revised the language of Section 2 in an attempt to diminish the possible consequences of the Supreme Court's decision in *City of Mobile v. Bolden*, which placed a heavy evidentiary burden of proof on the plaintiffs in vote-dilution litigation.[19] Congress also relied on the Supreme Court's previous decision in *White v. Regester* and the decision of the Fifth Circuit Court of Appeals in *Zimmer v. McKeithen* in drafting the 1982 amendment.[20]

In *Mobile*, the Supreme Court employed a strict constructionist interpretation of the Fifteenth Amendment, holding that it ensured only the right to register and vote, and offered no protection against vote dilution. Moreover, the Court concluded that the Fourteenth Amendment did prohibit vote dilution, but only in those cases where it could be proved that an electoral procedure had been established for racially discriminatory purposes.

Not only did the Court devise the "intent" standard in *Mobile*, it also distinguished between disenfranchisement and vote dilution. According to the Court, the former prevents or discourages a group from voting, while the latter may exist even though people are permitted to vote. The Court held that proof of intentional discrimination was necessary to successfully demonstrate the employment of discriminatory voting practices. This standard placed an evidentiary burden of proof on plaintiffs in vote-dilution lawsuits.

The *Mobile* Court also rejected the *Zimmer* test, devised by the Fifth Circuit Court of Appeals in *Zimmer v. McKeithen*, thus requiring plaintiffs to provide proof of invidious or intentional discrimination in order to prevail in vote-dilution claims.[21] In *Zimmer*, the Fifth Circuit augmented the Supreme Court's ruling in *White* by providing a list of guidelines to be met in proving a vote-dilution claim. It is specifically Section 2(b) of the amended Act that contains the language of both *White* and *Zimmer*. Proof of a "totality of circumstances" as outlined in *Zimmer* is required to prove that "a voting qualification or prerequisite to voting or standard practice, or procedure ... imposed by any State or political subdivision ... results in a denial or abridgment of the right of any citizen of the United States to vote...."[22] Section 4(f)(2) of the Act extended this coverage to language minorities.

According to the *Zimmer* test, unconstitutional dilution is proved when an aggregate of these factors occurs: 1) lack of access to the process of slating candidates, 2) unresponsiveness of legislators to the particularized interests of the minority community, 3) a tenuous state policy underlying the preference for multimember or at-large districting, and 4) existence of past discrimination that generally precluded the effective participation of minorities in the political process.[23] Additional *Zimmer* factors that may be considered by the courts are anti-single shot voting requirements, existence of unusually large districts, majority vote requirements, and omission of provisions for residency requirements in geographical sub-districts in at-large elections.[24]

Section 2 originally protected only the act of voting, but Section 2 as amended in 1981 provided for the right to participate at every level (e.g., nomination, election, holding political office) of the political process. In short, the overall purpose of revising Section 2 was to reinstate and re-inforce the legislative intent of the Voting Rights Act following the *Mobile* decision. According to the Senate report, "this amendment is designed to make clear that proof of discriminatory intent is not re-quired to establish a violation of Section 2." It thereby restores the legal standards, based on the controlling Supreme Court precedents, which applied to voting dis-crimination claims prior to the litigation involved in *Mobile v. Bolden*.[25]

Additionally, Congress was very much aware of the Court's past inconsistency in deciding challenges to at-large election structures, and sought in its 1982 amend-ments to eliminate that ambiguity.[26] Ac-cordingly, Congress devised a "results" standard to be utilized by the courts in re-solving voting rights claims. The compo-nents of this new standard were outlined in the Senate report.[27] In effect the results standard nullified the intent standard de-vised by the Supreme Court in *Mobile*.

According to Congress, if "as a result of the challenged practice or structure plaintiffs do not have an equal opportu-nity to elect candidates of their choice, such a practice will be considered in vio-lation of the Act, specifically Section 2."[28] Additionally, the language of Section 2 prohibited both vote dilution and disen-franchisement.

The Court's Interpretation of Section 2 as Amended

Congress's amendment of Section 2 resulted in the filing of numerous lawsuits. The first case to reach the U.S. Supreme Court involving allegations of a Section 2 violation following the 1982 amendments was *Thornburg v. Gingles.*[29] It is important to emphasize that prior to *Gingles*, the Court had adjudicated a case involving the sub-ject of minority vote dilution, but the com-plaint in that instance was based on con-stitutional grounds, not the Voting Rights Act.[30] The Court ruled in *Rogers v. Lodge* that an at-large election system utilized by Burke County, Georgia resulted in minor-ity vote dilution and was thus violative of the equal protection of the laws guaran-teed by the Fourteenth Amendment.

Gingles originally was a 1984 case filed by black registered voters in North Car-olina challenging one single-member dis-trict and six multimember districts in the state's reapportionment plan.[31] The Plain-tiffs alleged that the plan concentrated blacks into a majority-white multimem-ber district resulting in vote dilution. Re-lying on the Senate report factors, the Dis-trict Court upheld the plaintiff's Section 2 claim, concluding that the totality of cir-cumstances were consistent with vote di-lution. The court's ruling with respect to five of the multimember districts was ap-pealed by the State of North Carolina.

On appeal to the United States Supreme Court, the state alleged that the District Court incorrectly concluded that the legislative reapportionment plan vio-lated Section 2. The Court unanimously affirmed the District Court ruling in four of the five multimember districts, but the justices split on the evidentiary standard to be applied in vote-dilution cases. This split resulted in the filing of four separate opinions, indicating a continued lack of consensus in judicial review of key Voting Rights Act provisions.

Despite its lack of consensus, the *Thornburg* Court devised a three-pronged test — the *Gingles* test — to detect justifiable vote dilution in multimember/at-large districts. This test requires plaintiffs alleging vote dilution to meet three criteria: The protected minority must demonstrate that 1) it is sufficiently large and geographically compact to constitute a majority in one or more single-member districts, 2) it is politically cohesive and tends to vote as a bloc, and 3) the majority vote sufficiently as a bloc to defeat the minority's preferred candidate.[32] The Court ruled that the *Gingles* factors were prerequisites that must be met to secure a determination of vote dilution.

Using similar reasoning as the Fifth Circuit in *Jones* and *McMillan* and the Eleventh Circuit in *Marengo* and *Dallas County*, the *Gingles* Court placed importance on the degree of racial bloc voting in vote-dilution cases.[33] In each of these cases, the circuit courts emphasized the importance of a finding of racial polarization in voting and pointed out that Section 2 did not require a demonstration of the existence of all of the factors included in Section 2. According to the courts, a showing of racial bloc voting is a prerequisite for a vote-dilution claim.

Of significance in *Gingles* was the Supreme Court's distinction between *legally significant* racial bloc voting (i.e., the degree of bloc voting required to prove a dilution claim) and racial polarization per se. Legally significant racial bloc voting requires plaintiffs to provide evidence of the existence of racial polarization that results in the inability of minorities to elect candidates of their choice.

In rendering a definition of legally significant racial bloc voting, the Court rejected the contention that proof of racial bloc voting should rest on the ability of minority voters to elect *minority* candidates of choice. According to the Court, "the fact that race of voter and race of candidate is often correlated is not directly pertinent to a Section 2 inquiry. Under Section 2, it is the *status* of the candidate as the *chosen representative of a particular racial group*, not the race of the candidate, that is important."[34]

Gingles provided clarity with regard to the accepted definition of racial polarization. The Court accepted a less stringent definition than that accepted by the lower courts in *Collins* and *McCord*.[35] The *Gingles* Court accepted the definition provided by the plaintiffs' expert witness, Dr. Bernard Grofman. According to Grofman, racial polarization is "a consistent relationship between race of the voter and the way in which he votes ... [or when] black voters and white voters vote differently."[36]

The *Gingles* Court also addressed the question of whether bivariate or multivariate analysis should be utilized to prove vote dilution. The lower courts had employed both methods.[37] The Supreme Court rejected the requirement of multivariate analysis, or the consideration of multiple factors in proving differential racial voting patterns. According to the Court, the proper question to ask is *whether* voters have divergent voting patterns on the basis of race, not *why* they vote differently. The court concluded that "it is the *difference* between the choices made by black and white voters and not the reasons for the differences that leads to blacks' having less opportunity to elect their candidates of choice."[38] Despite the *Gingles* Court's attempt to specify criteria that must be met by plaintiffs alleging vote dilution, its actual decision in *Thornburg v. Gingles* resulted in numerous unresolved questions, which have catalyzed additional debate over voting rights.[39] Some of the questions posed as a result of the *Gingles* decision include:

1. Should the courts be interested only in the presence of racial bloc voting, and not explanations for such differences?

2. Did the three-pronged *Gingles* test replace or complement the "totality of circumstances" test incorporated into the amended Section 2?

3. Are plaintiffs required to provide evidence of the presence of any of the factors included in Section 2 as amended in 1982?

4. Since *Gingles* focused primarily on the second factor in Section 2, how should the courts adjudicate cases involving the other inclusive factors of Section 2?

These unanswered questions resulted in conflicting decisions rendered by lower courts.[40]

Post-Thornburg Interpretation of Section 2

The United States Supreme Court did not revisit Section 2 until the early 1990s, in cases involving challenges to judicial election structures and processes.[41] These lawsuits forced the Court to provide clarity on its interpretation of Section 2, since the Fifth and Sixth Circuits differed in their respective interpretations of the applicability of Section 2 to the election of judges. The Fifth Circuit concluded in *Chisom v. Roemer* that Section 2 coverage did not extend to judicial contests since the explicit language of the Section — "to elect *representatives* of choice" — did not include judges, who are now viewed as representatives.[42] On the other hand, the Sixth Circuit held that Section 2 did apply to the election of judges.[43] In response to these conflicting rulings, the Supreme Court held in a Justice Department appeal of the *Chisom* ruling that Section 2 does indeed apply to judicial elections, opining

that Section 2 "protected the right to vote … without making any distinctions or imposing any limitations as to which elections would fall within its purview."[44]

To a certain degree, *Chisom* lessened the evidentiary burden imposed by the Court in *Gingles*. Even though the Court's decision in *Chisom* did not over-rule *Gingles*, the fact remains that although the plaintiffs in judicial challenges provided the Court with evidence to fulfill the results standard of Section 2, the majority opinion of the Court focused primarily on whether judges were representatives, rather than the issue of vote dilution. By centering on statutory interpretation of the legislative intent of Congress in revising Section 2, the Court, in effect, shifted the question in cases involving the election of judges from a results standard proving vote dilution to the ability of minorities to elect their preferred candidates — an influence standard. As a result, the Court opened a Pandora's Box which eventually led to what is considered by a number of observers to be one of its most infamous voting rights determinations.[45]

In response to the Court's decision in *Chisom*, many jurisdictions devised majority-minority single-member election districts. Opponents of such districts challenged their constitutionality by relying on the equal protection clause of the Fourteenth Amendment. As a result, the Court was faced with the formidable task of interpreting and balancing the protections set out in section 2 of the Voting Rights Act with those provided by the Fourteenth Amendment. The result has been an unwillingness to provide definitive and consistent rulings with regard to voting rights.

The ambiguity leads to a discussion of the most recent case law involving vote dilution.[46] In *Growe*, the Court rendered a decision with negative implications for minority voting rights. Even though the decision was cloaked in a consideration of judicial federalism, with the Court holding that states should have autonomy in reapportionment, the overall ruling resulted in an attack on the creation of majority-minority legislative districts. This case represented the initial reluctance of the Court to render a decision involving its interpretation of either Section 2 or the *Gingles* standard. Then, in *Voinovich*, a unanimous court upheld the creation of black-majority voting districts,[47] but during the same term questioned the constitutionality of race-conscious districting in *Shaw v. Reno*.[48]

In *Shaw*, the Court was asked to determine the constitutionality of the actions of the United States Department of Justice in its efforts to secure minority voting rights. *Shaw* represented a departure from a reliance on the Voting Rights Act and the Court's own precedents, since the plaintiffs in this case were not required to provide any evidentiary proof under Section 2 or in compliance with the *Gingles* test to prove the existence of vote dilution.[49] The results standard was completely ignored by the *Shaw* Court.

In subsequent voting rights cases, the Court's fragmentation has continued, with the dissenters emphasizing the Court's tenuousness and disregard of precedents. In the *Johnson* and *Holder* cases, a splintered Court narrowed the scope of Section 2 by concluding, respectively, that minorities in Florida were not entitled to additional majority-minority districts and that a grant of ultimate power to a single white county commissioner in Georgia did not deny African-Americans a voice in local government policy.[50]

The Court's decision in *Johnson* to a certain degree mirrored its reasoning in *Voinovich*, in which the Court concluded that the creation of majority-minority districts was permissible if it did not diminish minority voting strength. The *Voinovich* Court, however, included a qualifier by opining that a case-by-case approach should be employed to determine the constitutionality of such districts because the facts and circumstances of each might differ. Nonetheless, *Johnson* dramatizes the unwillingness of the Court to declare *all* majority-minority districts unconstitutional after its controversial ruling in *Shaw*.

Holder provided a clear indication that the members of the Court differ in their interpretations of Section 2 of the Voting Rights Act. Justice Souter's reasoning in *Johnson* led to his dissension in *Holder*. In *Johnson*, Souter, writing for the Court's majority, held the creation of majority-minority districts permissible in order to increase minority representation. However, this same reasoning was not applied in *Holder*. Three justices provided separate concurring opinions. In fact, Justice Thomas, in his dissenting opinion, advocated judicial restraint in voting rights cases, a narrow judicial interpretation of the Act, and the overturning of *Allen*.

Holder had been brought by black plaintiffs challenging a single-member county commission form of government in Bleckly, Georgia. The Court of Appeals for the Eleventh Circuit, finding that the form of government constituted an obstacle to minority voting and thus violated Section 2, ordered an expansion of the county commission. The Supreme Court reversed the appellate court's decision, holding that changes to the size of the governmental body or organization are not covered by the Voting Rights Act.

In *Miller*,[51] the Court declared a majority-minority congressional district in Georgia unconstitutional. The opinion of the Court rested on constitutional grounds—the Equal Protection Clause of the Fourteenth Amendment—rather than an interpretation of Section 2 of the Voting Rights Act or the three-pronged *Gingles* test. The *Miller* Court contended that neither *Shaw* nor *Miller* involved vote dilution claims, but equal protection claims, because states had employed race as a basis for "segregating" voters.

In essence, the *Miller* Court failed to recognize that it is impossible to comply with the mandates of sections 2 and 5 of the Voting Rights Act without a consideration of race (in many cases race may be the paramount factor). The Court has therefore made it very difficult for jurisdictions to meet the requirements of the Voting Rights Act without violating the equal protection guarantees of the Fourteenth Amendment.

Conclusion

The United States Supreme Court has been consistently vague in its interpretation of Sections 2 and 5 of the Voting Rights Act. This ambiguity has resulted in both plaintiffs and defendants in vote-dilution cases attempting to meet evidentiary proof requirements as the Court continues to devise new modes of interpretation, ignores precedents, and fails to uniformly apply provisions of the Act.

In light of the fact that the Court has in many cases abandoned its own voting rights precedents, lower courts— as well as parties involved in vote-dilution claims— lack clear guidance to follow in such cases.

In addition, the Court's holdings in the most recent cases have had serious ramifications relative to the political gains of minorities. These decisions have carried minority voting rights back to the second era of vote-dilution litigation, during which the Court rendered its *Mobile* decision. In fact, the Court's interpretation and application of the three-pronged test in *Gingles* has resulted in a return to the "intent" standard of *Bolden*.

Additionally, an overwhelming impact of the Court's tenuousness on the issue of voting rights constitutes what this author refers to as "vote dilutigation," in which attorneys and others opposed to ensuring the full electoral participation of minorities have devised standards and statistical interpretations that serve the same purpose as earlier barriers to voting, such as large, multimember districts and anti-single-shot provisions.

It is time to refocus the voting rights debate on the proper role of the judiciary in extending and enforcing minority political access. Such a reframing of the debate will require legislative involvement, just as it did when the Supreme Court rendered its decision in *Mobile*. However, the ultimate question is this: Will a conservatively oriented legislative branch place limitations on a conservative court?

Notes

1. *Thornburg v. Gingles*, 478 U.S. 30 (1986).

2. H.R. Rep. Ser. No. 9, 99th Cong., 2d Sess. 11 (1986). See also, 28 C.F.R. Section 51.55. The amended Section 5 reads: "(a) Section 5 of the Voting Rights Act of 1965 as amended, 42 U.S.C. 1973c [1988], prohibits the enforcement in any jurisdiction covered by Section 4(b) of the Act, 42 U.S.C. 1973b(b), of any voting qualification or prerequisite of voting or standard, practice, or procedure with respect to voting different from that in force or effect on the date used to determine coverage, until either: (1) A declaratory judgment is obtained from the U.S. District Court for the District of Columbia that such qualification, prerequisite, standard, practice, or procedure does not have the purpose and will not have the effect of denying or abridging the right to vote on account of race, color, or membership in a language minority group, or (2) It has been submitted to the Attorney General and the Attorney General has interposed no objection within a 60-day period following submission. (b) In order to make clear the responsibilities of the Attorney General under Section 5 and the interpretation of the Attorney General of the responsibility imposed on other under this

Section, the procedures in this part have been established to govern the administration of Section 5."

3. Section 4(f)(2) reads: "(2) To assist the Court in determining whether to issue a declaratory judgment under this subsection, the plaintiff shall present evidence of minority participation, including evidence of the levels of minority group registration and voting, changes in such levels over time, and disparities between minority-group and non-minority-group participation." See also, C.F.R. Section 51.2.

4. *Allen v. State Board of Elections*, 393 U.S. 544 (1969).

5. *Georgia v. United States*, 411 U.S. 526 (1973).

6. *Georgia v. United States*, 411 U.S. at 534.

7. *Hadnott v. Amos*, 394 U.S. at 358 (1969).

8. *Perkins v. Matthews*, 400 U.S. at 379 (1971).

9. *Petersburg v. United States*, 410 U.S. at 962 (1973).

10. *City of Rome v. United States*, 446 U.S. at 156 (1980).

11. *City of Rome v. United States*, 446 U.S. at 156.

12. *City of Richmond v. United States*, 422 U.S. at 358 (1975); *Beer v. United States*, 425 U.S. at 130 (1976).

13. *City of Richmond v. United States*, 422 U.S. at 371.

14. This standard was developed by the Court in *Petersburg* and first applied in *Richmond*.

15. *Presley v. Etowah County Commission*, 112 S. Ct. at 820 (1992). *Presley* involved separate challenges by black commissioners of Etowah and Russell Counties, Alabama. These commissioners filed a single complaint alleging that the restructuring of the county commissions resulted in racial discrimination in violation of the U.S. Constitution, civil rights statutes, court orders, and Section 5 of the Voting Rights Act.

16. *Presley v. Etowah County Commission*, 112 S. Ct. at 828.

17. *Presley v. Etowah County Commission*, 112 S. Ct. at 836.

18. *Presley v. Etowah County Commission*, 112 S. Ct. at 839.

19. *Voting Rights Act of 1982*, 96 Stat. 131, 42 U.S.C.A. Section 1973.

20. *White v. Regester*, 412 U.S. 755 (1973) and *Zimmer v. McKeithen*, 485 F.2d 1297 (5th Cir. 1973).

21. *Zimmer v. McKeithen*, 485 F.2d 1297 (5th Cir. 1973).

22. See, *Voting Rights Act of 1982*, 96 Stat. 134, 42 U.S.C. Section 1973 (1988).

23. *Zimmer v. McKeithen*, 485 F.2d 1297 (5th Cir. 1973).

24. *Zimmer v. McKeithen*, 485 F.2d 1297 (5th Cir. 1973).

25. U.S. Senate, 1982, p. 2.

26. See, Senate Judiciary Report on the Extension of the Voting Rights Act, Rep. No. 97–417, 97th Cong., 2d Sess., pp. 19–27 (1982).

27. Senate Judiciary Report on the Extension of the Voting Rights Act, Rep. No. 97–417, 97th Cong., 2d Sess. at 19–27 (1982).

28. House of Representatives 1981 at 29; Senate 1982b at 28, 36–37.

29. *Thornburg v. Gingles*, 478 U.S. at 30 (1986).

30. *Rogers v. Lodge*, 458 U.S. at 613 (1982).

31. *Gingles v. Edmisten*, 590 F.Supp. at 345 (E.D.N.C. 1984), *aff'd. sub nom Thornburg v. Gingles*, 478 U.S. at 30 (1986).

32. *Gingles v. Edmisten*, 590 F.Supp. at 345 (E.D.N.C. 1984), *aff'd. sub nom Thornburg v. Gingles*, 478 U.S. at 30 (1986).

33. *Jones v. City of Lubbock, Texas*, 727 F.2d at 364 (5th Cir. 1984); *U.S. v. Marengo County Commission*, 731 F.2d at 1546 (11th Cir. 1984); *McMillan v. Escambia County*, 748 F.2d at 1037 (5th Cir. 1984); *Lee County Branch of NAACP v. City of Opelika*, 748 F.2d at 147 (11th Cir. 1984).

34. *Gingles v. Edmisten*, 590 F.Supp. at 345 (E.D.N.C. 1984), *aff'd. sub nom Thornburg v. Gingles*, 478 U.S. at 30 (1986).

35. *Collins v. City of Norfolk*, 605 F.Supp. at 377 (E.D. Va. 1984); *aff'd.* 768 F.2d at 572 (4th Cir. 1985); *rev'd.* 816 F.2d at 932 (4th Cir. 1987); 679 F.Supp. (E.D. Va. 1988); 883 F.2d at 1232 (4th Cir. 1989); *McCord v. City of Fort Lauderdale*, 787 F.2d at 1528 (11th Cir. 1986).

36. *Thornburg v. Gingles*, 478 U.S. at 53.

37. Bivariate analysis was utilized in *Jones*, *Marengo County* and *McMillan*. On the other hand, multivariate analysis was employed in *Opelika*, *Collins* and *McCord*.

38. *Thornburg v. Gingles*, 478 U.S. at 63.

39. See, Bernard Grofman, Lisa Handley and Richard Niemi, *Minority Representation and the Quest for Voting Equality* (Cambridge University Press, 1992). For a discussion of the unresolved issues flowing from the *Gingles* test, see, Robert Heath, "*Thornburg v. Gingles*: The Unresolved Issues," *National Civic Review*, January–February 1990, pp. 50–71.

40. *Buckanaga v. Sisseton Independent School District*, 804 F.2d at 469 (8th Cir. 1989).

41. See, *Georgia State Board of Elections v. Brooks*, 498 U.S. at 916 (1990); *Chisom v. Roemer*, 111 S.Ct. at 2354 (1991), and companion cases *United States v. Roemer*, 111 S.Ct. at 2354 (1991) and *Houston Lawyers' Association v. Texas Attorney General*, 501 U.S. at 419 (1991).

42. *League of United Latin American Citizens Council No. 4434 [LULAC] v. Clements*, 914 F.2d at 620 (5th Cir. 1990).

43. *Mallory v. Eyrich*, 839 F.2d at 275 (6th Cir. 1988).

44. *United States v. Roemer*, 111 S.Ct. at 2354 (1991).

45. *Shaw v. Reno*, 113 S.Ct. at 2816 (1993).

46. *Growe, Secretary of State of Minnesota v. Emison*, 113 S.Ct. at 1075 (1993). See also, *Shaw v. Reno*, 113 S.Ct at 2816 (1993); *In re Voinovich et al.*, 114 S.Ct. at 2156 (1994); *Johnson v. DeGrandy*, 114 S.Ct. at 2647 (1994); *Miller et al. v. Johnson et al.*, No. 94–631 (1995).

47. *In re Voinovich et al.*, 114 S.Ct. at 2156 (1994).

48. *Shaw v. Reno*, 113 S.Ct. at 2816 (1993).

49. See dissenting opinions of Justices White, Blackmun, Stevens, and Souter.

50. *Johnson v. DeGrandy*, 114 S.Ct. at 2647 (1994) and *Holder v. Hall*, 114 S.Ct. at 2581 (1994).

51. The *Miller* decision has not yet been published, but may be identified by its case number 94–631.

· *Chapter 4* ·

Redistricting and the Supreme Court

Richard L. Engstrom

Contiguity, compactness, and respect for both communities of interest and formal political subdivisions are districting criteria that have been elevated in importance recently by the United States Supreme Court. Although none of these criteria is required by the federal constitution or any federal statute, the Court identified them in *Miller v. Johnson* as "traditional, race-neutral districting principles" that, absent extraordinary justification, are not to be "subordinated" to racial considerations when representational districts are constructed.[1] These traditional criteria now serve, in Justice Sandra Day O'Connor's words, as "a crucial frame of reference" in the evaluation of districts.[2] If they are accorded less weight than race in the design of a district, the district must satisfy the strict scrutiny standard for compliance with the Fourteenth Amendment, which means the district must be "narrowly tailored" to further a "compelling governmental interest." Strict scrutiny is popularly described as "strict in theory but fatal in fact."

Miller involved a challenge to the Eleventh Congressional District in Georgia. The plaintiffs alleged that this majority African-American district was a "racial gerrymander." The allegation was not based on a claim that any racial group's voting strength had been diluted by the location of the district lines, but simply that this particular district had been deliberately constructed to have an African-American majority. The Court found that race had indeed been "the predominant factor" in the design of the district, and that this had occurred at the expense of the traditional districting criteria.[3] Strict scrutiny was therefore applied, and the district was found to be fatally flawed.

Miller is the progeny of *Shaw v. Reno*,

Originally published as "The Supreme Court on Redistricting," *National Civic Review*, Vol. 84, No. 4, Fall/Winter, 1995. Published by the National Civic League Press, Denver, Colorado. Reprinted with permission of the publisher.

a 1993 decision involving majority African-American congressional districts in North Carolina.[4] The Court held in *Shaw* that race-based districting could be challenged as a violation of the equal protection clause even though there is no allegation that the voting strength of any racial group is adversely affected by the districts. Although *Shaw* failed to resolve this new type of "gerrymandering" claim, it succeeded in attracting increased attention to the criteria for drawing districts by holding that strict scrutiny will be required when "traditional districting principles such as compactness, contiguity, and respect for political subdivisions" are disregarded in the design of districts.[5] *Miller* was the first application of the *Shaw* precedent by the Supreme Court. The principle of respecting "communities defined by actual shared interests" was added to the list of traditional districting criteria in *Miller*.[6]

The explicit recognition of these criteria will no doubt make them more important referents for future districting decisions. Those who design and/or adopt districting plans will not want to subject their product to strict scrutiny, and therefore will be less inclined to deviate from these criteria. This will not, however, make the districting task any easier. It is, in contrast, likely to make districting more difficult, because what exactly these criteria entail is far from certain.

The absence of clear definitions for some of these criteria, as well as clear standards for identifying when they have been "respected" and when they have been "subordinated," leaves districting cartographers, litigators, advocates, and judges in a conceptual thicket. This is already apparent in the post–*Shaw* decision of the lower federal courts. This ambiguity is exacerbated by the fact that these traditional criteria are often in conflict rather than in harmony. Emphasizing one criterion, quite simply, can interfere with implementing

another. Communities of interest, for example, may not be geographically distributed in a compact fashion and can be split by county and municipal boundaries. No agreed-upon hierarchy of these criteria exists to help resolve such conflicts.

Even assuming that these criteria can be clearly defined and readily measured, and therefore capable of providing an unambiguous "frame of reference," what exactly the standard for comparison will be also remains unclear. Will courts compare the respect accorded these criteria to some absolute standard, or to the respect actually accorded them in the past? Given that the Supreme Court has acknowledged that none of these criteria is constitutionally required,[7] it is not likely that some absolute standard will be judicially imposed. Nor, presumably, will the tolerance for deviations from these criteria be less because a gerrymandering allegation concerns race. Justice O'Connor's statement, in her concurrence in *Miller*, that "certainly the standard does not treat efforts to create majority-minority districts *less* favorably than similar efforts on behalf of other groups"[8] indicates that deviations tolerated in the past, for non-racial purposes, will continue to be acceptable in the racial context. If that is the law, then the frame of reference will have to allow substantial deviations in many states and local political jurisdictions, for the application of these criteria has not been particularly strict. Indeed, their subordination to political considerations has been substantial, even when explicitly required by state constitutions or statutes or by city charters.

The conceptual ambiguity surrounding these districting criteria, and the new subordination standard, is a cause for serious concern. Adherence to these traditional principles does not extricate those responsible for districting from the "political thicket," but rather confronts them with capricious definitions and contrasting measurements, as evident in the litigation spawned by *Shaw*. Elevating the legal importance of these criteria, without more precise guidelines for their application, will not bring us closer to the goal of "fair and effective representation."[9] While these criteria may be facially neutral, districting is, unfortunately, an activity in which "the potential for mischief in the name of neutrality is substantial."[10]

This chapter reviews the criteria identified in the *Shaw* and *Miller* decisions. Special attention will be given to their treatment by the federal district courts in the gerrymandering litigation following the *Shaw* decision, and to their new role as a "frame of reference" in the post–*Miller* districting process.

Contiguity

Contiguity and compactness are criteria widely invoked in the evaluation of districts. They are conceptually distinct criteria that concern different aspects of the geographical form of districts. Many state constitutions, statutes, and local charters required representational districts to be contiguous; far fewer require them to be compact.[11]

Contiguity is, or at least was, the most straightforward of the criteria identified by the Court. It is a simple dichotomous concept. A district is either contiguous or it is not. The test for determining this is not complicated, "A contiguous district is one in which a person can go from any point within the district to any other point [within the district] without leaving the district."[12] In short, contiguity requires that districts not be divided into discrete geographical parts.

The lack of confusion over what contiguity entails rarely has resulted in controversy. The major issue concerning contiguity involves whether the ability to travel throughout a district is a theoretical or a literal requirement. This usually arises when bodies of water serve to connect what are otherwise separate parts of a district. Some contiguity provisions require an actual transportation linkage across any water separating parts of a district, such as that in the New York City Charter, which specifies that "there shall be a connection by a bridge, a tunnel, a tramway or by regular ferry service."[13] Additional controversy has arisen over whether having parts of a district connecting only at a point satisfies the criterion of contiguity.

Until *Shaw*, it could be said that "Contiguity is a relatively trivial requirement and usually a noncontroversial one."[14] Lower court decisions following *Shaw*, however, have created confusion about what "contiguity" now requires. Some judges have not been convinced that districts that meet the traditional definition of contiguity satisfy this criterion. In a case involving Louisiana's congressional districts, for example, a federal court held that a majority African-American district that was only 80 feet wide in places complied with this criterion, "but only hypertechnically and thus cynically," and that "Such tokenism mocks the traditional criterion of contiguity."[15] The expression "technical contiguity" has been applied to other majority-minority districts in other post-*Shaw* decisions.[16] Some courts even have begun to treat contiguity as a continuous concept, as if some districts can be viewed as "more" or "less" contiguous than others.[17]

This approach to contiguity has been an unfortunate development. It commingles the notion of contiguity with that of compactness, treating the two as if they are synonymous. A district that is never less than 80 miles wide may well be more compact that one that is 80 feet wide at points, but it should not be considered "more contiguous" for that reason as well. These are distinct criteria that concern different aspects of the geographical form that districts can assume. A district should not be found to violate the contiguity criterion simply because its shape violates the compactness criterion.

Compactness

In contrast to contiguity, the compactness criterion has always been a matter of considerable ambiguity. It concerns the shape of districts, not whether they contain geographically discrete parts. Compactness is a continuous concept. Districts can be considered more or less compact, and therefore this criterion, unlike contiguity, has been the object of a great variety of quantitative measurements. In fact, there is "no generally accepted definition" of what exactly compactness entails, and therefore no generally accepted measure of it either.[18]

Compactness is legally required less often than contiguity,[19] and there is far less consensus about its importance in the design of districts. The linkage between the shapes districts assume and the quality of representation district residents receive has long been questioned. As candidly expressed by one set of commentators:

> It is, in truth, hard to develop a powerful case for the intrinsic value of having compact districts: If the representative lived at the center of a compact district, he or she wouldn't have to travel any more than absolutely necessary to campaign door-to-door or meet with constituents, but other than that, uncompactness does not seem to affect representation in any way.[20]

A compactness requirement is widely touted, however, as an impediment to gerrymandering. It will rarely preclude gerrymandering, at least the dilutive kind, because that type of gerrymandering is not limited to funny-shaped districts. Indeed, a compactness rule, in some circumstances, could even serve as an excuse for this type of gerrymander.[21] But it is at least a constraint on the way in which district lines can be drawn and therefore an impediment of the manipulation of those lines for political advantage. Odd-shaped districts do stimulate suspicions of deliberate manipulation, and therefore districting is an area, as Justice O'Connor observed in *Shaw*, "in which appearances do matter."[22]

Since *Shaw* elevated the concern for compactness, lower courts have been confronted with a wide array of quantitative indicators that supposedly reveal the relative compactness of districts.[23] These measures emphasize different aspects of shapes, however, and therefore can and do result in conflicting conclusions. Even bizarrely shaped districts can satisfy some of the tests. The measures also vary greatly in complexity. The simplest is based on the length of district boundaries. The shorter the length, the more compact a district is considered to be. Other measures examine the extent to which district shapes deviate from some specified standard, such as a circle or a square, or the extent to which a district fills the area of a polygon encasing it.

New measures have been proposed that depart from the notion of geographical appearances, focusing instead on the physical distances between the homes of the people residing within a district.[24] A federal court in California recently departed even further from the traditional concern for shape and adopted the notion of "functional compactness," holding [that] "Compactness does not refer to geometric shapes but the ability of citizens to relate to each other and their representatives and the ability of representatives to relate effectively to their constituency."[25]

The variation in approaches does not

end here, either. Just as the federal court in Louisiana commingled contiguity with compactness, the federal court handling the *Miller* case commingled communities of interest with compactness. After reviewing several approaches to measuring geographical compactness, that court chose to rely instead on a population-based approach that would "require an assessment of population densities, shared history and common interests; essentially, whether the populations roped into a particular district are close enough geographically, economically, and culturally to justify their being held in a single district.[26] The Supreme Court affirmed both the California decision (rejecting a *Shaw*-type claim) and the *Miller* decision without commenting on what compactness actually entails.

With this type of confusion over the concept of "compactness," requiring that districts not be subordinated to a compactness standard will not simplify the districting task. Districting decisions are likely to be more, not less, difficult in this context. Without some clarity concerning this constraint, those designing and/or adopting districts cannot be expected to know the limitations under which they must work.

Communities of Interest

Many sets of equi-populous districts can usually be created, even when contiguity is required and some type of compactness constraint is applied. Ideally, however, districts should be more than arbitrary aggregations of individuals. The use of geographically based districts is premised on the notion that people who reside close to one another share interests. Geographical proximity is assumed to either cause or reflect, distinct interests and policy preferences. When such "communities of interest" exist, it is often suggested that they be maintained intact within representational districts.

The communities of interest standard is unfortunately "probably the least well defined" criterion for drawing districts.[27] Serious problems arise in identifying such communities, as well as deciding which ones deserve to be recognized in the design of districts. This criterion was not listed among the traditional districting principles in *Shaw*, and therefore has not received as much attention from the lower courts as has compactness. Respect for "communities defined by actual shared interests" was added to the list in *Miller*, however, with little indication of how this concept is to be applied.

One of the principle questions in light of *Miller* is whether this criterion concerns "shared interests" among people living in geographical proximity to each other, or whether it concerns the degree to which districts themselves are homogeneous along some dimension or dimensions. In *Miller*, Justice Anthony Kennedy said that "A State is free to recognize communities that have a particular racial makeup, provided its action is directed toward some common thread of relevant interests."[28] The fact that this comment was immediately followed by a quote from *Shaw* indicating that it would be legitimate to concentrate minority group members in a single district—when they "live together in one community"—suggests that the concept may require geographic proximity.[29] But when Justice Kennedy concluded that the district at issue in *Miller* "tells a tale of disparity, not community," he was explicitly referencing "the social, political and economic makeup" of the district as a whole. African-Americans in the Savannah area had been joined with African-Americans in metropolitan Atlanta, thereby linking, according to Kennedy, African-Americans who were "worlds apart in culture."[30]

This issue is central to the North Carolina congressional districting case, which will be reviewed by the Supreme Court during its 1995–96 term. In North Carolina the district court identified the state's two majority African-American congressional districts as distinctive in character, one being rural and the other urban. This resulted from the legislature's concern that districts reflect "significant communities of interest."[31] The application of this criterion to these districts was very systematic; a guideline was adopted that at least 80 percent of the population of one district reside outside cities with populations exceeding 20,000, and at least 80 percent of the population of the other reside within cities exceeding 20,000. This resulted in districts that are far from compact, but which, according to the district court, have "substantial, relatively high degrees of homogeneity of shared socio-economic — hence political — interests and needs among [their] citizens."[32]

Justice Kennedy did not state that the "mere recitation of purported communities of interest" will not successfully invoke this criterion.[33] Simply referencing well known geographical place names presumably will not suffice. Identifying an area as containing people with particular traits, such as ethnic or religious identifications or life-style preferences, may be sufficient, provided the particular interest[s] shared are documented. But which "shared interests" deserve recognition in districting, and whether this recognition extends to people who share an applicable interest but do not reside in close geographical proximity to each other, remain to be determined. This is a districting criterion that has never been well specified, and is unlikely to be clearly defined prior to the next round of redistricting following the 2000 census.

Political Subdivisions

The final traditional criterion on the Supreme Court's list is respect for political subdivisions. Local units of government, especially counties, have often served as building blocks for state legislative and congressional districts. Prior to the Supreme Court's adoption of the "one person, one vote" principle, counties were even the units to which legislative seats were apportioned in many of the states.[34] Not dividing counties among districts, unless necessary to equalize populations, has been a common districting constraint.[35] Following established political boundaries such as these is said to keep districts more cognizable to voters.

Political subdivisions are recognized by law, and there should be no problem in identifying them and in determining whether or not they have been divided by representational district lines. This is a simple matter of counting. There may be arguments, however, over which political subdivisions to include in the count. Counties, as noted, had been the major focus prior to *Shaw* and *Miller*, but the treatment of other subdivisions could be examined as well. The district court in Louisiana, for example, referenced how the state's congressional districts divided "major municipalities" as well as counties.[36] The list could include other units as well, such as school districts, other types of special districts, or townships. Where the list ends is an issue in need of resolution.

Simply counting the number of units divided by a district or districts may not be the appropriate basis for evaluation, either. Whereas the court in Louisiana found the splitting of municipalities to be objectionable *per se*, the federal court in Texas congressional districting case responded very differently. The fact that cities in Texas had been divided between districts was not viewed as a negative, despite the divisions being along racial lines. The court noted instead that these divisions "gave the Congressmen a toe-hold in such cities and effectively doubled the cities' representation in Congress."[37] Other issues include such things as "How many splits are too many?" and "Is a little split from a single unit as bad as a big split?[38]

Another related issue is the respect to be accorded precinct lines. Precincts are not governmental jurisdictions, but merely administrative units for elections. It is often argued that precincts should not be divided by districts, but this is simply a matter of administrative convenience. Requiring districts to follow preexisting precinct boundaries can impede the achievement of other, more important districting goals, such as creating majority-minority districts, and courts should not allow this constraint to be a pretext for discriminatory districting. Precincts can be changed relatively easily to accommodate more important districting criteria.

Frame of Reference

Traditional race-neutral districting criteria are now supposed to provide a frame of reference for evaluating *Shaw*- and *Miller*-type gerrymandering allegations. The districting criteria discussed above are those that the Supreme Court has explicitly recognized as falling within that category. The Court made it clear in *Miller*, however, that it did not consider these to be an exhaustive list of such principles.[39] While the Court provided no indication of the other types of criteria that might be employed to evaluate these allegations, it did leave some of Georgia's expressed criteria off the list, perhaps indicating that these criteria are not to be included.

The Georgia legislature had adopted districting "guidelines" that included, in addition to contiguity and respect for political subdivisions, the protection of incumbent office holders. This was expressed through two separate guidelines. One was "avoiding contests between incumbents," the other was "preserving the core of existing districts," which functions largely as a euphemism for incumbent protection.[40] Georgia had elevated one of the venerable unwritten rules of redistricting — save the incumbents! — to the status of an explicit guideline.[41] Indeed, even the federal court in Georgia had included "protecting incumbents" among its list of "traditional districting principles."[42] The absence of this criterion in the Supreme Court's recitation of principles may reflect the fact that this criterion, while traditional, has hardly been "race-neutral" in application, given the over-representation of whites (or Anglos) in elected offices.

Another question concerning the use of the recognized criteria as a frame of reference concerns, as noted above, the standard for comparison. While protecting incumbents may not make the list of traditional criteria, it is not by itself an impermissible districting goal,[43] and has often been a reason for deviating from the other criteria. The federal court in Louisiana, for example, acknowledged that the compactness criterion, not required by any Louisiana law, had been trumped by incumbent protection considerations in previous congressional districting schemes of that state. The "Old Eighth" district, which the court described as "certainly bizarre" in shape, was admittedly "crafted for the purpose of ensuring the reelection of Congressman Gillis Long."[44] Will districts drawn to enhance the electoral opportunities of African-Americans in Louisiana therefore also be allowed to be bizarre or at least no more bizarre, or will such districts be held to a higher standard?[45]

Traditional districting principles often have been subordinated to nonracial political goals, of course, without any requirement that such subordination be justified. This is illustrated by another Supreme Court case, *Gaffney v. Cummings*, which involved districts for the lower house of the Connecticut state legislature.[46] The parallels between *Gaffney* and the *Shaw* and *Miller* cases are striking, except the issue in *Gaffney* is the deliberate manipulation of district boundaries for partisan rather than racial reasons.

In designing Connecticut's legislative districts, two of the traditional criteria cited in *Shaw* and *Miller*, compactness and respect for political subdivisions (the latter even a requirement of the Connecticut Constitution), were clearly subordinated to a purported goal of providing "proportional representation." The proportionality in this case concerned the representation of the state's Republican and Democratic voters. The Supreme Court found that "The record abounds with evidence, and it is frankly admitted by those who prepared the plan, that virtually every Senate and House district line was drawn with the conscious intent to create a districting plan that would achieve a rough approximation of the statewide political strengths of the Democratic and Republican Parties."[47]

While the Connecticut plan has been described as "a bipartisan gerrymander,"[48] it was not, in fact, the product of any bipartisan agreement. It was developed by the Republican party's representative to a three-person apportionment board, with the assistance of counsel to the state Republican party, and was vigorously opposed by the Democratic party's representative on the board. (The decisive vote was provided by the third member of the board, who had been selected by the two party appointees.) The plans were subsequently challenged by Democratic plaintiffs as "a gigantic gerrymander."[49] A large number of Republican party supporters were concentrated in one geographical area of the state, and therefore districts based on neutral districting principles would result in many Republican votes being wasted in safe Republican districts. The plaintiffs argued that the architects of the plan had deliberately gerrymandered the districts across the state in order to offset this unfavorable (for districting purposes) geographical pattern of Republican support.[50]

The federal district court in Connecticut found that districts in the plan had "highly irregular and bizarre outlines."[51] The state acknowledged the fact that districts had been made less compact than otherwise necessary in order to achieve the desired partisan balance among the districts. This was also "frankly admitted by those who prepared the plan."[52] Indeed, in defending the distorted shapes of the districts, the state rejected the notion that districts should be held to a compactness standard, of any type, stating:

> Compactness has no necessary relation to the devising of districts to provide fair and effective representation because the crucial variables are the residential patterns of the persons to be represented. Noncompactness could be the only way to provide even minimal representation of a scattered minority.[53]

Another neutral districting criterion, respect for political subdivisions, was also subordinated to the proportionality goal. In this case, the criterion was actually a state constitutional requirement. The Connecticut Constitution contained a prohibition against dividing towns when creating state assembly districts, and this criterion was also violated more than necessary so that districts would have particular partisan configurations.[54] This was also frankly acknowledged by the authors of the plan. Its chief architect testified, "We considered keeping the breaking of town lines within as reasonable limits as we could but where there were other considerations of fairness [proportional representation] that overrode that, I did not insist the town lines be maintained exact."[55] His assistant likewise testified:

A. I cut town lines which were in my opinion necessary.

Q. In order to achieve the political balance?

A. In order to achieve the balance, yes.[56]

The subordination of these traditional criteria in this context produced no adverse comment by the Supreme Court. They certainly did not constitute "a crucial frame of reference" for the Courts' evaluation of these state legislative districts.

The districting criteria the Court has recognized as constituting the frame of reference have not been rigidly adhered to in the past. They have, in contrast, often been subordinated to political considerations. In light of Justice O'Connor's comment that majority-minority districts will not be held to a higher standard, presumably past practices rather than political science texts will be the point of comparison. Whether deviations from these criteria resulting from nondilutive racial considerations will be no less tolerable than past, or even present, deviations due to other acceptable political considerations, however, remains to be seen. While Justice O'Connor's words no doubt were meant to reassure minority voters that a double standard was not being adopted, no other justice in the majority joined her in that gesture.[57]

Conclusion

The *Shaw* and *Miller* decisions have made several districting criteria the frame of reference for adjudicating allegations of racial gerrymandering. These criteria, unfortunately, are neither well defined nor easily measured; moreover, they have not all been strictly applied prior to these decisions. Even contiguity, which was once the clearest of the criteria, is now clouded in ambiguity and no longer readily distinguishable from compactness.

The confusion surrounding these criteria themselves, as well as the standards for determining when they are respected and when they are subordinated, are a cause for concern. The districting task is difficult enough without adding this additional complexity to the process. The Supreme Court will review cases concerning congressional districts in North Carolina and Texas during its next term. Hopefully the Court will see the need to begin clarifying the components and application of the new frame of reference it has created. Without such clarification, redistricting in the post-*Miller* era will indeed be, as Justice Ruth Bader Ginsburg has predicted, "perilous work for state legislatures,"[58] not to mention county boards, city councils, school boards, and any other person or group who may be responsible for structuring representational districts.

Notes

1. The decision in *Miller v. Johnson* has not yet been published but the "slip opinion" may be identified by the following case numbers: 94–631, 94–797 and 94–929.

2. *Miller*, sl. op. at 1 (O'Connor, concurring).

3. *Miller*, sl. op. at 17–18.

4. *Shaw v. Reno*, 113 S.Ct. 2816 (1993).

5. *Shaw*, sl. op. at 15.

6. *Miller*, sl. op. at 15.

7. *Shaw*, sl. op. at 15.

8. *Miller*, sl. op. at 1 (O'Connor, J., concurring) (emphasis in original).

9. *Reynolds v. Sims*, 377 U.S. 533, 565–566 (1964).

10. David Butler and Bruce Cain, *Congressional Redistricting: Comparative and Theoretical Perspectives* (New York: MacMillan Publishing Co., 1992), p. 150.

11. See Bernard Grofman, "Criteria for Districting: A Social Science Perspective," 33 *UCLA Law Review* (October 1985), pp. 177–183; Richard H. Pildes and Richard G. Niemi, "Expressive Harms 'Bizarre Districts,' and Voting Rights: Evaluation Election-District Appearances after *Shaw v. Reno*," 92 *Michigan Law Review* (December 1992), pp. 528–531; and W.E. Lyons and Malcolm E. Jewell, "Redrawing Council Districts in American Cities," 18 *State and Local Government Review*, (Spring 1986), p. 76.

12. Note, "Reapportionment," 79 *Harvard Law Review*, (April, 1966), p. 1284.

13. N.Y.C. Charter ch. 2, sec. 52 (2).

14. Bernard Grofman, "Criteria for Districting," p. 84

15. *Hayes v. State of Louisiana*, 839 F. Supp. 1188, 1200 (E.D. La. 1993).

16. *Shaw v. Hunt*, 861 F. Supp. 408, 468 (E.D. N.C. 1994) and *Johnson v. Miller*, 864 F. Supp. 1354, 1368 (S.D. Ga. 1994).

17. *Shaw*, at 452. See also *Vera v. Richards*, 861 F. Supp. 1304, 1338, 1342 (S.D. Tex. 1994). It has also been suggested that "...'contiguity' is not an abstract or geometric technical phase. It assumes meaning when seen in combination with concepts of 'regional integrity' and 'community of interest.'" *DeWitt v. Wilson*, 856 F. Supp. 1409, 1414 (E.D. Cal. 1994).

18. *Shaw v. Hunt*, at 452; see also *Johnson*, at 1388.

19. See Lyons and Jewell, "Redrawing Council Districts," at 76.

20. Charles Backstrom, Leonard Robbins, and Scott Eller, "Establishing a Statewide Electoral Effects Baseline," in Bernard Grofman (ed.) *Political Gerrymandering and the Courts* (New York: Agathon Press, 1990), p. 152.

21. See David Butler and Bruce Cain, *Congressional Redistricting*, pp. 149–150.

22. *Shaw*, sl. op. at 15

23. See especially *Johnson*, at 1388–1390, and *Vera*, at 1329–1330.

24. See generally Richard G. Niemi, Bernard Grofman, Carl Carlucci, and Thomas Hofeller, "Measuring Compactness and the Role of a Compactness Standard in a Test for Partisan and Racial Gerrymandering," 52 *Journal of Politics*, (November 1990), 1155–1181, and H.P. Young, "Measuring the Compactness of Legislative Districts," 13 *Legislative Studies Quarterly*, (February 1988), 105–115.

25. *DeWitt*, at 1414.

26. *Johnson*, at 1389; see also *Vera* at 1341.

27. *DeWitt v. Wilson*, (unsigned, one-paragraph order, issued by Supreme Court on June 29, 1995, upholding California's 1992 redistricting plan).

28. Richard Morrill, "A Geographer's Perspective," in Bernard Grofman, ed., *Political Gerrymandering and the Courts* (New York: Agathon Press, 1990), p. 215.

29. *Miller*, sl. op. at 18

30. *Shaw v. Reno*, sl. op. at 14.

31. *Shaw v. Hunt*, at 471.

32. *Shaw v. Hunt*, at 470.

33. *Miller*, sl. op. at 15, 18.

34. See Malcolm E. Jewell, "Constitutional Provisions for State Legislative Apportionment," 8 *Western Political Quarterly* (June 1955), 271–279.

35. See Grofman, "Criteria for Districting," at 177–183.

36. *Hayes*, (1993), at 1201, and *Hayes v. State of Louisiana*, 862 F. Supp. 119, 121 (W.D. La. 1994).

37. *Vera*, at 1345; compare, however, the same court's comments at 1334–1335 n. 43.

38. Backstrom, Leonard, and Robbins, "Establishing a Statewide Electoral Effects Base," at 153.

39. *Miller*, sl. op. at 15.

40. *Miller*, sl. op. at 4.

41. See, for example, Royce Hanson, *The Political Thicket: Reapportionment and Constitutional Democracy* (Englewood Cliffs, N.J.: Prentice-Hall, Inc., 1966), p. 35.

42. *Johnson*, at 1369.

43. See *Burns v. Richardson*, 384 U.S. 73, 89 n. 16 (1966) and *White v. Weiser*, 412 U.S. 783, 791 (1973).

44. *Hayes* (1994), at 122.

45. One judge on the *Hayes* court stated that the old eighth district "has no application to this case," presumably because it "was never challenged on constitutionality by any court in the United States," *Hayes* (1994), at 127 (Shaw, J., concurring). The main opinion in that case also mentioned that the old eighth was "before *Shaw* and never challenged." *Id.*, at 122. The grounds for such a constitutional challenge

remain unclear, however, given that the only features of the district referenced by the court were that it was (1) not compact and (2) protected an incumbent, neither of which violates the Constitution. See notes 7 and 44, *supra*.

46. *Gaffney v. Cummings*, 412 U.S. 735 (1973).

47. *Gaffney*, at 753.

48. *Davis v. Bandemer*, 478 U.S. 109, 154 (1986) (O'Connor, J., concurring).

49. Brief for a Appellees at 47, *Gaffney v. Cummings*, 412 U.S. 735 (1973).

50. See Richard L. Engstrom, "The Supreme Court and Equipopulous Gerrymandering: A Remaining Obstacle in the Quest for Fair and Effective Representation," 1976 *Arizona State Law Journal* (No. 2, 1976), 277, 301–304.

51. *Cummings v. Meskill*, 341 F. Supp. 139, 147 (D. Conn. 1972).

52. See depositions of Judge George A. Saden and James F. Collins, Appendix at 54–55, 100–101, 153–170, Record, *Gaffney v. Cummings*, 412 U.S. 735 (1973).

53. Brief for a Appellant at 51, *Gaffney v. Cummings*, 412 U.S. 735 (1973).

54. *Cummings v. Meskill*, at 148.

55. Saden deposition, *supra* note 50, at 53.

56. Collins deposition, *supra* note 50, at 99; see also deposition testimony at 92, 95, and 98.

57. Some courts have held that the "narrow tailoring" portion of the strict scrutiny test requires a majority-minority district to adhere as closely as possible to neutral districting criteria. See *Vera*, at 1343, and *Hayes* (1993), at 1208–1209. In *Shaw v. Hunt*, however, narrow tailoring is viewed as requiring only compliance with constitutionally mandated criteria. *Shaw v. Hunt*, at 449–454.

58. *Miller*, sl. op. at 17 (Ginsburg, J., dissenting).

Chapter 5

Voting Rights Remedies

EDWARD STILL AND ROBERT RICHIE

A municipality faced with a voting rights suit or just the desire to do the right thing before it is sued typically considers multimember districts (MMD)and single-member districts (SMD), or some combination of the two (if entire city is the district, the MMD can be called at-large voting). There are several other systems used in the United States now which may fit the needs of a community better than MMD or SMD. This chapter compares Preference Voting (PrV), Cumulative Voting (CV), and Limited Voting (LV) to the more usual alternatives by using a series of goals we believe should be fairly noncontroversial. For the rules of each system are described in the following pages. We suggest that the goal for any municipality ought to be choosing a system that works for minorities because it works for everyone.

1. Can our election system provide racial or ethnic minorities some representation on the city council?

The lack of such representation is probably why the city fears being sued. If the city now uses MMD voting, this will typically cause a severe under-representation of racial minority groups—perhaps even a complete exclusion of the minority group.[1]

SMDs may work if the city has a geographically concentrated minority that votes cohesively. On the other hand, the city may have a racial minority for which one district cannot be drawn. In many cities, for instance, Hispanics live in several areas of the city, but still have a distinctive and cohesive political agenda. Or the minority group may be cohesive in wishing to have its own representation, but different factions would like to have the upper hand in choosing the representative. Let's assume the city council has agreed to draw one black majority district, but not all blacks can be fitted into the district. Should the district start at the northern end of the black residential area leaving out the

---

Originally published as *Alternative Election Systems As Voting Rights Remedies*, 1995. Published by the Center for Voting and Democracy, Washington, D.C. Reprinted with permission of the publisher.

southern end — or vice versa? What if the Booker T. Washington faction wants different district boundaries than the W.E.B. DuBois faction? How does the city council make a decision between those plans?

An alternative election system would avoid most of these problems. CV and LV give minority groups a chance to have some representation on the council, while PrV gives each group a chance at fair representation. Because a minority group will want to undertake a cautious strategy of minimizing the number of its candidates so as to maximize the votes they receive, CV and LV are likely to result in only one minority representative. On the other hand, because PrV allows votes to be transferred according to the wishes of each voter, the minority group does not need to limit the number of its candidates and may be able to win several seats on the council.

2. Will the election system discourage racial vote dilution?

> Vote dilution is a process whereby election laws or practices, either singly or in concert, combine with systematic bloc voting among an identifiable group to diminish the voting strength of at least one other group. The idea is that one group, voting cohesively for its preferred candidates, is systematically outvoted by a larger group that is also cohesive.[2]

It is an unfortunate fact of life that racially polarized voting exists. Racially polarized voting simply means that two racial groups vote cohesively within the racial group and differently from the other group. The fact that the two groups vote differently and cohesively does not assign blame or even give us a reason for the difference. Racial polarization may be based on the different political interests of the two groups, or it may be based on their prejudices about the other group. It is really fruitless for election system designers

to try to decide why polarization occurs; instead, they should try to alleviate its pernicious effects.

Any "winner-take-all" election will allow racially polarized voting to have an effect. Assume, for instance, that a city had two polarized groups, the Blues and Greens. If the Blues win 51 percent of the vote in an at-large election, they will win all the seats. Many cities have adopted SMD as a method of ameliorating the effect of racially polarized voting. If the Blues and Greens were residentially concentrated, it would be a simple matter to draw districts in which one group or the other had a clear majority. For instance, the Blues with 55 percent of the city's population could be the majority in three districts, and the Greens in two. This result would please many of the Greens and Blues, but the minority group in each district might be dissatisfied.

On the other hand, PrV, LV, and CV do as well as, if not better than SMD in ameliorating the effects of racial bloc voting. Rather than drawing districts for each group, these alternative systems allow voters to group themselves into "voluntary constituencies." Such nondistricts groupings will allow the formation of bi-racial coalitions and racial crossover voting, both of which might have been frustrated by the rigid district lines imposed under SMD.

3. Will the election system allow everyone's vote to count?

If Joe Jones puts his money into a soft drink machine, he gets his money back if his selection is sold out. On the other hand, if he buys a lottery ticket and doesn't win, the money is not refunded. While we do not suggest that voters are "buying" candidates when they cast a vote, the present winner-take-all voting systems are more like a lottery than a commercial transaction. Winner-take-all inevitably leads to "wasted votes," which occur whenever a voter gets nothing back for his or her vote.

While the number of wasted votes may be diminished by districting, all the people in the minority political group in each district will still be wasting their votes—the election could have been held without their participation without changing the results. If the city creates a district with a voting majority of some minority group, it generally has to add enough voters from some other group to make the requisite number of people to meet the one-person-one-vote standard. Two law professors have called these added voters "filler people":

> These additional individuals must not be of the relevant demographic group (in order to avoid claims of packing [the district to reduce the minority group's influence in other districts]), and, in the interest of minority representation, they should not be expected to compete in any genuine sense for electoral representation in the district to which they are assigned lest they undo the preference given to the specified minority group.[3]

By avoiding both districts and winner-take-all elections, alternative election plans eliminate "filler people" and reduce wasted votes greatly. For instance, in a PrV election for five members of a city council, we know that at least ⅚ of the ballots will be counted for winning candidates. Many of the final ⅙ of the voters might have expressed a preference for one or more of the winners, so that the number of wasted votes will be even less than ⅙. Contrast that with the wasted votes in five SMDs: up to 49 percent of the voters in each district could have voted for a losing candidate.

Because of the way LV and CV work, it is much harder to predict the number of potentially wasted votes. An empirical study of the LV and CV elections in Alabama has shown that at least 73 percent of the voters in LV jurisdictions and at least 61 percent of the voters in CV jurisdictions have voted for winning candidates. The number of wasted votes will depend, of course, upon the particular conditions in the election. If there are many candidates with fairly even support in the electorate, the number of wasted votes could fall closer to or even exceed 50 percent of the electorate.

4. Can our election system encourage voter turnout?

Several political science and legal commentators have contended that SMDs depress voter turnout because of "incumbency lock." In a study of Latino politics, two political scientists said,

> Thus, in these [barrio] districts, incumbents have few electoral incentives to mobilize new voters; moreover, they are not indebted to their party for their office, and they have no reason to seek party support to win reelection. These districts are also safe districts for the incumbent's party. Thus, neither the incumbent nor the party is likely to try to mobilize voters in these districts. The design of these districts, therefore, may effectively eliminate the party's need to mobilize the grassroots.[4]

Professor Lani Guinier has taken her criticism a step earlier in time—to the creation of the district.

> [D]istricting decisions may simply reflect the arbitrary preferences of incumbent politicians who prefer packed, safe districts to ensure their reelection. Indeed, districting battles are often pitched between incumbents fighting to retain their seats, without regard to issues of voter representation. Because the choice of districts is so arbitrary, incumbents enjoy extraordinary leverage in self-perpetuation through gerrymandering.
>
> Thus, districting strategies often promote noncompetitive election contests, which further reduce voter participation and interest.[5]

Since alternative election systems do not use districts, they avoid the problems of incumbency lock and depressed voter turnout associated with districts. In LV, CV, and PrV elections, all candidates—incumbents and challengers alike — are running against each other. No incumbent has a "free ride," but must instead rally the faithful behind his or her candidacy.

In a recent study of municipal elections in four Massachusetts cities, George Pillsbury found that voters were like consumers of material goods—a larger set of available choices will lead to more consumption and greater satisfaction. Pillsbury found that voter turnout had declined in all four, but less in Cambridge (which uses PrV) than in the other three (which use plurality voting). Pillsbury concluded, "…the evidence certainly points to preference voting providing more incentive for voters to participate than plurality elections."[6]

5. Can we prevent a minority of the electorate from electing a majority of the council?

In some cities, a candidate can win an MMD or SMD seat by a plurality of the vote.[7] If several such candidates in an MMD election are all supported by the same group of voters, the minority of the voters can win a majority of the council. Similarly, in SMD elections, one group could win a majority of the seats with only a majority of the vote in those districts and no other votes at all — again, a plurality of the voters would have elected a majority of the council. For instance, consider the results in the 1993 Canadian election:

> In the election, Canadians clearly wanted to show the ruling Progressive Conservatives that [they] had lost confidence in them, and the party won only 16% of the popular vote. However, the workings of the voting system turned

a show of nonconfidence into a massacre. Rather than electing 46 of the 295 members that a proportional system would have provided, the Tories elected only two. By contrast, two regionally-based parties, the Bloc Quebecois and Reform, with 13% and 19% of the popular vote respectively, elected 54 and 52 Members. The voting system also turned the victorious Liberals' 41% of the vote into a very solid majority of 177 seats.[8]

LV and CV elections could also allow a minority of voters to control a majority of the council, although it is less likely than with an MMD or SMD. For instance, three of five council seats might be won by three different "single issue" groups, if each had the support of about 15 percent of the electorate, and the remainder of the electorate was fragmented in its choices for the council.

Minority control is extremely unlikely under PrV. Assume that a particular group with about 52 percent of the voters endorses five candidates for the five-member city council. If all the voters in the group cast their preferences for all five candidates of the group — in any order — the group should win three seats, since it has enough voters to fill three thresholds (each threshold would be $1/6 + 1$, so three seats would be elected by $3/6 + 3$ of all the votes).

6. How can we avoid gerrymandering?

Gerrymandering is defined as "political manipulation within the process of drawing district boundaries."[9] In essence, it is the effort by one group to force a disfavored group to waste its votes. Methods of gerrymandering include packing, stacking, and cracking. Cracking is splitting a political group's population concentration to prevent it from having a majority in a district. Stacking occurs when a group numerous enough to elect one representative is combined with an opposing group in a multimember district. Packing is the over-concentration of a group in one or a few districts to prevent its members from having an impact in adjoining districts.[10]

By definition, gerrymandering can only occur if there are districts. Therefore, eliminating districts eliminates gerrymanders.

Any of the non-SMD election systems may be run from the city at large or from smaller, multimember districts. A city electing fewer than a dozen members of a city council can easily run an election in the whole city. The alternative election systems have the advantage of completely eliminating the cost of redistricting.

7. Can we avoid inter-census malapportionment?

A city can spend a lot of money on a districting plan (including perhaps on a court challenge to the plan), but the plan will be malapportioned as soon as there are significant changes in the population of the city. For instance, the annexation of territory with occupied houses, the creation of new subdivisions or residential apartments in the city, the movement of people out of a decaying neighborhood — all these can cause changes in the population of the various districts. Even before the city reaches the next census, its districts can be malapportioned.

Any system without districts will avoid this creeping malapportionment problem.

8. Can the election plan provide women an equal opportunity to be elected to the council?

Studies of various types of electoral systems have shown that women do better in multimember plans than in single-member district plans.[11] Generally, the larger the number of members elected from a particular district, the more likely it is that women will be elected. Thus, any system electing several council members in the same election or district will probably elect more women than SMD.

9. Can we reduce the cost of campaigns and election administration?

There are several factors that may affect the cost of campaigns for the candidates. The first is the absolute number of people who are potential voters for a particular office. If the candidate wants to use direct mail or telephone banks to reach 5,000 voters, the cost will be less than reaching 50,000 voters by the same method. Similarly, a smaller district size may allow the candidate to make personal contact with all the voters, while she will have to use media or surrogates to contact everyone in a larger district.

The second is the number of votes the candidate expects to need to win. In a winner-take-all election, this will be one half of all the votes. This is true even if there are three or more candidates, since it is possible that some candidates could receive negligible numbers of votes. On the other hand, in the alternative election systems the usual number of votes needed is $1/n + 1$, where "n" is the number of seats being filled. Thus, if the candidate is able to target her direct mail, phone bank, or media campaign, she may be able to spend her money more effectively on voters who are likely to provide her margin of victory.

The third is the number of campaigns the candidate must endure to win office. For instance, a candidate will have to spend more money to run in a partisan primary, a possible runoff, and the general election than on a non-partisan election with no runoff. The alternative systems (LV, CV, and PrV) have the advantage that they can eliminate the necessity of having both partisan primaries and (general election or primary) runoffs.

Fourth, if the candidate must run a media campaign that will reach many voters who are not in her district, she might be able to share the cost with other candidates by running joint ads—for example, "Vote for the Cost-Cutting Team of Smith (District 1), Katzenbach (District 2), and Paglia (District 3)." These joint ads will be more effective if all the candidates listed are running in the same multimember district, as they would be under MMD, LV, CV, or PrV.

Fifth, candidates can win under an alternative system with the support of voters already inclined to support the candidate rather than needing the support of "swing voters" who by definition do not like either candidate. A disproportionate amount of money in SMD elections must be spent on either winning the support of these swing voters or keeping them from the polls with a negative campaign.

While there will be some tradeoffs in costs, a PrV election campaign is likely to be more cost-efficient for the candidate. She can target her campaign toward her potential supporters, wherever they live in the city, and not have to run multiple election campaigns.

Just as it costs more for the candidates to run in two or three primaries or elections, the cost to the city is greater also. By holding only one election, the city avoids the cost of the polling officials and election supplies (and in some places the rental cost of the polling places) for a second or third election.

In the past, one of the complaints about PrV has been that the counting of the ballots took too long. For instance, in Cambridge, Massachusetts, the election takes place on Tuesday and the count usually concludes on Saturday. However, the Center for Voting and Democracy has been developing a computer counting program for PrV which will allow a count within a matter of a minute or two after the computer has the choices from each ballot. The ballot information can be input manually or by using computer-readable ballots (such as computer punch cards or optical character readers). The "long count" will soon be no barrier to having the results of a PrV election by midnight on the day of the election.

10. What is a simple method for the voter to cast an effective ballot?

In terms of simplicity of marking the ballot, the "X" voting (winner-take-all) systems are likely to take the prize. But for whom should the voter cast his ballot? If he was a Perot supporter, should he stick with Perot and probably throw away his vote, or make a choice between Clinton and Bush? If he was pretty sure Perot would lose, he might switch to his least objectionable second choice.

In PrV elections the voter has only to mark first, second, third, ... (and so on) choices. Here he could have voted for Perot first and Clinton second with the assurance that his vote for Perot would "send those politicians a message" but still allow his vote to have an effect in choosing the winner.

CV voters are likely to suffer from the agonies of strategic voting, just as the winner-take-all voters do. If the voter has five votes, but thinks that her group can probably get only one or two candidates elected, should she plump all her votes behind one candidate or divide them among two candidates? If she divides her votes, which candidate gets three or four votes and which only one or two? All of these calculations have to be made trying to figure out what like-minded voters and the opposing voters are going to do. In short, the voter has to play a three-dimensional video game with a constantly moving target.

LV voters may have to make the same sort of strategic choice if there is more than one attractive candidate. Voting for a losing candidate is a wasted vote, and it is especially wasted if there was another candidate who could have been helped by the votes received by the loser.

Technical Points About Modified At-Large Voting Systems

Modified at-large voting systems describe systems in which candidates or parties win seats in close proportion to their share of the vote because as many voters as mathematically can elect candidates of choice.

Most democracies use modified at-large systems that result in nearly all votes counting toward representation. Although many of these systems allocate votes among parties rather than candidates, the following three systems are based on voting for candidates and are already used in some local elections in the United States. They require at lease some seats to be elected from districts with more than one representative.

Cumulative Voting

In cumulative voting, voters cast as many votes as seats. The most common form of cumulative voting allows voters to allocate their votes however they wish, including giving all their votes to their favorite candidate.

Because voters in a minority can assign all of their votes to one candidate, that candidate can win with support from fewer voters than in a traditional at-large election. The "threshold of exclusion" is the lowest percentage of support that ensures a candidate will win no matter what other voters do. With cumulative voting, this threshold is equal to $1/(\text{\# of seats} +1)$, which is 20 percent of a four-seat race and 10 percent in a nine-seat race.

A second form of cumulative voting may promote more coalition-building and provide easier voting instructions. Voters simply vote for as many candidates as they like, and votes are allocated equally among these candidates. In a five seat race, for example, a voter choosing two candidates would give each candidate 2.5 votes, while a voter choosing four candidates would give each candidate 1.25 votes. The Illinois State Legislature was elected by this form of cumulative voting from 1870 to 1980.

In recent years cumulative voting has been adopted to resolve voting rights cases in over forty localities, including Alamogordo (NM), Peoria (IL) and Chilton County (AL). A member of the covered minority won office in nearly every subsequent election.

Limited Voting

Limited voting is similar to traditional at-large elections, except voters must cast fewer votes than the number of seats or parties must nominate fewer candidates than there are seats. The greater the difference between the number of seats and the number of votes, the greater the opportunities for fair representation of those in the minority. In a race to elect five candidates in which voters had two votes, any cohesive group of voters comprising one-third of the electorate would be guaranteed to win one seat.

Notes

1. Richard L. Engstrom and Michael D. McDonald, "The Effect of At-Large versus District Elections on Racial Representation in U.S. Municipalities," in *Electoral Laws and Their*

Political Consequences, Bernard Grofman and Arend Lijphart, eds., 203–25 (New York: Agathon Press, 1986).

2. Chandler Davidson, "The Recent Evolution of Voting Rights Law Affecting Racial and Language Minorities," at 22, in Davidson and Grofman, eds., *Quiet Revolution in the South: The Impact of the Voting Rights Act, 1965–1990* (Princeton: Princeton Univ. Press, 1994).

3. T. Alexander Aleinikoff and Samuel Isaacharoff, "Race and Redistricting: Drawing Constitutional Lines after *Shaw v. Reno*," *92 Mich. L. Rev.* 588, 631 (1993).

4. Rodolpho O. de la Garza and Louis DeSipio, "Overview: The Link Between Individuals and Electoral Institutions in Five Latino Neighborhoods," in *Barrio Ballots: Latino Politics in the 1990 Elections*, ed. de la Garza *et al.* (Boulder, CO: Westview Press, 1994).

5. Lani Guinier, "No Two Seats: The Elusive Quest for Political Equality," *77 Va. L. Rev.* 1413, 1452–52, 1454–55 (1991) (footnotes omitted).

6. George Pillsbury, "Preference Voting and Voter Turnout," *Voting and Democracy Report* 1995, 79–80 (Washington: Center for Voting and Democracy, 1995).

7. A majority-vote requirement, along with at-large elections and nonpartisanship, was part of the Good Government reform movement initiated during the early part of the twentieth century. In 1986 Susan MacManus conducted a survey of all American cities that had a population of at least 25,000 in 1980.

Most of the 946 cities contacted had a runoff provision.

Charles S. Bullock III and Loch K. Johnson, *Runoff Elections in the United States* 24–5 (Chapel Hill: University of North Carolina Press 1992). See also, National Municipal League, *Model City Charter* 51–2 (New York: National Municipal League, 6th ed. 1964).

8. Henry Milner, "Prospects for Electoral Reform in Canada," *Voting and Democracy Report 1995*, 159 (Washington: Center for Voting and Democracy, 1995).

9. Michael D. McDonald and Richard L. Engstrom, "Detecting Gerrymandering," in *Political Gerrymandering and the Courts*, Bernard Grofman, ed. (New York: Agathon Press, 1990), 178–202, and 182.

10. Gus Tyler, "Court versus Legislature: The Sociopolitics of Malapportionment," 27 *Law and Contemporary Problems* 390, 400 (1962).

11. Wilma Rule, "Electoral Systems, Contextual Factors and Women's Opportunity for Election to Parliament in Twenty-three Democracies," 40 *Western Political Quarterly* 487 (1987); Wilma Rule and Pippa Norris, "Anglo and Minority Women's Underrepresentation in Congress: Is the Electoral System the Culprit?"; and Susan Welsh and Rebekah Herrick, "The Impact of At-Large Elections on the Representation of Minority Women," in *United States Electoral Systems: Their Impact on Women and Minorities*, Wilma Rule and Joseph F. Zimmerman, eds., 41–54 and 153–66 (Connecticut: Greenwood Press, 1992).

• *Chapter 6* •

The State of the Cities

ROGER L. KEMP

The rapid growth of cities was largely the consequence of the development of new technologies and their application to the industrial and agricultural sectors of the American economy. The location of industrial facilities in our urban centers, and the surplus of labor brought about by agricultural advances in rural areas, provided the necessary labor supply for our industrial expansion. During the latter part of the 19th century, the United States witnessed a population migration of unprecedented proportions from rural to urban areas. Cities grew in size and flourished as this trend continued during the ensuing decades.

As our metropolitan areas flourished, a rapidly growing population base created the need to greatly expand the level of existing municipal services, as well as ways to finance them. One of the first local taxes — the municipal property tax — helped to generate the necessary revenues for local governments to finance property-related services. They typically include police, fire, and public works services. The rapid urbanization of America during the late 19th century placed unanticipated demands on these municipal services. Local governments expanded services in these areas, and increased property taxes, in response to these new population demands.

New forms of taxes and fees evolved over the years to help finance a growing need for cultural and recreational programs. The decrease in working hours, evolving family patterns, and increased longevity created the need for new community programs in these nontraditional service areas. Communities, regardless of their size or geographic location, began to provide a full range of municipal services to their residents. The addition of these new services, and the expansion of traditional services, created the need for larger and more complex municipal service delivery systems. These factors led to the need for more professional management of America's cities to run the organizations that provided these services.

The magnitude of America's urban problems increased during the Great Depression to the extent that local governments could no longer provide meaningful and workable solutions to their local municipal problems. The states, because of their restricted financial capability, were limited in the financial assistance they could provide to solve these problems. The federal government expanded its programs to fill this service vacuum. The central government began by providing direct programmatic, technical, and financial aid to cities to help ameliorate America's pressing urban problems. The height of federal involvement with localities, both operationally and financially, reached its peak during President Johnson's Great Society movement in the 1960s.

Federal aid to communities continued relatively unabated until the advent of the so-called "taxpayers' revolt" movement in the mid–1970s. Because of the mismatch between urban problems and municipal revenues, federal grant programs filled the economic need of transferring tax monies from wealthier to poorer urban areas to balance the capability of local governments to cope with their urban problems. The growth of the taxpayers' revolt, Washington's preoccupation with balancing the federal budget, and the public pressure to eliminate the federal deficit all helped to form a change in the philosophical direction of the U.S. central government. Today, local problems mean local solutions. Local governments can no longer rely on higher levels of government for programmatic, technical, or financial support to tackle their urban problems.

This forced self-reliance has created the need for local elected officials to demand more of their management staffs, and for professional managers to seek out innovative and creative ways to reduce costs, increase productivity, and to maintain existing service levels. These tasks are particularly difficult in many urban communities that have witnessed an out-migration of their middle class population, an influx of low-income citizens demanding public services, and a declining property tax base. State governments, to some extent, have attempted to provide aid to their larger urban communities in an effort to counteract these negative trends. Because of limited state revenues, many pressing urban problems have gone unresolved, and are growing in both their enormity and complexity.

Changing societal trends and values over the past century have served to reshape municipal governments. As community governments grew in size to meet new service and population demands, three important national trends occurred simultaneously that facilitated our current form, structure, political processes, and administrative structures of America's contemporary municipal governments. These trends included the increasing popularity of business and corporate ideals, the progressive reform era, and the public administration movement. These three trends are briefly highlighted below.

Popularity of Business and Corporate Ideals. Business executives and the public concept of the corporation have been instrumental in determining public thought and values about the structure of community governments. The success of modern-day corporations in the private sector has had a significant influence on American political and administrative thought. Probably no political or administrative philosophy reflects business practices and corporate ideals more clearly than the growth of professional management in our nation's cities. Many citizens still compare the operation of their city government with that of the private corporation. The elected representatives are the board of directors, the city manager is the chief executive officer, and the citizens of the community are the stockholders of the government. Economy and efficiency, two primary values of the private sector, are foundations of the movement towards the professional management of our municipalities.

Progressive Reform Movement. Many

of the effects of rapid urbanization, particularly the early political machines and large monopolistic corporations, met with disfavor among many citizens, who were commonly called Progressives. These individuals, who formed a significant movement because of their large numbers, felt that the best interests of the public were frequently not being served by the existing political processes and some of the large corporations were perceived as being too strong and having too much power over common people. One of the most significant municipal reforms developed and supported by the Progressives was the council-manager plan. The management concepts embodied in the plan ideally suited the Progressive political philosophy of the early 19th century — a competent professional manager and public policy established by nonpartisan elected representatives. The manager's apolitical qualities suited the Progressive values, which favored impartiality and opposed personality politics and favoritism. Two key Progressive ideals — equality of participation in the political process and centralized administrative authority — were well balanced in this form of municipal governance.

Public Administration Philosophy. The modern city management profession also fit the emerging concepts of public management in the early 1900s. Many administrative scholars espoused a sharp division between policy determination and policy implementation. Highly respected scholars of the time drew a sharp distinction between "politics" and "administration." The council-manager plan incorporated the ideals of the separation of policymaking and the implementation of public policy. The elected representatives should be responsible for setting public policy, while the city manager should focus on its implementation. The separation of these two distinct tasks — policy setting and policy implementation — formed the

basis of the emerging trend to separate community politics from the operation of the municipal organization. This widespread public administration philosophy facilitated the growth of professional management in America's cities.

As the Progressive reform movement emerged and spread, the prevailing philosophy of public administration at the time and the increasing popularity of business and corporate ideals provided the positive background against which professional municipal management blossomed into national popularity. All of these ideological and social forces provided the supportive environment in which professional municipal management spread from city to city across the landscape of America's local governments. The many changes and challenges currently facing our cities — increased service demands, fewer financial resources, citizen aversion to increased taxation, and fewer funds from higher levels of government — have tested the abilities of governing bodies to adopt policies to improve the condition of their cities and, at the same time, hold professional managers accountable for their proper implementation.

Forms of Governance

There are several significantly different forms of local governmental structure that citizens can adopt to serve the needs of their community. The four most common types of municipal governance are the strong mayor form, the commission type, the mayor-council model, and the council-manager plan. Each structure's strengths and weaknesses are perceived differently by constituents, political officeholders, professional government managers, and the employees of the municipal organization. The particular form selected is not an easy decision for citizens to make. Elected leaders above all want to be responsive to their constituents. On the other hand most citizens find equal treatment, an apolitical and objective service delivery system, and cost-effective government to be most important. The characteristics of each of these models of municipal governance are briefly described below.

Strong Mayor. In many large cities in the United States, the mayor is elected to lead the city, usually through partisan municipal elections. The mayor serves as the chief executive officer, while the city council serves as the legislative body. The mayor typically manages the municipal organization through mayor-appointed department managers. The mayor may have the authority to appoint a deputy mayor or chief administrative officer to run the daily operations of the city. This plan has its advantages and disadvantages, depending upon the qualifications of the person elected as the mayor. A good political leader is sometimes not a good municipal administrator. Hiring professionally trained administrators has served to overcome this shortcoming.

Commission. This form of government, which usually employs non-partisan, at-large elections includes a board of commissioners. Collectively they serve as the legislative body of their municipal government. Individually each commissioner serves as the head of one or more administrative departments (e.g., public works commissioner, police commissioner, and parks commissioner). The municipal reform movement in the United States has led to the near-demise of this form of local government. This model of municipal governance fuses policymaking with implementation, since both roles are performed by the same officeholders. The other major weakness of this model is obvious, since few elected leaders possess the necessary requirements to professionally manage large portions of a municipal organization.

Mayor-Council. This form has a legislative body (city council) that is elected either at-large, by ward or district, or by some combination of the two (i.e., some at-large and others by district). There are two distinguishing characteristics of this plan. The mayor is selected separately through at-large elections and his office is officially designated as the formal head of the municipal government. Depending upon local laws, the powers of the mayor may vary greatly from limited administrative duties to full-scale authority to appoint and remove department managers. The mayor sometimes has veto power over the policies adopted by the city council. The mayor frequently has authority to appoint a chief administrative officer to run the daily operations of the city. The city council typically must confirm this appointment.

Council-Manager. This form of government typically has a legislative body selected by popular vote through nonpartisan elections. Although most council members are usually elected at-large, they are sometimes selected through some combination of at-large and district elections. They are responsible for setting policy, while the management of the municipal organization is under the direction of an appointed city manager. The city council appoints and removes the city manager by majority vote. The city manager usually has the power to appoint and remove department managers. The mayor, sometimes elected by the city council, is a voting member of the governing body with no special veto or administrative power. The mayor is, however, the community's recognized political and legislative leader and represents the city at all official ceremonies as well as civic and social functions.

Nearly 4,000 cities in the United States operate under the council-manager plan, which separates the policymaking duties of elected officials from the administrative role of professional managers.

This is the most successful and popular form of government in cities over 10,000 in population. This form of government has been adopted on the average of one each week by citizens in cities and counties throughout the nation since 1945. Because of its popularity among citizens, it is the fastest growing form of municipal governance in America. For this reason, the references made to mayors, city councils, and city managers refers to this governmental structure, although other titles such as city administrator, chief executive officer, and business manager may commonly be used in other forms of government to refer to the duties of the city manager.

The form of government that the electorate of a community selects should best serve the needs of its citizens. Voters elect their representatives based on their confidence in them to set the right policies, and to ensure that these policies are implemented into programs and services to serve their needs. If the council-manager plan best serves this goal, then it is the most desirable form of government. If another model of local governance is adopted, it should embody the type of governance desired by its citizens. The form of government best suited for a particular city should always be determined through the electoral process. No system of municipal governance is perfect, nor can any single system represent the wishes of all of the people all of the time. When the form of local government selected represents the wishes of the majority of the electorate, this is the form that best serves the democratic process and the will of the people.

Municipal Organizations

Every city government has a governing body consisting of a mayor and city council in some form. How the mayor is selected and the number of council members are determined by state laws for general law cities and by the electorate in charter cities. In many general law cities, for example, there are typically five council members elected at-large. The mayor is sometimes selected by majority vote of the governing body. In charter cities, on the other hand, the mayor is usually elected at-large, while the members of the council are elected through some combination of at-large and district elections. The number of council members in a charter city is usually seven or nine, but varies greatly and may even be based upon population. Some charter cities also require the election of other municipal positions such as the city clerk, treasurer, and auditor. The powers of the mayor, as well as these other positions, are set forth in the municipal charter. The term governing body refers to the mayor and members of the city council. It is also assumed that the governing body sets policy, while the city manager implements this policy, and that all department managers, with the exception of the city attorney, are appointed by the city manager.

The typical municipal government provides a variety of services to its residents. These public services are provided by individual city departments, which are organized by function. Each department performs those services related to its function. Some departments perform a narrow function, such as police and fire departments, while other departments encompass broader functions, like public works and health and human services. The type of services a city provides depends upon a number of different factors. Communities on coastlines, for example, may provide small craft harbors and public beaches, while larger cities may have museums, zoos, and golf courses. Some cities have municipal airports and also provide public transit services. To make matters more confusing, some states require certain functions to be performed by counties, such as health, welfare, property assessments, and tax collection. In many urbanized areas, some services are provided by special districts. These services may include public transit, water distribution, and wastewater treatment. Furthermore, many communities contract for certain services from other municipalities and counties, as well as the private sector.

A municipal organization can also be divided into line and staff departments. Line departments provide a direct service to the public, while staff departments serve the organization to keep it operating smoothly. For these reasons, the external services provided by line departments are more visible to the public than those internal services performed by staff departments. Typical staff departments include city clerk, city manager, finance, and legal. Common line departments encompass fire, health and human services, library, parks and recreation, planning and building, po-

lice, and public works. Some departments, like city clerk, perform both line and staff functions. That is, they serve the public (e.g., the sale and recording of public records, licenses, and permits) and also serve the needs of the organization (e.g., the preparation of meeting agendas, minutes, and staff reports, as well as the posting of public notices). Although the number of departments may vary from community to community, the above departments are so common that they are used to represent the typical municipal organization. Figure 1 graphically illustrates these departments.

Every department's operations can further be divided into specific programs, each related to a department's overall function. Each program represents a particular service and, taken together, these programs encompass those services provided by each municipal department. The number and types of programs in a municipal department may vary from department to department, as well as community to

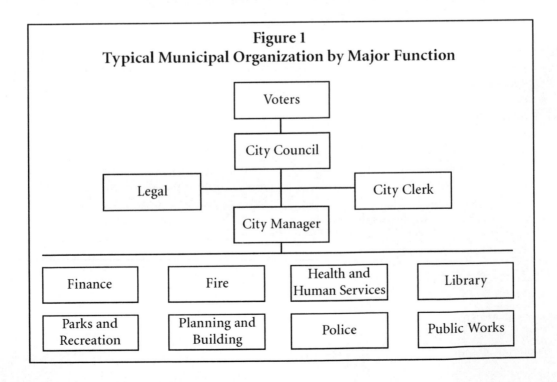

Figure 1
Typical Municipal Organization by Major Function

community. Variables that influence this phenomenon include each community's unique historical development, the existence of contract services, and how each department director organizes their respective departmental operations. Individual municipal charters may also alter this program arrangement, but these changes would be the exception to the typical municipal organization rather than the norm. The various programs indicated for each department are typical and common to its function. For these reasons, the programs shown in Table 1 represent the most common programs contained in each municipal department.

Table 1
Typical Municipal Organization
Major Functions and Programs

City Council
Office of the Mayor
Citizen Advisory Bodies
Financial Policies
Municipal Legislation
Legislative Advocacy
Standing Committees

Finance
Treasurer
Comptroller
Debt Management
Revenue Management
Assessment
Budget Preparation
Purchasing
Data Processing

Parks and Recreation
Recreation Services
Parks Management
Youth Services
Senior Citizen Services
Community Events
Special Programs

City Manager
Administration
Organizational Development
Financial Management
Personnel
Labor Relations
Citizen Inquiries
Policies/Procedures
Special Assignments

Fire
Fire Suppression
Fire Prevention
Fire Inspection
Emergency Services
Emergency Preparedness
Hazardous Materials

Planning and Building
Land-Use Planning
Zoning Control
Development Regulations
Affordable Housing
Building Inspection
Code Enforcement
Economic Development
Capital Improvements

City Clerk
Public Documents
Public Meetings
Records Management
Licenses/Permits
Vital Statistics
Election Administration
Registrar of Voters
Public Information

Health and Human Services
Health Services
Health Education
Environmental Services
Code Enforcement
Community Clinics
Social Services

Police
Patrol Services
Community Policing
Investigations
Crime Prevention
Officer Training
Records Management
Dispatching
Police Auxiliary

Legal
Legislation
Litigation
Legal Counsel
Legal Documents
Public Meetings
Safety and Risk

Library
Information Services
Technical Services
Children's Services
Community Services
Circulation Control
Literacy Programs

Public Works
Engineering Services
Transportation Systems
Solid Waste Management
Water Resource Systems
Buildings and Grounds
Central Garage

Sources and Limits of Power

The various sources of power for public officials and municipal governments are created by selected federal, state, and local laws, as well as numerous court decisions. Conversely, the limits placed on these same powers are also influenced by different types of federal mandates, state regulations local laws, and court decisions. The political and administrative environment of community governments is increasingly regulated by a number of conditions beyond the control of locally elected officials and their management staffs. While elected officials, city managers, and department managers may wish to implement new human resources practices, for example, existing employment laws, personnel regulations, and labor agreements may place restrictions on the use of such practices. Existing labor contracts, may place restrictions on privatizing or contracting for municipal services, as well as regulate the use of community volunteers. Figure 2 highlights many of the common sources and limits of power in our community governments.

The Future

This chapter began by describing the rapid growth of cities in the American intergovernmental system of governance. The three societal conditions facilitating this trend were the popularity of business and corporate ideals, the progressive reform movement, and the public administration philosophy of the time.

The four most common forms of community government — strong mayor, commission, mayor-council, and council-manager plans— were then examined. The council-manager plan is the fastest growing form of municipal governance in the United States. It retains popularity because its structure reflects the valued private-sector corporate model of organization.

The structure of a typical municipal organization was then examined, along with the most common programs found in community government. The major sources and limits of powers of local public officials were also discussed. The actions of the federal and state governments, as well as their court systems, continue to limit the powers of local officials— both elected and appointed.

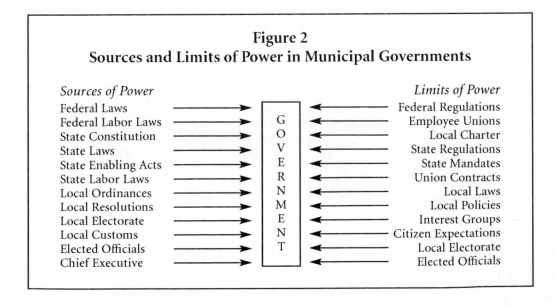

Figure 2
Sources and Limits of Power in Municipal Governments

Sources of Power		Limits of Power
Federal Laws		Federal Regulations
Federal Labor Laws		Employee Unions
State Constitution		Local Charter
State Laws	GOVERNMENT	State Regulations
State Enabling Acts		State Mandates
State Labor Laws		Union Contracts
Local Ordinances		Local Laws
Local Resolutions		Local Policies
Local Electorate		Interest Groups
Local Customs		Citizen Expectations
Elected Officials		Local Electorate
Chief Executive		Elected Officials

Chapter 7

City Government Forms

Charles R. Adrian

Poets, politicians, journalists, and sociologists have ridiculed form as an insignificant factor in the kind of government we experience. Political scientists and reformers have not been so certain. The most familiar comment on the subject is probably that of the great British poet of the Augustan age, Alexander Pope: "For forms of government let fools contest. Whatever is best administered is best."[1] True, public administration was not exactly Pope's strong suit, but he was not alone in his viewpoint. Edmund Burke, Lincoln Steffens, and many others agreed with him. Burke subscribed to a theory of history holding that the quality of leadership determined the quality of life. "Great men are the guideposts and landmarks in the state," he observed in 1774. In 1904 Steffens argued that corrupt leaders, and especially those who corrupted them, were responsible for bad government.[2]

The Significance of Structure

Though political scientists have studied city government and politics for many years, they are unable to make definitive statements about any autonomous effects of form or structure on the political system, especially about administrative considerations.

Some scholars, without clear evidence, have rejected the possibility of an autonomous influence coming from the structure itself. Some find the question uninteresting or unimportant. Although sociologists often picture structure as inhibiting function to one degree or another, some of them have expressed serious doubt about the effect of formal rules. Practicing politicians sometimes give short shrift to the idea,[3] especially reform opponents who do not wish to prepare a more substantial defense of the status quo. Marxians argue that power in the city is grounded only in

---

Originally published as "Forms of Local Government in American History," *The Municipal Year-book*, 1998. Published by the International City/County Management Association, Washington, D.C. Reprinted with permission of the publisher.

the control over the means of production. This kind of analysis can lead to a dismissal of form as irrelevant,[4] as can a conviction that informal political organizations outside the provisions of the charter, such as the boss-and-machine structure, are the dominating forces in allocating power.[5]

In addition to the traditional weak mayor-council forms, which served as the structural base for dozens of political machines, other forms of local government rarely hampered the bosses. Thus, bosses ruled under the strong mayor-council plan (Boston under James Michael Curley), the commission plan (Jersey City under Frank Hague and Memphis under Edward H. Crump), and the council-manager plan (Kansas City under Thomas J. Pendergast). Indeed, political machines could themselves be reformed or modified to allow the party to increase its efficiency or modernity or to give the boss greater control, without much affecting the way the governmental structure itself operated. Anton J. Cermak, a brilliant administrator, reorganized the Chicago machine in the early 1930s in order to concentrate power in the boss but without creating a new governmental system of operation.[6] Under George W. Olvany, Tammany Hall in Manhattan looked carefully at a modernization plan in the late 1920s.[7] It failed to adopt one for shortsighted reasons unrelated to the question of whether the machine structure was independent of that of the city government, but the machine, not the city charter, was the subject under study.

Despite other viewpoints, some political scientists have reached the conclusion that the structure of city government is important in helping to determine the content of policy, access to decision making, the image of the city held by outsiders, and the accomplishments of the goals of major interest groups.[8] Certainly reformers have long believed this or they would not have devoted, as many of them have,

years of effort and thousands of their own dollars in efforts to secure the adoption of new charters, to oust old machines, or to reach other difficult-to-achieve goals. (Some reformers have certainly been sophisticated enough to recognize that at least a part, and possibly a very large part, of their efforts have involved symbolic activities. But interviews with reformers virtually always reveal assumptions concerning the efficacy of structure itself.)

The question of the impact of structure on form upon government cannot be settled here. To some extent, participants in the debate have talked past one another, not actually discussing the same issues. Furthermore, too many variables exist to say anything definitive about their interaction patterns or about causality. Certainly some aspects of structure have been statistically measurable. The use of professional management, merit personnel systems, the executive budget, the initiative and referendum, nonpartisan elections, and quite a number of other reform goals or policies have surely not varied randomly among the various forms of city government. And the relative influence of specific interest groups or access to decision makers is certainly not the same for citizens generally or to certain categories of citizens from one structure to another.

Although it cannot be demonstrated formally, it seems eminently reasonable to assume that structure affects the policy processes and outcomes in some way. The question is not one of its existence but of the extent, form, and character of such effects. The 1986 *Form of Government* survey sheds some additional light on this.[9]

Unlike administration and policymaking, form undoubtedly affects *elections*. To a much greater degree than we may care to concede democracy as expressed through voting is a matter of *faith* in the process. No ideal election system exists; all involve, to some degree, arbitrary rules by which winners are determined. All have some "slippage" or inaccuracy in the counting process, although this is usually a result of inadequate financing or deliberate or accidental human error that the system permits though strictly speaking does not cause.

The growth of elections, suffrage, and ballot forms is reported in textbooks and monographs and need not be dwelt upon here.[10] In general, the beginning of modern democracy dates from the Glorious Revolution of 1688–89 in the United Kingdom, where the theory of parliamentary supremacy replaced the Stuart concept of the "divine right of kings." Subsequent developments spread to the 13 colonies that became the United States about 90 years later.

In this incipient democracy, the eligibility rules were derived primarily from two principles: (1) *The possession of a certain amount of property.* This supposedly ensured that the voter had a sufficient stake in an election to behave responsibly. The basic minimum rule was ownership of a 40 shilling freehold. (2) *The voter must have attained adulthood.* Originally restricted to an upper middle-class electorate with adult status based on the common-law rule of age 21, eligibility to vote was broadened gradually but inexorably. Merchants first assaulted the freehold rule and got it changed to property of a specific value, but the Jacksonians succeeded in abolishing most property requirements altogether in the 1820s and 1830s.

Court action in quite recent decades gradually eliminated late nineteenth-century rules designed to restrict voting to those who could read English. Rules in the South designed to disenfranchise blacks (and the white poor as well) were not finally overcome until the federal Voting Rights Act of 1965. The voting age was left at the traditional 21 until four states reduced it to 18 or 19 in the 1950s. In the late 1960s,

as a by-product of the social conflict surrounding the Vietnam war, the figure was dropped to 18, which corresponds to the age most people leave high school, take a job, or go to college, thus becoming more nearly autonomous from their parents. It was also the age of military draft eligibility. The Twenty-sixth Amendment to the United States Constitution (1971) established this as the universal voting age in the United States, and there seems little likelihood of its changing in the future.

The form of the ballot and rules for voting procedures have caused, and probably always will continue to cause, problems in elections. The voters' choices were given orally in early democracies, a time when even persons of considerable wealth might be illiterate. While our British friends were still voting *viva voce*, Americans introduced the written ballot, which became the standard practice by the 1780s. One need not dwell long on why an oral vote imposed strong pressures to conform to social expectations. But the ballot was not truly secret even with the adoption of the written form. As the political parties increased in importance in the early Republic, they aided those who identified with them (and the illiterate) by printing distinctive ballots, even premarking them with the "X" in the "right" places and perhaps with only the party's candidates listed so that one could not "split" the ticket. The Australians devised a truly secret ballot, uniform in size, color, and content, printed by the government at its expense, and available only at the polling booth from election officials, to be marked and folded in secret but deposited in public. This ballot was first used in the United States in Louisville, Kentucky, in 1888 and was rapidly accepted across the nation, though the last state to adopt it, South Carolina, held out until the 1950s.

The outcome of elections may also be, or once have been, altered by rules concerning citizenship, legal insanity, felony conviction, pauperism, literacy, and registration. In the era when property was an essential requirement, owners need not necessarily have lived in the locality or even city in which they voted, but residency rules were created and became universal after property ownership ceased to be a requirement. (The rule then became that each person was entitled to one legal domicile, with which he or she had some personal identification, though actual residence might be somewhere else for years, such as while one was away at college.) Registration was introduced in some large cities in the mid–nineteenth century and gradually became almost universal. Its stated and often actual purpose was, and still is, to reduce fraud in elections. But many forms of registration exist, and it is quite easy to devise one that will either maximize or minimize potential participation by the citizen who has low political information and a low interest level. The rules on registration as well as other rules may deliberately or fortuitously affect the pattern of participation in elections.

Problems of ballot form are compounded in the United States because since early in the twentieth century we have nominated by primary election. Every ballot has a built-in set of biases that potentially influence each election outcome. For practical purposes, some rules must be arbitrary. A common example of built-in biases may be found in the run-off primary common in the South, and the non-partisan "primary" election, used in thousands of local elections. In these, numerous persons may file for the first vote. The common result is that no candidate achieves a required majority (50 percent of the votes cast plus one). The candidate with a plurality, the most votes, could simply be declared the winner, as is common enough in ordinary partisan primary contests, even though more votes were cast against than for that person. The arbitrariness involved

does not seem to trouble the voting public, probably because a final outcome is not involved: a general, interparty election follows. Although the South is changing, voting rules from one-party days still are largely in use, in part because many offices continue to be settled as Democratic contests. In the traditional southern primary, the fact that a majority of votes were not cast for the candidate finishing first seemed wrong because it was in fact a final result. The first vote in non-partisan elections has always been considered to be a primary election (although technically, it is not). A second election in each case could easily produce a majority result. The obvious— but by no means necessarily most equitable —"solution" would be to have the two candidates with the highest number of votes compete in a second election. One's "common sense" says that this is fair. But it may be no more equitable than the first result if we make two assumptions about election conditions: (1) individual voters have an order of preference among two or more of the candidates, and (2) one of the two highest vote getters, although the first choice of many, is the second choice of very few. This could happen, for example, if one candidate were an extremist on certain matters, an eccentric, or an avowed ethnic-group candidate.

With one position to be filled, the result might look like this:

Candidate	Primary election	General election	Winner
A	37%	57%	A
B	28	43	
C	25	—	
D	10	—	

But suppose that instead of eliminating anyone at the primary, we were to consider all second choices, such as the following (third and fourth choices would also be possible):

Candidate	First Choice	Second Choice
A	37%	24%
B	28	16
C	25	44
D	10	3

Viewed from this aspect of voter choice, the elimination of Candidate "C" (and conceivably both "C" and "D" in another possible illustration that readers can easily construct for themselves) is arbitrary and contrary to popular will, if we assume that the winner should be preferred by more than one-half of the voters in the election, if not as a first choice, then by cumulative subsequent choices. This weakness in the structure of the ordinary ballot led to the adoption from its British origins of the use in some cities of proportional representation (PR) in the 1920s and 1930s. Several types of PR plans were already known, but the most accurate one was the Hare single transferable vote system, with Droop quota.[11] This approach, sparing the reader the details, would sidestep the problem some will have spotted in the above scenario of having to weight second choices without again being arbitrary.

PR received much publicity when it was made a part of the Cincinnati reform charter of 1925. New York City adopted the plan (with a different quota system) in the "LaGuardia" charter (effective in the 1937 election), and PR seemed to be on its way, but it was adopted by a total of only about 25 cities. It ran into trouble precisely because it did what it was designed to do — it distributed council seats on a proportional basis to various political parties or other discernible interests. In New York, this meant that after World War II, two council seats went to Communist party members and two more to fellow travelers. Growing opposition from newspaper editors and the major parties forced abandonment of the plan in 1947, with a subsequent return to an all-Democratic party city council.[12] In Cincinnati, the plan continued in use although it was opposed for many reasons, including its distribution of a proportionate share of council seats to blacks. Its representational strength was its political weakness. After much controversy, PR was abolished by charter amendment in Cincinnati in 1952. Within a little more than a decade, it had disappeared in all American cities.[13] It had been opposed consistently by those who could gain from its elimination and by others because its operation was not easy to understand. It required esoteric rules of centralized counting to determine the winners. Many people would not trust a system that complex. Others saw no beauty in making democracy so precise as to produce what they saw as unwanted council factions creating chronic conflict.

The rules of the game and the structure of the contest may have important effects in many ways. Although one of the enduring myths of democracy holds the simple majority sacred, it is often an elusive thing. That, perhaps, works to reinforce its symbolic value. Yet, the majority must often be constructed artificially. At the local level, the actual majority commonly consists of the registered nonvoters. The majority, however generated, is not always accepted as adequate for decision purposes. Although the practice is coming under increasing court scrutiny, we sometimes demand an extraordinary majority, especially for adopting charters, charter amendments, tax overrides, or bond issues. By requiring some extraordinary vote, we may sometimes defeat the majority preference, an irony that apparently is often accepted without much hesitation. (In the cases of demands for extraordinary majorities, advocates are seeking to achieve the closest approximation to total community consensus — unanimity, the community ideal. But the idea is often impractical.)

The Primary Election

The most important and a unique structural innovation in the United States is the primary election, used generally for nomination purposes now for about 75 years. Its origin can be found in limited use in Pennsylvania in the 1840s. Its revival came about in the 1890s in an effort to break up the monopoly political control of the Bourbon aristocracy in the South. Use spread rapidly in the early years of the twentieth century and especially in connection with the popularity of Progressivism before the outbreak of World War I. Prior to this time, caucuses and conventions were the standard method for nomination. The rules sometimes required an extraordinary majority. As an example at the national level, James Knox Polk became the first dark-horse candidate to win the presidency, in 1844, because the leading candidate, Martin Van Buren (who had been defeated for reelection four years earlier) could muster a majority, but not two-thirds of the delegates at the Democratic National Convention. So Polk, a compromise, was nominated on the ninth ballot and later elected president.

The arbitrary rule (it was designed to give the South a veto over the nomination) probably made an important difference historically. Polk was ready to fight Mexico over Texas and California; Van Buren opposed prompt annexation because he wanted to avoid the war that began two years later in April 1846. Franklin D. Roosevelt easily put together a majority of delegates in 1932 but scrambled to get the two-thirds vote needed for the nomination. (In 1936, at the height of his popularity, FDR persuaded the convention to adopt a simple majority rule. This aboli-

tion of the southern veto over the Democratic presidential nomination contributed later to the destabilization of the "Solid South" in presidential and congressional politics.).

The Early Years

The forms of government with which we as a nation began were, of course, inherited from England.[14] With the nation 97 percent rural by the first census in 1790, its leaders did not yet see forms of city government as a major concern, but experimentation and change soon began. The earliest American city governments possessed characteristics most of which are still familiar to us today, though there are a few surprises. Cities were legally public corporations, possessing what we would call special charters, but they were granted by the governor or proprietor acting in the name of the Crown, not by Parliament or the colonial legislatures. These few urban places were usually called *boroughs*, the traditional English term. A few were *cities*, in England an honorary title granted by the Crown, usually because the borough possessed a cathedral. (New York was a city from its first charter in 1686.) They had the right to exist in perpetuity, to sue and to be sued, to use a corporate seal, and to own property.

As in England, there was a unicameral council manned by aldermen and common councillors or assistant aldermen sitting together (the alderman sometimes also had judicial duties). Presiding was the mayor, who was a full voting member (except in Philadelphia). The mayor and recorder (corporation counsel or city attorney) were chosen annually, either by the council or the governor, but they were never elected as they were in England. There was no separation of powers. In addition to the aldermen, the mayor and recorder, or a combination of them, usually had more judicial powers, hence the "mayor's" and "recorder's" courts that still survive in some states. Several boroughs were "close" corporation, Philadelphia being the largest. In these, vacancies on the council were filled by the remaining members, and terms of office were for life. But in most of the boroughs, council members were elected by the freemen, freeholders of sufficient property, or other taxpayers who qualified as voters.

In colonial or revolutionary America, none of the urban places as yet provided municipal utilities or other services. The councils appointed officers to regulate trade and occupations (to supervise the fixed price of bread or to guard against the sale of very low quality pork, for example), to oversee the common land (and to lease some of it out to individuals), to manage the municipal markets and fairs, and to organize other activities.

The first two boroughs created in what became the United States were Maine coastal places, Agamenticus (1641) and Kittery (1647). Neither was ever organized, and all of New England operated under the town government system at the time of Independence and until long afterward.[15] New York, as Niew Amsterdam, was organized by the Dutch in 1656, taken over by the English nine years later, and operated as a municipal corporation. It received a charter upon local petition (the standard English procedure) in 1686. Philadelphia was chartered in 1691. About 20 other municipalities, many of them very small, were also incorporated between then and 1746, after which no additional charters were executed until after Independence, perhaps an indication of a growing reluctance on the part of the royal governors and the proprietors to grant more autonomy to the increasingly recalcitrant colonials.

A New Set Decision Makers

With the coming of independence, decision[s] about municipal governments were no longer made in London. The new leaders in the state capitals immediately asserted their claims to power. The legislatures quickly assumed control over municipal corporations, preempting the rights of the governors that would have existed by precedent. The practice of limiting legislative power over local government developed quickly, for in Massachusetts the new state constitution prohibited the legislature from imposing a municipal charter on a town without its own consent. (Such a charter could have been used to increase legislative influence as compared with the autonomy of the towns.)

The English model had never in fact existed in exactly the same form in the colonies as it did at home. In particular, the mayor was weaker in the colonies. Being appointed by the governor or proprietor, he was less trusted by local residents than were the council members, who kept the corporate powers in their hands, restricting the mayor to his vote and to presiding over the council. The governor, in naming the mayor, had potential influence over the municipality. But in England, there was no central government intervention possible, for the mayor was elected by the same electors as were council members.

Changes in the status and structure of cities began promptly after the Declaration was issued. Pennsylvania set aside the Philadelphia charter of 1701, ending the "close" corporation and providing for the election of council members, although a completely new charter did not go into effect until 1789. Close corporations in all states were soon abolished. Except for their necessary alterations to allow for elections, charter changes at first were small in scope.

A sharp new direction was taken,

however, in the Baltimore charter of 1797, which introduced for the first time at the local level the concept of separation of powers and checks and balances. This was borrowed, of course, from the new Maryland and United States constitutions. In the bicameral Baltimore council, the lower house consisted of two members from each of eight wards, elected for one-year terms. In the upper house, each ward elected one member (the at-large idea came later). The wards also chose members of an electoral college, which then selected the mayor. The most significant long-term provision, however, gave the mayor a *veto* power, which could be overridden by a two-thirds vote in each house.

There appear to have been no traumatic experiences or obvious threats to local government to inspire the establishment of these derivative institutions. They were no doubt thought of, however, as thoroughly American. At first the veto spread slowly, but it became a commonplace power of the mayor from the 1830s, with the Jacksonian-era charters. The electoral college idea, by contrast, never gained in popularity. This approach was perhaps just an imitation that produced no apparent benefits, or perhaps it reflected a general discontent with the manner in which the mayor had been chosen in colonial times and still was being chosen nearly a generation after Independence. After all, civic leaders were aware of the British precedent of election. Other changes soon took place. In 1821, selection of New York's mayors was shifted from gubernatorial appointment to choice by the council, but this did not produce a groundswell of demand for limitation. The Detroit (1806) and New Orleans (1815) charters, for example, had still left selection to the governors. Then in 1822, a great change occurred. Boston became the first New England town to give up its status and ask the state legislature for a charter. The re-

sult was to provide the settled, tradition-bound hub city with an elected mayor. And in that same year, out on the frontier, the St. Louis mayor was made subject to popular vote. Other cities followed in short order: Detroit (1824), Philadelphia (1826), Baltimore (1833), New York (1834), and then a flood of others. Jacksonian democracy, in the temper of the times, was carried from rural America into the cities.[16] It called for keeping government "close to the people," believing that almost anyone of goodwill could govern. By 1840, almost all mayors were chosen by popular vote.

Still more changes in form followed: The elected mayor in many cities continued to preside over the council and now, in addition, appointed some or all of the committees, sometimes making himself chair of the important ones and thus in a position to lead in shaping policy development. The mayor was reaching the level of policy leader at the very time that the functions and activities of cities were rapidly expanding. By the 1850s, there was a strong trend toward the separation of the mayor from the council.

Jackson called for further extension of the ballot. Administrators should be chosen not by the now-elected mayor but by the voters directly. This approach was first seen in the Detroit charter of 1824. The ward assessors, tax collectors, and constables were made elective. This idea spread rapidly and soon encompassed the clerk, treasurer, and corporate counsel or city attorney. Before long it included in some places the city engineer and the chief of police. Jacksonianism continued to spread. It appeared in full fig, Wild West style, in the San Francisco charter of 1851, which provided for the election of the mayor, assessors (three of them), city attorney, comptroller, marshal, recorder, street commissioner, tax collector, and treasurer. The powers of both the council and the mayor were being weakened, but decentralized power appealed to Jacksonians, and focusing administrative responsibility was not yet perceived as a problem.

Another development, essential to bringing frontier government "close to the people," was the loosening of the suffrage rules, which had not changed much since the late seventeenth century. Municipal suffrage was in some cases even more restrictive than was the general, which was determined by the amount of taxes paid or the amount of land owned. The rules were based on the firm and logical belief that property ownership generated in an individual a serious interest in community welfare, while a transient, propertyless population, if enfranchised, would be free to act irresponsibly. The rules remained in effect for two generations after Americans had been told that "all men are created equal." Suffrage eligibility was not yet seen as a human right that should be extended to all males, much less to females.

Nevertheless, the ideas of American democracy seemed, from the beginning, to call for a broad suffrage. Jefferson saw education, not property, as the sound basis for participation in government. Even before the Jacksonians, voting rights began to broaden. Universal white manhood suffrage was first extended by two rural New England states, Vermont (1791) and New Hampshire (1792), along with Kentucky (1792), on the frontier. The campaign for extending the vote to women got underway in the late 1840s, and the Wyoming Territory gave women full voting rights in 1869, but only three other states, all in the West, followed this path in the nineteenth century. However, 15 states had extended full voting rights before adoption of the Nineteenth Amendment in 1920, when 19 others, mostly in the Southeast, still allowed no female suffrage at all.

Free blacks owning property could generally vote with whites in the early years of the Republic, but this privilege was gradually withdrawn as the Civil War approached, and in some states this was done much earlier. Kentucky allowed "all free male" adult citizens to vote in 1792 but withdrew this privilege from blacks seven years later. For white males, the removal of property requirements generally came a generation or so after the three pioneering states, mostly in the 1830s, but sometimes later. Chicago, in its original village charter of 1833, had full traditional taxpayers' requirements, for example. These were reduced to $3.00 in annual taxes in the city charter of 1835. Universal manhood suffrage was not authorized for Chicagoans until 1841.

The Expansion of Services

From early times, city governments controlled the common land used for pasture and recreation, operated ferry boats, maintained cemeteries, graded streets, controlled use of public firewood and timber, fixed the price for bread and beer, licensed restaurants, taverns, and liquor stores, operated public markets and fairs, and occasionally performed other tasks. Cities relied upon fees, land rents, and income from businesses, rarely upon taxes. After Independence, the power to tax was gradually bestowed. Modern functions of government had their beginning in early America with elementary police and fire protection, the operation of public schools (beginning in New England in the seventeenth century), and some basic welfare ("relief") under the Poor Law of 1601. Water supply (though sometimes privately owned) was the first municipal utility. After about 1830, other functions were added with increasing frequency.

Charles W. Eliot, president of Harvard for 40 years, was born in Boston in

1834. He once said that as a boy he had lived in that city and remembered that it had no public water supply, no sewers anywhere in town (even when the population had reached 50,000), no street lights "to speak of," and only basic police and fire protection.[17] Yet when he died in 1926, Boston and other American cities had a line of services and functions virtually as complete, if not of the same quality, as those of today. It had all happened within the lifetime of one man (though it was a long lifetime).

Trends in Structure

By the 1840s, full-time municipal employees became necessary. The patronage system of personnel administration had always existed and had been tied to political parties at least since Jefferson's election in 1800. The simple, nontechnical tasks of the day really did make it possible to change personnel with each election. But this practice, together with the use of full-time employees, which became commonplace in the 1850s (a tumultuous and often lawless time in American cities) set the stage for the coming of the boss-and-machine system that flourished between the Civil War and World War I.

Early in the nineteenth century, the tasks of government were overseen by council committees. But as the population increased and city responsibilities expanded, council members had too little time or ability to serve as administrators, or their interests were in other things, like patronage. The New York charter of 1830 required the council to appoint administrators or boards to head various functions. This was the beginning of departments. (Today boards and commissions are interchangeable terms, but originally commissions were established on an *ad hoc* basis, for example, to build a new city hall

or install a water-supply system.) This plan was followed elsewhere, and soon the boards were made elective: in New York in 1849, in Cleveland in 1852, and then elsewhere during the remainder of the century. The extreme decentralization of city government that resulted together with the inability of the best-intentioned voters to identify able administrators, among other weaknesses in the rapidly growing cities, led to increasing dissatisfaction. The need for better administrative skills, coordinated programs and policies, sufficiently skilled employees, and less waste in government, was rapidly developing and becoming increasingly clear.

The one development in city government structure that supported better democracy during the last half of the nineteenth century was the growth in the size of councils as urban populations grew and the ethnic makeup of the nation became more complex. In cities with bicameral systems, more of them in the East than the West or South, the upper house was normally elected at large and represented *de facto* the downtown merchants, bankers, and developers. It brought citywide businesses and other economic interests into the political arena. The lower house was chosen by wards, which often were drawn along ethnic-group residential lines. Representation was more direct and specific than it is today. Council members did not, however, always simply satisfy themselves with being effective representatives of their constituents' interests as combined into an overall set of community values and goals. By seeking to gain narrow, short-range personal goals, pursue nepotism, and aid friends and neighbors by exploitation of municipal wealth, council members in many cities often demonstrated the characteristic interests that Americans had come to refer to contemptuously as "politics." Many persons, taught about democracy but not civic responsibility, had discovered that it was fun to spend other people's money for their own advantage. During this degenerate period, council members fouled the environment in which the councils existed. They provided one instead in which corruption and pettiness thrived, and they left behind an unwanted inheritance that is still with us.

As the century waned, reformers turned to the executive for leadership. The first charters using versions of the strong-mayor plan went into effect in Brooklyn (then a separate city) in 1880 and Boston in 1885. Gradually the idea spread, in large cities at first, then into others. The centralization of bureaucratic responsibility with the coordination of activities was a result. The plan helped overcome the waste and lack of focus or purpose of the old headless system, especially when the mayor was given full appointive powers, the item veto, and from early in the twentieth century, responsibility for the executive budget. But there were problems, too. The political role of the mayor as policy developer and as the person responsible for selling a program to the public was not always compatible with carrying responsibility for day-to-day operations. The voting public could not identify a candidate with the needed administrative skills, and there was nothing to keep the candidate with the fewest such qualifications from making the strongest claims of possessing them. In large cities, the mayor lacked the needed time for some tasks. And the plan was found to be less than a copy of the corporate model of decision making that many reformers sought. Something else was needed.

With the beginning of the twentieth century came first the commission plan, introduced at Galveston, Texas, in 1901, though there were precedents for it in America.[18] The council-manager plan followed, with the first manager in 1908 and the full plan in 1911, though again there were precedents.[19] Both plans called for small councils with typically seven or fewer members. Both bicameralism and the large, representative ward council were suddenly and almost completely rejected everywhere. Subcommunity representation was not an important consideration of reformers; some were hostile to the very idea. The stories of these developments, the general failure of the former plan, and the success of the latter, which finally was the long-sought reflection of the corporation's formal model, will be well known to most readers. They can, in any case, be reviewed quickly in textbooks and other writings.[20] The commission idea, with the populistic initiative, referendum, and recall added, became the "Des Moines plan." Commission government spread rapidly at first, extending to some 500 cities by 1917. It then went into a long, permanent decline, with very few adoptions after that and with 90 percent of all adoptions being eventually abandoned. The council-manager plan, on the other hand, started a climb on the popularity charts in a trend that still has not ended. Adoptions came particularly on three large waves: First it attracted the efficiency-and-economy reformers. Next came those who hoped to save tax dollars during the Great Depression. (The plan was designed for professional administration from top to bottom, which discourages waste but not necessarily at bargain-basement prices.) Then it became the model of choice for the great suburban movement after 1945. And still today it attracts reformers seeking professionalism and efficiency, as well as most of those who are dissatisfied with the current lot of their city.[21]

In the more than two centuries during which America has been developing its own forms of local governments, we have not sought to create a large number of fundamentally different approaches to government. Rather small differences are commonplace within what are in essence two systems.

The Later Mayor-Council Plan

The mayor-council plan has carried many Jeffersonian and Jacksonian traditions into the present day, including emphasis upon the political aspects of government, separation of powers, and in the early years, a large, often bicameral council featuring easy citizen access to a member, the representation of many ethnic, social, and economic groups, dependence on grass-roots management skills, and the political party as the coordinating agent with other governments at all levels.

Through the years, the plan has followed a definitive pattern of change: From the 1880s onward, the earlier deterioration of the executive structure was gradually halted and the mayor's administrative power increased, but only a few cities have ever accepted the truly powerful mayor that we find, for example, in Boston and Detroit. Something further toward the midrange of the weak-strong continuum is the rule, and in the largest cities, the voters (and sometimes the state legislatures as well) have generally kept the mayors quite weak.[22] The "strong" (or at least strengthened) mayor was expected to provide political and policy leadership, negotiated settlements among the many council members, and at least some degree of coordinated administration among the various departments.

Later another trend that strengthened the mayor as administrator allowed the appointment of a chief administrative officer (CAO). (Sometimes council approval was required.) This allowed the elected mayor to serve as chief executive officer of the city, to concentrate on political leadership, to maintain morale among officers and employees, and to plan policy and development. The CAO, a professional administrator, served as the chief operations officer, responsible for the daily management of the city. In practice, the powers of the CAO vary greatly from one city to another, but all adoptions recognized the unsuitability of reliance upon grass-roots administrations. The first use of this modification appears to have occurred in San Francisco in 1931, but it did not spread until after World War II. Los Angeles and Philadelphia added CAOs by charter in 1951, and gradually most large and many smaller cities did so, too.[23]

Political parties were the institution by which the Jacksonians believed they could coordinate the "bedsheet" ballot they had created. Gradually the need for leadership and coordinated policy became greater while the executive, because of the use of elective administrations, boards, and commissions, became ever weaker. The boss-and-machine system grew rapidly after the Civil War, and in the cities where it existed, the party did serve as a coordinating device. But where machines were weak or absent, the party never was effective for this purpose, and no substitute approach was found or devised. Furthermore, the possible cleansing action of party competition and turnover did not function because cities, especially machine cities, increasingly came under one dominant party. Two-party competition, except at the national level and in a few states, has always been a myth in this country.

The mighty machines, along with the capital-accumulating "robber barons," arose together with the urbanization that accompanied industrialization. The machines were villains to the middle classes, but to journalists, historians, and political scientists, they have always been glamorous, worth studying because they offered perhaps the ultimate in the pure exercise of power, at least within a democracy. But their history was short — about 80 years or three generations in all, by which time they had been defeated, not by middle-class righteousness, but because the need for them passed as the result of social change. By the mid–1950s, they were all gone except for the anomalies in Chicago and Albany, and these could not survive the deaths of their last leaders in the mid–1970s. Non-partisanship, which spread rapidly in the early twentieth century, affected mayor-council cities but not to the extent it did the reformed cities. In 1986, 60 percent of them had non-partisan elections, compared to 74.6 percent in commission and 81.9 percent in council-manager cities.

The councils changed greatly through time. With the beginning of bicameralism in 1797, councils began to increase in size. Although it never extended to as many as 50 percent of the cities, bicameralism suited the central business district elite, and the small, at-large upper house (usually called the select council) continued throughout its history to be dominated by community leaders. The lower house (usually called the common council) was elected by wards. The common council could expand indefinitely, indeed tended to do so, and especially along ethnic lines. Thus, as a city's population became more complex socially, its lower house grew in size.[24] Even quite small cities might have large common councils, especially those that had once been New England towns. The lower house had little incentive to concern itself with citywide problems, and its members frequently were parochial, selfish, wasteful of the city's resources, patronage oriented, and often enough, venal. Except for parochialism, the select councils were sometimes no better. Late in the century, James Bryce, in disgust, called cities dominated by such councils the "one conspicuous failure" in American democracy.[25]

Mutterings of discontent began to make themselves heard by the 1880s. Even in cities where "reform" did not become a war cry, the council came under sharp criticism. Change started slowly, first in attempts to strengthen the office of the mayor. Then the reformers of the second decade of the new century sought to change the structure to the new forms, and this was accompanied in the cities retaining the mayor-council form with a drastic reduction in the size of the councils. Often, though not always, with the resistance of the machines, change came slowly at first, but it had been an avalanche by the 1920s. By the end of the decade, the large councils were almost all gone. Bicameralism came under vigorous attack at the same time. Today, with 50 aldermen, Chicago has the only really good-sized council. (Even it had dropped from 70 members in 1921.) By the mid–1950s, bicameralism had disappeared, unless one counts the unusual arrangement in New York.[26] Today, in mayor-council cities, the mean size of the council is 6.88 members, barely larger than council-manager cities, with 6.13.[27] There was also a rush to abandon alignment with the political parties, although never with the same eagerness as in the reformed cities. With most all cities under the partisan ballot at the turn of the century, the figure dropped rapidly in the second and third decades and continued on its path until today's figure reads but 39 percent partisan elections in mayor-council cities. In some of these cases, state law rather than local preference established the partisan ballot.

Haste, in council reform, may have had, in some cities at least, its proverbial result. In the urgent desire (1) to eliminate corruption, parochialism, and the squandering of resources, (2) to replace the "errand runner" with the "community regarding councillor," and (3) to discourage the revival of faltering machines, access and representation were undervalued as part of the currency of democracy. The efficiency-and-economy reformers, people of influence and affluence, had no need to fear lack of access and representation, but the poor and members of ethnic groups did, and it was they who paid much of the cost in establishing the new councils. They were often excluded from direct access or representation on the council, and this was true whatever the form of government put into or kept in effect.

The Changing Council-Manager Plan

The beginning-of-the-century search for a new structure of government for cities was, in effect, an effort to return to the simplicity of the American colonial system, a system in which there was no separation of powers. More directly, however, the reformers wanted to emulate the highly successful corporate structure, thinking the form would help produce the same much-admired results. The first effort, the commission plan of the beginning of the century, was a false start. It was a serious effort at reform, but its initial use in Galveston evoked the familiar "Hawthorne effect"[:] its encouraging results led to false hopes. Its many weaknesses are well known and need not be discussed here.[28] Use of the plan is slowly disappearing today, with only about 185 cities still clinging to it. In some of these, attempts have been made to modernize it by using professional budget and personnel officers hired on a merit basis, but for some of the deficiencies, there is no solution.

The council-manager plan finally brought to cities a form that paralleled that of the private corporation. It seems surprising that it was not developed somewhat earlier, for the essence of it was also the basis for modern school administration (except that the school superintendent traditionally has had a written contract). In its conceptualization, the plan was Hamiltonian rather than Jeffersonian, and it sought professional efficiency over political leadership and subgroup representation. It consists of a small council (most commonly five or seven members) elected at-large on a nonpartisan ballot. The council hires (and fires) a professional manager who carries out policies through a professional staff. The plan has been so widely accepted that it is in effect in about 73 percent of all the nation's cities today. Its stability and its reflection of the American mainstream is shown in the slowly aging, largely middle-class councils it produces, the increasing number of women serving on councils, the increasing educational levels of council members (nationally, more than one-fourth are college graduates), and an increasing understanding of the theory of the plan, an understanding that was often lacking in earlier days.[29]

Though successful in terms of adoptions, continued support, rarity of abandonments,[30] and compatibility with modern expectations of local government, the council-manager plan is subject to some criticisms and continues to see some changes in its role and, to some degree, its form. The same is also true, of course, of the mayor-council plan. Most interesting of all, perhaps, is that the two urban forms are slowly converging, not with a collision the likely result but with excellent prospects for the further interchange of aspects of structure and function.

The Merging Forms

The organizational needs of one city are much the same as those of another if one controls roughly for size. It is to be expected, then, that cities might drift toward one another in structural pattern. Modern methods of transportation and communication especially make this the case. Today we can point to five distinct trends toward the convergence of the two primary forms:

1. Intergovernmental relations among bureaucrats at the three levels in a federal system and including both urban forms continue on a daily basis to provide coordination of functions and activities. This task was once considered to be that of the political parties, which never did it very well, and the administrators, with their shared values, standards, goals, and procedures, have taken over this job resulting in the further diminution of the functional utility of parties.

2. With the success and continuing expansion of the office of CAO and the ever-wider use of the merit system, differences in professionalism between the two forms continue to diminish. Andrew Jackson could argue in 1829 that public positions could be made "so plain and simple that men of intelligence may readily qualify themselves for their performance," but training is more complex and time-consuming today. The reformed structures once featured better-trained employees, but this is no longer so in relation to well run mayor-council cities. Suitable qualifications do not differ by form of government.

3. As the role of the CAO expands, that of the city manager becomes somewhat more focused, (a) moving away from nonconsensual functions that lack agreed-upon "solutions," or means of resolution, and concentrating upon those functions for which an efficiency expert is needed,[31] and (b) serving as the city's expert on the problems and opportunities of intergovernmental relations. The manager and CAO can both act within the federal government's version of local government, which is seen primarily as an administrative structure implementing policy after its principal characteristics have been delineated in Washington. The manager and CAO have another broad and important intergovernmental task — serving as negotiators and fund finders in hunting expe-

ditions among state and federal agencies. Despite efforts by the Reagan administration to reorient federalism, demanding and expecting the availability of funds for various purposes from Washington will remain important to cities simply because the marginal cost of raising additional funds is cheapest at that level. That economic fact of life will not change so long as the national government controls its own credit.

4. While the chief executive in mayor-council cities has always had some opportunity to function as a policy initiator or developer, this has not been the case with most mayors in council-manager cities. The indefinite responsibility for leadership other than by the manager had occasionally been a subject for criticizing the plan, especially in larger cities. Then in the late 1960s, or even a little earlier in some places, city governments came under pressure to broaden their activities into areas involving social issues having indeterminant modes of resolution, with a resulting lack of local consensus. In these areas, no experts exist (though there may be plenty of community volunteers for the role) and involvement in them can be risky for a manager because there are no likely professional payoffs and no assured peer support. But a mayor who seeks approval in the political realm rather than from peers in ICMA might find political profit in emerging as a leader on such issues, even if the problem has no known means of satisfactory resolution.[32] In cities in which this pattern of action has appeared, leadership has been divided along consensual and dissentual lines, contrary to the original conception of the plan. But this approach — we shall have to observe results for a time before deciding — may prove a strengthening factor, especially in larger cities lacking social homogeneity and values and thus make it more appropriate for today. Success will surely depend in part,

however, upon the mayor's ability and willingness to recognize the areas in which the manager can act as a professional or technical expert and accept the rule that these belong to the manager. The mayor-with-CAO plan is especially well suited, at least potentially, for the assignment of functions along the lines of local value consensus or conflict. The hierarchical lines are not so clear in the council-manager plan, but developments in recent years again show the tendency toward a common approach.

5. Originally, the council-manager approach was conceived of as having a council of amateurs, representing citywide interests, making broad policy that would be carried out in a disinterested manner by professionals. The founding father, Richard S. Childs, thought one of the plan's greatest features allowed for the elimination of the errand-runner councillor.[33] But at-large, nonpartisan elections also reduced the prospects for ethnic-group or dissenting representation. As small council-manager cities with socially homogeneous populations grew into large cities that were much more heterogeneous, problems of representation increased. With the social unrest of the 1960s, the broadening of the local agenda, the politicization of blacks, Hispanics, and others, agitation for change became effective.[34] Unfortunately minorities have needed to resort again to the federal courts in order to achieve fair representation, possibly at the further cost of local autonomy and control. Still, even though proposed changes call for a wider use of the ward system and, in some cases, the enlargement of the council, changes that threaten a return of the errand runner and parochial councillors, they also increase opportunities for better access and representation. These are matters of no small importance when one considers that the local level is the last remaining one in which "democ-racy" can have any real direct, participatory meaning for the ordinary citizen.

Today, the council-manager plan is used in almost one-half of all cities of 2,500 or more population. The reform cities still are revealed in the statistics, even though the convergence trend I discuss exists. The council-manager cities lack the separation of powers characteristics of the older mayor-council model. They are more likely to make use of the initiative, referendum, and recall. They are far less likely to have a partisan ballot. The mid–nineteenth century movement to remove the mayor from the council was so successful that today only one-third of the mayor-council mayors (most of them in weak-mayor cities) still are members, far fewer than in other forms. Their right to vote (except in case of ties) is therefore greatly restricted, but they are much more likely to have the power of veto.

The mayor in mayor-council cities, given the logic of the separation of powers and the tradition since the 1820s, would logically be elected, and 98 percent of them are. On the other hand, in council-manager cities with the mayor ordinarily a member of the council and not an independent executive, greater variety may correctly be expected, with only 61.8 percent directly elected as mayor, 35.5 percent selected by the council, and the others chosen on a rotation basis or by getting the highest vote in the general election. Similarly, with the emphasis on sharing the mayoralty, 9.3 percent of council-manager cities have limits on the number of consecutive terms that can be served in that office. Only 3.6 percent of mayor-council cities have such limits.

That most politically active persons in council-manager cities now understand the general theory of the plan can be determined, at least indirectly. Only 13.4 percent of mayors in council-manager cities have a veto power, and of these it happens that the same percentage can vote on all issues before the council. Thus, only 1.8 percent of the mayors in responding council-manager cities have what amounts to the powers of a mayor in a weak-mayor city. About three-fourths of the mayors having a veto power can vote only to break ties.

It is unlikely that one would find today a situation like that in Jackson, Michigan, in the 1930s. The city had been a pioneer in the council-manager plan, having adopted it in 1914, but much of the time the council had used local, nonprofessional managers, occasionally hiring a professional to build public works. In 1935, an unsatisfactory manager was dismissed, and his successor was hired as chauffeur for the council. (The mayor had wanted to dispense with the position altogether and use the money to build public toilets.) A reform slate, chosen in 1937, hired a professional manager who explained the theory of the plan to the council. Although council-managership had, at least formally, been in effect in Jackson for 23 years not one council member had ever before heard it explained.[35] We have come a long way from such times, at least.

Conclusion

The story of the struggle for the most desirable form of city government is a long and complicated one. It began with a simple, direct form, though one using a highly restricted suffrage. It grew more varied and complex through the nineteenth century as various new factors and pressures entered the picture. Then the trend reversed. It began to simplify and unify in the present century, though variation in detail continued to exist and perhaps always will.

As we near the beginning of another century, further convergence of the two forms seems likely, and further efforts will surely be made both to improve further the quality of the daily work of urban governments and to preserve the meaning for citizens of the democratic experience. State and national governments, except for the act of voting alone, have become for the vast numbers of people, spectator events to be witnessed on television screens. The task remaining for us all is to make certain that the opportunity is kept open for local government always to remain something more than that, something special.

Notes

1. Alexander Pope, *Essay on Man* (1734), various editions.
2. Lincoln Steffens, *Autobiography of Lincoln Steffans* (New York: Harcourt, Brace & World, Inc., 1931).
3. See Charles R. Adrian's *Governing Urban America*, 1st ed. (New York: McGraw-Hill Book Company, Inc., 1955), pp. 172–73.
4. Robert S. Lynd and Helen M. Lynd, *Middletown* (New York: Harcourt, Brace & World, Inc., 1925) and their *Middletown in Transition* (New York: Harcourt, Brace & World, Inc., 1937).
5. Charles R. Adrian, *A History of American City Government, 1920–1945* (Lanham, Md.: University Press of America, 1987).
6. Alice Gottfried, *Boss Cermak of Chicago* (Seattle: University of Washington Press, 1962).
7. Adrian, *History*, Chapter 8.
8. As partial evidence, see Robert L. Lineberry's and Edmund P. Foster's "Reformism and Public Policies in American Cities," *American Political Science Review* 61 (September 1967): 714–17.
9. The data used in this article were collected from the survey "Forms of Government —1986," conducted by ICMA.
10. Two classic sources are Joseph P. Harris' *Election Administration in the United States*

(Washington, D.C.: The Brookings Institution, 1934) and Kirk H. Porter's *A History of Suffrage in the United States* (Chicago: University of Chicago Press, 1918).

11. George H. Hallet, Jr. *Proportional Representation: The Key to Democracy*, 2nd ed. (New York: National Municipal League, 1940).

12. Belle Zeller and Hugh A. Bone, "The Repeal of P.R. in New York City: Ten Years in Retrospect," *American Political Science Review* 42 (December 1948): 1127–48.

13. Adrian, *History*, Chapter 9.

14. See William Anderson's *American City Government* (New York: Henry Holt and Co., 1925) and W.B. Munro's *Municipal Government and Administration* (New York: Macmillan Company, 1923).

15. See John F. Sly's *Town Government in Massachusetts* (Cambridge: Harvard University Press, 1930).

16. Arthur M. Schlesinger, Jr., *The Age of Jackson* (Boston: Little Brown and Company, 1945).

17. The story is repeated in Munro's *Municipal*, 99n.

18. See E.B. Schulz's *American City Government* (Pittsburgh: Stackpole and Hack, 1949), pp. 319–21 and also Charles R. Adrian's and Ernest S. Griffith's *A History of American City Government, 1775–1870* (Lanham, Md.: University Press of America, 1976), p. 161.

19. Charles R. Adrian, *Governing Urban America*, 1st ed. (New York: McGraw-Hill Book Co., Inc., 1955), pp. 195–206.

20. See Bradley R. Rice's, *Progressive Cities: The Commission Government Movement in America* (Austin: The University of Texas Press, 1977).

21. Heywood T. Sanders, "Governmental Structure in American Cities," in *The Municipal Year Book* (Washington, D.C.: International City Management Association, 1979).

22. See Sunder's "Government Structures," Tables 4/7 and 4/8.

23. Charles R. Adrian, *Governing Urban America*, 2nd ed. (New York: McGraw-Hill Book Company, Inc., 1961), pp. 210–14.

24. Adrian and Griffith, *City Government*, Chapter 9.

25. James Byron, *The American Commonwealth* (New York: Macmillan Company, 1888).

26. Charles R. Adrian, *Governing Urban America*, 1st ed. (New York: McGraw-Hill Book Company, Inc., 1955), p. 233.

27. Heywood T. Sanders. "The Government of American Cities: Continuity and Change in Structure," in *The Municipal Year Book* (Washington, D.C.: International City Management Association, 1982), Table 3/7.

28. Rice, *Progressive*..

29. Mary A. Schellinger, "Council Profile," *Baseline Data Report*, vol. 15, no. 5 (Washington, D.C.: International City Management Association, May 1983).

30. Arthur W. Bromage, *Manager Plan Abandonments*, 5th ed. (New York: National Municipal League, 1959).

31. Charles R. Adrian and James F. Sullivan, "The Urban Appointed Chief Executive, Past and Emergent," *The Urban Interest* 1 (Spring 1979): 3–9. It is worthwhile to contrast Clarence B. Ridley's, *The Role of the City Manager in Policy Formulation* (Washington, D.C.: International City Management Association, 1958) with Keith F. Mulrooney's "Can City Managers Deal Effectively with Major Social Problems?" *Public Administration Review* 31 (January 1971): 7–9; and R.J. Stillman's *The Rise of the City Manager* (Albuquerque: University of New Mexico Press, 1974).

32. See James H. Svara's "The Mayor in Council-Manager Cities: Recognizing Leadership Potential," *National Civic Review* 75 (September-October 1986): 271–83; David A. Booth's "Are Elected Mayors a Threat to Managers?" *Administrative Science Quarterly* 12 (March 1968): 572–89; and Robert P. Boynton's and Deil S. Wright's "Mayor-Manager Relationships in Large Council-Manager Cities," *Public Administration Review* 31 (January 1971): 35–42.

33. Richard S. Childs, *Civic Victories* (New York: Harper & Row, Publishers, 1952) and his *The First Fifty Years of the Council-Manager Plan of Municipal Government* (New York: National Municipal League, 1965).

34. See Tari Renner's "Municipal Election Processes: The Impact of Minority Representation," *Baseline Data Report*, vol. 19, no. 6 (Washington, D.C.: International City Management Association, November-December, 1987); Howard D. Neighbor's "The Case Against Non-partisanship: A Challenge from the Courts," *National Civic Review* 66 (October

1977): 447–51; and his "The Supreme Court Speaks, Sort of, on the 1982 Voting Rights Act Amendments," *National Civic Review* 75 (November-December 1986): 346–53.

35. Charles R. Adrian, *A History of American City Government, 1920–1945* (Lanham, Md.: University Press of America, 1987), pp. 477–79.

• *Chapter 8* •

City Government Structures

Tari Renner and Victor S. DeSantis

Public policy making within American city governments is an incredibly complex process. The local context (or political environment) and types of public officials necessarily differ among the country's nearly 20,000 municipalities. In addition, there is tremendous variation from community to community in the rules that define how public officials interact with each other; that is, who has what authority within the policy-making process? There are generally considered to be five basic forms of city government that structure these relationships in different ways.[1]

The two most widely used forms are, of course, the mayor-council and council-manager systems. The former is the only form of city government with an element of separation of powers that is typical in American federal and state governments. The chief executive is elected separately from the city council and exercises some distinctive executive authority (although the precise contours of that authority vary from jurisdiction to jurisdiction). Alternatively, the council-manager plan vests all authority in a popularly elected council, which, in turn, hires an appointed executive.

Powers are also unified in the commission form of government. The voters elect a legislature (the commission) in which each legislator also serves as an executive department head. The commission form is distinguished from both the mayor-council and the council-manager structures in that it has no provision for singular executive leadership. This has become an important point of criticism of the commission form and is one reason why that form has consistently declined in usage over the last several decades.

Town meeting and representative town meeting governments, often cited as the last remaining examples of direct democracy, are almost exclusively found in New England communities. Under the town meeting form, the annual mass public meeting in which all adult voters may participate is

Originally published as "Municipal Forms of Government: Issues and Trends," *The Municipal Year Book*, 1998. Published by the International City/County Management Association, Washington, D.C. Reprinted with permission of the publisher.

considered to be the local legislative body with the authority to pass bylaws and to raise and appropriate funds. State statutes typically mandate that each community have at least one town meeting each year but may hold as many additional (special) town meetings as deemed necessary. During the remainder of the year, the elected board of selectmen, with usually three or five members, is charged with running the daily operations of the town. Under the representative town meeting form, however, the voters elect a limited number of citizens to represent them at town meetings. All citizens may attend and participate in the debates, but only the duly elected representatives may actually vote. This structure, which is a more recent variation of the town meeting form, is an attempt by increasingly urban New England communities to keep many of the elements of direct popular democracy but, simultaneously, to promote greater efficiency in the policy process.[2]

There is considerable controversy among academics, practitioners, and community activists over the consequences of different city government structures. In the first systematic examination of the fiscal impact of different municipal forms of government, published in 1967, Robert Lineberry and Edmund Fowler found that reformed systems (council-manager or commission plans with at-large and nonpartisan elections) tend to tax and spend at lower levels that so-called unreformed systems (mayor-council governments with district and partisan elections).[3] However, they also found that political structure is a significant intervening variable affecting the relationship between a municipality's socioeconomic characteristics and its public policy outputs. Specifically, unreformed jurisdictions tend to be more responsive to the demographic characteristics of their communities than reformed jurisdictions. The authors concluded that "reformed gov-

ernments make public policy less responsive to the demands arising out of social conflicts in the population."[4]

Not all subsequent research, however, has supported these findings. In 1968, for example, Terry Clark used a somewhat different research design and found that the correlations between structure and spending were in the opposite direction.[5] And in the early seventies, Roland Leibert found that if the number of functions that cities perform is controlled, the relationship between structure and policy outputs disappears altogether.[6]

Although the above researchers used different sampling frames and statistical techniques, their studies were all cross-sectional in scope. More recent projects that have attempted to examine this controversy with longitudinal research designs have also produced contradictory results. William Lyons, for instance, found that as citizen demands and resource opportunities increase over time, unreformed jurisdictions tend to increase expenditures more rapidly than do reformed jurisdictions.[7] However, David Morgan and John Pelissero studied 11 cities that changed to reformed structures, matched them with a group of 11 cities that retained their unreformed structures, and found no significant differences in spending patterns between the two groups.[8] These are the most widely cited academic articles examining the consequences of city government structures in America. They not only illustrate the lack of consensus among scholars but also underscore the reality that structural change is absolutely no guarantee of public policy change.

One important limitation of the existing body of empirical research is that it tends to focus on the general form-of-government categories that have been found to be grossly oversimplified. Since "cities have adopted a myriad of structural arrangements that cannot easily be considered part of one model or the other, researchers must reflect this situation in order to be more useful from both a theoretical and practical standpoint."[9]

Methodology

This study does not attempt to sort out the controversies over the consequences of different forms of city government. Rather, its more modest goal is to examine the characteristics of these forms. Specifically, this study analyzes some of the cross-sectional patterns and longitudinal trends in ICMA's *Municipal Form of Government* survey. This landmark survey is conducted systematically every five years. The 1996 survey instrument was mailed to city clerks in all jurisdictions with populations of 2,500 or more and in 643 jurisdictions with fewer than 2,500 people that ICMA recognizes as providing for a position of professional management. In all, 7,331 jurisdictions were given two opportunities to respond.

Questionnaires were received from 4,555 jurisdictions for an overall response rate of 62.1 percent. The response patterns are similar across the population groups except that the rates are somewhat lower for the smallest and largest groups. Regionally, the highest response rates come from the West North Central and Pacific Coast divisions while the lowest are found in the Mid-Atlantic and East South Central divisions. There is less variation in response rates by metropolitan status. The rates for central, suburban, and independent municipalities are 54 percent, 62.4 percent, and 63.5 percent, respectively. However, the most substantial decline in responses from the 1991 to the 1996 surveys is found in central cities, which were the most likely to respond in the former year (74.8 percent) and the least likely to respond in the latter (54 percent).

Policy-Making Structures and Procedures

The responses for the five general municipal forms of government are also examined. Overall, there is a plurality of council-manager systems. A total of 48.5 percent of the respondents report this form, compared with 35.2 percent reporting the mayor-council form. The other three forms are each found in fewer than 5 percent of the responding communities. As discussed above, the commission system is the only minor form found in substantial numbers outside New England. In the 1996 survey, for the first time, ICMA gave city clerks the option of designating "not sure" when asked about their current form of government; 11 (0.2 percent) chose this category. A total of 429 (9.4 percent) did not report a form of government.

The cross-sectional patterns of municipal forms of government in the current survey are similar to those in previous years. Jurisdictions with the largest populations are the most likely to have mayor-council systems, with council-manager systems most prevalent in midsize communities. The decrease in the percentages reporting mayor-council structures is most precipitous between the 500,000–1,000,000 (71.4 percent) and the 250,000–499,999 (32 percent) categories. However, the highest proportions of council-manager governments are found among cities in the 100,000–249,999 (68.3 percent) and 50,000–99,999 (67.3 percent) categories. This form then consistently declines with population through the 2,500–4,999 category and then appears to increase in the smallest population category (under 2,500). However, it is important to remember that the jurisdictions with fewer than 2,500 people are unrepresentative of all jurisdictions in this population category because, to be included in the survey, they must provide for a position of professional management. In addition, there are thousands of cities with a population under 2,500. Consequently, the reported figures understate the proportion of mayor-council and other structures in this population category.

Predictably, there are substantial differences in city government structures by geographic division. In New England, a plurality of jurisdictions have the town meeting form of government (43.8 percent), followed by the council-manager (30.8 percent), mayor-council (10.5 percent), and representative town meeting (3.9 percent) forms. Mayor-council systems are found in a majority of East South Central communities (65 percent), as well as in pluralities of Mid-Atlantic (44.08 percent), East North Central (47.9 percent), and West North Central (47.5 percent) communities. Alternatively, the council-manager form is reported by majorities of South Atlantic (67.9 percent), West South Central (58.7 percent), Mountain (54.5 percent), and Pacific Coast (78.5 percent) communities. Commission governments are reported by 3.5 percent or less of the respondents in each of the nine geographic divisions.

The variations by metropolitan status are small compared with those by geographic division. There are proportionally more council-manager than mayor-council systems reported for each of the three categories. Central jurisdictions split 56.7 percent to 36.9 percent for council-manager over mayor-council systems. The comparable percentages among suburban jurisdictions are 50.5 percent to 32.8 percent, respectively, and those among independent jurisdictions are 44.3 percent to 38.2 percent, respectively.

Structural Change at the Aggregate Level

To obtain an accurate aggregate estimate of the ratio of council-manager to mayor-council forms of government among all American municipalities, two statistical adjustments were made in the data. First, since the unadjusted survey totals include an unrepresentative sample of jurisdictions with fewer than 2,500 people, these communities were removed. Second, those respondents who were not sure about their jurisdiction's form of government were removed to ensure comparability of results with previous surveys. However, these changes made very little difference in the percentage gap between the two major types of structures. The aggregate unadjusted survey results indicate a 48.5 percent to 35.2 percent split for council-manager over mayor-council jurisdictions. With the cities under 2,500 and unsure respondents eliminated, this split becomes 52.7 percent to 40.1 percent, respectively. The adjusted figures also indicate that commission, town meeting, and representative town meeting systems are found in 1.7 percent, 4.9 percent, and 0.6 percent of jurisdictions, respectively.

This study presents some longitudinal data to examine the changes in municipal government structures over time. It includes data from the last four ICMA *Municipal Form of Government* surveys (1981, 1986, 1991, and 1996) for jurisdictions with 2,500 people or more than reported having one of the three *national* forms (council-manager, mayor-council, or commission). (Recall that the town meeting and representative town meeting systems are almost exclusively found in New England communities.) Among jurisdictions with one of the three national forms, mayor-council municipalities declined from a slight majority in 1981 (51.7 percent) to minorities in 1986 (43.8 percent), 1991 (47.4 percent), and 1996 (42.4 percent). Council-manager governments increased from a minority in 1981 (45.5 percent) to majorities in the next three surveys, reaching a new peak (55.8 percent) in 1996. Alternatively, commission cities have consistently declined during this period. They were found in approximately 3 percent of the communities in 1981 and 1986, but fell to 2.1 percent in 1991 and to 1.8 percent in 1996.

However, the changes in aggregate responses in these surveys only indirectly indicate that there were corresponding changes among individual jurisdictions. Differences in response patterns from one survey to the next could produce some of the observed differences. It is also possible that some of the aggregate change is a result of a tendency among newly incorporated municipalities to adopt the council-manager plan. A large number of new municipal incorporations are occurring in southeastern and western states, where council-manager government is more prevalent. The ICMA survey instrument does, however, have several questions that directly address proposed and successful structural changes within the cities.

Proposed and Adopted Structural Changes

Respondents to the 1996 survey were asked whether there were attempts to change their city government structures since the previous ICMA survey in 1991. Overall, the proportion of municipalities reporting an attempt at structural change in the current survey is 14.6 percent. This represents a slight increase over the 12.7 percent reported in the 1991 survey. In 1991, however, city clerks were reporting on attempts at structural change since the 1986 survey. Consequently, the data indicate a slight increase in attempts at structural change from the 1987–1991 period to the 1992–1996 period.

There appear to be few differences in attempted changes by population group, geographic division, or metropolitan status. The variations by general form of city government, however, indicate that changes were most likely to be proposed in town meeting (22.1 percent) and representative town meeting (33.3 percent) systems.

This study reviewed the types of changes that were proposed and those that were actually approved, as reported in 1996 compared with both 1991 and 1986. In the most recent survey, the structural changes that were most likely to be proposed were changing the basic form of city government and adding the position of a chief administrative office (CAO); in both cases there are noticeable increases over the figures reported in 1991 and 1986. There are corresponding increases in the changes that were actually approved for both the form of city government and the addition of a CAO. The absolute numbers of cities reporting either a proposal or an approval to change forms of government in 1996 are approximately twice as large as those in 1991 or 1986. These data are consistent with the overall movement toward the council-manager form of government indicated earlier. Alternatively, there is also a very slight increase in the number of proposals and approvals to eliminate the position of CAO.

The data indicate that attempts to change election systems from at-large to ward or district during the same time period have been reduced. They also suggest that there has been a small decrease in proposals to increase the number of members serving on city councils.

Chief Administrative Officers

Respondents were asked whether their municipalities have the position of a CAO. This person may be called a city manager, city or town administrator, village administrator, or something similar. This position of professional management can be found in all forms of city government. These survey results are based on the relevant data from the 1996 survey. Overall, 77.5 percent of the jurisdictions report having a CAO position. The cross-sectional patterns predictably vary by population, geographic division, metropolitan status, and form of government.

There is an important longitudinal shift between the 1991 and 1996 surveys: the substantial increase in the overall proportion of communities that report having a CAO. The change from 67.1 percent to 77.5 percent between 1991 and 1996 represents an increase of 10.4 percentage points over the five-year period. Although some of this shift may be a result of differing response patterns between the two surveys, the near uniform increases by population group, geographic division, metropolitan status, and form of government strongly suggest that this trend is not primarily a product of sampling variation. The most substantial increases from 1991 to 1996 appear to have occurred among suburban cities (68.9 percent to 80.9 percent), mayor-council cities (36.9 percent to 50.8 percent), commission cities (33.7 percent to 48.5 percent), and communities with representative town meetings (45.0 percent to 70.8 percent). The trend among mayor-council cities is particularly interesting since the data indicate that a majority now report having a CAO. In these jurisdictions, however, the role of the CAO might be limited to assisting the elected mayor with budget preparation and per-sonnel management or conducting policy research and making recommendations; and the mayor alone, without a majority vote of council, may be able to fire the CAO. The authority and responsibility of the CAO in non-council-manager cities are usually not as substantial as those of a city manager under the council-manager plan.

This study reviews the method of establishing the position. A plurality of municipalities with CAOs established the position by charter (44.6 percent). Those positions established by ordinance or state statute constituted 40.6 percent and 10.6 percent of the total, respectively. The proportion created by charter varies with population. The largest municipalities are the most likely and the smallest are the least likely to establish by charter. The reverse is apparent for ordinances. State statute establishment does not appear to vary substantially by population, except that no jurisdictions of 500,000 and over indicate this source for the position of CAO. Charters are most likely to be the source in South Atlantic and West South Central cities. Ordinances are most often used in Mid-Atlantic and West North Central cities. State statute establishment is reported most frequently in New England. The overwhelming majority of central communities (77.7 percent) establish by charter, as do modest majorities of council-manager (54.6 percent) and representative town meeting (62.5 percent) communities.

The authority of appointed CAOs and elected mayors is compared in two critical areas: responsibility for budget preparation and appointment of department heads. Budget authority is much more likely to be solely vested in a CAO (64.2 percent) than in a mayor (12.9 percent). The two share this responsibility in 6 percent of jurisdictions, finance departments have it in 4.2 percent, and other procedures are used in 12.6 percent.

The proportion of jurisdictions in which the mayor has responsibility for developing the budget decreases with population size. This is consistent with the conventional wisdom that although mayor-council systems are most likely in the largest cities and those with a population from 2,500 to 4,999, the former group tends to have strong mayor versions of the plan whereas the latter tends to have weak mayor versions in which the executive has few formal powers.

Mayors appear to have somewhat more power in appointing municipal department heads than they do in developing the budget. CAOs are more likely to appoint department heads than are mayors, but the percentage gap is not as substantial as that for budgetary authority. CAOs have appointment power in 39.3 percent of responding jurisdictions compared with 20.2 percent for mayors. The mayor and CAO share the authority in 16.6 percent of jurisdictions, with other procedures used in 23.9 percent. The differences by population group indicate that mayoral appointment power is the greatest among cities with 500,000 or more people. Predictably, the CAO patterns are similar to those for the form-of-government data. CAOs are most likely to have the power to appoint department heads in midsize municipalities. The highest percentages are found among the 25,000–49,999 (59.2 percent), 50,000–99,999 (62.4 percent), and 100,000–249,999 (58.4 percent) categories. Except for one case in the 500,000-and-over group, the highest percentages of shared authority between the mayor and CAO are apparent in the smallest municipalities.

The form-of-government patterns indicate that mayors have the power to appoint department heads in a narrow majority of mayor-council municipalities (50.3 percent) and CAOs have the power in a solid majority of council-manager municipalities (65.7 percent). These somewhat predictable figures are substantially higher than the percentage of mayors with budget authority in mayor-council municipalities (30.3 percent) and substantially lower than the percentage of CAOs with budget authority in council-manager municipalities (92.6 percent).

This study also examines the changes in mayor and CAO powers from 1991 to 1996. The data suggest that CAOs have fared well compared with elected executives in terms of increased appointment and budgetary authority. The percentage of jurisdictions reporting that the CAOs have appointment authority increased from 31.4 percent to 39.3 percent over the time period. Even more striking, the percentage of jurisdictions reporting that the CAOs have budget authority increased from 46.8 percent to 64.2 percent over the same period. A large portion of this shift is from the "other" category to the CAO category, although the mayor's power has diminished slightly also.

Mayors

The role of the mayor in American municipalities changes depending on the structural relationship between the mayor and council, on whether the mayor's position is full or part time, and on formal authority.

Separation of Powers

One of the most important structural variations distinguishing the different forms of city government is the degree of separation of powers among the key actor[s] and institutions. Although distinctive branches of government are traditional in American state and national governments, they are comparatively rare at the local level. For example, the data revealed that 65 percent of the jurisdictions responding to the survey report that their mayor (or chief elected executive) is also a member of the legislative body. Mayors are somewhat less likely to be members of council in the largest communities and in those responding from the West North Central and East South Central geographic divisions. There are surprisingly few differences among suburban, independent, and central jurisdictions: the first group is only slightly more likely to report that the mayor is a member of council (69.6 percent) than either independent (59.5 percent) or central (61.4 percent) jurisdictions. While the response patterns by form of government are predictable, it is important to note that mayors are members of the legislative body in more than one-third of mayor-council jurisdictions (34.5 percent). This underscores the conclusion of previous research that the traditional models of American city and county forms of government are over-simplified.

Similar patterns are evident from the data, which indicate whether mayors are full or part time. Overall, the distribution of full- and part-time mayors (15.1 percent and 85 percent, respectively) is similar to that in previous surveys. In 1991, for example, the comparable figures were 15.5 percent and 84.5 percent, respectively. There are, however, clear cross-sectional patterns, the most dramatic of which is the consistent decline in the percentage of full-time mayors by population of the responding jurisdiction. Among the geographic divisions, full-time mayors are most likely to be reported in East South Central communities (34.4 percent) and least likely to be found in Mid-Atlantic communities (7 percent). The differences by metropolitan status suggest that central city mayors (38.8 percent) are much more likely to serve full time that either suburban (11.5 percent) or independent (15.7 percent) city

mayors. The response patterns by form of government are predictable. Council-manager communities report the lowest percentage of full-time mayors (5 percent). However, it is noteworthy that only 27.8 percent of mayors are full time in mayor-council communities.

Regarding the methods of mayoral selection used in American communities across the 1991–1996 time period, almost three-fourths of mayors are elected directly by the voters (73.7 percent), slightly lower than the percentage reported in the 1991 survey (77.1 percent). Although far fewer mayors are selected from among the council membership (23.3 percent), this percentage did increase by 2.2 percent over the five-year time frame. Only a very small number of jurisdictions rely on other methods of mayoral selection.

Mayoral Voting and Veto Power

In the traditional American separation-of-powers model, the elected executive is autonomous from the legislature. The executive's power typically includes a veto over legislative enactments as part of the checks and balances inherent in the system. These critical elements are absent from the policy-making process in most American municipalities, however.

This study reviewed the circumstances in which mayors are permitted to vote *within* the legislature. Overall, a majority of communities (54.6 percent) indicate that their mayors can vote on all issues before the city council. Another 35.9 percent allow the mayor to vote only when a tie must be broken. The remaining jurisdictions either do not allow the mayor to vote in council meetings (7.4 percent) or have some other procedure (2.1 percent). There are few patterns in the responses by population except that the largest cities are the least likely to have mayors voting on the council. Pacific Coast communities are the most likely to report having mayors with voting power on all council issues (80.4 percent) while West North Central communities are the least likely (40 percent). There is surprisingly little variation in the data by metropolitan status, but the form-of-government patterns are comparatively strong and predictable. However, the complexities of American municipal structures are illustrated by the fact that more than one-fifth (22.1 percent) of mayor-council cities report that their executive votes on all issues before the legislature.

An important source of executive power may come from the authority to veto legislation passed by the legislative body. This power often comes not only from an executive's actual ability to veto but also from the perceived threat that the executive may use his or her formal authority. Both the actual and potential use of the veto can significantly enhance a mayor's ability to influence council actions in a particular way. The survey data indicate that, overall, only 28.1 percent of jurisdictions give their mayor a veto, whether it be over entire ordinances, resolutions, or appropriations, or only over specific sections or line items of each. The total percentage of jurisdictions reporting mayoral vetoes has consistently declined from 34.6 percent in the 1986 survey to 31.2 percent in 1991 and to 28.1 percent in 1996. These changes are consistent with the apparent movement toward council-manager governments discussed earlier.

The cross-sectional patterns demonstrate that the presence of mayoral veto powers decreases with the population size of jurisdictions. By geographic division, it is most likely to be found in West North Central communities (47.4 percent) and least likely in New England communities (12.5 percent). There are comparatively few differences, however, by metropolitan

status. The form-of-government patterns, although generally predictable, provide further evidence of the complexities in American city government structures. While mayor-council jurisdictions are the most likely to report having an executive veto power (55.9 percent), nearly half of these systems (44.1 percent) do not. Alternatively, more than one out of ten (11.1 percent) of council-manager jurisdictions give their mayor a veto. These data illustrate that many American cities do not necessarily conform to one of the traditional form-of-government models.

City Councils

Next, we turn our focus to the legislative institutions that make public policy in American communities. While these institutions can vary in size, procedures, responsibilities, and traditions, the individual members of these bodies share a fundamental principle: all are directly elected and reelected by voters. Local legislative bodies are most commonly referred to as councils; however, a small number of communities may use the title of board, selectmen, or trustees. The most common size for local legislative bodies across the nation is 6, although this ranges from a low of 2 to a high of 50 council members. Generally, the average size of the council is positively related to population size.

Frequency of Council Meetings

How often the council meets in formal session may be one indication of the council's workload. Just over two-thirds of the responding communities reported that their councils meet twice each month (69.1 percent). Just over 10 percent reported that their councils meet more frequently than twice a month, with 7 percent meeting once a week or more and 3.4 percent meeting three times a month. Just over 20 percent of respondents reported monthly or fewer than monthly council meetings.

The frequency of council meetings is positively related to population size. Weekly council meetings are held in 71.4 percent of the 500,000–1,000,000 population jurisdictions and in 56 percent of the 250,000–499,999 population jurisdictions. Conversely, weekly council meetings fall below the 5 percent rate in the three population groups below 10,000. In these smaller communities, bi-monthly or monthly council meetings are much more common. Similarly, weekly council meetings are more likely in central communities (21.1 percent) than in either suburban (6.5 percent) or independent (3.9 percent) ones.

Although few noteworthy patterns emerge when the council meetings data are presented by geographic division, New England communities are again the outliers. Almost one-fifth (19 percent) of the respondents from this division report weekly council sessions. The next highest rate is among the jurisdictions of the Pacific Coast at 9.3 percent. Not surprisingly, 29.4 percent of town meeting communities and 25 percent of representative town meeting communities rely on weekly council meetings. This may again be an indication of political values and the desire to provide constant access and information to community residents.

Council Standing Committees

In addition to the frequency with which the council meets in formal session, the need for standing committees to handle legislative matters may be another indication of council workload. Standing committees are the most common type of committees used by legislative bodies.

Overall, 53.1 percent of all responding jurisdictions use standing committees in the policy-making process. This is a small increase over the percentage reported in the 1991 survey (52 percent) but is still below that reported in 1986 (54 percent).

The use of standing committees appears to be positively correlated with population size. All of the largest jurisdictions (500,000 and over) use them, as do 92 percent of the 250,000–499,999 population jurisdictions and 63 percent of the 100,000–249,999 population jurisdictions. Only the smallest population group (under 2,500) falls below the 50 percent mark of communities with standing committees. Similarly, the use of standing committees varies by metropolitan status. Nearly two-thirds (65.9 percent) of central jurisdictions report using standing committees. This drops to 54 percent for suburban and 49.8 percent for independent jurisdictions.

Local traditions are often important determinants of local government institutions and processes. Accordingly, geographic patterns often emerge in studies of how people relate to local government and how they design local charters. The data reveals there are substantial geographic differences in the use of standing committees by local councils. The greatest usage is seen among the East North Central (69.7 percent) and Mid-Atlantic (62.3 percent) jurisdictions, while the lowest usage is seen among the New England (37 percent) and West South Central (39.3 percent) jurisdictions.

Filling Vacant Council Seats

Although council members are normally elected through direct election by citizens, alternative systems are often used when a council seat is vacated before a term ends. A majority of responding jurisdictions allow a vacant council seat to be filled by council appointment (52.4 percent). Fewer jurisdictions use appointment by chief elected official (11.2 percent), special election (9.8 percent), or other methods (9.3 percent). Another 17.3 percent of communities reported that the method of filling a vacant council seat depends on the length of term remaining.

When data are presented by population size, no consistent pattern for council appointment of vacant seats emerges, although this method is somewhat more likely in smaller rather than larger communities. While the highest rate of council appointment is for communities under 2,500 (59.7 percent), the lowest usage can be seen among the 100,000–249,999 population group (42.5 percent). The highest rate for special elections can be seen in the 250,000–499,999 population group (24 percent), and the highest rate for appointment by chief elected official can be seen in the 2,500–4,999 population group (16.5 percent).

All the geographic divisions except New England report a majority (or close to a majority) of communities using council appointment to fill vacant council seats. New England communities rely less on council appointment than do other areas (34.7 percent) but also report a greater use of special elections (30.8 percent). Similarly, almost half of the town meeting and representative town meeting systems use the special election feature (40.5 percent and 34.8 percent, respectively). The form-of-government differences demonstrate that, as expected, council-manager jurisdictions, which tend to vest more power with their councils, rely more on council appointment (61.5 percent) than do any other form of government.

Term Limits

In recent years, term limitation for elected officials has garnered a great deal of attention among American voters. Feeling that many elected leaders have become too entrenched in their positions and that elected offices at all levels could use an infusion of new ideas, reform-minded citizens in many parts of the country have called for term limits. This movement has taken on great visibility during the 1990s with many state and local ballot items being placed before voters and winning passage.[10] Over the 1991–1996 time period, the use of mayoral term limits among responding jurisdictions almost doubled from 5.3 percent to 9.7 percent, and the use of council term limits more than doubled from 4.2 percent to 8.7 percent. Although term limits remain infrequently used at the local level, they have received much more widespread attention in the past five years and their use at the local level has certainly increased.

When mayoral term limits are distributed across population groups, the data show that their usage is positively related to population size. The larger cities tend to use this legal mechanism at higher rates, from 55.6 percent in the 500,000-and-over group, to 44 percent in the 250,000–499,999 group, to 28 percent in the 100,000–249,999 group. Related to population size, central communities (20.2 percent) use such mechanisms more often than suburban (9.2 percent) or independent (8.6 percent) communities.

Geographically, the highest frequency of use can be seen among the communities in the Mountain (30.4 percent) and West South Central (17.1 percent) divisions. This should not be surprising since some Mountain states (Colorado in particular) have seen public support for, and a host of ballot referenda on, term limits for many elected government offices in recent years. Also, term limits seem to be used more often in the reform-minded council-manager communities than in communities with the mayor-council form of government.

The data on council term limits reveal very similar patterns to those on the mayoral term limits. Council term limits are also positively correlated with population size. Among those jurisdictions with populations of 500,000 and above, 55.6 percent have this mechanism, compared with fewer than 10 percent of communities with populations of less than 25,000. As expected, central communities use council term limits at the highest rate (16.1 percent) among the metro status categories.

Geographically, council term limits appear to be most popular in the Mountain (28.3 percent) and West South Central (15.7 percent) areas. Of course, these were the two geographic divisions where the mayoral term limit was also the most popular. The council term limit is used least often by communities of the East South Central area (2.7 percent).

Election Systems

Although the last decade has seen a substantial legal battle surrounding the use of at-large elections in local governments around the country, this type of election method remains entrenched at the local level. This study revealed that 60.9 percent of responding jurisdictions rely on at-large systems to elect their local leaders. Previous analysis of the ICMA survey results showed an aggregate decline in the percentage of jurisdictions reporting the use of at-large elections, from 66.5 percent in 1981 to 60.4 percent in 1986 to 59 percent in 1991.[11] While this slight increase back over 60 percent might be due to specific respondent variations from survey to survey, the data suggest that the shift away from at-large elections has leveled off over the 1990s. Historically, the largest shift was apparently toward mixed or combination plans, in which some members of the city council are elected by district and some are chosen at-large. However, mixed systems, which increased from 26.8 percent in 1986 to 29.3 percent in 1991, decreased to 22.3 percent in 1996. The 1991–1996 time frame showed a noticeable increase in the use of district systems, from 11.7 percent to 16.8 percent.

When analyzed in the context of population size, the proportion using at-large elections decreases as population size increases. The reverse is true for mixed systems. The presence of district elections does not appear to vary substantially by population levels. The one clear outlying group is the under-2,500 population category: the distribution of election system types among these smallest communities is 80.7 percent at-large, 8.8 percent district, and 10.6 percent mixed.

The differences by geographic division and metro status are generally consistent with the conventional wisdom regarding the types of cities in which the municipal reform movement was the strongest. At-large elections are most prevalent in Pacific Coast (85.5 percent) and suburban (69.7 percent) jurisdictions. Mixed systems are most likely to be found in West South Central (32.5 percent) and central (44.6 percent) jurisdictions. District elections are most prevalent in West North Central (29 percent) and central (23.2 percent) jurisdictions.

Partisan and Nonpartisan Elections

Just as at-large elections were an important component of the municipal reform movement of the Progressive Era, so too were non-partisan elections. The data from the 1996 survey confirm that nonpartisan election has been one of the most successful reforms. Overall, 76 percent of the responding cities report having nonpartisan elections compared with only 24 percent for partisan elections. This distribution is similar to the 74.5 percent to 25.5 percent and 70.2 percent to 29.8 percent splits reported in the 1991 and 1986 surveys, respectively. The 1996 and 1991 data are slightly higher because they include valid responses from the entire sample, whereas the earlier survey figures exclude the jurisdictions with under 2,500 people and those with either town meeting or representative town meeting forms of government — groups that are overwhelmingly nonpartisan in their election procedures. Therefore, the slight differences between the data presented here and those in previous ICMA publications should not be construed as representing a recent trend toward nonpartisan systems. In fact, given the changes in election systems over the past decade, the nonpartisan election data have been remarkably stable over time.

The distribution patterns of partisan versus nonpartisan elections are predictable. As with at-large elections, the patterns generally reflect the types of jurisdictions in which the reform movement was strongest and weakest. There are few consistent differences by population size, but the variations by geographic division are rather dramatic. Virtually all jurisdictions in the Pacific Coast (98.1 percent), West North Central (94.8 percent), and Mountain (94.8 percent) divisions have non-partisan systems. On the other hand, 89.2 percent of Mid-Atlantic jurisdictions use partisan elections. The differences by metropolitan status are small but mildly surprising. Suburban communities are the most likely to have partisan elections (28.8 percent), followed by central (21 percent) and independent (18.1 percent) communities.

Provisions for Direct Democracy

A variety of provisions for direct democracy, in which voters can influence public policy through their vote, exist across the country. Among these mechanisms are the initiative, the binding and nonbinding referenda, and recall and petition procedures. Splitting the referendum category between binding and nonbinding was new to the 1996 *Municipal Form of Government* survey; the difference between these two provisions is that the binding referendum enacts a ballot measure while the nonbinding referendum may be more advisory in nature and does not specifically change policy or force governmental action. A petition is sometimes called a protest referendum as it allows voters to delay enactment of a local ordinance or by-law until a referendum is held.

As this study revealed, the initiative is reported in 58.1 percent, binding referendum procedures in 41.6 percent, nonbinding referendum procedures in 39.8 percent, recall elections in 68.5 percent, and petitions in 35.7 percent of jurisdictions. When analyzed within the context of population size, the presence of initiative, recall, binding referendum, and petition elections declines with population; however, the nonbinding referendum pattern is relatively consistent. When broken down by metro status, it appears that central jurisdictions are more likely than either suburban or independent ones to have these direct democracy provisions in place (with the exception of the nonbinding referendum).

The geographic division differences are also more dramatic for initiatives and recall elections than for either referendum elections or petitions. The presence of initiatives ranges from 83.3 percent in the Pacific Coast to 25.3 percent in the East

South Central division. Recall elections range from 95.8 percent in the Pacific Coast to 40.2 percent in East South Central division. The amount of variation among geographic divisions is much smaller for the other three types of direct democracy methods.

Conclusion

This research examined the cross-sectional patterns for the 1996 *Municipal Form of Government* survey and analyzed several longitudinal shifts from previous surveys. It appears that there has been a modest, but consistent, movement over the last 15 years toward council-manager and away from mayor-council and commission forms of government. The 1996 survey reports the largest gap to date between the two main systems. This is supported by the trends of increasing structural changes toward council-manager governments, increasing percentages of communities with CAOs, increasing budgetary and appointment powers of the CAO relative to the elected mayor, and decreasing percentages of jurisdictions that report giving their mayor a veto power over council actions. However, the 1996 data also suggest that local election systems, one of most volatile features of municipal government in recent decades, have begun to stabilize over the past five years.

While this research attempts to shed some additional light on the characteristics of policy making and electoral structures in American municipalities, there are substantial controversies that are not addressed regarding the consequences of alternative systems. Future research in the field should seek to make substantive contributions by examining the impact of separate structural elements (such as the location of budgetary authority or the presence of a mayoral veto) rather than just the broad form of government categories, which this study has found to be oversimplified. A more accurate understanding of the linkage between political structures and public policies is still illusive but nonetheless very important to practitioners and reformers as well as to academics.

Notes

1. The term *city* refers also to towns, townships, villages, and boroughs.
2. For an analysis of recent trends in town meeting and representative town meeting forms of government, see Victor S. DeSantis and Tari Renner, "Democratic Traditions in New England Town Meetings: Myths and Realities" (paper presented at the 1997 Midwest Political Science Association annual meeting, Chicago, Ill., 10 April 1997).
3. Robert Lineberry and Edmund Fowler, "Reformism and Public Policy in American Cities," *American Political Science Review* 61 (September 1967): 701–16.
4. Lineberry and Fowler, "Reformism and Public Policy," 714.
5. Terry Clark, "Community Structure: Decision-Making, Budget Expenditures, and Urban Renewal in 51 Cities," *American Sociological Review* 3 (August 1968): 576–93.
6. Roland Leibert, "Functions, Structure and Expenditures: A Re-analysis of Recent Research," *Social Science Quarterly* 54 (March 1974): 765–83.
7. William Lyons, "Reform and Response in American Cities: Structure and Policy Reconsidered," *Social Science Quarterly* 58 (June 1978): 118–32.
8. David Morgan and John Pelissero, "Urban Policy and City Government Structure: Testing the Mediating Effects of Reform," *American Political Science Review* 74 (December 1980): 999–1006.
9. Tari Renner, "Elected Executives: Authority and Responsibility," *Baseline Data Report* 20 (Washington, D.C.: International City Management Association, May/June 1988): 8.
10. Victor S. DeSantis and Tari Renner, "Term Limits and Turnover among Local

Officials," in *The Municipal Year Book* (Washington, D.C.: International City/County Management Association, 1994), 36–42.

11. Tari Renner, "Municipal Election Processes: The Impact on Minority Representation," in *The Municipal Year Book* (Washington, D.C.: International City Management Association, 1988), 13–22.

• *Chapter 9* •

Separating the Powers

Michele Frisby

From the alderman and councillors of colonial America to the mayors, councilmembers, commissioners and managers of the 20th century, local government in the United States has passed through a variety of incarnations. The history of city and county management is rooted in parliamentary England, but it has evolved into a uniquely American balancing act between elected and appointed officials.

In the Beginning

The first American cities were legal corporations with special charters granted by the governor or a proprietor who acted in the name of the English Crown. Those early boroughs (a traditional English term) or cities (an honorary title granted to boroughs that possessed a cathedral) operated under a unicameral council consisting of:

• an alderman and councillors or
• assistant aldermen presided over by a mayor who typically had full voting privileges.

The mayor and the recorder (a city attorney or corporation counsel) were chosen annually by the council or the governor, and they often had limited judicial powers. Councilmembers, on the other hand, were elected by property holders or other taxpayers who qualified as voters.

At the same time, the open town meeting was being employed in Connecticut, Rhode Island, New Hampshire, Maine, Massachusetts and Vermont. Originating in the Massachusetts Bay Colony of the late 1620s, the town meeting form of government functioned unquestioned until the 1780s, when Boston began to explore incorporation and the establishment of a town council. In 1822, the city adopted a charter that replaced the open town meeting with a mayor and council, and other Massachusetts jurisdictions followed suit. Nevertheless, town meetings are still prevalent in New England.

From *American City & County*, Vol. 114, No. 13, November, 1999. Published by the Intertec Publishing Corporation, Atlanta, Georgia. Reprinted with permission of the publisher.

By 1746, roughly 22 municipalities, including New Amsterdam (New York) and Philadelphia, had been incorporated, but no additional charters were granted until after the Revolutionary War. At that time, new state leaders asserted their claims to power, and state legislatures pre-empted the rights of English governors and took control of the municipal corporations. In Massachusetts, for example, the state constitution prohibited the imposition of municipal charters on towns that did not give their consent — an act that paved the way for home rule charters.

Direct Elections

While the mayor-council hierarchy was in place at America's inception, separation of powers and a system of checks and balances were not introduced until 1797, when Baltimore established the country's first bicameral council. The lower house consisted of 16 members — two representatives from each of eight wards — who were elected for one-year terms. Additionally, one representative was elected in each ward to form the upper house.

Baltimore's voters also chose members of an electoral college who selected a mayor. The mayor had the power of veto, which could be overridden by a two-thirds vote in each house of the council. Although the concept of the mayoral veto spread slowly, it was commonplace by the 1830s. However, Baltimore's method of selecting a mayor through an electoral college did not catch on.

In fact, despite their newfound autonomy, during the early 1800s, many U.S. municipal governments still followed the English practice of gubernatorial selection of the mayor. That began to change in 1822, when St. Louis revised its charter to provide for direct election of the mayor. It paved the way for direct elections in De-troit (1824), Philadelphia (1826), Baltimore (1833) and New York (1834).

Corruption and Change

Along with direct elections came new power for the nation's mayors. For example, mayors began to appoint committees, and, combined with their authority to preside over councils, the mayors had significant influence in policy development. With the advent of Jacksonianism, however, municipalities sought to decentralize their governments, separating powers between the mayor and the council and extending public ballots to allow direct election of administrative officials (e.g., ward assessors, tax collectors, clerks, constables, treasurers and corporation counsel/city attorney).

Services changed, too. Initially, taxes funded fire and police protection, public schools, and basic welfare and water provision. By 1860, however, as local governments faced a half-century of unprecedented growth, they juggled demands for road construction, development and building code enforcement — specialized expertise that could not be provided by councilmembers alone.

Seemingly overnight, partisan city bosses emerged, indulging in nepotism, patronage and the exploitation of the municipal funds over which they were granted control. In response to public discontent (primarily voiced by citizens in rural towns and the small communities that surrounded the cities), progressive reformers fought for — and won — a series of reforms that prompted a number of organizational experiments in local government.

In the 1870s, New York's Committee of Seventy — one of the country's earliest nonpartisan "good government" associations — overthrew the corrupt Tweed Ring that controlled Tammany Hall, the dominant political organization in the city.

Philadelphia later formed a similar group, and the two organizations met at the Conference for Good Government in Philadelphia in 1894. That meeting paved the way for the establishment of the National Municipal League in 1895, which joined 46 reform groups from across the country.

In an attempt to stem the corruption and waste that characterized many city governments, reformers began developing charters that centralized bureaucratic responsibility with the mayor. The National Municipal League endorsed that practice when, in 1898, it approved the first model city charter, which concentrated municipal power in the elected executive.

Under that model, mayors were given full appointing authority, a line item veto and budget responsibility. However, policy duties often were incompatible with the mayor's operational duties, prompting reformers to experiment further with the local government hierarchy.

A Push for Commissions

In particular, reformers began looking for ways to incorporate the administrative organization of U.S. corporations into that of local government. The commission form of government, which was formally introduced in 1901 in Galveston, Texas, was one of the first — and initially one of the most popular — models to emerge from that search.

Applying the organizational and administrative techniques of private business, the unicameral commission rejected the large, ward-selected council in favor of a smaller group of seven or fewer members elected at large on a nonpartisan basis. Reformers later added the populistic initiative, referendum and recall that became known as the Des Moines version of the commission plan.

The Des Moines plan garnered sup-

port from the National Short Ballot Organization, a group founded by a young Yale graduate and advertising executive, Richard Childs. Childs fervently believed that the power of the boss machines could be overthrown by significantly reducing the size of party ballots, thus limiting the number of administrative positions that could be elected and forcing citizens to focus on just a few officials directly responsible for the government's administration.

The concept spread quickly and was adopted by nearly 500 cities by 1917. However, despite its popularity, the commission form was flawed; it discarded all the checks and balances established under the executive-mayor-council form. Furthermore, the commissioners — usually elected for their political rather than administrative skills — assumed full-time administrative roles as department heads, despite their lack of qualifications.

Eventually, the prevalence of the commission plan declined. The number of new commissions dwindled, and nearly 90 percent of cities that had adopted the model abandoned it.

Birth and Rebirth

As many cities experimented with the commission concept, others looked for ways to incorporate the practices of private sector management into a system that preserved separation of powers. Staunton, Va., would be pivotal among that group.

In 1906, Staunton became a first-class city under Virginia state law and reorganized its government as a bicameral council — the Common Council — consisting of 22 members. However, the municipal government was placed under the direction of numerous committees, which brought the city's capital projects to a complete standstill.

John Crosby, former clerk of the

board of supervisors in Augusta County, Va., served on the Common Council and suggested a remedy to Staunton's local government bottleneck. "I was a clerk of the Board of Supervisors, which is the governing body of the county," Crosby later wrote. "As I kept the records and attended to all the business under the jurisdiction of the board, reporting directly to them in carrying out its instructions for the government of the county, I was in a sense the general manager or executive officer for Augusta County.

"I could see no reason why the business affairs of the city should not be managed in the same manner as that of the county," he explained. "If the affairs of Augusta County were operated with a governing board of six members and an executive secretary, why was it necessary to have a bicameral council of 22 members and 12 standing committees to operate the affairs of the city of Staunton?"

Crosby encouraged the Common Council to recommend that the city hire a general manager, and, in 1908, the mayor approved an ordinance that put the council's report into effect. That year, Charles Ashburner became Staunton's—and the country's—first city manager.

Recognizing that delegating administrative duties to a trained individual could be the key to reviving his commission model, Childs reintroduced the commission plan. Under that plan, all local government power was concentrated in an elected, part-time council. Citizens became stockholders; councils became boards of directors; and a principal elected official—usually the mayor—assumed a significant role of activism and coordination. The manager was appointed and terminated at the will of the council.

In 1912, Sumter, S.C., became the first city to adopt the commission-manager form of government. Within one year, 11 other cities adopted the model.

The first formal gathering of U.S. city managers was held in Springfield, Ohio, in 1914. It led to the establishment of the City Managers Association, which was designed to address the needs of individual managers who wanted to share their expertise and the challenges of managing the day-to-day operations of the country's communities.

A Question of Authority

Under the first council-manager and commission-manager plans, the manager was granted the authority of administrative functions, including the development of related policy, free from interference of the elected body. The difficulty was in structuring the system to compel councils to let the manager exercise that authority.

Eventually, the National Municipal League and the City Managers Association jointly developed the Model City Charter, which mandated that the council allow the city manager to exercise certain responsibilities without interference. That position differed from the one put forth by the National Short Ballot Organization, creating a schism between the three organizations.

At the same time, the mayor-council form of government was undergoing similar changes. Most mayor-council municipalities expected their chief executive to coordinate some administration among departments. However, as the 1800s came to a close, cities began appointing chief administrative officers, sometimes subject to council approval, to serve as operations officers. That move afforded the mayor more time to focus on political leadership and policy development, and it ensured the continued growth of the mayor-council model.

Through the Years

In its first 100 years, city and county management — in all its forms — was marked primarily by the struggle to clearly define local government responsibilities[:] preserve a system of checks and balances[,] and ensure that policy, services and operations were administered by qualified officials. That era ended with the establishment of government models (mayor-council; manager-council/commission; etc.) that have remained essentially unchanged. However, another century of social and economic shifts have further shaped the manager's role.

1920s

The 1920s heralded the "cult of efficiency" among local governments. Based on the recommendations of the Taft Commission on Economy and Efficiency, scientific budgeting, personnel management, classification systems and efficiency ratings techniques used in federal government experiments were adopted by locals.

In 1924, the City Managers Association changed its name to the International City Managers Association [ICMA] and adopted its first Code of Ethics. The code required members to commit to providing quality public services for all citizens and to support representative democracy, as directed by the community's elected officials.

1940s and 1950s

After World War II, the cult of efficiency and the local government obsession with business and corporate ideals had waned. At the same time, Americans moved to suburbia, stretching the boundaries of core cities and ratcheting up the demand for new infrastructure and service delivery.

A notable shift also occurred in the way citizens viewed their civic responsibility. Unlike John Adams' deliberative public, which had worked together to achieve a shared community vision, the post-World War II suburbanites quickly became focused on the maintenance of their own communities. The suburbanization of the country sowed the first seeds of democratic discord as citizens looked less frequently beyond the immediate boundaries of their own neighborhoods.

1970s

Following the turbulence of the 1960s, neighborhood activism became an even greater force throughout the country. According to a Christian Science Monitor poll, by the late 1970s, 20 million Americans belonged to neighborhood organizations. Those groups — generally organized as a result of a specific incident or situation taking place within the community — worked directly with their local governments to solve problems.

The effort to help neighborhood groups find their voice in public decision-making also led to one of the most controversial vehicles in local politics.

In 1976, Howard Jarvis, a representative of a group of apartment building owners, formed a partnership with a real estate agent and former car salesman to establish the framework for one of the country's most renowned tax-revolt initiatives, California's Proposition 13. The initiative signified the beginning of the popular referendum.

Ongoing Challenges

In its final report, issued in 1995, an ICMA-established task force of local government managers, assistant managers, academics and other participants articulated a vision of the future of local government:

"The trend toward government by initiative and by state and federal mandate will continue. Metropolitan development patterns will continue to change what we think of as a city. Economic, racial and age diversity will exert increasing pressure on the political process, and the perception of the effectiveness of various forms of government."

According to the task force, managers would become highly sensitive to political issues and would help mayors deal with councils more effectively. The partnership between manager and mayor would become essential to the community's political and administrative future, including citizen involvement in local government decision-making.

The task force's predictions appear to be accurate. During the past several years, observers have witnessed dramatic changes in local government structures that affect the responsibilities, duties and authorities granted to mayors and appointed professional managers. For example:

• Citizens in Oakland, Calif., recently supported their newly elected mayor's proposal to abandon the city's 68-year history of council-manager government while entrusting responsibility for day-to-day operations to a nationally recognized professional manager.

• In Miami, a major scandal involving numerous city officials (including the city manager) dominated the headlines a few years ago. The newly elected mayor immediately appointed a veteran city manager to serve as interim chief administrative officer.

• In Cincinnati, following the second form-of-government challenge in four years, voters adopted a proposal to retain the city's 73-year tradition of council-manager government while strengthening the mayor's role to become one of the most empowered mayoral positions among council-manager communities.

Today, of the U.S. communities with populations of 2,500 or more, roughly 3,285 have adopted the council-manager structure of government, and 2,978 operate under the mayor-council form. The remaining 543 employ the commission, town meeting or representative town meeting forms.

As the demand for services and global competition among communities continues to rise, the need for visionary political leadership and effective administrative management will as well. In the end, what happens to local government in the United States will be determined by the unique needs of the communities served.

• *Chapter 10* •

The Council-Manager Plan

William H. Hansell, Jr.

The 20th century could well be called the century of local government in American democracy. The American system of governance is based on a federal system, which divides the powers of sovereign governance between, on the one hand, a central or national government and, on the other, 50 state entities. The powers of the national government are limited to those specifically delineated in the United States Constitution. All other powers are reserved for the people or given to each of the 50 states.

This preference for decentralized government has been advanced by the 50 states as they empower their local governments, resulting in the strongest and most decentralized local governments in history. Throughout the 50 states, for example, there are 27 large consolidated cities/counties, 3,043 independent counties, 19,279 municipalities, 16,656 towns and townships (in 20 of the states), 14,422 independent school districts educating American children, and 31,555 special districts.

This is a significant amount of local government for 275 million people. But as the French observer Alexis de Tocqueville said in the early 1830s, "Local institutions are to liberty what primary schools are to science: they put it within the people's reach; they teach people to appreciate its peaceful enjoyment and accustom them to make use of it. Without local institutions, a nation may give itself a free government, but it has not got the spirit of liberty."[1]

Stability and Change

By the end of the 20th century, local governments in the United States had become the most trusted level of American government. Year after year, citizens ranked local government higher than state or national government as the level from which they felt they got the greatest value for their money.

Originally published as "Evolution and Change Characterize Council-Manager Government," *Public Management*, Vol. 82, No. 8, August, 2000. Published by the International City/County Management Association, Washington, D.C. Reprinted with permission of the publisher.

Table 1
Professional Management Continues to Grow Among U.S. Counties

CAO Status	2000	1999[1]	1994	1990	1986
With Chief Administrative Officer	1,151[1] (37.8%)	1,032[1] (33.8%)	705 (23.2%)	677 (22.2%)	650 (21.4%)
Without Chief Administrative Officer	1,897[1] (62.2%)	2,020[1] (66.2%)	2,338 (76.8%)	2,367 (77.8%)	2,393 (78.6%)
Total	3,048	3,052	3,043	3,044	3,043

Form of Government	2000	1999[2]	1994	1990	1986
Council-Administrator	371 (12.2%)	371[2] (12.2%)			
Council-Elected Executive	480 (15.7%)	481[2] (15.8%)			
Commission	2,197 (72.1%)	2,200[2] (72.0%)			
Total	3,048	3,052	3,043	3,044	3,043

[1]Statistics were obtained by pulling the number of counties with CAO positions listed in ICMA's database. These data do not appear in the Cumulative Distribution of Counties published annually in ICMA's *Municipal Year Book.*
[2]The first year in which ICMA published county form-of-government data using this breakdown was 1999.

Source: The Municipal Year Books *1986–2000, published by the International City/County Management Association (ICMA), Washington, D.C.*

This has not always been the case. During the 1900s, local governments evolved from holding the dubious distinction as the most troubled component of the American system of governance to becoming the most trusted. This evolution has been accomplished through a series of radical changes that began in the early part of the century, continued throughout it, and is generally known as the progressive reform movement. The reforms have included:

• Instituting civil-service personnel systems.
• Promoting personnel on a merit basis.
• Mandating competitive tendering or purchasing of goods and supplies.
• Requiring performance budgeting and measurement.
• Ensuring open, transparent government that is fully accessible to citizens and the media.
• Implementing alternative service-delivery mechanisms, including contracting, volunteerism, franchising, and privatization.

• Developing the council-manager system of organizing and operating local government.

Of the reforms, the development of the council-manager system may have been the most significant step in improving the performance and credibility of local government.

The Flexible System

The council-manager form continues to prove its adaptability. The system's developers originally conceived elected councils as consisting of only five to seven members, elected at large on a nonpartisan basis. The council would select one member to serve as mayor. Initially, elected councilmembers received little or no compensation for what was viewed as volunteer service to the community.

Data collected by ICMA in 1996 show

that council-manager communities in the United States elect an average of six councilmembers; however, councils consisting of 12 to 13 members have become increasingly common among larger jurisdictions. Often, some or all councilmembers are elected to represent a particular section of the community.

Seventeen percent of council-manager communities nominated and elected council members by ward or district; an additional 18.5 percent used a combination of at-large and by-district elections. Seventeen percent of responding council-manager communities also held partisan elections.

To fulfill development needs in public works and capital infrastructure, local governments initially recruited managers with engineering backgrounds or undergraduate degrees. In the book *The Rise of the City Manager*, author Richard Stillman reported that in 1934 77 percent of responding managers with college degrees had majored in engineering and that 51 percent listed a bachelor's degree as their highest level of educational attainment.

According to information in Stillman's book and in ICMA's *1996 Municipal Year Book*, appointed managers often are trained in the general management field of public administration, and the proportion of managers with a graduate or professional degree has risen steadily, from 27 percent in 1971 to nearly 73 percent in 1995. A manager's course of study may include such diverse topics as public finance, resource allocation, economic development, technology, intergovernmental relations, planning, public policy, and environmental and human resource management.

Level and type of education have not been the only changes among appointed local government managers. In 1971, researchers reported that virtually all city managers surveyed were white and male. The *1996 Municipal Year Book* directories indicated, however, that by 1995 12 percent of reporting managers were women and that an increasing number of minorities had joined the profession.

While managers continue to serve without a guaranteed term or tenure, the number of managers with employment agreements—which set the terms and conditions of employment and separation and give clear guidelines for performance evaluation—continues to grow. The results of

Table 2
Council-Manager Government:
The Fastest Growing Form of U.S. Local Government Structure

Form of Government	2000	1998	1996	1992	1988	1984
Council-Manager	3,302 (48.3%)	3,232	2,760	2,441	2,356	2,290 (34.7%)
Mayor-Council	2,988 (43.7%)	2,943	3,319	3,635	3,686	3,686 (55.8%)
Commission	143 (2.1%)	146	154	168	173	176 (2.7%)
Town Meeting	334 (4.9%)	333	365	363	369	370 (5.6%)
Representative Town Meeting	65 (1.0%)	65	70	79	82	81 (1.2%)
Total	6,832[1] (100%)	6,719[1]	6,668[1]	6,686[1]	6,666[1]	6,603[1] (100%)

[1]Totals for U.S. local governments represent those municipalities with populations of 2,500 and greater. There are close to 30,000 additional local governments with populations of less than 2,500. Only those that have been recognized by ICMA as having a professional manager or administrator are included in the Association's database; therefore, municipalities with populations of less than 2,500 have not been included in this calculation.

Source: The Municipal Year Books *1984–2000, published by the International City/County Management Association (ICMA), Washington, D.C.*

Figure 1
Fast Facts

• More than 75.5 million individuals live in communities operating under council-manager governments.
• During the past 16 years, an average of 63 U.S. communities per year have adopted the council-manager form.
• Sixty-three percent of U.S. cities with populations of 25,000 or more have adopted the council-manager form.
• Fifty-seven percent of U.S. cities with populations of 10,000 or more have adopted the council-manager form.
• Fifth-three percent of U.S. cities with populations of 5,000 or more have adopted the council-manager form.

---

a 1998 ICMA survey showed that nearly 80 percent of responding local government managers and chief administrative officers reported having a contract or letter of agreement with their councils, compared with 14 percent in 1974.

Roles and Responsibilities

An appointed manager constantly must be aware that the powers of the local government belong to the council. Any authority or responsibility assigned to the manager by the council or by the citizens through a local charter can be removed at any time, for any reason. The illusion of power that may appear to rest with a manager must be accepted as a temporary acquisition based on the manager's knowledge and expertise.

Managers who serve a jurisdiction for an extended period come to understand this community's values, traditions, and goals. Yet, the manager must remember that the *council* represents the community, and she or he must defer to the elected officials as reflecting the policy wishes of the citizenry.

Elected Leadership

In most communities, the citizens perceive their mayor as their most visible leader, and the elected leaders of council-manager communities are no exception. In this way, mayors are analogous to corporate board chairpersons.

Mayors in council-manager communities fulfill two critical leadership functions. The first is that of consensus building: the mayor coalesces the community's disparate constituencies so they can work together successfully. The second role held by the mayor in council-manager communities is to guide the development and implementation of policies that improve community service delivery.

Over the past 86 years, the position of mayor within council-manager communities has been strengthened in a variety of ways. Under the original understanding of the form, the mayor was selected annually by the council from among its members. Councillors frequently rotated into the

---

Figure 2
C-M Facts

For the past 86 years, the choice of U.S. communities has been council-manager government. Since the early 1900s, the council-manager form has become the most popular system of local government for communities with populations of 5,000 or more.

By 1918, there were 98 council-manager localities; in 1930, ICMA recognized 418 U.S. cities and seven counties as operating under the council-manager form. And by 1985, the number of council-manager communities had grown to 548 cities and 86 counties in the United States. Currently, 3,302 U.S. cities with populations greater than 2,500 and 371 U.S. counties operate under this system of local government.

---

mayor's position, over time leaving no clearly identifiable political leader. But ICMA's 1996 form-of-government survey showed that 62 percent of all council-manager communities now elect their mayors directly by a vote of the citizens, for a two- or four-year term. The people elect their political leader, and the council must accept that selection.

In recent years, some communities have chosen to strengthen the mayor's authority, providing the mayor with one or more of these powers:

- Veto actions of the council that require an extraordinary majority to overturn.
- Organize the council by assigning councilors to chair or serve on committees and assign matters to these committees.
- Appoint citizens to serve on advisory or quasi-judicial authorities, boards, or commissions.
- Receive the annual budget prepared by the manager and to present that budget, with comments and suggestions, to the council for their consideration.
- Make an annual report to the council and the citizens on the state of the community.
- Initiate the hiring and/or involuntary termination of the person serving as manager.

The manager remains the chief executive officer with clear authority to:

- Hire and terminate all senior officers and staff.
- Purchase all goods, supplies, equipment and services required by the government.
- Prepare an annual budget and financial plan for consideration by the council.
- Administer and enforce all contracts involving the local government.
- Enforce all laws adopted by the council.

Communities with a delegation of authority to an appointed manager and a strongly empowered mayor might be seen as working under a mayor-council-manager form. Under this scenario, the elected leadership comes "from the people" via the election process. The citizens oversee the operations of the government through an open and transparent system that guarantees that it will continue to be "by the people."

Day-to-day management of the government is directed by an experienced professional manager who is selected by the elected officials and who facilitates the government by operating "for the people" who live in the community and who will live there in the future. Here are the values these managers add to the system of governance for the communities they serve:

- Establishment of policy and service delivery strategies on a basis of need rather than of demand.
- An emphasis on the long-term interests of the community as a whole.
- Promotion of equity and fairness.
- Recognition of the interconnection among policies.
- Advancement of broad and inclusive citizens' participation.

For nearly 90 years, the council-manager form has successfully adapted to American community needs. Cities and counties are not static and the changes taking place in them involve the core of our values. Professional managers and the council-manager form, however, continue to evolve so that today, as in the early 20th century, this system offers government of the people, by the people, and for the people. In short, council-manager government is a system of reform that will continue to serve communities well in the 21st century.

Today, more than 75 million Americans live in council-manager communities, and, because of the system's compatibility with modern expectations of local government, continues to grow and flourish in nations dedicated to improving the quality of life in their communities.

Note

[1]*Hypertexts in American Studies.* "Democracy in America: Alexis de Tocqueville"; Web site found at http://www.xroads.virginia.edu.

• *Chapter 11* •

Overview of County Governments

TANIS J. SALANT

Discussion of the American county typically generates diverse views on the usefulness and role of county government that range from praise as the regional government of the 21st century to ambivalence as the sleeping giant of the 1990s to judgments of obsolescence. Opinion has often reflected misconceptions and outdated perceptions; indeed, county government has endured a barrage of jaundiced assessments for decades. Attempts to reform counties have been occurring since the beginning of the century, and home rule and consolidation movements continue today.

Until recently, however, little was actually known about county government. Academic research tended to focus on the federal, state, and municipal governments or to lump counties together with municipalities as "local governments."

This chapter traces the origins and development of county government from an administrative arm of the state into a vital and integrated unit of the intergovernmental system.

Origins

County government's lineage can be traced to the English shire of a thousand years ago. Throughout its development in England, two opposing traditions unfolded and were later transported to this country: the county as an administrative arm of the national government and the county as a local government.[1] Primitive counties delivered the principal services of the royal government through justices of the peace who were appointed by the king, but local officials, particularly the sheriff, also were important. Early responsibilities included judicial, military, and public works functions.

Originally published as "County Governments: An Overview," *Intergovernmental Perspectives*, Vol. 17, No. 1, Winter, 1991. Published by the U.S. Advisory Commission on Intergovernmental Relations, Washington, D.C.

The English county remained as the leading unit of local government, but the parish and borough also became providers of local services. Parishes generally were formed in small rural areas as a unit of church and civil government to furnish elementary education, poor relief, and highways, while boroughs were established in more urban areas to provide police and judicial services.

Early settlers in North America crafted a host of adaptations to conform to their own economic and geographic needs. In Virginia, initial jurisdictions were modeled after the parish, but because the state was agricultural with a dispersed population, larger areas were called for, and eight counties were superimposed to serve as election, judicial, and military districts.[2] These first counties were governed by a plural executive form called the county court, a model replicated extensively in other counties, especially those in the South.

New York and New Jersey adopted a third form of local government. These states were divided into counties, but elected township officials automatically became members of the county board of supervisors, and a penchant for large county governing boards commenced. In Pennsylvania, the county became the primary unit of local government because of the state's widely dispersed population, and county governing bodies, called boards of commissioners, were elected at large.

These colonial origins show the diversity of rationales for counties, but the dual tradition of the county as an arm of the state and as a local government persisted. Virginia's strong county form was followed throughout much of the South. Massachusetts' form, which provided fewer services, spread throughout New England. The county supervisor form originating in New York and New Jersey surfaced in parts of Illinois, Michigan, and Wisconsin, while Pennsylvania's county commissioner form was transported to many midwestern and western states.

Historical Development of County Government

Colonial counties were not altered significantly by the American Revolution, and in the quest for a balance of power between the federal government and the states, the framers of the new Constitution did not include provisions specifically for local governments. Early state constitutions generally conceptualized county government as an arm of the state, declaring it to be "nothing more than certain portions of the territory into which the state is divided for more convenient exercises of the powers of government,"[3] and left the prime responsibility of serving local constituencies to municipalities.

By the Civil War, however, counties were assuming more responsibilities. Many states fashioned them into election districts, paving the way for their becoming a significant political unit for party machines and placing them in the center of the "spoils system." County governing bodies also were gaining more elective positions, and the potential for corruption increased along with the expansion in their political power, planting seeds that eventually resulted in a deeply tarnished image and subsequent cries for reform.

Following the Civil War, populations grew, and both cities and counties experienced greater demands for urban services. After World War I, three trends helped strengthen the secondary role of counties as units of local government: (1) population growth, (2) suburbanization, and (3) the reform movement to streamline governmental structure.[4] By World War II, urbanization and the reform movement were bringing changes to county government that broadened its role further: changes in organization, more autonomy from the state, a greater number of intergovernmental linkages, more resources and revenues, better political accountability, and a "cleaner image."[5] Newer services joined the more traditional ones, such as responsibility for libraries, airports, hospitals, other health services, planning, zoning, and fire protection.

Diversity in Size, Governance and Authority

There are 3,042 county governments in the United States, with another 22 city-county consolidations and 44 "independent cities" that perform county activities. Forty-eight states are divided into functional county governments (called "boroughs" in Alaska and "parishes" in Louisiana). Connecticut and Rhode Island are divided into "unorganized areas" for the purpose of elections, but they have no functional county governments. The number of counties per state ranges from 3 in Delaware to 254 in Texas. Eight states have fewer than 20 counties, and 7 have 100 or more; the average number is 64. Counties range in area from 26 to 159,099 square miles, and the average is between 400 and 599 square miles. County populations range from as low as 164 in Loving County, Texas, to eight million in Los Angeles County; the average is between 10,000 and 25,000 residents.

Counties, like cities, are created by the state, but primarily for the purpose of providing state services. As such, counties are considered quasi-corporations. Their powers are derivative, but counties have always been recognized as units of local government as well. With few exceptions, the county governing body and most line officers are elected locally, and have some authority to provide optional local services and raise additional revenues which makes local autonomy a reality, though limited. Many observers point out, however, that counties often have huge responsibilities but little real authority beyond local police powers, an anomaly often frustrating to county officials.

All counties were created originally as general law units of government subject to almost unlimited state control. Since the home rule movement was launched in California with passage of a state constitutional amendment in 1911, 35 other states have given counties the option of having discretionary authority through home rule.[6] Home rule provisions vary from state to state, but typically focus on changes in governmental structure as the avenue for modernization and autonomy. A few states also grant additional authority in functional and fiscal areas, and even some of the 12 states without home rule have granted extra authority through special legislation.

The most common type of home rule is charter government, offered to counties by 24 states. Charter home rule permits counties to frame and adopt their own charter and generally brings greater autonomy than other types of home rule, particularly in functional and fiscal domains. In 1988, Iowa became the most recent state to provide for charter adoption, while Texas remains the only state to have repealed such a provision.

Of the 1,307 counties eligible to adopt a charter, 117 have succeeded in doing so. Charter adoption tends to have more appeal in urban counties and in areas with reform-minded constituencies. The failure of charter adoption has been attributed to lack of a compelling need for structural change, little interest among voters in reform issues, or the opposition of county constitutional officers, whose elective positions are often transformed into appointive ones or consolidated with other offices.[7]

Approximately 2,924 counties, or 95 percent, remain general law counties. The others operate under charter, as city-county consolidations, or as variations attained through special legislation. Regardless of status, however, all counties are still obliged to perform traditional state services, and their original rationale as administrative arms of the state survives intact.

All functional county governments are governed by locally elected executive bodies. The composition and title vary greatly across states and sometimes within, but boards of commissioners and boards of supervisors with three to five members are the most common. There are about 17 different titles, and board size ranges from one member to over fifty in New York.[8] Titles often reflect their origins, such as "Judge Executives" in Kentucky, reflecting that state's initial emphasis on delivering judicial services.

In most counties, board members serve in both legislative and executive capacities. Boards have overall fiscal responsibility for the county, approving the budget, and setting the property tax rate as well as levying other types of taxes. Most counties elect additional officers to head constitutionally mandated departments, such as the sheriff, attorney, recorder, assessor, and treasurer. Often referred to as "row officers," constitutional officers are elected countywide and have functional authority independent of the governing board.

County Government Today

In addition to traditional duties and other programs mandated by the state, counties perform a growing list of optional services once largely reserved for municipalities. Despite the limits and controls imposed by the state, many counties now enjoy a large measure of autonomy. Yet, in spite of dramatic changes in scope, authority, and level of resources, many scholars and "reformists" still hold that county government is anachronistic, rigid, and ill-equipped to meet the needs of a rapidly changing society. This position perpetuates the view of counties as an arm of the state and further obscures the real changes that have been occurring. Laments are frequently heard in state legislatures that county government is difficult to understand. Confusion and ambivalence on the part of taxpayers as well as legislators have hurt the efforts of county officials to secure tax increases from voters and to plead their case in state capitols.

A more contemporary view recognizes the county as a major provider of local services as well as an arm of the state. This view is an outgrowth of urbanizing and suburbanizing trends and dwindling federal support to states and localities, where counties are called on to deliver more services both within and outside of municipal boundaries. Recent research has led to the development of a *quadruple* role concept of county government, an amplification designed to reflect its growing importance in the intergovernmental system.[9] These roles can be defined as follows:

Administrative Arm of the State. Under this role, counties deliver services that are state programs, typically client- or formula-driven and beyond the control of counties. Indigent services are in this category, and state mandates under this role are generally the most onerous.

Traditional Government. These services also are (constitutionally) mandated and are performed generally by elected constitutional officers. Usually, however, counties have discretion in the level of service provided. These include countywide services performed by such officers as assessor and treasurer, and traditional services in unincorporated areas, such as law enforcement. Other services can include the county hospital, the superior court, and road construction and maintenance.

Local Government. These functions can be divided into three categories: municipal-type services in the unincorporated area, such as planning and zoning, libraries, and parks and recreation; services provided jointly with cities and towns (or for them) through intergovernmental agreements; and responses to individual constituent requests by elected supervisors or commissioners (a function that can consume more time than their "formal duties").

Regional Government. This role is perhaps the fastest growing, and includes such functions as transportation, air quality, conservation, landfill and toxic sites, growth management, and economic development. These functions are typically environmental or "quality of life" issues that address long-range problems. Rural and medium-size counties also play this role, especially in landfill siting, growth management, and economic development. In this role, counties often become the dominant government in the region.

Contemporary Issues

Traditional government roles likely claim the greatest portion of county budgets today, particularly because of escalating expenditures for law enforcement, corrections, and courts. But new roles as "local" and "regional" governments are not likely to diminish, and recognizing this trend would help state legislatures address county issues, particularly the financial ones. Legislators frequently point to the diversity among counties as problematic in crafting uniform legislation, but while the nature of county government has changed dramatically since its inception and demographic shifts continually place

new strains on existing structures and resources, diversity should not be overemphasized or cited as an obstacle to problem solving. Recent research concludes that, with respect to "major" problems, there are more similarities than differences among counties.[10] Special circumstances, such as demography, geography, economy, and spending traditions, determine more the *severity* of problems and the way they are handled than the *type*.

Recent surveys of county officials, legislative hearings in state capitols, and a growing body of literature point to the relationship with the state as the most critical component of county viability. Insufficient revenues have become the biggest headache for county officials, and the spiraling costs of state-mandated programs, particularly those for indigent services and long-term health care, are cited as the primary cause. These mandates are handed down without accompanying funds, or sufficient funds, to finance them, and client-driven state formulas keep costs beyond the control of counties. Unfunded state mandates are now widely recognized as unworkable, especially in light of the restricted revenue-raising capacity of counties, and many states are searching for alternatives.

Urban problems are no longer confined to communities with population concentrations. Environmental concerns and the shift of indigent populations from inner cities to outlying areas have superimposed urban problems on rural structures. Urban, suburban, and rural counties alike are grappling with common concerns. Affordable housing, solid waste management, clean air, water quality, AIDS, refugee resettlement, juvenile justice, hazardous material transportation, energy alternatives, cable TV, urbanizing parks systems, and managing natural disasters are just a few of the concerns of county officials—concerns that reflect intergovernmental complexity and a greater role for counties in societal problem solving.

It should be in the best interests of both the federal and state governments to have healthy county governments, particularly since economic development and urban growth issues have become so prominent. The state of counties across the nation is only now beginning to receive more attention, and the double jeopardy of spiraling mandated costs and revenue and expenditure caps makes the fiscal future of all but the wealthiest counties look grim. Counties have assumed and been given a multiplicity of roles, however, even in less populated areas of the country, and the performance of these roles will require authority, resources, energy, and creativity.

Notes

1. Laura Kaifez, John Stuart Hall, and Albert K. Karnig, "Counties in the National Context," in *County Government in Arizona; Challenges of the 1980s* (Phoenix: Arizona Academy, 1984), p. 2.

2. Herbert Sydney Duncombe, *County Government in America* (Washington, DC: National Association of Counties, 1966), p. 20.

3. *State of Maryland v. Baltimore and Ohio R.R.*, 44 U.S. 534, 550 (1845) cited in Ibid., p. 23.

4. Duncombe, p. 28.

5. John C. Bollens, *American County Government* (Beverly Hills, California: Sage, 1969), p. 41.

6. Tanis J. Salant, *County Home Rule: Perspectives for Decision Making* (Tucson: University of Arizona, 1988), Chapter II.

7. *Ibid.*

8. Blake Jeffery, Tanis J. Salant, and Alan L. Boroshok, *County Government Structure: A State-by-State Report* (Washington, DC: National Association of Counties, 1989), pp. 8–14.

9. Tanis J. Salant, *Arizona County Government: A Study of Contemporary Issues* (Tucson: University of Arizona, 1989), pp. 160–162.

10. *Ibid.*, p. 152.

• *Chapter 12* •

County Governments and Change

VICTOR S. DESANTIS

County government in the United States has undergone tremendous change during the last century. In one of the most well-known early studies of county governments, H.S. Gilbertson depicted them, unfortunately, as the "dark continent[s]" of American politics.[1] The characterization stemmed from the rampant corruption and incompetence that was associated with the political machines and boss rule at the turn of the century. By mid-century however, Clyde Snider, a prominent scholar of county government, reported optimistically about the modernization of the county government organizations and the expansion of the county role in the federalist state.[2] By the mid–twentieth century, counties were asked to take on more functional responsibility and were better equipped to handle their new role. The period since the mid-century assessment of the state of the county can also be seen as a continuation of more-significant involvement from county government in the operation of American democracy. Indeed, many of the recommendations offered by Snider to enhance county government further, such as authority centralized in a chief administrative officer position and increased power to conduct county business, have been instituted.

Historically, one of the most remarkable features of county government has been its stability as an American institution. The number of county units reported in the 1987 Census of Governments stands at 3,042.[3] This number has changed little from the 1942 total of 3,051 and the 1962 figure of 3,043. When viewed beside the steady increase in the number of municipal and special district governments over the same time frame, the stability appears even more dramatic.

Originally published as "County Government: A Century of Change," *The Municipal Year Book*, 1989. Published by the International City/County Management Association, Washington, D.C. Reprinted with permission of the publisher.

Roots of the American County System

The evolution of the American county can be traced back to its use in Britain as an administrative arm of the national government.[4] The tradition of county government was well ingrained in the lives of the British colonists as they began to settle in North America, though the role of the county differed slightly depending on the region of the country. Regardless of the different roles delegated to the county, it is not surprising that the county unit as a layer between town and state governments should become a permanent fixture in America from its inception.

During the early colonial days, towns and counties were the basic units of local government in New England. While the towns were at the heart of local decision making with the annual town meeting, counties were established to carry out a variety of functions not performed by the smaller towns. Counties were responsible for such functions as judicial, military, and fiscal administration. However, even in the early days of the nation, the county operated in the background of the town government and failed to achieve the same level of importance. This tradition has remained throughout the history of New England. In fact, Connecticut and Rhode Island function without the existence of counties as organized units of government. Thus, the impression of the county as the "lost child" of local government was visible quite early.

The counties of the middle colonies held a position somewhat more important than those in New England and grew to be more instrumental in the delivery of public services. While performing the same duties as their New England counterparts, the counties of the middle colonies also became involved in law enforcement, with the county sheriff a principal focal point. The more important status of these counties allowed them to further their functional responsibilities to include road construction and maintenance and many welfare programs for the poor. In New York and New Jersey, one supervisor with taxation duties was elected from each town or township. In addition this taxation supervisor served on the county board of supervisors (or board of chosen freeholders as they became known in New Jersey). This county board had control over many of the county administrative functions. This arrangement of county government became the most traditional form of county government and later evolved into what is now known as the commission form. As the population spread westward, this pattern of county government became widely adopted by Midwestern areas.

Quite different from the system of local government adopted in either New England or the Middle Atlantic states was the system established in Virginia by the early settlers of the Tidewater region. Since the county covers a much larger geographic area, it performed better as the basic unit of local government in this region. This was primarily a reflection of the predominantly agricultural society with its widely dispersed rural population. This made it necessary to establish the county government as the primary unit of local government in the delivery of public services with much more importance than the smaller units of municipal government.

The early models of county government that developed in the different regions of the original colonies set forth the basic patterns of county government still in existence. Many of the foundations set out in these early forms continue to affect the ongoing administration of American counties.

Evolution of Modern County Government

Like other units of local government, counties are essentially creatures of the state government and have only derivative powers. As such, they have often been limited in the amount of freedom to conduct their internal affairs. The ability of a county or municipality to bring about more autonomy or self-government is acquired through home-rule provisions. The primary argument behind such provisions stems from the feeling that the local government has a better understanding of local needs and traditions and is better suited to handle such requests.

Historically, the movement toward greater autonomy and home-rule authority has come much slower for counties than for cities in many states. This is not to suggest, however, that all states have moved at a constant pace. Today, the National Association of Counties (NACo) reports that 36 of the 48 states with county governments grant those units some form of home-rule authority, either in the form of home-rule charters or optional forms of government.[5] Of those 36 states, 23 offer counties the ability to adopt a home-rule charter, while the remaining 13 offer counties limited autonomy through limited home-rule provisions or optional forms of government.

Regardless of the form of government, the trend toward such legal grants of authority from the states reached a peak during the period between 1972 and 1974, when nine of these provisions were passed.[6] However, autonomy is a much more recent phenomenon in most counties. As recently as 1965, only 18 states granted counties the right to choose from among optional forms or charter government.

While the scope of authority granted under these provisions varies widely, the powers can be divided into the general areas of structure, functional responsibility, and fiscal administration.[7] In the structural area, home-rule authority gives counties the authority to have a position of appointed manager, or the position of elected executive, or both. It gives counties the ability to change the method of electing commissioners and the size of the legislative board. Additionally, it enables counties to move away from the tradition of electing many of the other county administrative officials and to fill these positions by appointment instead.

The ability to change the basic structural arrangements in counties is based on the idea that there is not one best way to organize the governmental machinery. The newer demands placed on counties require that there be some flexibility in their operation. As Florence Zeller points out, movement away from the traditional structure allows for greater professionalism and more centralization and accountability through the addition of a county manager or county executive.[8] The charges of lack of professionalism and accountability are those most often leveled against the commission form of county government still mandated in some states. Giving counties the authority to institute changes through home-rule charters or optional forms have greatly enhanced their ability to deal with the growing complexity of local government.

In the area of functional responsibility, granting home authority can allow counties to increase their level of efficiency in public service provision. The ability to exercise independence in choosing alternative approaches for delivering public services has enabled some counties to better manage their resources. In addition to outright city-county consolidation, the use of intergovernmental service arrangements has allowed counties and their cities to avoid the duplicated and uncoordinated efforts that confront many neighboring jurisdictions. As Joseph Zimmerman points out, in 1974 only ten states had the constitutional or legislative authority to transfer voluntarily functional responsibility among units of government.[9]

Several types of functional arrangements can be used in the delivery of public services. The first involves a complete transfer of functional responsibility from one governmental unit to another. This has become more popular as many cities, under circumstances of fiscal stress, began realizing that the larger county unit may be better prepared to handle certain services. The other alternatives are to provide for an intergovernmental service contract or a joint service agreement. Under a service contract one or more cities can enter into a voluntary contract with the county to provide any number of services. A joint agreement may be entered into by a city and county for the joint financing and implementation of a service. A 1983 study by ICMA and ACIR showed that a substantial number of counties were using all three of these approaches, and the trend has increased over the previous decade.[10] Regardless of the approach used, counties are now handling the provision of more services than ever before. Clearly, this new responsibility indicates the growing role of the county in the intergovernmental framework.

The last area of powers granted under home-rule authority relates to fiscal administration. The ability of counties to control their own finances and promote budgetary stability is greatly enhanced when the rules governing county debt and revenue raising are loosened by the state government. Historically, counties were not free to issue bonds and raise debt limits on their own authority. Counties were also limited in their ability to raise revenue through taxation. Although there are wide differences, grants of fiscal control that accompany home-rule provisions allow counties greater financial flexibility to operate in the changing society. The current revenue data for counties point out the increased use of approaches that were not available to many counties until the last 20 years.

The trend toward greater autonomy suggests that counties have improved their position vis-à-vis the states over the past several decades. Interestingly, however, the rush toward adoption of home-rule charters has not proceeded quickly. Few counties in states that allow full home-rule charter provisions have attempted to institute such new forms. While this may suggest that many counties have made better use of the states optional forms without going the full route toward self-determination that a home-rule charter would bring, it may also indicate other obstacles faced by counties in establishing home rule. One of the major obstacles involves the nature of charters themselves, which call for local approval. Many counties in the pursuit of local self-governance have tried and failed to establish home-rule charters. As Tanis Salant notes, "It appears an easier task for states to pass relevant proposals than it is for individual counties to adopt charters."[11]

Legally, the home-rule movement for counties has come far in affording counties a more-substantial degree of self-governance. This may be the most important ingredient in promoting county modernization. According to Alastair McArthur, the ability of counties to move beyond the constitutional requirements mandated by the states is an important provision if counties are to confront the many demographic and economic changes that continue to occur.[12]

The City-County Consolidation Movement

One of the areas of change in intergovernmental relations has been the use of city-county consolidations. While this approach received popular support during the 1960s and early 1970s, the practice dates back to 1805 with the consolidation of New Orleans and Orleans County. A number of other large city and county areas also took this step by the turn of the century. Among them were New York, Boston, Philadelphia, and San Francisco.

A city-county consolidation involves the merger of one or more municipalities with a county to form a metropolitan government performing the functions of both cities and counties. Such consolidations can be established through voter referendum or state legislative action. Along with the governmental unification comes a merger of the geographic boundaries of the consolidated area. The current number of city-county consolidations stands at 21.

While the first half of the twentieth century saw few consolidations, the move toward this approach began to pick up again in the early 1960s. Unfortunately, while interest in this alternative had picked up, political and social realities confronting many areas trying to consolidate made success hard to come by. Some states have made consolidation difficult through restrictive provisions in the state constitution and statutes.

The benefits of consolidating an area come mainly in the provision and delivery of public services and the advantages that accrue from the consolidation of functional responsibility. Specifically, some of the frequent arguments in favor of consolidation are that it promotes efficiency and coordination in the provision of services, reduces the amount of governmental fragmentation, provides for greater re- sources by combining those of both areas, and reduces the need to establish special district governments.[13]

An independent city is one that performs the functions of both the city and the county but operates independently of any county unit. Though this phenomenon is found primarily in Virginia, in which there are 41 independent cities, several others also exist: St. Louis, Missouri; Baltimore, Maryland; and Washington, D.C.

Virginia is a special circumstance because it allows incorporated communities the ability to seek state legislative approval for designation as an independent city when the city reaches 5,000 in population and meets the requirements of the law to become a city. Such cities, if granted the designation, operate independently of any county governmental unit.

Form of Government

While a variety of different arrangements exist for the organization and administration of American counties, there remain three basic forms of county government: commission, council-administrator, and council-elected executive. Historically, the commission, or plural executive, form of government has served as the most extensively used form of county government. It has only been because of the more recent home-rule movements and optional form passages that county government has begun to use the alternative forms.

In order to gain precise information about the use of different forms of county government, ICMA conducted a "County Form of Government Survey" during the summer and fall of 1988. The survey included questions related to form of government, the county legislature, the chief elected officer, and the election process.

The results of that survey form the database for this section.

The Commission Form. The commission or plural executive form of government in counties is the oldest and most traditional organizational structure. It is characterized by a central governing board with members usually elected by district. Though a variety of names exist for this board, among the favorite are the board of commissioners or supervisors and the county court (sometimes known as the levying court). Most often, the board selects one of its members as the presiding officer. Members of the governing board may act as department heads. The governing boards share administrative and, to an extent, legislative functions with independently elected officials: the clerk, the treasurer, the sheriff, the assessor, the coroner, the recorder, etc. No single administrator oversees the county's operations. In some counties with the commission form, the structure includes an official (generally full-time), such as the county judge, who is independently elected at-large to be the presiding officer of the governing board. As noted previously, many disadvantages associated with the commission form stem from the usual lack of a chief administrator to provide more professionalism, executive leadership, and accountability.

Among those counties that responded to the survey, the highest percentage use the commission form of government (39.7 percent). This is a relationship between form of county government and both population and metro status. The smaller and more rural counties are those that most frequently choose to remain under the traditional commission form. There would also appear to be substantial variation among the geographic divisions in the use of the commission form.

The Council-Administrator Form. Interestingly, the survey results point to increased usage of the council-adminis-trator form and the council-elected executive form. While these findings may be partly a result of biases in the survey response group, the overall trend toward these two forms cannot be masked. In the past few years, counties have made dramatic leaps in moving toward these alternative structural arrangements.[14] Indeed, as noted previously, the overall trend toward professional management in counties can be seen by the ever-increasing number of counties recognized by ICMA as providing for the manager form of government.

The council-administrator form of government for counties is similar to the council-manager form for cities. But three distinct variations are identifiable. In its strongest variation, the council-administrator form provides for an elected county board or council and an appointed administrator. The county board adopts ordinances and resolutions, adopts the budget, and sets policy. The administrator, appointed by the board, has responsibility for budget development and implementation, the hiring and firing of department heads, and recommending policy to the board. In some counties, where a weaker version of the council-administrator plan is in place, the administrator usually has less direct responsibility for overall county operations and less authority in hiring and firing, and may consult with the board on policy issues.

There is more widespread use of the council-administrator plan among the more populated counties. This may be a result of the need for more professional management on a continual basis to accompany the complexity of governing large counties. While over half of the counties use this plan in each of the population groups above 50,000, none of the population groups below 50,000 use it with more than a 44.9 percent frequency. Counties with suburban status use this form most often, followed by counties with central status. The geographic breakdown reveals quite a high degree of variation also, with the South Atlantic counties having the highest percentage (75.6 percent) and the West South Central counties having the lowest rate (16.4 percent). Admittedly there is some degree of correlation between these variables. For example, the counties of the West South Central region are also those in Texas and other states that have a larger percentage of smaller rural county governments. In addition, the 254 Texas counties are mandated by state law to operate under the traditional commission form of government.

Another variation of the council-administrator form used in some areas combines elements of the council-administrator plan and the commission form. Here, an assistant to the presiding officer may serve in the capacity of administrator. For example, in Michigan the auditor, or controller, appointed by the governing board to audit the county's finances, may serve as an administrator; in other states, the county clerk, who is by statute clerk to the governing board, may have some administrative responsibility.

The Council-Elected Executive Form. The third form of county government is the council-elected executive form. This system has two branches of government — legislative and executive — and more clearly resembles the strong mayor form of city government. Here the county council or board assumes responsibility for county policies, adopts the budget, and audits the financial performance of the county. The elected at-large executive is considered the chief elected official of the county and often has veto power, which can be overridden by the council. The executive prepares the budget, carries out the administration of the county operations, appoints department heads (usually with the consent of the council), and suggests

policy to the governing board. In addition, this official carries out appropriations, ordinances, and resolutions passed by the board and generally acts as the chief spokesperson for the county. When the executive is considered the chief political spokesperson, the executive often delegates the administrative responsibility for the daily county operations to a chief administrator.

This form, along with the council-administrator form, has begun to receive more popular support over the past several decades. In 1977, only 142 counties or about five percent operated under this form of county government, and those that did use it were often the larger more-populated counties.[15] A total of 269 (22.1 percent) of the responding counties reported operating under this form. Additionally, some noteworthy variations appear when this figure is broken down by population, region, and metro status. The counties in the population group between 500,000 and 1,000,000 put this form to use most frequently, with a percentage of 45.8 percent. None of the population groups below 250,000 reported using this form at a rate any higher than 24.9 percent. Regardless of such differences, the fact remains that this form has received much greater usage over recent years and has helped to push counties forward in their quest toward modernization.

Among the responding counties, 37.7 percent indicated that the county had established the position of chief administrative officer. When broken down by population group, it becomes clear that the larger counties are those that use the chief administrative officer most frequently. Not surprisingly, these results are similar to those for the council-administrator form of government. The majority of the counties report that the position was established through state statutes that allowed for the optional form. As noted previously, few counties have chosen to use the home-rule charter as a route to alter their form of government. Indeed only 7.3 percent claimed to have established the position through a charter adoption. Additionally, of those that did use the charter as a means of acquiring a CAO, the highest percentage (53.8 percent) came in the second largest population group.

The Elected Head of County Government

While the official title of the presiding officer in counties has long been a traditional title such as county judge, county supervisor, or county board president, this has begun to change. The movement toward independently elected executives has made the title of county executive much more prevalent. Though the terms of office for the top official vary somewhat, almost all serve terms of less than five years. The greatest percentage of terms (58 percent) are only one year in duration. This is mostly an artifact of the plural executive form of county government in which the county council selects the presiding officer from among its members. This selection process may be a council vote or some rotational scheme. The rise in the number of two- and four-year terms may be a result of the increased use of the council-executive form, which allows the popularly elected executive the pleasure of a longer term.

The most popular method of selecting the elected head of county government is from the commission or council membership. While 69.1 percent use this method, only 22.2 percent of presiding officers are elected directly by the voters for that position. Few counties use an alternative method such as the rotation of a commission member to select their presiding officer.

Though the powers of the elected head of the county government vary among jurisdictions, one indication is the ability of the elected head to veto measures passed by the county council. The data shows few (8.1 percent) of the elected heads of government can veto council-passed measures. The breakdown by population group indicates that larger counties grant this right with the greatest frequency indicating this may be a function of the form of government, particularly the elected executive.

The County Legislature

One of the traditional aspects of county commissions is the smaller size of most legislative boards. Close to two-thirds (63.6 percent) of the county boards have sizes that range from three to five members. Another 15.2 percent range in size from six to ten members. A small percentage of county boards (5.6 percent) have over 20 members. The ability to increase the size of the county board is one of the reforms associated with the home-rule movement. The tradition of small councils is one that was long mandated by state requirements.

As previously mentioned, the presiding officer or elected head of the county government is often a member of the county board or council. As the data reflects, 93 percent of the responding counties indicated that the elected head of the government is also a member of the county board. This high percentage suggests that even under the council-executive form, the elected head may serve on the council in some capacity.

The length of the term for commission members is broken down between those elected from at-large and ward systems. Under both methods of election, the majority of commission members are elected to serve four-year terms. For those elected from at-large systems, 82.9 percent of commission members have four years to serve, while 75.9 percent serve four-year terms under ward systems. While there are small percentages of two-, three-, and over six-year terms in the at-large systems, the only substantial percentage of respondents (21.5 percent) in the ward system are those using two-year terms.

Use of overlapping terms in legislative bodies is one way of providing stability and continuity in the legislative process. The data indicates 69.5 percent of the responding counties allow for the overlap of commission member terms. The breakdown by population group reveals little relationship between the size of the county and overlap of commission member terms. However, it is noticeable that the overlap mechanism is used most often in the smaller counties (those under 5,000 in population).

The results indicate that there is substantial variation in overlap between geographic divisions. While the Mid-Atlantic and East South Central divisions use overlapping terms the least frequently, the West North Central and Pacific Coast use overlap most frequently. Metro status does not seem to be relevant to the use of overlapping terms.

The type of election system used in counties was also examined. The highest percentage of counties (45.5 percent) that responded indicated the use of district elections. For many counties without home-rule authority, the district plan is required under state law. While 30.1 percent use a system that mixes the at-large and district plan, only 24.4 percent use the pure at-large system. The predominant use of district elections in counties may stem from the larger size and more diverse nature of counties. While some geographic variations exist, there seems to be little correlation between either population or metro status. Populations under 2,500 report use of at-large systems at a rate of 51.2 percent, an amount that is 15.9 percentage points higher than the next highest frequency at 35.3 percent.

One of the political reforms instituted in an effort to break the control of party organizations in local government was the establishment of nonpartisan elections. But only 17.6 percent of the responding counties have opted to exclude party labels from the election ballot. Further analysis of the partisan election phenomenon reveals that for those counties that have partisan elections, over 60 percent allow for the presence of both national and local party labels on the ballot. These election trends are surprising in light of the more widespread use of both at-large and nonpartisan election systems at the city level. Possibly the political reform movement that occurred so profoundly at the city level has never been felt as great at the county level.

County Finances

While the effects of fiscal stress on local governments is now a well-known reality, the problem remains an important aspect of managerial decision making. The tough decisions that are made to keep expenditures in line with revenues while citizens beckon for increased service levels remain with city and county administrators. While most managers have discovered new tools for dealing with such macrobudgetary issues, the impact of eight years of "new federalism" has been quite dramatic. One of the most detrimental policy changes may have been the demise of general revenue-sharing funds. In addition, many local government administrators have found their options limited in the wake of citizen initiatives to curtail the use of property taxes. Such efforts to hold down property tax rates have forced local governments around the country to look for alternative sources of revenue.

One of the most widely accepted alternatives has become current charges, or user fees as they are known. Current charges accounted for nearly one-quarter (24.8 percent) of the total county revenues in 1985–1986.[16] In contrast, current charges made up roughly 16 percent of the total county revenue as recently as 1976–1977. While the future promises continued growth in the use of current charges, increases in functional assignments to counties may spell even more widespread use of this mechanism. Current charges, though somewhat controversial, can work to offset the costs of both delivering the public service and determining the level of service demanded by the citizens. Without question, however, the popularity of current charges as a revenue mechanism should continue to increase in the future.

In spite of the policy shifts at the federal level, intergovernmental fiscal transfers remain the greatest single source of county revenues. In 1985–1986, such revenue accounted for slightly over 35 percent of the total revenue pool. The revenue data from 1976–1977 show that intergovernmental revenue accounted for roughly 44 percent of the total county revenue. These figures point to a much reduced role for the federal and state government in their fiscal assistance to county governments.

The 1988 presidential election may have bolstered the hope of many local governmental officials, however. Many of them are taking an aggressive role in determining their economic fate. Such groups as the National Association of Counties, the National League of Cities, and the U.S. Conference of Mayors joined forces to lobby many of the presidential and congressional candidates long before the election in the hopes of getting local government support higher on the list of priorities in the upcoming years.[17]

Another trend in county revenues is the decreased reliance on property taxes as a revenue source. Though property taxes accounted for 26.2 percent of total revenue in 1985–1986, this amount represents a decline since 1976–1977 when over 30 percent of total revenue was acquired through property taxes. Offsetting this decline, however, has been the increase in non-property tax revenue over the same time period. While such taxes accounted for a mere seven percent of total revenue in 1976–1977, they made up nine percent of total revenue by 1985–1986.

Examination of the data reveal that counties have responsibility for provision of a variety of public service functions. The top three expenditure areas for county government in 1985–1986 are health and hospitals, public welfare, and education, in that order. This trend has remained consistent since 1979–1980.[18] The greatest percentage of county expenditures (15.9 percent) goes toward the maintenance and operation of hospitals and implementation of various health programs. This percentage has increased since 1979–1980 when the health and hospital expenditures accounted for 15.6 percent. While 14.3 percent of county expenditures was devoted to public welfare programs in 1985–1986, this represented a decrease on a percentage basis from the 1979–1980 figure of 15.3 percent. This decrease indicates the overall trend that has been seen as county spending in the area of public welfare decreases. During the early 1970s, the percentage of direct expenditures toward public welfare was roughly 25 percent.

The 1985–1986 expenditures in education account for 13.8 percent of total expenditures, down from 15 percent in 1979–1980. Importantly, these aggregates do not reveal the variations among the different states in county expenditure patterns.

County educational expenditures, for example, are relatively high in those states in which counties are responsible for the direct administration of that function.

In the aggregate, county expenditures have increased dramatically during the 1980s. While counties spent over $56 billion in 1979–1980, the total expenditure increased to over $92 billion for 1985–1986. This represents an increase of 65.3 percent over the six-year period. However, revenues have increased at a slightly higher rate. While the total revenue amount in 1985–1986 was over $96 billion, in 1979–1980, the total revenue was just over $56 billion. The percentage-increase in revenues between those time periods was 72.6 percent.

The date for the start of new fiscal years and the settling of the various revenue and expenditure reports required in modern government also shows some variation. While the highest percentage of counties (45.9 percent) opts for 1 January as the start of the new fiscal year, a large percentage also relies on the mid-year date of 1 July as a start of the fiscal cycle. Interestingly, only a small percentage of counties (11.2 percent) coordinates its fiscal cycle with the federal government's.

Conclusion

If counties were in a period of flux at the time of Snider's mid-century review, the same can be said of today's county government. The county government has grown in importance and plays an increasingly integral role in the intergovernmental framework. This can be seen most emphatically in the amount of service responsibility that has been granted to the county. While providing more services, they have also found new approaches to enhance their revenue base to cover the costs of delivering these services. Addi-

tionally, and most importantly, counties have been given more discretion in the organization and structure of their government through grants of home-rule charters and optional forms. These factors add up to a county government that is more professional, more flexible, and better equipped to handle the complexities that confront local governments in today's political and social environment. While much more remains to be accomplished at the county level, they clearly are an integral part of American politics.

Methodology

The data used in this survey were collected through ICMA's 1988 County Form of Government survey. The survey was mailed to county clerks in 3,044 counties in the United States. Counties not responding to the first request were sent a second survey. A total of 1,295 counties (42.5 percent) responded to the survey.

Notes

1. H.S. Gilbertson, "The Dark Continent of American Politics," in *The County* (New York: The National Short Ballot Organization, 1917).

2. Clyde Snider, "American County Government: A Midcentury Review," *American Political Science Review* 46 (March 1952): 74.

3. 1987 Census of Governments (GC87-ICP), November 1987, 1.

4. Herbert S. Duncombe, *Modern County Government* (Washington, D.C.: National Association of Counties, 1977): 20.

5. National Association of Counties, (telephone interview with Research Department), 15 November 1988.

6. Duncombe, 51.

7. Tanis Salant, "County Home Rule: Perspectives for Decision Making in Arizona," in *County Issues* (University of Arizona, 1988), 10.

8. Florence Zeller, "Forms of County

Government," in *County Year Book* (Washington, D.C.: International City Management Association, 1975), 28.

9. Joe Zimmerman, "Transfers of Functional Responsibilities," in *County Year Book* (Washington, D.C.: International City Management Association, 1976), 59.

10. Harry P. Hatry and Carl F. Valente, "Alternative Service Delivery Approaches Involving Increased Use of the Private Sector," in *The Municipal Year Book* (Washington, D.C.: International City Management Association, 1983), 201.

11. Salant, 41.

12. Alistair McArthur, "3,049 Labs for Local Government Testing," *Public Management* (April 1971): 3.

13. From *America's Counties Today 1973* (Washington, D.C.: National Association of Countries, 1973).

14. Zeller, 28.

15. *Ibid.*

16. *County Government Finances in 1985–1986*, U.S. Bureau of Census, 1988, 1.

17. Kim Beury, "Counties Hopeful for New Deal," *American City and County* (August 1988): 31.

18. *County Government Finances in 1979–1980*, U.S. Bureau of Census, 1981, 5.

Chapter 13

City-County Consolidations

Julianne Duvall

City and county officials have been discussing issues of consolidation for years in hopes of increasing services, productivity, and savings by having one local government preside over both former jurisdictions. In fact, local officials have been attempting to streamline local government for greater efficiency and cost savings since 1805, when the city of New Orleans and Orleans Parish, Louisiana merged in the first city-county consolidation in the United States. Since that time, cities and counties have attempted complete consolidation more than 84 times, with a success rate of only approximately 29 percent. Currently, 25 consolidated cities and counties exist, with 18 of those having merged after World War II.

In recent years, cities and counties have pushed the issue of consolidation more frequently as a way of answering the growing problems of local government, such as revenue losses in terms of intergovernmental transfers and increased service demands. However, the influx of new consolidation proposals faces a declining success rate because citizens typically resist the idea. Many times, the mere prospect of consolidation explodes into a volatile issue among the citizens of both jurisdictions. The division among citizens over city-county consolidation stems from citizens' desire to have local government operate responsively and efficiently. In a democracy, however, this is difficult to achieve without some type of local government coordination.

The consolidation issue also relates to the roles cities and counties play in providing services. Counties, as administrative arms of the state, must provide services with state limitations on the amount and source of revenue.[1] Therefore, with restrictions on funds, counties and cities often view consolidation as an appropriate measure to meeting increasing citizen expectations as well as regional planning needs. Some form of consolidation can indeed

Originally published as "City-County Consolidation: An Answer to Local Government Efficiency," *Issues Brief*, January, 1989. Published by the National League of Cities, Washington, D.C. Reprinted with permission of the publisher.

help local governments fulfill their obligations.

Pressures to Consolidate

In these days of tighter purse strings for local governments, there are more incentives for cities and counties to attempt consolidation. City incorporations have been on the rise because of conflicts between unincorporated areas and counties over the organization of government services, limited sources of local revenue, regional planning efforts, and land-use control.[2] Unfortunately, as more cities incorporate, counties cannot meet service needs with the declining revenue base. Counties must then look for alternatives in providing services for lower cost. And, as the number of incorporations within a county increases, fragmented systems develop, ignoring areawide issues. Cities take over planning and zoning powers from the county while city land-use decisions can create problems regionally.[3]

The proliferation of fragmented local government systems has economic implications as well. Local governments have a difficult time attracting new business if the geographic area is divided into different tax structures, rules, and regulations. In fact, the prospect of new business often spurs the consolidation movement. York 2000, a governmental reorganization commission in York County, Pennsylvania, has been studying consolidation of its 72 political divisions in order to revitalize its economy and compete for business on a larger scale. Floyd Warner, chairman of York 2000, sees that "there is no coordination among municipalities. That is paramount to economic development."[4] County officials in St. Louis County, Missouri, want to dismantle its 90 jurisdictions and combine them into 21 as a way to continue prosperity and attract out-of-state com-

panies to its growing business corridor. The city of Georgetown and Scott County, Kentucky, are also reviewing consolidation to keep a planned Toyota plant interested in the area. New business can revitalize an area's economic system and even change its image. When Indianapolis and Marion County, Indiana, merged most government functions in order to become the futuristic-sounding UNIGOV in 1978, Indianapolis' image and economy boomed. UNIGOV's success has brought in $850 million in private development and the highest Moody Bond Rating of AAA. Among the results of the new government operations, Indianapolis was named one of "America's Most Livable Cities" by Partners for Livable Places.

Revenue limits combined with the loss of federal funds that local governments previously enjoyed have reduced the service capabilities of both cities and counties, forcing them to search for new methods of delivering services. Duplication of services by the county and city governments has led to increased costs and inefficiency. Combining services and facilities seems to offer the cities and counties a way to balance area needs with area supply capabilities.

State laws, such as Proposition 13 in California and Proposition 24 in Alaska, which limit the amount of taxes that local governments can impose upon their citizens, also force local governments to search for new ways to save money. Proposition 13, which promoted city incorporations after it passed in 1978, is pushing some counties in 1988 to consider abolishing themselves because of the loss of revenue areas to incorporated cities; counties cannot provide the state-mandated services. Because of this problem, the chances for city-county consolidation in California are on the rise. Martin Nichols, Administrator of Butte County, California, says that his county is considering turning its functions over to specialized community service districts with more financial flexibility.[5] And in Alaska, the state assembly has cut municipal budgets by $7 million, forcing cities to consider the options of local cooperation.[6] Both Fairbanks and Ketchikan, Alaska, are reviewing unification commissions and proposals.

Finally, cities and counties consolidate to address the regional and metropolitan problems that affect the jurisdictions, such as air pollution, water pollution, and transportation needs. When jurisdictions deal with these issues in fragmented sections, they produce narrow solutions to larger problems. Officials sometimes choose consolidation as a method of dealing with environmental and area concerns.

Of course, not all the pressures to consolidate would warrant a full consolidation; many could be solved through partial consolidation of specific public services. So, when determining whether or not to consolidate fully or partially, there are many considerations having both advantages and disadvantages.

Full City-County Consolidation

Full consolidation has different meanings as defined by different state statutes. Generally, cities and counties consolidate fully by disincorporating the city and absorbing it into the county, or by passing a law to establish one body which governs over the city and county. Most states share this definition. Florida, however, lists full consolidation as a dissolution of all jurisdictions within a county. If some cities remain independent, the consolidation is not complete.

Because it requires dismantling one or more local governments in exchange for another, full consolidation becomes an emotional issue with the citizens of both city and county. Voters must approve the referendum to consolidate, and, as previously stated, these attempts rarely succeed. Counties surrounding urban areas tend to oppose consolidation because they fear cities are trying to rob revenue rich suburban areas. Minorities, also, tend to fight consolidation attempts because they feel the strength of their vote will be diluted in a larger election. Due to the controversy, local governments should take into account several issues before weighing the rewards and liabilities of consolidation.

Planning, zoning, levels of service, and facility logistics are important considerations, of course, but the political environment with regard to state regulations, political feelings, taxing and debt limits, and community emotions determines the feasibility of total consolidation.

Most state statutes dictate that a consolidated government charter cannot affect the status of nonparticipating entities, abolish courts, or repeal any general laws, while it must accept the debts and contracts of the former jurisdictions and put the proposal in front of the citizens of both entities for a majority vote. These requirements do not, in any way, limit the prospect of consolidation except in states where the requirements contradict each other or are not clear. Confusion over state regulations can make consolidation an impossible task from the beginning. For example, in Pennsylvania, the General Assembly may have the right to order mergers, yet the Pennsylvania constitution guarantees the voters a choice in the matter. Officials feel that the state must take the lead and provide a uniform law in order to make attempts legally possible.[7]

Proponents of consolidation should also consider the political situation and congruity of the areas. The Indianapolis-Marion County UNIGOV excludes three cities within Marion County — Speedway, Beechgrove, and Southport — because the political sentiment in those areas would have defeated the entire UNIGOV proposal.

Full consolidation requires the creation of special tax districts in order to match taxes with services received and debts incurred. In a consolidation proposal, especially those with more than two participants, it becomes difficult to assess tax rates so that citizens who received services in the previous government pay for the debt that that jurisdiction suffered while it provided the services. The UNIGOV consolidation, although hailed as a great success, does not operate simply. It retains 56 tax districts and 101 tax bill combinations so that citizens will not be taxed for other entities' outstanding financial obligations. Most areas, as a way to appease citizens, cannot allow taxes to increase in a consolidated government, but must find other ways to increase the revenue base. Research Atlanta, a group which has been studying city-county consolidation measures, found that property taxes did actually fall in consolidated governments, while the tax base increased because of higher sales taxes, income taxes, and federal aid.[8]

The biggest and most divisive consideration is community feeling toward consolidation. In nine instances, six of which occurred in the 19th century, the state legislatures ordered consolidation; in all other cases, consolidation proposals live or die at the polls. Many times, the voter approval becomes a matter of public relations. The demise of the effort, according to Linda C. Strutt in her article "The Okeechobee Experience: Florida's First Rural City/County Consolidation Effort," is due in most part to opposition from officials, confusion over government roles, confusion over the taxing system, emotionalism and community identity, as well as lack of understanding of the problems of the existing government.[9] Two sides always emerge in consolidation proposals and the forceful arguments in favor and against consolidation reflect the community values of efficient government performance and responsive local officials. Notwithstanding the benefits of consolidation, voters have rejected proposals more than once. Voters in Fairbanks, Alaska, have defeated attempts two times, while officials in Athens and Clark County, Georgia, failed three separate times to convince the citizens of the merits of consolidation. Many other jurisdictions have given up on consolidation attempts after many unsuccessful tries.

Advantages and Disadvantages of Full Consolidation

For local governments interested in efficient streamlining in order to cut costs and gain greater revenues, proponents argue that total consolidation has many advantages. First, consolidation into a larger political body could allow the consolidated government greater political power in the state to control outcome and protect its interests. Secondly, municipalities can solve the problems within their own boundaries, but eventually cause problems outside their borders through uncoordinated regional planning. Small political subdivisions cannot effectively address such large scale issues as environmental protection and development. Finally, consolidation matches the entire area's needs with its resources, rather than having an excess of a needed resource in one jurisdiction and a lack of it in another; cities and counties can share their assets and lessen their liabilities.

Opponents of consolidation tend to have emotional arguments on their side.

They argue that efficiency is not guaranteed in a consolidated government, while losing the responsiveness of a smaller local government inevitably occurs in a merged situation. Consolidations are supposed to cut costs when actually larger governments have greater per capita expenditures. Moreover, citizens lose the "local" aspect of local government; the opportunities for participation may decrease and the merger weakens community identification. Voters expect services to rise when, in fact, the larger governments often have more service delivery problems than before the consolidation. Also, political problems arise when one jurisdiction absorbs another, leaving power struggles in the new government. Consolidation may dilute the political strength and representation of minorities and create new majorities, while political leaders retain their ties to the area from which they came. And, most important, consolidations change the status quo for the unknown.

In an impartial study, Research Atlanta compiled some results on consolidated governments and concluded that the benefits actually outweighed the disadvantages.[10] They found that consolidated governments made more of an effort to provide services to previously underserved areas. In addition, an increase in black representation on the new council compensated for the expected decrease in black voting strength. Consolidation generated savings and costs, but due to inflation and expanded services, it did increase governmental expenditures.[11]

The volatility surrounding consolidation issues makes proposals political taboo; yet, local governments need to cooperate in some way to respond to fiscal and regional issues. Given the success rate of consolidation attempts, local government officials may wish to pursue alternative methods of cost savings and planning through cooperation.

Partial Consolidation

Partial consolidation involves agreement between local governments to consolidate one or more functions of government while participating entities retain their own identity. The extremes of partial or functional consolidation range from minimum to radical, from simple cooperation to incorporated counties. The authors of *An Analysis of State-Local Relations in Florida*, a 1987 report on governmental reorganization and intergovernmental interaction, concluded:

> In lieu of consolidation, governments have been engaged in less comprehensive reforms such as functional consolidation and intergovernmental service agreements…. [T]hese incremental changes, rather than governmental consolidation, are more feasible now and probably will continue to predominate in the future.[12]

When two or more governments wish to consolidate certain functions, they need to consider several items. The proximity of the areas, the social distance of the communities, the political influence of the officials within the jurisdictions, and the structure of government can be important factors depending on the aspects the governments wish to consolidate. The different types of partial consolidation do not need voter approval and therefore are easier to implement.

Cooperation, the simplest "consolidation," revolves around a brief issue or a time of crisis during which entities commit their support to one another in order to solve an immediate problem. Formal cooperation can develop on long-range issues of interest to both parties. These interlocal agreements tend to address policy and service issues much more than administrative ones.

Contractual service agreements, in which one government provides a service for another, work effectively in 52 percent of all cities and counties.[13] Maintenance delivery, fire and police protection, solid waste services, utilities, and health services operate well under these agreements.

Functional transfers occur when cities and counties decide to reassign control over some services among themselves. Counties may opt to provide services other than state statutes require in exchange for city responsibility of other services county-wide. These transfers usually become permanent after they are included in the city and county charters. Fulton County and Atlanta, Georgia, reassigned functions between them and established urban service tax districts in unincorporated areas where additional service levels were in demand. A commission recommended various services and obligations which should be transferred in order to reduce duplication and improve service delivery.

County Study Commission

Fifty-five percent of all cities and counties, although primarily the more populous areas, enter into joint service agreements for planning or financing.[14] By contracting out to a third party or by jointly financing projects, smaller areas receive more service and larger areas pay less money for the same service. Public safety and health departments most frequently function under joint service agreements, although the controversy surrounding consolidated police and fire services mirrors the arguments supporting and opposing total consolidation. Proponents argue that consolidation increases public safety officers' efficiency, specialization, resources, and training, while opponents insist that a larger force promotes a loss of community control and accountability.

The Sacramento Local Government Reorganization Committee, which is studying the possibilities of consolidation in Sacramento County and the city of Sacramento, recommends the metropolitan-federalism system of partial consolidation to best solve the local and regional problems.[15] The consolidation operates on two tier levels which handle regional or local interests. The first tier consists of a series of local governments which provide local services, planning and functions. One member from each local council represents the area on the second tier, which is a metropolitan or county-wide government with jurisdiction over regional issues. In addition to its recommendation, the Sacramento committee lists regional services or agencies which should function on the second tier, such as transportation systems, air pollution, drainage and flood control, regional sanitation, and parks and open space planning. The local entities retain control over their own local problems, while the regional board addresses the concerns of the entire area. Herbert H. Hughes and Charles Lee, in their article "The Evolutionary Consolidation Model: A Response to Revenue Limits in Growing Metropolitan Areas," argue that cities and counties "should consolidate ... only under a federated approach, in which authority is shared between the central city and other areas in a consolidated jurisdiction."[16]

Miami and Dade County, Florida, function in a complicated system which some experts label a modified metropolitan-federal approach,[17] and which others describe as a comprehensive urban county.[18] The local governments within Dade County have autonomy on local issues, while an eight member at-large county commission presides over the county-wide issues. The incorporated cities function in the two-tier model, but the unincorporated areas are the responsibility of the county commission. The county provides many services to the cities in exchange for tax revenues, prompting the use of the title of comprehensive urban county.

The comprehensive urban county consolidation involves the county provision for an agreed upon number of services to the cities within the county or the county incorporation of all its unincorporated areas. St. Louis County proposals for consolidation include one in which the entire county would incorporate so the county would not lose revenue by providing services to the unincorporated areas. Some states, however, regulate the formation of a comprehensive urban county in their statutes on government reorganization, due to minimum population density requirements for incorporation. Virginia, for example, prohibits counties from incorporating and merging services with their cities. Kentucky, on the other hand, allows cities to abolish all existing governments within a county in order to develop an incorporated charter county.

The evolutionary model of consolidation, coined by Hughes and Lee, yet described by other experts, occurs when cities and counties cooperate on some issues and over time develop more formal relations. The model seems to work well for areas experiencing controversy over consolidation. Many researchers on consolidation believe that merger attempts that evolve from cooperation through the states of partial consolidation stand a better change of eventually succeeding.[19] Hughes and Lee say "Local governments should consolidate only when strong evidence shows that the collective government and community capacity will increase."[20] Many local governments feel comfortable using any one of these partial consolidations permanently or experimenting with different services without reorganizing the structure of the entities. The advantages and options of evolving into a partial consolidation stage attract

local governments into considering cooperation. The effects of a partial consolidation are not irreversible, while officials can even experiment with service levels, department mergers, and joint contracts. At the same time, community identities of the participating areas remain intact while the voters do not offer roadblocks to the effort. Partial consolidations can function effectively between dissimilar governments, while standardizing service and costs between the areas. Finally, if the governments choose, partial consolidation can lead to a total merger.

Conclusion

Consolidation of city and county government will always remain a divisive issue as long as citizens expect both efficiency and responsiveness from local government. Local governments, however, are realizing the need for cost saving techniques and regional planning which consolidation may provide. Not all services in a full consolidation are better or even more economically delivered on an areawide basis, while citizens wish to retain local control over their government. At this point, due to the opposition involved in enacting a full consolidation proposal, varying degrees of partial consolidation seem to be the most politically and economically feasible solution to meeting areawide problems and revenue squeezes.

Notes

1. Barbara P. Greene, "Counties and the Fiscal Challenges of the 1980's," *Intergovernmental Perspective*, vol. 13, n. 1, Winter 1987, p. 15.

2. Robert Feinbaum, "Counties Lose: Climate Right for Creating New Cities," *California Journal*, vol. 18, n. 10, October 1987, p. 497.

3. Feinbaum, p. 499.

4. Michael Argento, "Weight of Numbers Intimidating," *York Daily Record*, 16 June 1987, sec. A, p. 1.

5. Rebecca LaVally, "Proposition 13, Ten Years Later," *California Journal*, vol. 19, n. 4, April 1988, p. 175.

6. "The Budget Crisis in the Years Ahead," *Anchorage Daily News*, opinion editorial, 24 June 1988.

7. Michael Argento, "Consolidation Too 'Hot' to Handle Politically," *York Daily Record*, 15 June 1988.

8. Kenneth Town and Carol Lambert, *The Urban Consolidation Experience in the U.S.* (Atlanta, Georgia: Research Atlanta, 1987), cited by Richard W. Campbell, "City-County Consolidation: Learning from Failure," *Urban Georgia*, April 1988.

9. Linda C. Strutt, "The Okeechobee Experience: Florida's First Rural City/County Consolidation Effort," cited by Florida House of Representatives Committee on Community Affairs. *Getting Together: The Forming and Reshaping of Local Government in Florida* (Tallahassee, Florida: Florida House of Representatives, March 1988).

10. Town and Lambert, cited by Campbell, p. 28.

11. *Ibid.*

12. Wayne A. Clark, J. Edwin Benton, and Robert Kerstein, *An Analysis of State-Local Relations in Florida* (Florida State University: 1987) p. 43, cited by Florida House of Representatives Committee on Community Affairs, *Getting Together: The Forming and Reshaping of Local Government in Florida* (Tallahassee, Florida: Florida House of Representatives, March 1988) pp. 4–9.

13. Lori M. Henderson, "Intergovernmental Service Arrangements and the Transfer of Functions," *Baseline Data Report*, vol. 16, n. 6 (Washington, D.C.: International City Management Association, June 1984) p. 1.

14. Henderson, p. 3.

15. Joint Commission of the County of Sacramento and the City of Sacramento, Sacramento Committee Report, *City-County Local Government Reorganization Commission, Volume I: Observations and Recommendations* (Sacramento: Joint Commission, June 1988) p. 26.

16. Herbert H. Hughes and Charles Lee, "The Evolutionary Consolidation Model: A Response to Revenue Limits in Growing Metropolitan Areas." *Urban Resources*, vol. 4, n. 2, Winter 1987, p. 6.

17. Joseph F. Zimmerman, "Dade County Reviews Charter," *National Civic Review*, vol. 71, n. 5, May 1982, p. 265.

18. Glen Sparrow and Lauren McKinsey, "Metropolitan Reorganization: A Theory and Agenda for Research." *National Civic Review*, vol. 72, n. 9, October 1983, p. 493.

19. Hughes and Lee, p. 3.

20. *Ibid.*, p. 6.

Bibliography

Argento, Michael. "Weight of Numbers Intimidating," *York Daily Record*. 16 June 1987; and "Consolidation Too 'Hot' to Handle Politically, *York Daily Record*. 15 June 1987.

"The Budget Crisis in the Years Ahead." *Anchorage Daily News*, opinion editorial. 24 June 1988.

Clark, Wayne A., J. Edwin Benton, and Robert Kerstein. *An Analysis of State-Local Relations in Florida*. (Florida State University: 1987) cited by Florida House of Representatives Committee on Community Affairs. *Getting Together: The Forming and Reshaping of Local Government in Florida* (Tallahassee, Florida: Florida House of Representative, March 1988).

Feinbaum, Robert. "Counties Lose: Climate Right for Creating New Cities." *California Journal*, 18, n. 10. October 1987.

Greene, Dr. Barbara P. "Counties and the Fiscal Challenges of the 1980's." *Intergovernmental Perspective*, 13, n. 1. Winter 1987.

Henderson, Lori M. "Intergovernmental Service Arrangements and the Transfer of Functions." *Baseline Data Report*, 16, n. 6 (Washington, D.C.: International City Management Association, June 1984).

Hughes, Herbert H. and Charles Lee. "The Evolutionary Consolidation Model: A Response to Revenue Limits in Growing Metropolitan Areas." *Urban Resources*, 4, n. 2. Winter 1987.

Joint Commission of the County of Sacramento and the City of Sacramento, Sacramento Committee Report. *City-County Local Government Reorganization Commission. Volume I: Observations and Recommendations* (Sacramento: Joint Commission, June 1988).

LaVally, Rebecca. "Proposition 13, Ten Years Later." *California Journal*, 19, n. 4. April 1988.

Sparrow, Glen and Lauren McKinsey. "Metropolitan Reorganization: A Theory and Agenda for Research." *National Civic Review*, 72, n. 9. October 1983.

Strutt, Linda C. "The Okeechobee Experience: Florida's First Rural City/County Consolidation Effort." Cited by Florida House of Representatives Committee on Community Affairs. *Getting Together: The Forming and Reshaping of Local Government in Florida* (Tallahassee, Florida: Florida House of Representatives, March 1988).

Town, Kenneth and Carol Lambert. *The Urban Consolidation Experience in the U.S.* (Atlanta, Georgia: Research Atlanta, 1987) cited by Richard W Campbell. "City-County Consolidation: Learning from Failure." *Urban Georgia*. April 1988.

Zimmerman, Joseph F. "Dade County Reviews Charter." *National Civic Review*, 71, n. 5. May 1982.

• *Chapter 14* •

The Evolutionary Consolidation Model

HERBERT H. HUGHES AND CHARLES LEE

For growing metropolitan areas facing new and changing demands for complex urban services and infrastructure, federal, state, and local revenue limits pose a serious problem.[1] Management solutions, such as privatization and productivity improvement, abound,[2] but only local government consolidation directly confronts the issue of local interjurisdictional fragmentation, which many feel is a major contributor to the problem of revenue limits in metropolitan areas.[3] Full administrative and political consolidation has pitfalls and, judging from the low number of consolidations reported nationwide, is seldom seen as a realistic solution.[4] Nevertheless, consolidation can be an appropriate and practical solution if it is allowed to evolve from minor cooperative arrangements among local governments into consolidated administrative or policy efforts whenever these interjurisdictional solutions are called for. This notion of consol-

idation as an evolutionary process is entirely consistent with the general philosophy and practice of local government in our country and with the strong tendency for individual local governments to cut across local jurisdictional boundaries through cooperative policy or administrative arrangements.[5]

Conceptual Framework

The Evolutionary Consolidation Model has been conceived and developed chiefly from experience with efforts to cooperate and consolidate in the Albuquerque/Bernalillo County metropolitan area and from ideas on local government capacity set forth by Gargan.[6] Although possibly unique in its small number of local government units (six), the Albuquerque/Bernalillo County area resembles other metropolitan areas in two important

From *Urban Resources*, Vol. 4, No. 2, Winter, 1987. Published by the Division of Metropolitan Studies, University of Cincinnati, Cincinnati, Ohio. Reprinted with permission of the publisher.

ways. Through annexation the area has experienced the same rapid central city growth through annexation characteristic of metropolitan areas nationwide,[7] and it reflects many of the same patterns of local interjurisdictional service transfers and cooperative service provisions reported in the nationwide Advisory Commission on Intergovernmental Relations study.[8]

Metropolitan Capacity. Metropolitan capacity and metropolitan government capacity are the foundation of the Evolutionary Consolidation Model. Metropolitan capacity may be defined simply as "the ability of a metropolitan community to solve its problems." Metropolitan government capacity, a subset, may be defined as "the collective ability of local governments in a metropolitan community to solve their problems." Metropolitan capacity is a function of expectations and resources, both concepts of John Gargan,[9] and harmony. All three are appropriate to interlocal community situations, but "harmony" is the key ingredient necessary to address fully the complicated environment of a metropolitan community and its governmental units. According to Gargan, *Expectations involve perceptions and attitudes on "adequate" levels of public services, appropriate styles of political leadership, and accepted ways of conducting public affairs. Expectations are based in local practices, traditions, and cultures.*[10] Expectations may be heavily influenced by resources available to adjacent local governments and communities in a metropolitan situation. *Resources involve those community elements that can be brought to bear on community problems. Resources include, but are not limited to, money, knowledge, administrative skills, private sector associations, neighborhood organizations, and political popularity.*[11] Limits on resources may create an imbalance in the metropolitan situation where expectations are high. *Harmony* involves the appropriate balance between community expectations and resources to solve problems in a metropolitan area. The timing of the mixture of resources and expectations is essential for appropriate balance. Harmony is critical to the effective marshalling of resources to cope with expectations in a metropolitan situation.

Evolutionary Consolidation. Evolutionary Consolidation may be defined as *the persistent tendency of local governments and communities to build metropolitan government capacity through progressively more centralized, cooperative arrangements as a metropolitan area urbanizes.* In this model, both revenue and jurisdictional limits have significant potential to create disharmony among the community expectations and government resources in metropolitan settings. Evolutionary Consolidation is the major solution precisely because it directly addresses the disharmony commonly found in a metropolitan situation.

The Evolutionary Consolidation Process. Figure 1 on page 146 depicts the entire evolutionary consolidation process starting at Stage 1, Informal Discussion, with occasional cooperation among adjacent local governments, and ending at Stage 5 with Consolidation of the governments in a metropolitan area. Maximum capacity is most attainable at Stage 1, before intense interdependence among communities in a metropolitan situation has occurred. Communities are sufficiently isolated to minimize disharmony from divergent, interlocal expectations; and resources, expectations, and limits are simple to evaluate, thereby allowing expectations within a given community to adjust easily to the level of resources. During Stage 1, only an occasional, informal discussion with adjacent local governments is necessary because harmony is high, limits are not a critical concern, and no jurisdiction fears losing control of resources to adjacent governments. For the same reason, annexation is not perceived as a high priority unless some very specific problem forces the issue.

In Stage 2, growing populations of adjacent communities are creating new urban problems which sharpen awareness of revenue and jurisdictional limits and require consideration of local government resource control through aggressive annexation and possibly other means. Resources are not yet strained to the point that they are unable to meet the still moderate level of expectations in the area communities, but the clear emergence of a central city is beginning to draw attention to common, rising expectations for urban services despite apparent resource variations among the area's local governments. In such an environment, local governments begin to explore the possibilities of cooperation.

During Stage 3, most communities in developing metropolitan areas are struggling to meet converging and rising expectations for urban services. Limits on operational revenue and bonding capacity, compounded by jurisdictional fragmentation, are severely limiting the ability of local governments to keep pace with the support and infrastructure expected in these rapidly growing areas. General disharmony throughout the metropolitan government structure is common during this period. With metropolitan government capacity at a low point, adjacent local governments are forced to explore every avenue of interlocal cooperation in order to cope with the service expectations of their constituents.

Stage 4, Trial Consolidation, begins a trial marriage period between the central city and one or more other major local governments in a metropolitan area. After considerable experience with earlier contractual arrangements, these governments have decided that the inconveniences of living together may be worth a try, particularly since severe revenue limits and jurisdictional fragmentation are making it very difficult to live alone. Annexation is fading as a realistic means for the central city to control resources, and the emphasis is shifting to building comprehensive policy and administrative cooperation which provide permanent solutions to metropolitan problems. Some rights are retained, however, for the cooperation to terminate without going to the voters.

Figure 1
The Evolutionary Consolidation Model as a Process in the Metropolitan Situation

Stage 1 Informal Discussion
Informal Joint Policy Discussion
    limited period, one issue
    extended period, multiple issues

Stage 2 Formal Cooperation
Cooperative Joint Policy Body
    one or multiple minor issues
    one or multiple major issues
Formal Contractual Arrangements
    part-time services, equipment
Formal Policy Arrangements
    zoning or other authority

Stage 3 Contract Consolidation
Policy or Management Sharing
    Equipment Sharing
    Facility Sharing
    Policy Delegation
    Management Delegation

Stage 4 Trial Consolidation
Master Joint Powers Agreement
    some major policy
    some major administrative
    formal joint decision body

Stage 5 Consolidation
Partial, Full Consolidation
    federated
    centralized

Finally, in Stage 5, local governments in a metropolitan area join in the most permanent cooperative arrangement, partial or full consolidation. This final stage is not inevitable, nor is it always desirable; disharmony and significant decreases in metropolitan capacity may result from premature or inappropriate centralization. Local governments should consolidate only when strong evidence shows that the collective government and community capacity will increase. They should also consolidate only under a federated approach, in which authority is shared between the central city and other areas in a consolidated jurisdiction.

Evolutionary Consolidation in One Metropolitan Situation

Named as one of the nation's ten new cities of great opportunity,[12] Albuquerque and the Bernalillo County metropolitan area provide an excellent laboratory for the study of the evolutionary consolidation process. Since 1940, Albuquerque's population has shown a continual urbanizing trend, growing from 35,000 or 50 percent of Bernalillo County to about 341,000 or 78 percent of the 1982 Bernalillo County population of about 433,000.[13] During this time, the community has been transformed from a small town with moderate expectations to an urban community whose citizens expect the delivery of a variety of complex urban services by both city and county governments. Basic structural changes affecting revenue limits and jurisdictional powers in city government have also taken place at the state level, and aggressive annexation, extensive interlocal cooperation, and consolidation have each been prominent in attempts to solve local government problems. Further, revenue

limits on local government are firmly embedded in the state constitution, and jurisdictional limits are now surfacing as a problem due to incorporation efforts on the fringe of the metropolitan area.

The following is an examination of the evolutionary consolidation process in the Albuquerque/Bernalillo County area since 1940. The *Albuquerque Data Book* (1985), *City of Albuquerque Budget* (1985), *Bernalillo County Official Budget* (1985), and *Albuquerque City Charter* (1983) are sources for the demographic and financial data.[14] Other data come from the junior author's staff research for the recent Albuquerque/Bernalillo County Unification Task Force[15] and the senior author's observations from participation in civic, governmental, and political affairs at both the state level and in Albuquerque.

Stage 1: Informal Discussion. In 1940, most of the population outside the Albuquerque city limits resided in the rural Rio Grande River Valley areas on the north and south edges of the city. Most of the annexation in the 1940s was in the East Mesa area between the city and the Sandia Mountains, where the major population growth was occurring, and in the populated area of the North Valley. Until the early 1950s, city and county governments felt little pressure to move beyond the information discussion stage of evolutionary consolidation. Possibly because of the relatively low expectations for complex urban services, the clear separation of roles between city and county government, and the abundance of vacant land within the metropolitan area, they found little need to cooperate in overcoming the revenue limits imposed by the state constitution and related statutes. Major annexation by the city was occurring, but primarily in previously uninhabited areas on the East Mesa or in the North Valley adjacent to downtown. Annexation may well have been perceived as a mutually beneficial decision for neighborhoods, developers, and city government rather than an aggressive encroachment of urban development on rural areas to gain revenue and to control life style.

Stage 2: Formal Cooperation. In 1949, the first signs of formal cooperation between the governments of the city of Albuquerque and Bernalillo County appeared. At that time, the county commission passed a formal resolution requiring that all proposed plats or subdivisions of land within five miles of the city limits be approved by the city planning board before the county commission acted on them. Although the city had approval authority through a 1947 state statute, the 1949 county commission resolution was significant because its language was cooperative in tone and it was formulated in cooperation with the city planning board.

During the 1950s, annexation and development on less expensive land on the East Mesa toward the Sandia Mountains began creating urban sprawl, and the accelerated population growth, which would push the city's population to 200,000 in 1960, was rapidly urbanizing the entire area. A major indication that metropolitan government capacity was indeed becoming a serious concern came in 1953, when the city and county commissions appointed a joint citizen's committee to study consolidation of city and county governments under enabling legislation passed by the state legislature in 1952. The consolidation committee worked for six years, and in 1959 the question of consolidation and a proposed new charter were put before the electorate. The vote failed almost 2 to 1 in the city and over 20 to 1 in the unincorporated area. The major issues in that election illustrate the complex relationships between the cooperative efforts of interlocal governments and capacity building in the metropolitan situation. On the one hand, the central governing bodies of both the city of Albuquerque and Bernalillo County supported consolidation as a way to meet rising expectations for urban services under existing revenue limits. On the other hand, opponents (mostly unincorporated area residents and some full-time county elected officials) were convinced neither that a problem existed nor that centralization would solve it. Opponents were particularly incensed that consolidation would achieve increased revenue through a property tax increase for unincorporated area residents and would require participation in retiring the bonded debt of the city. Zoning authority in the unincorporated area was also an issue, as was control of the resource priorities in the proposed new government.

During the 1960s, the 107 percent growth rate in the city during the 1950s declined to about 21 percent. Combined with the major influx of federal aid during the 1960s, the slower growth rate provided a breathing spell for the metropolitan area. With the exception of joint agreements on airport zoning and parks and recreation, few major cooperative efforts between city and county governments occurred until the late 1960s. With the Council of Governments (COG) providing significant joint transportation planning capability and direct federal aid flowing to both city and county for a variety of services, there was less pressure to build capacity through interlocal cooperation. Both the airport zoning and parks and recreation agreements, however, may have reflected some local government capacity concerns. The airport zoning agreement addressed an overall metropolitan area problem by assigning administrative responsibility to the city, while for the sake of efficiency the parks and recreation agreement consolidated all such services in the county under the city.

Stage 3: Contract Consolidation. In the mid–1960s, the city and county governments in Albuquerque were edging into the Contract Consolidation stage. Then a 1969 contract for city government to provide all planning services for the county, followed by a flurry of joint agreements in the early 1970s, ushered in contract consolidation on a broad scale. Aggressive annexation was continuing but was limited by the boundaries of Indian jurisdictions on the north and populations already established in some unincorporated areas. City growth was accelerating to a rate of 35 percent in the 1970s and the 1980 population of 332,000 was 75 percent of the population of Bernalillo County. A 1969 effort to revise the state constitution, city charter revisions in 1971 and 1974, another consolidation attempt in 1973, a state-sponsored study of city financing in 1976, and the service priorities addressed in the many cooperative agreements all clearly reflect the struggle of citizens and officials in the metropolitan area to overcome limits on the ability to meet rising urban service expectations.

The results of the 1973 consolidation referendum were similar to those of 1959. In 1973, unincorporated area residents voted about nine to one against, and both the proposed new charter and consolidation passed with a slight majority in the city. A post-election study discloses some other similarities between the 1973 and 1959 efforts.[16] Much like 1959, the major issues in 1973 were tax increases, rural lifestyle (zoning authority), and control of the new government. Another finding in the post-election study, that expectations for better services from consolidation correlated highly with a positive consolidation vote, reinforces the significance of expectations. But why, in the midst of a period of thriving cooperative activity, does consolidation fail? From an evolutionary consolidation view, the answer is simple. Full consolidation puts the major emphasis on increasing metropolitan government capacity, sometimes to the detri-

ment of overall metropolitan community capacity, which requires harmony among community expectations, resources, and governments.

An analysis of the formal cooperative agreements between the two governments since 1969 confirms that significant cooperation became a critical concern at that time. Of the approximately 70 formal joint agreements since 1949, 33 were signed in the 1969–1979 period. At least 10 of the 33 involve major sharing of policy and resource control:

1. City provides planning services for county government.

2. City and county governments jointly contract out ambulance services.

3. City government manages adult jail facilities throughout the county.

4. North Valley unincorporated area gains access to city water system.

5. South Valley unincorporated area gains access to city water system.

6. City government provides animal control facilities for the county.

7. City government establishes sanitary sewage disposal system for valley unincorporated areas.

8. City and county governments, through COG, jointly sponsor general aviation facility planning for the county.

9. City government is designated lead agency in waste water treatment plan for the county.

10. County government issues General Obligation (GO) bonds for new adult jail facility.

An examination of these ten formal agreements reveals that in Agreements 1, 3, 4, 5, 6, 7, and 9 county officials granted major administrative control to city government in exchange for constituent-expected services which revenue limits in county government would not readily permit. In the case of ambulance services

(Agreement 2) and aviation facility planning (Agreement 8), which required relatively low expenditures, service expectations were more critical than revenue limits. The construction of the jail facility (Agreement 10) is an excellent example of using interlocal government agreements to cope with revenue limits. In Bernalillo County, city government has remained at or near the GO bonded debt limit and county government at or near the operational millage limit since the 1960s; city government has had access to major gross receipts and enterprise fee revenue for operational purposes while county government has seldom exceeded under 50 percent of its GO bonding capacity. Under the two major jail facility agreements, city government has assumed responsibility for 50 percent of the operational funding, and county government has floated the bond issue for construction of the new jail facility.

Frequent communication between city and county governments now occurs during the planning of bond projects, and, in particular, county bond issues have broadened to include major urban concerns such as roads and bridges related to industrial developments and a new criminal justice center in the downtown area. A trend in recent bond elections is to take pressure off the city bonding capacity limits by use of county GO bonding capability in exchange for joint ownership in physical facilities built by the bond issue proceeds, or shared administrative control of the service involved, or operational revenue and fee arrangements which reduce the pressure of operational revenue constraints. The advantages to the city of using county government bonding capability are obvious. The advantages to the county are also obvious where operation revenue relief is obtained. In the case where the county government receives only ownership rights in the tradeoff, the increase in

political capacity resulting from the leverage of ownership can be substantial.

Stage 4. Trial Consolidation. Perhaps the single most important step along the path of evolutionary consolidation for the Albuquerque/Bernalillo County metropolitan area was the creation of the city-county Intergovernmental Committee (IGC) during the 1970s. Although the idea was a natural outcome of the growing cooperation between city and county government, it was recommended by a 1976 state-sponsored study on the financing of urban services in Albuquerque.[17] The IGC is a permanent body consisting of three county commission members, three city council members, and the mayor. Meetings are routinely covered by the press, and both the city and county governing bodies delegate considerable authority to the IGC. The IGC provides a forum for joint discussion of metropolitan area concerns and has been involved in most of the major cooperative arrangements between city and county governments since the late 1970s.

Most departments in city and county government are now involved in some type of cooperation with the other government, either formally or informally. About 36 formal agreements of cooperation between city and county government have been signed since 1980. At least seven of these agreements involve major sharing of policy and resource control:

1. County government designs and constructs key street expansion.
2. City government designs key street expansion.
3. County Sheriff Department leases space in City Police Building.
4. City and county governments jointly construct/occupy new building.
5. City and county governments jointly use city mainframe computer.
6. County government GO bonds fund City Police Building addition.

7. Regional Solid Waste Authority is formed by the city and county.

Together, these agreements illustrate the depth of the cooperation between the two governments. To be more specific, in Agreement 2 (key street expansion), administrative control is granted to the city government in exchange for constituent-expected services which revenue limits in county government would not readily permit. Agreement 3 exchanges some loss of control of the space in which the sheriff is housed for a very low lease fee; both governments stand to improve service through increased communications between their law enforcement officers and to gain political capacity from the perception that attempts are being made to eliminate duplication. Agreements 5 (joint computer use) and 7 (Regional Solid Waste Authority) were signed on the assumption that both parties would benefit financially due to economies of scale, but the gain in political capacity from elimination of duplication was strongly anticipated, especially in Agreement 5. Although severely criticized, both agreements continue in effect. Agreement 2 involves street improvements which had long been expected by many residents both in and outside the city limits, and Agreement 1 is a key street expansion critical to major new city and county industrial development and to the use of a bridge which has been a major issue in the metropolitan area for over ten years. Both city and county governments should gain political capacity and outside matching revenues from these joint efforts.

The joint construction of the new city/county building (Agreement 4), and the issue of county GO bonds for joint construction of a new addition to the city police building (Agreement 6), may well represent the most significant movement along the path of evolutionary consolidation since the formation of the IGC. The addition to the city police building enabled city government, which is near the limit of its bonding capacity, to use available county government bonding capacity to obtain additional space for both city and county law enforcement agencies. The county will obtain joint ownership of the building, thereby saving operational revenue previously required to lease space in it. Originated by the IGC, which had full responsibility for design and construction, the new city/county building was financed by county government GO bonds and city government revenue bonds. Thus, the county was able to trade use of available bonding capacity for savings in its severely limited operational revenue; similarly, the city government could thus conserve its limited bonding capacity by paying the major share of the revenue bond obligation with more readily available operational revenue. Ownership of the building is shared under this arrangement. Even deeper concern for revenue limits can be found in the events which led to the agreement to fund this building. The original idea for a joint city/county building was generated principally from earlier county-wide voter rejection of a bond issue for a new county government office building. Since city voters overwhelmingly voted against that proposal, a joint city/county building provided the means to gain support of city and unincorporated area voters for county and city government office space. In terms of metropolitan government capacity, this project provides another example of how interlocal cooperation can maximize harmony among community expectations, resources, and local governments.

One other major cooperative effort occurring in 1985 was the Albuquerque/Bernalillo County Unification Task Force, formed by the city and county governing bodies to investigate the feasibility of policy and administrative consolidation.

The task force deliberations reinforced the premise in the Evolutionary Consolidation Model that revenue limits are significant in consolidation considerations. The task force suggested the "municipal," rather than "county," form of combined government because New Mexico municipalities have higher gross receipts tax limits and broader bonding, enterprise fee, and home rule options than do counties. The task force endorsed eventual consolidation and immediate expansion of the IGC concept into a sixteen-member Intergovernmental Council comprised of the mayor, all city councillors, and all county commissioners. It also recommended the adoption of a City/County Master Joint Powers Agreement to serve as a charter for the Intergovernmental Council. Each governing body received and discussed the recommendations in early 1986, but no further action has been taken since then. In the meantime, the IGC continues to function as the major organizational link between city and county governments.

Concluding Remarks

Evolutionary consolidation may well be the major solution to revenue limits in growing metropolitan areas because it directly addresses the appropriate balance between diverse community service expectations and resources necessary to increase capacity in complex metropolitan environments. The common emphasis nationwide on interlocal government cooperative arrangements, rather than full consolidation, suggests that the Albuquerque/Bernalillo County experience may have general application to many other metropolitan situations. Now the Evolutionary Consolidation Model needs to be tested in a variety of urban communities to determine its value in understanding and solving metropolitan problems.

Notes

1. Roy Bahl, *Financing State and Local Governments in the 1980s* (New York: Oxford University Press, 1984).

2. Charles H. Levin, "Citizenship and Service Delivery: The Promise of Co-production," *Public Administration Review*, 44 (March Special Issue, 1984), 178–89.

3. Herbert H. Hughes and Dan Weaks, et. al., *Albuquerque Municipal Financing: Final Report* (Governor's Albuquerque Municipal Financing Task Force, 1976), 3–10; David B. Walker, "Localities under the New Intergovernmental System," in L. Kenneth Hubbell, ed., *Fiscal Crisis in American Cities: The Federal Response* (Cambridge, MA: Ballinger Publishing Company, 1979), 25–57; Advisory Commission for Intergovernmental Relations, *State and Local Roles in the Federal System* (Washington, DC, 1981); Robert E. Firesline, Bernard I. Weinstein, and Shelley M. Hayden, "Inter-governmental Fiscal Cooperation in Growing Metropolitan Economies," in James H. Carr, ed., *Crisis and Constraint in Municipal Finance*, (New Brunswick, NJ: Center for Urban Policy Research, Rutgers, 1984), 221–29; Bahl, 1984.

4. Governmental Research Institute, *Reorganizing Our Counties* (Cleveland, OH: Cleveland Foundation, 1980).

5. Advisory Commission on Intergovernmental Relations, *Intergovernmental Service Arrangements for Delivering Local Public Services Update 1983* (Washington, DC, 1985).

6. John J. Gargan, "Consideration of Local Government Capacity," *Public Administration Review*, 41 (November/December 1981), 649–58.

7. Robert D. Thomas, "Metropolitan Structural Development: The Territorial Imperative," *Publius*, 14 (Spring 1984), 83–115.

8. Advisory Commission, 1985.

9. Gargan.

10. *Ibid.*, 652.

11. *Ibid.*

12. John Naisbitt, *Megatrends* (New York: Warner Books, 1982).

13. City of Albuquerque Municipal Development Department, *Albuquerque Data Book* (1985).

14. Bernalillo County Department of Finance, *Bernalillo County Official Budget* (1985);

City of Albuquerque, *Albuquerque City Charter* (1983); City of Albuquerque Department of Finance and Management, *City of Albuquerque Budget* (1975).

15. Joint Albuquerque/Bernalillo County Unification Task Force, *Final Report*, (1985).

16. Dan Weaks, *An Analysis of the Consolidation Effort in Albuquerque/Bernalillo County*, (1974).

17. Hughes, Weaks, et al., 1976.

• *Chapter 15* •

Counties in Transition

ROBERT D. THOMAS

When confronted by changing socioeconomic, demographic, and governmental conditions, county officials often
face critical problems without authority to
legislate locally, raise sufficient revenues,
or engage in areawide or neighborhood
planning and land use management. Such
problems vary dramatically across the
spectrum of counties, from the most urbanized (e.g., Los Angeles County, California, and Cook County, Illinois) to the
most rural (e.g., Loving County, Texas,
and Hillsdale County, Colorado). Many
counties are confronting economic shifts,
changing residential patterns, and more
governments delivering public services
and issuing regulations. These transitions
intensify demand for traditional county
services and also compel consideration of
how county government should respond
to the changing environment. The issue,
of course, is framed partly by the county's
legal powers, or lack thereof.

Five Counties in Transition

The five counties of the Houston Metropolitan Statistical Area (MSA)—Ft.
Bend, Harris, Liberty, Montgomery, and
Waller—provide an example of counties
in transition. These counties serve
3,247,000 people (1986) within 5,345
square miles of the upper coastal plains of
Texas. MSA employment increased from
300,000 in 1945 to 1.6 million in 1988. Harris County has 85.8 percent of the MSA's
population, with 60.8 percent of its population living inside the city of Houston.
Thus, the city and Harris County form the
core of the area's economy.

Growth Trends

From a metropolitan perspective, with
population increasing 74.6 percent and personal per capita income rising 314 percent
from 1970 through 1988, Houston's MSA
counties underwent a massive face-lift.

Originally published as "Counties in Transition: Issues and Challenges," *Intergovernmental Perspective*, Vol. 17, No. 1, Winter, 1991. Published by the U.S. Advisory Commission on Intergovernmental Relations, Washington, D.C.

Growth varied among the counties, however, arraying them along an urban continuum: Harris County on the urbanized side; Ft. Bend and Montgomery moving in an urbanizing direction; and Waller and Liberty the least urbanized.

During the 1980s, the populations of Ft. Bend and Montgomery counties skyrocketed (72 percent and 42 percent, respectively), mainly because they became bedroom communities of Houston.[1] Comparatively, population growth in Harris, Liberty, and Waller counties was modest (17 percent or less).

Population growth also brought new residential, commercial, and industrial developments in each county. New single-family housing, building permits, capital expenditures, and value added by manufacturing — as well as other elements of urban growth — rose sharply in the 1970s and 1980s. As the area experienced an economic boom in the late 1970s and early 1980s, the landscape of each county began to change. While the total number of houses increased by an average of 107 percent (1972–1982), the size of farms decreased by an average of 25 percent. In Montgomery and Waller counties, urban conditions seemed to replace rural conditions. Ft. Bend County, however, became more bifurcated, experiencing the greatest increase in housing and substantial increases in manufacturing simultaneously with the smallest decrease in farm sizes and the greatest increase in the value of farm products.

Changes in the Tax Base

How did these growth trends affect tax valuations? The data provides some insight. Given that growth has had an impact on the tax value of land, we might expect such changes to result, eventually, in a shift of county government's priorities from rural to urban concerns. However, the growth effects on tax values are not uniform. While Harris County's tax base in the 1980s was substantially urban (e.g., residential and commercial/industrial property valuations averaged about three-fourths of total valuations), the other counties presented a mixed picture. Waller and Liberty were consistently skewed toward farm, ranch, and acreage. Ft. Bend and Montgomery were more bifurcated, relying both on urban-type sources and on farm, ranch, and acreage sources.

Governmental Responses

Governmental complexity seems to mirror urbanization and taxation trends. As counties change, more governments are created to provide an urban infrastructure for new residential, commercial, and industrial developments or for servicing these developments once they are in place. Municipal utility districts (MUDs) and, to some extent, independent school districts (ISDs), but counties only secondarily, are the vehicles used in the Houston MSA to support new developments in unincorporated areas. (Numerous MUDs exist in Harris County, and MUDs are especially important in rapidly developing Ft. Bend and Montgomery counties.)

The State Connection

Governmental complexity in the five counties is linked directly to the structure of state authority for local governments. Consider how the state forms the legal parameters for MUDs and ISDs.

The legal antecedent of MUDs is a 1917 Texas constitutional amendment. That amendment was the foundation for state statutes allowing landowner initiative in the creation of taxing entities to fund improvements on undeveloped land.

Originally, farmers and ranchers used these authorities to finance land improvements to protect against hurricanes and floods and to have higher productivity.[2] State statutes subsequently expanded the constitutional concept, allowing such financing to be used for urban infrastructure improvements supporting residential, commercial, and industrial developments.[3]

Likewise, because the Texas Constitution provides authority for independent school districts and explicitly authorizes the legislature to form ISDs embracing "parts of two or more counties," education services can emerge around land development patterns rather than being corralled inside either cities or counties.[4] Thus, many school districts have overlapping boundaries, especially in the most urbanized and urbanizing counties.

Who Pays for Urban Development? The Debt Picture

The Texas Constitution makes counties first and last administrative arms of the state government.[5] A review of public indebtedness for the governments of the five counties shows how this role shapes not only county responses but also other governments' responses to change. The study revealed that MUDs have the largest share of debt in the most urban county (Harris) and in the most urbanizing counties (Ft. Bend and Montgomery). In these counties, as well as in the least urbanized counties, ISDs are also key entities in establishing an urban infrastructure through debt financing.

These data suggest that the county is generally a secondary player in debt financing, but there are interesting exceptions on each end of the urban continuum. One of the least urbanized counties, Liberty, bears relatively more indebtedness in relation to its other local governments than the most urbanized counties. On the other side, in Harris County, special purpose authorities, which are either quasi-county agencies (e.g., Toll Road Authority and the Flood Control District) or closely allied with the county (e.g., Port Authority), have 18 percent of the total indebtedness for all governments in Harris County, thus making them significant actors in areawide developments.

Consequences and Challenges: Whence Counties?

What do these trends imply for county governments? Perhaps a football analogy illustrates the implications. In Texas, as in many other states, counties operate substantially as administrative arms of state government. As a result, counties are often placed in the position of being second or even third stringers in responding to changing patterns of growth and decline. If local circumstances warrant it, the state may allow the county to play an important skilled position, although not always one that is central to the challenges at hand.

Harris County is a case in point. The state has permitted the creation of quasi-county agencies and authorities closely allied with the county to respond to public needs where other local governments cannot or do not take action. Still, there are limits to the county's ability to respond to growth. Of course, county governments also carry out state administrative services that are an integral part of metropolitan governance (e.g., criminal justice administration). However, the state does not provide counties with sufficient statutory authority or legal latitude to be first-team players able to shape responses to permanent and transitional needs arising from urbanization.

Instead, statutory embellishments of selected provisions of the Texas Constitution have placed MUDs and ISDs at the forefront in providing counties with an urban infrastructure and delivering important services. This differentiated structure of local service provision has given rise to a free-market atmosphere in which land use patterns are shaped largely by land ownership and by what the market will bear. Given that MUDs and ISDs are formed around or along with developments, the initial, if not always final, urban infrastructure created in counties is financed mainly on a neighborhood-specific basis, not by the county's entire population.

A recent ACIR report argues that a cluster of local governments inside and overlapping counties, such as that found in the Houston MSA, can be viewed as a "local public economy." This economy is created by local actors, public and private, within a "framework of rules ... supplied largely through state constitutions and laws, not by metropolitan or regional governments."[6] For the Houston MSA, the multiplicity of governments emerging with urbanization does seem to serve "a number of useful purposes: it increases the sensitivity of local government to diverse citizen preferences; it increases efficiency by matching the distribution of benefits more closely to the economic demand of communities; and it enables citizens to hold public officials accountable to a specific community of interest."[7]

In the Houston area and across the nation, however, the "rules" for local governments are not static, nor are they framed only by the state's constitution and statutes. Increasingly, the U.S. Constitution and statutes also have come to overlay local governance. Sometimes, perhaps often, what works at one time must later be altered to deal with new circumstances.

The problem, though, is that the "rules" established by the state and federal governments do not always allow counties and other local governments to respond adequately to challenges in order to build a more functional local public economy where conditions are dysfunctional. In the Houston MSA, for example, a number of local governance challenges will have to be addressed in the near future.

For one, Texas faces major questions of equity in the financing of public education. With ISDs created to serve economic enclaves, as opposed to citywide or countywide jurisdictions, many differences in fiscal capacity exist among school districts, although with urbanization, the creation of more ISDs does give metropolitan residents more choices. Of course, such disparities are not confined to the Houston MSA; they exist statewide. Thus, how this issue is finally resolved will require changes in state "rules." The political challenge will be to equalize funding under state court orders largely within the present structure of ISDs. Two possibilities, each with consequences for local governance, are interjurisdictional transfers from rich to poor districts or statewide financing based on uniform assessments.

Several intergovernmental questions also need resolution. For example, many MUDs in the Houston MSA use groundwater and have small wastewater treatment plants that were built to meet population projections that were too low. Eventually, MUDs will have to be supplied by surface water because of depletion and subsidence problems, and their treatment plants will have to be upgraded or integrated regionally.[8] In resolving these issues, local government boundary questions will arise around the complex issues of incorporation and annexation.

Through incorporation, MUD costs and benefits can be absorbed by existing cities. Such incorporations are unlikely, however, because all Harris County MUDs and most MUDs in Ft. Bend, Montgomery, and Waller counties are inside the city of Houston's extraterritorial jurisdiction (ETJ), which extends five miles beyond the city's corporate limits.[9] State law prohibits new incorporation within a city's ETJ unless the city grants permission. Given that Houston is not likely to grant such permission, incorporations are out of the question. The surrounding counties, therefore, have little leverage under the existing rules to help fashion a more functional local public economy.

Ironically, the state's ETJ rules were intended, in part, to allow municipalities to respond to growth. Indeed, since World War II, Houston has dissolved many MUDs and taken over their liabilities and assets through large-scale annexations. (A home-rule city may annex by simple ordinance action within its ETJ.) This annexation power, however, has been complicated by two major factors. One is the *Voting Rights Act of 1965* and its later amendments. This act, which is applicable to Houston, prohibits boundary changes that dilute minority voting strength.[10] The second factor is the 1963 Municipal Annexation Act that requires cities to provide equivalent city services to annexed areas within three years of annexation — a hurdle that is sometimes difficult for cities. Thus, these federal and state statutes — which have laudable equity objectives — have some counter-equity consequences, while they also limit the ability of the city and its surrounding counties to respond to growth challenges.

How county governments can fit more effectively into the overall pattern of local governance in the future will require a thorough reshaping or at least fine tuning of existing state rules, and perhaps, some federal rules. On the educational equity question, for example, county governments are not even in the picture.

On many intergovernmental questions, county governments can only react and adapt to the actions of other governments. At this time, moreover, county governments can only venture selectively from their traditional service responsibilities.

Hence, county empowerment needs to be addressed in Texas as well as in many other states, especially where the challenges to local governance posed by urbanization are stretching the limits of existing governments. Such empowerment, moreover, can be seen as a logical extension of the traditional service responsibilities of counties, an extension that does not require the county to take over and centralize all functions, but rather an extension that allows a county to serve its local communities by facilitating the development of a functional local public economy.

Notes

1. A 1989 Missouri City (Ft. Bend County) survey, for example, found that 61 percent of the city's residents worked in Houston.

2. The 1917 amendment gave landowners *unlimited and unrestricted* debt financing for flood control, drainage, irrigation, and power projects — financial latitude not available to cities and counties.

3. Under the 1917 amendment, the legislature has authorized 13 different types of districts, but only 3 have been used to support urban developments. As forerunners of MUDs, Fresh Water Supply Districts and Water Control and Improvement Districts were used to finance urban improvements. The Municipal Utilities Act of 1971 applied the concept directly to urban developments, authorizing MUDs to provide all types of water supplies, waste disposal services, and drainage. MUDs were also authorized to alter land elevations, provide parks and recreation facilities, as well as other functions. Combined, these functional responsibilities made MUDs "small" towns. Cf. Lee Charles Schroer, "The Water Control and Improvement District: Concept, Creation and Critique," *Houston Law Review* 8 (March 1971):

712–738; and Texas Water Code, Chapter 54.201, p. 297.

4. The Texas Constitution (Art. VII, Sec. 3) also authorizes cities to constitute separate school districts; however, there are 1,064 ISDs in Texas and only a few city districts.

5. Art. XI of the Texas Constitution creates counties as legal subdivisions of the state (Sec. 1), and then controls their authorities through general laws (Sec. 2).

6. U.S. Advisory Commission on Intergovernmental Relations, *The Organization of Local Public Economies* (Washington, D.C., 1987), p. 35.

7. *Ibid.*, p. 1. See also U.S. Advisory Commission on Intergovernmental Relations, *Metropolitan Organization: The St. Louis Case* (Washington, DC, 1988).

8. See also Virginia Lacy Perrenod, *Special Districts, Special Purposes: Fringe Govern-* ments and Urban Problems in the Houston Area (College Station: Texas A&M University Press, 1984).

9. Home-rule cities in Texas have ETJs of one-half mile to five miles beyond their corporate limits, depending on their population, as follows: more than 100,000, five miles; 50,000 to 100,000, three and one-half miles; 25,000 to 50,000, two miles; 5,000 to 25,000, one mile. Municipal Annexation Act, General and Special Laws of the State of Texas, 57th Legislature (1963), Ch. 160, pp. 447–545.

10. See also Robert D. Thomas and Richard W. Murray, "Applying the Voting Rights Act in Houston: Federal Intervention or Local Political Determination?" *Publius: The Journal of Federalism* 16 (Fall 1986): 81–96.

• *Chapter 16* •

Models of Regional Government

RICHARD SYBERT

This chapter reviews four models and examples of regional government: (1) one-level; (2) two-level; (3) cooperative; and (4) metropolitan council.[1]

Nashville-Davidson County provides an example of the first model, where the city and county governments are consolidated into one. In this case, the new government was able to save its taxpayers an estimated $18 million in the first ten years by providing a more efficient government and cutting duplication of services. The one government could represent both local and regional interests through a combination of district and at-large representation. However, this model has never been successful in metropolitan areas that extend over more than one county or have populations of over one million people, limiting its usefulness in California.

Miami-Dade County's two-level comprehensive government has successfully integrated and coordinated the county's previously disorganized departments and agencies. "Metro" was successful in financing water and sewer treatment, transit, a seaport, traffic, and law enforcement projects in its first two decades. It also established a South Dade Governmental Center to make services such as public works, pollution control, traffic and transportation, water and sewer, and housing and urban development, more accessible. Metro's main problem is that the growth of the region is extending beyond the Dade County line. With no governing power outside the county, Metro is facing difficulties dealing with the region's problems. This is possibly a problem for California as well, with its urban regions often crossing multiple county lines.

Another two-level model is federation. Through government reorganization, Toronto's Metro, like Miami-Dade County, has been successful in finding solutions considered unachievable in the previous government system. Metro has successfully stabilized the region's governmental finances

From *Models of Regional Government*, October, 1991. Published by the Governor's Office of Planning and Research and the Governor's Interagency Council on Growth Management, Office of the Governor, State of California, Sacramento, California. Reprinted with permission of the publisher.

and resolved specific service crises. Its accomplishments include: water and sewer facilities, a regional highway network, a coordinated public transportation system, a traffic control system, and the establishment of a large parks system. One problem facing Toronto's Metro is factionalism. The Metro Council is often divided by local interests, limiting its ability to deal with regional problems.

The Lakewood–Los Angeles cooperative approach is an efficient and effective form of government whereby the county provides needed services— generally fire, sanitation, and police services— to the city of Lakewood and others in the Los Angeles County without unnecessarily duplicating government agencies. Opponents say the plan limits a city's powers to land use decisions. Further, Lakewood was a new, small city with no previous service capabilities; the approach may not be applicable to California's existing, large urban regions.

Finally, there is the model of metropolitan councils. Two examples are the Twin Cities Metropolitan Council in Minneapolis-St. Paul and the Portland, Oregon Tri-County Metropolitan Council. Both these plans are examples of regional governments in multi-county areas. Through legislation passed in the Minnesota Legislature, the Twin Cities Metropolitan Council was formed in 1967. Although it possesses rather weak powers, the Council was originally successful in developing regional approaches for sewers, transportation, airports, housing, parks, and open space. However, the Council later encountered difficulties in its effectiveness as a governing body. Portland's Tri-County Council was an evolution of regional agencies. Although it too has weak powers, it has increased its effectiveness through popular support.

One-Level Alternative

Since the beginning of the 20th century, many urban reformers have contended that the entire metropolitan area or "sphere of influence" of the modern city should be brought within its actual legal boundaries. These reformers believe that the creation of a single or "one level" governments for an entire urban region would be more efficient, effective, and economical than multi-level governments. However, opponents of this model maintain that it results in the loss of local control, decreased citizen access to public officials, and reduced attention to local services. This is because one-level urban government in a metropolitan area necessarily is on a larger scale than traditional local government.

The one-level alternative can be accomplished by three basic techniques: (1) annexation (the absorption of nearby unincorporated territory); (2) municipal consolidation (the merger of two or more incorporated units); and (3) city-county consolidation (the union of one or more municipalities with the county government).

This chapter focuses on city-county consolidation because it is the most dramatic or strongest of these techniques. To achieve city-county consolidation, two legal battles normally must be won. First, a state constitutional amendment or legislative enabling act must be passed to permit the metropolitan areas to pursue the consolidation. Second, the consolidation must win the approval of the local voters, usually by separate majorities of the city or cities and the unincorporated part of the county.

An example of the one-level alternative through city-county consolidation is Nashville-Davidson County in Tennessee.

Nashville-Davidson County

Background. The metropolitan government of Nashville-Davidson County is located in the north central area of the State of Tennessee. Prior to consolidation, Davidson County had 12 governments within its boundaries: the county, the city of Nashville, six incorporated suburbs, and four special utility districts.

The Nashville region faced problems similar to those of many other medium or small metropolitan areas in the country. There existed a single urban area with overlapping governments—one, the city, with substantial authority but little area; and the other, the county, with substantial territory but little power. This situation created constant attempts between local governments to "pass the buck" and avoid responsibility, with each government trying to keep its own taxes low by taking advantage of the other's services.

The Nashville region also provided an example of a tax dispute often seen between the city government and its "daytime citizens"—i.e., commuters—from the suburbs. Most citizens in the region paid taxes only in their resident communities, despite the fact that their jobs were located in and arguably depended upon the city of Nashville. Suburban commuters also used many city-supported services. While county residents argued that they contributed to the city's wealth, the city believed that its own citizens were effectively subsidizing services to county residents in this manner. The city tried to correct this perceived inequity by overcharging county residents for city-supplied water and electricity. In addition, the city levied a "wheel tax" on all motor vehicles using the streets of Nashville for 30 days or more. However, the strict enforcement of these taxes created considerable resentment on the part of county residents. As an example of conflict, city and county police with-

held information from each other. Also, the two school systems fought over how to split state education funds. Additionally on some roads where the city-county line went down the middle, the speed limit was 35 mph in one direction and 45 mph in the other.

These conflicts made it increasingly evident that the needs of the residents in the Nashville-Davidson County area were not being efficiently and effectively met by the existing multi-level government arrangement. Accordingly, in 1957 the Tennessee State General Assembly enacted enabling legislation permitting city-county consolidation.

A first attempt to approve a county-city consolidation failed in 1958. It was supported by the mayor of Nashville, the Nashville Chamber of Commerce, the Tennessee Taxpayers' Association, labor, and a variety of other groups. Opponents, including suburban private fire and police companies, some suburban businessmen, and members of the county legislature, argued that the consolidation would mean bigger government, higher taxes, and city control over the suburbs. In 1962, a new "Metro" charter election was called for in the Nashville-Davidson County region. This time, with a greater grass roots effort (telephoning, doorbell ringing, and neighborhood coffees), the charter won approval both in the city and the county, by margins of 57–40 percent and 55–44 percent respectively.

The System. The metropolitan government of Nashville-Davidson County merged the functions previously held separately by the city of Nashville and Davidson County. The six suburbs were frozen at their existing boundaries, and given the opportunity to use Metro's services, which most did.

The Metro government has a strong mayor-council system. The chief executive is the "metropolitan mayor," who is elected by the area's voters to a four-year term. His tenure in office limited to three consecutive terms. The mayor is responsible for the supervision, administration, and control of the executive departments, agencies, boards, and commissions. The mayor is authorized to approve or disapprove council ordinances, subject to an override by two-thirds of the council. The mayor may also veto line-item budget expenditures, again subject to a two-thirds override by the council.

The legislative branch consists of two parts: the metropolitan council and the urban council. The metropolitan county council is comprised of 40 councilmembers and the vice mayor. Thirty-five of these councilmembers are elected from single-member districts of approximately equal population, and five councilmembers are elected at large. The charter provides for a high number of councilmembers to ensure that local concerns [are] represented. The five at large members were included to make sure that regional problems were addressed.

The charter designates two separate service-tax districts with[in] the metropolitan government's geographic limits: the general services district (GSD) and the urban services district (USD). The GSD comprises the total area of Davidson County and provides such services as general administration, police, courts, jails, health, welfare, schools, transit, and parks and recreation. The USD provides additional services, such as urban level fire protection, trash collection, street lights, storm drainage, and additional police protection. Separate taxes are levied in each district to support the level of services within the respective district.

The USD may be expanded whenever areas in the GSD need additional urban services, and when the metropolitan government is capable of providing such additional services within one year after the additional USD tax rate is imposed. While there is no formula to determine when additional services are needed, expansion usually occurs when enough local support is gathered to join the USD and pay the additional taxes. If the USD is not capable of providing the services within the one-year deadline, Metro can delay the application until the services are ready to be provided.

Two-Level Alternative

The two-level alternative of regional reorganization is based on the theory of federalism. With this technique, area-wide functions are delegated to area-wide governments, while purely local functions remain with the local units, creating a two-tier system.

The two-tier system can take three basic forms:

1. Metropolitan district: A governmental unit that usually encompasses all or a substantial part of the entire geographic metropolitan area, but is normally authorized to perform only one function or a few closely related activities of an area-wide nature. California examples would be school districts, water districts, air quality and transit districts and the like. The existing city-county structure is retained.

2. Comprehensive urban county plan: The simultaneous transfer of selected functions from municipalities and other local units to the county governments. The existing city-county structure is retained, with the county performing a number of municipal functions county-wide.

3. Federation: The establishment of a new area-wide government that is assigned new responsibilities and customarily replaces the existing county government.

Again, the upper tier performs a number of municipal functions region-wide.

Because metropolitan districts are single-interest entities, with no general jurisdictions to address metropolitan-wide problems, this section will focus on the other two systems.

All of these forms are structural variations and may accomplish the same functional result.

Comprehensive Urban County Plan

Under a comprehensive urban county plan, a county assumes those functions that are determined to be area-wide in nature, while the municipalities continue to administer those functions considered to be of purely local concern. Thus, the county is transformed into a metropolitan government, with the simultaneous reallocation of a variety of functions from all municipalities to the county.

Politically, such a plan can have considerable appeal if the county is viewed by the public as an acceptable unit of local government. Unlike other techniques of reform, the urban county plan does not require the creation of still another unit of government. Instead, it merely strengthens the county to serve as a second tier. The success of this type of regional government in California is questionable because most major metropolitan areas often cross county lines.

An example of a comprehensive urban county plan is Miami-Dade County in Florida.

MIAMI-DADE COUNTY

Background. Dade County, located in the southeast corner of Florida, covers approximately 2,300 square miles. It encompasses all of the Miami area and stretches westward to the Everglades. Population growth in Dade County over the last few decades has been high, increasing six-fold in the 45 years after World War II to over 1.9 million people. Historically, the county had experienced a series of municipal incorporations by the core city, Miami, and its surrounding suburbs.

Metropolitan government, or "Metro," was created in 1957. Prior to this, there was no effective countywide agency responsible for long-range regional planning in such areas as economic development, welfare, recreation, and the environment. Local planning boards did exist, but were ineffective because of relatively poorly trained technical staffs, inadequate financial support, and what some believed to be lack of appreciation by local officials and the general public of the need for adequate planning.

The needs of the unincorporated areas of Dade County, home to one-third of the total county population, constituted a particularly serious problem. These unincorporated areas frequently entered into informal agreements with incorporated municipalities for provision of essential services, such as fire protection and police communication and training, to rapidly growing populations. The major problem with these agreements was that larger cities were burdened with the expenses of providing the services to the smaller areas.

A number of proposals to consolidate Dade County with the city of Miami and a varying number of smaller communities failed in the late 1940s and early 1950s. However, the closeness of a referendum in 1953 led to the formation of the Metropolitan Miami Municipal Board (3M Board) to study the feasibility of governmental reorganization.

In November 1956, the citizens of the State of Florida by a two to one margin, passed a home rule constitutional amendment, thus freeing Dade County and its cities from dependence on the state legislature for the enactment of local laws. The home rule amendment also permitted the county's voters to create a metropolitan government. Following this approval, the 3M board developed a proposal for a metropolitan system.

The principal recommendation of the 3M Board was creation of a two-tiered form of government of the Dade County Region. The city level would be responsible for local functions, such as zoning and police and fire protection, the minimum standards for which would be set by the county. The second level would be a reorganized and enlarged county government, responsible for such regional functions as water, sewage, solid waste disposal, all public transportation construction and operation, traffic control, and overall metropolitan planning.

Prior to the referendum election, a Dade County League of Municipalities committee established to study the proposal returned a negative report. In spite of the League's opposition, Dade County voters narrowly approved (51–49 percent with only a 26 percent turnout) a charter based on the 3M recommendations in May 1957.

The System. The powers of the county government under the terms of the charter are separated into four distinct categories: (1) municipal-type functions, (2) responsibilities in unincorporated areas, (3) responsibilities for setting minimum standards, and (4) elastic powers.

The municipal-type functions include transportation systems, traffic control, police and fire protection, county development plans, health and welfare programs, parks and recreation, housing, water supply, waste disposal, and taxing. County government's responsibilities in unincorporated areas include the same municipal-type functions, such as police and fire protection and waste disposal, plus other functions performed by municipalities, such

as licensing and regulation of the limousines and taxis, and establishing and enforcing regulations for the sale of alcoholic beverages.

To provide local control of municipal services, the county government is empowered to set minimum performance standards for services provided by all local governmental units. If a municipality does not comply with such standards, the county government is empowered to take over and perform or contract out to other organizations to operate the service. Finally, under the so-called "elastic" provisions of the charter, the county government is authorized "to exercise all powers and privileges granted" to municipalities and counties under the Florida Constitution to "adopt such ordinances and resolutions as may be required in the exercise of its powers" and to "perform any other acts consistent with laws which are required or which are in the common interest of the people of the county."

Although the division of powers under this scheme is strongly weighted on the county government's side, the individual municipalities are given certain protections and prerogatives. The county cannot abolish an incorporated municipality without the express permission of the municipality's voters, nor can the county rearrange municipal boundaries. Municipalities retain the right to change their respective charters, provided the provisions do not conflict with the county charter. Each city can exceed county minimum standards for zoning, and, subject to county standards, regulate taxis and other rental vehicles, determine hours for sale of alcoholic beverages, and provide for fire and police protection.

A board of county commissioners is designated under the terms of the charter to serve as the legislative and governing body of the county and to oversee the entire metropolitan system. The board consists of nine commissioners, with eight elected by the voters of the county at large, subject to the requirement that each commissioner must reside in a different county commission district. The ninth member, who serves as the mayor and chairman of the board, also is elected by a county wide vote. All commissioners serve four-year terms.

Federation

Another variation of the two-level alternative is a federation. This approach involves the creation of an entirely new area-wide government with either multi-county or one-county territorial limits. The newly created unit is usually designated as the metropolitan government and is charged with carrying out numerous area-wide functions. The original municipal units continue to operate and perform local functions that are not performed by the new metropolitan government.

Most of the federation plans proposed in the United States have called for the metropolitan legislative body to be made up of local representatives from the municipalities. Thus, federation, as a metropolitan concept, requires replacing the existing county government with a new metropolitan unit, while the previous urban county plan involves retaining the county unit as the area-wide tier.

TORONTO

Background. An example of federation is Toronto, Ontario. Metropolitan Toronto is situated on the northern shore of Lake Ontario in the Canadian province of Ontario. Prior to governmental reorganization in 1953, the 240-square mile metropolitan area contained 13 municipal jurisdictions.

Between 1945 and 1953, there was an exodus of business firms and middle-class citizens from central Toronto to the outlying districts and a steady in-migration of lower-income families. At the same time, new industries were locating in the suburbs rather than the central city. This population shift generated rising concerns over the city's ability to finance and provide water, sewage disposal, housing, and other municipal functions to its residents. To finance these increasing needs, the city was forced to increase its tax rate. However, the smaller, established suburbs, located between the city and the growing industrialized suburbs, benefitted from using Toronto's hospitals, libraries, and parks without taxation, and felt no pressure to expand their facilities or raise their low tax rates. Needless to say, this scenario is strikingly similar to situations faced by the older U.S. central cities in the wake of post-war suburbanization.

The Ontario Municipal Board (OMB), a provincial board, was requested by the province to create an area for joint administration of municipal services in order to redress this situation. In January 1953, the chairman of the board, submitted a report calling for the creation of a metropolitan federation. Although the proposal was controversial, the premier of Ontario's support ensured that the report's recommendations would be adopted by the Ontario provincial legislature.

The System. Under the terms of the 1953 Act for the Toronto Region, a Metropolitan Council was created to serve as both the executive body of metropolitan Toronto ("Metro"), and the legislative body for the 13 represented municipalities. The Metropolitan Council was comprised of 25 members: 12 from the city of Toronto, the mayors from each of the 12 suburbs, and an independent chairman to be elected by the council. Toronto's delegation consisted of its mayor, two controllers, and an alderman from each of the nine city wards.

The chairmanship of the Metro Council was assigned little formal power under the Act, being limited to such functions as presiding over meetings, interpreting the rules of procedure, and casting a vote only in the case of a tie. However, unlike the members of the council, the chairman was a full-time official who could devote his total time and energy to Metro matters, and thereby acquire considerable influence with other council members.

The council's first chairman used these limited powers to successfully influence the decision process. The chairman succeeded in convincing the council that it could work more effectively through a smaller group. A seven-member executive committee was chosen by the entire council and possessed all of the powers of boards of control in municipal governments—preparing budgets, nominating department heads, awarding contracts, etc. Some believe that the chairman knew that the smaller committee could also be more easily controlled by him.

For the most part, the metropolitan government dealt with the more critical regional problems, particularly finances to build schools, transportation, and water facilities, while such matters as police, fire, public health, and public welfare were left primarily in the preserve of the 13 municipalities. A system of shared responsibilities was set up among the municipalities under Metro in such areas as street construction, road maintenance, traffic control, public assistance, zoning and planning. Only public transportation became a fully Metro function.

While the local communities retained the right to assess taxes, Metro was given the power to cope with regional problems through exclusive borrowing authority for all of the municipalities and independent boards of the region, thereby obtaining very favorable interest rates. It also secured the power to apportion revenue it raised through assessment among the 13 communities, utilizing a formula whereby each municipality's share was based upon a total assessment area.

Cooperative Alternative

The "cooperative" alternative model of regional government, also referred to as "inter-local agreements," calls for greater cooperation between existing governments without the creation of new ones. This approach represents a voluntary technique to address regional problems while maintaining local control.

Supporters of the cooperative alternative view themselves as political realists, because cooperative proposals appear and probably are less radical than other proposed metropolitan structures. Proponents also favor dispersed local government and argue for the right of public choice between competing community locations, services, and tax bases. Proponents argue that the cooperative alternative, although maintaining existing structures, still contributes to greater governmental efficiency and lower costs, since through the possibility of interjurisdictional agreement, it can eliminate the necessity of each local government's hiring its own personnel or constructing new facilities for particular services.

Interjurisdictional cooperation is a broad concept with numerous variations. These range from verbal agreements which may consist merely of the exchange of information, to formal agreements that relate to specific functions or services. Agreements can take the following basic forms:

1. A single government performs a service or provides a facility for one or more other local units.

2. Two or more local governments administer a function or operate a facility on a joint basis.

3. Two or more local governments assist or supply mutual aid to one another in emergency situations.

The cooperative approach has been the subject of considerable criticism. First, critics argue that it is a piecemeal approach since each service agreement normally involves only two governments and one service or facility, resulting in a patchwork of agreements that usually relate to noncontroversial matters. Second, and perhaps the most serious criticism, is financial inadequacy. Cooperative agreements are not devices that equalize public resources among localities within a metropolitan area. Although most interjurisdictional agreements call for provision of services by one local unit in exchange for payment by another, some local governments do not have sufficient financial resources to pay for needed services.

The county of Los Angeles provides an excellent example of the cooperative approach to metropolitan government.

Los Angeles County–Lakewood Plan

Background. Millions of Americans migrated to Southern California to work in aircraft plants and shipyards after World War II. The population of the Los Angeles–Long Beach metropolitan area expanded rapidly during this period.

California state law gives counties control over services vital to all governments, and cities in particular. These include relief for the poor, public hospital care, property tax assessments, registration of voters, the administration of elections and support of the trial court system including jails, prosecution, probation administration, courtroom facilities and staffs. California counties also provide unincorporated areas with many municipal services, including water, sewage, roads, street lighting, and fire [and police] protection.

County provision of such services helped moderate the trend of incorporation of suburban areas within Los Angeles County, which is California's largest county (indeed the nation's) by far in population. Since the county provided services, pressure to incorporate was reduced. However, city-county relations were not always amicable. There had been charges that the county had effectively subsidized unincorporated areas with dollars raised through the county's general fund, which was funded in part by taxes on city residents. In 1950, a study by a League of California Cities committee found that a large part of city residents' county tax dollars were going to provide services to the unincorporated areas of the county. As a result, the county reduced the number of its services available to the unincorporated areas.

The System. Lakewood began as an unincorporated planned housing development within Los Angeles County in 1950. The development was built on land that the city of Long Beach planned to annex to help provide services and increase its tax base. In 1953, Long Beach began a series of annexation proceedings and successfully annexed a part of Lakewood Village with a population of 24,000.

Residents of the remaining unincorporated area of the Lakewood area began a drive to incorporate in order to save it from annexation. An election was set that would have allowed a choice between incorporation and annexation to Long Beach. Pro-incorporation forces argued that incorporation would ensure local control at low costs. On March 9, 1954, the voters approved the incorporation petition.

A new state law, permitting a newly incorporated city in California to contract with its county for all essential services, enabled Lakewood to have a wide variety of services available immediately through Los Angeles County. These services included the county-administered special districts (fire, library, sewer, and lighting), self-governing special districts (sanitation, recreation, and mosquito abatement), and county contracts for general services (animal regulation, assessment and collection of taxes, health services, industrial waste regulation, jails, law enforcement, planning and zoning staff services, street maintenance and construction, and treasury and auditor services).

By contracting with the county for needed services, the new city of Lakewood was able to function with only ten employees and a very reasonable tax rate. While the county lost some tax revenues as a result of incorporation, by contracting with Lakewood it was able to maintain its departments, such as law enforcement and sanitation, at strength.

The Lakewood plan was so successful that it spurred new incorporations within Los Angeles County. Most of the new cities entered into similar agreements with the county for provision of services. However, ultimate control over service levels remained with each city, because each city purchased only specific services that it believed were both needed and affordable. Effectively, this arrangement allowed smaller cities to pool their needs for services and purchase them on a "volume discount" basis from a single, cost-effective provider, the county.

The Lakewood plan eliminated the need for additional municipal service departments and duplication of services. However, it did not attempt to address other pressing regional concerns of planning, water supply, sewage, and education. Further, as the county is the actual producer of the services, the county tends to dominate any bargaining process with the cities over the quality of services and their costs.

Metropolitan Council Alternative

A fourth category of regional or metropolitan government is the metropolitan council. Metropolitan councils are permanent associations of governments that meet on a regular basis to discuss and seek agreement on various issues. While metropolitan councils can be classified as variations of the cooperative approach, there are some key differences. A metropolitan council can be defined as a voluntary association of governments designed to be an area-wide forum for key officials to research and discuss issues and eventually determine how best to address common problems. However, because of its lack of authority, the council mechanism cannot be classified as a true metropolitan government.

Examples of a metropolitan councils are Minneapolis–St. Paul in Minnesota and the Tri-County/Portland area in Oregon.

Minneapolis–St. Paul

Background. The Twin Cities Metropolitan Council in the Minneapolis–St. Paul area of Minnesota was created in 1967. It is comprised of 7 counties, 25 cities, 105 villages, 68 townships, 77 school districts, and 20 special service districts.

The problems leading to creation of the Twin Cities Metropolitan Council arose from the usual causes: an expanding population, changing population patterns, scattered and uncontrolled growth, and the accompanying need for services such as sewers, waste disposal, housing, and transportation.

There were three main reasons why existing local governments seemed unable to handle all issues. First, some problems, such as pollution, tended to spill over into other jurisdictions. Second, some of the proposed solutions to these problems were potentially very costly and beyond the means of a single local jurisdiction. Finally, no single existing jurisdiction, including any of the involved counties, possessed the authority to make decisions for the entire metropolitan area. Minnesota counties have been traditionally weak, and in this case the metropolitan region crossed county lines.

Unlike many other metropolitan areas, when Twin Cities area leaders recognized that the problems needed to be dealt with from a metropolitan perspective, there was an almost even balance between the central cities and the suburban areas both in population and property value. This prevented either area from dominating the other and made it politically easier to proceed.

The System. Between 1965 and 1967, a consensus was built among metropolitan leaders that an area-wide government body should be created to handle such issues as sewer works, open space, transit, airports, and a zoo. These functions had previously been provided by special purpose districts, not individual municipalities, so that this consensus implied consolidation of various single-purpose agencies or districts.

A group of civic leaders was formed to study regional government in the Twin Cities. By 1967, the group presented its proposal to the Minnesota Legislature. The legislature considered two alternative pieces of legislation, one calling for an elected council with planning and operating control of regional functions, and one creating a council appointed at large by the governor and responsible for planning and coordinating the operation of regional agencies. The latter proposal was passed to establish the Twin Cities Metropolitan Council.

The Council is composed of 16 members appointed by the governor for staggered six-year terms. Each member represents two state senate districts of equal population size. The chairman is selected at large and serves at the governor's pleasure.

The Council's powers are mostly of a coordinating nature. Specifically, the Council is directed to perform three functions. First, it must review all regional plans and projects affecting the Council's metropolitan systems plans for airport, parks, transportation, and sewers, against development guidelines developed by the Council. Within 60 days of submission of such plans, the Council may indefinitely suspend, in total or part, any project that it finds to be inconsistent with the guidelines. While the Council has the power to delay a project, it uses its powers mainly to leverage changes in projects, not to prevent their development.

Second, the Council reviews and comments on long-term municipal comprehensive plans and any other matters that the Council determines may have a "metropolitan effect," such as a project that would have an effect on the entire Twin Cities region. These local plans must be consistent with metropolitan systems' plans developed by the Council for airports, parks, transportation, and sewers, and which together function as the regional comprehensive plan.

Local plans do not have to be updated at any specific time interval, but rather when they affect the regional systems plan, as determined by the Metropolitan Council. The plans are required to include current and future land use; community facilities, such as transportation, airports, sewers, and parks; and implementation — how the plan will be carried out. Local plans are not subject to council veto, although as a practical matter the existence of the Council with its powers generally leads local governments to be consistent with the regional plans. If one local unit objects to the plans of another unit, the Council may hold hearings and mediate any differences.

Finally, the Council performs an advisory evaluation of applications for federal grants emanating from local governments, boards, and agencies.

The Twin Cities Council can be classified as a metropolitan government because it is comprised solely of local representatives, and it is concerned only with regional interests, decisions, services, and needs. Moreover, the Council is empowered to levy an area property tax to finance its operations. It can be viewed in one sense as a state agency, since the governor appoints the representatives who comprise the Council. In addition, it is the legislature that assigns the Council its powers, controls its finances, determines its structure, and requires it to submit reports.

At the forefront of regional governance in the late 1960s, the Metro council has more recently become less relevant in many regional issues. In its early years, the Council succeeded in creating a region-wide sewer system, founding the Minnesota Zoo, and blocking the construction of an unneeded airport. However, with an ambitious legislature, which did not want to provide the Council with substantial power, and an uninterested governor, the Council's powers dwindled. In recent years, the Council has been left out of the site selection and project definition of the Metrodome, the site selection of a horse racing track in the suburbs, and the consideration of a light-rail system between the two cities. In addition, it was unable to determine a site for a new landfill.

Most of the blame for the Metro Council's recent failures center on its lack of public support: because the Council is appointed by the governor, not elected by the people, citizens and public officials do not believe it has the clout to make necessary changes. In 1985, the Citizens League, a Minneapolis non-partisan research group, concluded that the Council was "in danger of sliding into irrelevance" because it was considered by state and local officials as just another level of bureaucracy. Recognizing the troubles facing the Council, Governor Arne Carlson recently instructed his nine new appointees to revitalize the agency.

Portland

Background. Regional government in the Portland, Oregon, area has evolved over the past six decades. In 1926, in response to rapid and unplanned suburbanization of the area caused by the invention of the automobile, the state established a committee to examine the problems facing the various local governments in the Portland area. The 1944 conference of the League of Oregon Cities passed a resolution that "sporadic, scattered, and unregulated growth of municipalities and urban fringes has caused tremendous waste in money and resources" and requested legislative action at the state level to permit "the creation of metropolitan or regional planning districts and the establishment of metropolitan or regional planning commissions." The state legislature responded by enacting legislation authorizing county planning commissions and county zoning to complement municipal planning programs.

The Metropolitan Planning Commission (MPC) was created in 1957. The Commission had a four-member board representing the city of Portland and the three surrounding counties (Multnomah, Washington, and Clackamas) and was funded by federal grant money. Although it was created to provide planning, the Commission actually provided information and reports on population and industrial sites and assisted local planning departments rather than prepare long-range plans for the region.

In the early 1960s, activists contended that the studies and work produced in the 1950s had done nothing to address the problems of public services in the region. In the 1940s and 50s, the number of special districts in the three counties increased from 28 to 218. In a 1960 study, *A Tale of Three Counties*, the League of Women Voters reported that the local agencies were inefficient and unaccountable, which resulted in poor services. Civic leaders joined together to request that regional options for government services be examined. In response, the state legislature created the Interim Committee on Local Government Problems, whose primary recommendation was the creation of a "metropolitan study commission," later called the Portland Metropolitan Study Commission (PMSC).

The PMSC's *Interim Report* of December 1966 made ten recommendations for more efficient service, including:

- Special district consolidations where possible.
- Legislation authorizing the creation of metropolitan service districts.
- Formation of a regional council of governments with memberships from counties, cities, and port districts.
- Organization of an area-wide air quality control program.
- Development of intergovernmental cooperative agreements among cities and counties for health, planning, law enforcement and engineering services.

The PMSC's work toward a more regional approach to government services helped produce the Columbia Region Association of Governments (CRAG) in 1966. Structured similar to the MPC,

CRAG was a council of governments representing the region's cities and counties. All of the participating city and county governments were represented in CRAG's General Assembly, but its Executive Board was comprised of three county representatives, a Portland representative, and three representatives from other cities in the three counties. CRAG was charged with studying, recommending, rendering technical assistance, and adopting comprehensive metropolitan plans. Although it carried out its duties regarding studies and reports, intergovernmental rivalries slowed its work to develop a comprehensive land use plan. After failing to pass plans in 1970 and 1974, CRAG adopted a general set of goals and objects as a plan.

Another proposal of PMSC was the creation of the multi-purpose Metropolitan Service District (MSD). The MSD governing board was made up of seven elected officials, one from Portland, one from each of the three counties, and one representing the other cities in each of the three counties. While the voters approved the District in May of 1970 (54–46 percent), they overwhelmingly rejected a district-wide tax in November of 1970. Thus the new agency was presented with a wide range of problems, with few resources to address them.

In 1975, several regional government supporters applied to the National Academy for Public Administration for an 18-month grant to study the possibilities of multi-level government in metropolitan areas. In November and December of 1975, the "Ad Hoc Two-Tiered Planning Committee," the official recipient of the grant, transformed itself into the Tri-County Local Government Commission. The Tri-County Commission set out to design "an upper tier system of government that will attend to the common needs of the entire Tri-County community." The Commission established a goal of drafting specific legislation for the 1977 Legislative Session.

In 1976, the Commission decided to propose a reorganization of the MSD. Some of the key components to provide a strong and responsive regional government were:

1. Combining the planning functions of CRAG and the regional services of MSD.
2. Direct election of the regional policy makers.
3. A relatively large number of councilors (15) to be elected from relatively small districts.
4. Direct election of the executive director.

The legislature made a number of changes to the proposal, reducing the size of the Council to 12 and deleting a proposed veto for the executive director, before passing it in June 1977. In May 1978, the proposal, Measure 6, passed by 20,000 votes in the three-county area. The new Metropolitan Service District (Metro) was officially established on January 1, 1979.

The System. The enacting legislation did not stipulate any formal relationship between the Council and executive, instead leaving it to them to decide. At the outset, the executive acted more like a city manager, supplying information, setting agendas, and offering recommendations, with the Council being similar to a large city council. However, the relationship gradually changed to one where the Council acted as a miniature legislature, establishing its own policies and programs, with the executive director much like an executive branch, carrying out the Council's policies and programs.

As with most newly established programs, Metro made a number of mistakes in its early years. Its overambitious plan, for example, to address flooding in the Johnson Creek watershed produced one of its first defeats. In 1981, Metro proposed establishing a basin-wide Local Improvement District to fund flood control measures. Although the proposal was technically sound and fiscally creative, it was politically unachievable. Residents on higher lands in the basin were upset that they were, for all intents and purposes, paying assessments to help property owners on the valley floor. Metro's arguments that their paved streets, driveways, and parking lots increased runoff and directly contributed to the flooding in the basin were scientifically correct but politically unacceptable. Metro later withdrew its proposal.

Metro has seen its share of successes as well, both major and minor. In 1979, the Oregon Land Conservation and Development Commission accepted the Portland area's Urban Growth Boundary as designed by Metro. Under Metro's control, the Washington Park Zoo has grown in visitors and national reputation. Metro was able to solve a dispute over the selection of a new landfill site by identifying an alternative site. Metro was also successful in the siting, construction, and operation of the Oregon Convention Center in Portland.

Except for siting regional facilities and accepting or denying the region's Urban Growth Boundary, Metro has not infringed on local jurisdictions' land use powers. Cities and counties also continue to provide municipal services, except for solid waste disposal which is overseen by Metro.

In response to its success, Metro has gained expanded powers. In 1987, the legislature restored the executive veto power that had originally been part of the Tri-County Commission proposal. The Council has also set up a committee structure, hired a legislative staff, and produced independent policy initiatives. The legislature also passed a measure that now permits Metro to collect an excise tax on its operations to fund its central administration and planning.

Conclusions

This chapter analyzed several different forms of regional structure and consolidated government. All of the models have been valuable in varying degrees in their respective jurisdictions and regions. The variety of options reaffirms the need for flexible state policy in California, allowing maximum local choice to address local needs, priorities, and state goals.

None of the examples in this chapter dealt with regions as large, complex, or diverse as California's. However, there are regions in the state which reflect comparable situations to each of the noted examples. City/county consolidation has been considered and rejected in Sacramento, and is being discussed in Stanislaus County. Models proposed by cities and the county under the auspices of San Diego Area Association of Governments (SANDAG) resemble the structure in Miami/Dade County. Coordinated planning between multiple counties, similar to the Twin Cities approach, can be anticipated as one option in the nine Bay Area counties, as per the recommendations of Bay Vision 2020.

However, the similarities and differences between these examples also raise a number of considerations in dealing with regional problems. First, a common element in all models is recognition that there are regional problems that need to be addressed. Regional entities were created to deal with specific problems that existing local governments could not or did not appropriately address.

Second, each model was implemented with assistance from the state (or provincial) legislature. There were different levels of involvement, ranging from legisla-

tion forming or authorizing the government (Twin Cities), to requesting that a board review regional problems and governments (Miami-Dade County and Toronto), to removing possible roadblocks (Nashville-Davidson County and Lakewood).

Beyond recognition of a problem and the need for some form of regional solution, the models go in separate directions. One key difference is in the varying selection methods for representatives selected to the regional body. While Nashville-Davidson County had districts and at-large representatives to ensure local and regional responsiveness, the Twin Cities had gubernatorial-appointed representatives to ensure regional responsiveness. Toronto had city representatives, while Portland's Tri-County Council members were elected directly by the people, in both cases to ensure local responsiveness. It appears that directly elected officials, such as in the Portland area, have proven to be more successful than appointed officials, such as the Twin Cities.

Another notable difference between the models is the scope and powers of the regional body. These were often dependent on the pre-existing government structures and the size of the region. Nashville-Davidson County was able to consolidate all the powers and responsibilities into one government; Toronto and Miami-Dade County had strong powers to deal with regional problems, leaving other "local" matters to the cities; Lakewood decided to temporarily contract out some of its powers to Los Angeles County; the Twin Cities Council had only advisory powers on limited regional issues; and the Tri-County Council assumed the planning and service responsibilities of existing agencies.

Finally, each body's finances were determined by the problems that each specific region faced and the form of the government it decided to pursue. While most of the governments received tax funds directly from the taxpayers, regional governments can also be financed by the state or by participating cities or cities and counties.

As one model was not appropriate for all the cited examples, so too one model may not be right for all or any of California's regions. While many of the state's urban areas face similar problems, such as traffic, air pollution, and housing, their differences, including population and geographic size, could lead to solutions using different or variable models.

Although it is possible for the state to determine whether a regional government is needed, and the appropriate structure, choosing whether or which approach is best for a given region may also be left to the individual areas. California has a long history of home rule, and the state can continue to respect this concept by giving local jurisdictions the opportunity to solve regional problems on their own. Under this approach, only after giving local governments in a region a reasonable opportunity to deal with problems should the state intervene and impose some form of regional approach on specific issues.

This need not mean the state necessarily must take a hands-off approach. General goals can be set for the entire state. Each region would then be responsible for establishing its own more specific goals consistent with the state's, and a specific plan, including means of meeting stated goals and the structure of regional governance if any; goals might also be met through local cooperation. The state would be responsible for certifying that each region's goals were consistent with the general state goals, and that the regional plan [was] feasible. Alternatively, a regional plan could be self-certified against state

goals. If not consistent or not achievable, the plan would be returned by the state for adjustment. Plans would also be reviewed and updated periodically.

The strengths of this proposal are that it provides regions with local control to deal with regional problems, while the state oversees the process. It emphasizes that the state has a role in determining the regional problems that need to be addressed, but provides local jurisdictions the opportunity to develop their own solutions. This is, of course, a general notion. Other details, such as financing, state oversight agency, region composition, and default regional governments, would still have to be addressed.

Ultimately, the effectiveness of any regional structure will be up to the credibility and effectiveness of the leadership in each region. The "local heroes" who can convene a political constituency for change, and bring together the interests which must cooperate for solutions, will provide the leadership and direct the structure of the region. Even now, within the cities and counties of California, there are many local differences in program administration and structure. Nothing in the state's growth management policy should restrict the ability of strong local leaders to work within their own agencies and organizations to form whatever planning or service delivery system meets the needs of the local area best, so long as state goals are reasonably met.

Note

1. These models were developed in *Experiments in Metropolitan Government*, James F. Horan and G. Thomas Taylor, Jr., Westport, Conn.: Praeger Publications, 1977.

• *Chapter 17* •

Regional Cooperation

Theodore Hershberg

Will metropolitan Philadelphia be better off in the global economy if the city at the core of the region collapses? If you live in the suburbs, do you believe that what happens to Philadelphia is without significant consequence for you and the community in which you reside?

Let us be clear about the argument. It is not that the suburban communities surrounding a failed Philadelphia will be wiped out by virtue of their proximity to ground zero in an atomic blast. They won't. But suburban residents are wrong if they think they won't suffer any fall-out. The fact is they have a compelling economic interest in Philadelphia's viability.

Ample evidence documents that suburbs surrounding healthy central cities are better off than those surrounding unhealthy ones, and proof is mounting that regions—not cities or counties—will be the preeminent competitive units of the global economy. The issue is not whether the city and suburbs are tied together in a regional economy—they are—but how to ensure that the region will prosper in the future.

The fear and frustration felt by so many suburbanites about the problems of big cities is understandable, but their economic interests are not well served by turning their backs and ignoring the troubles next door. Such a course guarantees that problems will grow, opportunities will be lost, and, in the long run, everyone will be worse off. The time has come to recognize the mutual interests across the region and to begin a rational dialogue about what is required to work with each other to shape a prosperous future.

Regional cooperation spins on two axes, not one. Although the focus of this chapter is on the more familiar and difficult *city-to-suburb* relationships, *suburb-to-suburb* cooperation remains an important part of the larger challenge facing the region. Southeastern Pennsylvania has 239 municipalities and 63 school districts.

Originally published as "The Case for Regional Cooperation," *The Regionalist*, Vol. 1, No. 3, Fall 1995. Published by the National Association of Regional Councils, Washington, D.C. and the University of Baltimore, Baltimore, Maryland. Reprinted with permission of the publisher.

These units of government offer citizens highly valued local control, but they also give rise to a cloud of parochialism that obscures the necessity for change that is demanded by the competitiveness of the new global economy.

New Global Economic Realities

There is an apocryphal story about an American in the 1930s who grew weary with the world rushing off to war. To get away from the madness, he sold all his possessions in the states and bought a piece of land on a remote South Pacific isle known for its beauty and tranquillity. Unfortunately, he settled on Guadalcanal, the site, as World War II buffs know, of the fiercest fighting in the Pacific theater. The moral of the story is that the past is not always a useful guide for the future.

The global economy ensures the future will differ from the past. International trade, which equaled only 11 percent of America's gross national product (GNP) in 1960, reached 25 percent in 1990 and is growing rapidly. Already 25 percent of agricultural produce is exported, 30 percent of autos sold in America are produced by foreign manufacturers, 40 percent of corporate profits among Fortune 500 companies and 20 percent overall are derived from international activities, and 40 percent of all commercial loans in the United States are made by foreign banks. Ten percent of American pension funds, $500 billion, are invested in Asian companies alone.

Many Americans, particularly those in leadership positions who came of age between 1945 and 1970, still do not fully understand the nature of this change. The subconscious assumptions they hold about America's place in the world order were formed when we were the world's undisputed leader after World War II decimated the economies of our friends and enemies alike. In the late 1940s, America's GNP was half of the world's; in 1950, American per capita GNP was 4 times that of West Germany and 15 times that of Japan.

But world dominance was temporary, and it gave way rapidly in the years following 1970. By the late 1980s, America accounted for only 23 percent of the world's GNP, and by 1990, Japan's per capita GNP slightly exceeded America's. Since 1970, dominance has been lost in industries that were once synonymous with America — steel, machine tools, chemicals and autos — while consumer electronics has been virtually wiped out.

As the rest of the developed world caught up with us in these difficult decades, the lives of working men and women were affected. Real wages have been flat since 1970; only the top 20 percent of American male workers have improved their standing, 20 percent were stagnant, and 60 percent actually experienced a decline. Our standard of living did not fall at the same time, largely because women entered the labor force in record numbers, but absent polygamy there will be no third spouse to send into the labor force to bail us out in the future. Moreover, since 1989, even median *household* income has fallen despite the fact that Americans now work longer hours and a greater proportion now hold at least two jobs than in the last half century. According to Lester Thurow (1995), income inequality also is growing — among men working full time the earnings gap between the top and bottom quintiles doubled in the last 25 years — and the distribution of wealth is worsening, with the share of wealth held today by the top one percent of the population — more than 40 percent — rising to what it was in the late 1920s. Although these troubling statistics result from many factors, including new labor-saving technologies and the decline of unions, it is clear that America must adapt to the competitive challenges of the global economy.

The global economy has already affected the lives of all Americans in powerful ways, and its impact will increase as barriers to free trade continue to fall, global capital markets become more fluid, and telecommunication technologies accelerate the flow of information. If we understand the future, we greatly increase our chances of successfully adapting to the changes it will bring.

The Regional Implications of the Global Economy

The starting point is to recognize that the competitive unit of the global economy is the *region*— not the city, suburb, or county. Victor Petrella, director of science and technology forecasting for the European Union, believes:

> Within fifty years, such nation states as Germany, Italy, the United States, and Japan will no longer be the most relevant socioeconomic entities and the ultimate political configuration. Instead, areas like Orange County, California; Osaka, Japan; the Lyon region of France; or Germany's Ruhrgebeit will acquire predominant socioeconomic status. The real decision-making power of the future … will be transnational companies in alliance with city-regional governments [quoted in Toffler and Toffler 1993].

Kenichi Ohmae (1995), former senior partner at McKinsey & Company and leader of a Japanese reform movement, put it this way in his new study, *The End of the Nation State*:

> The noise you hear rumbling in the distance is the sound of the later twentieth century's primary engine of economic prosperity — the region-state — stirring to life. No longer will managers organize the international activities of their companies on the basis of national borders. Region-states have become the primary units of economic activity. It is through these region-states that participation in the global economy actually takes place.

Neal Peirce, nationally syndicated columnist and, with Curtis Johnson and John Stuart Hall (1993), coauthor of *Citistates: How Urban America Can Prosper in a Competitive World*, contends, "Only when the central city and its surrounding counties work together will they be able to compete effectively. It won't be America versus Japan or Germany, but Greater Philadelphia versus metropolitan Tokyo or Stuttgart."

It is not difficult to understand why this is true. Only regions have the necessary scale and diversity to compete in the global marketplace. Only regions have an asset profile capable of projecting overall strength, in sharp contrast to the much less attractive profiles of individual counties or cities that lack either key infrastructure or a sufficiently skilled labor force.

Regions, moreover, are the geographic units in which we create our goods and services. We hire from a regional *labor force*. We count on a regional *transportation system* to move the people and the materials involved in their production. We rely on a regional *infrastructure* to keep the bridges and roads intact and our sewers and pipelines functioning. We live in a regional *environment* whose water and air do not recognize political boundaries.

Finally, although most people don't realize it, regions have always been the geographic units of economic competition. The national economy is a set of summary statistics drawn from the performance of distinct regional economies.

The global economy has important

implications for regions. Let us consider three: develop human resources, lower the costs of goods and services, and use scarce investment capital wisely.

Develop Human Resources

The source of comparative advantage in the future will be human capital. Future competition, argues Lester Thurow (1992) in *Head to Head: The Coming Economic Battle Among Japan, Europe, and America*, will be characterized by competition over seven "brain intensive" industries—computers and software, robotics and machine tools, civilian aviation, microelectronics, material sciences, biotechnology, and telecommunications—that offer high paying jobs to their workers and bring prosperity and world prestige to their countries. But even jobs requiring lower skills will be far more demanding than in the past. While only 30 percent of the jobs in the year 2000 will require college degrees, fully 89 percent will require post-secondary training.

Employers may recruit their top managers from a national labor pool, but they must rely on the regional labor force for the lion's share of their workers. If the region's schools and training institutes are not producing workers with adequate skills, the premium that employers will have to pay to attract qualified labor from outside the region will erode their competitiveness. Even though big corporations have the resources to compensate by retraining their workers, such a strategy unavoidably adds to their costs. Small businesses, utterly dependent on the quality of local institutions, lack even this option.

The central argument of *America's Choice: High Skills or Low Wages*, the report of the Commission on the Skills of the American Workforce (1990), was summarized by William Brock, a commission co-chair and former U.S. labor secretary. If

companies in every country in the world can now buy "idiot-proof machinery" to compensate for workers with terribly deficient skills, and if there are people elsewhere in the world who will work for $5 per day with the same equipment as Americans who want $10 or $15 per hour, then we cannot compete on the basis of wage. We can compete only on the basis of skill.

Suburban schools generally have lower dropout rates, better achievement scores, and higher college enrollment rates than city schools, but there should be no comfort in this comparison. Nor does it matter if our schools are somewhat better than they were 20 years ago. The appropriate comparisons are first to schools in the rest of the developed world, and the results are sobering.

On average, American students are measurably far behind students in other nations—their future competitors—in math, science, and critical thinking skills. Only the top 10 to 20 percent of our children can be considered truly competitive.

The second comparison — how does the human capital of our children match up with the skill requirements of twenty-first century jobs—is equally troubling. Of new entrants to the nation's labor force between 1985 and 2000, roughly 80 percent have the skills for only the bottom 40 percent of the jobs, and only five percent have the skills for the top 40 percent of the jobs.

As corporate leaders well understand, America cannot succeed in the global economy unless every able-bodied citizen has the skills required by the demanding jobs of the new economy. The results of the recent *National Adult Literacy Survey* (Kirsch et al. 1993) are shocking: half the adult population in the United States is ill-equipped for the job requirements of the twenty-first century global economy. Although this makes clear that the challenge is national rather than solely urban, the fact remains that great efforts to improve human capital must be made in our cities. Here is where a disproportionate number of the fastest growing segment of new labor-force entrants— immigrants and minorities— reside, which means they are attending some of the nation's worst schools and living in some of our worst environments.

The cost of supporting people who are unable to contribute to the economy— those without skills, on welfare, or in prison— will hold us down just as surely as a weight tied to a kite's tail. The suburbs cannot be sealed off from the city or the world. The future standard of living of the children of the *haves* will be determined to a significant extent by the productivity of the children of the *have-nots.*

The region—city and suburbs together— must work to adopt rigorous academic performance standards for its students and schools, benchmarked against the toughest in the developed world; greatly expand training for high school graduates not going to college; make admission to its colleges and universities far more demanding; and increase the availability of advanced on-the-job training in the workplace.

Lower the Costs of Goods and Services

The good news is that the global economy means vast new markets; with 5.5 billion people, the world has more than 20 times the population of the United States. The bad news is that our goods and services must now compete with those from firms around the world. As the latest round of corporate downsizing suggests, the competition is fierce, in part because of a dramatic shift that is making commodities out of what used to be specialized products. A decade ago an IBM personal computer was unique. Today many man-ufacturers produce high quality clones, making computers a commodity, like so much rice, wheat, and potatoes. The result in industry after industry is rapidly falling prices, and the message is clear: firms that can keep costs down will remain competitive; others will fade away.

Grasping how global competition differs from domestic competition is absolutely essential. For 30 years, critics have pointed out the inefficiency of duplicated services, facilities, and personnel that result from too many local governments. Others have lamented the inadequate management of regional resources such as labor force, transportation, infrastructure, and environment. But despite the higher costs resulting from inefficiencies found outside the firm and beyond the direct control of company managers, reformers found few supporters.

These inefficiencies did not matter very much when the competition was *domestic* for two reasons. First, the inefficiencies noted above did not cut into profit margins because producers passed their costs to their customers as higher prices. Second, since all domestic producers did the same thing, no one derived competitive advantage.

But when the competition is *international*— and for whatever reasons the prices of foreign goods and services are lower than our own— inefficiencies that spring from domestic practices undercut our competitiveness. Thirty years ago, 20 percent of General Motors' assembly line workers were illiterate, but it didn't matter, as David Osborne and Ted Gaebler (1992) remind us, because 20 percent of Ford's and Chrysler's workers were illiterate as well. Today, when 100 percent of Toyota's workers are literate, it matters a great deal. When voters understand that to maintain the competitiveness of American goods and services in a global economy, the choice is either to lower their wages or to find ways outside their firms of more efficiently reducing costs and managing resources, they will, not surprisingly, choose the latter. Behaviors and governance structures considered sacrosanct today, I contend, will change far more rapidly than most people currently think.

The time has come to scrutinize a host of current behaviors. In metropolitan Philadelphia, for example, fiscal policy, land use, growth management, and zoning decisions are being made by municipalities— 239 in Southeastern Pennsylvania and 100 in southern New Jersey— rather than at the level of multiple municipalities, the county, or the region. But the response should not assume that the regional scale is automatically best. Rather, the political smog that obscures our choices should be blown away by an objective cost-benefit analysis to determine what size "service shed"— on a geographic scale — is appropriate for what service and, for that matter, whether government should produce the service or contract it out to the private sector. The issue before us, as Richard Nathan (1994) has argued, is not *structural*— requiring the consolidation of local governments into larger units, but *functional*— offering services at the most efficient geographic scale.

Use Scarce Investment Capital More Productively

When crime, drugs, homelessness, and other social problems spill over into adjacent suburban communities, the response of those who can afford it has been to move even farther away to more pristine areas at the peripheries of our regions. This process is embedded in the concentric rings of growth that emanate outward from our central cities.

Very troubling signs in the older, inner-ring suburbs suggest that the pace of out-migration and other indicators of deterioration — job loss, housing depreciation, drugs, crime, and related social problems— are accelerating faster than in the central cities they surround. The reason is that these small communities lack the basic resources the big cities use to slow down and mediate the process of decline. These inner-ring communities do not have large central business districts generating substantial tax revenues to underwrite essential services in the neighborhoods; they do not have large police forces to maintain safety and a sense of social order as the crime rate climbs; and they do not have the sizable public and not-for-profit human and social service agencies to address the needs of the poor and disadvantaged.

This out-migration from the cities and the inner-ring suburbs leads to new development in the exurbs requiring new roads and highways, water mains and sewer lines, schools and libraries, homes and shopping centers, and offices and sports complexes. When this happens, we end up spending our scarce investment dollars redundantly because we are essentially duplicating an infrastructure that already exists in older suburbs and central cities. Such growth also often represents a highly inefficient use of land. In Southeastern Pennsylvania between 1970 and 1995, for example, while population declined by 140,000, one-quarter of the region's prime farmland was lost to development.

This redundant spending imposes heavy opportunity costs because these dollars are not available for vital investments in productivity. To improve our competitive position in the global economy, America's regions would be far wiser to undertake more cost-effective development by adopting metropolitan growth rings, increasing residential and job densities in existing suburbs and cities, and investing the savings in research and development, plant and equipment, and human capital. The current practice of redundant spending is akin to eating our seed corn. America can ill afford public policy that leads to throw-away cities, throw-away suburbs, and throw-away people.

"It's the economy, stupid" read the now famous sign on James Carville's wall, announcing the central message for the 1992 Clinton presidential campaign. For those of us who want to see our metropolitan areas prosper in the twenty-first century, the sign should be amended to read "It's the *global* economy, stupid!" In sum, the global economy has forever changed the rules of competition. Either we adapt intelligently, or we face a significant deterioration in our standard of living and an increasingly worrisome unequal distribution of wealth within our regions that threaten the stability of our democracy.

Economic Linkages Between the City and the Suburbs

The nation's economy is an aggregate of metropolitan economies in which the fortunes of the cities and suburbs are intertwined. Here are just a few examples of the economic linkages that bind them together. We'll first consider relationships between cities and suburbs in general and then review some of the specific linkages between Philadelphia and the surrounding suburban counties.

Detroit and Its Suburbs

Skeptics about regional cooperation often pose the "Detroit question": if cities and suburbs are so interdependent, then why are Detroit's suburbs doing well while the city is an economic wasteland? While the Detroit suburbs are doing well relative to the city, it turns out this is a misleading comparison. According to a Philadelphia Federal Reserve Bank study (Voith 1992) of 28 metropolitan areas in the Northeast and Midwest, the better off the central city is, the better off its suburbs are. The Detroit suburbs have experienced considerably slower job, population, and income growth than the suburbs surrounding healthier central cities. For example, although the population of the Detroit suburbs grew two percent between 1980 and 1990, the average for the northeastern suburbs studied for that period was almost seven percent.

National League of Cities

In its recent study, *All in It Together: Cities, Suburbs, and Local Economic Regions* (Ledebur and Barnes 1993), the National League of Cities documents that in each of the 25 metropolitan areas with the most rapidly growing suburbs, central city incomes also increased from 1979 to 1989. "No suburb in this high growth set experienced income growth without corresponding growth in their central city.... For every $1.00 increase in central city household incomes, suburban household incomes increase by $1.12." Cities and suburbs are not two distinct economies, the report concludes, "but a single highly interdependent economy.... Their fortunes [are] inextricably intertwined. Cities and suburbs grow or decline together."

Cities Without Suburbs

In *Cities Without Suburbs*, David Rusk (1993), former mayor of Albuquerque, New Mexico, describes a fascinating set of differences between *elastic* cities (those that have been able to annex or merge with their suburbs so they are "without" suburbs) and *inelastic* cities (those whose growth stopped at their historic political boundaries and therefore are surrounded by suburbs). In elastic cities, income distributions are more equal, poverty is less concentrated, crime rates are lower, residential segregation is lower, and schools are less segregated. By contrast, Rusk argues, inelastic cities like Philadelphia "are programmed to fail." He does not write off the Philadelphias of the world, however, because he believes public policies promoting regional responses can produce greater social and economic equity.

Citistates

In *Citistates: How Urban America Can Prosper in a Competitive World*, Peirce, Johnson, and Hall (1993) argue that the true economic units of the global economy are *citistates*, a new name for metropolitan areas. With the end of the Cold War, the battleground of the future will be economic, not military, a shift that will diminish the role of nations and enhance the importance of regions. Based on case studies of metropolitan areas that included Baltimore, Dallas, Phoenix, and Seattle, Peirce contends that only when the central city and the surrounding suburban communities work together will they be in a position to compete effectively against the metropolitan economies of Frankfurt, Milan, and Osaka. Peirce urges metropolitan residents to recognize the indivisibility of the citistate, find a niche for the region in the global economy, focus on workforce preparedness, plan for a multicultural future, fight for fiscal equity, and build a sense of regional citizenship.

The consequences of continued urban decline will be felt well beyond city borders. A 10 percent decline in the value of real estate in just nine of America's largest cities would mean losses of $160 billion, reports Joseph Gyourko (Gyourko and Summers 1994), real estate professor at the University of Pennsylvania's Wharton School. This amount roughly equals the cost of the entire savings and loan bailout. A great many suburbanites—shareholders in the banks, insurance companies, and pension funds that own these properties—would be among the losers.

The evidence from around the nation, then, is compelling, but does it hold true for Southeastern Pennsylvania? Despite the striking growth of the suburbs in past decades, research done here strongly suggests that many economic ties bind Bucks, Chester, Delaware, Montgomery, and Philadelphia counties together.

Commuting Patterns in Metropolitan Philadelphia

Although most people live and work in a single county and suburb-to-suburb commuting is on the rise, a great many people cross Philadelphia's borders as part of the journey to work. Each day 395,000 commuters are on the move in and out of the city. Fifteen percent of suburban residents come into the city (down from 20 percent in 1980), and altogether, Philadelphia imports almost one-third of its labor force. Meanwhile, 20 percent of city residents commute to jobs in the suburban counties (up from 15 percent in 1980). These commuting patterns are important linkages between the city and surrounding counties that are experienced by real people in very real ways.

Purchases of Goods and Services

A 1991 survey of more than 1,000 area firms conducted by the Center for Greater Philadelphia revealed that despite considerable suburban economic growth, the region's economy remains tightly integrated.

For example, nearly 20 percent of all goods and services purchased by firms in Bucks, Chester, and Delaware counties are acquired from Philadelphia firms. Overall, when direct and indirect purchases are considered together, roughly one-quarter of Southeastern Pennsylvania's $110 billion gross metropolitan product in 1991 was a function of city-county business transactions.

Best-Case and Worst-Case Scenarios for the Year 2000

When Philadelphia was at the brink of bankruptcy in 1991, leaders of the Pennsylvania General Assembly asked the Center for Greater Philadelphia to consider the question "what would happen to the suburbs if the city went down the tubes?"

Two regional job scenarios were constructed for the Sixth Southeastern Pennsylvania State Legislators' Conference (Hershberg 1991). The *worst case* was based on the 1970s when the city lost 40 percent of its manufacturing jobs, 18 percent of its total jobs, and 13 percent of its population. The *best case* was based on the 1980s when the city ended the decade with roughly the same number of jobs it had at its start and population loss slowed to less than half the prior decade's rate.

The difference between these two scenarios in the year 2000 is 268,000 fewer jobs in Bucks, Chester, Delaware, and Montgomery counties and 178,000 fewer jobs in Philadelphia. This would represent a loss to the region of $11.6 billion in wages and a loss to the state treasury of $585 million in personal income, corporate net income, and sales taxes (in 1990 dollars).

It Won't Be a Zero-Sum Game

Nor would Philadelphia's deterioration be a zero-sum game for Pennsylvania in which city jobs move to the suburbs and the state treasury breaks even because only the location of economic activity changes. Although many city firms would move to the suburbs, some would close rather than relocate, others would downsize, and still others would leave the region entirely. One study of manufacturing firms in the 1970s estimated that at least 30 percent of jobs eliminated in the city did not relocate. Such losses are shared by everyone.

Suburban Housing Values are Affected by Philadelphia's Economy and Access to Commuter Rail

Another glimpse into the integrated regional economy comes from the work of Richard Voith (1993), senior economist at the Federal Reserve Bank of Philadelphia. Voith set out to learn whether access to commuter rail service in the suburban counties boosts home values. In a careful study that controlled for access to highways and the quality of homes, Voith found that residences in neighborhoods with rail service — about 258,500 owner-occupied houses — enjoy a premium of 6.4 percent in housing values over those areas without service. This amounts to $1.45 billion in the value of residential real estate over the five-county region. In examining the value of homes in Montgomery County located near commuter rail lines, Voith found that prices fell in the 1970s as the city's manufacturing economy collapsed and rose sharply in the mid–1980s when the Philadelphia economy, especially downtown jobs, rebounded.

Good Things Happen When the City and Suburbs Cooperate

The case for regional cooperation is solid. Intense new competition in the global economy makes regions the strategic units of future economic competition. Moreover, economic linkages between the city and the suburbs make cooperative strategies in everyone's self-interest. But there is a third basis for this approach, and that is, simply put, good things happen when the city and the suburbs cooperate. Let's consider three of the leading achievements of regional cooperation in Southeastern Pennsylvania in the last decade.

Regional Success Stories

Pennsylvania Convention Center: The new center, the most important economic development project in Philadelphia's modern history, functions as the cornerstone of an ambitious, multi-pronged effort to make Philadelphia a "Destination City" in the burgeoning global hospitality industry. The suburban counties are now working with the city to develop a regional tourism strategy. The $525 million facility was made possible with a contribution of $185 million from the Commonwealth of Pennsylvania, an investment that required cooperation between political leaders from both parties across the region.

Philadelphia Regional Port Authority (PRPA): In 1990, the General Assembly created the PRPA, a partnership between the state and Bucks, Delaware, and Philadelphia counties. PRPA has been a "win-win" proposition: the city was freed from a multi-million drain on its annual budget; $60 million was made available for port capital and marketing projects, including Philadelphia's first intermodal facility; and

PRPA was instrumental in attracting a new rail line to the region. The port's competitive position will be greatly improved by the recent affiliation of PRPA and the South Jersey Port Corporation under the auspices of Delaware River Port Authority.

SEPTA Capital Funding: In a historic breakthrough in 1991, the Pennsylvania General Assembly provided a source of predictable capital funding for all 37 of the commonwealth's mass transit agencies. Numerous studies have documented the significant impact the Southeastern Pennsylvania Transportation Authority (SEPTA) has on the region's economy, and the guarantee of a reliable funding stream allows SEPTA to continue its rebuilding process. Once the region's leaders reached consensus on ensuring SEPTA's future capital needs, the debate between city and suburbs gave way to the search for a politically viable funding formula.

Southeastern Pennsylvania Commands Considerable State Power

The reason good things like these can happen when city and suburban state leaders cooperate is that Southeastern Pennsylvania is the most powerful region in the state. John Stauffer, the former majority leader of the Pennsylvania State Senate from Chester County, recognized this at the first regionwide conference of elected officials in 1985 when he said, "If we in Southeastern Pennsylvania ever flexed our political muscle on *both* sides of the aisle, we'd be a formidable force to be reckoned with in Harrisburg."

While Bucks, Chester, Delaware, Montgomery, and Philadelphia counties are only 5 of the state's 67 counties, they account for 31 percent of the state's population, 33 percent of its jobs, and 36 percent of its income. The five counties, moreover, are home to many leaders of the General Assembly. As of November 1995, these include House Speaker Matthew Ryan (R-Delaware County); House Majority Leader John Perzel (R-Philadelphia); Senate Majority Leader Joseph Loeper (R-Delaware County); and all four appropriations committee chairmen — Rep. Dwight Evans (D-Philadelphia), Sen. Vincent Fumo (D-Philadelphia), Rep. Joseph Pitts (R-Chester County), and Sen. Richard Tilghman (R-Montgomery County).

Philadelphia Rebounds

The 1990s are critical years for Philadelphia and the region. The decade began with a national recession, which in conjunction with an accumulated deficit of $250 million, brought the city of Philadelphia to the brink of bankruptcy. But in November 1991, Edward G. Rendell won election as the city's new mayor and has led Philadelphia in a remarkable comeback.

Central to his success was a political alliance with John Street, president of the Philadelphia City Council. This partnership has meant that for the first time since 1980, the city's mayor and city council have worked in tandem to promote Philadelphia's best interests. Since Rendell is white and Street is African-American, it has also meant that highly divisive racial politics have been avoided in a city where whites and non-whites share political power.

Working together, Rendell and Street produced a five-year fiscal plan that won approval from the Pennsylvania Inter-governmental Cooperation Authority, the fiscal oversight committee created by the state with the power to issue bonds on Philadelphia's behalf. Bankruptcy was avoided, budgets were balanced, and new labor contracts containing remarkable wage, health benefits, and work rule concessions were signed with all four of the city's municipal labor unions. The public financial markets have responded by buying Philadelphia's bonds at low, prevailing market rates of interest. In 1995, the city reported an $80 million surplus, and Rendell was reelected by a 77 percent margin.

The restoration of Philadelphia's fiscal image has been paralleled by other events with high national visibility:

- metropolitan Philadelphia was ranked third in overall livability by the 1993 *Places Rated Almanac.*
- *Fortune* magazine rated Philadelphia among the ten "Best Cities for Knowledge Workers" (November 15, 1993), and
- FBI statistics documented that the Philadelphia region is the safest of the twelve largest U.S. metropolitan areas.

The city's long-term economic prospects hold real promise. The city and region have considerable strength in higher education, with 80 institutions granting degrees in higher learning and 50,000 college graduates annually. The region has enormous strengths in health care, medical education and research, biotechnology, and pharmaceuticals. Organized venture capital companies can now be found throughout the region, and they support synergies among universities, entrepreneurs, and the growing base of companies in what promoters call "Medical Valley" and "America's High-Tech Mainstreet."

The $525 million Pennsylvania Convention center opened in downtown Philadelphia in 1993, and by all measures is living up to its advance billing as the anchor institution for the city's growing hospitality industry that promises to become a major sector of its economy. Efforts valued at several hundred million dollars are now underway to develop the *Avenue of the Arts* on South and North Broad Street as lively settings for the performing arts, and entertainment-based development is proceeding smartly on the Delaware River waterfront. Along with the city's unique comparative advantage as the birthplace of American democracy, these multiple developments are helping transform Philadelphia into an exciting "Destination City" in a global economy marked by extensive travel, tourism, and trade.

Serious Social Problems Remain

Despite these strengths and the mayor's *Economic Stimulus Plan*, Philadelphia's prospects are not without serious threats. The city's tax base has eroded precipitously, as Philadelphia lost 10 percent of its jobs between 1990 and 1993. Although the city added jobs in 1994, other significant weaknesses endure. One family in five is mired in poverty, and unemployment, particularly for non-whites, remains high. The 1980s saw the rise of new and costly social problems, including AIDS, homelessness, and the crack epidemic. The condition of public housing is disgraceful, and the past performance of public schools has been dismal (although it is gratifying to see the efforts of the new school superintendent, David Hornbeck, to implement fundamental reform through his "Children Achieving" agenda).

So it can be argued that despite all the positive trends described above, Philadelphia and America's other big cities are on greased skids. What distinguishes one from the other is the angle of descent. Aid is needed at least to help level the fiscal playing field so that cities can stabilize their revenues by holding on to their job and population base. But without intervention from federal and state governments, America in the long run may well lose all its big cities, Philadelphia included. The time has come to get the suburbs involved.

Toward a Dialogue Between the City and the Suburbs

If I've convinced you that the region's best chance for success in the global economy requires city-suburb cooperation, it should also be clear that the counties' and state's best interests are to help Philadelphia survive in the face of declining federal aid, an eroding local tax base, and mounting social problems. Philadelphia's neighboring suburban counties can help in three important ways.

First, modest county funds are needed for varied *regional* projects. Bucks, Chester, Delaware, Montgomery, and Philadelphia counties should undertake joint strategic planning, expand regional marketing strategies, embrace tax base sharing for *new* economic development, promote regional tourism, dedicate funds for the region's arts and cultural institutions, protect open space, and create a regional airport authority. While the details and the politics behind each initiative differ, they share the common notion that regional opportunities require regional responses.

This agenda was advanced by the 2,000 business, civic, and political leaders, as well as concerned citizens, who gathered at the Call to Action Conference on May 25, 1995, which was organized by the University of Pennsylvania's Center for Greater Philadelphia, the Greater Philadelphia Chamber of Commerce, and Greater Philadelphia First. They heard addresses by Pennsylvania Governor Tom Ridge, Philadelphia Mayor Ed Rendell, and Neal R. Peirce and considered 89 regional initiatives collected in the *Greater Philadelphia Investment Portfolio*.

Second, Philadelphia will need political support from suburban legislators in the General Assembly to provide additional state funding for the social costs associated with the support of the disadvantaged.

Fairness dictates that these costs should be shared more equitably by citizens across the Commonwealth. These disadvantaged people are Pennsylvanians, not just Philadelphians, and their problems are not of the city's making. To overcome the perception that "giving additional funding to Philadelphia is like throwing the money down a hole," most Philadelphians would likely accept some form of state control over social programs in return for adequate state aid to meet needs. Neither economic nor moral ends are served by balancing the city's budget on the backs of the poor or by driving Philadelphia into bankruptcy in a futile attempt to meet social needs beyond its fiscal capacity. Cities cannot solve social problems because they cannot redistribute income without driving out businesses and middle-income taxpayers.

The devolution of federal authority to the states in the form of block grants also presents an excellent opportunity for the states to stimulate regional approaches. Instead of distributing all block-grant funds directly to individual counties, states would reserve portions only for counties that joined together as regions and submitted strategic plans defining how they would allocate funds for health care, welfare, job training, education, environment, and the like. In *New Visions for Metropolitan America*, Anthony Downs (1994) calls for the creation of "regional allocation agencies" to decide how such funds would be spent. Their members could be popularly elected as in Portland, Oregon, or appointed by the governor and the state legislature as in the Minneapolis–St. Paul area, or designated by local governments.

Third, and perhaps most importantly, political leverage from the suburban counties is needed to help the city continue government reform and to use more effectively the large sums of money it already spends on education and government operations.

I am not suggesting that the suburbs should come to the table with a blank check — that would be both counterproductive and politically impossible. But the time has come to begin a candid dialogue about what can be done to keep central cities like Philadelphia fiscally stable and economically viable. Voters in the city and suburbs must ask Republicans and Democrats to stop the histrionics and get on with the difficult task of finding solutions because partisan politics is not a luxury neither the region nor the nation can afford.

If suburban residents believe state funds have been put to poor use in Philadelphia, this is the moment to sit down and agree on the changes that need to be made to use these funds more effectively. If further aid is required in the city, suburban political support could be conditioned on the adoption of fundamental reforms. A possible model is the Wharton Real Estate Center's "New Urban Strategy," which proposes no new net funding for urban America. However, Joseph Gyourko and Anita Summers (1994) argue that cities that undertake serious reform should be rewarded with additional dollars, while those that refuse to make the tough political choices should receive fewer dollars. In short, many desired changes in cities may prove impossible without this new politics of leverage from the suburbs.

Although there is no line item in the federal budget for "cities," as HUD secretary Henry Cisneros (1995) has pointed out, the aggregate impact of the cuts proposed by Congress for Medicaid, food stamps, welfare, Head Start, education, job training, mass transit, and the earned income tax credit will have a devastating impact on urban America because this is where those in poverty and with low incomes disproportionately reside. Suburban leaders need to understand that these cuts will further destabilize the cities they surround, with serious consequences for their communities as well.

We also must not become captives of our own language. Words such as *city* and *suburbs* suggest monoliths where none exist; they give rise to false but powerful images of we/they and us/them. The images are reinforced with census data, and the political numbers favor the suburbs: nationwide one-quarter of Americans live in cities and one-half live in suburbs.

Yet many older, inner-ring suburban communities more closely resemble the cities than they do the affluent suburbs where the wealthiest 20 percent of Americans live. During the 1980s, these older, inner-ring suburbs generally lost population, had little or no job growth, saw housing values stagnate or decline, and watched urban social problems such as homelessness, crime, and drugs spill over into their communities. The city-suburb duality distorts reality, buttresses partisan approaches, and complicates the cooperative arrangements that should follow economic self-interest.

Not too long ago *regional cooperation* was an oxymoron, but efforts by a great many people and organizations in the last decade have made it a strategy taken seriously by business, civic, and political leaders. Although substantial progress has been made, much of what remains to be done will be more controversial. When asked to move in these more difficult directions, elected officials in the city and suburbs first look over their shoulders to see if their constituents are behind them. For those of us who believe in regional cooperation, it is time to build a host of parades.

Of course the barriers of race, class, and politics that divide the city and suburbs are formidable. But we must accept the fact the global economy is putting Americans on the same team. The economic realities of the 1990s make clear that we are in this together and that cities and suburbs must work cooperatively. In our region people must recognize that Philadelphia bashing is *old* politics. The failure to respond to the fiscal factors that undermine the city's competitiveness is *old* economics. It is time to change. It is time for city dwellers and suburbanites to develop a quid pro quo—to ask what they expect from each other and to explore what they will do if each fulfills the respective commitments.

Although a compelling argument based on morality and social justice can be made to bring the city and suburbs together, the case presented here is based on economic self-interest. This is not an exercise in what we *should* be doing but in what we *have* to do to be competitive in the global economy.

Lest this task seem overwhelming, it is good to recall in closing that truly radical changes can occur: the Soviet Union has collapsed, the Berlin Wall has come down and the Germanys have united, Arabs and Israelis are making peace, and black and white South Africans are peacefully building a new nation together. Surely we can have regional cooperation in metropolitan Philadelphia.

References

Cisneros, Henry G. 1995. "Aid to the Cities Is Being Chopped into Little Pieces by Republicans." *Philadelphia Inquirer*, 4 October, Op-Ed.

Commission on the Skills of the American Workforce. 1990. *America's Choice: High Skills or Low Wages*. Rochester, NY: National Center on Education and the Economy.

Downs, Anthony. 1994. *New Visions for Metropolitan America*. Washington, D.C. and Cambridge, MA: The Brookings Institution and the Lincoln Institute of Land Policy.

Gyourko, Joseph, and Anita A. Summers. 1994. *Working Towards a New Urban Strategy for America's Larger Cities: The Role of an*

Urban Audit. Wharton Real Estate Center, University of Pennsylvania.

Hershberg, Theodore. 1991. At the Crossroads: The Consequences for the City, Region and Commonwealth of Economic Stability or Decline in Philadelphia. Pre-conference report for the Sixth Annual Southeastern Pennsylvania State Legislator's Conference, Center for Greater Philadelphia.

Kirsch, Irwin S., Ann Jungeblut, Lynn Jenkins, and Andrew Kolstad. 1993. *Adult Literacy in America: A First Look at the Results of the National Adult Literacy Survey.* Washington, DC: National Center for Education Statistics.

Ledebur, Larry C., and William R. Barnes. 1993. *All in It Together: Cities, Suburbs and Local Economic Regions,* National League of Cities.

Nathan, Richard P. 1994. Reinventing Regionalism. Keynote Address for the Regional Plan Association Meeting, 26 April, New York.

Ohmae, Kenichi. 1995. *The End of the Nation State: The Rise of Regional Economies.* New York: Free Press.

Osborne, David, and Ted Gaebler. 1992. *Reinventing Government: How the Entrepreneurial Spirit Is Transforming the Public Sector.* New York: Addison-Wesley Publishing Company, Inc.

Peirce, Neal R., with Curtis Johnson and John Stuart Hall. 1993. *Citistates: How Urban America Can Prosper in a Competitive World.* Washington, DC: Seven Locks Press.

Rusk, David. 1993. *Cities Without Suburbs.* Baltimore: Johns Hopkins University Press.

Thurow, Lester. 1992. *Head to Head: The Coming Economic Battle Among Japan, Europe, and America.* New York: Morrow.

_____. 1995. "How Much Inequality Can a Democracy Take?" *The New York Times Magazine,* 19 November.

Toffler, Alvin, and Heidi Toffler. 1993. "Societies at Hyper-Speed." *The New York Times,* 31 October, Op-Ed.

Voith, Richard. 1992. "City and Suburban Growth: Substitutes or Complements?" *Business Review,* September-October.

_____. 1993. "Changing Capitalization of CBD-Oriented Transportation Systems." *Journal of Urban Economics* 33.

• *Chapter 18* •

Regional Government and Regional Councils

J. Eugene Grigsby III

Data from the 1990 census indicate that the United States had 39 metropolitan areas of at least one million people. The combined population of these areas was 124.8 million, or approximately half of the nation's total population. In 1950, there were only 14 metropolitan areas of this size, and their total population was about 45 million, which was less than 30 percent of the nation's total. Thus, in a span of 40 short years, a significant proportion of the country's population steadily migrated from small towns and rural settings to more densely populated urban centers.

During this same 40-year period, two significant shifts were also occurring within these metropolitan areas. The first involved middle- and upper-income whites migrating away from central city areas to suburban locations. This resulted in an increasing number of low-income minorities, particularly African Americans, being confined to central cities. The second shift taking place during this period was the deindustrialization of the economies in many of these areas, resulting in an exodus of jobs from central cities to suburban locations.

The rapid population growth followed by population redistribution and economic restructuring have given rise to what is often referred to as "urban problems": traffic congestion, smog, polluted water, urban development encroaching on open space, crime, poorly funded school systems, and increasingly low income minority populations trapped in decaying inner-city locations.

It is within this context — rapid metropolitan growth and metropolitan restructuring — that planners and elected officials have sought to develop and implement strategies designed to: 1) induce growth and manage it simultaneously by focusing on

Originally published as "Regional Governance and Regional Councils," *National Civic Review*, Vol. 85, No. 2, Spring/Summer, 1996. Published by the National Civic League, Denver, Colorado. Reprinted with permission of the publisher.

infrastructure capacity, 2) respond more effectively to growing social service demands through coordinated delivery systems, and 3) seek ways to be competitive in a rapidly changing economic climate while not exacerbating inequalities between the poor and those with means.

Regional councils have emerged as one of the mechanisms thought capable of meeting challenges posed by these changing conditions. While the success of regional organizations in effectively meeting these challenges has been mixed, there is little doubt that the changing dynamics which metropolitan areas will continue to face will demand more regional approaches to problem solving. In the past, the federal government has been the primary driver behind formulating regional strategies. In the future, it will be states prompted by the private sector and community-based groups who forge the types of partnerships required for regional organizations to become more effective.

The Role of the Federal Government

In the 1950s, few people ever heard of regional councils because there were fewer than 50 nationwide. The number of regional councils reached a peak high of 669 in 1976.[1] The primary factor accounting for this rapid growth in the number of regional councils was the federal government.

During the 1960s, the federal government offered many incentives to local jurisdictions to create and or enhance the position of regional councils. This was achieved by making additional funding available through categorical grant programs and giving preferential treatment in legislation or regulations to regional councils as eligible recipients. The federal government also required the preparation of a regional plan, or formation of a regional planning agency as a pre-condition for receipt of certain types of funds. The objective of coordination was first introduced in 1959 under Section 701 of the Housing Act as amended. Greater emphasis was added in Section 204 of the Demonstration Cities and Metropolitan Development Act, which established a regional review requirement for projects proposed under 30 different federal grant and loan problems. The Intergovernmental Cooperation Act of 1968 and OMB's associated A-95 grant-review procedures extended coordination requirements to 50 federal programs, and in 1971 it was further expanded to cover almost 100 federal programs.[2]

By the mid–1960s, federal government promotion of regional planning rapidly accelerated. In addition to the extension of Section 701, new legislation authorized regional conservation and development districts. In 1962, Metropolitan Planning Organizations (MPOs) for comprehensive transportation planning were initiated and required, where feasible, to plan for entire urban areas on an inter-jurisdictional basis. In 1965, economic development districts were authorized, and local development district legislation followed in 1966. The number of federal grant programs supporting state and local planning efforts increased from 9 in 1964 to 160 by 1977.[3]

In a 1992 article in the *National Civic Review*, Patricia S. Atkins and Laura Wilson-Gentry suggest that the cumulative effect of these 1960s era federal programs was the widespread use of regional councils for comprehensive land-use and economic development planning.[4]

It should be noted, however, that not all councils during this era were initially formed to function as coordinating agencies; a number of them were first created as single-purpose organizations and later emerged into a broader coordinating entity. The Metropolitan Council of the Twin Cities, for example, was established in 1967 to address a water-pollution crisis, and the catalytic agent in creating Seattle's Metro was pollution in Lake Washington.[5] Over time these single-purpose agencies have evolved into multi-service agencies which combine planning and operating responsibilities, often by absorbing existing single-purpose organizations.[6]

In the 1970s, the focus of regional organizations broadened to include efforts at coordinating fragmented human services delivery systems. Amendments to existing legislation created criminal justice coordination councils (CJCCs) to administer comprehensive regional law enforcement and criminal justice programs. In 1973, legislation was passed allowing "prime sponsor" designations for regional councils and other entities to provide job training and employment improvement for the unemployed and underemployed. Areawide agencies on aging (AAAs) were also authorized by legislation in 1973 to provide comprehensive, coordinated social service networks for the elderly. Legislation passed in 1975 created health systems agencies (HSAs) designed to enhance economies of scale and quality in regional health services delivery systems, and authorized social service agencies to extend a wide selection of social services to the eligible poor.[7]

Even though much emphasis was focused on coordinating human services programs during the 1970s, physical and economic planning programs initiated in the 1960s, were also augmented by federal legislation during this period. New pollution-mitigation initiatives in coastal zone management, resources planning, and noise pollution control legislation were enacted in 1972, and legislation related to disaster assistance planning passed in 1974. In 1976, solid waste management planning was created. In 1977 came water pollution control legislation, followed by air pollution control with air quality control regions (AQCRs) and airport systems planning was authorized.[8]

By the end of the 1970s, there were nearly 48 federal programs which required a regional plan or regional planning organization as a condition of funding, or which gave preference to regional councils within any pool of eligible recipients. Thus, the very essence of regional councils was derived from the strong push of federal policy decisions. But there were signs that things were beginning to change. The U.S. Advisory Commission on Intergovernmental Relations turned from being a champion of strong regional governance to an advocate of public choice with its tacit acceptance that fragmentation is good.[9]

Too much reliance on federal funding, however, ultimately proved to be the Achilles' heel of regional councils. The dependence of most regional councils on the federal government was significant by the close of the 1970s. According to a 1989 report by Richard Hartman, three-fourths of their budgets came from federal programs.[10]

Turning Off the Federal Spigot

As a part of his campaign strategy, Ronald Reagan promised that if elected, his administration would place more control and authority in the hands of states and reduce the size of the federal budget. Once elected, Reagan moved with all deliberate speed to implement his earlier promises. Reduction in federal spending was felt almost immediately by the nation's regional councils. The number of regional councils declined from a high of 669 in 1976 to 529 in 1991. Staff sizes dropped from an average of 21 in 1977 to 17 in 1988.

The number of federal programs administered by regional councils averaged around 4 from 1977 to 1983, but decreased to 2.5 by 1988. The federal contribution to the regional council budget, as a share of the total budget, plummeted from 75 percent in 1977 to 45 percent in 1988.[11]

The federal government shifted the locus of regionalism to the state — through block grants and changed categorical grants — permitting much discretion as to how regional councils should be used. The transfer of the A-95 review-and-comment responsibilities to the states was accomplished through Executive Order 12372. This shift enabled states to accomplish intergovernmental review of federal project applications, with the option of deferring participation or, if maintained, doing so without the regional council as the mechanism. By 1992, ten states, Alaska, Idaho, Kansas, Louisiana, Minnesota, Montana, Nebraska, Oregon, Pennsylvania, and Virginia conducted reviews without the benefit of a regional process.[12] The federal government was rapidly distancing itself from sub-state regional agencies by establishing the state as the preeminent connection. By 1991, only 13 of the 48 federal programs promoting sub-state regionalism that were founded in the 1970s were still funded. The only new federally sponsored legislation which still promotes a strong role for metropolitan planning councils has been the Intermodal Surface Transportation Efficiency Act (ISTEA) which was enacted into law in late 1991.

Because of the reduction of federal monies during the 1980s, regional councils found that they had to diversify their activities, shift from federally mandated comprehensive planning to membership and contract services, become more attuned to customer preferences, enhance their coordination with state policy and administrative cost concerns, establish active advocacy agendas in the state capitals,

do more with less funding, and learn how to compete with an expanded pool of recipients of federal funds.[13]

While it is true that much of this shift resulted from direct reduction in federal expenditures, other forces were also in play, influencing this change in strategy. The strongest was the growth of suburban areas as the new locus of power. This shift increasingly called into question the necessity for having a suburban-urban linkage. The majority of metropolitan growth which occurred during the decade of the 1980s occurred in non-central city locations. At the same time, industrial restructuring meant a greater decentralization of the work place, with more new jobs being created outside of central city areas. In a sense, one could argue that the initial strength of the federal government's support for regional councils emanated from the strength of central city elected officials. By the same token, the rapid disengagement of the federal government during the 1980s reflects the shifting of power from central city constituents to the emerging suburban constituent base. Ironically, constrained resources at the metropolitan level resulting from both a nationwide recession and global competition may once again focus more attention on regional councils as viable entities for addressing urban problems. Only this time, the federal government will not be the dominant player.

Emerging New Directions

Some scholars have suggested that regional councils as we know them today are not inevitable beyond the 1990s. From their perspective, what is more likely to emerge are increasingly effective integrated networks of intercommunity problem-solving and service delivery mechanisms.[14] There seems to be growing evidence that this view may prevail.

Allan Wallis, for example, identifies two strategic arenas in which these new networks, or alliances as he calls them, will occur. The first arena is economic development. Competition in the global economy is forcing these regional alliances to take place. Examples include Seattle, Detroit, Hartford, Cleveland, Houston, Orlando, Philadelphia, and Pittsburgh.[15] Capitalizing on the work initiated by RLA, a public/private/nonprofit partnership created in 1992, the city of Los Angeles is currently engaged in creating alliances to focus on what the city has identified as major regional growth sectors. Common to these efforts is an agenda requiring public sector participation but with a focus which is primarily business oriented. Typical of these efforts is the attempt to engage in strategic planning explicitly designed to capitalize on growing market opportunities.

The second strategic arena identified by Wallis is social equity and fiscal disparity. Here the questions are what constitutes fair share, whether or not a focus of the planning process should be on redistribution, and of course who pays and who benefits. For Wallis, it is nonprofits who must play a major role in resolving these dilemmas. According to him, providing solutions to these problems cannot fall solely on the shoulders of the public sector. A number of different efforts such as the Atlanta Project, the Federation of Community Planning in Cleveland, the Regional Fair Housing Compact Pilot Program in Connecticut, the East Suburban Council for Open Communities in Ohio, and the Scientific and Cultural Facilities District in Denver are identified as examples of how the non-profit sector and business together can help to develop a regional response to these problems.[16]

Much of the strategy being designed to foster economic development and social equity hinges on the question of whether or not prosperity can exist within suburban locations independent of healthy central cities. Few doubt that major inequities continue to exist between these two geographic locations. What to do about these disparities has been a continuing dilemma since the early days of regional councils. On the one hand, there are the regional economic growth proponents who argue that if you grow the region, then you will lessen the inequalities. Advocates of this position seem to agree that less centralization and less federal involvement will enable this regional economic growth to take place. There is growing empirical evidence that this may not necessarily be the case.

David Rusk, for example, described cities as either elastic or inelastic.[17] He finds that elastic cities "capture" suburban growth and inelastic cities "contribute" to suburban growth. Furthermore, elastic cities tend to expand their city limits, while inelastic cities do not. Not a new finding but one which should be uppermost in our thinking, is that racial prejudice continues to shape city growth patterns. Based upon Rusk's criteria, inelastic areas are more segregated. He also found that city-suburban income gaps were more critical a problem than overall income levels in metropolitan areas (a finding similar to that of Myron Orfeld),[18] and that poverty is more concentrated in inelastic cities than in elastic cities. Most important is his finding that the smaller the income gap between city and suburb, the greater the economic progress for the entire metropolitan community.

Rusk's findings are also interesting relative to their implications for future regional problem solving efforts. For example, he found that fragmented local government fosters segregation, and unified local government promotes integration. Dispersed and fragmented public education is more segregated than centralized and unified public education.

Rusk's findings, as well as those of Neal Peirce[19] and Oliver Byrum,[20] suggest regional decision making is critical, and more of it, not less, is better. Furthermore, his findings suggest that no matter how regional councils evolve, two critical issues will have to be addressed: 1) How to assure that future suburban growth does not occur at the expense of central city areas; and 2) How to facilitate growth and development while simultaneously narrowing the gap between the poor and the non-poor.

Strategies for the Future

It should be fairly evident at this point that the role that regional councils play has changed significantly over the past 30 years. In the coming years, they undoubtedly will undergo even more changes. John Kirlin[21] and Allan Wallis[22] both seem to agree that one of the central thrusts of the new change will be a shift from the concept of metropolitan government as a separate entity to a focus on governance. This belief is supported by a number of recent surveys which indicate that while there is some general support for regional government, most respondents question the ability of regional government to solve problems or respond effectively to local issues. Indeed, the extent to which regional governments are perceived to interfere with local self-interest appears to be directly correlated with the degree of opposition to such entities.[23] Attempts to strengthen regional structures by giving them more authority or by changing the selection process of governing board members to make them more representative have not been successful. And there is little likelihood that stronger regional government structures will emerge in the foreseeable future.

On the other hand, there is growing support for organized entities that promote a return to a collective sense of civic mindedness. The extent to which the influential business leaders effectively promote this vision of the future will be the degree to which the general public believes that it has some chance of succeeding. Earlier indications in cities like Atlanta, Philadelphia, and Denver suggest that there may be a great deal of merit to this new form of regional problem solving.

But what seems more likely to occur is that a clearer distinction will be drawn between regional agencies that continue to function as governmental entities because their mission is to plan and implement regional infrastructure requiring massive capital investment (or because they are carrying out a federal mandate such as pollution control) and the emerging entities which function as loose affiliations. Local interest will reluctantly continue to support the more structured government entities because in the long run it is more cost effective. But successful as many of these agencies have been in influencing the infrastructure development process, they simply have not been capable of addressing issues of social equity, and thus the need to explore alternative structures to address these problems will become even stronger.

Regional entities which are emerging as partnerships between the business sector and non-profit institutions have the potential to address social equity concerns more directly. In no small part, this is because influential business people supporting these partnerships see that growing income and class inequalities within a region simply do not bode well for the future economic health of that region, let alone for promoting a more civil society.

Regional government is here to stay. As long as its primary function is to provide infrastructure capacity and implement federal or state regulatory mandates, it will receive tacit support from local municipalities and contribute little to the growing problem of regional inequalities. Regional organizations working both in concert with and independent of regional governments have a much higher probability of tackling the more politically volatile social equity issues facing every metropolitan area in the country. In the final analysis, however, dedicated leadership resolved to address these difficult social equity issues will be the factor which makes the difference.

Notes

1. Atkins, Patricia S. and Laura Wilson-Gentry, 1992: "An Etiquette for the 1990s Regional Council" *National Civic Review*, Volume 81, Number 4, Fall-Winter, p. 466.

2. Wallis, Allan D., 1994: "Inventing Regionalism: The First Two Waves" *National Civic Review: Realizing Human Potential*, Volume 83, Number 2, Spring-Summer, pp. 168–169.

3. Wallis, op. cit., p. 170.

4. Atkins and Wilson-Gentry, op. cit., p. 469.

5. Wallis, op. cit., p. 170.

6. ACIR, 1973–74: *Substate Regionalism and the Federal System*, Washington, D.C., U.S. Government Printing Office.

7. Atkins and Wilson-Gentry, op. cit., p. 469.

8. *Ibid.*, p. 470.

9. McDowell, Bruce as cited in *Substate Regional Governance: Evolution and Manifestation Throughout the United States and Florida* (Tallahassee, Fla.: Florida Advisory Commission on Intergovernmental Relations, November 1991), p. 28.

10. Hartman, Richard, 1989: *A Report to the Membership*, Washington, D.C., National Association of Regional Councils, p. 1.

11. *Ibid.*, p. 4.

12. Symonds, Richard N., Jr., 1992: "Montana Discontinues Process," SPOC-NET, Vol. 7, No. 7, 19 February 1992, p. 1.

13. Atkins and Wilson-Gentry, op. cit. p. 468.

14. Dodge, William R., 1992: "Strategic Intercommunity Governance Networks" (Signets of Economic Competitiveness in the 1990s), *National Civic Review: Partnerships for Regional Cooperation*, Volume 81, Number 4, Fall-Winter, p. 412.

15. Wallis, Allan D., 1994: "The Third Wave: Current Trends in Regional Governance" *National Civic Review: Renewing America*, Volume 83, Number 3, Summer-Fall, p. 294.

16. *Ibid.*, p. 303.

17. Rusk, David, 1995: *Cities Without Suburbs*, Second Edition, The Woodrow Wilson Center Press, Washington, D.C.

18. Lecture presented to the Graduate School of Architecture and Urban Planning, Spring 1995.

19. Peirce, Neal R. with Curtis W. Johnson and John Stuart Hall, 1993: *Citistates: How Urban America Can Prosper in a Competitive World*, Seven Locks Press, Washington, D.C.

20. Byrum, Oliver E., 1992: *Old Problem in New Times: Urban Strategies for the 1990s*, American Planning Associates, Chicago, Illinois.

21. Kirlin, John J., 1993: "Citistates and Regional Governance" *National Civic Review: Tales of Turnaround*, Volume 82, Number 4, Fall.

22. Wallis, op. cit., 1994.

23. Baldassure, Mark, Joshua Hassol, William Hoffman, and Abby Kanarek, 1996: "Possible Planning Roles for Regional Government: A Survey of City Planning Directors in California" *Journal of the American Planning Association*, Volume 62, Number 1, Winter, pp. 179–183.

• *Chapter 19* •

Fiscal Regionalism

David Miller

Metropolitan regions across the United States are faced with the need to design governance systems that preserve and protect their constituent communities while maintaining or developing a more competitive economic climate. In the face of a globalizing world economy, most regions are seeking to rationalize their local government structure, but effectively adapting to the changing nature of the global economy has proven elusive.

Regionalist Neil Peirce, who popularized the term "citistates," has identified two overarching issues. The first is physical sprawl, defined by Peirce as "the alarming environmental and social consequences of America's inability or unwillingness to contain urban growth within reasonably compact geographic areas." Indeed, the social and environmental impact of sprawl has resurfaced as an important regional and national issue. Traffic congestion and crowded schools are leading to a renewed call for more rational strategies that do not lead to growth occurring in areas unable or unprepared to deal with its consequences. The second issue, Peirce argues, is "America's hesitation, one might say their paralysis, in creating effective systems of coordinated governance for citistates." America has one of the most diffuse, or decentralized, systems of government in the world. This chapter will focus on this second issue of decentralization.

American Governance

Governance in metropolitan areas is, fundamentally, built around local governments. Although many reformers would argue such an assumption is invalid and leads to inappropriate outcomes, the monopoly position of local governments in two key policy areas makes the assumption a practical reality. The first is local governments' exclusive ability to locally raise public funds through taxation. Although

Originally published as "Fiscal Regionalism: Metropolitan Reform Without Boundary Changes," *Government Finance Review*, Vol. 16, No. 6, December 2000. Published by the Government Finance Officers Association, Chicago, Illinois. Reprinted with permission of the publisher.

regulated by state governments, this power helps organize how public funds are allocated. The second factor is local governments' exclusive ability to make land-use decisions through the exercise of, primarily, zoning powers. As with taxation power, this monopoly position is tempered by state regulatory responsibility.

Efforts to improve governance in metropolitan regions, therefore, must deal with one or both of these issues and recognize that local government participation in designing improvements is essential for any change.

The Missing Link

More than 40 years ago, Arthur Maas defined the structure of local governance in the United States as an "areal" division of power. By that, he meant that the territorial-bounded local governments were, by culture and practice, an integral part of a system of organization that divided power between the federal, state, and local governments. The "missing link" in this division of power, Maas argued, was a general process to address governmental issues at the metropolitan level. Such a missing link required the development of four separate processes. They were:

- a last resort way to settle inter-jurisdictional disputes and questions of jurisdiction;
- a process of inter-jurisdictional cooperation;
- a process by which the governments in a region can act separately and independently; and
- a process of change that cannot be dictated or stopped by a minority of the jurisdictions.

The need to work together in a cooperative fashion in this "areal" environment has never been greater. The Metropolitan Initiative, a partnership between national foundations and the Center for Neighborhood Technology, conducted a series of workshops with key leaders in 12 regions across the United States. The purpose of the workshops was to identify public policy problems associated with growth and regional competitiveness. These 1997 sessions identified eight common themes which every region shared with every other region; namely:

- regions and the communities within them cannot deal with transportation, housing, environment, and economic issues in isolation;
- the large number of governmental jurisdictions in a region makes it very hard to work together. Indeed, participants, regardless of the region they were from, argued that governmental fragmentation and fiscal disparities in their region were the worst;
- individual jurisdictions do not want to lose their identity;
- metropolitan approaches to governmental reorganization require support of state governments and legislators and that is often seriously lacking;
- this is a pivotal time for regional cooperation in each region, but most regions have experimented with regional cooperation in the past with only marginal results;
- sprawl and its dysfunctional effects exist in every region and pose a serious threat to quality of life;
- any success a region is experiencing in metropolitan cooperation is in its early stages; and
- crisis seems to be the strongest motivator for regional cooperation.

Strategies for Regional Reform

Few regions have been idly standing by as the need for reform has emerged. Indeed, a number of cooperative strategies have historically been used, representing a range of options from relatively modest to extensive, highly controversial changes. Perhaps the most controversial of regional strategies involve consolidation/merger and annexation. In annexation, one government takes over part or all of the territory of another government. Today, it is a strategy used primarily in metropolitan areas in the south and west. For instance, through annexation, Charlotte, North Carolina, has grown from 30 square miles to 200 square miles since the end of World War II.

Consolidation/merger is a process by which a government actually goes out of business. One government merges into another existing government, or two or more governments consolidate to form a new government. It was a heavily used process in the 19th century. Many of the great cities of today — like Boston, New York, and Pittsburgh — were formed through the absorption of contiguous municipalities. Because of the implications associated with a government actually ceasing to exist, it is now considered a historical artifact and an infrequent event. Since World War II, voters have adopted only 20 out of 120 consolidation/merger efforts.

Councils of Governments (COGs) are a more modest effort at regional cooperation. They are voluntary associations of local governments that work on issues of common interest to their members. Because they are voluntary, most COGs require unanimity before they can enter a policy area. As a result, they have most commonly focused on non-controversial and non-threatening issues. Joint purchasing and sharing of capital-intensive equipment and services represent primary areas of COG activity. Although every region should, and most do, have a COG, its presence may have limited value in addressing the broader public problems facing the region.

A stronger form of intergovernmental organization is the Metropolitan Council. A council may or may not be a council of governments. Although deeply dependent on the support of the local governments in the region, some councils have moved into a broader role in their respective regions. In the Portland, Oregon, region, the council is directly elected and delivers services in areas such as growth management and transportation development. The Twin Cities Council (Minneapolis and St. Paul, Minnesota) has assumed responsibilities in the areas of wastewater and regional transit.

Although the development of metropolitan councils or other organizations that have some ability to compel local governments to act consistent with a regional plan has broad implications on local governments, a more promising category of regional cooperation is "fiscal regionalism."

Fiscal Regionalism

Fiscal regionalism is a set of cooperative strategies that recognize the governmental structure of the existing configuration of local governments but create regional funding mechanisms for a wide variety of public purposes. As such, they are relatively recent innovations in metropolitan cooperation. There are three broad forms of fiscal regionalism that will be discussed in this chapter: cultural asset districts, tax and revenue sharing programs, and peaceful coexistence plans.

Taken as a broad set of strategies, fiscal regionalism addresses a number of important metropolitan policy issues. Initially, strategies that create a metropolitan government with taxing authority appear or are perceived to lessen or eliminate local decision-making authority. Fiscal regionalism approaches create the fiscal equivalent of a regional government without the government. Second, fiscal regionalism mechanisms or institutions create the capacity or the authority to distribute benefits from economic growth or to develop growth policies that reflect the distribution of benefits across the metropolitan region. Third, fiscal regionalism mitigates the worst effects of fiscal mercantilism. Local government reliance on property tax revenues requires those governments to engage in competitive fiscal mercantilism — encouraging only the location of net revenue-producing developments within their boundaries. Such practices have the effect of exacerbating the difficulties associated with the location of undesirable or marginally desirable land uses within a region. Fourth, costs for economic development are not always borne by the government within whose boundary the growth has occurred. Although every government would like to derive economic benefit without cost, the opportunity itself is dysfunctional because a government is rewarded for "free-riding."

Fiscal regionalism approaches allow for a more equitable distribution of both costs and benefits. Few means exist whereby governments in an urban environment can share in the region's growth, as the only determinant of benefits is location within a particular jurisdiction. Fiscal regionalism approaches create means by which such sharing can occur. In addition, annexation laws create a "win-lose" outcome for governments— the government getting the new territory wins, but at a significant loss to the government losing the territory. Fiscal regionalism allows for the development of "win-win" outcomes. Finally, wealthier jurisdictions are able to provide services with lower tax rates than less affluent jurisdictions. This disparity results in a vicious circle of greater disparity as wealth gravitates to wealth, and the poorer jurisdictions become even less competitive. Over time, the gap between rich and poor communities in a region grows wider. Fiscal regionalism aids in "leveling the playing field."

Cultural Asset Districts. One form of fiscal regionalism is the Cultural Asset District. This institutional arrangement has emerged in the last several years as a direct result of the dispersion of population. Even after World War II, the majority of Americans lived and worked in the center city of our metropolitan areas. Cultural and civic activities were usually, and appropriately, financed by the center city. For instance, in 1948, 73 percent of business activity in Allegheny County, Pennsylvania, took place within the City of Pittsburgh. For the City of Pittsburgh to be financing the zoo, as an example, was consistent with its economic base and its fiscal capacity. However, by the late 1980s, only 38 percent of business activity conducted within Allegheny County occurred within the City of Pittsburgh. As people and business disbursed to the suburbs, however, they continued to utilize the civic facilities financed by the center city. But the city no longer had the fiscal base to support those services, and non-city residents were becoming the primary users of those facilities. Cultural Asset Districts are a way to finance civic institutions by the regional public.

Denver and Kansas City are representative of regions that have adopted cultural asset districts. In 1988, the Denver region approved the "Scientific and Cultural Facilities District." It is an example of the first wave of this regional approach to public services. Approved with a 65 percent positive vote at a referendum, the district is financed by .1 percent increase in the sales tax. The district supports institutions like the zoo, museums, performing arts, and a wide variety of local and regional arts organizations.

The Kansas City region enacted (again by referendum) a "Bi-State Cultural District" in 1997 to finance the capital and operating costs associated with historic Union Station. Unlike Denver, this district goes out of business in six years. In this respect, it represents the next generation of districts in that it is organized for a specific purpose and, when that purpose is served, the district ends.

Tax and Revenue-sharing Programs. The second form of fiscal regionalism is tax or revenue-base sharing. Tax-base sharing is a simple idea—take a regional resource of revenue, such as the property tax or sales tax, and distribute the proceeds to constituent local governments on some other basis that reflects the needs of the region, taken as a whole. Its asserted benefits are its more effective and equitable impact on economic development and growth. To the degree that the fragmentation of government services and decision making in an urban area prevent any rational approach to the distribution of the gains and benefits from development and growth policies, tax-base sharing can help mitigate the adverse effects of that fragmentation.

The largest, and perhaps most well-known tax-base sharing plan is in the Twin Cities of Minnesota (Minneapolis and St. Paul). The Minnesota model of tax base sharing has been in place for about 25 years. Today, the program covers 2.5 million people, 7 counties, and 200 local jurisdictions, and involves $200 million in tax proceeds. The Metropolitan Council administers the program.

In its simplest form, 40 percent of a municipality's growth in commercial and industrial real estate valuation is diverted from the municipality's direct control to a "pool" shared by all municipalities in the region. A uniform millage is applied to this "pooled" value, and the proceeds are distributed back to the municipalities on a need-based formula. Figure 1 outlines the Minnesota tax-base sharing model. The amount a government contributes to the pool has no relation to what it will receive in distributions—a participating government may receive much less than it contributes to the pool, and conversely, it may receive substantially more than it contributes. In this fashion, tax-base sharing serves a redistributive function. Since its inception, the plan has reduced fiscal disparities between jurisdictions. For the period 1987 to 1995, measured inequality in total tax base per capita between jurisdictions was reduced by 20 percent. By some

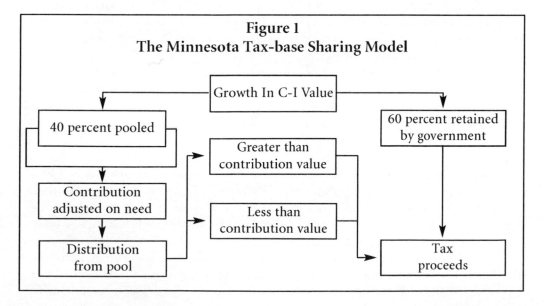

Figure 1
The Minnesota Tax-base Sharing Model

estimates, it has significantly reduced disparities from a ratio of 50:1 to a ratio of 12:1.

Most of the arguments used to develop the fiscal regionalism program in Minnesota were included in the enabling legislation. Although reduction in fiscal disparities has become one of the major benefits of tax-base sharing as implemented in Minnesota, it was not mentioned in the legislation. The explanation for this omission centers on the difficulty associated with the "selling" of redistributive programs at the local level. The arguments that were used to develop the tax-base sharing program in Minnesota are identified below.

First, the plan was a means to allow local governments to share in the growth of the area without taking away any resources that local governments currently enjoy. By taking a percentage of future or new revenues, governments were not giving up resources that they were currently receiving. Second, the plan would create more rational urban development by minimizing the fiscal impact of locational decisions. Third, the plan would create an incentive system that would encourage all parts of the regions to work for the growth of the whole. Fourth, and perhaps most important, the plan would develop regional strategies that employed the existing structure of local governments and local decision making. Fifth, the plan would assist those communities either in the early stages of development or those facing disinvestments by allocating additional resources to them. In summary, the proponents of this form of fiscal regionalism were supporting the existing structure of local government in the area while recognizing a need to minimize some of the dysfunctions associated with that structure.

Although the fiscal success of the Minnesota plan is documentable, as a form of fiscal regionalism, it continues to come

under attack locally and has yet to be totally replicated in other areas. Based on the Minnesota Plan, jurisdictions in Montgomery County, Ohio, have agreed to pool a portion of future growth in exchange for revenues from an economic-development fund. Unlike Minnesota, where some jurisdictions lose more than they contribute, the Ohio plan guarantees, through an economic-development fund, that every jurisdiction will be a net beneficiary. If contributions to the tax-base sharing pool exceed distributions from the pool, the jurisdiction will receive more from the economic-development fund to compensate.

The Meadowlands Area in New Jersey represents a planned commercial and economic development area that spans 14 separate jurisdictions. In 1972, the State of New Jersey established a commission to develop a master plan for the site. Recognizing that not all jurisdictions would benefit equally from the developments, particularly if open and public spaces were to be incorporated, a property tax sharing program was developed for the affected jurisdictions.

A program that captures both of the first two forms of fiscal regionalism has been developed and adopted in Allegheny County, Pennsylvania. Mirroring Denver, an asset district has been created to help finance many of the region's cultural and civic institutions; mirroring Minnesota, a redistributive tax base-sharing plan has been adopted that assists in reducing fiscal disparity between rich and poor local governments.

There were a number of issues confronting Allegheny County and the City of Pittsburgh in the early 1990s. Initially, there was a need to correct inequities caused by the City of Pittsburgh bearing a significant financial burden for regional assets. For instance, less than 15 percent of attendees at Pittsburgh Pirate games were city residents, even though the city was the sole public underwriter of the stadium. A second problem was the growing fiscal disparity between the county's richer and poorer communities. Research had demonstrated that the gap had been accelerating. Third, many public- and private-sector leaders believed that, to be economically competitive, the region needed to address the issue of over-reliance on certain taxes such as those on amusement events, real property, and personal property. Fourth, given the deteriorating fiscal condition of the city, there was a need to stabilize and perhaps increase funding for maintenance of existing assets. In addition, the region had no real mechanism for the funding or development of new assets. Lastly, given the highly fragmented governance structure of the region, it was necessary to establish precedent for future cooperative approaches to the resolution of public problems.

The Allegheny County Regional Asset District was created and funded through an additional 0.5 percent on the sales tax. This funding stream generates more than $60 million annually to provide funding to the region's shared assets. Facilities like the zoo, aviary, libraries, parks and stadiums are now the fiscal responsibility of the region.

Two important regional funding issues have been addressed through this program. First, approximately $40 million is provided to the region's assets directly from the sales tax proceeds, replacing funding that previously had been provided to the assets by individual local governments. This transfer of funding responsibility, primarily away from the City of Pittsburgh and Allegheny County, has helped to make those governments more fiscally sound and competitive than they would be otherwise.

Second, the asset district provides a more stable and elastic funding base for the region's assets. Initially, approximately $13 million was available annually to increase funding to new or existing assets. This discretionary portion of the program has grown to more than $20 million in several years.

The "other half" of the legislation created in the first form of fiscal regionalism also brought into existence the second form. This less visible reform has created a tax-base sharing program second in size only to the Minnesota plan. Through an additional 0.5 percent on the sales tax, more than $60 million is available annually to assist Allegheny County Governments in shifting a portion of their funding requirements away from the property tax and other taxes.

The distribution is as follows: 50 percent goes to the Allegheny County government, and 50 percent is shared among the participating municipalities in the county. Although all municipalities in the county have a right to participate, the formula used for this distribution targets the less affluent. Per capita distribution under this program ranges from $9.81 in the county's wealthier communities to $18.86 in the most fiscally distressed of the county's communities. The dynamics of the Allegheny plan are presented in Figure 2.

Peaceful Coexistence Plans. The third form of fiscal regionalism involves peaceful coexistence strategies. Particularly in states where territory is divided between incorporated areas (usually run by cities) and unincorporated areas (generally run by counties or townships), fiscal equity arrangements have emerged to address the problems surrounding the economic loss of one governmental jurisdiction when a territory transfers from one government to another.

The City of Louisville and Jefferson County, Kentucky, entered into a 12-year agreement in 1986 (which was subsequently renewed in 1998) that has become known as the Louisville Compact.

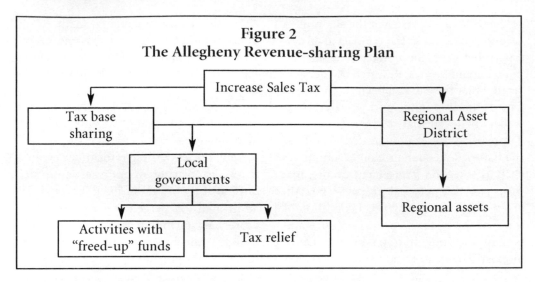

**Figure 2
The Allegheny Revenue-sharing Plan**

As a center city, Louisville was faced with severe fiscal problems and repeated attempts to consolidate the city and county had been rejected by voters. Although it was a difficult legal process, the city was poised to engage in a significant annexation campaign that would have serious financial implications for the county. Rather than conduct an adversarial battle with each other, both parties agreed to negotiate a plan for the delivery of services and the funding of those services. Predicated on the assumption that there would be a moratorium on annexation, the parties divided service delivery between them. Services like air pollution control, public health, and planning were assigned to the county. Services such as the zoo, museums, and emergency services were assigned to the city. The glue that held the compact together was an agreement to share tax revenues. The resulting agreement has been beneficial to both the city and the county and has led to an institutionalizing of cooperation.

Laws in Virginia represent another example of governments working together to avoid adversarial battles over territory. Agreements entered into by the City of Franklin with Southampton and Isle of Wight counties are representative. In areas of the counties that are experiencing significant commercial and industrial growth, the city has agreed to no annexation in perpetuity, but has agreed to deliver essential utility services in exchange for a percentage of all local tax revenues collected in the designated areas.

In Michigan, several peaceful coexistence strategies have been developed that create "win-win" outcomes for the state's cities and townships. One in particular is Michigan's Land Transfer Act. Rather than annexation, the township conditionally transfers the land that would have otherwise been the subject of annexation to the city in exchange for a share of the tax revenues and state aid. Typically, the agreements are for a 50-year period at which point the land is scheduled to revert back to the township.

Conclusion

A review of the fiscal regionalism approaches taken by local governments demonstrates how they are addressing a number of important regional issues. As such, they represent pragmatic responses to the need for cooperation within a metropolitan area. Given the difficulties associated with altering the governmental boundaries within a region, the strategies identified in this article are creating the equivalent of what a regional government would do fiscally were it to be created. Fiscal regionalism mechanisms or institutions are distributing benefits from economic growth across the metropolitan region.

They are mitigating fiscal mercantilism while creating a more equitable distribution of both costs and benefits to participating jurisdictions. They share an ability to level the playing field and create win-win solutions that improve the overall fairness and competitiveness of the regions in which they occur.

• *Chapter 20* •

Regional Government and the Post-Industrial Economy

Allan D. Wallis

In 1991 Denver lost out to Indianapolis in a competition to win construction of a $250 million United Airlines maintenance facility. After a speech in Denver a year later, former Indianapolis mayor Bill Hudnut was asked why Indianapolis had been successful even though Denver's incentive package was more generous. His answer was that in his city when negotiations took place with a major corporation, only three people had to be in the room: the corporate executive, the mayor, and someone from the governor's office. Because of Unigov — the consolidated city-county government — the mayor could speak for the region.[1]

A story with similar implications is told by Clarke County (Georgia) commissioner Tal DuVall. Several times the county and its core city of Athens attempted to win voter approval of a consolidation plan.

The primary rationale presented to the voters had always been economical service delivery and infrastructure development. Although analysis demonstrated that consolidation would achieve significant savings, the voters weren't buying.

But in 1992, a consolidation referendum passed. Success resulted from a change in strategy. Rather than using an argument based on service and infrastructure cost savings, commissioners justified consolidation this time as a way of improving economic competitiveness. DuVall said,

> When you have a corporation that wants to locate, they want to know that you can provide the necessary permits and deliver the services they need. If you can't give them an answer quickly, then they start to look elsewhere. It's easier to provide a timely response when you're speaking as one government.[2]

Originally published as "Regional Governance and the Post-Industrial Economy," *The Regionalist*, Vol. 1, No. 3, Fall 1995. Published by the National Association of Regional Councils, Washington, D.C. and the University of Baltimore, Baltimore, Maryland. Reprinted with permission of the publisher.

Across the country communities are beginning to realize that economic competitiveness requires a regional approach. The real competition is not among communities of the same region, but among regions here and abroad. Even regions long divided by bitter rivalries among local governments are finding common cause in the threats of job and population loss. This shift in attitude is evident in places like the Mon Valley that previously comprised the heart of Pennsylvania's steel producing region. The mills are now closed, and the 37 local governments in the valley are having to learn to cooperate regionally in efforts to restore their economy (Ehrenhalt 1995).

The desire to achieve economic competitiveness has always been one of the basic reasons for strengthening regional government (Wallis 1994a). In the nineteenth century city, size was equated with economic strength. The rapid expansion of central cities to encompass their populated suburbs was justified as making the city more competitive. Size assured an adequate labor supply, as well as the capacity to deliver the services and infrastructure necessary to support industrial growth.

In today's economy, size does not necessarily result in strength. Instead, competitiveness comes from the ability to mobilize regional resources in response to rapidly changing demands. Most regions in the United States have not figured this out yet. Communities within the same region continue to compete with one another for economic base, and in cases where metropolitan communities do unite, it is often against the central city, which is seen as a common enemy. This internal competitiveness assumes that the United States maintains economic hegemony among nations. By contrast, regions in other advanced industrialized nations are reorganizing to become effective competitors in a global economy. They realize that in such an economy national policy may be less important than effective regional governance.

Characteristics of the Global Economy

In a mass-production economy, wealth is made by transforming raw materials into consumer products—for example, coke and iron into steel, and steel into automobiles. The process is labor- and resource-intensive. In a post-industrial economy, wealth is generated by the exchange of information and the transformation of ideas (Reich 1991). Microsoft has become one of the wealthiest corporations in the world by manufacturing information-organizing products for a market that did not exist 20 years ago. U.S. communities may compete for a Japanese automobile assembly plant, but the real wealth of the parent corporation is generated by its design, engineering, and marketing side, which it is not likely to ship overseas.

A post-industrial *global* economy is characterized by three interrelated trends (Accordino 1992):

- **Globalization of Production.** In a mass-production economy, manufacturing is concentrated in metropolitan regions, especially in central cities. But in a post-industrial economy, routine production activities are transferred to rural areas and or less developed countries. Such relocation is motivated by the search for lower labor and land costs in a politically stable environment. It is made possible by such technological changes as wide-body cargo jets, which reduce transportation costs, especially for valuable electronic goods, and by electronic communications, which allow a high level of production control from remote headquarters.
- **Globalization of Consumption.** In a mass-production economy, efficiency requires a market that demands large quantities of a standard product. If the market can

be controlled by a few major manufacturers, they can regulate the product obsolescence cycle to assure profits. In a post-industrial economy, the product obsolescence cycle is accelerated as consumers in advanced industrial nations seek newer products from an ever broadening range of suppliers. Shorter product obsolescence cycles place pressure on manufacturing to become more flexible and market responsive, while remaining cost competitive. Lowering or eliminating tariff barriers also served to promote a global flow of products.

• **Globalization of Investment.** In today's economy, capital is increasingly free to move around the world, seeking the highest return. This mobility has significantly increased with the free-floating exchange rate system that was initiated in the early 1970s. Moreover, participation in global capital markets is no longer restricted to large-scale investors. Today, anyone with an interest can become involved.

Globalization of the economy has been occurring for several decades, but the end of the Cold War, combined with a lowering of international trade barriers, has accelerated the pace. A recent study sponsored by the German Marshall Fund of the United States (1992, 6) concludes, "As national trade barriers are lowered ... 'city-regions' in the European Community and the North American Free Trade Area are [becoming] the real arenas of global economic competition...." Similarly, urbanologists Richard Knight and Gary Gappert (1989, 11–12), writing about city-regions, observe,

> With the advent of the global economy, nation building is becoming more and more synonymous with city building. Cities serve as the nexus of the global society. As the global society expands, a nation's welfare will be determined increasingly by the roles its cities play in the global society.

Effects on the Structure of Regions

The global shifts just described have produced a significant restructuring of what economic geographers refer to as the "system of cities" that consists of the patterns of production and labor dependencies among metropolitan centers (Bourne and Simmons 1978). A mass-production economy results in a system characterized by dominant central cities and, in later phases, polycentric regions. By contrast, because a post-industrial economy depends more on the flow of information that on the movement of material goods, the system of cities it produces is less dependent on spatial proximity (Castells 1984). Consequently, the vitality of suburban and "edge-city" employment centers has become less dependent on the health of the central city, or cities, in their region. Instead, they may depend on the vitality of corporations located in wholly different regions.

One manifestation of changing employment locations is that incomes for central-city residents, which historically have been higher than those of suburban households, today are significantly lower and declining (Rusk 1993; Barnes and Ledebur 1994). Another manifestation is that an increase in vehicle miles traveled in urban areas is now primarily generated by intra-suburban trips rather than in commutes between central cities and suburbs (Federal Highway Administration 1990).

The transformation of the system of cities is also evident in the restructuring of labor markets within regions. In the mass-production era, metropolitan regions with an economic base of heavy industry supported a high proportion of blue-collar employment. Workers in this segment — often benefiting from organized-labor negotiated wage agreements —

could expect to achieve relatively high salaries that outpace inflation. By contrast, the service-based economy of a post-industrial era consists of significantly fewer blue-collar workers on one end and a growing number of highly skilled service professionals and semi-professionals at the other. This labor market reflects a dual economy in which employees in the low-skilled segment have little opportunity to earn wages comparable to those in the skilled segment (Noyelle and Stanback 1981).

The loss of middle-income jobs in both manufacturing and services has produced a widening gulf between classes, with fewer bridges of opportunity. It has also produced a socially isolated "underclass" with extremely poor access to new job markets (Kasarda 1989). Again, in socio-spatial terms, this earnings gap manifests itself in the form of suburban alienation from the central city.

These changes often are used to question the central city's significance in the region's economy. But that debate draws attention away from a more fundamental point — the importance of the interdependency of all of a region's communities for its economic competitiveness. The implication of the foregoing analysis is not that a post-industrial economy allows all communities to function as free agents, independent and indifferent to their neighbors. Rather, it suggests that the communities of a region are now bound up in a far more complex set of interdependencies, and the relationship between central cities and their suburbs is only one aspect (Savitch 1992).

Pathways through the Post-Industrial Economy

Over the last 20 years, regions across the country have been struggling to keep pace with the trends associated with globalization of the economy. Some regions, faced with factory closings, offer extremely attractive incentives to keep existing manufacturing plants and lure new ones. Others have abandoned efforts to maintain their old industrial base and seek either to attract or incubate firms capable of competing in the new high-tech service sector (Miller and Cotes 1987). Some approaches clearly are predicated on a desire to restore the old economic order, while others attempt to comprehend emerging trends and apply them in their plans. Major corporations similarly are engaged in prognostications on how best to restructure.

How a region chooses to respond to the changing economic realities reshaping it depends very much on how current trends are interpreted and future directions are perceived. At this point in its evolution, the post-industrial economy appears to have at least two distinct pathways through it. Each has very different implications for the competitive mobilization of regions and, in turn, for their governance.

The Neo-Fordist Path

Many of the largest corporations in the United States continue to adhere to mass-production, or "Fordist," principles. These corporations are attempting to extrapolate those principles on a global scale by promoting an international division of labor on one hand and an international organization of markets on the other. This is especially evident among automobile manufacturers (Barnet and Cavanagh 1994). Such corporations continue to be structured hierarchically, with a strong division between upper-management decision makers and line production workers. Neither trust nor power flows downward through their organizational structure.

Variants of the neo–Fordist approach,

however, accept a degree of decentralization. In some cases, individual factories or firms are encouraged to diversify. More power is given to the worker on the line, especially where total quality management principles have been adopted.

Large firms also create smaller subsidiaries focusing on specialized production and innovation. For example, major steel manufacturers have created or acquired subsidiaries that produce relatively small batches of special allow steels. These mills often are built in new locations, rather than replacing older mills that have been closed due to technological obsolescence and changing demands. Likewise, chemical companies have subsidiaries specializing in products ranging from new fibers to insecticides (Sabel 1982; Bianchi 1992).

Some analysts suggest that the neo-Fordist approach contains inherent contradictions. Its attempts to achieve greater flexibility to respond to rapidly changing consumer demands require a redistribution of power and responsibilities that is antithetical to the corporate hierarchies that continue to concentrate control (Sabel 1982; Lorenz 1992).

The Regional Industrial-Districts Path

In the early phases of the industrial revolution, efficient production occurred in districts where skilled artisans learned to employ machines to increase their output of traditional goods. Some shops produced only components of a finished good — fabric but not cloth, cloth but not clothing — but the district as a whole created market-competitive products. Such districts maintained a high level of craft, but they also provided an environment conducive to continuous, if relatively modest, innovation. In addition to a shared ethic

for quality craftsmanship, such districts cultivated strong social solidarity. Indeed, analysts of such districts emphasize the importance of trust and reciprocity in structuring social relations (Sabel 1982; Lorenz 1992).

The manufacturing districts of early industrialization were largely displaced by mass production techniques that sought to reduce reliance on craftsmanship by dividing production tasks into small steps that could be reproduced, without variation, by machines. But the idea of industrial districts never wholly disappeared. The production of highly specialized goods, especially those sufficiently high priced to cover rising labor costs (e.g., musical instruments), continues in a district form of organization. In some cases, districts have developed a symbiotic relationship with mass producers. The fashion industry, for example, still relies on highly specialized districts to create new designs that subsequently provide the basis for mass-produced imitations.

In addition to traditional industrial districts such as those associated with the garment industry, new high-tech districts have grown in prominence since the end of World War II. The Draper Labs of MIT helped provide the knowledge base for many of the firms that now dot Route 208 west of Boston. Similarly, Stanford University helped give rise to Silicon Valley. These high-tech districts have several characteristics of their traditional counterparts. They, too, rely on shared craft knowledge that can best, and perhaps only, be gained by being immersed in the environment of production — an environment that typically includes proximity to major research universities (Miller and Cotes 1987).

The vitality of both traditional and high-tech districts relies on orderly competition among local firms, but this internal competition limits itself to maintaining and enhancing a competitive advantage over similar districts located elsewhere. Both types of districts develop strong reciprocal relationships among firms— relationships built on trust and mutual advantage.

Implications for the Governance of Regions

Each path through the post-industrial economy has significant implications for the definition and conduct of governance, especially at the regional and even at the neighborhood level.

Governance Supporting the Neo-Fordist Path

Under a neo–Fordist regime, large firms become even larger through mergers and acquisitions and more global in their expanse. In effect, they operate in a "borderless world" (Ohmae 1990). As such, it might be expected that they would want an end to all government regulation of trade. In fact, they lobby for streamlining and or eliminating certain forms of regulation that are costly to large corporations, such as those pertaining to environmental protection, workplace safety, and minimum wage and benefit levels. Nevertheless, such firms continue to support national policies offering specific market protections, production subsidies, funding for research and development, and advantageous tax policies.

Since neo–Fordist firms benefit from the flexibility to relocate where labor-market conditions are most favorable, they presumably support federal policies that are non-place specific — for example, policies that favor accelerated obsolescence of capital investment in factories. Conversely, they oppose funding that is directed toward the problems of declining cities or regions.

In many cases, winning a bid for a new industry can result in downstream losses. The public sector may be left with debts from up-front incentives if companies move out within the payback period (Faux 1987). States have tried to protect themselves by implementing "clawback" provisions, requiring corporations to pay back incentives if they relocate before a specified period (Ledebur and Woodward 1990). But if such policies have real talons, they can act as disincentives to locating in those states. Alternatively, some neighboring regions and states have agreements not to compete to avoid bidding wars, but these agreements have proven to be conspicuously nonbinding when a large relocation prospect is highly prized. In short, although competition for jobs can result in increased inter-governmental cooperation, especially at the regional level, it is just as likely to result in predatory competition.

Even when public-sector cooperation is achieved, the private sector may maintain a tenant-at-will mentality, failing to commit itself to the region's long-range future. If firms are not committed to being regional citizens, neither are their executives. Local nonprofit institutions have long been dependent on the involvement of such executives to raise funds and lend expertise. But executives in neo–Fordist corporation are more likely to identify with their firm's worldwide network, rather than the local social networks of the communities in which they are located. When the Rockefellers left Cleveland they still felt a strong civic obligation to the community, leaving it with a significant endowment. Will British Petroleum feel a similar obligation?

All this is not to suggest that corporations are totally footloose. Many have significant plant investments, as well as concentrations of skilled employees, at specific locations. Consequently, they continue to have a strong vested interest in the ability of local and regional governments to deliver essential public services and infrastructure in an efficient and timely manner. One potential implication for governance growing out of this demand is increased use of single-purpose regional authorities, for example, port and or airport authorities, water districts, sewage districts, and the like. Such authorities overcome local fragmentation, and corporations can work with them easily.

However, many corporate requirements are not amenable to such an approach. For example, providing an adequate supply of affordable housing so that skilled employees can be attracted to and retained in an area often involves working with local governments on reform of their land-use policies. In this case, corporate interests may promote regional governance designed to override local controls that limit the supply of needed goods and services (Association of Bay Area Governments et al. 1990; Danielson and Doig 1982).

Similarly, corporations may find it necessary to become involved in issues of public education to assure an adequately trained workforce. Again, promoting regional governance to address the problem may be more attractive to corporate interests since it provides an organized forum through which to influence performance. By contrast, social equity issues, such as concentrated poverty and fiscal disparities among communities of a region, are not likely to be issues of central concern to neo–Fordist corporations (Mollenkopf and Castells 1991). The collective implication for regions is a somewhat strengthened form of governance, but in areas of narrow and strategic corporate interest.

Governance Supporting the Industrial-Districts Path

In contrast to the neo–Fordist path, which focuses attention on federal policies

that can promote mobility, the industrial districts path is much more concerned with developing effective regional and local policies. Likewise, whereas the neo–Fordist path prefers policies that are not place-specific, the industrial-districts path is firmly rooted to place and emphasizes building local capacity.

Nevertheless, advocates of an industrial-districts path see a strong role for federal policy if it is structured to support and enhance local and regional efforts at strengthening the industrial-districts approach (Accordino 1992). Developing a national industrial policy could have this effect, depending on how it is crafted. Likewise, a federal enterprise zone program could be structured to support industrial districts. Unfortunately, the current empowerment zone/enterprise community program, although emphasizing the importance of community capacity building, does not embrace an industrial-districts philosophy.

Since the industrial-districts approach emphasizes development of local production networks, advocates of this position see benefit in creating a regional government capable of providing a wide variety of public goods ranging from training and education to support for research and development, medical care, and housing (Lorenz 1992; Clavel 1986).

Economists Piore and Sabel (1984, 301) conclude,

> Successful industrial reorganization in the United States will require reinvigoration of local and regional government — not necessarily its supersession in favor of an expansion of corporate autonomy. Industrial policy will have to be regional policy; to be effective, the coordination of training programs, industrial research, transportation networks, credit, marketing information, environmental protection, and other elements of infrastructure will have to be done at the regional level.

In addition to suggesting a strong role for regional governments, the industrial-district paradigm also suggests a restructuring of *governance*, defined as participation in the processes of public decision making. In this conception, governance involves considerable interaction between the public, private, and nonprofit sectors. This restructuring goes beyond the creation of partnerships, focusing more broadly on achieving genuine collaborations in which all sectors— public, private, and nonprofit— provide distinct services and capacities in pursuit of a common regional vision (Wallis 1994b).

The type of governance advocated to support industrial districts also emphasizes neighborhood/community participation in decision-making processes (Peirce et al. 1993). Interest in neighborhood-level governance is indicative of the place-based orientation of an industrial-district approach, as distinct from the "borderless world" of the neo–Fordist alternative.

Emphasis on cross-sectorial governance also recognizes the importance of strengthening local civic infrastructure as an integral aspect of economic development. Robert Putnam (1993a, 106), drawing from his research on regions in Italy, observes,

> Of two equally poor Italian regions a century ago, both very backward, but one with more civic engagement, and the other with a hierarchical structure, the one with more choral societies and soccer clubs has grown steadily wealthier. The more civic region has prospered because trust and reciprocity were woven into its social fabric ages ago.

Part of the effort to strengthen civic infrastructure involves reengaging the poor living in isolated neighborhoods, as well as tapping into the talents available from new immigrants. The justification for placing resources in these populations of a region is that they represent human capital, which if abandoned creates inertia to competitive development.

Comparing the Paths

The two paths through a post-industrial economy, which are briefly described here, are ideal types. Most U.S. regions are of a scale and complexity that elements of both types are evident, but neither exists in a pure form. Nevertheless, distinguishing between these two paths may help regions in thinking about their current economic structure, how it is changing, and where it might be heading.

Each path through the post-industrial economy has very different implications for regional government and governance. The neo–Fordist alternative, based on the growing dominance of large multinational corporations, requires regions with the capacity to deliver necessary infrastructure and services. This demand could be met by developing and or strengthening special regional authorities or by enhancing the capacity of existing organizations, such as metropolitan planning organizations and councils of government.

In many regions, a neo–Fordist alternative also would benefit from strengthening regional capacity to override local government opposition to siting various supportive land uses, ranging from power plants to landfills to affordable housing. None of these requirements necessitate a radical reinvention of regional government or governance, but all involve a degree of state and interlocal commitment that to date has been very difficult to achieve.

By contrast, the industrial-districts scenario implies a substantial restructuring of regional government and governance. Few if any U.S. regions have developed an effective means to analyze adequately the linkages of industries comprising their current or nascent industrial districts, and few have the ability to connect such analysis to the formulation of a complementary, strategic policy agenda.

If the emerging global economy favors industrial districts, then U.S. economic competitiveness will be substantially disadvantaged by its lack of governance capacity to support such development. European and non-western regions appear to be ahead of the game in this respect, not simply due to recent efforts at "harmonization," a term for reducing local government fragmentation (van den Berg et al. 1993), but because of well established political cultures in many regions that already support the types of governance conducive to industrial districts (Lorenz 1992; Putnam 1993b; Sabel 1982; Piore and Sabel 1984).

Which Path?

Global restructuring of the economy is no longer an esoteric phenomenon confined to specialized conferences and journals. It has become material for the evening news. Increased awareness of change can motivate desire for shared dialogue and eventually for collective action.

Asking the question "Which path?" assumes a deliberative process by which interest groups in a region get together and think about what is happening to their economic structure and what they need to do to change it. In some cases this does occur, but only rarely. There are many efforts at visioning, but few engage in the kind of rigorous economic analysis necessary to generate informed conclusions. Several regions have developed coalitions of corporate interests dedicated to developing strategies to enhance regional economic competitiveness.[3] Some of these coalitions even include public agency members, but more often community

dialogue occurs in an environment of crisis defined by the threat or a factory of military base closing.

If the question "Which path?" is to be asked, several things have to happen:

- **Identity.** If interests from different sectors within a region are to enter into dialogue, they must first identify themselves as active participants in the life of their region.
- **Citizenship.** People not only need to see themselves as part of a region, they need to develop a sense of citizenship for its well being (Cisneros 1995).
- **Dialogue.** Once identity is established, opportunities must be provided for genuine dialogue. Coming together in dialogue helps reinforce identity with the region.
- **Vision.** Beyond dialogue, visioning involves a structured attempt to think about the future. It works best when it is strategic (about specific, pressing issues) rather than general (Dodge 1992).
- **Mobilization.** If visioning is effective, it should lead to mobilization to implement elements of the vision.

Realistically, regions do not have the capacity to control global economic forces, but they can actively decide how they want to respond to them. In formulating their responses, alternative forms of regional governance should be a central consideration.

Notes

1. William Hudnut, keynote speech at Town Meeting West (Denver, Colorado), April 3, 1992.

2. Personal interview with Commissioner DuVall, April 21, 1993.

3. Examples of such coalitions include Cleveland Tomorrow, Greater Philadelphia First, and the Greater Seattle Trade and Development Alliance.

References

Accordino, John. 1992. *The United States in the Global Economy*. Chicago: American Library Association.

Association of Bay Area Governments et al. 1990. *Bay Area Housing*. The Local Housing Element Assistance Project.

Barnes, William, and Larry Ledebur. 1990. *Toward a New Political Economy of Metropolitan Regions*. Washington, DC: National League of Cities.

_____. 1994. *Local Economies: The U.S. Common Market of Local Economic Regions*. Washington, DC: National League of Cities.

Barnet, Richard, and John Cavanagh. 1994. *Global Dreams: Imperial Corporations and the New World Order*. New York: Simon and Schuster.

Bianchi, Patrizio. 1992. "Levels of Policy and the Nature of Post-Fordist Competition." In *Pathways to Industrial and Regional Development*, edited by Michael Stroper and Allen J.Scott. New York: Routledge.

Bourne, Larry S., and James W. Simmons, eds. 1978. *System of Cities*. New York: Oxford University Press.

Castells, Manuel. 1984. "Space and Society." In *Cities in Transformation: Class, Capital and the State*, edited by Michael Smith, Vol. 28, Urban Affairs Annual Reviews.

Cisneros, Henry. 1995. *Regionalism: The New Geography of Opportunity*. Washington, DC: U.S. Department of Housing and Urban Development.

Clavel, Pierre. 1986. *The Progressive City*. New Brunswick, NJ: Rutgers University Press.

Danielson, Michael N., and Jameson W. Doig. 1982. *New York: The Politics of Urban Regional Development*. Berkeley: University of California Press.

Dodge, William R. 1992. "Strategic Intercommunity Governance Networks." *National Civic Review* (Fall-Winter).

Ehrenhalt, Alan. 1995. "Cooperate or Die." *Governing* (September): 28–32.

Faux, Jeff. 1987. Industrial Policy and Democratic Institutions. In *The State and Local Industrial Policy Question*, edited by Harvey Goldstein. Chicago: American Planning Association.

Federal Highway Administration. 1990. *Personal Travel in the United States*. Washington, DC: U.S. Department of Transportation.

German Marshall Fund of the United States. 1992. "Divided Cities in the Global Economy" (November).

Hanson, Royce, ed. 1983. *Rethinking Urban Policy: Urban Development in an Advanced Economy*. Washington, DC: National Academy Press.

Kanter, Rosabeth Moss. 1994. Collaborative Advantage. *Harvard Business Review* (July-August): 96–108.

Kasarda, John. 1989. Urban Industrial Transition and the Underclass, in *The Annals of the American Academy of Political and Social Sciences*, v. 501.

Knight, Richard V., and Gary Gappert. 1989. *Cities in the Global Society*. Newbury Park, CA: Sage.

Ledebur, Larry, and Douglas Woodward. 1990. "Adding a Stick to the Carrot: Location Incentives with Clawbacks, Rescissions and Calibrations." *Economic Development Quarterly* 4(3): 221–237.

Lorenz, Edward H. 1992. "Trust, Community and Cooperation: Toward a Theory of Industrial Districts." In *Pathways to Industrial and Regional Development*, edited by Michael Stroper and Allen J. Scott, New York: Routledge.

Miller, Roger, and Marcel Cotes. 1987. *Growing the Next Silicon Valley: A Guide for Successful Regional Planning*. Lexington, MA: Heath and Company.

Mollenkopf, John, and Manuel Castells. 1991. *Dual City: Restructuring New York*. New York: Russell Sage.

Noyelle, Thierry J. 1983. "The Implications of Industry Restructuring for Spatial Organization in the United States." In *Regional Analysis and the New International Division of Labor*, edited by Frank Moulaert and Patricia W. Salinas. Boston: Kluwer/ Nijkoff Publishing.

_____ and Thomas Stanback, Jr. 1981. *The Economic Transformation of American Cities*. New York Conservation of Human Resources, Columbia University.

Ohmae, Kenichi. 1990. *Borderless World: Power and Strategy in the Interlinked Economy*. New York: Harper Collins.

Peirce, Neal, Curtis Johnson, and John Stuart Hall. 1993. *Citistates: How Urban America Can Prosper in a Competitive World*. Washington, DC: Seven Locks Press.

Piore, Michael J., and Charles F. Sabel. 1984. *The Second Industrial Divide*. New York: Basic Books.

Putnam, Robert D. 1993a. "What Makes Democracy Work." *National Civic Review* (Spring): 101–107.

_____. 1993b. *Making Democracy Work: Civic Traditions in Modern Italy*. Princeton, NJ: Princeton University Press.

Reich, Robert. 1991. *The Work of Nations*. New York: Random House.

Rusk, David. 1993. *Cities Without Suburbs*. Baltimore: Johns Hopkins.

Sabel, Charles. 1982. *Work and Politics: The Division of Labor in Industry*. New York: Cambridge University Press.

Savitch, Hank. 1992. "Ties That Bind." *National Civic Review* (Summer-Fall).

van den Berg, Leo, H. Van Klink, and J. Van Der Meer. 1993. *Governing Metropolitan Regions*. Brookfield, VT: Avebury.

Wallis, Allan. 1994a. "Regionalism: The First Two Waves." *National Civic Review* (Spring).

_____. 1994b. "Inventing Regionalism: A Two-Phase Approach." *National Civic Review* (Fall-Winter).

• *Chapter 21* •

The State of the States

DAG RYEN

By almost every measure, the state of the American states as we approach the new millennium is strong. Having weathered the fiscal woes of the late 1980s and early 1990s, with the welcome assistance of a general turnaround in the national economy, and having reached a new accommodation with the federal government on key domestic issues, the states face the turn of the century with growing resources, increased organizational sophistication, added responsibilities and considerable flexibility in making policy and program choices.

The favorable conditions have led to an air approaching jubilation in the corridors of many state capitols. As West Virginia Gov. Cecil Underwood said in his 1998 address to the legislature in Charleston, "I can't remember a time brimming so completely with optimism and opportunity."

The general euphoria may be a well deserved reward to those state officials who have labored many years to hold the line on state government expenditures and to implement results-oriented state programs. However, in public service there is seldom rest for the weary. There remain a number of daunting challenges to policymakers and in our rapidly changing and highly interconnected world, new problems are sure to emerge.

A Quiet Evolution

Recent state government success builds on an unusual confluence of circumstances. Developments over the past decade had not only created an environment conducive to state activity, but in many ways forced state officials to look at their efforts in new ways. The last recession brought many states to their fiscal knees. As a result, executive and legislative decision-makers were forced to consider options that in better times would have been

Originally published as "These Are the Good Old Days: The State of Governance in the American States," *The Book of the States*, Vol. 32, 1998–99 Edition, 1998. Published by the Council of State Governments, Lexington, Kentucky. Reprinted with permission of the publisher.

unthinkable. Faced with billion dollar budget shortfalls, state governments from coast to coast responded with massive layoffs and drastic program cuts. During these often gut-wrenching times, state officials also began to question many of their conventional solutions and methods. Borrowing heavily from management theories prevalent in the private sector, they sought to rethink their approach to public issues. The result was a spate of structural analyses and strategic planning processes, many linked to trends such as quality management, public/private partnerships, reengineering or privatization. Not all these initiatives were equally successful in streamlining government or its services, but they uniformly improved communication from top to bottom in various state government hierarchies and led to considerable consensus on the need for government programs to be more directly responsive to citizen needs.

During this time, the federal government underwent a painful metamorphosis of its own. Without a constitutional mandate for balanced budgets, the president and Congress were less inclined to take dramatic steps to resolve increasingly perilous fiscal problems. Moreover, while the budget deficit ballooned, the political debate in Washington, D.C., deteriorated into partisan bickering. States often found it necessary to fill the vacuum created by inaction or gridlock at the federal level. And state leaders began to take a more active role in lobbying the president or members of Congress to break through the gridlock when vital state interests were at stake. Following the failure of President Clinton's health initiative, for example, a bipartisan coalition of governors in 1995 hammered out a comprehensive Medicaid reform plan.[1] Although Congress failed to enact major portions of the plan, it did provide an impetus for several new initiatives, pilot programs and federal waivers

that have helped ease the health care burden in certain states. Through this and similar discussions, state leaders became more adept at influencing decisions at the national level. Today, they are gradually being accorded a stronger voice in the national debate. In recent months, state leaders have been called in to help determine major changes in national education policy and welfare reform legislation.

Another element in recent state success is the so-called information revolution. On the one hand, the explosion in electronic technology made it easier for constituencies to communicate their wants and needs to representatives in state capitals. On the other hand, increased access to data of all kinds gave state officials what they needed to address citizen concerns better and faster. No longer is information held on a proprietary basis exclusively by national governments or independent interest groups. No longer do decision-makers have to go to Washington to get the briefings and statistics they need for effective program management. The data is available to state (and local) officials in their home offices through high-tech sources that place a premium on speed and ease of access. State officials can tap into these resources and craft specific proposals to meet local needs.

Finally, state officials are doing more and doing it better because they have enhanced their own skills when it comes to policy development and implementation. The growing complexity of the world in general has forced officials at all levels to new heights of sophistication. Today, state governments can tap into expertise and institutional resources that weren't available a decade ago. Drawing from research institutes, universities, government contractors and their own extensive staff, states can bring knowledge and skills to bear on a vast number of public policy issues. At the same time, with the general increase in mobility in our society, the job market for qualified researchers and managers in public policy has become national, if not international. And states have begun to realize that they must compete not only with each other but with the private sector to secure the human resources necessary for the business of governing.

Fiscal Strength

The most significant element in the current positive state of the American states and American island commonwealths is fiscal stability. For the most part, constitutional mandates have forced states to make the necessary adjustments to ride out the latest recession. Severe cuts left many government programs wounded in the late 1980s and early 1990s, but the enforced frugality served the states well in the subsequent economic spurt. Today, revenues are running higher than estimated and many states are enjoying a rare opportunity to accomplish all three things that voters constantly ask for: increased spending on programs, heftier budget surpluses and lower taxes.

The fiscal status of the states on the eve of the millennium is a marked contrast to the situations 8–10 years ago, when states were laying off tens of thousands of workers and struggling to meet budget shortfalls in the billions of dollars. In 1991, California alone faced a shortfall of $14 billion. That summer, New York Gov. Mario Cuomo laid off 5,700 workers and launched a campaign to trim the state payroll by an additional 13,000 jobs. During these difficult times, state welfare rolls were increasing, revenues were lagging and federal mandates were placing additional burdens on state coffers.

The extent of the turnaround in the ensuing years is remarkable. State revenues ran 2.7 percent above estimates in fiscal

1997 and 3.9 percent above estimates in fiscal 1998. A majority of states have taken advantage of this windfall by rolling back taxes. In fiscal 1998, 31 states gave their citizens breaks on fees or taxes. The most common option was a reduction in automobile excise taxes or registration fees. At the same time, the 50 states and Puerto Rico combined to increase year-end balances to their highest level since 1980. In many states, surpluses exceed 10 percent of annual expenditures. Combined, states now have ending balances of about $12.5 billion, or nearly five percent of annual expenditures, creating a good cushion for the somewhat less vigorous economic growth expected around the turn of the century.[2]

Cautious budget and program management continues to be the trend. Despite the surpluses, states are reluctant to increase payrolls. In fact, total state employment remained relatively flat in fiscal 1997 and 1998, with 15 states actually reducing the number of employees. While total state spending continues to increase by about five per cent annually, this represents actual annual growth adjusted for inflation of about two percent. Areas toward which states are applying additional revenues include aid to local governments, early education programs and increased compensation and benefits for employees. States are making adjustments to other mainstream programs, but the emphasis is generally on changes to increase efficiency rather than expansion of services.

Unfortunately, the dramatic improvements in the general economy and fiscal soundness of state governments are not universal. There are still jurisdictions struggling to shake off the effects of recession, military base closings or fluctuations in international markets. In Hawaii, unemployment has reached an all-time high. In Alaska, a glutted oil market has had a serious impact on the state economy. And in pockets of some Northeastern states, structural changes in manufacturing continue to create difficulties. But even these hard-hit areas are beginning to see light at the end of what once seemed a very dark fiscal tunnel.

The Age of Devolution

One of the most significant catch-words in government circles during the 1990s has been "devolution," the practice of turning over the development, implementation and management of government programs to state and local governments. This is not just an American phenomenon, but a global one. Particularly in the developed and industrialized nations, subnational and constituent jurisdictions have developed their organizational infrastructure and expertise to the extent that they now can act as full partners with national governments. And throughout the world, there is a growing recognition of the varied needs of regions and localities as well as the advantages of having decisions made by officials who are closest to the problem. In the European Union, where the comparable term "subsidiarity" is more in vogue, greater autonomy is being granted regional and municipal governments. In Japan and Korea, where strong central control has been the hallmark, regional and local governments, through "decentralization" initiatives, have recently been given autonomous taxing authority. And in the Federal Republic of Germany, the constituent länder are given primary responsibility for most domestic issues.

Over the past decade in the United States, we have witnessed increased state-federal interaction. The relationship between federal officials and state leaders has been cordial at times, adversarial at others. But through the decade, both sides have come to a new understanding of how different levels of government can work together. The decade began with a hue and cry from state officials about the unfunded mandates that were being loaded onto already strained state budgets. At times, the states went to the courts to seek redress. Suits initiated by Florida, California and others in 1993 sought to recoup costs incurred by states in providing services, primarily health care and education for undocumented aliens. Similarly, a year earlier, several states went to court to prevent the federal government from forcing states to provide repositories for low-level radioactive waste. Supreme Court Justice Sandra Day O'Conner wrote the opinion for the majority in the radioactive waste case, New York v. U.S., asserting that "state governments are neither regional offices nor administrative agencies of the federal government." But a federal appeals court dismissed the Florida suit on the grounds that it involved a political dispute between the states and the federal government and was therefore not subject to judicial review.

The administration of President Clinton, a former Arkansas governor, and the Republican dominated Congress first elected in 1992 seem to have taken some of the criticism to heart. Under President Clinton's directive, federal officials eased the process through which states can get waivers to implement new ideas in health care and welfare programs. And under the leadership of Sen. Dirk Kempthorne of Idaho and Sen. John Glenn of Ohio, Congress in 1996 finally passed the Unfunded Mandates Bill that set new standards for dealing with the programmatic and fiscal transactions between the federal and state governments.

The combination of budget surpluses, added political influence and increased autonomy have left states in a rare and enviable position. As William Pound, executive director of the National Conference of

State Legislatures recently remarked, "States generally have much greater flexibility in shaping economic and social policy than they've had for quite some time."[3]

Welfare Reform: Devolution in Practice. Perhaps no other issue typifies the new relationship between the federal and state governments as welfare reform. The reform act adopted by Congress in 1996 established a radically new approach to dealing with the nation's welfare recipients. Through the Temporary Aid to Needy Families (TANF) block grants, states have considerable leeway to devise programs that meet specific state needs.

In many ways, the changes were long in coming. Saddled with burgeoning welfare rolls and diminishing funds during the lean years of 1988–92, many states campaigned for fundamental changes in the welfare law. Early advocates of reform included Michigan's Gov. John Engler and the minority leader of the New Jersey house, Wayne Bryant. But state adjustments to the system remained piecemeal until the block grant measure was enacted by Congress.

Early results of the new system have been remarkable, thanks in part to a healthy national economy. Just 18 months after implementation of the TANF program, welfare caseloads have been reduced by 27 percent nationally. In Indiana, for instance, caseloads have fallen by half. Other states in the South, Midwest and West have experienced similar declines. The new federal law, however, requires that states continue to spend at a certain level compared with the baseline years 1992–95. With fewer people to take care of, there is more money to go around. In fact, in its initial year, TANF funding was seven percent higher than the federal programs it replaced. Consequently, states are able to increase benefits for recipient families, expand services and at the same time establish reserve accounts to meet future needs.

States are also allowed to shift up to 10 percent of TANF funds to other social services, an option some have already implemented and many others are considering. If caseload levels remain at their current low levels, states may be able to bolster child care, job training, housing subsidies or substance abuse treatment programs without increasing state appropriations.[4]

The real test of the block grant system may come in the new century, if and when the national economy stumbles and welfare rolls increase once more. Having argued for greater autonomy, state leaders will find it difficult to extract increased support from the federal government once welfare budgets get tight again. Critics of the legislation argue that the accountability and documentation requirements place a tremendous burden on state officials even though there is considerable flexibility on the programmatic side. And some analysts are concerned that the new state-managed system is generating a class of working poor and shifting their problems to other program areas. They argue that making the poor work at low wage jobs will only lead to a need for increased spending on public housing, education (especially early education), health care and transportation.

The federal law also contains provisions limiting TANF benefits to non-citizens. To date, most states with large immigrant populations continue to maintain levels of support to these families. However, as the phase-in period comes to an end, states may be faced with the challenge of providing assistance to sizeable immigrant populations without federal support.

Another consequence of the welfare block grant reform is that states have begun to revamp their assistance delivery systems. One method being tested is additional "in-state devolution," as states establish partnerships with cities and counties and set up local offices to coordinate all public social services. In Minnesota, for instance, where block grants for social services have been provided to localities since the 1970s, additional measures are being considered to move greater responsibility for children's services to cities and counties.[5]

The Tobacco Trials. Another development that will have an enormous impact on the evolution of federal-state relations is the effort to reach agreement with American cigarette manufacturers on regulation of tobacco products. A consortium of 40 state attorneys-general made history when they reached agreement with tobacco companies in 1997 on a $368.5 billion proposed settlement. The deal was remarkable in a number of ways. It constituted the most restrictive set of regulations ever imposed on an industry and its total reimbursement value was greater than any settlement in American legal history.

Of equal importance is the fact that the deal emanated from suits brought by state officials to recoup health care costs caused by smoking. It represents one of the most significant steps ever taken by states to deal with a major national public policy issue. And it marks one of the first instances in the modern era in which officials from the American states were placed in a position to negotiate matters that will have broad-ranging consequences for federal regulatory agencies. The accord would give tobacco companies some protection from future civil lawsuits, including a cap on legal payouts, a ban on class-action suits and immunity from punitive damages in future suits. In exchange, the pact would require the industry to restrict advertising and make a series of substantial payments to government entities.

As of this writing, several aspects of the tobacco negotiations remain uncertain. Through the winter of 1997–98, Congress continued to debate whether the deal punishes tobacco companies enough for knowingly damaging public health, whether restrictions on future suits against the tobacco companies are unfair to individuals who have suffered from smoking-related illnesses and whether the proposed agreement sufficiently addresses the impact on tobacco farmers. Also subject to controversy is how the monies that tobacco companies have promised to pay will be distributed. In testimony before Congress, state officials have argued adamantly that the bulk of compensation should go directly to the states, which initiated the suit.

Problems and Priorities: A Children's Crusade

A notable portion of current activity at the state level is directed at preserving viable opportunities for future generations. As a follow-up to changes in the welfare system and in response to new research on the importance of early child development, states are going through an intensive review of programs for children during the first few years of life.

Particular attention is being paid to the needs of two-income families. With both parents in the work force, often at low paying jobs, many families find it difficult, if not impossible, to find affordable child care. States are trying to address this need in a variety of ways. To begin with, a dozen or more states are extending child care support to low income families beyond current federal requirements. Utah has established "crisis nurseries" that provide around the clock service to families undergoing difficult transitions or hit by a health crisis. Other states are putting the squeeze on private corporations to establish child care centers for their employees or to help finance public child care centers within the community.

The quality of child care is also a major concern. Most states monitor facilities for threats to health and safety, but there are few regulations on skills or educational background for the employees. Care providers earn an average of only $11,000 per year and turnover in the industry runs 41 percent annually.[6] Some states are offering special training in children's needs at various age levels. Others are earmarking funds specifically for the expansion of care for infants and toddlers. Still others are expanding their Early Start programs to include extended training to first-time mothers. While states are reluctant to establish stricter criteria for child care operations for fear of driving costs out of the reach of low income families, quality improvement remains a priority. In New Mexico, officials are trying an innovative program that will increase reimbursement to child care facilities that achieve higher levels of quality and performance.

Another approach being tested by some states is the establishment of comprehensive support programs for parents. By linking health, day care, pre-school and parental education initiatives, states such as Delaware and Vermont hope to get the most out of their programs and achieve the highest possible levels of pre-school child development.

Finally, states are bolstering children's health programs. Recent amendments to Title XXI of the Social Security Act has freed up considerable federal funding for expanded health insurance for children and the Americans with Disabilities Act has allowed states to significantly increase services for disabled youngsters. These programs, combined with state initiatives merging home health services and parental education, greatly improve the states' ability to ensure that younger citizens are receiving appropriate medical attention.

Back to Education Basics. As part of the general effort to improve the lives of the nation's children, states continue to invest in education. Across the country, states are expanding pre-school options, after school programs, career planning services and college scholarship programs. Also, a number of states have initiated "back to basics" campaigns to enhance the quality of K-12 education. A major component of these efforts is statewide testing of students at the elementary, junior high and high school levels. And state education officials

---

Figure 1
Other State Policy Priorities

Health Care— Refinement of state regulations on managed care providers to ensure client options and enhance quality. Increased privatization of mental health services.

Environment—Intensified consideration of new EPA air standards for ozone and particulate matter, including extension of California standards to other areas. Likely to include discussions of market systems for pollution quotas.[8] Establishing ecoshed management techniques.

Transportation—States continue to rebuild aging transportation infrastructure. Emphasis on regional planning, connector highways and transportation corridor refinements as envisaged in federal ISTEA legislation. Public transit improvements in major metropolitan areas.

Workers Compensation—Restructured workers compensation systems, setting payout limits and streamlining claims and reimbursement procedures.

Corrections—From 1990–95, states spent $15 billion to add 400,000 beds to state prisons, greatly alleviating overcrowding. Now, states face the problem of crowded city and county jails. A priority in coming years will be to help local communities renew their corrections facilities.[9]

Public Safety—Continued interest in community policing and drug interdiction techniques.

are seeking to eliminate the practice of "social promotion," advancing students who are not ready academically so as not to stunt their social development. In recent addresses to legislatures, several governors took direct aim at this practice, arguing that it sends an extremely harmful message to our youngest citizens.[7]

The Productivity Agenda

Throughout the history of our country, states have actively dealt with matters of commerce and employment within their jurisdictions. However, as the new millennium approaches, demands on the states to ensure economic prosperity are escalating. Partly by design and partly by default, the federal government has ceded a central role in the economic development arena to states and localities. While officials in Washington, D.C., continue to manage the macro-economic affairs of the nation, more and more it is state and local officials who deal with the nuts and bolts of job creation and plant siting.

Today, states have a multitude of tools at their disposal to bolster local economies. Using incentive packages, economic empowerment zones, job training programs and infrastructure enhancements, states can attract prospective employers and employees. But subtle changes are taking place. The vigorous smokestack chasing of the 1970s and 80s, marked by intense competition between states and extravagant tax incentives, seems to have lost a great deal of its appeal. States have begun to look more closely at the social, environmental and infrastructure costs involved with major industrial expansion. And they have become aware of the extensive role small and medium-sized businesses play in sustaining economic health.

As a result, states are refining their economic development strategies, reducing the tax and regulatory burden on all businesses, and looking to build a more diversified economic base. At the same time, they are becoming more sensitive to the types of employment opportunities available to workers. The fastest growing sectors in the national economy include both low paying service industries and high paying technology industries. In an attempt to tap into the higher end of this development, states are establishing corporate office and research parks aimed at luring rapidly growing high-tech companies. Competition for this "silicone sector" is becoming as intense as the battle for automobile manufacturing factories once was.

State leaders have also recognized that the availability of a well educated work force is critical to getting and keeping high-tech jobs. Consequently, improvements to the education system have become an important element in the long-term economic development strategy of many states. In Kentucky, for instance, a higher education reform package enacted in 1998 will lead to greater coordination between the traditional college and university system and technical education institutions across the state. These reforms are expected to enhance the state's ability to provide job training opportunities geared to specific industrial needs in the future.

Another area in which states are taking an increasingly active role is international trade. The importance of global ties can scarcely be overestimated. Sales abroad of American goods and services account for more than 10 percent of our gross domestic product. Imports and exports combined total almost one-third of our domestic product, and more than 12 million American jobs are directly dependent on international trade.

Today, 38 states operate some form of overseas office, including posts in such exotic venues as Kuala Lumpur and Harare. On average, each American state spends almost $1.5 million on trade promotion efforts, including trade missions, product fairs, export loan services, port tax credit programs, tax exempt export companies, shared foreign sales corporations, translation services, trade newsletters and export procedures training.[10]

A recent trend in this field has been the establishment of public/private non-profit corporations to coordinate international trade activities. The Empire State Development Corporation and Enterprise Florida are examples of such initiatives. However, most states continue to fund specific agencies, usually within the economic development cabinet, whose role is to promote international trade and assist companies entering the global market.

An important challenge facing the states with respect to international trade is educating the public about the need for direct contact with businesses and investors abroad. Governors and other state officials are often reluctant to embark on trade missions or other visits to foreign capitals for fear that the trips be portrayed by local media as wasteful junkets. Yet support and involvement from leadership at the highest levels is critical to a successful international trade and investment promotion effort. In the coming years, state officials must find ways to revitalize communication links with the media and the general public and to lay out the benefits of active involvement in the global economy.

Conclusion: Trends for the Future

The relatively strong health of the American states at the close of the 20th Century can be attributed in part to sound decision-making, in part to good fortune. A strong national economy coming on the heels of substantial belt-tightening at the state level has created agencies and programs that are efficient and for the most part adequate to their mission. In almost every policy area, states have greater flexibility and greater incentive to test innovative ideas than at any time in the post–World War II era.

The state officials who are faced with this enviable situation represent in some ways a new generation. The term limits enacted in a majority of states have led to the retirement of many experienced legislators and executive officials. At the same time, the rigors of campaigning and political fund-raising have led others to retire from public life. As a result, state capitols and many state agencies are filled with a younger set of officials. Some analysts argue that the current focus on family and children's issues is a direct result of this generational shift.

There are indications that the new generation of leaders is more representative of the population as a whole. After a period of stagnation, the number of women legislators is once again rising, comprising 27 percent of the total membership in state legislative chambers.[11] Minority representation is also on the upswing.

In terms of organizational structure, the picture is fairly constant. Given the fiscal constraints imposed during the past decade, there is little room for experimentation. To the contrary, states continue to eliminate some agencies or departments and to merge others as cost-saving or downsizing initiatives. The mergers most often involve agencies in health and human services or in labor and job training. There is also a trend toward a more comprehensive approach to juvenile justice.

Perhaps the most prevalent development in the structure of state governments is toward performance-based or outcome-based budgeting. A number of states are moving in this direction, either through statewide implementation of a performance budgeting system or through a specific emphasis on outcomes during budget deliberations.[12]

All of these factors should ultimately increase the ability of states to deal with future problems and emerging issues. The combination of broadened institutional experience and relative fiscal prosperity places the states as a strong partner in the American governance system. But the good times can evaporate as rapidly as they appeared. Unless the states move in partnership with the federal government now when the resources are available to address some of the endemic and structural problems that exist in our society, such as the growing disparity between the poor and wealthy, the shrinking middle class, the disconnect between education, skills and job opportunities, the overdependence on fossil fuels or the specter of a bankrupt social security system, all may have been for naught. The newly discovered vitality at the state level could deteriorate rapidly in the face of even a minimal economic downturn. And the prospect of significant action at the federal level remains as dim as ever.

State leaders have worked hard to get their governments where they are. But the eve of the new millennium is no time to lose vigilance. There will be golden opportunities ahead to further improve conditions in the American states. State leaders should remain prepared to take advantage of them.

Notes

1. For a discussion of the governor's plan and the negotiations that led to it, see *State Government News*, March 1996, pp. 6–7 and 30–31.

2. See *The Fiscal Survey of States*, National Governors' Association and National Association of State Budget Officers, December 1997.

3. "*NCSL Inside*," March 1998, p. 1.

4. Tweedle, Jack, "Welfare Spending: More for Less," *State Legislatures*, March 1998, pp. 12–18. See also State Reports issued by the Urban Institute as part of its *Assessing the New Federalism* initiative. And Mennin, Gorden and C. Eugene Stuerle, "The Impact of TANF on State Budgets," No. 18 in the series *New Federalism: Issues and Options for States*, The Urban Institute, 1997.

5. Burt, Martha R., et. al., "Income Support and Social Services for Low-Income People in Minnesota," The Urban Institute, 1997.

6. Statistics provided by Sharon Lynn Kagan, senior associate at the Yale University Bush Center in Child Development and Social Policy, in a presentation to the National Governors' Association annual winter meeting, Washington, D.C., Feb. 23, 1998.

7. See Moyes, Howard, "Let the Good Times Roll," *State Government News*, March 1998, pp. 13–14, and 35–36.

8. Dale, Jeff, "New National Air Standards for Particulate Matter and Ozone," *NCSL State Legislative Report*, March 1998, Vol. 23, No. 6.

9. Freyman, Russ, "Jails in a Jam," *Governing*, March 1998, pp. 30–31.

10. Ryen, Dag and Susan W. Zelle, *The ABCs of World Trade*, The Council of State Governments, 1997.

11. Center for the American Woman and Politics, Rutgers University.

12. See *The Fiscal Survey of States*, op. cit., p. 17.

· *Chapter 22* ·

The Structure of State Government

Edwin Meese III

When the Founding Fathers wrote the Constitution in 1787, the United States only had 13 states. The Founding Fathers believed that more states would want to join the Union in the future. They saw that it would be important for new states to have the same type of government as the original states had. There were 50 states as of 1987, all of which have these characteristics:

- state government is based on a state constitution;
- state has a republican form of government;
- state constitution does not contradict the U.S. Constitution; and,
- there are three branches of government — legislative, executive, judicial:
  — separation of powers,
  — checked and balanced by each other and by the federal government.

Authority

The states have primary responsibility for many aspects of government. Often the state and federal government work together to provide services. Sometimes the state receives federal aid for specific programs. Some services for which the state has primary responsibility include:

- protection of lives and property by maintenance of a police force;
- regulation and improvement of transportation within the state;
- regulation of business within the state; and,
- education.

In providing services the federal and state governments work as partners. Often the federal government provides most of the funding while the state primarily provides distribution though it varies from

Originally published as "State Government," *U.S. Government Structure*, 1987. Published by the Immigration and Naturalization Service, U.S. Department of Justice, U.S. Government Printing Office, Washington, D.C.

program to program. Some of these services include:

- health care;
- public assistance for persons in need;
- protection of natural resources; and,
- improvements in living and working conditions.

The Constitution **delegates** any authority not specifically given the federal government in the Constitution to the states. Since the early years of the country, the role of the federal government has grown. Technical advances, such as the telephone, airplane and computer, have brought people and places closer together than they were in 1787. The expanded role of the federal government reflects those changes. State governments, however, serve an important purpose. They are closer to the people than the federal government and can be more responsive to the specific needs of the people in their states.

The Constitution puts one major limitation on state authority. Article VI states that the Constitution, federal laws, and treaties between the U.S. and other countries make up the supreme law of the country. If state or local laws **contradict** any of those, the state or local law can be declared **unconstitutional** by the Supreme Court. Recently, the Supreme Court has used this authority to help guarantee that people's **civil rights** are protected. It has declared laws unconstitutional if they discriminate against people for reason of race, religion, political beliefs or national origin.

Structure

State governments are set up through state constitutions, which usually have four sections. These sections are the:

- preamble;
- bill or declaration of rights;
- outline of the structure of the government; and,
- methods for changing the constitution.

These sections are similar to those in the U.S. Constitution, in form and often in content. The sections usually consist of a:

- preamble:
  — states the purpose and that the authority of the government comes from the people;
- bill of rights:
  — includes many of the same rights as in the U.S. Constitution's Bill of Rights;
  — sometimes additional rights, such as the right to work, are included;
- structure section:
  — sets up the three separate branches: the executive, judicial and legislative; and,
- methods of change:
  — states the procedure for amending or redrafting the constitution.

State constitutions sometimes set up procedures or guarantee rights not mentioned in the U.S. Constitution. Some states guarantee that workers will not lose their jobs if they do not belong to a union or have a special statement on equal rights for women. States also must establish procedures for local governments within the state, such as the process for granting a city **charter**. Some states provide their citizens with opportunities for **direct democracy**. The federal government could not easily do this because the number of people and size of the country would make it difficult to implement. The states, being smaller and more able to respond to local needs than the federal government, often provide one or more types of direct democracy. The major types are the

- initiative;
- referendum; and,
- recall.

The *initiative* usually is used to pass laws or amend the state constitution. A group of concerned citizens draws up a **petition**. The petition states the problem and a solution. If the required number of people signs the petition, the issue is put on the ballot and the people vote on it. At least 50 percent (or half) must vote in favor of the issue for it to pass.

Referenda work in a slightly different way. There are three different types: the *compulsory referendum, optional referendum,* and *petition* or *protest referendum.* Some states require that certain issues, such as amendments to the state constitution, be submitted to a popular vote. This is the *compulsory referendum.* State legislatures sometimes use the *optional referendum* to settle a highly controversial issue. When the citizens vote, that tells the legislature what the people believe should be done about the issue. The *protest referendum* gives citizens who are not pleased with a law a chance to overturn the law. A certain number of citizens must sign a petition to submit the issue to popular vote. The outcome of the vote determines whether the law remains or is overturned.

The *recall* provides citizens with a chance to remove an official from office. Sometimes judges and appointed officials are exempt from recall. In other states the citizens can vote to remove any public official who they believe is not serving the best interests of the government and people. As with the initiative and the protest referendum, a certain number of people must sign a petition to put the recall issue on the ballot. These examples of direct democracy — the initiative, referendum, and recall — provide citizens with the opportunity to be involved in issues which they consider very important.

State and local government, like the federal government, is based on the principle of **representative democracy**. Though many states provide opportunities for direct democracy, most governing is done by elected representatives. One of the most important functions of the state constitution is to establish the structure of the state government. All state governments have three branches — the executive, legislative and judicial. Details of government structure vary among states, but the basic structure is similar. For information about a specific state, contact its *League of Women Voters*, the *National Municipal League*, or another civic group.

Executive Branch

The head of every state government is the governor. The qualifications, term of office and powers of the governor are listed below:

- Qualifications vary, but candidates for governor of a state usually must be qualified voters, citizens of the U.S., of a certain age (usually more than 30) and have lived in the state a certain period of time (often five years).
- The term of office varies, usually either two or four years.
  - In some states, there is a limit to the number of times the governor can serve.
- The powers of the governor are similar in all states:
  - Advise the state legislature on the laws needed;
  - Call special sessions of the state legislature;
  - Serve as head of the state's National Guard;
  - Pardon or decrease sentences of people convicted in state courts, when appropriate.
- If the governor dies or is unable to serve, the lieutenant governor, whose position is similar to that of the Vice President, becomes governor.

The governor has a group of advisers, similar to the President's Cabinet, who perform special services for the state. In some states, voters elect these officials, and in others the governor appoints them. Some of these are:

- Secretary of State, who keeps official records and publishes state laws;
- Attorney General, who represents the state in court;
- Treasurer, who receives tax money and pays bills for the state from that money;
- Auditor or Comptroller, who keeps track of the financial matters in the state; and,
- various commissioners, who are concerned with such issues as labor, banking, public utilities, and health.

The governor and his/her advisers not only carry out the laws passed by the state legislature, but propose new laws. Governors often are elected on a specific **platform** and try to get the legislature to pass their new proposals.

Legislative Branch

Each state has a legislature similar to the federal government. Forty-nine of the states have bicameral legislatures, meaning they have two houses, similar to the federal government. (Nebraska is the exception — it only has one house.) The two houses usually are called the house of representatives and the senate. Each state sets its own requirements and structure for its legislature.

- The purposes of all state legislatures are:
  — to make laws about state matters, and
  — to represent the interests of its citizens.
- The term of office varies from state to state. Usually, a term is four years in the senate and two years in the house of representatives. However, it can be four years or two years in each.
- Distribution of representatives differs by state.
  — Some states have a set number of representatives for a set geographic area, such as one representative for every 10 square miles.
  — Some states have representation based on population, such as a representative for every 20,000 people.
  — In some states, representatives are *at-large*, and all voters help elect all representatives.

- The procedure for making laws is similar to the procedure followed in the federal government.

Judicial Branch

The state courts have a **hierarchy** which is similar to the federal system. (See Figure 1.) The structure, from lowest to highest, is:

- justice of the peace, municipal, county or special courts;
- district, superior, circuit or common pleas courts;
- intermediate appellate courts (not in all states); and,
- state supreme court.

There are two kinds of cases: **civil** and criminal. Judges, who usually are elected, preside over all cases. Most cases also have juries. Trial by jury is guaranteed by the U.S. Constitution in most cases. Juries consist of citizens who listen to the lawyers argue both sides of the case and to the judge's instructions. Then the jury decides, by a vote, whether the accused person is guilty or innocent. The jury also may make recommendations about punishment of those found guilty, but the judge has the final authority on punishment and sentencing.

State courts only hear cases that involve state or local laws, so they have somewhat different duties than federal courts. Some of their duties are:

- to explain state laws;
- to tell how state laws apply;
- to settle disagreements between citizens in a state;
- to decide guilt or innocence of breaking a state law; and,
- to decide if state laws are unconstitutional.

Responsibilities

Citizens and state governments have important responsibilities to each other.

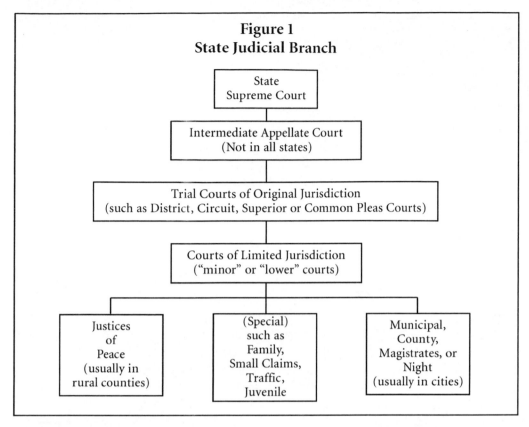

Figure 1
State Judicial Branch

State Supreme Court

Intermediate Appellate Court (Not in all states)

Trial Courts of Original Jurisdiction (such as District, Circuit, Superior or Common Pleas Courts)

Courts of Limited Jurisdiction ("minor" or "lower" courts)

Justices of Peace (usually in rural counties)

(Special) such as Family, Small Claims, Traffic, Juvenile

Municipal, County, Magistrates, or Night (usually in cities)

Since states have fewer people than the country, citizens have more personal contact with their state governments. Usually it is easier for the citizen and state to remind each other of their responsibilities. Citizens in the state have a responsibility to:

• obey state laws;
• pay their state taxes;
• vote in all state elections; and,
• be informed and participating citizens.

States have responsibilities to their citizens to:

• protect the lives and property of people in the state;
• provide certain basic services, such as education; and,
• provide government and justice according to state and federal laws.

Chapter 23

The States and the Federal Government

Richard P. Nathan

The 1994 election, which gave Republicans control of both bodies of the 104th Congress, is likely to represent a historic realigning moment for our governmental system comparable to realignments of the past. In 1800, the first Republicans (Jefferson and Madison) established a new party, which weakened the Hamiltonian system; 1828 saw the populist Jacksonian revolution capture the presidency; and 1860 saw the national emergence of Lincoln's new northern-based Republican party. The Bryan-McKinley election of 1896 and, in 1912, Wilson's election to the presidency and the maturation of the Progressive Movement, could be included on this list of realigning moments, as could Franklin Roosevelt's first election to the presidency, the emergence of his New Deal program in 1932, and the advent of Lyndon Johnson's Great Society in 1965. In each instance, historic shifts occurred that had strong manifestations in governmental structures not unlike what is happening right now as a result of actions by the 104th Congress to change the basic character of American federalism.

This chapter is divided into five parts: the first defines federalism as a governmental form and assesses the current condition of American federalism; the second discusses the "Devolution Revolution" encompassed in the changes in domestic policy and intergovernmental relations pressed forward by the leaders of the 104th Congress; the third considers issues for state governments in their relationship with the national government; the fourth discusses the role of state governments; and the fifth offers concluding observations.

Originally published as "The Role of the States in American Federalism" in Carl E. Van Horn, Editor, *The State of the States*, 1996. Published by CQ Press, Washington, D.C. Reprinted with permission of the publisher.

Defining Contemporary American Federalism

American federalism emerged out of frustration with the earlier arrangement under the Articles of Confederation, which none other than the magisterial George Washington called "a shadow without substance."[1] Our brand of federalism was unique when it was created in precisely the sense that the word "unique" means—*one and only*. U.S. federalism, said the brilliant Madison (a proponent of centralization in 1787 at the Philadelphia Convention), was created as a "great composition"—partly federal and partly national (*Federalist No. 39*). Unlike earlier confederal forms, which were essentially leagues of states, under the U.S. Constitution each citizen is a citizen of both the national government and the state. Over the two centuries of our history, the great battles of federalism have been fought over which citizenship—federal or state—should predominate. In this century, the clear victor has been the national government. There have been flurries of state activism—the Progressive Movement in the 1920s, under Richard Nixon's New Federalism, and during the Reagan years—but the great movement of government has been toward the center.

The "Devolution Revolution"—Why Now?

Now, however, we are in the midst of a dramatic shift toward what many political leaders believe is a correct, limited interpretation of the "enumerated powers" assigned to the national government in Article I of the U.S. Constitution and a correspondingly broad interpretation of the Tenth Amendment, which assigns residual (nonenumerated) powers to the states, or to the people. This shift is likely to involve basic changes at the core of the nation's governmental system.

Why is this happening now? Governors are demanding more responsibility and budget pressures are acute. Early in 1995, Republican leaders in Congress decided federal deficit reduction targets could best be met by striking a deal whereby governors received more power in exchange for going along with cuts in spending. No matter what happens on headline-level policy disputes about block grants and budget cuts, a power shift is already under way that is not likely to be reversed soon. Congress passed and the president signed into law the Unfunded Mandates Reform Act of 1995 limiting the federal government's power to adopt future mandates for state, local, and tribal governments without paying them. This was promise "Number 8" in the House Republicans' "Contract with America," The law also requires a study of all existing mandates, and in other areas Congress is pulling back from regulatory regimes, notably for environmental programs.

The federal government is not simply loosening the regulatory apron strings, it is also tightening the purse strings. Cuts in discretionary spending for many domestic programs with be 15–20 percent or more for fiscal year 1996. Looking down the road to 2002, the reductions being discussed average 30 percent at the end of this seven-year period. Not only is federal spending being cut, it is no longer the *modus vivendi* of Washington to discover problems and provide money to solve them. The federal money machine is turned off. This is not just a fiscal event; it shifts the social policy agenda to others—mainly to the states.

The states are exhibiting a new readiness and capability for action. Republican governors (now 31 in number) are linked arm in arm with leaders of the Congress. Many governors are re-engineering state government, modernizing its administrative machinery, and taking steps to overhaul and integrate social programs. Many state governments are also hard at work on the "nuts and bolts" of good government, redesigning their civil service, procurement, training, and information systems and revising management procedures.

This devolutionary shift is rooted in frustration over stagnant wages. Voters, responding to their straitened circumstances, are supporting conservative economic policies aimed at reducing the size and cost of government. Part of the economic reason as to "Why now?" is international, tied to steps private corporations have taken in recent years to re-engineer and downsize their operations. The increasingly global economy puts pressure on not just private-sector costs, but on the cost of government as well. The Devolution Revolution can be seen as a way to push all of America's governments to cut costs and achieve efficiencies. A more political interpretation as to why the Devolution Revolution is under way relates to an idea emphasized in the political science writing of Robert D. Putnam.[2] Putnam believes that community identity matters. Neighborhoods, villages, cities, and states represent identities that give meaning to people's lives. Federalism as a device for reconciling unity and diversity is an instrument for enhancing this sense of belonging to a community.

American federalism, of course, is not just about the national government and the fifty states. There are 20,000 municipal governments, 17,000 towns and townships, and 3,000 county governments. In fact, a criticism of American federalism is that it is too diverse and fragmented and that this layering of multiple small governments frustrates the citizenry. But multiple governmental identities are intrinsic to who we are. The sense Americans have of living and self-governing with other people in communities is not a small item on the scale of values that citizens of the United States consider important.

In the literature on federalism, some scholars have taken the position that American federalism has three parts— national, state, and local. Roscoe Martin argued in the 1950s that U.S. federalism should be viewed as a three-cornered stool, unable to stand if there is not strength in all three legs.[3] However, while it is a mistake to ignore the role and importance of local units, federal systems of government should *not* be viewed this way.

Crucial Role of the Middle Level

What distinguishes federal systems of government from unitary systems is the existence of a middle level. It is the role and character of these governments (states in the United States, Australia, and India; Länder in Germany; provinces in Canada) that differentiate federalism from a unitary form of government. The relative strength of the role of these middle-level governments is what determines the overall strength of federal systems. A variety of aspects of the role of state governments should be the basis for assessing the strength of the federal form in different settings— for example, according to the relative strength of these governments in terms of their fiscal, legal, and programmatic role and powers; the strength of their political and cultural identity; the structure of the federal-state relationship; and the authority (both formal and informal) state governments exercise over local units.[4] In the United States, some states assign extensive home rule powers to local units. These are the powers local governments have to set their own tax rates, policies, and regulations. The critical point here is that this is basically (though not fully) each *state's* decision. It is to states that we must look to understand the balance of contemporary American federalism. The story line in recent years for the federalism changes now under way — and accelerating — has been the rising role of the states. At the outset of American history, states were the dominant governments in our political system. Today, they are coming into their own again.

Rising Role of the States

Five factors undergird this ascendance of the American states. One is the conservative and devolutionary policies adopted under the Reagan administration. A second, long-term factor underlying state activism is the modernization movement in state government, which first appeared in the mid–1960s. The phrase refers to reforms adopted by states to increase their managerial and technical capacity to take on new and expanded functions. In a 1985 report, the Advisory Commission on Intergovernmental Relations concluded that "state governments have been transformed in almost every facet of their structure and operations."[5] A third factor is the effect of the Supreme Court decision in *Baker v. Carr* (1962). This decision reduced the rural-urban political imbalance of state legislatures and increased public support for a stronger role for state governments. A fourth and related factor is "the end of southern exceptionalism." Martha Derthick believes that the civil rights revolution and integration in the South created a situation in which "the case for the states can at last begin to be discussed on its merits."[6] Finally, the strong recovery of the U.S. economy from the 1981–1982 recession contributed to the resurgence of the states in the 1980s. This factor interacted in an important way with Ronald Reagan's devolutionary policies to highlight the role of the state. Typically, state governments

overreact to national recessions, battening down their fiscal hatches by cutting spending and raising taxes to balance their budgets. In late 1982 the strong recovery from recession meant that state coffers were filling up just as Reagan's federal aid retrenchment policies were being felt. This high volatility of state finances put state governments in a position to spend more and do more in those functional areas from which the federal government under Reagan was pulling back or signaling its intention to do so.

Taken together, these trends have produced a resurgence of the state role in American federalism. Evidence of this change appears in the states' response to Reagan's domestic budget cuts, his creation of new block grants, and related changes in federal grant-in-aid programs.[7] Data compiled by the U.S. Bureau of the Census show in the aggregate that state governments increased their role during the Reagan years. From 1983 to 1986, as the Reagan retrenchment and federalism policies took effect, state aid to localities increased by an average of 5.6 percent a year in real terms, that is, adjusted for inflation.[8] Total state spending rose by nearly the same percentage. Prior to that, from the mid–1970s to 1983, both state aid to localities and total state spending had been level in real terms. Considerable variation exists, however, in the character and mix of state expenditure increases, reflecting U.S. Supreme Court Justice Louis Brandeis's famous characterization of state governments as laboratories that can "try novel social and economic experiments without risk to the rest of the county."[9]

There are no ready calipers for measuring the activism and innovativeness of individual states. Studies by political scientists Jack L. Walker and Virginia Gray indicate that over time it has been the larger, older, and ideologically most liberal or pro-government states that have tended to be most innovative.[10] Other research suggests a broader distribution of state innovation in response to increasingly conservative national fiscal policies and devolutionary initiatives.[11] Southern and western states contributed to the rising role of state governments in the 1980s.

In the middle of the twentieth century, when state governments were in the doldrums, political scientist Morton Grodzins and other scholars downgraded their importance. In a famous essay, Grodzins said federalism is not a layer cake. Instead, he introduced the metaphor of a marble cake "characterized by an inseparable mingling of differently colored ingredients, the color appearing in vertical and diagonal strands and unexpected swirls." Continuing, Grodzins said, "As colors are mixed in the marble cake, so functions are mixed in the American governmental system."[12] Even for its time, this theory downgrading the role of the states seemed a serious exaggeration. It is patently wrong today to ignore the distinctive and crucial role of states in American federalism. Events occurring now in national policy making in Washington are highly likely to enhance further the role of state governments in American federalism. State governments are challenged today to take on new roles and responsibilities as never before in the twentieth century.

Building Blocks of the "Devolution Revolution"

The best description of the domestic program of the Republican leadership of the 104th Congress is one of a "Devolution Revolution." A major aim of this revolution is the creation of block grants. Block grants are fixed amounts of money distributed to state (and sometimes local) governments on an automatic formula-allocation basis that can be spent flexibly within major functional areas of government. There are two ways to create block grants. One is the conventional way, by consolidating existing, narrower so-called "categorical" grants into lump-sum formula allocations to states and localities. The second way, new and more important, is to create block grants by closing the end on what had previously been open-ended grants-in-aid to the states, thereby placing a limit on federal aid payments. The two biggest block grants proposed in the 104th Congress are for Medicaid and the Aid to Families with Dependent Children (AFDC) program. Together Medicaid and AFDC account for half of total federal grant-in-aid spending. (The purpose of Medicaid is to provide health care services for the poor, including nursing home and other types of institutional care for the elderly and disabled. The AFDC program provides cash assistance to poor families with children.) Under both programs, the federal government pays the states a share of the benefits they provide to eligible families and individuals. Republican leaders in the Congress seek to convert these two programs into lump-sum payments to the states allocated on a formula basis with aggregate caps on their annual spending.

In addition to converting Medicaid and AFDC into block grants, leaders of the Congress have proposed measures to convert other entitlement-type grants (for example, for foster care, school nutrition, and welfare-related child care) into block grants; to convert food stamps (now federal vouchers) into a block grant; to create block grants in the conventional consolidation mode, as in the case of work force development, combining nearly ninety existing programs into a three-part block grant; and to reduce the size of other grants-in-aid, that is, grants that are not currently block grants or recommended to be converted into block grants.

The 104th Congress, as noted, has also cut back on the regulatory requirements of federal aid programs— that is, the conditions Congress places on the receipt of federal grant funds. These conditions, often referred to as mandates, can involve requirements that are not intrinsic to the purpose of the funds provided. The mandates issue has created bad blood between national and state and local officials.

Taken together, this push to decentralize presents a challenge to the states. It rivals in historic importance the shifts made earlier in this century to centralize American governmental responsibilities during the New Deal era and the years of the Great Society. We don't know what the consequences will be. Predictions tend to be more influenced by ideology than by scholarship. Liberals predict a "race to the bottom," with states competing with each other to slash social benefits. Conservatives see a golden opportunity to integrate social programs, tone down social engineering, and generally enhance the efficiency of domestic government.

There is only one prediction that can be made with confidence, and that is that the response of state governments to the Devolution Revolution will be *varied*. Moreover, the effects of the changes in domestic policy now being contemplated in Washington are likely to shift over time.

History of Grants

One can go back to the pre–Constitutional period to find intergovernmental subventions to the states. During the period when the United States operated under the Articles of Confederation, the Continental Congress adopted the first grants-in-aid to the states, putting aside land for the support of public schools in territory west of the Ohio River. However, cash grants-in-aid were not significant until the twentieth century. The years of Woodrow Wilson's presidency started a slow and steady rise in cash grants to the states for major programmatic purposes. But even after Franklin Roosevelt's New Deal, federal aid accounted for only 10 percent of total state and local spending. It was under Lyndon Johnson that federal aid jumped to where it is now; from the mid–1960s to the present, federal grants-in-aid have represented about 30 percent of total state and local spending.

Federal grants-in-aid to states, localities, and nonprofit groups were estimated at $238.5 billion in the federal budget submitted for the fiscal year that began October 1, 1995. This included fifteen programs classified as block grants by the General Accounting Office and the Advisory Commission on Intergovernmental Relations (See Table 1). Over half of total outlays for current block grant programs is for surface transportation, provided as federal aid on a much more flexible and discretionary basis that in the past under the Intermodal Surface Transportation Efficiency Act of 1991.

The block grants now being debated in the 104th Congress represent a significant change in U.S. domestic policy because they mark a break with the past fifty years of steady accretion of entitlement-type federal grants-in-aid that operated on a fiscally open-ended basis. Under entitlement programs, states automatically receive payments equal to a fixed proportion of the income transfers (both cash and in-kind) they provide to poor families and individuals. These entitlement grants were actually entitlements to states. The states in turn determined the benefits eligible individuals and families received within the framework of federal laws and regulations.

Looked at on an across-the-board basis, there are three types of federal

Table 1
1995 Block Grants

Block Grant	Millions of Dollars (estimated)
Surface Transportation	18,773
Community Development Block Grant	3,186
Social Services Block Grant	2,800
Federal Transit Capital and Operating Assistance	2,284
CDBG States' Program	1,246
Low Income Home and Energy Assistance Program	1,319
Prevention and Treatment of Substance Abuse	1,234
Job Training Partnership Act, Title II-A	1,055
Child Care and Development Block Grant	935
Maternal and Child Health	684
Education (Federal-State-Local Partnerships)	370
Community Services	392
Community Mental Health Services	275
Preventative Health and Health Services	152
Assistance for Transition from Homelessness	29
Total	34,834

Source: Budget of the U.S. Government, Fiscal Year 1996, Budget Information for the States (Washington, D.C.: Government Printing Office, 1995).

grants-in-aid: those for operational purposes (education, child care, etc.), those for capital purposes (surface transportation, wastewater treatment), and entitlement grants for income-transfer to families and individuals (Medicaid and AFDC). Figure 1 illustrates the dramatic shift that would occur with the blocking of entitlement (income transfer) grants.

Block Grants Emerge

It was during the Johnson administration that block grants first emerged in the modern era. Johnson saw the writing on the wall in the form of growing state and local government resentment towards narrow-gauged and particularistic federal grants. The idea of block grants began to take hold in answer to what chairman of Johnson's Council of Economic Advisors, Walter Heller, called "the hardening of the categories."

Responding to pressures from gover-nors and mayors, President Johnson in 1966 proposed a block grant that would consolidate several public health grants into a single comprehensive grant for public health services. In 1967 Johnson took a bigger leap into grant blocking (although not enthusiastically) when his administration, with Republican urging, backed the creation of the law enforcement assistance grant. These funds were distributed on a formula basis to states with a requirement that 75 percent of the funds provided be passed on to localities.

Nixon's New Federalism

As already noted, contemporary block grants have generally been created through the consolidation of pre-existing categorical grants into broader grants with the combined stream of grant funds from the folded-in programs allocated to states and/or localities on an automatic formula basis. President Nixon's New Federalism

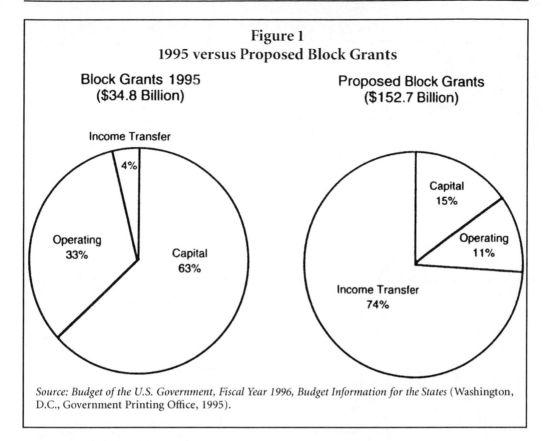

Figure 1
1995 versus Proposed Block Grants

Block Grants 1995
($34.8 Billion)

Income Transfer
4%

Operating
33%

Capital
63%

Proposed Block Grants
($152.7 Billion)

Capital
15%

Operating
11%

Income Transfer
74%

Source: Budget of the U.S. Government, Fiscal Year 1996, Budget Information for the States (Washington, D.C., Government Printing Office, 1995).

successfully advocated the creation of several such block grants, notably for community development, employment and training, and social services. Nixon also won passage of a general revenue sharing program in 1972, which provided flexible aid on a formula basis to states and localities. But this was not called a block grant, because the use of this aid was not limited to a particular function of government (for example, law enforcement or community development).

Among the three basic types of federal grants mentioned earlier (entitlement grants, operating grants, and capital grants), Nixon's New Federalism called for blocking two types of grants— operating and capital grants— but not entitlement grants. Nixon was a spender when it came to grants and domestic policies in general. Besides his revenue sharing program (which involved distributing $5 billion per

year in new funds to states and localities), Nixon's block grants included funds known as "sweeteners." The term referred to extra funds provided on top of the money contained in the categorical grants bundled together in a new block. Nixon added these sweeteners as an inducement to state and local officials to support his initiatives.

Again, Nixon did *not* recommend blocking entitlement grants. In advocating the sorting-out of functions in American federalism, Nixon argued that income transfers (cash, health care, foster care, school lunches, food stamps) should be made more — not less— national to assure equal treatment of the needy and to share this fiscal burden on a national basis. The consensus is that the community development block grant was the most successful of the block grants created under Nixon, moving away from huge renewal and slum clearance projects to more selective, targeted local development initiatives. Neither Nixon's Family Assistance Plan (FAP) for welfare reform nor his Family Health Insurance Plan (FHIP, which was similar to Clinton's 1993 health-reform proposal) was enacted.

Reagan's New Federalism

President Reagan's brand of "new federalism" (he didn't use the term, but the press did) departed from Nixon's approach on the idea of blocking entitlements. Reagan was much less committed to the idea that what have come to be referred to as "safety net" functions should be exclusively or mainly carried out by the national government. In 1982 Reagan advanced a "swap and turnback" plan, which proposed that the national government take over Medicaid. In exchange, the states would pick up the responsibility for the AFDC program. In short, Reagan was on the fence on this federalism issue. He proposed centralizing one income transfer program (Medicaid) and devolving another (AFDC). As it turned out, Reagan's "swap and turnback" plan was not even introduced in Congress.

In the 1981 Omnibus Budget Reconciliation Act (OBRA), Reagan won enactment of nine new programs dubbed "block grants" by his administration. Like Nixon's block grants, they extended to operating and capital functions, and *not* to entitlement-type programs. Three were mainly in the health field — for the prevention and treatment of substance abuse and mental health, preventive public health services, and maternal and child health care. None of these programs were especially large, and four of the "blocks" contained only one pre-existing categorical grant. Reagan's reputation as a grant blocker is overrated. However, his block grants have one important point in common with Nixon's. These grants lost value over time, both in nominal dollars and in real terms (that is, adjusted for inflation).

Enter the New(t) Federalism

The House Republican majority in the 104th Congress is decidedly not on the fence when it comes to block grants for welfare-type programs. Early on in the "First 100 Days," Speaker Newt Gingrich and his Republican colleagues set about creating block grants for entitlement grant programs with a vengeance. This is in sharp distinction to the policies of Nixon and Reagan. In effect, the new Republican majority in the Congress favors repealing the national "safety net" aspect of grants that provide aid in cash and in kind to poor families and individuals on an open-ended basis.

These devolutionary policies of the new majority in Congress do not stand alone. They are part and parcel of the strong movement in the country towards conservatism and limiting government, which is being played out in the legislative and budget processes. Some cynics see the new devolution as a tactic (even a cover) for conservatism and budget reduction. This doesn't gainsay the point that the new devolution is distinctive historically and likely to cause powerful shifts in the balance of federalism.

Essential Questions

James Madison is mis-characterized by conservatives who attribute to him the idea of devolving national programs to the states. Madison's constitutional purpose in 1787 was nation building — in effect, centralization. Indeed, his opening gambit at the Constitutional Convention was a plan that would have given the national government an absolute veto power over state laws. By the same token, classical public finance theory in the modern period assigns redistributional functions to the broadest population group to achieve equal (or close to equal) treatment for the needy and to share this fiscal burden widely. As a nation, we have done this (or at least moved strongly in this direction) since the 1930s. The United States is by no means first among the industrial democracies in centrally providing this safety-net function. However, in our own distinctive, incremental way of making policy, Americans have spent the last six decades building alliances, striking bargains, and forging political compromises that gave the federal government a leading role in setting, administering, and financing a wide range of social policies. Nowhere has this process been more inexorable than in the steady increase in the federal role in social welfare policy. Thus, blocking income-transfer programs to the poor represents a basic change in direction both for American federalism and for social policy.

Issues of Federal-State Relations

This is an exciting, fluid time for American federal-state relations. A recent report by the Advisory Commission on Intergovernmental Relations (ACIR) expressed the view that the U.S. Supreme Court is unlikely to alter its present interpretation of the Tenth Amendment, which reserves the powers not assigned to the national government as reserved to the states or to the people:

> By virtue of the Supreme Court's opinion in *Garcia v. San Antonio Metropolitan Transit Authority*, reversing *National League of Cities v. Usery*, states are virtually powerless to challenge federal action

in the courts on Tenth Amendment grounds.[13]

In a similar vein, recent ACIR reports have highlighted legislative preemption by the national government of state and local authority. The commission in 1992 called attention to "an ever widening range" of federal statutes in the commercial, monetary, civil rights, environmental, health, and safety fields.[14] Referring to the number of federal preemptions, the commission said they have

> *increased to the point that over half of all such preemptions in the nation's constitutional history have been enacted by the Congress only since 1969.* These preemptions include prohibitions of economic regulation and other activity by the state and local governments, as well as requirements that states enforce federal laws, conform their own laws to federal standards, and take on new responsibilities. Federal preemptions also may override state and local decisions and prevent states and local governments from pursuing policies preferred by their citizens.[15] (Italics added.)

However, there is now movement towards the states in all three branches of American government on these and other federalism issues. This is reflected in the Court's decision in *United States v. Lopez* and Justice Clarence Thomas's dissent in the term limits decision (*U.S. Terms Limits, Inc. v. Thornton*), both of which were handed down in 1995.[16] In the *Lopez* case the Court held that Congress did not have the power to make it a federal crime to possess a gun near a school. Going even further, Justice Thomas's dissenting opinion in the *Term Limits* decision, concurred in by Justices William Rehnquist, Sandra Day O'Connor, and Antonin Scalia, would have strikingly limited the power of the federal government and given the states extensive new authority. The Court found state-imposed term limits for elected members of the House to be unconstitutional since "the power to add qualifications was not within the original powers of the states, and thus was not reserved to the states by the Constitution's Tenth Amendment." The two events— one a decision overturning a federal law and the other a powerful dissent — have renewed the debate in the Court about the relative roles of the enumerated powers of the federal government in Article I of the Constitution and the reserved powers of the Tenth Amendment. The Tenth Amendment states, "The powers not delegated to the United States by the Constitution, nor prohibited by it to the States, are reserved to the States respectively, or to the people."

Indeed, the rhetoric of federal-state relations needs to be reassessed today. This rhetoric has a familiar ring to it. The problem of federal government domination of the states is lambasted as "Leviathan." It is derided as "Mother Knows Best." It is described in terms of intrusion by "pointy-headed" federal bureaucrats in state and local affairs. It is discussed in terms that emphasize mandates without money. It is depicted as the "proliferation" of categorical grants-in-aid. Data provided by the ACIR show an increase from 1993 to 1995 in the number of federal grants-in-aid from 594 to 634.[17] While I have always been skeptical of such raw counts of aid categories, certainly it is fair to say that new block grants will slow such proliferation, although it has to be added that old habits die hard.

Other federal-state issues involve organizational requirements. Federal laws and regulations often tell states how to structure their government, requiring them to set up agencies in certain ways and to create regional and other special bodies that may or may not be the way state and local officials and the public want to operate. On this question, as on others, the situation could change with block grants, but it is unlikely to change the whole picture. In the transportation field, for example, the 1991 Intermodal Surface Transportation Efficiency Act prescribes a regional structure for planning, public participation, and decision making. On the other hand, in the environmental field, a rollback has begun as Congress overhauls laws and changes federal agency roles and staffing, though again it is not clear what the eventual outcome will be. As for federal-aid waivers, they can be thought of in a way suggested by Martha Derthick: "as reversing the historic presumption in intergovernmental relations."[18]

> The historic presumption is that the states are the primary, the bedrock, governments. Domestic functions fall initially to them. Over time, the federal government constrained them by attaching conditions to aid, but it was still up to them in the first instance to decide what to do. The constitutional presumption was in their favor. They were free to do things unless, after the fact, the federal government said they couldn't.
>
> Waivers have reversed the presumption. They assume that power and discretion rest initially with the federal government. It is the primary domestic government. It makes the rules, and if the states want to do something, they must begin by asking its permission.[19]

These are *structural* and *process* issues. We also need to look at issues involving *functions* of government. Increasingly in the twentieth century, particularly in the middle part of the century and continuing up into the 1970s, the national government seemed willing, even eager, to step into any and all functional areas of domestic public affairs. During this century, especially in a response to the Great Depression, with the enactment of welfare-state policies, and under the civil rights revolution and in the environmental movement, a heightened role was assigned to the central government. In the Great Society period, Medicaid was the "400 pound gorilla" in terms of federal intervention in a functional area. State officials often claim Medicaid is not a grant-in-aid; it is a mandate to serve and spend. Maybe it is a good one. Nonetheless, it is portrayed as a federal government initiative that has reduced the fiscal flexibility of the states, growing rapidly in the 1980s, in some years by as much as 19.5 percent. The other side of this argument claims that Medicaid has been used by the states as a way to shift health and health-related activities into the federal aid stream.

In essence what is involved in the debate over changes in Medicaid and AFDC is a tradeoff between *policy goals* and *federalism goals*. Both programs represent mechanisms for aiding needy groups in the society. These programs, as noted, are not an entitlement to individuals or families, because the states set the eligibility rules and benefit amounts. Rather, they require that states serve certain groups along with setting other requirements about the way these functions have to be carried out. People of good will can argue (and many have) that the social purposes encompassed in these two programs are best advanced centrally and that the desirability of advancing them outweighs concerns about the role of states in American federalism.

Some readers may object to the focus on "welfare-type" functions in this analysis. But note the wording. These functions refer to the broad field of social policy. A similarly intense debate is now going on in one other broad functional area — environmental policy. The rollback efforts in environmental policy now underway raise equally profound questions about how states will perform if greater discretion is assigned to them. In other major areas of domestic affairs — for example, transportation and law enforcement and corrections — federalism issues are more settled.

The Intermodal Surface Transportation Efficiency Act of 1991 has quieted debate in this field, pending how the new law works, which is not yet known. In the law enforcement and corrections fields, federalism issues that involve the courts are regarded by many state officials as sufficiently serious to require strong remediation. In any event, the issues here are different from those in the arena of social policy. To sum up, there are bound to be differences of view in the body politic that on the one hand reflect a strong concern about some functional area that advocates believe should be centralized and on the other reflect a strong concern that state and local officials may be undercut by such centralization policies. These questions never will be settled for all times. There is no magic arrangement for sorting out responsibilities in American federalism.

Strategies for Strengthening the States

It is useful to consider next different strategies that can be taken to strengthen the role of the states in American federalism. One is legislative and relates to the functional realignment just discussed. A second is constitutional and focuses on structural changes in the basic relationship of the national government and the states. A third is operational.

Functional Realignment

Functional realignment in American federalism is often portrayed as a "sorting-out" process— that is, sorting out functions of government between the national government and the states. Candidates for political office often use this metaphor to indicate their theory of American government. The positions taken in this sorting-out debate involve more than matters of political structure. They involve assumptions about how much money should be spent for particular purposes, how policies should be formed and implemented, and what the results will ultimately be in the lives of citizens. For example, the current debate about welfare block grants can be viewed in terms of federalism and governmental structures, but the more important consideration for many observers involves the amount of money that will be spent on the poor.

There is, as just stated, no one intrinsic way to view the proper alignment of functions in American federalism. Take as an example the function of welfare. It is common among people who write about federalism to argue that welfare should be primarily or exclusively a national government function. The reasons for this appear to be good ones: transferring income should be national because people move from state to state and all eligible people in the country should be treated the same way; also, there are efficiency and equity benefits from sharing the burden of the treatment of the poor across the whole fisc. Indeed, what has come to be known as classical Musgrave public finance theory reflects this position.[20]

Yet, welfare today is hotly debated in terms that suggest it is viewed by the public and most politicians as far more than a check-writing function. Unlike social security retirement benefits, for example, there has been an escalation of the rhetoric about transforming welfare policies from payment systems into *service* systems. The welfare debates of the past ten years have been predominantly about *social-service interventions* to change behavior. This was the aim of the Family Support Act of 1988. The welfare debate currently is not, as it was in the 1970s, about minimum payment levels, benefit disregards, and marginal reduction rates along the lines of arguments

for the so-called "negative income tax" approach to welfare reform. More than anything else, the debate today is about how to prevent teenage pregnancy and reduce the number of children born out of wedlock to fathers who are unwilling to take responsibility for them in the kind of traditional family setting that, like it or not, is strongly favored by a sizable majority of the people who participate in elections in America. To a great extent, these welfare debates are about interventions that can prevent dependency on the part of poor parents (mostly single women) through regulatory requirements and remedial services and activities such as job placement and counseling, training, education, and the provision of child care to enable welfare family heads to participate in the labor market.

Whether this behavior-modification function focusing on social services should be assigned to the national government or to the states is not an easy question to answer. Generally speaking, the literature on federalism suggests that income-transfer functions should be centralized, whereas service-type functions should be decentralized. The point is often made that the provision of services (e.g., education, job training, child care) is not a type of activity that can be orchestrated, and even more so that can be managed, by the central government in a nation as vast as the United States. One benefit of federalism is that it allows for the flexibility of state and local action to assess and deal with social service needs in ways that reflect different regions representing a variety of conditions, attitudes and aspirations. One can object to this argument, but it needs to be noted that the main body of writing about federalism has treated this decentralized service attribute of the genre as an advantage of the federal form.

One can also argue that health care for the poor under Medicaid is more of a service function that a check-writing function. Although it is not the aim of this chapter to make a case for a particular way of realigning functions in American federalism, it should be clear that there is no one sorting-out of function in federalism for all times. Ideas and purposes change. Whereas in the 1970s, many people (both experts and non-experts) viewed welfare and health care for the poor as basically an income-transfer function, this is not the case today. In short, the way one views a function has a lot to do with where one puts it.

Structural Change

Another way to change the balance of American federalism is by altering its constitutional structure. Although the framers rejected the idea, the U.S. Constitution could be amended to institute a state veto of federal laws or a process that would require their reconsideration. There was sentiment to do so on the part of Anti-federalists at the Philadelphia Convention; however, James Madison at the time was in precisely the opposite camp, favoring "a sweeping veto by the national government on all state laws."[21] Madison the politician recanted a decade later, consorting with his fellow Virginia, Thomas Jefferson. He then urged a realignment of American government, ironically in much the same way that today's new majority in the Congress is using the party machinery to devolve responsibilities. In the Kentucky Resolution, which Madison authored (Jefferson authored the Virginia Resolution in the same year, 1798), he asserted that the Constitution (his very own handiwork) created a *compact* of the several states. This interpretation came to haunt Madison's legacy when it was used as an argument for succession by southern states in the middle of the nineteenth century.

Similar to proposals to allow some proportion of the states (usually two-thirds) to veto national laws, recommendations have been advanced to add the word "expressly" to the reference to "delegated" powers assigned to the national government in the Tenth Amendment. It is also possible to follow the lead of other federal countries, for example Canada, Australia, and Germany, where regional governments have a formal role in national government policy making. In Canada and Australia, there are official "Premiers' Conferences" that participate in central government policy making. They meet regularly, share information on common problems with national government officials, and consider and take joint actions. The intergovernmental specialists who staff these bodies have a role in central government decision making on a continuing basis, especially in periods when the Premiers' Conferences are not in session. In Germany, the Länder have strong, explicit administrative responsibilities with less rigorous oversight powers available to the Federal Council than is the case of the national government under U.S. federalism.

Another avenue for structural reform is to change the amendatory process to permit the states to initiate constitutional amendments. Now, the Congress has the power to do this. Indeed, the framers intended that there should be a state route to amendatory reform in crafting the Convention process, which arguably never worked as intended. (The Advisory Commission on Intergovernmental Relations recently recommended that there be a constitutional provision for the call for amendatory conventions that are limited to particular issue areas or proposals.) Still another constitutional avenue for change would add specific constraints to Article I limiting the conditions under which the national government could influence activities of the states. A proposal to do this by legislative action has been advanced by Sen. Hank Brown, R-Colo. and others. Other, less fundamental institutional changes could be accomplished by law, for example, by strengthening the unfunded mandates law enacted in 1995, or by executive action. The unfunded mandate law only applies to future mandates and even then is not high powered.

Using Clout

A third strategy for strengthening the role of the states can be viewed as operational. States already have consequential powers for influencing both the character and execution of domestic programs. Few things demonstrate this more clearly than the emergence in 1995 of the block grant strategy in the House. It was Republican governors who originally pressed for the block grants at a meeting with Speaker Newt Gingrich and Senate Leader Robert Dole at the November 1994 Republican governors conference in Williamsburg, Virginia. Governors as a group — Republicans and Democrats alike — have been pushing since then for these kinds of devolutionary changes in domestic policy. Across the board the organizations representing state governments, such as the National Governors' Association and the National Conference of State Legislatures, have become stronger and smarter. The officials of state government are talented men and women anxious and able to wield strong influence in many areas of domestic public affairs. It used to be assumed that the national government had a monopoly on talented governmental experts and executives. Whether this was ever true, it is not true today. States have won a place at the table, more precisely at the many tables where decisions are made about the character and execution of domestic policy. They are using this clout right now to reshape American federalism.

Conclusion

The jury is out on how the Devolution Revolution will be encompassed in laws that realign functions in American federalism. Some observers have concerns about the functional realignment plans. The essential point here is that this functional realignment may be so great in the final analysis that state government officials may decide that structural and institutional change strategies are no longer as important as they once were seen to be. A major question for federal-state relations is whether to push for constitutional changes to re-balance federalism or to wait and see what happens in the wake of the functional realignment processes currently under way.

In my view, the constitutional route is the wrong road to travel. Devolutionary policy changes and structural and administrative reforms by the states should be the focus of attention for governors, legislators, and other state officials and their partisans. Everyone who cares about the role states play in our governmental system will have an overflowing plate in responding to the new challenges being put to them. In this setting, it would not be wise to devote the time and energy necessary to educate the public and press for constitutional change.

What is more, the constitutional route is not an easy one to take. Opening up the Pandora's box of constitutional change could stimulate efforts that involve divisive, emotional issues that should not be added to the Constitution. The U.S. Constitution is general and short. This is part of its genius. State governments have their moment in the sun right now. They should seize it rather than commit huge amounts of energy and argumentation to constitutional change.

Notes

1. Stanley Elkins and Eric McKitrick, *The Age of Federalism: The Early American Republic, 1788–1800* (New York: Oxford University Press, 1993), 43.

2. See Robert D. Putnam, "Bowling Alone: America's Declining Social Capital," *Journal of Democracy* 6 (January 1995): 65–78.

3. Roscoe C. Martin, *The Cities in the Federal System* (New York: Atherton Press, 1965).

4. See Richard P. Nathan, "Defining Modern Federalism," in *North American and Comparative Federalism Essays for the 1990s*, ed. by Harry N. Scheiber (Berkeley, Calif.: Institute of Governmental Studies Press, 1992).

5. Advisory Commission on Intergovernmental Relations, *The Question of State Government Capability* (Washington, D.C.: Advisory Commission on Intergovernmental Relations, January 1985).

6. Martha Derthick, "American Federalism: Madison's 'Middle Ground' in the 1980s," *Public Administration Review* 47 (January/February 1987): 72.

7. See Richard P. Nathan and Fred C. Doolittle, *Consequences of Cuts: The Effects of the Reagan Domestic Program on State and Local Governments* (Princeton, N.J.: Princeton University Press, 1983); and Nathan and Doolittle, *Reagan and the States* (Princeton, N.J.: Princeton University Press, 1987).

8. Steven D. Gold and Corina L. Eckl, "State Budget Actions in 1984," Fiscal Affairs Program, National Conference of State Legislatures, Legislative Paper 45, September 1984. See also Steven D. Gold, "Developments in State Finances, 1983 to 1986," *Public Budgeting and Finance*, 7 (Spring 1987).

9. *New State Ice Co. v. Ernest A. Liebmann*, 285 U.S. 262–311 (1931).

10. Jack L. Walker, "The Diffusion of Innovation among the American States," *American Political Science Review* 63 (September 1969) 880–899. Walker's analysis is for the period 1960–1969; Virginia Gray, "Innovations in the States: A Diffusion Study," *American Political Science Review* 67 (December 1973): 1174–1185.

11. See Nathan and Doolittle, *Consequences of Cuts*, and *Reagan and the States*.

12. Morton Grodzins, "The Federal System," in *Goals for Americans: The Report of the President's Commission on National Goals* (New York: Columbia University Press, 1960), 265.

13. Advisory Commission on Intergovernmental Relations, "Federal Regulation of State and Local Governments: The Mixed Record of the 1980s," A-126, July 1993, iii.

14. Advisory Commission on Intergovernmental Relations, "Federal Statutory Preemption of State and Local Authority: History, Inventory, and Issues," A-121, September 1992. See also "Federal Regulation of State and Local Governments: The Mixed Record of the 1980s," A-126, July 1993; and "Intergovernmental Decisionmaking for Environmental Protection and Public Works," A-122, November 1992.

15. *Ibid.*, 1.

16. *United States v. Lopez* (No. 93-1260) 1995. *U.S. Term Limits, Inc. v. Thornton* (No. 93-1456 and 93-1828) 1995.

17. Advisory Commission on Intergovernmental Relations, "Characteristics of Federal Grant-in-Aid Programs to State and Local Governments: Grants Funded FY 1995," M-195, June 1995.

18. Letter to the author, August 29, 1995.

19. *Ibid.*

20. Refers to the work of economist Richard A. Musgrave who pioneered public finance theory. See *Public Finance in Theory and Practice*, 3d ed. (New York: McGraw-Hill, 1980), 524.

21. Elkins and McKitrick, *The Age of Federalism*, 83.

Chapter 24

The States and the City Governments

DAVID R. BERMAN

Several decades ago, political scientist William Anderson wrote a book entitled *The Nation and the States, Rivals or Partners?*[1] The question embedded in this title — whether the relationship between the national government and the states should be one of rivalry or partnership — has long divided scholars and politicians alike. Similar controversy attends the relationship between state and local governments. Just as states raise the banner of "states' rights" in trying to fend off what they see as overextensions of federal power, localities rally to the cry of "home rule" in an effort to protect themselves from what they view as state intrusions on the local domain. When it comes to money, states and local governments, like states and the federal government, fight over spending responsibilities and access to tax resources. And the problems that state and local officials encounter when dealing with the federal government — mandates, preemptions, and lack of assistance with pressing financial needs — are mirrored in state-local relations.

Although not all shifts in federal-state power relationships have been in this direction, the federal government is generally moving toward greater devolution of authority, the welfare reform legislation of 1996 being the most dramatic example. The emerging pattern of state-local relations is, in many respects, one of greater centralization at the state level. Over the past few decades, economic, political, and legal pressures have intensified state officials' interest in matters — such as education and land use planning — that have traditionally been addressed at the local level. Local governments worry constantly about the threat to their authority posed by mandates and preemptions, and often find themselves in conflict with their states

Originally published as "State-Local Relations: Authority, Finance, Policies," *The Municipal Year Book*, 2000. Published by the International City/County Management Association, Washington, D.C. Reprinted with permission of the publisher.

over specific areas of policy, such as welfare and environmental protection.

State financial assistance to local government, ordinarily a matter for dispute, has been on the upswing. With improved economics bringing both an increase in revenues and a decline in Medicare and welfare expenditures, several states have increased their aid to local government. Nevertheless, aid to general-purpose local governments (cities, towns, and counties) has had to compete with demands for tax relief as well as with increased demands for spending in various areas, particularly education, health care, and corrections. One approach to both managerial and financial difficulties—used successfully by many local governments—is the creation of interlocal partnerships for service delivery.

General Developments and Patterns

Local governments are part of a complex intergovernmental system in which actions taken by one unit of government often have direct or indirect effects on the others. Within this system, decisions made by federal officials often have a ripple effect on state-local relations sometimes increasing and sometimes decreasing local governments' dependence on the states. Local officials also are function in an environment where battles are being fought in the state legislatures and the state courts—for example, over control of the telecommunications industry, the taking of private property. Internet taxation, and the regulation of tobacco—could at any moment be greatly altered by preemptive federal action.

The Federal Context

Two changes in federal grant and regulatory policies—the decline in federal aid

and the increase in federal mandates— have dramatically rearranged the broad pattern of state-local intergovernmental relations. From the 1960s to the late 1970s, the nation experienced what one observer described as the "galloping intergovernmentalization" of nearly all governmental functions.[2]

As part of this trend, the number of federal aid programs rose from 132 in 1960 to more than 540 by 1980; the number of dollars involved grew from $7 billion to more than $90 billion during the same period. A robust economy that fed federal revenues made this explosive growth in federal aid possible. Life began to change drastically in the late 1970s when, as the federal government's fiscal strength began to wane, Congress began to scale down the growth of federal aid programs. In 1978, federal aid made up approximately 27% of state-local spending, a figure that had fallen to 17% by 1989. Although federal grants have increased since 1989 and are now up to about 22% of state-local spending, much of the increase in federal aid has gone to state rather than to local governments.

Beginning in the mid–1970s, the federal government shifted from the use of subsidies to the use of mandates in its efforts to encourage states and localities to take various courses of action. Since then, costly federal mandates have made matters doubly difficult for state and local officials. Although in 1995, through the Unfunded Mandates Reform Act, Congress took a step toward making federal mandating more difficult, some authorities doubt — on the basis of the history of similar legislation in the states— that the federal mandate law will be effective,[3] and implementation has indeed been fraught with difficulties— from controversy over how mandates are defined to difficulties estimating costs;[4] moreover, Congress can waive the requirement for full federal funding by a majority vote of the Senate or House.[5]

Although a renewed federal-local partnership seems a long way off, there have been some bright spots in this regard. In 1999, for example, President Clinton signed a new executive order on federalism that greatly strengthened state and local officials' ability to influence proposed federal rules that affect their authority. Later in the year, Congress was considering legislation that would require it to consult with state and local officials on such matters. Nevertheless, local officials have reason for continued concern about their ability to influence state policy, and basic changes in the intergovernmental system in recent years have made this concern, if anything, more pronounced.

Politics and Policy in the States

Given state officials' importance in shaping the environment in which local governments operate, it comes as no surprise that some of the most active lobbying at the state level is on the part of local officials or individual cities and counties. Local officials are concerned about many issues, but none is more important than state actions that affect local financial capacity.[6] Quite simply, local officials want more revenue authority, more state aid, more discretion in spending funds, and fewer costly mandates.

For local officials, timely involvement in state decision making — that is, having the opportunity to express the local point of view before decisions are made — is always the goal. Although they are often successful in securing a change or preventing some unwanted action (though in the latter case they sometimes have to depend on a gubernatorial veto), local officials do not think they enjoy a privileged position. Indeed, many feel that legislators regard them as special interests seeking favors, rather than as partners in the governing system.[7] From time to time, legislators have proposed laws to limit the lobbying and electoral activities of organizations, such as municipal leagues and county associations, that are partially supported by public funds.

Although local officials focus much of their attention on state legislatures, other individuals and entities — governors, administrative bodies, state courts, and the voters who participate in initiatives and referendums — are not to be overlooked in the politics of state-local relations. Governors set the agenda for taxing and spending programs and are often able to influence the fate of legislation that affects localities. Much of the state government's day-to-day involvement in local affairs occurs through administrative supervision. Nearly every state now has an office of community or local affairs that functions as an information clearinghouse and, at the request of local governments, provides technical assistance on matters such as local finance and planning.

Over the years, state courts have built up an enormous body of case law regarding what local governments can and cannot do — and thus play a major role in determining the parameters of home rule (or general discretionary authority) on the local level. State courts have also had an increasingly important impact on local taxing, spending, and regulatory powers in general as well as in a number of specific policy areas, such as education, environmental protection, land use planning, and housing.

Traditionally, state courts have made it difficult for municipalities and counties to challenge state governments in court. Over the past few years, however, state courts have become more inclined to regard local governments as "judicial persons" with standing to sue their "parent" state governments on a number of matters, such as the state's failure to meet constitutional funding obligations. In addition, state courts have become more willing to examine basic legal questions, such as whether state actions violate state constitutional bans on special or local laws.[8]

Voters have come to exert a strong direct influence on decisions affecting local finance and operations. One type of reform currently being put before voters prohibits a legislative body from increasing taxes or spending unless two-thirds or more of its members agree to do so. Another popular reform requires voter approval for tax and spending increases above a certain level. In addition to influencing local finances, voters have often approved measures that strip local control over other matters. Interest groups have been able to circumvent local authority by putting proposals on statewide ballots that are designed to negate ordinances enacted by a few municipalities. Even though residents of particular localities have shown their support for certain local actions (e.g., controlling rents, extending legal protections to homosexuals), their decisions have been reversed by the wishes of voters in the rest of the state.[9]

Local Authority

Although judges have at one time or another expressed the view that local self-government is an inherent right, by far the dominant legal view is that cities, counties, and other local governments are the "legal creatures" of their states. Applying Dillon's Rule (after John F. Dillon, a 19th-century Iowa jurist and authority on municipal law), state courts have also commonly concluded that (1) local governments have only those powers expressly granted them by the state and (2) courts must construe those powers narrowly. In Dillon's Rule

states, local governments must obtain specific legislative authority for virtually everything they wish to do. As a result, state legislators—busy passing bills that affect one or a few local governments—are kept immersed in minor local matters at the expense of policy issues of statewide interest. For example, in 1999 in Virginia—a state that has long operated under Dillon's Rule—the general assembly took the time to pass a bill authorizing a specific county to appoint eight members to its local industrial authority, rather than the seven allowed by general law.

Home Rule

To circumvent Dillon's Rule, several states have constitutional provisions or statutes that allow local governments to obtain home-rule authority, which gives them the right to make decisions without specific grants of authority. Home-rule provisions not only give local governments the authority to adopt their own policies but also limit the states' power to intervene in local affairs. Although some state constitutions or laws give local governments exclusive authority to deal with "municipal" or "local" matters, courts have found it difficult, in practice, to distinguish between local affairs and issues of statewide concern — and have usually resolved uncertainties in favor of the states. In other states, statutes or constitutional provisions avoid the problem of distinguishing between state and local concerns by taking a devolution of powers approach — that is, by authorizing local units to carry out any function or exercise any power not expressly forbidden or preempted by the state (in essence, an approach that is the reverse of Dillon's Rule).

In addition to the protections afforded by home rule, laws in most states now require that state legislatures deal with municipalities and counties through general rather than special legislation: in other words, states are prohibited from enacting laws that affect only a particular local jurisdiction. In practice, however, the protection afforded by such laws may be limited. Many states, for example, assign classifications to municipalities (e.g., first-class city, second-class city) on the basis of factors such as population or total property value. Such classifications determine the form of government and the powers of the municipality, and once a municipality is classified, it is subject to all state laws that apply to that classification. Although the practice of classifying municipalities should work to support prohibitions on special legislation, general laws sometimes amount to special laws because only one municipality falls into a certain classification.

The scope of local authority in every state is highly influenced by judicial decisions. Even when home-rule laws are essentially the same, state courts' interpretations of local authority vary widely. Wyoming's experience provides an example: in the hope that Wyoming courts would interpret the law liberally, as Kansas courts had, Wyoming patterned its home-rule provision on the one used in Kansas. Wyoming courts, however, did not follow the precedent set by Kansas courts, choosing instead to keep Dillon's Rule alive in the state.[10]

Over the years, the view that local governments should have home rule or greater discretionary authority has gained ground: some degree of home rule is available for municipalities in 48 states, and county governments have such powers in 37 states.[11] The fact that home rule is authorized, however, does not mean that local governments will opt to apply for it — or indeed, that they will exercise the authority that home rule gives them. Some cities, for example, have not sought home-

rule status because the legislature has already given them the discretion to do many of the specific things they want to do — which makes securing a charter seem less necessary. Even in Dillon's Rule states, legislatures may have adopted a large number of statutes giving local governments discretion on a broad range of matters. Particularly — but not exclusively — in jurisdictions that have recently attained home rule, both county and municipal officials are often uncertain about how much authority they have, and therefore feel more comfortable receiving specific grants of authority from the legislature. Thus, despite some progress in achieving increased local discretion, many local officials are still caught up in a pattern of constantly approaching the legislature for authority or assistance or to head off unwanted action.

Scope of State Involvement

On average, about one-fifth of the hundreds of measures introduced yearly in state legislatures significantly affect local governments. State laws affect local authority, structures, procedures, and finances. Of the laws affecting procedures, open meeting and open record requirements are among the most common. The first of these has posed particular difficulties for local officials, and some critics have argued that open meetings legislation has effectively hamstrung local officials and their staffs, preventing them from doing their work and creating unreasonable criminal offenses.[12] Other types of state laws affecting local government concern elections, incorporation, annexation, consolidation, and intergovernmental service agreements. In the areas of finance and personnel, state laws often set debt limits, mandate public budget hearings, require a referendum for bond issues, and outline property assessment methods; and most local governments must abide by state laws requiring employee training and workers' compensation.[13]

In nearly every session, state legislators tinker with laws that they believe will improve local government operations or service delivery. Legislative efforts sometimes stem from a genuine desire to make local government more accountable, effective, and efficient. In the case of mandates, however, the motivation may be to shift program costs to local governments. In the case of prohibitions or preemptions, legislative action is often a matter of acceding to the demands of private groups that are eager to avoid local taxes or regulations.

In extreme cases, state governments may suspend local autonomy and take over local government operations: in some cases, the takeover has taken on the aura of a crusade on the part of state officials, who feel that they are coming to the rescue of citizens faced with incompetent local officials or corrupt local governing systems.[14] Though states are cautious about taking such action, there have been several takeovers of school districts and general-purpose local governments in recent years. Because such a level of intervention clearly conflicts with the norms of local autonomy and runs the risk of considerable resistance — not only from local officials but from community residents as well — states generally make a point of very carefully justifying their actions.

The Mandate Problem

State governments often rely on their legislative and regulatory authority to compel local units to assume responsibility for various programs— along with the costs. Individual states impose many more mandates on their local governments than does the federal government, although some of the most expensive mandates are federal mandates that states have passed on to localities. The costs of mandates are likely to be substantial. A Connecticut study, for example, found that some 700 statutory state mandates and a host of additional administrative regulations accounted for half of all municipal expenditures.[15] On the basis of a range of studies, localities appear to devote from 20 percent to 90 percent of their expenditures to the implementation of federal and state mandates.

Even when local officials are in sympathy with the goals of state mandates, they are nevertheless aware that all mandates distort local priorities, restrict managerial flexibility, and impose costs that have to be paid through local revenues. The extent of the unfunded mandate problem varies from state to state. For example, a study of Ohio estimated that about 1 in 12 laws passed in that state in recent years imposed an unfunded mandate on local governments.[16] A similar study in Tennessee put about one in four laws into this category.[17]

Mandates address matters ranging from the important to the inconsequential. A study of Kansas suggests that the state had a compelling interest in the adoption and enforcement of only about 100 of the 941 mandates it had imposed on local governments. About 300 of the mandates are obsolete and widely ignored; for example, one mandate, more than a century old, requires counties to pay the burial expenses of Civil War veterans and limits the payment to $20 per headstone. The remaining mandates evidence excessive intervention, prescribing in detail what has to be done, how it is to be done, or both. For example, one mandate requires that county stationery be of uniform design; others describe how local officials are to get rid of noxious weeds, build sidewalks, or construct culverts. In Kansas, state intervention through mandates has not been deterred by home rule but has actually increased since cities (in 1960) and counties (in 1974) were granted this protection.[18]

Local officials have little objection to the goals of many mandates; they may even welcome the political "cover" that mandates provide for the implementation of programs that are unpopular with some segments of their communities (e.g., low-income housing).[19] Moreover, local officials themselves are sometimes responsible for mandates. In 1997, for example, county executives and county commissioners asked the Tennessee legislature to require that counties adopt certain personnel policies. From the local point of view, these policies did not impose extra burdens and were necessary to ensure that all county officials are in compliance with state and federal laws. Mandates may also be the result of conflicts among city and county officials: when city officials want to make county officials assume particular responsibilities or county officials want to shift some costs to city governments, one side or the other may make a successful appeal to the legislature that results in a mandate.[20] In addition, some mandates are the project of "end runs" by local government employees who succeed through state legislation in securing benefits that they could not obtain through collective bargaining: for example, some states require local governments to pay police officers and firefighters what some observers consider overly generous pension benefits. In 1999, for example, the Florida legislature enacted an unfunded mandate for more than 100 cities that increased municipal police and fire pension benefits at an estimated cost of at least $55 million per year.

Because local governments are financially dependent on state legislators, local officials are reluctant to alienate legislators by opposing state mandates.[21] Nevertheless, local officials have been anything but passive on this issue. They have compiled comprehensive assessments of the financial impacts of mandates, intensified their lobbying activities for mandate relief, taken their complaints directly to the public through media campaigns, attached notices to tax and utility bills that blame mandates for increased taxes, sponsored ballot measures opposing mandates, and brought court suits challenging the validity of mandates. Because courts have been inclined to defer to the judgment of the legislatures in such matters and to make it difficult for localities to bring suit, local governments have had only limited success in challenging state mandates through the judicial system.[22] They have, however, had some success in securing voter support for measures that attempt to reduce the number of mandates or that require the states to pick up the implementation costs. Local governments have also succeeded in securing other types of anti-mandate legislative and administrative reforms.

Strategies for Coping with Mandates

Local officials and their lobbying organizations constantly seek state support to cover the costs of new mandates. Sometimes they succeed, but at other times the legislatures simply give local governments more authority to raise the necessary revenues to meet the costs of new mandates. This is a less desirable outcome, because it means that local officials run the risk of incurring the wrath of their taxpayers.

Other strategies for coping with mandates center on the mandate process. More than 40 states have fiscal note requirements, which require that state agencies (in some places, commissions on intergovernmental relations) estimate the costs that state laws or regulations impose on localities. In several states, fiscal notes are combined with a requirement that the state reimburse localities for the expense of undertaking the mandated activity. In other states, fiscal notes are used simply to call attention to the costs to be incurred by local governments.

When employed alone (i.e., without a reimbursement requirement), fiscal notes appear to have only a limited effect on legislative behavior. Even if legislators are made more aware of the financial burden that they are passing on to local governments, they will not necessarily refuse to impose the costs—which are, after all, assumed not by the state but by the local governments. The primary value of fiscal notes as an anti-mandate strategy seems to be in providing local governments with lobbying ammunition.[23]

Several states have adopted statutory or constitutional limits on their ability to impose mandates on local governments, and some laws call for full or partial state reimbursement of the cost of new mandates. In some states, such as California, the state must either pick up the costs for mandated programs or give localities the authority to raise taxes to finance them. Most laws have a "safety valve" allowing the legislature to pass an unfunded mandate through a supermajority (two-thirds or three-fourths) vote. In several states, mandates have been restricted through voter-approved constitutional amendments. Voters appear more likely to approve such measures when proponents link them to the goals of reducing local property taxes and preserving local control over spending priorities.[24]

As a deterrent to unfunded mandates, a statutory or constitutional requirement for reimbursement appears to be more effective than a fiscal note. And, at least initially, reimbursement requirements added to the constitution with the backing of the voters may be more effective in influencing legislative behavior than those created

by statute. Over time, however, the deterrent effect brought about by the expression of public opinion may diminish. Extensive funding for mandates does not appear to be the major effect of reimbursement provisions; instead, the provisions seem more likely to deter the creation of mandates or to bring about modifications that render them less expensive.[25]

In several states, such as Florida, Maine, New Hampshire, and North Carolina, anti-mandate laws appear to have helped reduce the total number of mandates. Legislatures in some states, however, have simply ignored reimbursement requirements (there is no penalty for doing so) or have gotten around them by earmarking as mandate reimbursement a part of the funding already allocated for state aid to localities—in effect, deducting mandate reimbursement costs from local aid programs.[26]

Perhaps the most effective way to deter mandates is to require a two-thirds vote to impose one.[27] But as one expert has warned, "despite the stringency of the anti-mandate legislation, when a state legislature has a will to pass an unfunded mandate, a way will ultimately present itself."[28] And even if a state decides to relinquish a long-standing requirement that localities provide a particular service, municipalities or counties may have no choice but to fund and provide the service anyway, because their citizens want it continued.

In addition to fiscal notes and reimbursement requirements, states have considered or adopted a variety of other anti-mandate measures, including the following:

- Requiring an agency (such as the state advisory commission on intergovernmental relations) to compile and annually update a catalogue of all mandates; such a catalogue would include assessments of the fiscal impact of new mandates.
- Requiring state agencies to review current

mandates regularly to determine whether any of them can be relaxed or eliminated.

• Encouraging agencies to implement new mandates on an experimental basis to determine their effectiveness and impacts before implementing them in all localities.

• Enabling the governor to suspend mandates on the request of local governments (acting individually or together), should the mandates be found to impose an unreasonable burden.

In 1999, mandate reforms were made in two states. In Nevada, the existing mandate statute was amended to require that a notice stating that the bill is an unfunded mandate be printed on the front of any mandate bill. In Virginia, where the state Commission on Local Government reviews proposed new state mandates, the legislature increased the scope of the commission's review so that it is now required to review bills that would restrict local revenue authority as well as those that would impose net additional expenditures on localities.

Prohibitions and Preemption

In addition to being subject to demands that they do certain things, local governments must concern themselves with "thou shalt not" directives. Legislative acts prohibiting local governments from taking certain actions often reflect a particular group's desire to minimize — if not completely avoid — government taxation or regulation. State legislators are particularly attracted to proposals for tax exemptions, which are politically popular and can be adopted without affecting state revenues, but tax exemption bills pose a serious threat to local government treasuries.[29]

In recent years, efforts to circumvent local authority have been especially intense with respect to smoking, rent control, and gun control. Tobacco companies have encouraged states to replace municipal and county nonsmoking ordinances with state legislation: because of industry pressure, statewide regulations are often less demanding than the local ordinances they replace. Commonly, states have preempted local action through the passage of statewide clean-indoor-air bills. Tobacco industry groups have also challenged proposed local bans on cigarette vending machines, arguing that any regulation of this business is reserved for state authority.[30]

Landlords in various states have long worked through the courts to contest local governments' authority to impose rent control; they have also lobbied at the state level to prohibit local action. Thirty-three states now prohibit local governments from adopting rent control measures,[31] and, in recent years, opposition to rent control has made some significant gains in Massachusetts, California, Illinois, and New York.

Thanks in large part to the efforts of the National Rifle Association (NRA), close to 40 states prohibit local gun control ordinances, and a majority of the states have deprived local governments of the authority to regulate the carrying of concealed weapons. Some states prevent local jurisdictions from imposing firearm ordinances that are more restrictive than the state laws; other states rescind local ordinances and impose statewide firearms laws in their place. In five states, preemption has come about through judicial rulings rather than by statute.

The school shooting in Littleton, Colorado, in April 1999 prompted gun rights proponents in Colorado and elsewhere to suspend, at least temporarily, efforts to reduce local control over firearms. In Arizona, the governor vetoed a bill that would have barred municipalities and counties from enacting a range of local gun-control ordinances. In West Virginia, however, the legislature passed and the governor signed a bill that prohibits municipalities and counties from placing any restrictions on the sale of guns, although the legislation grandfathered two cities with existing ordinances.

During 1999, several cities' efforts to sue gun makers to recover the costs of gun-related violence prompted the NRA to lobby state legislators to prohibit local governments from taking such action. The NRA was successful in several states—including Georgia, where suits had been initiated, and Maine, where localities had not even contemplated suing gun makers. The Georgia law prohibits any municipality or county from filing product liability suits against the firearms industry, reserving that right to the state. In Florida, a legislative proposal, which was later withdrawn, would have made it a felony for any local official to sue the gun industry.

Local Finances

As a consequence of general improvements in the economy as well as local officials' efforts to improve their jurisdictions' long-term fiscal health, many local governments have seen improvements in their overall financial picture in recent years. And the state aid picture has also been improving: some states have decided to fund the cost of mandates and to eliminate various tactics adopted during the recession to shift costs to local governments. Some have even agreed to fully fund the costs of homestead and other tax exemptions. Nevertheless, local efforts to have state aid restored to previous levels or to shed burdens that had been imposed during periods of state fiscal stress have not been altogether successful. In 1999, for example, despite a multibillion-dollar state budget surplus, the Minnesota legislature

refused to repeal a 1992 extension of the sales tax to include purchases made by local units of government, which had been adopted when the state was faced with a severe budget shortfall.

Many municipalities, moreover, continue to experience budgetary pressures from a wide range of sources, including infrastructure and capital projects, unfunded federal and state mandates, employee health benefits, and greater demand for criminal justice expenditures.[32] Because of structural changes in their economies, some large cities have a particularly strong need for continued intergovernmental aid.[33] Many counties are also under financial pressure. A spring 1999 survey found that nearly one-third of the 500 counties surveyed had had to raise their property taxes in each of the previous three fiscal years in order to meet growing expenditures. And many smaller, rural counties reported that their revenue bases were declining.[34] As states have pursued "get tough on crime" policies, counties have had to assume much of the bill—housing an increasing number of criminals and dealing with growing juvenile justice caseloads. In over half of the states, counties pick up a major share of state Medicaid costs,[35] and many counties have had to shoulder welfare costs as well.

Financial Controls

Local governments' ability to raise and spend revenues is limited by state constitutional and statutory limitations on property tax rates, property tax revenues, assessment increases, and general revenue or expenditure increases. State laws also prohibit certain types of local taxes entirely (e.g., a sales tax or a graduated income tax). In some states, the amount of revenue that can be raised is tied to such measures as inflation, population, or growth in personal income, and revenue that exceeds the limit must be refunded to the taxpayers. In several states, total expenditures are limited by being tied to a growth index. Some states have truth-in-taxation laws that require full public disclosure and public hearings on proposed tax increases.

Many of the more recent restrictions result from the success of statewide initiatives set in motion by citizens' groups. Although loss of local revenues has been the most immediate effect of the limitations on property and other taxes that have been adopted in California and other states during the past two decades, some jurisdictions have experienced a secondary effect: because local governments have found it more difficult to meet matching requirements for state and federal grants, they have been less able to attract intergovernmental aid. Often, however, local officials have successfully used productivity improvements or targeted revenue increases— such as new or increased fees— to reduce their losses.

Although tax expenditure limitations (TELs) appear to have had little effect on total spending, they have affected the composition of local revenues; specifically, TELs have decreased local governments' reliance on the property tax (although property taxes have increased) and increased their reliance on state aid and on locally collected fees and sales taxes. Overall, TELs appear to have encouraged centralization of authority at the state level and local dependence on more regressive revenue sources.[36]

The Revenue Base

In the mid–1980s and early 1990s, local tax revenues increased rapidly — more rapidly, in fact, than state revenues— to offset the loss or slow growth of inter-governmental aid and to meet the increased costs of unfunded mandates and local service demands.[37] Among local governments, counties experienced the largest tax revenue increases— about 58 percent between 1985 and 1990. This increase reflected, in part, (1) the growth in demand for county-administered health and social service programs and (2) a tendency to shift responsibilities from cities and towns to counties. (Such shifts sometimes occur by mutual agreement between localities; at other times, they are imposed by the state.)[38] Because cutbacks in federal aid hit them especially hard, counties also had greater incentive than municipalities to raise taxes.[39]

The property tax accounted for much of the growth in local revenues during the 1980s. From 1980 to 1990, local property tax revenues increased nationally by an astounding 128 percent, and during the 1990s, they continued to outpace inflation. Measured as a share of personal income, property taxes were 4.1 percent in fiscal year 1978 and 3.6 percent in fiscal year 1979, dropping in part because of the adoption of Proposition 13 in California. As the property tax rebellion spread to other states, property taxes fell to 3.2 percent of personal income. The percentage, however, slowly rose after 1982 and, with the help of the 1990–91 recession, had returned to the pre–Proposition 13 level by 1992.[40] As a result of state relief efforts, property taxes appear to be generally stabilizing, although they continue to be on the increase in various parts of the country.[41]

Not surprisingly, the property tax has been among the most unpopular taxes in the country.[42] In 1998, for example, Arkansas citizens initiated a proposed constitutional amendment that would have abolished all property taxes in the state; because of violations of the law that occurred while signatures were being collected, this proposal was thrown off the ballot — but the same group appears willing to try again. In an effort to take the steam out of the anti-property tax campaign, the Arkansas legislature came up with (1) the Property Taxpayer's Bill of Rights, which clarifies how the property tax system works and what taxpayer rights are in challenging assessments and tax bills; (2) a circuit-breaker tax limitation measure to provide relief for older or disabled property owners; and (3) proposed constitutional changes that would limit property tax increases.

In some cases, property tax reform has taken the form of added discretion for local officials, many of whom have nevertheless been reluctant to use this authority. In South Carolina, for example, despite considerable pressure from state lawmakers to take action, county officials have hesitated to employ powers that they were granted under a state law passed in 1999 that allows them to delay property tax assessments and cap property value increases on homes.

Faced with public demands for property tax relief, some state officials have imposed tax freezes and capped assessment rate increases. In 1997, the Minnesota legislature imposed a two-year limit on property tax levels in all counties and in municipalities with populations over 250. Some states, including Connecticut, Indiana, and Kansas, have decided to phase out automobile property taxes. Still others, including Ohio, South Carolina, and Utah, have provided property tax relief by expanding homestead exemptions. Several states have reduced pressure on the property tax by shifting much of the burden of financing education to other taxes, such as sales. In the past few years, revenue increases have allowed some states to provide property tax relief without cutting programs or increasing other taxes to offset the lost revenues.

In California, property taxes continue to be bones of contention between the state and local governments. In the early 1990s, the legislature shifted more than $2 billion in property taxes from local governments to the state education budget. Without this transfer, the state would have had to raise taxes or take money out of the general fund to pay for education, which would have meant cutting the level of other state services. In making the tax shift, the legislature effectively brought an end to the "bail-out" it had given counties and municipalities after the adoption, in 1978, of the property tax-limitation measure Proposition 13. Since 1992, California cities, towns, counties, and special districts have lost some $2.6 billion a year in property taxes (although the losses have been partially offset by the addition of nondiscretionary funds earmarked for public safety).

California county governments have been particularly hard hit by the loss of property tax revenues. Some counties reacted dramatically to the "tax grab," directing their auditors not to turn the money over to the state and challenging the state in court, on the grounds that the tax shift violated county rights under the state constitution. After several years of struggle, in 1999 local officials secured legislative support for a cap on the amount of revenue transferred to the state and for a reform that requires the state to pick up more of the cost of administering the property tax. Both changes, however, depend on voter approval of a constitutional amendment on local government structure. Late in the year, a county superior court judge came down on the side of the 54 counties that had sued the state and declared that the property tax shift violated the state constitutional requirement that local governments be reimbursed for state-imposed mandates.

As noted earlier, state-enacted exemptions limit the usefulness of the property tax in many jurisdictions by reducing the property tax base: counties often find, for example, that 60 percent or more of the property tax base has been exempted,[43] and in some states, such as New York, figures are nearly as high for many municipalities. Although states commonly make payments in lieu of taxes (PILOTs) for property tax exemptions, PILOTs are often far lower than what local governments would have collected in taxes had property not been exempt.

Many local governments have tried to move away from reliance on the property tax toward a more diversified revenue structure that includes the sales tax, user fees, and local income taxes. In some jurisdictions, additional revenues are available from state or locally owned enterprises or through legalized gambling. Proposals to give municipalities a major alternative revenue source, such as a sales tax, have been repeatedly rejected in some states, Mississippi being an example. Generally, however, states have in recent years allowed local governments more discretion in raising revenues, granting new or enlarged authority to levy new taxes—particularly on sales—and to impose fees for various services, such as special police patrols or ambulance service. Legislatures have usually made the adoption of new taxes subject to voter approval. Although in many states, increased urbanization and suburbanization have blurred the distinction between municipal and county services, county governments lag behind municipal governments in their ability to raise revenues. In recent years, proposals to expand the taxing powers of counties, rendering them comparable to those enjoyed by municipalities, have failed in Alabama, Florida, Maryland, North Carolina, and Virginia.

During the past two decades, user fees have become a popular means of financing water, sewer, transportation, and other services. Because the idea that the direct user of a service should pay for it is popular throughout the country, user fees are a relatively acceptable way of raising revenues, and the fact that they can generally be levied without a grant of permission from state legislatures makes user fees even more attractive to local officials. However, some courts have declared user fees (such as transportation utility fees) to be disguised taxes—and therefore invalid in the absence of specific state authorization.[44]

Nationwide, the number of exactions (required improvements, property set-asides, impact fees, and taxes) imposed by local governments on developers has increased greatly in the past two decades. To some extent, the increase in exactions reflects widening acceptance of the principle that growth must pay for itself. The increase has also stemmed, however, from the financial difficulties of many localities. Just as the federal and state governments tried to cope with their own economic problems by passing costs on to local governments, local governments have attempted to ease their economic difficulties—and the burden on current taxpayers—by passing costs on to developers. That developers have not offered more resistance may stem from the fact that they can, in turn, pass the costs on to residential or commercial buyers.[45]

One area of continued difficulty is infrastructure financing, particularly transportation financing.[46] Local governments nationwide are financing transportation improvements by tapping local general revenues and gasoline taxes, establishing special-benefit assessment districts, and seeking voter approval for sales tax increases. Some jurisdictions have turned to bonds—general obligation bonds, revenue bonds retired by special taxes or user fees, or a hybrid of both types—to raise capital for highway projects. To help municipalities and counties pay for highway and bridge projects, states have increased the amount of shared taxes (especially those on motor fuels) distributed to local governments. In addition, state and local governments have turned to private funding of toll roads, bridges, and tunnels.

State Assistance

In recent years, localities have often had to fight to avoid revenue losses caused by cuts in taxes that they share with the state. In 1999, for example, the League of Arizona Cities and Towns organized grass-roots opposition to a proposal from the state's joint legislative budget committee that would have reduced the municipal share of state income tax collections from 15.8 percent to 15.0 percent. Cutting their share to 15.0 percent would have cost Arizona municipalities nearly $40 million over two years. In the end, cities and towns wound up retaining about 15.4 percent of the state income tax monies, thus sustaining a $20 million reduction. To protect themselves from future cuts in revenues that they share with the state, Alabama local officials proposed that the state-local revenue-sharing agreement be made part of the state constitution so that it could not be eliminated or modified simply by an act of the legislature.

Because state aid is so important, reductions in aid normally require a reduction in local services or an increase in local revenue sources, such as property taxes. Overall, state aid has a modest equalizing effect, somewhat reducing the revenue gap between poorer and wealthier localities.[47] Only a handful of states, however, make a conscious effort to target funds on the basis of local need.[48]

With improved economies, which have brought both increases in revenues and a decline in pressures for Medicare and cash assistance expenditures, several states have recently increased direct aid to local government, especially for education and public safety.[49] Still, the prospect of continued improvement is limited because aid to general-purpose local governments (cities, towns, and counties) has had to compete with demands for tax relief as well as with increased demands for spending in various areas—particularly education, health care, and corrections. Moreover, state legislators, as a matter of ideology or philosophy, may simply not be inclined to see the need for greater state aid to localities. Responding last year to a request from several Wisconsin municipalities and counties for more aid, the chair of the legislature's joint finance committee declared, "I don't view my role as being an ATM machine for local governments."[50] In Alaska, where the economy is troubled, it took an intensive lobbying effort on the part of mayors to restore two-thirds of a proposed $48 million cut in aid to local governments.

Considering the level of state financial aid in isolation, however, gives a somewhat misleading picture of state efforts to ease fiscal pressures on local governments. A state that provides minimal direct financial aid to local governments, for example, may actually be providing more indirect aid to local governments than many or most states, because it has assumed the cost of expensive functions that are borne in other states by local governments.[51] In recent years, several states have taken on more financial responsibility for education, courts and corrections, indigent health care, mental health care, and cash welfare assistance. State assumption of expenditures could both (1) reduce the disparities in local government spending that result from local governments' reliance on the property tax and (2) free property tax revenues for other local functions. Although shifting financial responsibility for a program to the state provides financial relief to local governments, the price is likely to be loss of local control — and perhaps even a decline in service quality.

In some states, the provision of state aid is secondary to efforts to cut local costs—by, for example, eliminating mandates, fostering greater efficiency at the local level, or encouraging greater cost-sharing cooperation among local governments. Municipalities, counties, and school boards in several states have taken advantage of the services of state management specialists to identify cost savings. Moving in this direction in 1999, the Florida legislature passed enabling legislation (but no funding) for a local government financial technical assistance program for smaller municipalities and independent special districts throughout the state. Some state lawmakers around the country have also considered encouraging local governments in a given region to share revenues rather than depend on state aid or enlarged revenue authority.[52] The financial strain on central cities and hard-pressed smaller communities in many places could also be relieved by burden shifting — if, for example, various functions were moved from the municipal to the county level. States can also help in other ways. Legislation adopted by the 1997 Georgia legislature, for example, allows cities and counties to ask the state revenue department to withhold unpaid local taxes, fees, and fines from an individual's state income tax refund. A similar program in South Carolina has been highly successful.

Proactive Steps to Aid Distressed Local Governments

States began in the 1970s to adopt policies to assist financially distressed local governments, and came under increasing pressure to do so during the 1980s, when nationwide economic difficulties set in and some cities—such as Bridgeport, Con-

necticut—threatened to go into bankruptcy. In keeping with traditions of local autonomy, much state intervention in the affairs of individual local governments occurs only after (1) it is clear that there is a problem and (2) the locality asks for assistance.

States have often adopted legislation for specific towns, cities, or counties in dire financial straits, putting them into state receivership or giving them financial and technical assistance and imposing various controls on their activities. Several states have more formal and comprehensive programs for fiscally distressed substate entities: these programs measure and monitor distress, and, as certain criteria are met, the states provide assistance and/or impose regulations to execute a fiscal recovery plan.[53]

States have tended to look to managerial changes as the source of long-term solutions for financially distressed local governments: that is, the emphasis has been on correcting the behavior of local officials and the procedures or practices they follow. Although management improvements and greater internal efficiencies are desirable in their own right, fiscal distress more often stems from economic conditions—such as demographic shifts and structural changes in the economic base — that are largely beyond local control.[54]

If the underlying problem in a distressed municipality is, indeed, the inadequacy of the locality's economic base, the state should be thinking in broader terms: state laws could, for example, (1) make it more difficult to form (incorporate) new municipal governments in urbanizing areas; (2) make it easier for municipalities to expand their boundaries through annexation; and (3) make it easier to consolidate local governments.

Some states already give cities and towns considerable power to annex contiguous land. In North Carolina, for example, this can be done without the owner's consent. North Carolina and about a dozen other states also give municipalities the ability to veto the incorporation of new municipalities forming outside their boundaries. Consolidation, however, has met with significant voter opposition in suburban areas. Many states require that voters in each affected jurisdiction approve consolidation—a legal requirement that has often discouraged action. Even in states that require voter approval of consolidation, however, the state is free to order consolidations.

Although the likelihood of more state-directed consolidations is remote, states have shown increased interest in plans calling for local governments in metropolitan areas or sub-state regions to share burdens and revenues. For example, some state legislatures and courts require each municipality to assume its share of responsibility for providing low-income housing. The Regional Tax Base Sharing Program, in Minneapolis-St. Paul, is an example of neighboring governments pooling resources: a portion of the increase in the areas' industrial tax base is placed in a regional pool, from which all jurisdictions in the area draw revenues.

Policy Areas

Among the policy areas in which state actions have become of increasing importance to local governments are education, welfare, telecommunications and electricity deregulation, environmental protection, and land use regulations and planning.

Education: Financing and Equity

In some parts of the country, much of the responsibility for financing the grow-ing costs of education continues to rest with local governments—principally, independent school districts—and the local property tax. In the nation overall, however, the share borne by state governments has increased over the past several years.[55] State aid to education has increased for two primary reasons: first, citizen dissatisfaction with the property tax has encouraged the states to reduce reliance on local property taxes for education funding and to replace property taxes with state aid drawn from other sources. Second, in about half of the states, shifting education funding to the state has been part of an effort to address court demands to remedy inadequacies in education or to equalize expenditures among school districts.

Among the most notable developments in recent years was Vermont lawmakers' adoption, in 1997, of a reform measure that created a new, statewide property tax to finance elementary and secondary schools and remedy funding inequities among school districts. The state supreme court had held that the old system—in which local property taxes paid 70 percent of education costs and the state 30 percent—was unconstitutional because of large funding disparities among districts. The Vermont plan has been controversial because it conflicts with the state's tradition of local authority and calls for a redistribution of tax money from rich communities to poor ones. In 1999 the New Hampshire legislature, responding to a state court order that made it illegal to use widely varying property taxes as the primary source of education funding, passed legislation under which the state will pay more than 60 percent of the cost of education. Prior to the act, New Hampshire had raised over 90 percent of its funds for schools from local taxes.

One disadvantage of largely state-funded education is that it links the financial support of education to the state's overall fiscal health — and, often, to revenue sources that are less dependable than the property tax. Second, it forces education funding to compete with a host of other demands on state funds. Finally, as states have picked up a larger share of education expenditures, local officials have had reason to worry about the dependability of state aid for areas other than education.

As part of the move toward greater centralization, 23 states now have academic bankruptcy programs under which low levels of performance trigger some type of state intervention in specific school districts. Under this legislation, a state education agency periodically evaluates the governance, management, fiscal operations, and education programs of each of its school districts. Early intervention may simply consist of warnings of the need for corrective action. To encourage compliance, state education departments may withhold state aid from districts or revoke their accreditation. State officials, as the ultimate remedy, may take direct control over the district, dismissing elected school board members and local administrators. In the past six years, there have been more than 20 takeovers in at least 10 states, but it is unclear whether state takeovers adequately address underlying problems. Intervention may improve management and curricula, but when it comes to educational achievement, there may be little reason to believe that state administrators can do a better job than local administrators.[56] Particularly in large urban systems, underlying economic or social problems — which are unlikely to disappear through changes in school personnel and operating practices — are the real barriers to academic achievement.

Many mayors view the quality of public schools as essential to their cities' survival and have become advocates for education as well as catalysts in bringing about improvement. As one mayor has put it: "We're going to get blamed for the schools anyway, whether we're responsible for them or not, so we might as well try to fix them."[57] The Illinois legislature, for example, in 1995 gave Chicago's Mayor control over the Chicago school district, the nation's third-largest public school system (410,000 students), which was faced with chronic financial and academic problems. In addition to takeovers, cities have initiated several types of partnerships with independent school districts.

Welfare: A Challenge for the Counties

Although the economy has been strong in recent years, poverty is still entrenched in many cities. A 1999 survey indicated that poverty and homelessness was increasing in several cities and that many cities (34 percent of those contacted) had experienced a need for more "survival services" — food, clothing, shelter, and health care — in their jurisdictions.[58] In the area of welfare, local officials have been concerned that the Personal Responsibility and Work Opportunity Reconciliation Act passed by Congress in 1996 will eventually shift more of the welfare burden to local governments and the local property tax. Thus far, however, financing problems have not generally surfaced, largely because an improved economy has reduced welfare rolls. Moreover, because block grants to the states are based on past state expenditures (at a time when welfare rolls were higher), they have been more than adequate. And because the same amount of money has to be shared with fewer welfare recipients, the average state has received over 50 percent more per family than it did before welfare reform. Nevertheless, welfare reform could turn out to be a budget-buster for counties and cities, boosting not only the cost of welfare but also the costs of making changes in transportation systems so that people can get to jobs, child care, homeless shelters, and affordable housing.

Particularly in states that already had state-supervised, county-administered welfare systems—such as California, Colorado, Maryland, New York, North Carolina, Ohio, and Wisconsin—much of the responsibility for welfare programs has been turned over to county governments. Although the states generally set basic policies regarding, for example, eligibility and benefits standards, counties have considerable discretion in designing plans to meet federal work requirements and are also given financial incentives to get recipients into the workforce. Some states take a block-grant approach, subjecting counties to performance standards but giving them considerable flexibility as to how a fixed amount of money is to be spent.

The late 1990s brought a large reduction in the number of people on welfare. This decline, which actually began before the federal welfare law took effect, was due in large part to a strong economy, although the new state requirements may have accelerated the reduction. What remains unclear is how many of the people who have left welfare have actually found employment. Many were dropped from the rolls not because they found jobs but because they violated new rules and regulations— failing, for example, to attend job readiness classes. Many of those who have left welfare are unemployed, living on the streets or with relatives or charities. Studies suggest, moreover, that many of those who have found jobs are likely to lose them six to nine months later and wind up back on welfare.[59]

Analysts predict, moreover, that the difficulty of finding employment for those on welfare assistance is only likely to increase: one reason is that the people who have found jobs thus far tend to be most employable, whereas those who remain have lower levels of education, fewer skills, and relatively little work experience—factors that will make them more difficult to place.

Telecommunications and Utilities Deregulation

Among other recent changes troubling local officials are the potential effects of the federal Telecommunications Act of 1996, which was designed to increase competition in the communications sector. As implemented by the states, the law could have a devastating effect on local zoning, land use, and right-of-way authority; local control over telecommunications firms (e.g., those that install cable services, satellite dishes, or cellular antennas); and local ability to tax telecommunications operations. In some states, such as Colorado, legislation already limits local governments' compensation for right-of-way use and local governments' ability to tax telecommunications firms.

Under the federal law, communities may build and operate their own communications infrastructures, but some states are attempting to limit or prevent direct or indirect provision of certain telecommunications services by municipalities and municipally owned utilities. Arkansas, Missouri, and Texas have already made it illegal for municipalities or municipal electric companies to go into the telecommunications business. Other states, however, such as Georgia and Tennessee in 1999, have established ground rules for local governments to offer cable television services.

Another set of complicated problems that stem, in part, from federal activity concern the national movement toward electric utility deregulation. The theory is that competition among power producers will bring down power rates. But as states have begun to deregulate, giving consumers a choice among competing producers of electric power, localities have been concerned about the adverse revenue impacts of such actions—in particular, about (1) declines in property tax revenues as power plants drop in value and (2) the loss of franchise fees that electric utilities currently pay for use of the public right-of-way. State legislatures are attempting to come up with revenue-neutral tax alternatives that keep all electric competitors on a level playing field. States and localities may either have to change their franchise fee structure or face the loss of franchise fee revenues: it may be necessary, for example, to regard the franchise fee as a fee on consumers regardless of where and from whom they purchase utility services.[60] As indicated in a 1998 Florida state supreme court decision, right-of-way fees charged to a private company may be invalidated as unauthorized taxes because the amount charged is not related to the value and use of the right-of-way and to the cost of regulation.

In addition to worrying about tax revenues, some localities have reason to be concerned about the viability of municipally owned power systems, which often bring in a large amount of income. Some large municipally owned power companies have encountered financial trouble because of investments in nuclear power plants. Few municipals, moreover, appear to have the resources to compete in markets outside their current sphere of operation. On the other hand, in some cases, the private power industry has encouraged municipal governments to get into the power business as way of broadening competition and lowering costs. In some states, municipal electric companies have been allowed to opt in or out of offering retail choice to their customers.

On the plus side, local governments stand to get cheaper electricity through deregulation. If state law permits, local governments may enter into agreements to jointly purchase energy. In 1999, for example, 148 of Connecticut's 169 cities and towns formed a massive buying pool to purchase electricity and natural gas. Local governments may also have the authority to enter into contracts with suppliers to purchase electricity on behalf of their residents. In California, for example, the city of Palm Beach is aggregating for its residents and buying power on their behalf. Such arrangements help ensure that all consumers will obtain electricity at competitive prices. Although aggregation is generally permitted, some states do place limitations on it: in Maryland, for example, 1999 electric deregulation legislation included a provision that forbids local governments from acting as aggregators for their citizens or businesses unless it is determined that no competition exists in that jurisdiction. In New Jersey, in contrast, despite the efforts of organizations representing local officials, the legislature forced cities, towns, and counties to go through a complicated and costly process to form buying groups among themselves and with their residential, commercial, and industrial energy users.

Land Use: Takings and Planning

Several state courts are currently examining cases challenging the regulatory authority of state and local governments. Property-rights advocates, realtors, and developers have also pushed for state legislation requiring compensation for the limitations placed on the use of private property by various types of state or local regulations. Some states simply require that regulatory agencies, drawing upon guidelines developed by the state attorney general, estimate the potential impact of a proposed regulation on private property before taking action. Other states require cash payments for declines in property value caused by regulatory action.[61] So far, however, the flood of property rights activity in the courts and legislatures has not succeeded in persuading local governments to refrain from enacting land use regulations.[62]

During the past decade, a growing number of local governments have become concerned about growth and its associated problems, such as pollution and traffic congestion. But in 1999, nearly half of all city officials surveyed felt that their states were not supportive of municipal growth management needs. Many of these officials, moreover, felt that development in their area had been poorly planned.[63]

In many parts of the country, problems originating with poor planning have created pressure to shift much of the responsibility for planning from localities to states and broad-based planning agencies. A growing number of states, for example, require local governments to draw up comprehensive land use plans that are consistent with state comprehensive plans. Under such legislation, local governments must often work together to prepare metropolitan or regional plans that address the interrelated goals of controlling growth, combating environmental problems (e.g., air and water pollution), and providing adequate infrastructure. Although states with such laws generally review local plans to ensure their consistency with statewide planning goals, states give local governments varying degrees of control over the specific details of plan content. All state growth management legislation, however, rests on the premise that the states can more effectively guide development than local governments can. Some states, including Florida, New Jersey, and Washington, have laws that limit new development

to places where adequate infrastructure is already in place or will be in place concurrent with the development being considered. Since 1973, as part of its statewide land-use planning program, Oregon has required all cities to define urban growth boundaries to contain urban development, leaving enough room for 20 years of growth and moving the boundary as the urban area fills up. In 1998, Tennessee followed the Oregon example and passed landmark legislation requiring cities to establish 20-year urban growth boundaries.

State planning mandates have generally improved the amount and quality of local planning and brought local planning more in line with state and regional concerns in such areas as environmental protection.[64] State-imposed planning, however, has also generated considerable costs for local governments—and in some places, state and local governments have struggled over their respective roles in growth management, especially with respect to infrastructure financing.[65] A more general problem with state-imposed comprehensive planning is that it takes a one-size-fits-all approach, ignoring the diversity among local governments: in particular, state-imposed comprehensive planning ignores variations in professional and financial resources, which largely determine a local government's ability to plan successfully.[66]

Setting off in still new directions, in 1999 the Georgia legislature created a superagency in the Atlanta region, which, under the control of the governor, has broad powers to attack problems of traffic, smog, and sprawl. Known as the Georgia Regional Transportation Authority, the agency can, among other things, control highway building in the 13-county area and build and operate a mass transportation system for the region. The state's action was a response, in part, to a warning from the federal Environmental Protection

Agency that Atlanta's air quality problems are so serious that it risks losing federal funds for new highway projects. Feeling that they had no choice, elected local officials from suburban areas—despite being likely to lose influence over how land in their jurisdiction will be used — appeared willing to go along with the creation of the new superagency. As the chair of one of the state's county commissions put it, "Ten years ago ... whoever was sitting in this seat would have taken it as a threat to local authority. Now most of us look at it as a blessing."[67]

Partnerships and Responsibilities

In recent years, local officials throughout the country have voiced their concerns about the quality of state-local relations. Late in 1993, 28 percent of the municipal officials who responded to a National League of Cities survey felt that relations with the federal government has worsened since 1990. Even more respondents— 30 percent — felt that relations with their state government had deteriorated or worsened during the same period.[68] Early in both 1998 and 1999, 20 percent of the respondents to the same survey again reported that state-city relations had worsened during the previous year.[69] In these and other surveys, local officials—county as well as municipal, appointed as well as elected — have lamented the loss of local government authority, the lack of sufficient discretion to generate revenues, the lack of state financial aid and technical assistance, the lack of support from state agencies, and — most of all — the growth of unfunded mandates.[70]

Over the years, the tensions and uncertainties of dealing with the federal and state governments have encouraged local officials to look to each other for support and to come together to address common problems. Thus, while evidence suggests that local officials have soured on their relations with the federal and state governments, local officials see improvements in their relations with other local officials in the same geographic area.[71] Local governments are increasingly entering into agreements for joint planning, financing, or delivery of services, and examples of increased efficiency of service delivery through interlocal cooperation or "interlocal self-governance" can be found throughout the nation.[72] Along these lines, a great deal can be accomplished under state joint powers acts, which give broad authority for such cooperative efforts. Interlocal contracts, through which one local government unit purchases services (such as police or fire protection) from another local government, are also popular. Although such cooperation has been driven principally by cost considerations, local governments are also using formal and informal cooperative efforts as a means of combating areawide problems.[73] In the mid–1990s, in Connecticut alone, there were 900 instances in which services were being delivered through intermunicipal cooperative ventures.[74] For local governments, the cooperative approach is a means of retaining their identities while still addressing problems that transcend their boundaries.

Indeed, metropolitan or regional cooperation may be the wave of the future, in part because of the voluntary actions of local officials, but also because the federal government and various state governments have encouraged this approach to problems that require comprehensive, areawide planning. Such efforts could be strengthened, however, if local officials were brought more directly into the state policy-making process, if "top down" management were reduced, and if local governments were given more discretion in achieving broad state or regional goals.

In addition to authorizing and encouraging cooperative ventures, states have a positive role to play in fostering interlocal cooperation by ironing out disputes between local governments. In California in 1998, for example, the California State Association of Counties and the League of California Cities got behind a bill that establishes a process—including the use of a neutral third party—for working out disputes between municipalities and counties with respect to property tax-sharing agreements on proposed annexations.[75] Georgia has also acted to address the issue of city-county disputes over annexation. States such as Maryland and Wisconsin have been concerned with establishing a framework in which municipalities and counties can address the problem of double taxation (i.e., city residents paying for city services as well as for similar services that the county does not provide in the city).

At the beginning of 1999, a National League of Cities survey found that nearly half (47 percent) of local officials surveyed felt that the unfunded mandate problem had worsened over the previous year, while only 8 percent said that the situation had improved.[76] Mandates have by no means disappeared, and both federal and state legislators continue to have a considerable incentive to pass them, despite rules and regulations that attempt to curb them.[77]

Generally, states generally need to clarify and strengthen home-rule authority. State governments also could do much to help financially strapped local governments. Courses of action include eliminating unnecessary mandates, increasing financial aid (and targeting it to the places where it is most needed), helping to improve local government management practices, encouraging the consolidation of services, encouraging regional burden- and tax-sharing, assuming the costs of programs currently financed out of local revenues, and allowing local governments greater discretion in raising revenues.

The recurrent disputes between state and local governments over authority and finances are not likely to abate in the immediate future. Each state might well consider a new sorting out of functions between the state and local units. In any given state, one can find instances in which problems of considerable importance to the state as a whole are being addressed by local officials who lack the perspectives and resources to cope with them. At the same time, in any given state, one can no doubt find decisions being made at the state level that should be made at the local level, in light of the needs and priorities of particular communities. While sorting out responsibilities is a difficult task, positive steps toward this and toward the overall improvement of state-local cooperation is imperative as both levels of government attempt to cope with the demands placed upon them.

Notes

1. William Anderson, *The Nation and the States, Rivals or Partners?* (Minneapolis: University of Minnesota Press, 1955).

2. Mavis Mann Reeves, "Galloping Intergovernmentalization as a Factor in State Management, *State Government* 54 (1981): 103–108.

3. Janet M. Kelly, "Lessons from the States on Unfunded Mandates," *National Civic Review* (spring 1995): 133–139.

4. See *An Assessment of the Unfunded Mandates Reform Act in 1997* (Washington, D.C.: Congressional Budget Office, February 1998).

5. For commentary on the legislation, see Timothy J. Conlan, James D. Riggle, and Donna E. Schwartz, "Deregulating Federalism? The Politics of Mandate Reform in the 104th Congress," *Publius* 25 (summer 1995): 23–39; and John Novinson, "Unfunded Mandates: A Closed Chapter?" *Public Management* (July 1995): 17–19.

6. William De Soto, "Cities in State Politics: Views of Mayors and Managers," *State and Local Government Review* 27 (fall 1995): 188–194.

7. *Ibid.*

8. U.S. Advisory Commission on Intergovernmental Relations (ACIR), *Local Government Autonomy: Needs for State Constitutional Statutory and Judicial Clarification* (Washington, D.C., October 1993).

9. For a recent account, see David B. Magleby, "Ballot Initiatives and Intergovernmental Relations in the United States," *Publius* 28 (winter 1998): 147–163.

10. Kathy Hunt, *Wyoming Home Rule: A Current Status Report* (Cheyenne: Wyoming Association of Municipalities, 1994).

11. See ACIR, *Local Government Autonomy.*

12. Charles Mahtesian, "The Endless Struggle over Open Meetings," *Governing* (December 1997): 48–51.

13. ACIR, *State Laws Governing Local Government Structure and Administration* (Washington, D.C., March 1993).

14. David R. Berman, "Takeovers of Local Governments: An Overview and Evaluation of State Policies," *Publius* 25 (summer 1995): 55–70.

15. Connecticut Conference of Municipalities, *The State of Municipalities in Connecticut: A Public Policy Report* (New Haven, February 1995): 17.

16. State and Local Government Commission of Ohio, *Unfunded Mandates: Regaining Control at the Local Level* (Columbus, 8 December 1994).

17. Harry A. Green, "State Mandates to Local Governments," memorandum to the Tennessee Advisory Commission on Intergovernmental Relations commissioners, 28 August 1995.

18. Edward Flentje, "State Mandates as Family Values?" *Current Municipal Problems* 22 (1996): 510–512.

19. Michael Fix and Daphne Kenyon, eds., *Coping with Mandates: What Are the Alternatives?* (Washington, D.C.: Urban Institute Press, 1990): 21.

20. ACIR, *Mandates: Cases in State-Local Relations* (Washington, D.C., September 1990): 21.

21. Edward A. Zelinsky, "Unfunded Mandates, Hidden Taxation, and the Tenth Amendment: On Public Choice, Public Interest, and Public Services," *Vanderbilt Law Review* 46 (November 1993): 1355, 1366.

22. Robert M. M. Shaffer, "Comment: Unfunded State Mandates and Local Governments," *University of Cincinnati Law Review* 64 (spring 1996): 1057.

23. See Ann Calvares Barr, "Cost Estimations as an Anti-Mandate Strategy," in Fix and Kenyon, *Coping with Mandates*, 57–61. See also U.S. General Accounting Office, *Legislative Mandates: State Experiences Offer Insights for Federal Action* (Washington, D.C., 1988); and Kelly, *State Mandates*, 42.

24. Susan A. McManus, "Mad about Mandates: The Issue of Who Should Pay for What Resurfaces in the 1990s," *Publius* 21 (summer 1991): 59–75. See also Shaffer, "Comment: Unfunded State Mandates."

25. Virginia Legislature, Joint Legislative Audit and Review Commission, *Intergovernmental Mandates and Financial Aid to Local Governments*, House Document no. 56 (Richmond, 1992).

26. See Richard H. Horte, "State Expenditures with Mandate Reimbursement," in Fix and Kenyon, *Coping with Mandates*; and Kelly, *State Mandates*.

27. Joseph Zimmerman, quoted in States Take Lead in Mandate Relief," *State Trends Bulletin* (February/March 1996): 8.

28. Kelly, "Lessons from the States," 136.

29. Research suggests that the impact of prohibitions on raising revenue can be as devastating to local finances as that of mandates requiring local governments to spend funds on various activities. On this point, see, e.g., Paul Flowers and John T. Torbert, *Mandate Costs: A Kansas Case Study* (Topeka: Kansas Association of Counties, 1993). On the definition of mandates and the different forms they may take, see Janet M. Kelly, *State Mandates: Fiscal Notes, Reimbursement, and Anti-Mandate Strategies* (Washington, D.C.: National League of Cities, 1992); Kelly, "Unfunded Mandates: The View from the States," *Public Administration Review* 54 (July/August 1994): 405–408; Max Neiman and Catherine Lovell, "Federal and State Mandating: A First Look at the Mandate Terrain," *Administration and Society* (November 1982): 343–372; Neiman and Lovell, "Mandating as a Policy Issue: The Definitional

Problem," *Policy Studies Journal* (spring 1981): 667–680; ACIR, *State Mandating of Local Expenditures* (Washington, D.C., 1978); Georgia Municipal Association, *Calculating the Cost of State and Federal Mandates: Getting Started* (Atlanta, March 1993); and Joseph F. Zimmerman, "Some Remedies Suggested for State Mandated Expenditure Distortions," *Current Municipal Problems* 21 (1994): 93–110.

30. See the overview by Patricia S. Biswanger, "Preserving Democracy in the Face of Special Interest Might: Local Initiatives to Ban Cigarette Vending Machines," *Current Municipal Problems* 21 (1994): 67–92.

31. Christopher Swope, "Rent Control: Invisible No More," *Governing* (January 1998): 28–29.

32. Michael A. Pagano and Andrew Dudas, "Reports of Growth by Cities Reflect Improved Policies and Long-Term Planning," *Nation's Cities Weekly*, 10 July 1995, pp. 1, 10; and Michael A. Pagano, "Fiscal Trends Help Develop Overall Picture of Cities' Fiscal Health," *Nation's Cities Weekly*, 15 July 1996, pp. 1, 9.

33. See, e.g., Helen F. Ladd, "Big-City Finances," in *Big-City Politics, Governance, and Fiscal Constraints*, ed. George E. Peterson (Washington, D.C.: Urban Institute Press, 1994): 201–269.

34. Survey by the National Association of County Officials, released 23 April 1999.

35. See "County Participation in State Medicaid Costs in 1986," *County News*, 29 April 1996, p. 11.

36. ACIR, *Tax and Expenditure Limits on Local Governments* (Washington, D.C., March 1995). See also Phillip G. Joyce and Daniel R. Mullins, "The Changing Fiscal Structure of the State and Local Public Sector: The Impact of Tax and Expenditure Limitations," *Public Administration Review* 51 (May/June 1991): 240–253; Daniel E. O'Toole and Brian Stipak, "Coping with State Tax and Expenditure Limitations: The Oregon Experience," *State and Local Government Review* 30 (winter 1998): 9–16; and Alvin D. Sokolow, "The Changing Property Tax and State-Local Relations," *Publius* 28 (winter 1998): 165–187.

37. For an analysis of this growth, see Steven D. Gold, "Local Taxes Outpace State Taxes," *PA Times* (July 1993): 15, 17; and "Passing the Buck," *State Legislatures* (January 1993):

36–38. Gold has also noted that the slow growth of local aid is one of the primary reasons that local taxes have been increasing more rapidly than state taxes: see Steven D. Gold, "State Aid to Localities Fares Poorly in 1990s," in *State Fiscal Brief* (New York: Rockefeller Institute of Government, Center for the Study of the States, June 1994): 1–5.

38. Gold, "Local Taxes."

39. Steven D. Gold, "The State of State-Local Relations," *State Legislatures* (August 1988): 17–20.

40. Scott Mackey, "Keeping a Lid on Property Taxes," *State Legislatures* (March 1997): 10–11.

41. *Ibid.*

42. ACIR, *Changing Public Attitudes on Government and Taxes* (Washington, D.C., 1990, 1991, 1992).

43. John P. Thomas, "Financing County Government: An Overview," *Intergovernmental Perspective* (winter 1991): 12.

44. Reid Ewing, "Transportation Utility Fees," *Government Finance Review* (June 1994): 13–17.

45. Alan A. Altshuler and José A. Gómez-Ibáñez with Arnold M. Howitt, *Regulation for Revenue: The Political Economy of Land Use Exactions* (Washington, D.C., and Cambridge, Mass.: Brookings Institution and Lincoln Institute of Land Policy, 1993).

46. National League of Cities, *City Fiscal Conditions in 1998* (Washington, D.C.: NLC 1998).

47. See Thomas R. Dye and Thomas L. Hurley, "The Responsiveness of Federal and State Governments to Urban Problems," *Journal of Politics* 40 (February 1978): 196–207; and John P. Pelissero, "State Aid and City Needs: An Examination of Residual State Aid to Large Cities," *Journal of Politics* 46 (August 1984): 916–935. For more pessimistic views, see Robert M. Stein and Keith E. Hamm, "A Comparative Analysis of the Targeting Capacity of State and Federal Intergovernmental Aid Allocations: 1977, 1982," *Social Science Quarterly* 68 (September 1987): 447–477; and David R. Morgan and Mei-Chiang Shih, "Targeting State and Federal Aid to City Needs," *State and Local Government Review* 23 (spring 1991): 60–67.

48. See, e.g., Robert M. Stein, "The Targeting of State Aid: A Comparison of Grant Delivery Mechanisms," *Urban Interest* 2 (1981):

47–60; Stein, "The Allocation of State Aid to Local Governments: An Examination of Interstate Variation," in ACIR, *State and Local Roles in the Federal System* (Washington, D.C., 1982): 203–226; Theda Skoepol, "Targeting within Universalism," in *The Urban Underclass*, ed. Christopher Jencks and Paul Peterson (Washington, D.C.: Brookings Institution, 1991): 411–435; and Robert M. Stein and Keith E. Hamm, "Explaining State Aid Allocations: Targeting within Universalism," *Social Science Quarterly* 75 (September 1994): 524–540.

49. National Association of State Budget Officers, "Executive Summary," in *The Fiscal Survey of the States* (Washington, D.C.: NASBO, April 1997).

50. Amy Rinard, "State Lawmakers Cool to More Local Funding," *Milwaukee Journal Sentinel*, 9 April 1999.

51. See Gold, "State Aid to Localities," 1–5.

52. Allan D. Wallis, "Governance and the Civic Infrastructure of Metropolitan Regions," *National Civic Review* (spring 1993): 125–139. See also the overview by David Rusk, "Bend or Die: Inflexible State Laws and Policies Are Dooming Some of the Country's Central Cities," *State Government News* (February 1994): 6–10.

53. See, generally, Anthony G. Cahill, Joseph A. James, Jean E. Lavigne, and Ann Stacey, "State Government Responses to Municipal Fiscal Distress: A Brave New World for State-Local Intergovernmental Relations," *Public Productivity and Management Review* 17 (spring 1994): 253, 264; Anthony G. Cahill and Joseph A. James, "Responding to Municipal Fiscal Distress: An Emerging Issue for State Governments in the 1990s," *Public Administration Review* 52 (January/February 1992): 88–94; and Scott R. Mackey, *State Programs to Assist Distressed Local Governments* (Denver: National Conference of State Legislators, March 1993).

54. See, e.g. Helen F. Ladd and John Yinger, *America's Ailing Cities* (Baltimore: John Hopkins University Press, 1989).

55. In 1971–72, state governments contributed about 38 percent of all revenues for public elementary and secondary schools. By 1986–87, this proportion had increased to nearly 50 percent, and in actual dollars, state governments spent four times as much in 1986–87 as they had in 1971–72. While total state expenditures for education have continued to grow, the state percentage had declined to about 46 percent by 1993–94 (the latest available figures).

56. See, generally, Berman, "Takeovers." Under the preclearance provisions of the Voting Rights Act of 1965, such takeovers may require U.S. Justice Department review. See Lynn Olson, "State Takeovers Run Afoul of Voting Rights Act," *Education Week* (11 September 1996): 22. An overview of state takeovers is found in Caroline Hendrie, "Ill Will Comes with Territory in Takeovers," *Education Week* (12 June 1996): 1, 12, 13.

57. "Strengthening Public Schools," *Nation's Cities Weekly*, 1 July 1996, p. 4.

58. "State of the Cities: 1999, Special Report," *Nation's Cities Weekly*, 25 January 1999, pp. 5–9.

59. See an ongoing series of Urban Institute studies assessing the new federalism (http://www.urban.org).

60. Lawrence C. Walters and Gary C. Cornia, "The Implications of Utility and Telecommunications for Local Finance," *State and Local Government Review* 29 (fall 1997): 172–187. See also David Berry, "Local Impact of Electric Industry Restructuring," *Public Management* (July/August 1999): 18–21.

61. See the overview by Kirk Emerson and Charles R. Wise, "Statutory Approaches to Regulatory Takings: State Property Rights Legislation Issues and Implications for Public Administration," *Public Administration Review* (September/October 1997): 411–422.

62. Jonathan Walters, "The Property Rights Bust," *Governing* (June 1999): 38–41.

63. "State of the Cities: 1999," 5–9.

64. See, generally, Raymond J. Burby and Peter J. May, *Making Governments Plan: State Experiments in Managing Land Use* (Baltimore: Johns Hopkins University Press, 1997); Linda C. Dalton and Raymond J. Burby. "Mandates, Plans, and Planners," *Journal of the American Planning Association* 60 (autumn 1994): 444–461; and Donald R. Porter, "State Growth Management: The Intergovernmental Experiment," *Land Use Law Reporter* (October 1993).

65. Robyne S. Turner, "Intergovernmental Growth Management: A Partnership Framework for State-Local Relations," *Publius 20* (summer 1990): 79–95.

66. See, generally, Jane Elizabeth Decker, "Management and Organizational Capacities

for Responding to Growth in Florida's Non-metropolitan Counties," *Journal of Urban Affairs* 9 (1987): 47–61; and Turner, "Intergovernmental Growth Management."

67. Quoted in Alan Ehrenhalt, "The Czar of Gridlock," *Governing* (May 1999): 20-24, 27.

68. See "Unfunded Mandates Rank as Highest-Priority Concern of Local Officials," *Nation's Cities Weekly* 10 January 1994, p. 8.

69. See Jamie Woodwell, *The State of America's Cities* (Washington, D.C.: National League of Cities, January 1998); and "State of the Cities: 1999, Special Report," *Nation's Cities Weekly*, 25 January 1999, pp. 5–9.

70. Victor S. DeSantis, "State, Local, and Council Relations: Managers' Perceptions," *Baseline Data Report* 23 (ICMA, March-April 1991). Relevant survey data are also found in William L. Waugh and Gregory Streib, "County Capacity and Intergovernmental Relations," and Tanis J. Salant, "Shifting Roles in County-State Relations," both in *County Government in an Era of Change*, ed. David R. Berman (Westport, Conn.: Greenwood Press, 1993).

71. See, e.g., "Unfunded Mandates," 8.

72. See, e.g., ACIR, *Metropolitan Organi-zation: The Allegheny County Case* (Washington, D.C., February 1992); Ronald J. Oakerson and Roger B. Parks, "Metropolitan Organization: St. Louis and Allegheny County," *Intergovernmental Perspective* (summer 1991): 27–30, 34; and Roger B. Parks, "Counties in the Federal System: The Interlocal Connection," *Intergovernmental Perspective* (winter 1991): 29–32.

73. David R. Morgan and Michael W. Hirlinger, "Intergovernmental Service Contracts: A Multivariate Explanation," *Urban Affairs Quarterly* 27 (September 1991): 128–144.

74. Connecticut Advisory Commission on Intergovernmental Relations, *Local Government Cooperative Ventures in Connecticut: Executive Summary* (Hartford, June 1996).

75. For background on these disputes, see Alvin D. Sokolow, "State Rules and the County-City Arena: Competition for Land and Taxes in California's Central Valley," *Publius* 23 (winter 1993): 53–69.

76. "State of the Cities: 1999," 5–9.

77. Edward A. Zelinsky, "The Unsolved Problem of the Unfunded Mandate," *Ohio Northern University Law Review* 23 (1997): 741.

• *Chapter 25* •

The Power Struggle Continues

CARL E. VAN HORN

Thirty years ago, in *Storm over the States*, Terry Sanford, former governor of North Carolina and later a U.S. senator, described profound changes that swept state governments in the 1960s as they adjusted to federal statutes and Supreme Court rulings that forced them to modernize.[1] Today, the state government scene seems more like a tornado of political, administrative, and policy change. The whirling activism of state governments in the 1980s was followed by a crash of the American economy in the early 1990s and diminished federal government involvement in domestic policy innovation.

The economic recovery that followed has not renewed federal government aid to the states. Instead, a Republican-controlled Congress has taken bold steps to curb government spending and put states at the cutting edge of radical social policy reform. It is, arguably, the most significant domestic policy development in at least thirty years. States will be struggling to absorb this rapid pace of change in the foreseeable future—change that is likely to further batter the foundation of state political institutions and threaten not only incumbent officeholders but also the representative functions of governors and state legislatures.

Political Reform

For many years, state government leaders were in the driver's seat of political activism. The origins of this enlarged state role in domestic politics and policy were changes in representation, governmental organization, and professionalization spawned in the late 1960s. The states' activism was tested when federal officials began cutting aid to states and local governments in the late 1970s. Interest groups shifted their focus from Washington, D.C., to the state capitals, repeating a phenomenon that has occurred before in American history.

Rewriting state constitutions, restructuring political institutions, and assembling

Originally published as "Power to the States," *The State of the States*, 1996. Published by CQ Press, Washington, D.C. Reprinted with permission of the publisher.

professional expertise enabled state governments to design and implement far-reaching public policies.[2] Furthermore, the policy-making circles—in legislatures, courts, bureaucracies, and governors' mansions—were no longer exclusively filled with the upper-middle class white males that dominated government for most of American political history.

Landmark reapportionment decisions and changes in social attitudes transformed state governments from unrepresentative, homogeneous institutions to more representative bodies.[3] The U.S. Supreme Court in *Baker v. Carr* and *Reynolds v. Sims* removed barriers to direct representation of voters and reapportioned legislatures according to the principle of "one person, one vote." The Voting Rights Act of 1965 eliminated obstacles to full political participation by African-Americans. Black registration in the deep South grew by more than one million between 1964 and 1972, an increase from 29 percent to 57 percent of eligible voters.[4]

State legislatures and administrative agencies today have greater numbers of women and minorities than twenty years ago but still far fewer than men or Caucasians. Women holding legislative office, for example, increased from 4 percent in 1969 to 20.6 percent in 1995.[5] In Arizona, Colorado, Nevada, Vermont, and Washington, women hold 30 percent or more of the seats in the legislature. Women's participation in state government positions also has risen at the appointive policy-making levels. Women have been less successful in obtaining statewide elected office. In 1996, only one woman was serving as a governor — Christine Todd Whitman of New Jersey.[6]

Minority participation in elected and appointed policy-making positions in state government also has grown, but very slowly. Even so, blacks, who account for 12 percent of the U.S. population, held no governorships and just five percent of the state legislative positions in 1992. In 1970, none of the governors was black and less than two percent of legislators were black.[7] Hispanics increased their share of elected positions in several states where they make up a significant part of the population — Arizona, California, Colorado, and New Mexico. Florida and New Mexico have elected governors of Hispanic origin.

Representatives of these newly empowered groups demanded greater government intervention to ameliorate social and economic problems in their communities. Elected officials' policy priorities reflect their life experiences and professional training. More teachers and working women in elected and appointed positions encouraged greater attention to family leave programs, child care, and women's and children's health care.[8]

Business, labor, local governments, school boards, and other traditionally powerful groups still wield the most influence in state politics, but environmentalists, consumer advocates, and senior citizens have become more effective. Citizen participation in state policy making has exploded since the early 1970s. State agencies now routinely allow citizens to voice concerns through public boards and commissions, ombudsmen, public advocates, and public hearings. Newly active groups raise money and contribute to candidates, advertise in the mass media, and exert considerable influence over governors and legislatures.[9]

The initiative process has been employed with increasing frequency by political leaders, interest groups, and citizens groups. Ballot initiatives doubled between 1976 and 1990. Sometimes the initiative is used as a method of circumventing the legislative process. In other cases, the mere threat of mounting such a campaign is used to spur the legislature to act.

In 1990, 236 ballot questions appeared

in forty-three states—the largest number since 1914. Sixty-seven proposals were launched by citizens groups. In recent years, voters weighed important and controversial proposals, including the regulation of pornography, acid rain, abortions, drug use, and the length of time legislators may remain in office.[10] Some state officials have concluded that joining initiative battles is better than fighting them.

Political institutions also have expanded their staffs to achieve their policy agendas and to compete with rival institutions in the struggle for power. Governors expanded staffs overseeing the bureaucracy, monitoring developments in Washington, D.C., and shepherding the flock of legislative proposals in the statehouse. Legislatures bolstered staffs to keep a watchful eye on the executive branch and to provide more effective service to constituents.

The cumulative impact of state governments acquiring more expertise and the renewed focus on state government has been dramatic. State officials now are able to fulfill their ambition and to meet the expectations of others in carrying out their responsibilities in the federal system. States now plan and execute complex policy initiatives: water supply and quality improvement programs, pollution prevention programs, education reform, science and technology development, and energy conservation initiatives.[11]

To some extent, the concern of some federal lawmakers that states are not up to the task of carrying out large-scale governmental reforms is unwarranted. The capacity to make complex choices and to implement difficult programs exists already in many states. States have been managing such large federal programs as welfare and Medicaid for decades. Steve Gold, director of the Center for the Study of the States, offers a balanced observation about the states: "They have more ability

to make the important decisions, but that doesn't mean they're magicians."[12]

What is more controversial, and a source of concern to some and celebration for others, is the matter of what state governments will do with programs that used to be ruled by the federal government establishment. Proponents of greater state control, such as Illinois' Republican governor Jim Edgar, assert that the states "can run the programs at less cost than it costs us now."[13] Opponents of broad decentralization, such as Democratic senator John Breaux of Louisiana disagree: "We might as well just throw the money up in the air and hope it falls down and does good."[14]

State courts matched the activism of legislators and governors. The courts hired more judges, law clerks, and administrative officers to meet the rising demands for court review of policy and administrative cases. They took aggressive action on several public policy fronts, including expanding the rights of women, minorities, and criminal defendants. In doing so, state judges often relied upon state constitutions to establish rights that the U.S. Supreme Court has not found in the U.S. Constitution. State courts also expanded the rights of individuals to recover for personal injuries and imposed strict liability rules for faulty products. However, the conservative backlash now resident in many state legislatures has also found its way into the courtrooms around the country.

From Entrepreneurship to Crisis

During the 1980s, state governments brimmed with an entrepreneurial spirit. No longer passive partners in the federal system, states eagerly became a driving force in American politics. They levied and spent vast sums of money, hired hundreds of thousands of new employees, managed tough public problems, and sought out new policy frontiers to conquer. The states aggressively set policy agendas for the nation and fashioned innovative solutions for some of the most important policy problems.

State governments were imperialistic in the 1980s. Governors and legislators clamored for new ideas and expanded government spending and regulation. State officials displayed no sustained interest in controlling government's spiraling costs. State leaders were more concerned with improving public education, protecting the environment, and rebuilding roads, bridges, and sewers.

The rosy fiscal picture became clouded when the U.S. economy lapsed into a long and deep recession in the early 1990s. Because the federal government was unable to prime the state government pump with new dollars, the burden of the recession fell squarely on the states. Following the path taken in the 1982 recession, states responded to the 1991 recession by raising $16 billion in additional taxes and by cutting $10 billion in state programs. States scaled back their plans for greater government intervention. Unlike the federal government, which can defy fiscal gravity by borrowing money, state budgets are tethered to the reality of declining revenues. States cannot spend what they do not collect.

With the new ideological winds sweeping the nation, governmental activism at the state level is no longer in vogue. State government spending continues to grow for such basic services as education, prisons, health care, and transportation. But large-scale innovations that come with big price-tags have been shelved — at least for now. The election of 1994 brought in the largest number of Republican legislators and governors since 1968. Republicans are more likely than Democrats to stake their political futures on

government downsizing or at least holding the line against rapid expansion. In 1995, for the first time in a decade, state tax cuts exceeded state tax increases: twenty-five states cut taxes by $2.1 billion and fourteen states increased taxes by $910 million.[15]

The changes adopted by the Republican-controlled Congress in 1994 are likely to help deepen the ideological divisions between Republicans and Democrats running state governments. Issues such as policies about welfare programs and environmental regulation are likely to join tax policy as matters that deeply divide representatives of the two parties. This is a change worth noting. In the 1980s, state government leaders were characterized more by pragmatism than partisanship. For example, Democratic and Republican governors and legislators developed similar strategies for reforming welfare programs for the poor.[16] Today, however, partisan disagreements about the purpose of government action are rising.

Consider the reactions of two Florida legislators — one Republican and one Democrat — to proposed revisions in the Medicaid program. Republican senate president James Scott said: "We'll now have the challenge and opportunity to be creative, to do more with less, without all these federal restrictions." His Democratic counterpart in the Florida House, speaker Peter Rudy Wallace, disagreed: "Certainly in Medicaid there is the prospect that reductions are going to mean very, very difficult decisions between funding for Medicaid nursing home beds and funding for health services for children and younger people in this state."[17]

Fiscal Policy Squeeze

State officials operate in a volatile environment with a public concerned about both taxes and spending. Unfortunately, the public remains ambivalent about fiscal policy. Most voters want lower taxes, but they also support higher spending for most programs. State officials are constantly buffeted by the need to reconcile competing priorities. When revenues declined, as in the 1990s, the pressures on state officials grew more intense.

In the early 1980s, tax-limitation initiatives, most notably California's Proposition 13, were adopted by several states. The reigning government buzzwords were zero-based budgeting, executive reorganization, and cutback management. But the "limited government" movement, the love affair with curbing government growth, did not last through the decade. State government spending soared at rates higher than inflation through the 1980s. Ironically, this spurt of government growth was rooted in the economic crisis of 1982. Faced with the prospects of greater social welfare spending and reduced tax collections, twenty-eight states increased their income taxes, and thirty increased sales taxes.[18] Even without additional tax increases, these actions eventually would have yielded a fiscal bonanza. But nineteen states raised either their income or sales taxes again in 1984 and 1985. In addition, the 1986 federal tax reform law brought millions of additional dollars rolling into state treasuries.

The 1980s-style budgets could not be balanced with the revenues collected during the depressed economy of the 1990s. Facing a rising tide of red ink, more than thirty-five states turned to tax increases and program cuts to bring their budgets into balance. Despite these drastic measures, states had difficulty achieving equilibrium. Within six months of enacting the largest tax increases in decades, more than half the states were still facing budget deficits in their current year budgets.[19]

The sustained economic recovery of the mid–1980s contributed to reduced spending on some government services, such as unemployment insurance and welfare, and increased revenue collections. When the state treasuries bulged, most states spent the windfall instead of giving it back to the taxpayers. Several states established so-called rainy-day funds to cushion the shock of another recession, but typically the increased state revenues were quickly committed to new or expanded programs.[20]

The economic troubles of the 1990s reversed the trends of the 1980s and resulted in fewer revenues but increased demands for government spending. As the recession deepened, states spent more to meet the swelling demand for social services. Revenues dropped sharply as unemployment rose and as the corporate bottom line changed from profit to loss. The economic recovery that began in mid–1992 and continued through 1995 created a fiscal windfall. But a 1980s-style spending binge did not occur this time. Why? Because state policy makers are now more conservative in their outlook about the role of government. In addition, policy makers are mindful of the past and wary of repeating the mistakes of the 1980s when rapid expansion brought a heavy price when recession gripped the economy.

Power Struggles

Reforms fashioned in the 1960s and 1970s to strengthen the competence of state government simultaneously encouraged governors, legislators, judges, and bureaucrats to boldly assert power. As power fragmented, state politics became more conflict-ridden. Policy makers who wanted to tackle tough problems struggled to find consensus for specific actions. Distrust deepened as governors, judges, legislators, and administrators jealously guarded their prerogatives.

Unfortunately, the positive developments that made state governments more democratic and responsive also caused some troubling problems. Personal conflicts often escalated into battles for institutional control and the agenda of government. Fragmented policy making sometimes blurs clear lines of responsibility and thus decreases institutional accountability.

The reforms that fostered modern political institutions carved up power into bits and pieces and undermined the ability of any one institution or political leader to dominate state politics. Individualism was encouraged at the expense of institutional responsibility. With more at stake in the governance of states, everyone has a greater incentive to seek power and control.

Prevailing attitudes about the responsibilities of legislators also changed during the 1980s and 1990s. Modern legislators are much more likely to pursue their own agendas instead of those dictated by party leaders. Legislators feel they must aggressively champion their districts' interests even if they come in conflict with county party organizations, governors, and legislative leaders.[21] With their antennae tuned to the voters back home and campaign contributors, legislators often feel free to ignore appeals for party discipline.

The dispersion of power within political institutions has resulted in fierce battles for the control of policy agendas and outcomes. More intense competition is apparent in all phases of state political life from elections to state budget decisions. More legislators, judges, bureaucrats, and interest groups have sufficient clout to engage in the struggle, but few have enough power to rule.

The desire to hold on to power strongly shapes the political process within institutions, especially in legislatures where electoral considerations are paramount. The quest for power is hardly a new phenomenon, but career-oriented politicians are more intent on winning because they are more intent on remaining in office for a long time. "Permanent" legislators must constantly deliver benefits, claim credit for accomplishments, and attack opponents in the executive branch or elsewhere.[22] They undertake new legislative initiatives, examine administrative rules and regulations, scrutinize the state budget, and investigate government agencies. Clearly, these strategies serve their intended purpose; incumbents rarely lose.[23]

Incumbents and challengers also have stepped up the intensity of campaigns. Costs are rising because people are willing and able to spend huge sums of money to gain elective office. The staples of modern campaigns— media consultants, pollsters, and television advertising — are expensive. Statewide candidates must collect substantial sums of money or have a large personal fortune. Even legislative candidates now are required to assemble substantial resources, except in the smaller states.

A candidate who cannot afford to participate in high-cost elections is less likely to be heard. Those who form political action committees and contribute money or political support or both get special attention from the candidate and from officeholders who want to keep their jobs. Educators, dentists, senior citizens, labor leaders, builders, and others are effective advocates for their interests because they supply the campaign funds and the reliable voters that keep incumbent politicians around to serve them another day.

State politics is locked in a spiraling institutional "arms race." Governors, legislators, bureaucrats, judges, and interest groups are employing new techniques and strategies to achieve their goals. Governors assert greater control over the bureaucracy. Legislatures step up efforts to oversee executive government agencies. Interest groups bypass representative institutions and pursue goals through the initiative process. State courts adjudicate disputes between legislators and governors and make policy independently.

Nothing is inherently wrong with conflict. Representative government and deliberation are well served by sharp clashes of strongly held views. Few observers of American politics are nostalgic for a return to an era when a handful of party bosses and top ranking elected officials called the shots. But, unfortunately, many political conflicts result from ambiguous authority and personal political ambition instead of from disputes over competing policy visions. Institutional conflicts have sidetracked the policy process into a round-robin policy game as the court, legislature, and governor fight with one another for leadership.

The more strident politics of the 1990s has soured many incumbent officeholders and led to a rash of early retirements. Consider the remarks of Democratic governor Bruce Sundlun of Rhode Island:

> It's not fun to be governor. You can't have fun shutting the state down, abolishing positions, laying off personnel, and balancing the budget by cutting expenditures. Nobody likes any of these things.[24]

Divided party control of the legislature and governorship exacerbates institutional conflict. Voters in most states do not seem to be bothered, however. A remarkable increase in split-ticket voting has taken place in the last thirty years. Split control of state legislatures has increased from four states in 1982 to twelve states in 1994. In thirteen states in 1996 where one party dominated the entire legislature, the governor was from the other party.

As battles for power intensify, others are drawn into the fray. When legislators

and governors cannot reach clear decisions, they often delegate hard choices to the bureaucracy or create new administrative entities. This policy-making-by-other-means has caused a proliferation of commissions and "independent" authorities created through legislative and gubernatorial appointments. State courts, as a result, frequently are forced to mediate between the other branches of government. For example, courts have ruled recently on the authority of governors to exercise their line-item veto and extent of gubernatorial appointment and removal powers.

By entering into disputes between representative institutions, the courts allocate political power, shed the role of referee, and become policy makers.[25] For example, the state courts have handed down dozens of liberal decisions in civil rights cases and other fields. But this activism has come with a price. Many legislators, governors, and voters perceive that courts have thwarted majority preferences. And they have sought to reverse the courts by amending the constitution, passing new laws, or removing judges from office.

State courts have become a battleground for competing ideologies and policy agendas. Interest groups, legislators, and governors have tried to overturn court decisions. The courts successfully have fended off challenges to their authority in the interpretation of constitutional law. But their power to interpret common law has not been so well defended. For example, state legislatures have narrowed the rights of injured parties, but they have been less successful in curbing the state courts' support for the rights of women in sex discrimination cases.

Recently, liberal judges have been challenged in judicial confirmation elections as a way of reining in the courts. Decisions on hot-button issues, such as the death penalty, frequently are central issues in campaigns to oust judges. Spending on judicial elections and the number of direct challenges have risen substantially. Ballot initiatives have overturned liberal court decisions affecting criminal defendant rights. While the defeat of incumbent judges and anti-court initiatives still are rare, the fear of defeat may curb the courts' liberal leanings. In California, the defeat of three supreme court justices resulted in new appointees who affirmed more death penalty sentences— the outcome sought by voters in statewide referendums.

Bureaucracies also are embroiled in disputes over their activities, purposes, and performance. Legislatures have sharpened their oversight of agency decisions through sunset laws and reviews of administrative rules and regulations. Governors have exerted greater control through executive reorganizations, a reduction in the number of boards and commissions, centralization of budgeting techniques, and executive orders mandating direct accountability to the governor.

Governing During a Revolution

State governments are facing unprecedented challenges in the 1990s. The "Devolution Revolution" will make effective governing extremely difficult. Republicans in Congress are cutting federal aid to the states, consolidating programs and turning control over to governors and legislators. Republican governors and legislatures appear to be unwilling to raise taxes to fill the void. Interest groups— from environmentalists to advocates for the poor— are girding for new battles in the state capitals. State government officials are going to have to do more with less and to make dozens of new choices that previously were settled elsewhere. According to political scientist Don Kettl, states are being asked to "do things that no American government has ever done before.... The governors and legislatures will not only have to figure out how to manage these programs. They will have to learn to dance the intricate minuet of connecting them."[26]

The rise of governmental, institutional, and individual entrepreneurship makes meeting these new challenges more difficult. Institutional accountability has been overshadowed by individual accountability. When incumbent governors and legislators deny responsibility for the actions of their own governments or institutions, they are trying to avoid responsibility. When no one is willing to accept responsibility, people are less willing to act responsibly.

Legislators have tried to insulate themselves from executive domination, party leaders, and legislative leaders. Governors increasingly portray themselves as the clarion of the people, not the head of state government. They play to the press and go over the heads of party and legislative leaders. Political parties have been shoved aside by candidate-centered politics, where the incumbent, not the party, is judged. Partisanship is on the rise, but responsible party governance is on the decline. Even judges now are more wary of voter reactions to their judicial decisions.

When political officials act like independent agents in the political system, leadership becomes difficult. Legislative leaders serve at the pleasure of the partisans who selected them, so they wield influence by distributing campaign funds rather than through persuasion. Legislators and governors used to be primarily concerned with governing. Now, they are more likely to be preoccupied with power. And they are dismantling local party organizations and taking over electoral functions through leadership caucuses and political action committees.

The high price tag of elections means that elected officials are more accountable to those with money and less accountable to the public at large. The deep public resentment of special interest politics helps explain why proposals to limit the terms of officeholders have caught fire in more than twenty states.

Political fund raising diverts time from governing responsibilities and compromises elected officials. Legislators and governors commonly hold large fund-raising events while important policy issues are under consideration. Elected officials regularly solicit and receive campaign contributions from companies that either have contracts with the state or want to do business in the future. Partisan staff in the executive and legislative branches are routinely deployed to work on election activities.

Warfare between legislatures and governors enhances the power of bureaucracy and courts and thus reduces accountability to the public. More decisions are delegated from democratic institutions to administrative agencies. While these agencies are somewhat more responsive to the public than before, they are less responsive than governors or legislatures. And bureaucracies often obscure clear lines of responsibility and make establishing who is in charge difficult. Ultimately these conflicts may generate more contradictions, delay, rigidity, and uncertainty. As more decisions are thrown into the courts, the "judicialization of state administration" may result.

The new state politics also puts its stamp on public policy. As the power of narrow special interests rises, policies serving the public interest suffer. Policy makers concerned with their political survival are likely to choose the safest course and are less likely to confront difficult choices.

When governors and legislators are driven by short-run political needs, they may ignore the long-term needs of their state. Electoral expediency crowds out other important values. State officials may ensure their reelection but undermine their state's future and further cripple democratic institutions.

If more fiscal restraint had been exercised in the 1980s when the economy was booming, the 1990s recession would not have wreaked so much havoc on state budgets. Unlike the federal government, the states cannot borrow their way out. So when they raised taxes and cut programs, voters were angry. Incumbent officeholders paid the political price for the loose-money politics of the 1980s; many are declining to run for reelection.

The reliance on statewide initiatives to resolve public policy disputes represents a troubling development. In some of the nation's more populous states, such as California and Florida, state elected officials are passing the responsibility for tough decisions to initiative campaigns. These "issue elections" seldom are grass-roots citizens' movements. Instead, they are dominated by interest groups that spend lavishly on television advertising, direct mail, and tracking polls. For example, the insurance industry and its opponents spent $80 million on campaigns for and against a proposal to cut insurance premiums in California.

The erosion of accountability raises serious implications for the ability of political institutions to effectively handle public policy problems. Expansion and innovation are popular, but power struggles reduce the possibilities for reaching consensus on matters involving difficult trade-offs. The fragmentation of power and the reluctance to assume responsibility produce policy gridlock and delegation of the hard choices to administrative agencies.

How will state leaders manage the difficult realities of the late 1990s? Opponents of enhancing power to the state paint a grim picture. They claim that the safety net for poor people will be shredded and that incompetence and corruption will run rampant.[27] Advocates of greater state control naturally envision a different future. They see innovative and efficient programs operated by officials who have greater understanding of the needs of intended beneficiaries. They say it is high time for states to take over responsibility for problems that the federal government has been unable to solve.

Both proponents and opponents of devolution are exaggerating their positions to score political points with voters and interest groups. Giving greater responsibility to state governments while cutting federal aid will not usher in the dark ages. Nor will it be a panacea. It is difficult to predict what will happen because the scope of reform is unprecedented and because states are so diverse. It is safe to say, however, that the late 1990s will be chaotic for state governments as they adjust to expansions in responsibilities, reductions in federal resources, and higher expectations from various constituencies. As we near the end of this century, basic assumptions about the size and standard operating procedures of state governments are ripe for challenge and change. State governments are going to endure the tornado of policy reform, but not without sustaining serious damage to the reputations of state government officials and institutions.

Notes

1. Terry Sanford, *Storm Over the States* (New York: McGraw-Hill, 1967).

2. *Ibid.*; Larry J. Sabato, *Goodbye to Good-time Charlie: The American Governorship Transformed* (Washington, D.C.: CQ Press, 1983).

3. Timothy G. O'Rourke, *The Impact of Reapportionment* (New Brunswick, N.J.: Transaction Books, 1980).

4. Charles S. Bullock and Charles M. Lamb, eds., *Implementation of Civil Rights Policy* (Monterey, Calif.: Brooks/Cole, 1984), 20–54.

5. Center for the American Woman and Politics, National Information Bank on Women in Public Office, Eagleton Institute of Politics, Rutgers University, November 1995.

6. *Ibid.*

7. Personal communication from the Joint Center for Political Studies, Washington, D.C., December 5, 1992.

8. See, for example, Alan Ehrenhalt, "In Alabama Politics, The Teachers Are Sitting at the Head of the Class," *Governing* (December 1988): 22–27.

9. William T. Gormley, Jr., "The Representation Revolution: Reforming State Regulation through Representation," *Administration and Society* 18:2 (August 1986): 179–196.

10. Patrick B. McGuigan, *The Politics of Direct Democracy in the 1980s* (Washington, D.C.: Free Congress Research and Education Foundation, 1985); Patrick B. McGuigan, ed., *Initiative and Referendum Report* (Washington, D.C.: Free Congress Research and Education Foundation, December 1986/January 1987); Carol Matlack, "Where the Big Winner Was the Status Quo," *National Journal*, November 10, 1990, 2748–49.

11. See, for example, Advisory Commission on Intergovernmental Relations, *The Question of State Government Capability* (Washington, D.C.: Advisory Commission on Intergovernmental Relations, 1985).

12. Same Howe Verhovek, "State Lawmakers Prepare to Wield Vast New Powers," *New York Times*, September 24, 1995, 24.

13. David Rosenbaum, "Governors' Frustration Fuels Effort on Welfare Financing," *New York Times*, March 21, 1995, B7.

14. E.J. Dionne, Jr., "50 Ways to Waste Money," *Star-Ledger*, October 10, 1995, 15.

15. Robert Pear, "Federal Impasse Saddles States with Uncertainty," *New York Times*, January 2, 1996, A1.

16. Julie Rovner, "Welfare Reform: The Issue That Bubbled Up from the States to Capitol Hill," *Governing* (December 1988): 17–21.

17. Verhovek, "State Lawmakers Prepare to Wield Vast New Powers."

18. David S. Broder, "States Make Hard

Decision as Reagan Fantasies Wane," (Raleigh) *News and Observer*, August 5, 1987, A17.

19. National Association of State Budget Officers, *Looking for Light at the End of the Tunnel: States Struggle with Another Difficult Budget Year* (Washington, D.C.: National Association of State Budget Officers, January 1992), 2.

20. Steven D. Gold, ed., *Reforming State Tax Systems* (Denver, Colo.: National Conference of State Legislatures, 1986).

21. See, for example, Malcolm Jewell, *Representation in State Legislatures* (Lexington: University of Kentucky Press, 1982).

22. See, for example, Joel A. Thompson, "Bringing Home the Bacon: The Politics of Pork Barrel in the North Carolina Legislature," *Legislative Studies Quarterly* (February 1986): 91–108.

23. Richard Niemi and L.R. Winsky, "Membership Turnover in State Legislatures: Trends and Effects of Redistricting," *Legislative Studies Quarterly* 12 (1987): 115–124.

24. David Sherman, "Governors of Fiscally Strapped States, Seeing No Sign of Relief, Yearn for the Good Old Days," *Wall Street Journal*, August 19, 1991, 12.

25. Dave Frohnmayer, "The Courts as Referee" (Paper delivered at the State of the States Symposium, Eagleton Institute of Politics, Rutgers University, December 15–16, 1988).

26. Robert Pear, "Shifting Where the Buck Stops," *New York Times*, October 29, 1995, 4–3.

27. See, for example, Richard Cohen, "States Aren't Saints, Either," *Washington Post Weekly Edition*, April 3–9, 1995, 28.

• *Chapter 26* •

Overview of the Federal Government

Edwin Meese III

The Constitution defines, directly or indirectly, the structure and responsibilities of the federal government. According to the Constitution, any power not specifically given to the federal government is a power of the states. The country has changed tremendously since 1787 when the Founding Fathers wrote the Constitution. Changing circumstances have made it necessary to amend or change the Constitution and to expand the federal government. The principles behind the government have not changed even though the federal government has grown.

The Executive Branch

Of the three branches of the government, the executive branch is perhaps the most complex. Its job is to enforce the laws of the United States. It is made up of:

• the President;
• the Vice President;
• the executive departments; and,
• the independent agencies.

Each has special powers and functions. These are the general powers:

• The President acts as leader of the country and Commander in Chief of the military. He or she directs the federal government and enforces federal laws.
• The Vice President presides over the Senate and votes in case of a tie. He or she becomes President if the President is disabled or otherwise cannot serve.
• The departments, and their heads, the Cabinet members, advise the President on specific policy issues and help carry out those policies.
• The independent agencies help carry out policy or provide special services.

Originally published as "The Federal Government," *U.S. Government Structure*, 1987. Published by the Immigration and Naturalization Service, U.S. Department of Justice, U.S. Government Printing Office, Washington, D.C.

The President

The Presidency is the highest office in the country. According to the Constitution, the President must:

- be a natural-born citizen of the United States;
- be at least 35 years old by the time he/she will serve; and,
- have lived in the United States at least 14 years.

If a person meets these qualifications, he or she may run for President in the election.

Presidential elections occur every four years. Presidential candidates are chosen by their political parties in the months before the election. A political party is a group of people who have similar ideas about how the government should be run. Each party chooses its candidates in the following way:

- Each party holds primary elections, conventions or caucuses in every state.
  - The candidates campaign and
  - The people who belong to each party vote for the person they believe would be the best candidate; and,
- Each party holds a national convention.
  - Party members meet to choose the candidates for President and Vice President.
  - The Presidential candidate is usually the person who has won the most primary elections or conventions.
  - All states are included in the national convention of the party.

Some parties are too small to have primaries. They hold conventions to choose their candidates. The Republican and Democratic parties are the largest in the United States, but there are many smaller political parties. Candidates for public office also may be independent; that is, they do not have to belong to a political party.

After all candidates are chosen, the campaign begins for the general election. The winner of that election becomes President. The procedure for the general election is as follows:

- It is always held on the first Tuesday *after* the first Monday in November;
- People in each state vote *indirectly* for their choice for President:
  - the Electoral College actually elects the President;
  - the people vote to choose electors who will vote for the Presidential candidate;
  - the number of electors is the same as the number of Representatives plus the number of Senators the state has;
  - in this way, the states keep their **influence** over the election of the President;
- The electors from each state meet on a specified date:
  - they do not vote for the person they want to be President;
  - they vote for the choice of the largest number of people in their state; and,
- The candidate with more than half of the electoral votes wins. (If no candidate has more than half of the electoral votes, the House of Representatives chooses one of the candidates.)

The newly elected President is inaugurated on January 20, two months after the November election. Each President may serve only two terms. Each term is four years.

The President has many duties and responsibilities, most of which are listed in the Constitution. The main ones are:

- to enforce laws and treaties of the United States;
- to conduct foreign policy (subject to certain limits placed by Congress and the Constitution);
- to serve as Commander in Chief of the armed forces;
- to approve or veto the bills which Congress passes;
- when appropriate, to pardon people found guilty of breaking federal law;

• to appoint people to certain positions, subject to Senate approval:
— heads of executive departments, or Cabinet members;
— heads of independent executive agencies;
— Supreme Court justices and judges of other federal courts; and,
• to advise Congress on his/her perception of the nation's needs.

The Vice President

The Vice-Presidency is the second highest office in the country, next to the Presidency. If the president dies, leaves office, or cannot perform his/her duties, the Vice President becomes President. For this reason, the Vice President must meet the same requirements as the President:

• be a natural-born citizen of the U.S.;
• be at least 35 years old by the time he or she will serve; and,
• have lived in the United States at least 14 years.

The Constitution established that the Vice President would be the person who received the second highest number of electoral votes, but that did not work well. Often the person who received the second highest number of votes had been the **opponent** of the person who had the most votes. When they became President and Vice President, they could not always work well together. The 12th amendment, in 1804, established separate ballots in the Electoral College for President and Vice President. First the electors vote on the President and then the Vice President. The President and Vice President run together in the general election.

The Vice President has special duties and responsibilities, most of which are listed in the Constitution. The most important ones are:

• to serve as Acting President if the President is disabled, for example, during an operation;
• to preside over the Senate, and vote in case of a tie;
• to act as a link between the President and the Senate;
• to participate in Cabinet meetings; and,
• to serve as a member of the National Security Council.

Laws also have been passed to establish a **succession** to the Presidency, in the event that both the President and the Vice President are unable to serve. The next in line, after the Vice President, is the Speaker of the House of Representatives, then the President **pro tempore** of the Senate, then the Secretary of State. The **line of succession** then includes the other Cabinet members in a set order. This order makes certain that the country will never be without a leader. The descriptions of the executive departments which follow are in the same order as the line of succession.

The Cabinet

The members of the Cabinet are the heads of the executive departments and usually are called Secretaries. (The head of the Department of Justice is the Attorney General of the U.S.) The Constitution did not set up a Cabinet, but every President, beginning with George Washington, has had a Cabinet to advise him and to carry out his instructions. The Cabinet and the departments are very helpful in carrying out the policies of the government which affect almost everyone living in the United States.

During George Washington's Presidency, there were only four Cabinet members: Secretary of State, Secretary of Treasury, Secretary of War, and Attorney General. As of 1987 there were 13 departments, showing how much the nation has grown and changed. Perhaps in the future more departments will be added or some will be abolished. This will depend on the needs of the nation. The 13 departments and their main responsibilities are:

Department of State

- Advises the President in making and conducting foreign policy.
- Provides information and advice about other countries.
- Provides services to Americans traveling or living abroad.
- Conducts consular affairs and services, such as providing visas.
- **Negotiates** treaties and agreements with other countries.

Department of the Treasury

- Advises the President on financial matters.
- Operates the Customs Service which regulates exports from and imports to the U.S.
- Designs and prints currency and makes coins.
- Maintains the Secret Service which provides protection to high-ranking government officials.
- Finds and arrests banking and currency law violators.
- Operates the Internal Revenue Service which collects income taxes.

Department of Defense

- Advises the President on military matters.
- Provides military forces to protect national security.
- Responsible for national defense.
- Directs the Army, Air Force and Navy, including the Marine Corps.

Department of Justice

- Advises the President on legal matters.
- Protects rights guaranteed by the Constitution.
- Represents the United States in all legal matters.
- Conducts cases in the Supreme Court if the U.S. is involved.

- Through the Immigration and Naturalization Service, enforces immigration laws and provides information and processes applications for immigrants who wish to become citizens.
- Maintains the federal prison system.

Department of the Interior

- Advises the President on conservation issues.
- Maintains most nationally owned public lands and natural resources.
- Administers programs for Native American groups.
- Works to identify, protect and restore endangered species of fish, wildlife and plants.
- Administers the national parks, monuments, historic sites and recreation areas through the National Park Service.

Department of Agriculture

- Advises the President on problems of farmers.
- Researches efficient agricultural methods.
- Provides loans to help family-size and smaller farms.
- Inspects and grades agricultural produce, such as meat and poultry, which appears in the grocery store.
- Provides nutrition programs for low-income persons.
- Helps farmers get a fair price for their crops.
- Operates national forests.

Department of Commerce

- Advises the President about the country's business matters.
- Promotes and develops domestic and foreign trade.
- Conducts the **Census** every 10 years.
- Issues patents.
- Studies transportation and travel.
- Provides weather reports to the public.

Department of Labor

- Advises the President on the welfare of workers.

- Administers labor laws to ensure safe and healthful working conditions, minimum wage laws, overtime pay rates, freedom from employment **discrimination**, unemployment insurance, and workers' compensation.
- Administers job training programs to help disadvantaged persons attain self-sufficiency.
- Protects rights of union members.

Department of Health and Human Services

- Advises the President on health and welfare policies and programs.
- Works to improve health services.
- Works to prevent and control disease.
- Administers assistance programs, such as Social Security, Aid to Families with Dependent Children, Aid to the Blind, and refugee assistance programs.

Department of Housing and Urban Development

- Advises the President on housing programs and community development.
- Works to improve housing and living conditions.
- Provides low interest loans to promote home ownership and development of low cost housing.

Department of Transportation

- Advises the President on transportation matters.
- Develops policies and programs to promote safe, fast, convenient and efficient transportation.
- Maintains the Coast Guard which enforces safety regulations for vessels, and saves lives and property at sea.
- Promotes development of air transportation, highways, and railroads.

Department of Education

- Advises the President on education programs and plans.

- Works to improve education in the U.S.
- Provides support for special education.
- Publishes reports on the condition of education.
- Administers programs providing educational services, such as bilingual, vocational and adult education.
- Assists many students in paying for postsecondary schooling through grants, loans and work study programs.

Department of Energy

- Advises the President on energy planning and policy making.
- Researches new, efficient and cost-effective forms of energy.
- Promotes conservation of energy.
- Researches and provides information on energy trends.
- Regulates energy rates and grants licenses.

Department of Veterans Affairs[1]

- Advises the President on matters relating to veterans affairs.
- Provides services to veterans of all branches of the armed services.
- Services include burial and memorial benefits; health benefits and services, compensation and pension benefits, vocational rehabilitation and employment services, home loan and guaranty services, life insurance programs, and educational benefits.
- Administers all special veterans programs, such as those for disabled veterans, homeless veterans, military veterans, minority veterans, and women veterans.
- Supervises all federal agencies that provide government services to veterans.
- Protects the rights of veterans under all laws pertaining to their services and benefits.
- Manages and processes appeals of veterans under the Board of Veterans Appeals.

Independent Agencies

In addition to the departments, there are independent agencies in the executive branch. They are not departments because they serve a very specific need or they are intended to be temporary. There are dozens of agencies, and they change more frequently than departments. Some of these agencies and their main responsibilities are:

- **Commission on Civil Rights** tries to prevent discrimination on the basis of race, color, religion, sex, age, handicapping condition, or national origin.
- **Consumer Product Safety Commission** investigates and reports on the safety of consumer products.
- **Environmental Protection Agency** sets standards for clean air and water; helps industry and local government clean up polluted areas.
- **Federal Deposit Insurance Company (FDIC)** insures the money deposited in banks which belong to the FDIC system.
- **Federal Election Commission (FEC)** tries to keep elections to federal office honest and fair.
- **Federal Reserve Board** helps the nation's economy grow, by controlling the money. The Federal Reserve loans money only to banks.
- **Federal Trade Commission (FTC)** promotes fair competition in the economy.
- **National Aeronautics and Space Administration (NASA)** promotes and develops programs which are devoted to the peaceful use of space. NASA plans and carries out all space flights, including the space shuttle, and works to develop the space station program.
- **National Labor Relations Board** attempts to protect the rights of both employer and employee to have fair labor relations.
- **Small Business Administration (SBA)** counsels, assists and protects small business interests. The SBA provides loans, education and assistance to small businesses.
- **United States Information Agency (USIA)** publicizes aspects of U.S. culture, policy and opinions abroad to encourage understanding of the U.S. in other countries. It produces Voice of America and Radio Marti broadcasts.
- **United States Postal Service** is responsible for delivering nearly 150 billion pieces of mail throughout the U.S. each year.

- **Veterans Administration (VA)** provides services to men and women who served in the U.S. armed forces. The VA helps veterans and their families with education, loans, medical services, and **compensation** to disabled veterans or to the families of those who died.

The Legislative Branch

The legislative branch, or Congress, makes the laws which govern the nation. Congress is divided into two houses, the Senate and the House of Representatives. This is called a bicameral legislature. The House and Senate have some separate and some shared responsibilities. The shared duties and responsibilities as written in the Constitution are:

- regulating money and trade, including
  - printing or coining of money,
  - borrowing of money by the government,
  - levying and collecting taxes, and,
  - regulating trade between states and with foreign countries;
- providing for the national defense, including
  - maintaining the Army, Navy and Air Force, and
  - declaring war;
- making laws regarding naturalization of persons seeking citizenship;
- establishing post offices;
- regulating the system of weights and measures; and,
- passing laws to govern the District of Columbia, the nation's capital.

The separate responsibilities, as written in the Constitution, are:

- **House of Representatives:**
  - introducing bills about the budget or taxes,
  - impeaching officials; and,
- **Senate:**
  - determining if impeached officials are innocent or guilty,
  - confirming Presidential appointments, and

— ratifying treaties between the U.S. and other governments.

The Constitution also lists some things Congress may never do:

- tax exports;
- pass trade laws which do not treat all states equally;
- spend tax money without a law to authorize it;
- authorize any title of nobility;
- pass a law to punish someone for an act which was legal when the person did it; and,
- pass any law which takes away a person's right to a trial in court.

Passing a Law

Congress spends most of its time passing **legislation** or laws. A complex procedure is followed to make sure that many different people have a chance to discuss the **bill**, ask questions about it, and change (amend) it if they think it needs to be changed. The procedure is as follows:

- Either a Senator or a Representative may introduce a bill which he/she wants to become a law.
  - The *exception* is that only Representatives may introduce tax or budget bills.
- A committee of the House of Congress in which the bill was introduced studies the bill. The bill can be:
  - amended,
  - rewritten,
  - recommended for passage without changes,
  - tabled or ignored, or
  - reported back to its House with no recommendation, after which it usually does not become law.
- Unless tabled the bill goes to its House of Congress for debate.
  - The committee makes a report on the bill.
  - The House debates and amends the bill, if needed.
  - The House either passes or defeats the bill.

- If the bill passes the first House, it is sent to the other House.
  - The second House debates the bill.
  - If the bill is amended, it must be sent back to the first House. Both Houses of Congress must agree on the amendments.
- If the bill passes both Houses in the same form, it is sent to the President. He can:
  - sign it. Then it becomes law.
  - do nothing. After 10 days, if Congress stays in session, it becomes law.
  - do nothing. If Congress adjourns within 10 days, it does not become law.
  - veto it. It does not become law.
- Congress may pass the bill over the President's veto by a two-thirds vote of both Houses.

Structure

The two Houses of Congress are set up very differently. The Senate is the smaller House. Its structure and requirements for serving are explained below.

- The Senate has 100 members (Senators).
  - There are two from every state.
  - Each Senator represents the whole state.
  - Members are elected for six-year terms.
  - Elections for one-third of the Senate seats are held every two years.
  - There is no limit to the number of times a Senator may be re-elected.
- Its officers include:
  - the Vice President, who presides and votes only in case of a tie, and
  - the President pro tempore, a Senator chosen to preside when the Vice President is not there.
- To be a Senator, a person must be:
  - at least 30 years old,
  - a citizen at least nine years, and,
  - a resident of the state he/she represents.

The House of Representatives is set up differently from the Senate. It also has different qualifications.

- The House of Representatives has 435 members (Representatives).

— The number of Representatives from each state varies, and this number is based on the population
–Each state has at least one Representative.
–The District of Columbia has one Representative who does not vote.
— Most states are divided into districts. A Representative of the people is chosen in each district.
— Members are elected for two-year terms.
— There is no limit to the number of times a Representative may be re-elected.
• The Speaker of the House presides.
— The Speaker of the House is elected by the other Representatives.
— The Speaker is usually a member of the majority party.
• To be a Representative, a person must be:
— at least 25 years old.
— a citizen at least seven years, and
— a resident of the state he/she represents.

The Constitution established that the Congress must meet regularly. A new Congress begins every two years, with the election of new Senators and Representatives. The time they meet to make laws is called a session. Congress meets in the Capitol Building in Washington, D.C. The House of Representatives has a large room, the Senate a smaller one, and the President has some offices for his/her use. Many people visit the Capitol Building each year to see where their members of Congress make laws.

The Judicial Branch

The judicial branch is made up of different federal courts. It is responsible for explaining and interpreting the laws. People take cases to court to preserve the rights guaranteed to them in the Constitution and by law. They also can take cases to court if they believe the laws passed by Congress or by a state are unconstitutional.

Structure

The court structure in the United States is **hierarchical**. There are local, state and federal courts, as well as different courts for different purposes. The establishment of the federal courts is provided in Article III of the Constitution, but most of the structure was decided later.

• The **Supreme Court** is the highest court in the country.
— It was established by the Constitution.
— Its **ruling** is the final decision on a case.
• **Circuit Courts of Appeals** are the second highest courts, a step below the Supreme Court.
— There are 11 Circuit Courts in the United States.
— They hear appeals from lower courts, when people believe something was unjust about the decision of the lower court.
• **District Courts** are the lowest level of federal courts.
— As of 1987, there were 94 district courts in the United States.
— If a person is accused of breaking a federal law, he/she will be tried in a district court.
• CONGRESS also has set up some special courts:
— Court of Claims,
— Customs Court,
— Court of Customs and Patent Appeals, and
— Court of Military Appeals.

The federal courts have special duties:

• to explain the meaning of the Constitution, laws of the United States and treaties;
• to settle legal disputes between citizens of different states;
• to settle legal disagreements between two or more states;
• to settle legal questions between states and the federal government;
• to settle legal disagreements between individuals and the federal government;
• to settle disagreements between states and foreign governments or their citizens; and,

- to naturalize persons as United States citizens.

The Supreme Court

The Supreme Court—the highest court in the United States—cannot be abolished except by amending the Constitution. Nine judges, called Justices, sit on the Supreme Court in Washington, D.C. One of the judges is chosen as Chief Justice, who acts as the leader. The Supreme Court has two types of authority:

- As an appellate court, it can overturn decisions made by lower courts.
  — Most cases it hears are appeals, in which people believe the decision of a lower court was not fair.
  — The *exception* is that cases involving foreign diplomats originate in the Supreme Court.
- As the Supreme Court, it can declare a state or federal law unconstitutional.
  — That means the law disagrees with the Constitution and must be abolished.
  — The decision is final.

Appeals

One of the most important rights in the United States is the right to a fair trial. The appeals process is set up to help make sure that people have as fair a trial as possible. Sometimes a person believes justice was not served at his/her trial because he/she believes:

- his/her rights were violated;
- a rule of law was not properly followed; or,
- all the evidence was not available.

That person may try to appeal his/her case to a higher court. The judge may agree with the:

- person and overturn the lower court's decision; or,
- lower court and uphold the decision.

The person may try to appeal again if he/she still is not satisfied. Courts will not always hear appeals, however. The Supreme Court does not hear all appeals because:

- the Supreme Court is busy, and wants to be able to give enough time to each case;
- it usually hears cases which involve complex questions about the protection of rights; and,
- sometimes the Justices decide in a **preliminary** review that the lower court gave the right decision.

Making It Work

The United State government seems complicated to many people because it has so many parts. Each branch has its specific functions. The branches work together to make a government which can best serve the interests of all the people. The three branches make the system of government by law work:

- the **legislative branch** makes the laws;
- the **executive branch** puts the laws into effect; and,
- the **judicial branch** applies and explains the laws.

Just as the three branches work together, they also serve to check and balance each other. This important principle was written into the Constitution so that the branches would have the same amount of power. There are several ways the branches check and balance each other:

- The Supreme Court can declare a law passed by the Congress or an action by the President to be unconstitutional.
- The President can veto a law passed by Congress.
- Congress can pass a law overriding the President's veto.
- The President appoints Supreme Court Justices.
- Congress can refuse to confirm appointments made by the President.

Responsibilities

Both citizens and the government have responsibilities to each other. It is important for each to fulfill their responsibilities. Some citizen responsibilities are to:

- be an informed and regular voter;
- obey laws;
- pay taxes honestly and on time; and,
- express concern and requests about the government in a peaceful and helpful way.

Some government responsibilities are to:

- protect and enforce the rights guaranteed in the Constitution;
- spend people's tax money wisely; and,
- be responsive to citizens' requests.

Note

1. The US Department of Veterans Affairs was established as a Cabinet-level position by Congress on March 15, 1989. Since the date of this chapter is 1987, the information about this new federal department was added to this chapter to make it as accurate as possible. Much of this information was obtained from the Department of Veterans Affairs Home Page (http://www.va.gov/).

• Chapter 27 •

The Complexity of the Federal Government

Roger L. Kemp

The traditional three branches of government at the federal level — legislative, judicial, executive — by themselves encompass nearly thirty offices and agencies within the national bureaucracy. This is in addition to the fourteen major executive agencies under the executive branch of government. Also, the American national government includes a plethora of independent organizations and government corporations; including numerous boards, commissions, and committees; and a host of multilateral, bilateral, and quasi-official organizations and agencies. While most of these entities are created by Congress, many have been created by presidential actions throughout the years.

In order to educate the reader about the many layers and organizational units within the American federal system of government, this chapter highlights these entities using four general categories. These include the organizational structure of the three branches; independent organizations and government corporation; boards, commissions, and committees; and multi-lateral, bilateral, and quasi-official organizations and agencies. This is a hierarchical ranking, based on the importance of these agencies and organizations within the federal government bureaucracy. The information contained in this chapter was obtained from *The United States Government Manual 2000/2001,* compiled by the Office of the Federal Register and the National Archives and Records Administration in June of 2000.[1]

Organizational Structure of the Three Branches

The three branches of the federal government — legislative, executive, and judicial — each include several important offices of the federal organization. The legislative branch, in addition to the House of Representatives and Senate, encompass six organizational units. The executive branch, in addition to the offices of the President, Vice President, and Executive Office of the President, includes ten offices and councils. Additionally, the judicial branch, which includes the Supreme Court of the United States, is over eleven specialized courts. The various organizational units of these three branches of the federal government are shown below by branch of government.

Legislative Branch:
Architect of the Capitol
United States Botanic Garden
General Accounting Office
Government Printing Office
Library of Congress
Congressional Budget Office

Judicial Branch:
United States Courts of Appeals
United States District Courts
Territorial Courts
United States Court of International Trade
United States Court of Federal Claims
United States Court of Appeals for the Armed Forces
United States Tax Court
United States Court of Appeals for Veterans Claims
Administrative Office of the United States Courts
Federal Judicial Center
United States Sentencing Commission

Executive Branch:
White House Office
Council of Economic Advisers
Council on Environmental Quality
National Security Council
Office of Administration
Office of Management and Budget
Office of National Drug Control Policy
Office of Policy Development
Office of Science and Technology Policy
Office of the U.S. Trade Representative

Executive Departments and Agencies:
Department of Agriculture
Department of Commerce
Department of Defense
  Department of the Air Force
  Department of the Army
  Department of the Navy
  Defense Agencies
  Joint Service Schools
Department of Education
Department of Energy
Department of Health and Human Services
Department of Housing and Urban Development
Department of the Interior
Department of Justice
Department of Labor
Department of State
Department of Transportation
Department of the Treasury
Department of Veterans Affairs

Independent Organizations and Government Corporations

The federal government includes some fifty-five independent organizations and government corporations. These government entities have been created by Congress throughout the years to typically carry out single programs or to grant a new program autonomy from the existing bureaucratic structure of the federal government. These groups range from such new organizations such as the African Development Foundation to the traditional mainstays of the federal government like the U.S. Postal Service.

African Development Foundation
Central Intelligence Agency
Commodity Futures Trading Commission
Consumer Product Safety Commission

Corporation for National and Community Service

Defense Nuclear Facilities Safety Board

Environmental Protection Agency

Equal Employment Opportunity Commission

Export-Import Bank of the U.S.

Farm Credit Administration

Federal Communications Commission

Federal Deposit Insurance Corporation

Federal Election Commission

Federal Emergency Management Agency

Federal Housing Finance Board

Federal Labor Relations Authority

Federal Maritime Commission

Federal Mediation and Conciliation Service

Federal Mine Safety and Health Review Commission

Federal Reserve System

Federal Retirement Thrift Investment Board

Federal Trade Commission

General Services Administration

Inter-American Foundation

Merit Systems Protection Board

National Aeronautics and Space Administration

National Archives and Records Administration

National Capital Planning Commission

National Credit Union Administration

National Foundation on the Arts and the Humanities

National Labor Relations Board

National Mediation Board

National Railroad Passenger Corporation (Amtrak)

National Science Foundation

National Transportation Safety Board

Nuclear Regulatory Commission

Occupational Safety and Health Review Commission

Office of Government Ethics

Office of Personnel Management

Office of Special Counsel

Overseas Private Investment Corporation

Peace Corps

Pension Benefit Guaranty Corporation

Postal Rate Commission

Railroad Retirement Board

Securities and Exchange Commission

Selective Service System

Small Business Administration

Social Security Administration

Tennessee Valley Authority

Trade and Development Agency

U.S. Agency for International Development

U.S. Commission on Civil Rights

U.S. International Trade Commission

U.S. Postal Service

Boards, Commissions, and Committees

The following is a listing of federal boards, commissions, councils, and other federal organizational units, which were established by congressional or presidential action, whose functions are not strictly limited to the internal operations of a parent department or agency and which are authorized to publish documents in the *Federal Register*. Federal advisory committees, as defined by the Federal Advisory Committee Act, as amended (5 U.S.C. app.), have not been included here.

Administrative Committee of the Federal Register

Advisory Council on Historic Preservation

American Battle Monuments Commission

Appalachian Regional Commission

Architectural and Transportation Barriers Compliance Board

Arctic Research Commission

Arthritis and Musculoskeletal Interagency Coordinating Committee

Barry M. Goldwater Scholarship and Excellence in Education Foundation

Chemical Safety and Hazard Investigation Board

Citizens' Stamp Advisory Committee

Commission of Fine Arts

Committee on Foreign Investment in the United States

Committee for the Implementation of Textile Agreements

Committee for Purchase from People Who Are Blind or Severely Disabled

Coordinating Council on Juvenile Justice and Delinquency Prevention

Delaware River Basin Commission

Endangered Species Committee

Export Administration Review Board

Federal Financial Institutions Examination Council

Federal Financing Bank

Federal Interagency Committee on Education

Federal Laboratory Consortium for Technology Transfer

Federal Library and Information Center Committee

Harry S. Truman Scholarship Foundation

Illinois and Michigan Canal National Heritage Corridor Commission

Indian Arts and Crafts Board

Interagency Committee on Employment of People with Disabilities

Interagency Savings Bonds Committee

James Madison Memorial Fellowship Board

J. William Fulbright Foreign Scholarship Foundation

Japan-United States Friendship Commission

Joint Board for the Enrollment of Actuaries

Marine Mammal Commission

Medicare Payments Advisory Commission

Migratory Bird Conservation Commission

Mississippi River Commission

Morris K. Udall Scholarship and Excellence in National Environmental Policy Foundation

National Commission on Libraries and Information Science

National Council on Disability

National Occupational Information Coordinating Committee

National Park Foundation

Navajo and Hopi Relocation Commission

Northwest Power Planning Council

Panama Canal Commission

Permanent Committee for the Oliver Wendell Holmes Devise

President's Committee on Employment of People with Disabilities

President's Council on Integrity and Efficiency

President's Foreign Intelligence Advisory Board

Presidio Trust

Social Security Advisory Board

Susquehanna River Basin Commission

Textile Trade Policy Group

Trade Policy Staff Committee

United States Holocaust Memorial Museum

United States Nuclear Waste Technical Review Board

Veterans Day National Committee

White House Commission on Presidential Scholars.

Multilateral, Bilateral, and Quasi-Official Organizations and Agencies

The United States government participates in many organizations in accordance with existing treaties, other international agreements, congressional legislation, or executive arrangements. In some cases, no financial contributions are involved. Various commissions, councils or committees subsidiary to the organizations listed are not named separately. This list of organizations and agencies include the international bodies for narcotics control, which are subsidiary to the United Nations. Multilateral organizations include agreements between three or more countries, or central government subsidiaries of countries. Bilateral organizations, on the other hand, include agreements between only two countries, or central government agencies thereof. Lastly, quasi-official agencies includes those organizations that are not executive agencies under the definition of 5 U.S.C. (105), but are required by statute to publish certain information on their programs and activities in the *Federal Register*.

Multinational Organizations

United Nations, Specialized Agencies, and International Atomic Energy Agency:
Food and Agricultural Organization
International Atomic Energy Agency
International Civil Aviation Organization
International Labor Organization
International Maritime Organization
International Telecommunication Union
United Nations
Universal Postal Union
World Health Organization
World Intellectual Property Organization
World Meteorological Organization

Peacekeeping
United Nations Disengagement Observer Force (Golan Heights)
United Nations Force in Cyprus
United Nations Interim Force in Lebanon
United Nations Iraq-Kuwait Observer Mission
United Nations Military Observer Group in India and Pakistan
United Nations Mission in Bosnia-Herzegovina
United Nations Mission in the Democratic Republic of Congo
United Nations Mission in Kosovo
United Nations Mission in Sierra Leone
United Nations Mission of Observers in Tajikistan
United Nations Mission to Prevlaka
United Nations Mission for the Referendum in Western Sahara

United Nations Observer Mission in Angola
United Nations Observer Mission in Georgia
United Nations Transitional Administration in East Timor
United Nations Truce Supervision Organization (Middle East)

Inter-American Organizations
Inter-American Indian Institute
Inter-American Institute for Cooperation on Agriculture
Inter-American Tropical Tuna Commission
Organization of American States
Pan American Health Organization (PAHO)
Pan American Institute of Geography and History
Postal Union of the Americas and Spain and Portugal

Regional Organizations
Asia-Pacific Economic Cooperation
Colombo Plan for Cooperative Economic and Social Development in Asia and the Pacific
North Atlantic Assembly
North Atlantic Treaty Organization
Organization for Economic Cooperation and Development (OECD)
South Pacific Commission

Other International Organizations
Bureau of International Expositions
Commission for the Conservation of Antarctic Marine Living Resources
Customs Cooperation Council (CCC)
Fund for the Protection of the World Cultural and Natural Heritage
Hague Conference on Private International Law
International Agency for Research on Cancer
International Bureau of the Permanent Court of Arbitration
International Bureau for the Publication of Customs Tariffs

International Bureau of Weights and Measures

International Center for the Study of the Preservation and the Restoration of Cultural Property (ICCROM)

International Commission for the Conservation of Atlantic Tunas

International Copper Study Group

International Cotton Advisory Committee

International Council for the Exploration of the Seas (ICES)

International Council of Scientific Unions and Its Associated Unions (20)

International Criminal Police Organization (INTERPOL)

International Hydrographic Organization

International Institute for Cotton

International Institute for the Unification of Private Law

International Lead and Zinc Study Group

International Natural Rubber Organization

International North Pacific Fisheries Commission

International Office of Epizootics

International Office of Vine and Wine

International Organization for Legal Metrology

International Rubber Study Group

International Seed Testing Association

International Tropical Timber Organization

International Union for the Conservation of Nature and Natural Resources (UNC)

International Union for the Protection of New Varieties of Plants (UPOV)

International Whaling Commission

International Wheat Council

Interparliamentary Union

North Atlantic Ice Patrol

North Atlantic Salmon Conservation Organization

Organization for the Prevention of Chemical Weapons

Permanent International Association of Navigation Congresses

Permanent International Association of Road Congresses

United Nations Compensation Commission

World Trade Organization (WTO)/General Agreement on Tariffs and Trade (GATT)

Special Voluntary Programs

African Development Bank

Asian Development Bank

Colombo Plan Drug Advisory Program

Consultative Group on International Agricultural Research

Convention on International Trade in Endangered Species of Wild Fauna and Flora (CITES)

Inter-American Defense Board

International Atomic Energy Agency Technical Assistance and Cooperation Fund

International Atomic Energy Agency Voluntary Programs

International Civil Aviation Organization (ICAO) Aviation Security Fund

International Contributions for Scientific, Educational, and Cultural Activities

International Fund for Agricultural Development (IFAD)

International Organization for Migration (IOM)

Korean Peninsula Energy Development Organization

Montreal Protocol Multilateral Fund

Organization of American States Fund for Strengthening Democracy

Organization of American States Special Cultural Fund

Organization of American States Special Development Assistance Fund

Organization of American States Special Multilateral Fund (Education and Science)

Organization of American States Special Projects Fund (Mar del Plata)

Pan American Health Organization Special Health Promotion Funds

United Nations Afghanistan Emergency Trust Fund

United Nations Center for Human Settlements (Habitat) (UNCHS)

United Nations Children's Fund (UNICEF)

United Nations Development Fund for Women (UNIFEM)

United Nations Development Program (UNDP)

United Nations Environment Program (UNEP)

United Nations/Food and Agricultural Organization World Food Program (WFP)

United Nations Fund for Drug Abuse Control (UNFDAC)

United Nations High Commissioner for Refugees Program (UNHCF)

United Nations Population Fund

United Nations Relief and Works Agency (UNRWA)

United Nations Volunteers (UNV)

World Health Organization Special Programs

World Meteorological Organization Special Fund for Climate Activities

World Meteorological Organization Voluntary Cooperation Program

Bilateral Organizations

International Boundary Commission, United States and Canada

International Boundary and Water Commission, United States and Mexico

International Joint Commission — United States and Canada

Joint Mexican-United States Defense Commission

Permanent Joint Board on Defense — United States and Canada

Quasi-Official Agencies

Legal Services Corporation

Smithsonian Institution

State Justice Institute

United States Institute of Peace

Retrospective Commentary

Compared to the other levels of government in America's intergovernmental system, the federal bureaucracy is the most complicated layer when compared to city, county, regional, and state government organizations. In fact, the book that provides a brief overview of our federal government, *The United States Government Manual 2000–2001*, is about 700 pages in length. The goal of this chapter is to make sense out of the many organizational units within the federal system, and to present them in a hierarchical order, showing their importance within the federal government system.

In summary, the many layers of the federal government, and the number of organizational entities within each, are highlighted below.

Branches (3)
   Legislative Branch (7)
   Judicial Branch (10)
   Executive Branch (14)
   Executive Departments and Agencies (19)

Independent Organizations and Government Corporations (55)

Boards, Commissions, and Committees (57)

Multilateral Organizations (115)

Bilateral Organizations (5)

Quasi-Official Agencies (4)

Note

1. *The United States Government Manual* is an annual publication by the federal government, compiled by the Office of the Federal Register and the National Archives and Records

Administration, and published by the U.S. Superintendent of Documents, Washington, D.C. The 2000/01 volume was selected for this analysis in an effort to reflect the complexity of the U.S. federal government as our society enters the 21st century.

• *Chapter 28* •

The Congress

Lydia Bjornlund

The 106th Congress began its term embroiled in the impeachment hearings of President William Jefferson Clinton. As the Senate hearings dragged on, public opinion polls revealed Americans' increasing frustration with the proceedings and a desire for Congress to "get back to business"—even as the public clung to every word of the trial. When the Senate acquitted President Clinton of the charges of perjury and obstruction of justice on February 12, both houses returned to the same legislative issues that had plagued them over the past several years—years during which they had been dubbed the "do-nothing Congress."

As in 1998, partisan bickering got in the way of making progress on key legislation, including health care reform, bankruptcy legislation, and plans to close loopholes in campaign finance laws. Lawmakers did make progress on some other bills of interest to state and local governments, however, and as the first session closed, the debate on several issues became increasingly non-partisan in nature, suggesting a smoother path for the second session.

Electric Utility Restructuring

Electricity deregulation has been before Congress since the 1992 Energy Policy Act, which gave independent power producers equal access to power lines. The act divided deregulation responsibility between the Federal Energy Regulatory Commission (FERC), which has authority over the sale of electricity in the wholesale market, and Congress, which has authority over retail sales to the consumer. FERC issued an order to deregulate the wholesale market in April 1996, mandating that utilities open access to their transmission lines. Most states have already passed or are in the process of passing legislation to

Originally published as "The First Session of the 106th Congress: Actions Affecting Local Government," *The Municipal Year Book*, 2000. Published by the International City/County Management Association, Washington, D.C. Reprinted with permission of the publisher.

enable customers to choose their electricity suppliers. Furthermore, the U.S. Treasury Department issued temporary guidelines to clarify how municipally owned electric utilities can participate in a deregulated electric utility market without jeopardizing existing or future tax-exempt municipal bonds. Until Congress enacts legislation, however, it is unclear how local governments will be affected by deregulation of the industry.

Restructuring of the electric utility industry presents local officials and municipal utility managers with both economic and technological challenges and opportunities. Deregulation is expected to reduce greenhouse gases and to save billions of dollars a year, but there is no guarantee that all consumers will benefit. Large users, such as manufacturing plants, may reap cost savings at the expense of smaller businesses and individual consumers, while regions of the country that already have low electricity prices may witness price increases. In addition, some local governments are concerned that there may be areas with such limited profit potential that no company would be willing to provide service. Local government lobbying organizations insist that all consumers should share in any resulting cost savings.

Local governments are affected not only as consumers of electric power but also, in many cases, as suppliers and franchisers. Deregulation has an impact on local governments' authority over such issues as land use and zoning, revenue generation from taxes and franchise fees, the issuance of bonds for the repair or maintenance of electric power transmission plants, and control over rights-of-way. Cities and counties are wary of federal or state government preemption of local authority over the location of electric transmission lines, poles, and towers.

Local governments maintain that Congress should leave electric utility

deregulation to states and localities. They have intently followed congressional debates regarding the issue, maintaining that — at the very least — they must be involved as partners in any national restructuring plans. Last year, a number of bills were introduced and hearings held. Some bills (such as H.R. 1230) were designed to restrict state and local governments from regulating who may legally sell electricity as well as the pricing and terms that electric service providers can set. Others (such as H.R. 655) mandated that states implement deregulation within a specific time frame. Major legislation on utility restructuring floundered in committee, however.

The Clinton administration introduced its proposal to the 106th Congress in April 1999. The administration's plan encourages states to adopt a competitive system but stops short of mandating such action. It would give retail customers the right to choose an electricity supplier by January 1, 2003, unless the state or non-regulated utilities within the state choose to "opt out" of competition.

Late in the session, the House Energy and Power Subcommittee approved and sent to the full Commerce Committee H.R. 2944, which would give states the option of determining whether restructuring should apply. The bill would not require utilities to generate a portion of their electricity from renewable sources, however, which sparked opposition from the Clinton administration. Although Congress is expected to consider this or similar legislation, there was no further action on the issue of utility deregulation during the first session.

"Takings" Legislation

Yet another threat to local government authority was "takings" legislation introduced in both houses (H.R. 2372 and

S. 1028). Supporters argue that a local zoning or regulatory decision that limits the development of property is a "taking" by the government that deserves just compensation under the Fifth Amendment to the Constitution. The bills respond to criticism by homebuilders, developers, and others that the current court process used to determine when a property rights claim is ready to be adjudicated is unpredictable and burdensome, and that it severely hinders a property owner's access to federal court. The proposed legislation would remedy this problem by giving property owners expedited access to federal courts for a regulatory taking of their property.

Local governments oppose takings legislation, arguing that it infringes on local land use decision making and authority to balance the rights of property owners against the greater good of the community. Local officials also contend that it would reduce the incentive for developers and property owners to negotiate with planning commissions, zoning boards, and elected officials before filing suit. Finally, the bills would require small communities to spend taxpayer dollars to hire outside legal counsel to defend themselves in federal court.

Environmental organizations have joined with local governments in opposition. In addition, the president has expressed concern that such legislation would create an undue burden on both local governments and the federal courts and has promised to veto the bills if they reach his desk.

Y2K

Early in the first session, legislation was introduced in both the House and the Senate to address liability issues related to the "Year 2000 (Y2K) problem," or the millennium bug. The Y2K problem stems from an inability of many computers to differentiate between the years 2000 and 1900 because they recognize only the last two digits of any year. Municipalities and counties throughout the nation have devoted significant resources to fixing the computer glitch in order to prevent such problems as the failure of emergency systems, malfunctions of computerized mechanisms that control public transit systems, and interruptions in commerce. However, local governments continued to worry about the potential consequences of failing to fix the Y2K problem and sought assurance that they would not be inundated with lawsuits. In July, local governments breathed a sigh of relief with the passage of the Y2K Act (P.L. 106-37). Among the provisions in the legislation, which is designed to address a host of Y2K liability issues, are exemptions for local governments and public agencies from punitive damages in Y2K-related litigation.

Public Safety and Emergency Response

A number of problems are inherent in enhanced 911 systems today. Some local governments have no E-911 systems; others have systems that are outdated and unable to handle an increasing number of calls. In addition, there are "dead zones" in which mobile phones cannot connect to emergency response systems because there are no antennae nearby to transmit the calls. To remedy problems, legislation regarding enhanced 911, the Wireless Communication and Public Safety Act of 1999 (P.L. 106-81), was signed into law on October 26.

P.L. 106-81 is designed "to promote and enhance public safety through the use of 911 as the universal emergency assistance number, further deployment of wireless 911 service, support of states in upgrading 911 capabilities and related functions, [and] encouragement of construction and operation of seamless, ubiquitous, and reliable networks for personal wireless services." The law designates 911 as the universal emergency service number and requires wireless carriers to offer 911 to subscribers as an emergency number. In addition, the legislation is designed to encourage better coordination among levels of government and the telecommunications industry, enabling local governments to more readily upgrade and modernize enhanced emergency response services. Unlike the bill introduced during the 105th Congress, the law does not include provisions that would preempt local zoning authority in siting wireless facilities on federal property.

Congress has also sought to remedy problems associated with the definition of a "firefighter" under the Fair Labor Standards Act (FLSA). Late in the session, the House of Representatives approved H.R. 1693, an amendment to the FLSA that essentially would eliminate the distinction between firefighters and emergency medical technicians (EMTs). This would allow local governments to establish a 28-day work period for EMTs and paramedics so that over-time compensation would not be owed until they had worked 212 hours. Under the legislation, an employee could be considered a firefighter if he or she (1) is a firefighter, paramedic, EMT, rescue worker, ambulance worker, or hazardous materials worker; (2) is trained in and is permitted to engage in fire suppression; (3) is employed by a fire department of a municipality, county, fire district, or state; and (4) is engaged in the prevention, control, and extinguishing of fires or the response to emergency situations in which life, property, or the environment is at risk. Senate action on the bill, which generated

bipartisan support in the House, is expected early next year.

Juvenile Justice Legislation

The federal role in juvenile justice has largely revolved around funding and setting standards and funding programs. Congress passed the Juvenile Delinquency Prevention and Control Act in 1968, a law later revised in 1972 and renamed the Juvenile Delinquency Prevention Act. The stated purpose of the act is to assist states and local communities in providing community-based preventive services to youths in danger of becoming delinquent, to help train individuals in occupations providing such services, and to provide technical assistance in the field. The federal Juvenile Delinquency Act defines juvenile delinquency (any criminal act committed by someone under 18 years of age) and sets forth rules by which state laws must comply with regard to juvenile court procedures and punishments.

Although juvenile crime has decreased slightly in the past few years, the continuing high rate and widely publicized occurrences of violence perpetrated by youths have prompted much conversation in Congress, and a number of bills were debated in both houses during the 105th Congress. As no legislation was passed before adjournment, however, discussion continued during the first session of the 106th Congress. In the wake of the tragic shootings at Columbine High School, Congress fell under increasing pressure to address related problems of gun control and mental health. But as the National Rifle Association stepped up its lobbying efforts, Congress was unable to come to agreement on even moderate gun control measures or other key issues before adjourning.

In June, the House passed the Consequences for Juvenile Offenders Act of 1999

(H.R. 1501) by a vote of 287–139. This bill would authorize $1.5 billion in block grant funding to state and local governments over a three-year period. It would also establish a $500 million Juvenile Accountability Block Grant (JABG) program and provide a pass-through of at least 75 percent of these block grant funds to local governments by formula. To be eligible for the block grants, states and localities would have to impose a system of graduated interventions for every delinquent or criminal act and establish a criminal history record system for serious violent juvenile offenders.

H.R. 1501 incorporated key provisions of H.R. 1150, which was passed by the House Subcommittee on Early Childhood, Youth, and Families. These provisions include the reauthorization of the Juvenile Justice and Delinquency Prevention Act (JJDPA) of 1974, the removal of juveniles from adult facilities, and a modest state-administered prevention block grant program. The Senate version of the bill, the Violent and Repeat Juvenile Offender Accountability and Rehabilitation Act of 1999 (S. 254), passed the Senate in May by a vote of 73–25. Like the House bill, S. 254 would provide for the reauthorization of the JJDPA. In addition, for cases in which juveniles are prosecuted for federal crimes, it proposes reform procedures that would make it easier to prosecute juveniles as adults, allow increased access to juvenile criminal records, and strengthen antigang statutes.

The Senate bill also contains a number of gun control measures, including a ban on the importation of high-capacity ammunition clips, a mandatory background check at gun shows and pawn shops, a prohibition on the sale of semiautomatic assault weapons to persons under age 18, and a requirement that all handguns be sold with child safety devices. Other provisions of the Senate bill would

- Increase penalties for crimes committed by gang members and by offenders wearing body armor
- Allow some juvenile offenders age 14 and older to be tried in adult courts on serious violent felonies and drug offenses
- Enforce laws prohibiting the interstate transportation of liquor
- Allow schools to offer prayers and build memorials in honor of students and teachers slain on their grounds
- Create a national Commission on Character Development that would report to Congress on the effect of cultural influences on society and recommend legislation.

Several provisions drawn from the Mental Health Juvenile Justice Act (S. 465) were also approved. The provisions would loosen the requirements of JABG funds to facilitate coordinated efforts across systems serving children and adolescents (e.g., law enforcement, mental health, substance abuse, juvenile court judges, and public defenders' offices); to "cross train" mental health and justice system personnel on appropriate linkages to community-based treatment programs that provide mental health and substance abuse services; and to allow states to use federal funds for projects that provide intake screenings for all youth entering the juvenile justice system and that administer mental health services for juveniles with serious emotional disturbances. The bill further requires the Office of Juvenile Justice and Delinquency Prevention to conduct a comprehensive study of all mental health services that are being administered to juveniles in the justice system. One amendment that was proposed would establish a parenting support and education program to help treat children who are victims of physical or sexual abuse or are witnesses to violence in their homes or communities. Another amendment — to require states to evaluate whether a disproportionate number of minority children are incarcerated — failed to pass the Senate.

S. 254 would authorize $1 billion per year for five years for juvenile justice. Of these funds, $450 million are slated for JABGs (to help states and cities perform drug tests and build detention centers), with 25 percent of this funding targeted to primary prevention. Prevention programs under the JJDPA would receive $435 million (including $200 million for Juvenile Delinquency Prevention Block Grants, of which 80 percent must be devoted to primary prevention; $200 million for Part B Formula grant programs; and $35 million for Gangs, Mentoring, and Discretionary grant programs). The bill would also include $75 million for states to up-grade and enhance juvenile felony criminal record histories and $40 million for National Institute of Justice research and evaluation of the effectiveness of juvenile delinquency prevention programs. Whereas the House bill would allow states to keep 25 percent of the grant monies, the Senate would allow states to keep up to 30 percent.

In August, the House and Senate named conferees to resolve differences between their juvenile justice proposals, but the committees tabled discussion until next year.

Law Enforcement Appropriations

President Clinton vetoed the Commerce, Justice, and State appropriations measure sent to him on October 25 because it included only $325 million for the Community-Oriented Public Safety program — well below the administration's request for $1.2 billion and last year's funding level of $1.4 billion. In response, congressional and administration leaders agreed to fund the COPS program at $800 million. The authorization bill also restored last year's funding for the JABG at

$250 million, the Violent Offender Incarceration program at $686 million, and the Local Law Enforcement Block Grant at $523 million.

As in the 105th Congress, legislation to reauthorize the Local Law Enforcement Block Grant at $750 million per year over six years was introduced in the Senate (S. 899). The block grant currently funds the following areas: law enforcement support (law enforcement personnel, overtime, equipment, and technology), security enhancement in and around schools, drug courts, adjudication of violent offenders, establishment of a multijurisdictional task force, crime prevention programs, and defrayment of the cost of indemnification insurance. S. 899 would expand the allowable uses of the block grant, including programs geared toward early prevention and multijurisdictional collaboration. However, it would not change the block grant formula — a reform that local governments have been seeking. Based solely on the volume of serious crime in various municipalities and counties, the current formula fails to take into consideration expenditure data, the division of responsibility between municipalities and counties in dealing with violent crime, and the importance of other components of the criminal justice system. No similar legislation has been introduced in the House, and the bill has not yet reached the Senate floor.

Financial Services and Bankruptcy Reform

In an attempt to encourage U.S. banks to become more competitive in the global market, both houses of Congress overwhelmingly voted for the Financial Services Modernization Act, which was signed into law on November 12, 1999 (P.L. 106-102). The legislation repeals the

Glass-Steagall Act of 1933 and the Bank Holding Company Act of 1956, thereby permitting banks to expand their operations by engaging in securities and insurance activities.

Of particular interest to local governments are provisions that address the Community Reinvestment Act (CRA) of 1977. The CRA required banks to make loans in low-income urban and rural areas. Since it was passed 22 years ago, the law has produced almost $400 billion in lending in underserved communities and has played a key role in the revitalization of thousands of communities nationwide. Although the Financial Services Modernization Act does not fully repeal the CRA, it does curb existing CRA requirements. Specifically, the final legislation contains a "sunshine" provision that requires community organizations to make detailed reports of how they use monies received under CRA agreements. Opponents of the requirement worry that this could make banks more hesitant to enter into agreements with community organizations. Several other CRA provisions have been well received by local governments: the legislation encourages the sound management of CRA institutions and prohibits a financial holding company from beginning any "new" financial activities unless its subsidiary depository institutions have a satisfactory CRA rating.

As in the 105th session, Congress was again unable to address the skyrocketing numbers of personal bankruptcy claims despite the introduction of legislation in both houses. Key provisions of both bills include limits on the homestead exemptions that would be allowed. The Senate's bankruptcy reform bill (S. 625), which stalled on the Senate floor after debate on several unrelated amendments, would put a $100,000 cap on homestead exemptions. The House bill (H.R. 833), which passed in May by a vote of 313–108, would cap these

exemptions at $250,000 but would allow states to pass legislation to opt out of the exemption. Tax provisions included in both pieces of legislation would give a higher priority to the payment of tax liens in bankruptcy proceedings. Bankruptcy courts would also have to follow state and local laws on property assessments, determining the amount of property taxes due and the interest rates on unpaid taxes. The issue is expected to be taken up again early in the next session.

Environmental Legislation

Since the Republicans took Congress by storm several years ago, environmental legislation has been much discussed but not much has been done. Congress has made little progress on issues related to the reauthorization of the Comprehensive Environmental Response, Compensation, and Liability Act of 1980 (CERCLA), known as Superfund. Major legislation to address brownfields, which include thousands of industrial and commercial sites that have been abandoned because of real or perceived contamination, also stalled. At the same time, local government lobbyists have been hard at work convincing legislators of the importance of issues related to stormwater runoff, which the Environmental Protection Agency (EPA) is expected to address, and waste flow control, which has remained a pressing issue for local governments since the 1994 Supreme Court case, *Carbone v. Town of Clarkstown.*

Superfund and Brownfields

Congress's authorization to fund CERCLA expired in 1995. The original legislation was intended to address uncontrolled releases of hazardous substances and established a $1.6 billion trust fund (largely financed by a tax on chemical and petroleum products). It provided joint and several liability for "potentially responsible parties" and gave the Environmental Protection Agency (EPA) authority to clean up sites and sue to recover its costs. In 1986, with the Superfund Amendments and Reauthorization Act (SARA), Congress established detailed rules for the selection of remedies. In 1990, Congress extended Superfund's authorization and taxing authorities (an additional $5.1 billion) through December 31, 1995.

Since then, Congress has made little headway in reauthorizing funding for CERCLA. There remain some funds for continued cleanup, but local governments worry that these funds will soon dry up. Superfund continues to be a hotly debated issue in Congress, with votes breaking primarily along party lines. During the first session of the 106th Congress, several pieces of legislation were considered in subcommittee.

In September, the House Transportation and Infrastructure Committee passed H.R. 1300, the Recycle America's Land Act of 1999, a Superfund reauthorization bill that also would provide funding for brownfields. The bill includes liability relief for local governments owning Superfund sites and shields them from Superfund liability for garbage disposal at those sites. It would also provide loans for the cleanup of brownfields. Democrats and the Clinton administration oppose the bill, however, because they believe that its provisions would fail to adequately protect against groundwater contamination and would slow the current pace of Superfund cleanups.

Less than a month later, the House Commercial Committee amended and adopted a different bill—again along virtually partisan lines. (Only two Democrats voted for the bill.) Along with provisions

for municipal and small-business liability relief from H.R. 1300, the Land Recycling Act of 1999 (H.R. 2580) would reauthorize the Superfund program for five years at $1.5 billion for the first three years, declining to $1.35 billion in the final year. It would also eliminate requirements that Superfund cleanups meet state standards that are more stringent than federal law and that groundwater be restored to "beneficial use." Local governments that own landfills on the Superfund list would receive liability protection, depending on their population: those under 100,000 in population would be subject to a maximum of the cost of cleaning up a regular landfill or 10 percent, whichever was less; the cost for larger jurisdictions would be capped at 20 percent. Localities that only deliver municipal solid waste or sludge to a landfill on the Superfund list would be exempt from liability for cleanup costs already paid.

If there is no compromise reached between the Transportation Committee and the House Commerce Committee regarding differences in the two bills, the House leadership will likely decide early in the next session which of them will reach the floor.

The Senate's Superfund reauthorization legislation, S. 1090, would provide liability caps for local government Superfund landfills as well as for local government generators, transporters, and "arrangers" of solid-waste disposal. It would also (1) require EPA to pay for any shortfall in cleanup costs from the Superfund Trust Fund, rather than shifting the costs to industrial parties at the site; (2) authorize $100 million annually for brownfields remediation grants, a significant improvement over other bills with revolving loan funding only; and (3) provide permanent liability protection once a state cleans up a brownfields site. The most controversial provision of the draft bill is the phasing out of the Superfund program by opting not to reinstate the corporate taxes that fund it. S. 1090 failed to reach committee during the first session of the 106th Congress.

Stormwater Runoff

Of concern to local governments is a proposal by EPA that would require local governments with separate storm sewer systems inside census-designated urbanized areas to institute minimum controls (including the mapping of storm sewer systems, provision of training to local government employees, adoption of erosion and sediment control ordinances, and mandated street sweeping) in an attempt to reduce the amount of sediment and pollutants that enter the drains. The proposed regulation also would impose restrictions on some construction projects, requiring permits to be obtained in some cases. State and federal permitting agencies may also require stormwater discharges to meet water quality standards.

EPA's proposal, which is in accordance with the Clean Water Act of 1987, would represent the most expensive water quality regulation in our country's history. EPA has heard testimony and reviewed its findings on the proposed regulations; however, local government lobbyists have already rallied to garner the support of Congress to overturn or revise the anticipated EPA regulations.

Waste Flow Control

Waste flow control is yet another issue that continues to hamper local governments. Flow control enables a local government to designate the facilities that will handle municipal solid waste and thereby guarantee a dependable supply of waste. This, in turn, provides landfill facilities with a predictable source of revenue to repay outstanding debt. In the 1994 decision *Carbone v. Town of Clarkstown*, the Supreme Court found that Congress has sole authority over the regulation of interstate commerce, undermining the authority of local governments to maintain control over the flow of waste leaving their communities for cheaper landfill sites.

Since the 1994 decision, local governments have called for congressional action to protect existing solid-waste facilities and bonded indebtedness adopted in accordance with legal flow control authority. Congress has neglected to address this problem, however, primarily because House and Senate negotiators have been unable to strike a deal on interstate waste restrictions, and attempts to move a separate flow control bill have failed. Bills addressing both interstate waste restrictions and flow control were once again introduced in both houses during the 106th Congress: S. 872, S. 663, and H.R. 1190 would each grandfather waste disposal facilities that relied on flow control authority for debt repayment prior to the 1994 Supreme Court decision. Yet, once again, Congress has not moved the legislation forward, and its inability to act puts local governments at risk of lawsuits and undermines their ability to provide and control an essential public service.

Transportation

As guaranteed under the Transportation Equity Act for the 21st Century (TEA-21), the FY 2000 Transportation Appropriations bill funded the highway and transit programs at substantial increases. The highway program is funded at $27.701 billion, which includes a $1.456 billion bonus owing to more funds than anticipated coming into the Highway Trust Fund. The transit program is funded at $6.088 billion.

The Airport Improvement Program (AIP), which began in 1982, provides funding for capital improvements and infrastructure projects at public airports. The AIP is funded by the Airport Trust Fund, which derives its revenue from a ticket tax (currently set at 9 percent), a passenger flight segment fee, various aviation fuel taxes, and an international departure and arrival tax.

The AIP expired on September 30, 1998. In addition to the overall authorization, at issue in Congress were proposals for increasing funding for the program, perhaps by increasing the passenger facility charge (PFC), currently capped at $3 per passenger, or by including a new program to help small airports provide additional passenger service. First introduced in the early 1990s, the PFC is an important source of local revenue for local governments to upgrade their airport facilities. Airports claim that nationally they have a multibillion-dollar shortfall in funding for capital projects and need an increase in the PFC.

Unable to enact reauthorization legislation before adjourning the following month, Congress passed a $1 billion, six-month extension of AIP funding, which expired on March 31, 1999. Still unable to settle the issue, Congress then enacted several additional extensions, and $1.95 billion was spent on the AIP program during FY 1999.

Bills to reauthorize the AIP and the Federal Aviation Administration were introduced in both the House and the Senate during 1999. The Senate version of the bill, the Air Transportation Improvement Act of 1999 (S. 82), was approved by the Senate Commerce Committee in February. The bill would reauthorize the AIP program for two years at an annual level of $2.4 billion. A main focus of the bill is competition and expansion of service to small communities. The Small Community Aviation Development Program, a four-year pilot program, would fund incentives and projects helping communities improve their access to major hub airports and overcome economic, geographic, and marketplace factors that inhibit the availability of quality affordable air service to small communities. The original version of the bill also included a controversial provision that would allow for additional flights at Washington's Reagan National Airport, as well as at Chicago's O'Hare and New York's La-Guardia and Kennedy Airports. However, S. 82 does not include a provision for increasing the PFC.

In June, the House passed its version of the bill, the Airport Investment and Reform Act for the 21st Century (H.R. 1000), by a vote of 316–110. The House proposal would reauthorize the AIP for six years at $19 billion and recommends an increase in the AIP budget to $4 billion beginning in 2001. Further, H.R. 1000 would take the Airport Trust Fund off budget, a provision opposed in the Senate. The House bill also proposes a $3 increase in the maximum PFC that a local government could charge but only if the AIP were unable to provide for the needed capital improvements. In addition, the bill includes a funding program to help small, underserved airports market and promote their services, authorizing $25 million annually to help improve facilities and increase passenger service in small communities.

Despite the progress that was made, House and Senate conferees could not agree on important budget issues associated with the reauthorization of the federal airport program. No agreement was reached on taking the Aviation Trust Fund off budget, on handling General Fund contributions, and on increasing the PFC. The legislation is expected to be revisited in 2000.

Social Services and Medicare

As the Republican Party took hold of spending initiatives, social services was among the categories to feel the pinch. The Social Services Block Grant (Title XX of the Social Security Act), which is part of the Labor, Health and Human Services, and Education appropriations bill, was appropriated $1.775 billion for FY 2000—well below the $2.38 billion authorized for 1999, which in turn was a reduction from previous years. In addition, transfer authority from the Temporary Assistance for Needy Families (TANF) Block Grant to Title XX was reduced from 10 percent to 4.25 percent. Advocates for the cost-cutting measures argued that TANF no longer needs to be funded at previous levels because of the drastic reduction in welfare caseloads nationwide.

Title XX is allocated to states through a formula based on population. Many states have chosen to allocate these funds to counties. The block grant program gives states and counties considerable flexibility in determining how to spend this money; some of the most common uses include adult protection, child care, and child welfare.

In an effort to remedy the severe cuts made to the Medicare program in the Balanced Budget Act of 1997, Congress struggled to agree on Medicare legislation. In the first week of November, the House passed Medicare relief legislation (H.R. 3075). The Senate Finance Committee approved a similar bill (S. 1788), but that bill has not reached the Senate floor. Both bills would provide this relief to a variety of health care providers and facilities, including hospitals, home health agencies, skilled nursing facilities, managed care plans, and teaching hospitals. Among the provisions in the legislation under discussion are a two-year freeze of the $1,500 therapy caps, an increase in compensation for teaching hospitals that have low rates, a boost in indirect medical education payments for hospitals with high resident-to-patient ratios, and a freeze in a scheduled cut for disproportionate share payments. Right before adjourning, House and Senate lawmakers were working on a compromise bill that would total $11.9 billion in Medicare "givebacks" over five years.

Bills to address issues surrounding Social Security Disability Insurance (SSDI) were passed by overwhelming majorities in both the Senate and the House. The Senate unanimously (99–0) passed the Work Incentives Improvement Act (S. 331) in June. The bill would allow states to extend Medicaid coverage to the working disabled and would extend disabled workers' eligibility for Medicare coverage up to six years. Then the House passed the Ticket to Work and Work Incentives Improvement Act (H.R. 1180) by 412–9 in October. The proposed legislation would provide Medicare coverage for SSDI recipients for ten years after their return to work, rather than for the four years in effect under current legislation. Advocates of the legislation argue that the relatively short period for coverage discourages workers from returning to work because they do not want to lose Medicaid and Medicare benefits. The legislation would also allow states to authorize disabled workers to "buy in" to Medicaid on a sliding fee basis, create a voucher system that would give workers access to job training and rehabilitation services, and authorize grants for states that create programs to assist disabled workers.

Still at issue is how to pay for the bill. Senate Majority Leader Trent Lott has pledged to work with the House during conference committee negotiations to find the needed spending cuts to offset the bill's cost, which is estimated at $1 billion over five years.

Welfare to Work

Efforts by local governments to convince the 106th Congress to reauthorize federal funding for the welfare-to-work program and to change eligibility requirements proved unsuccessful. The welfare-to-work program was part of the 1997 Balanced Budget Act (P.L. 105-33) and was intended to help states move hard-to-employ welfare recipients into the workforce. Because of eligibility restrictions, only $2.7 billion of the $3 billion appropriated has been spent. Local government advocates lament that millions of dollars in welfare-to-work program funds are going unused because the program eligibility guidelines are so strict that most municipalities and community groups cannot find clients who can be served. Welfare-to-work advocates fear that Congress may rescind much of the money it has authorized for the program if eligibility requirements are not changed to make funds easier to spend.

Late in the session, the House Committee on Education and the Workforce approved H.R. 3172, a bill designed to loosen eligibility requirements for the welfare-to-work program for people who are long-term recipients of welfare or whose benefits would end within a year. Applicants would have to meet just one of the other eligibility criteria, rather than three as required under current law. (These eligibility requirements address barriers to work, such as homelessness, not having a high school diploma, and being a victim of domestic violence.)

The House Ways and Means Committee also considered a bill that contained several amendments to the welfare-to-work program. Like H.R. 3172, the provisions would reduce the number of criteria that individuals must meet to participate in the program. It would also simplify reporting requirements, allow some welfare-to-work funds to be used for job training activities, and create a new program targeted for noncustodial parents.

Housing and Homelessness

Community Development Block Grants (CDBGs) remain the primary tool whereby the federal government supports local economic development, neighborhood stabilization, and revitalization initiatives. CDBG funds must be used for activities that meet national objectives, including providing benefit to low- and moderate-income persons. The federal government mandates that CDBG grantees spend 70 percent of the appropriated funds on programs that benefit persons at 80 percent or below the median income, but since the block grant program was established 25 years ago, CDBG grantees have far exceeded this minimum requirement, spending more than 90 percent of the funds on this target audience.

During the last few years, funding for the CDBG program has increased slightly. Set at $4.6 billion from FY 1995 through FY 1997, funding was increased to $4.675 billion in FY 1998 and to $4.750 billion in FY 1999. Despite this slight increase, allocations to local and state governments decreased by about 10 percent on average because of a growing trend toward set-asides for special-purpose grants, which increased from $90 million to $526.8 million during this same period.

The FY 2000 VA-HUD and Independent Agencies Appropriations Act (P.L. 106-74), which was signed into law on October 20, 1999, includes further increases for the CDBG program. The additional $50 million over current funding levels brings the total funding to $4.8 billion.

The HOME Investment Partnerships Program provides local governments with the flexibility to design and implement strategies for expanding the supply of affordable homes and rental housing through acquisition, rehabilitation, new construction, and tenant-based rental assistance. More than 500 jurisdictions nationwide have participated in the HOME program, committing funds for over 280,000 affordable housing units, the majority of which are targeted to low-income people. Recent data reveal that approximately 54 percent of HOME-assisted rental housing (including tenant-based rental assistance) helps families with incomes at or below 30 percent of area median income, and more than 90 percent of this housing benefits families at or below 50 percent of area median income. Sixty percent of HOME funds are allocated to counties and cities, and 40 percent are allocated to the states.

Over the past few years, funding for HOME had increased slowly — from $1.4 billion in FY 1995–FY 1997 to $1.5 billion in FY 1998 and $1.6 billion in FY 1999. The president proposed an additional $10 million for HOME for FY 2000, but the House recommended cuts. In the end, the funding level was held steady at $1.6 billion. An additional $1.02 billion was authorized for HUD's homeless assistance program and $11.03 billion for HUD's Housing Certificate Fund to renew existing Section 8 contracts and to fund new vouchers.

Editor's Note

The actions of the 106th Congress were included in this volume in order to reflect the significant impact that the U.S. Congress has on our nation's fifty state and numerous local governments. This chapter shows the dramatic impact that this body has on our nation's lower-level governments as our nation enters the 21st century.

• Chapter 29 •

The Supreme Court

CHARLES WISE

In the 1998–99 term, the U.S. Supreme Court decided a number of cases that significantly affect state and local governments. This chapter reviews the major holdings of these cases, which are in the following areas: immunity of government from suit, disabilities and public services, sex discrimination, federal employees and local taxes, sexual harassment, the federal census, ordinances against loitering, disability in employment, union security, employee retirement plans, medical care, municipal land use regulation, search and seizure, and prisons and jails.

Immunity of Government from Suit

The Supreme Court took up three cases involving the right of individual citizens or firms to sue states pursuant to federal legislation authorizing them to do so. In *Alden v. Maine*, the Court took up the question of whether Congress, under authority granted to it by the Constitution's Commerce Clause, could pass legislation authorizing private parties to sue a state in state court without the state's consent. The Court had already determined, in *Seminole Tribe v. Florida*, 517 U.S. 44 (1996), that such suits are not allowed in federal courts.

The case involved a suit brought by probation officers alleging that the state of Maine had violated the overtime provisions of the Fair Labor Standards Act, 52 Stat. 1060, as amended, 29 U.S.C. § 201 *et seq.* The probation officers sought compensation and liquidated damages. The Court held that the powers delegated to Congress under Article 1 of the Constitution do not include the power to subject states, without their consent, to private suits for damages in state courts. The majority held that Congress could not enable private individuals or firms to sue states by means of a federal statute that was

---

Originally published as "Recent Supreme Court Cases Affecting Local Government," *The Municipal Year Book*, 2000. Published by the International City/County Management Association, Washington, D.C. Reprinted with permission of the publisher.

beyond the power of Congress to enact: neither the Supremacy Clause nor the enumerated powers of Congress confer authority to abrogate the states' immunity from suit in federal court. Recalling the Court's decision in *Seminole Tribe*, which applied to suits brought in federal court, the majority stated that the logic of the decision did not turn on the forum in which the suits were brought but extended to suits in state courts as well (67 U.S.L.W. 4609 [1999]).

The majority also pointed out that recognizing the states' immunity from suits brought by individuals did not deprive the federal government of a means of enforcing its regulatory will as specified by Congress: the federal government could still pursue an offending state in federal court by means of a suit brought by the Justice Department in the name of the United States. Unfortunately for local governments, the Court also stated that the principle of sovereign immunity on which the majority rested its conclusion does not bar suits for damages against lesser entities— such as a municipal corporation or other governmental entity that is not an arm of the state (67 U.S.L.W. 4615 [1999])— when such suits are authorized by Congress.

Another case involved suits for damages against state entities that engage in commercial activities. In *College Savings Bank v. Florida Prepaid Postsecondary Education Expense Board*, 67 U.S.L.W. 4590 (1999), a bank sued Florida Prepaid Postsecondary Education Expense Board under the Trademark Remedy Clarification Act, which subjects states to suits for false and misleading advertising. The plaintiff claimed that the brochures and annual reports of Florida Prepaid had misrepresented its tuition prepayment program. In support of their suit, the plaintiffs asserted that Congress had, in passing the Trademark Remedy Clarification Act, acted pursuant to its power to enforce the Fourteenth Amend-ment, which would abrogate the state's Eleventh Amendment immunity from suit by individuals. The plaintiffs further alleged that failure to allow their case to go forward would deny them their property without due process of law, in violation of the Fourteenth Amendment. According to the plaintiffs, Congress has enacted the act to remedy and prevent state deprivations of due process of two species of property rights protected by the Fourteenth Amendment: (1) a right to be free from a business competitor's false advertising about its own product, and (2) a more generalized right to be secure in one's business interests.

The Court's majority concluded that neither of these rights qualifies as a property right protected by the Constitution's Due Process clause. With regard to the first alleged right, the Court said that the hallmark of a protected property interest is the right to exclude others, and the act's false-advertising provisions bear no relationship to any right to exclude. With regard to the second alleged right, the Court found that business— in the sense of *the activity of doing business* or *the activity of making a profit*— is not property in the ordinary sense and that there was therefore no deprivation of property at issue.

The plaintiffs had further argued that even if Florida Prepaid was adjudged to enjoy immunity under the Eleventh Amendment, it had "impliedly" or "constructively" waived its immunity by voluntarily engaging in a field in which Congress had passed regulatory legislation (the Trademark Act) and by engaging in interstate marketing and administration of its program despite the fact that the Trademark Act had made it clear that such activity would subject Florida Prepaid to suit. The Court declared that it would not subscribe to a principle of implied waiver: a state's consent to be sued would have to be unequivocally expressed (67 U.S.L.W.

4595 [1999]). In so holding, the Court explicitly overturned a precedent set out in a previous case, *Parden v. Terminal R. Co. of Ala. Docks Dept.*, 377 U.S. 184 (1964), on which the plaintiffs had relied and which held that under certain circumstances, states could be found to have impliedly waived their immunity from suit. As in the case of *Alden v. Maine*, this ruling does not protect municipal corporations from suit.

Another Florida case applies the test the Court pronounced in *City of Boerne v. Flores*, 521 U.S. 507 (1997), for identifying "appropriate" legislation that would be recognized as abrogating state sovereign immunity. In that case, the Court had said that under Section 5 of the Fourteenth Amendment, states may be sued by individuals when such suits are authorized by Congress and if the legislation is appropriate to the Fourteenth Amendment. Legislation will be adjudged appropriate if the statute can be demonstrated to show "a congruence and proportionality between the injury to be prevented or remedied and the means adopted to that end" (521 U.S. 519–520 [1999]).

In *Florida Prepaid Postsecondary Education Expense Board v. College Savings Bank and United States*, 67 U.S.L.W. 4580 (1999), the attempt by Congress to abrogate the states' Eleventh Amendment immunity from suit under the Patent and Plant Variety Protection Remedy Clarification Act, 35 U.S.C. § 271(h), 296(a), was challenged. College Savings Bank sued Florida Prepaid, a subdivision of the state of Florida, under the act for directly and indirectly infringing on the patent held by College Savings Bank on its financing methodology.

The majority reminded the parties of its test, enunciated in *City of Boerne*, for "appropriate legislation" under Section 5 of the Fourteenth Amendment and stated that for Congress to invoke Section 5, "it must identify conduct transgressing the Fourteenth Amendment's substantive provisions, and must tailor its legislative scheme to remedying or preventing such conduct" (67 U.S.L.W. 4583 [1999]). The Fourteenth Amendment evil or wrong in question was the alleged "unremedied patent infringement" by the state. The Court found, however, that in enacting the Patent Remedy Act, Congress had identified no pattern of patent infringement by the states, let alone a pattern of constitutional violations. The Court pointed out that in procedural due process claims, a state depriving a person of a constitutionally protected interest is not in itself unconstitutional: what is unconstitutional is a state depriving the person of such an interest without due process of law (67 U.S.L.W. 4584 [1999]).

The Court found that Congress had barely considered the availability of state remedies for patent infringement, and that the record of Congress's consideration of the act offered scant support for Congress's conclusion that states, by being immune from suit in federal court, were depriving patent owners of property without due process of law. Because of Congress's lack of consideration of state remedies, the Court concluded that the provisions of the act were so out of proportion to the intended remedy that they could not be considered to be designed to prevent unconstitutional behavior on the part of the states (67 U.S.L.W. 4585 [1999]). Thus, the Court found that the act did not meet the test for "appropriateness" that would be required to sustain it under the Fourteenth Amendment. Therefore, Florida Prepaid retained state immunity from suit.

The Court's holding can apply to other entities of state governments that are sued by businesses who believe that the entities have violated their Fourteenth Amendment rights. In order for federal statutes used as the basis for such suits to be adjudged constitutional, however, they will have to meet the Court's test for "appropriateness." As is true of the other cases, this standard does not apply to cases involving municipal corporations.

Disabilities and Public Services

In *Cedar Rapids Community School District v. Garret*, 67 U.S.L.W. 4165, the Court addressed the issue of what services public schools would be required to provide to disabled students under federal law. Under the Individuals with Disabilities Education Act (IDEA), 20 U.S.C. § 1400(c), states receive federal funds on the condition that they agree to provide disabled children with special education and "related services." The act further states that school districts are not required to provide for medical services other than for diagnostic and evaluation purposes (20 U.S.C. § 140[a][17]).

The question the Court examined was whether the definition of "related services" required a public school district in a participating state to provide a ventilator-dependent student with certain nursing services during school hours. According to the Department of Education's regulations defining "related services," schools must provide "school health services" through a "qualified school nurse or other qualified person" but need not provide "medical services," which are defined as those that are provided by a licensed physician. The school district argued that the act did not require it to provide the student with "continuous one-on-one nursing services" during the school day.

The majority referred to one of its earlier decisions and asserted that the phrase *medical services* in the IDEA does not embrace all forms of care that might loosely be described as medical in other contexts (67 U.S.L.W. 4167) and that the requested services thus did not come under the statute's medical services exclusion. Therefore, as a condition of receiving IDEA funds, the district had to provide the service to the student. The decision opens the door to other students who require services that can be found to be "school health services"—that is those not requiring administration by a medical doctor—to demand that school districts supply such services.

In another case, which involved access to community mental health services, the Court's holding applies to local as well as to state governments. Two women sued various Georgia officials under Title II of the Americans with Disabilities Act (ADA) of 1990, 42 U.S.C. § 12131 *et seq.* Both women are mentally retarded, and one was diagnosed with schizophrenia and the other with a personality disorder. They were voluntarily admitted to a Georgia state hospital, where they were confined for treatment in a psychiatric unit. Both women subsequently sued, claiming that Georgia had violated Title II by failing to place them in a community-based program despite the fact that (1) their treating professionals had determined that such placement was appropriate and (2) the women had requested such placement.

The court of appeals had held that the state must transfer the women and also refused to allow the state's defense that, under the regulations, it could not be forced to do so because such a transfer would involve excessive costs. The court of appeals stated that the federal regulation permitted a cost-based defense "only in the most limited of circumstances" (138 F.3d at 902).

The Supreme Court held that states are required to provide community-based treatment for persons with mental disabilities when the state's treatment professionals determine that such placement is appropriate, the affected persons do not oppose such treatment, and the placement can be reasonably accommodated, taking into account both the resources available to the state and the needs of others with mental disabilities (119 S.Ct. 2190 [1999]).

Addressing the "reasonable modifications" regulation, which allows states to resist modifications that entail a "fundamental alteration" of the state's services and programs (28 C.F.R. at 35.130[b][7] [1998]), the Court turned down the court of appeals' interpretation and directed lower courts to consider, in view of the resources available to the state, not only the cost of providing community-based care to the litigants, but also the range of services that the state provides to others with mental disabilities and the state's obligation to mete out those services equitably.

Another case involving the ADA focused on its relationship with the disability provisions of the Social Security Act. In *Cleveland v. Policy Management Systems*, 67 U.S.L.W. 4375 (1999), the Court sought to determine whether a recipient of Social Security Disability Insurance (SSDI) may simultaneously pursue an action for discrimination under the ADA, claiming that with reasonable accommodation she could perform the essential functions of her job. In this case, a corporate employee who had had a stroke applied for SSDI benefits, then returned to work when her condition improved, only to be fired by the corporation months later. Her SSDI application was initially denied but was granted retroactively after the employee filed an action alleging that the corporation had violated the ADA by refusing to reasonably accommodate her disability.

The federal district court granted summary judgment in favor of the corporation on the theory that (1) the employee, by applying for and receiving SSDI benefits, had conceded that she was totally disabled and (2) this concession stopped

her from proving that she could perform the essential functions of her job as required by the ADA. The Fifth Circuit Court of Appeals ruled that the application for or receipt of Social Security benefits creates a rebuttable presumption that the claimant or recipient is judicially stopped from pressing an ADA claim.

The Supreme Court, however, ruled that an individual who applies for Social Security disability benefits is *not* automatically barred from suing an employer under the ADA; moreover, the application for or receipt of benefits does not even constitute a strong presumption against the ADA claim. The Court observed that when the Social Security Administration determines whether an individual is disabled for purposes of the SSDI program, it does not take into account the possibility of reasonable accommodation. So an ADA suit claiming that the employee can perform the job with reasonable accommodation may well prove consistent with an SSDI claim that the employee could not do his or her own job (or other jobs) without it. Nonetheless, the Court made it clear that the employee, in order to block a summary judgment motion to dismiss an ADA suit, will have to explain how the Social Security disability claim is consistent with the ADA claim.

Sex Discrimination

In the case of *Kolstad v. American Dental Association*, 67 U.S.L.W. 4552 (1999), the Supreme Court addressed the availability of punitive damages for employees who sue employers for sex discrimination. In this case, a woman who had formerly been employed by a professional association and who had applied unsuccessfully for a promotion filed an action against the association in federal district court, alleging that the decision of the association officers to promote a male applicant constituted employment discrimination, in violation of Title VII of the Civil Rights Act of 1991.

The district court denied the woman's request for a jury instruction on punitive damages and submitted the case to the jury, which (1) found that the association had discriminated against the women on the basis of sex and (2) awarded her back pay. However, the court of appeals expressed the view that before the question of punitive damages could go to the jury in a Title VII case, the evidence must show not only intentional discrimination but also that the defendant had engaged in some "egregious misconduct."

The Supreme Court disagreed, holding that punitive damages may be awarded in Title VII cases without a showing of "egregious misconduct." The Court observed that Section 1981a(b)(1) of the 1991 Civil Rights Act requires that the employer must have acted "with malice or with reckless indifference to the federally protected rights of an aggrieved individual." The Court stated that this standard addresses the employer-defendant's state of mind, rather than the degree of its misconduct, and requires that the employer discriminate in the face of perceived risk that its actions will violate federal law. The Court said that under this subjective test, an employer that intentionally discriminates would not be liable if it was unaware of the relevant prohibition or if it believed that its discrimination satisfied a bona fide occupational qualification defense.

Finally, the Court also refused to recognize the vicarious liability of employers for the discriminatory acts of managerial employees if the employers acted in good faith. The Court said that in the punitive damages context, an employer may not be vicariously liable for the discriminatory employment decisions of managerial agents where these decisions are contrary to the employer's good faith efforts to comply with Title VII.

Federal Employees and Local Taxes

Pursuant to an Alabama state statute, an Alabama county enacted an ordinance that imposed an occupational tax on persons employed in the county and declared it unlawful to engage in a covered occupation without paying the tax. Included among those subject to the tax were any federal, state, county, or city officers whose services were rendered within the county. Two federal judges did not pay the tax, and the county instituted suits in Alabama small claims court to collect them. The judges removed the suit to federal court under 28 U.S.C. § 1442(a)(3), which authorizes the removal of a civil action or criminal prosecution commenced in any state court against any "officer of the courts of the United States, for any act under color of office or in the performance of his duties."

The judges argued that they were not required to pay the tax because it violated the doctrine of intergovernmental tax immunity. The Eleventh Circuit Court of Appeals had held that the county tax was a direct tax on the federal government or its instrumentalities, in violation of the intergovernmental tax immunity doctrine. The Supreme Court stated that the Eleventh Circuit Court's holding extended the doctrine of intergovernmental tax immunity beyond the limits that the Supreme Court had set and was inconsistent with the controlling federal statute.

The judges had also argued that the occupational tax was a thinly veiled licensing scheme that violated the Court's previous precedents and the Public Salary Tax Act. The Court rejected this argument and said that the county's tax was a tax on "pay or compensation," which was permitted under the Salary Tax Act, 119 S.Ct. 2076 (1999). The Court said that Jefferson County's tax does not discriminate against federal judges in particular, or against federal officeholders in general, on the basis of the federal source of pay or compensation. The Court concluded that there is no sound reason to deny Alabama counties the right to tax with an even hand the compensation of federal, state, and local officeholders whose services are rendered within the county (119 S.Ct. 2077 [1999]).

Sexual Harassment

Davis v. Monroe County Board of Education, 67 U.S.L.W. 4333 (1999), was the first case to come before the Supreme Court in which a school was being held liable for the alleged sexual harassment of one student by another. The mother of a fifth-grade girl sued the county board of education for money damages, alleging that her daughter had been sexually harassed by another student in her class. The Court had to decide whether, under Title IX of the Education Amendments of 1972, 20 U.S.C. § 681 *et. seq.*, which prohibits discrimination in educational programs that receive federal assistance, such private suits may go forward in cases of student-on-student harassment.

A previous *en banc* ruling in the case by the Eleventh Circuit Court of Appeals relied on the Supreme Court's Spending Clause principle, according to which the statute must provide potential recipients of federal education funding with "unambiguous notice of the conditions they are assuming when they accept it." The court found that the statute fails to provide a recipient with sufficient notice of a duty to prevent student-on-student harassment (120 F.3d at 1401).

The majority of the Supreme Court justices concluded that a school district "subjects" its students to discrimination when it knows of peer harassment but fails to respond appropriately (67 U.S.L.W. 4333–4334 [1999]). The majority so found on two grounds: first, the "regulatory scheme" surrounding Title IX has long provided funding recipients with notice that they may be liable for their failure to respond to the discriminatory acts of certain non-agents; moreover, the Department of Education requires recipients to monitor third parties for discrimination in specified circumstances and to refrain from particular forms of interaction with outside entities that are known to discriminate (67 U.S.L.W. 4333 [1999]). Second, the Court concluded that the common law has put schools on notice that they may be held responsible under state law for their failure to protect students from the tortuous acts of third parties.

The Court then proceeded to hold that school districts may be held liable for damages under Title IX "only where they are deliberately indifferent to sexual harassment, of which they have actual knowledge, that is so severe, pervasive, and objectively offensive that it can be said to deprive victims of access to the educational opportunities or benefits provided by the school" (67 U.S.L.W. 4335 [1999]). The Court went on to assert that whether schools can be held liable for damages for student-on-student harassment depends on a "constellation of surrounding circumstances, expectations, and relationships including, but not limited to, the ages of the harasser and the victim and the number of individuals involved." In addition, the Court stated that the phrase in Title IX "under any educational program or activity" means that the behavior has to be serious enough to have the systemic effect of denying the victim equal access to an educational program or activity (67 U.S.L.W. 4336 [1999]).

The language of the decision would appear to restrict damage suits to a limited number of cases in which student-on-student sexual harassment was serious and pervasive and school officials did almost nothing to stop it. The Court stated that it was not requiring schools to "remedy" peer harassment and to ensure that students conform their conduct to certain rules. Instead, the Court stated, recipients must merely respond to known peer harassment in a manner that is not clearly unreasonable (67 U.S.L.W. 4335 [1999]). The Court also said that damages are not available under its ruling for simple acts of teasing and name-calling among schoolchildren.

In *Saenz v. California Department of Social Services*, 67 U.S.L.W. 4291 (1999), a California statute that limits the maximum welfare benefits available to newly arrived residents was challenged under the Fourteenth Amendment. For those who had resided in the state for less than 12 months, the statute limited benefits to the amount that the recipient would have received in his or her prior state of residence. Citing a provision of the Fourteenth Amendment that "no State shall make or enforce any law which shall abridge the privileges or immunities of citizens of the United States," the Court said that what was at issue was the "right to travel": although the word *travel* is not specified in the Constitution, the Court's own jurisprudence had upheld it on the basis of the Fourteenth Amendment and other constitutional provisions (67 U.S.L.W. 4294 [1999]).

The majority stated that the Citizenship Clause of the Fourteenth Amendment expressly equates citizenship with residence and therefore does not permit length of residence to determine degree of citizenship (67 U.S.L.W. 4296 [1999]). The majority concluded that the state's legitimate interest in saving money provides no justification for its decision to discriminate against equally eligible citizens.

The state had relied on congressionally enacted amendments to the Social Security Act as a basis for its own statute. The Temporary Assistance for Needy Families (TANF) program of the Personal Responsibility and Work Opportunity Reconciliation Act of 1996, 110 Stat. 2105, expressly authorizes any state that receives a federal welfare block grant to "apply to a family the rules (including benefit amounts) of the [TANF] program ... of another State if the family has moved to the State from the other State and has resided in the State for less than 12 months" (42 U.S.C. § 604[c] [1994 ed., Supp. II]). The Court did not find, however, that congressional authorization for California's practice served to save the state's statute. The majority simply declared that Congress may not authorize the states to violate the Fourteenth Amendment (67 U.S.L.W. 4296 [1999]).

The case has implications for other services that depend on residence, although the Court did not say that all residence requirements may be challenged. It remains to be seen which other such requirements may be successfully challenged.

The Federal Census

In *Department of Commerce v. U.S. House of Representatives*, 119 S.Ct. 765 (1999), an important case with significant implications for local governments, four counties challenged the Clinton administration's decision to use two forms of statistical sampling that it claimed would improve the accuracy and reduce the cost of the decennial census. In particular, the administration argued that sampling would help reduce undercounting of minorities, children, and renters.

The administration relied on a 1976 amendment to the Census Statute, 13 U.S.C. § 141(a), which authorizes the secretary of commerce to take a decennial census "in such form and content as he may determine, including the use of sampling procedures and special surveys." In disallowing the procedure, the district court held that the sampling would violate 13 U.S.C. § 195, which provides that "except for the determination of population for purposes of apportionment of Representatives in Congress among the several States, the Secretary shall, if he considers it feasible, authorize the use of the statistical method known as 'sampling' in carrying out the provisions of this title."

The Supreme Court stated that in the provision that the district court had relied upon, the "except clause" could technically be read as either permissive or prohibitive with regard to the use of sampling for apportionment purposes. However, in light of a 200-year-old statutory prohibition on sampling, the Court observed that the only plausible reading is that the statute prohibits sampling in the context of apportionment while mandating it in assembling the myriad demographic data that are collected in connection with the decennial census, such as unemployment and household characteristics. Thus, the Supreme Court disallowed the administration's plan to use sampling in the conduct of the census. For apportionment purposes, a complete enumeration would have to be used.

Ordinances Against Loitering

In 1992, in *City of Chicago v. Jesus Morales*, 67 U.S.L.W. 4415 (1999), a city ordinance prohibiting "criminal street gang members" from "loitering" with one another or with other persons in any public place was challenged. The ordinance's definition of loitering was "to remain in any one place with no apparent purpose." The ordinance further provided that

whenever a police officer observes a person whom he reasonably believes to be a criminal street gang member loitering in any public place with one or more other persons, he shall order all such persons to disperse and remove themselves from the area. Any person who does not promptly obey such an order is in violation of this section.

The question the Court considered was whether the ordinance violates the Due Process Clause of the Fourteenth Amendment. The Court's opinion, which had a majority only for some parts, stated that a law fails to meet the requirements of the Due Process Clause if it is so vague and standardless that it leaves the public uncertain as to the conduct it prohibits. The opinion concluded that the ordinance was unconstitutionally vague. The Court also found that the broad sweep of the ordinance violates the requirements that a legislature establish minimal guidelines to govern law enforcement. The Court said that the "no apparent purpose" standard for making the decision is inherently subjective because its application depends on whether some purpose is "apparent" to the officer on the scene. As such, it requires no harmful purpose and applies to non-gang members as well as to suspected gang members (67 U.S.L.W. 4420 [1999]).

In a concurring opinion, Justice O'-Connor indicated that narrower ordinances— such as those that require loiterers to have a harmful purpose — that apply only to gang members or that incorporate limits on the area and manner in which they may be enforced, are not vulnerable under the Court's decision (67 U.S.L.W. 4422 [1999]).

Disability in Employment

Four closely related decisions interpreting the ADA, 42 U.S.C. at 12102 (2), affect local governments as employers.

In the cases of *Sutton v. United Airlines Inc.*, 67 U.S.L.W. 4537 (1999), and *Murphy v. United Parcel Service*, 67 U.S.L.W. 4549 (1999), the Court acted to resolve a dispute among the lower courts with regard to whether people should be evaluated in their corrected or uncorrected state under the ADA.

In *Sutton*, twin sisters who had uncorrected visual acuity of 20/200 were refused employment as airline pilots because they did not meet the airline's requirement of uncorrected visual acuity of 20/100 or better. With corrective measures, the sisters functioned identically to individuals without similar impairments. They filed suit under the ADA, which prohibits covered employers from discriminating against individuals on the basis of their disabilities. Among other things, the ADA defines disability as a "physical or mental impairment that substantially limits one or more ... major life activities" or as "being regarded as having such an impairment."

The district court, which dismissed the women's complaint, held that they (1) were not actually disabled under the terms of the act because they could fully correct their visual impairments and (2) were not regarded by the airline as disabled under the act.

The guidelines of the federal government's Equal Employment Opportunity Commission (EEOC) had directed that people be evaluated for disability in their uncorrected or unmitigated state. The Supreme Court rejected the EEOC's guidelines and declared that evaluating people in their uncorrected state is an impermissible interpretation of the ADA. The Court stated that the statute is properly read as requiring that a person be currently — not potentially or hypothetically — substantially limited in order to demonstrate a disability. The Court went on to say that the congressional findings underpinning the act reflect an understanding that those whose impairments are largely corrected by medication or other devices are not "disabled" within the meaning of the ADA.

With respect to the airline's rejection of the women for positions as pilots, the Court stated that the ADA specifically allows employers to prefer some physical attributes over others and to establish physical criteria. The Court concluded that employers are free to decide that physical characteristics or medical conditions that do not rise to the level of impairment — such as height, build, or singing voice — are preferable to others, just as they are free to decide that some limiting, but not *substantially* limiting, impairments may make individuals less than ideally suited for the job.

In *Murphy v. United Parcel Service*, a truck mechanic whose job required him to drive commercial vehicles was fired because his high blood pressure prevented him from meeting Department of Transportation (DOT) health certification requirements, which his employer — United Parcel Service (UPS)—claimed was necessary for a person in his job. The mechanic sued under the ADA. The Supreme Court stated that the issue of whether Murphy was disabled had already been resolved by its decision in the *Sutton* case: the fact that UPS may have regarded Murphy as unable to be a mechanic in jobs that require a commercial driver's license is not enough to prove that he was regarded as disabled in the major life activity of working. The Court observed that Murphy could still work as a diesel or automotive mechanic, a gas-engine repairer, or a gas-welding equipment mechanic.

The third ADA case involved a truck driver who was fired for failing to meet federal vision standards for truck drivers. In *Albertsons, Inc. v. Kirkingburg*, 67 U.S.L.W. 4560 (1999), a driver with monocular vision had applied for — and received — a waiver of the vision requirements under the Federal Highway Administration Program. However, the employer refused, on safety grounds, to accept the waiver, and the driver brought suit under the ADA. The Ninth Circuit Court of Appeals held that (1) the waiver program was on a par with DOT safety regulations and (2) the driver's impairment is a covered disability because the manner in which he sees differs significantly from the manner in which most people see.

The Supreme Court reversed the circuit court's ruling, stating that the lower court should not have treated monocular vision as sufficient by itself to establish a disability; the Court also noted that the appeals court had paid little heed to the statutory obligation to determine the existence of disabilities on a case-by-case basis. The Court also disagreed with the lower court's conclusion that the waiver program was on a par with the federal regulation for visual acuity. The Court found that the waiver program's regulations did not change the content of the DOT's regular vision standard in a way that deprived the employer of the right to insist on it. Accordingly, the employer's adherence to the DOT vision standard protects it from ADA liability.

In *Wright v. Universal Maritime Service Corp.*, 67 U.S.L.W. 4013 (1998), a longshoreman went on permanent disability after being injured on the job. Three years later he briefly returned to work, but the employer informed him that, having settled a claim for permanent disability, he was not qualified to work under the collective bargaining agreement (CBA). The employer relied on a CBA clause providing that the agreement was intended to cover all matters affecting wages, hours, and other terms and conditions of employment. The employee filed suit under the ADA. The district court dismissed his suit because of his failure to exhaust the CBA's grievance procedure, and the Fourth Circuit Court of Appeals affirmed.

The Supreme Court disagreed, stating that an employee could not be compelled to arbitrate an ADA claim through a CBA. Arbitration of claims under CBAs does not extend beyond the reach of the principal rationale that justifies it: namely, that arbitrators are in a better position than courts to interpret the terms of a CBA. The Court said, however, that this dispute was not about the application or interpretation of a CBA but about the meaning of a federal statute. The Court also said that in order to be free from antiunion discrimination, any collective waiver of the right to litigate a statutory discrimination claim — such as an ADA claim — must meet the standard for waiver of a statutory right: that is, it must be clear and unmistakable. The clause in the CBA that the employers had relied on did not meet that standard.

Union Security

The case of *Marquez v. Screen Actors Guild*, 67 U.S.L.W. 4001 (1998), involved the application of the National Labor Relations Act and a union's duty to provide fair representation. An actress successfully auditioned for a one-line role in one episode of a television series produced by Lakeside Productions. The labor contract that the Screen Actors Guild had entered into with Lakeside included a standard union security clause that required any performer to be a member of the union in good standing. Because the actress had previously worked more than 30 days in the industry, union rules required that she pay approximately $500 in union fees before taking the job. She sought a delay in paying the union fees until she was paid for the performance. The union eventually agreed to allow the actress to take the job before paying the fees, but Lakeside had already hired another actress. The actress then sued the union for breach of the duty of fair representation.

The Supreme Court held that a union does not breach its duty of fair representation by negotiating a union security clause that requires membership in good standing and payment of dues and initiation fees. It also found that the actress had failed to prove that the Screen Actors Guild's conduct toward her was arbitrary, discriminatory, or in bad faith — requirements set down under previous Supreme Court decisions to prove breach of the duty of fair representation.

Employee Retirement Plans

The case of *Hughes Aircraft v. Jacobson*, 67 U.S.L.W. 4122 (1999), concerned the limits of employers' freedom to alter employee pension plans. Beginning in 1955, Hughes Aircraft Company had provided a defined benefit plan for employees, and both employees and the company had made contributions to the plan. By 1987, however, the plan had surplus assets of almost $1 billion, and Hughes ceased making contributions. In 1989, Hughes amended the plan to create an early retirement program that provided significant additional retirement benefits to certain eligible active employees. In 1991, it again amended the plan to prohibit new participants from contributing to it; new participants would thereby receive fewer benefits. Current members could continue to contribute or opt to be treated as new participants.

In 1992, retirees filed a class-action suit alleging that Hughes had violated the Employment Retirement Income Security Act (ERISA) (29 U.S.C. § 1103[c][1]). The retirees claimed that Hughes had breached its fiduciary duties by amending the plan in 1989 to fund a program outside the plan's purposes, amending the plan in 1991 to create the noncontributory structure, and using the surplus assets to fund noncontributory benefits for those who had never contributed to the plan.

The Supreme Court held that ERISA's non-forfeiture and anti-inurement provisions do not apply in this case. The retirees' claims under these provisions were based, the Court found, on the erroneous assumption that the retirees had an interest in the plan's surplus. The Court stated that a defined benefit plan establishes a general pool of assets—rather than individual dedicated accounts, as is the case in a defined contribution plan. While both employee and employer may contribute, the employer typically bears the entire investment risk in a defined benefit plan. Conversely, if the plan is overfunded, the employer may suspend contributions. Given the employer's obligation to make up any shortfall, no plan member has a claim to any particular asset within the plan's pool of general assets. The retirees thus had no entitlement to share in the plan's surplus.

Medical Care

In *Roberts v. Galen of Virginia Inc.*, 67 U.S.L.W. 4062 (1999), the Supreme Court dealt with hospitals' liability under the Emergency Medical Treatment and Active Labor Act, 42 U.S.C. § 139dd(b). This case should be of interest to local governments responsible for hospitals.

Under the act, hospitals are required to "stabilize" individuals who come to the hospital with an emergency medical condition. In *Roberts*, a woman who had sustained severe injuries in a motor vehicle accident alleged that a hospital had violated the statute by transferring her to another medical facility before her condition had stabilized. Extending an earlier ruling that required proof of improper motive to establish a violation of the statute's "appropriate medical screening" provision (42 U.S.C. § 1395dd[a]), the Sixth Circuit Court of Appeals held that in order to recover damages for a violation under the statute, the plaintiff must show that the hospital acted with an improper motive.

The Supreme Court disagreed, holding that hospitals can be held liable in federal court for violating the act's "stabilization" requirement without proof that they acted with an improper motive. The Court pointed out that the stabilization provision contains no express requirement of appropriateness. In addition, the Court stated that the stabilization provision cannot reasonably be read to require an improper motive. The Court's ruling reinstated the woman's suit for further proceedings by the district court. This interpretation of the act makes it easier for individuals to successfully bring suit in federal court against hospitals that they allege violated the stabilization requirement.

Local governments that contract with group health insurance companies will be interested in *Humana, Inc., v. Forsyth*, 67 U.S.L.W. 4085 (1999), in which the issue was whether plaintiffs could sue the managed care firm Humana, Inc., in federal court under the Racketeer Influenced and Corrupt Organizations (RICO) Act, 18 U.S.C. § 1961 *et. seq.*

In a class-action suit, 84,000 plaintiffs in Nevada claimed that they had overpaid millions of dollars in medical copayments under the employer-based group health policies sold by Humana in Nevada. The policies provided that, after meeting a certain deductible, beneficiaries would be responsible for a 20 percent copayment on medical bills, and Humana would pay 80 percent. The employees alleged that Humana had negotiated a secret agreement with a Humana-owned hospital that entitled Humana — but not the beneficiaries — to substantial discounts. As a result, the beneficiaries ended up paying more than 20 percent and Humana less than 80 percent.

At issue was whether another federal statute, the McCarran-Ferguson Act, 15 U.S.C. § 1012(b), precluded the plaintiffs from bringing the suit under RICO. Under that act, federal statutes other than those that specifically relate to insurance shall not be construed to "invalidate, impair, or supersede" state insurance laws. The question was whether the use of RICO violated this provision: the Supreme Court said that it did not.

The Court held that under the standard definitions of *invalidate*, *impair*, and *supersede*, the use of RICO would not frustrate any declared state policy or interfere with the state's administrative regime. Instead, the Court found that RICO's private right of action appeared to complement Nevada's law. Thus, beneficiaries who feel that they have been cheated by such companies' schemes have the additional option of pursuing their claims in federal court under RICO.

Municipal Land Use Regulation

A California case focused on the question of whether jury trials were available to landowner plaintiffs in suits against municipalities for unconstitutional takings of property pursuant to city regulations. In *Monterey California v. Del Monte Dunes at Monterey Ltd.*, 67 U.S.L.W. 4345 (1999), a developer sued the city for its decision concerning his housing development proposal. In his original proposal, submitted in 1981, the developer sought to build 344 residential units on a 37.6-acre parcel zoned for multi-family residential use under the city's general zoning ordinance. Although 344 was well within the number allowed for the entire parcel — 1,000 — the planning commission rejected the plan. The developer then scaled back the proposal to 224 units, which was followed by more rejections and increasing demands by the city.

After five years, five formal decisions, and 19 different site plans, the developer decided that the city would never permit development of the property under any circumstances and filed suit under the federal Civil Rights Act, 42 U.S.C. § 1983, for an unconstitutional regulatory taking. A jury awarded him $1.45 million. The Supreme Court engaged the issue of whether the matter was properly submitted to the jury.

The Court first found that precedent recognizes that Section 1983 creates a tort-like claim; thus, the suit is an action at law within the meaning of the Seventh Amendment. The Court then stated that in actions at law, predominantly factual issues are in most cases allocated to a jury. According to previous Court precedents, the question in regulatory takings cases is whether the property owner was denied "all economically viable use of his property." In this case, the Court held that the issue of whether the landowner had been deprived of all economically viable use of his property is predominantly a factual question: the narrow question submitted to the jury was whether, when viewed in light of the context and protracted history of the development application process, the city's decision to reject a particular development plan bore a reasonable relationship to its proffered justifications. This question is essentially a "fact-bound" one, and the Court concluded that it was proper to submit this narrow, fact-bound question to the jury.

The city had argued that allowing a jury trial would undermine the uniformity of the law and eviscerate state and local zoning authority by subjecting all land use decisions to plenary — and potentially inconsistent — jury review. The Court stated that its decision raises no such specter. The plaintiff had not brought a broad challenge to the city's zoning ordinance and policies but had argued that the city's final denial of the final development permit was inconsistent not just with the city's general ordinances but with the shifting, ad hoc restrictions that it had previously imposed. The Court concluded that, as is often true with Section 1983 actions, the disputed issues were whether the government had denied a constitutional right by acting outside the bounds of its authority and, if so, the extent of the resulting damages. The Court stated that these were the questions for the jury.

Search and Seizure

The Supreme Court decided several cases that involve the Fourth Amendment's protection against unreasonable searches and seizures. These cases will be of interest to local government law enforcement agencies and those agencies that deal with them.

The issue in *Wyoming v. Houghton*, 67 U.S.L.W. 4225 (1999), was whether police officers violate the Fourth Amendment when they search a passenger's personal belongings inside an automobile that the officers have probable cause to believe contains contraband. In this case, a Wyoming highway patrol officer stopped an automobile for speeding. In the front seat were the driver (a man) and two women passengers. While questioning the driver, the officer noticed a hypodermic syringe in the driver's shirt pocket; when questioned about it, the driver admitted that he used it to take drugs. In light of this admission, the officer had probable cause to believe that there were illegal drugs in the car, so he searched the passenger compartment for contraband. On the back seat, he found a purse, which one of the women passengers claimed was hers. Inside the purse, he found a brown pouch and a black wallet-like container, both of which contained illegal drugs and drug paraphernalia. The owner denied that these were hers, and she was placed under arrest.

The Wyoming Supreme Court held that the search of the purse violated the Fourth and Fourteenth Amendments because (1) the officer knew or should have known that the purse did not belong to the driver but to one of the passengers and (2) there was no probable cause to search the passengers' personal effects and no reason to believe that contraband had been placed within the purse.

The Supreme Court reversed the Wyoming court's decision, stating that once probable cause exists to support a search of an automobile, the automobile exception allows a warrantless search of all containers in the vehicle capable of holding the object of the search. The Court said that the determining factor is whether the container could hold the object of the search, not the ownership of the container. The Court observed that a passenger may be pursuing the same illegal activity as the driver — or a driver might, upon being approached by a police officer, hide contraband in a container belonging to a passenger, with or without the passenger's knowledge. It would be nearly impossible for an officer to know whether this had happened, and making the legality of the search of a container depend on such a determination would create an unworkable rule, the Court concluded. The best rule, the Court stated, is that any container may be searched as long as it can contain the object of the search, regardless of whether its owner is present or is a passenger.

Another case focused on whether an officer may conduct a search after issuing a traffic citation. According to Iowa law, a police officer's decision to issue a citation rather than make an arrest does not affect the officer's authority to conduct an otherwise lawful search. In *Knowles v. Iowa*, 67 U.S.L.W. 4027 (1999), a police officer stopped a driver for traveling at 43 miles per hour on a road with a speed limit of 25 miles per hour. After issuing the driver a citation, the officer conducted a full search of the car and found, under the driver's seat, a full bag of marijuana and a "pot pipe." The driver was then arrested. Before trial, the defendant moved to suppress the evidence, arguing that under the "search incident to arrest" exception that the Supreme Court had recognized, the search could not be allowed.

The question was whether issuing a citation rather than conducting an arrest authorizes an officer, consistent with the Fourth Amendment, to conduct a full search of the car. The Supreme Court held that it does not. The Court observed that in a previous case it had noted two rationales for the "search incident to arrest" exception: (1) the need to disarm the suspect in order to take him into custody and (2) the need to discover and preserve evidence for later use at trial. In this case, the Court found, neither rationale applied. With regard to the first, the threat to the officer is a good deal less in issuing a traffic citation than in conducting a custodial arrest, and the officer has other lawful ways to minimize risk. With regard to the second — the need to discover and preserve evidence — once the driver was stopped for speeding and issued a citation, all evidence necessary to prosecute that offense had been obtained. No further evidence of speeding was going to be found.

In another Fourth Amendment case, *Florida v. White*, 67 U.S.L.W. 4311 (1999), the issue was whether the police must obtain a warrant for the seizure of vehicles for purposes of civil forfeiture. The issue arose in the context of a criminal prosecution. Police officers had seized a defendant's car from his employer's parking lot; during an inventory search, they found drugs. On appeal of his conviction, the defendant argued that the seizure of the car without a warrant violated his Fourth Amendment rights. The Florida Supreme Court ruled that the automobile exception to the warrant requirement applies only when the police have probable cause to believe that there is evidence in a car, not when they have probable cause to believe that the car itself is subject to seizure.

The Supreme Court reversed the decision of the Florida court and held that officers who have probable cause to believe that a car is subject to forfeiture (1) need not obtain a warrant before seizing the automobile from a public place and (2) are then free to conduct an inventory search of the car without a warrant. The Court also stated that because the police seized the defendant's vehicle from a public area, the seizure of the car without a warrant did not involve any invasion of the defendant's privacy.

In *Minnesota v. Carter*, 67 U.S.L.W. 4017 (1999), the issue was whether the Fourth Amendment protects the privacy of individuals who are in someone else's home if they are engaged in a common task with their host. In this case, a woman gave two men permission to use her apartment to engage in a cocaine-bagging operation; the woman was promised a share of the drugs. The two men were in the apartment for two and one-half hours and had never been to the apartment before. While walking by a window to the apartment, a confidential informant observed the two men putting white powder into bags. The informant notified a police officer, who looked into the same window through a gap in a closed blind and observed the bagging operation for several minutes; the officer then informed headquarters. After leaving the apartment, the two men were stopped in a car and arrested for possession of illegal drugs.

At trial, the men moved to suppress the evidence, arguing that the officer's initial observation of their drug packaging was an unreasonable search in violation of the Fourth Amendment. The Minnesota Supreme Court held that the Fourth Amendment does protect the privacy of individuals when they are in someone else's home if they are engaged in a common task with their host, and thus the officer's observation without a warrant constituted an unreasonable search.

The Supreme Court reversed the decision of the Minnesota court. In reviewing previous Court decisions, the Court found that the principle is that an overnight guest may claim the protection of the Fourth Amendment, but one who is merely present with the consent of the householder may not. The Court observed that the defendants were obviously not overnight guests but were essentially present for a business transaction and were only in the home for a matter of hours. Property used for commercial purposes is treated differently for Fourth Amendment purposes than residential property. The Court stated that given the purely commercial nature of the transaction, the relatively short time on the premises, and the lack of any previous relationship between the defendants and the householder, the defendants' situation was closer to that of individuals who are simply permitted on the premises. Therefore, the Court held that any search that may have occurred did not violate any Fourth Amendment rights.

Two other Fourth Amendment cases focused on whether the news media could be invited along when police officers conduct an otherwise legal search of a home with a search warrant. The two cases— *Wilson v. Layne*, 67 U.S.L.W. 4322 (1999), and *Hanlon v. Berger*, 67 U.S.L.W. 4329 (1999)— both resulted in the holding that it is a violation of the Fourth Amendment for police to bring members of the media or other third parties into a home during the execution of a warrant when the presence of the third parties in the home is not in aid of the execution of the warrant.

In the *Wilson* case, which produced the main opinions, county officers obtained a warrant to arrest a fugitive in what they believed to be the fugitive's home but which turned out to be his parents' home. They executed the warrant in a team operation with U.S. marshals, who (pursuant to the "ride-along" policy of the U.S. Marshals Service) invited a photographer and a reporter from the *Washington Post* to accompany them for the arrest. The warrant made no mention of media presence or assistance.

Early in the morning, the county officers and marshals entered the home of the fugitive's parents, who were still in bed when they heard the officers enter the home. The father confronted the officers in his living room and angrily demanded that they state their business. Believing that the father was the fugitive, the officers quickly subdued him. After conducting a protective sweep and learning that the fugitive was not in the house, the officers departed. The reporter was in the house at the time of the arrest and the photographer took several pictures, which were never published. Neither was involved in the execution of the arrest warrant. (In *Hanlon*, a television crew recorded the execution of a search warrant by officers at a ranch.)

The home owner and his wife sued the county officers for money damages under 42 U.S.C.§ 1983 and the marshals under a comparable Court precedent, *Bivens v. Six Unknown Fed. Narcotic Agents*, 403 U.S. 388 (1971), for the officers' action in bringing members of the media to observe and record the attempted execution of the arrest warrant, which they contended violated their Fourth Amendment rights. The Supreme Court stated that even when police officers are in a home under the authority of a warrant, what they do in the home must be related to the objectives of the authorized intrusion, and that that standard was not met in this case. The media representatives did not take part in the execution of the arrest warrant, which was the justification for the officers' entry into the home. The Court stated that the possibility of good public relations for the police is not in itself enough to justify a ride-along intrusion into the home.

However, the Court did not permit the awarding of damages to the home owner. Both Section 1983 and the *Bivens* precedent (1) grant qualified immunity to government officials, such as police officers, who are performing discretionary functions and (2) shield them from liability for civil damages insofar as their conduct does not violate clearly established statutory or constitutional rights of which a reasonable person would have known. The Court concluded that it was not unreasonable for the officers to believe that bringing along media observers during the execution of an arrest warrant was lawful. Therefore, the officers in this case (and in *Hanlon*) would not be liable for damages. Nonetheless, officers in the future would be so liable because the Court has now laid down the standard for ride-alongs.

In *West Covina v. Perkins*, 67 U.S.L.W. 4058 (1999), the issue was whether the Constitution requires a state or its local entities to give detailed and specific instructions or advice to owners who seek return of property that was lawfully seized but is no longer needed for police investigation or criminal prosecution. In this case, police officers with a valid search warrant searched a home when the owner was not present. During the search, they seized some personal property that belonged to the owner of the home rather than to the boarder for whom the police were looking. The officers left the home owner a form stating their authority for the search, listing the items taken, and providing the names of detectives to contact for further information. Because the warrant was under seal to avoid compromising the investigation, the officers did not leave the search warrant number. In a public index maintained by the court clerk, however, the issuance of the warrant was recorded by the address of the home and the search warrant number. The home owner made some inquiries and tried to have a judge (other than the one who had issued the warrant, who was on vacation) issue an order to release his property, but was told that the court had nothing under his name.

Rather than continue to pursue a court order for release of the property, the owner filed suit in U.S. district court against the city and the officers who had conducted the search, claiming that the officers had violated his Fourth Amendment rights by conducting a search without probable cause and exceeding the scope of the warrant. The district court granted summary judgment for the city and its officers but invited supplemental briefings on the issue of whether the available remedies for the return of the seized property were adequate to satisfy the due process requirements of the Fourteenth Amendment. The district court ultimately awarded summary judgment for the city on the due process question, but the Ninth Circuit Court of Appeals reversed that decision, holding that the city was required to give the home owner notice of the state procedures for recovering the property as well as any information he needed to invoke those procedures.

The Supreme Court reversed that decision and held that due process does not require individual notice of state law remedies that are established by published, generally available state statutes and case

law, as were those in this case. The Court stated that once a property owner is informed that his property has been seized, he can turn to these public sources to learn about the remedial procedures available to him, and the city need take no further steps to inform him of his options.

In another search case, *Conn v. Gabbert*, 67 U.S.L.W. 4222 (1999), an attorney who represented a witness in the first trial of the Menendez brothers in California challenged the search of his person. The prosecutors had directed a police detective to obtain a warrant to search the attorney for a letter that one of the brothers had written to the witness. As the attorney and the witness entered the courthouse, one of the prosecutors directed a special master to search the attorney while another prosecutor called the witness to the stand before the grand jury. The witness was unable to consult with the attorney during her testimony and asserted her Fifth Amendment right not to testify for fear of self-incrimination. The attorney filed suit under 42 U.S.C. § 1983, alleging that the handling of the search violated his Fourteenth Amendment right to practice his profession without unreasonable government interference.

The Supreme Court held that the attorney did not have a legal cause of action. The Court recognized that people have a liberty interest under the Fourteenth Amendment that includes a generalized right to choose one's work. Nonetheless, the Court found that the case law makes clear that an individual's right to pursue a vocation is not absolute but is subject to reasonable government regulation. The Court concluded that the brief interruption of the attorney's work that occurred in this case was not extensive enough to rise to the level of a constitutional deprivation.

Prisons and Jails

The one prison case that the Court decided applies to local jails as well. The issue in *Martin v. Hadix*, 67 U.S.L.W. 4500 (1999), was how to apply a statute to cases that were pending when the statute became effective. The case arose in the context of a lawsuit brought by prisoners in Michigan years before the Prison Litigation Reform Act, 110 Stat. 1321 § 803(d), which amended 42 U.S.C. § 1997e(d), was passed.

The act, which limits attorneys' awards in several ways, places a cap on the hourly rate of attorneys who litigate prisoners' claims. The prisoners' case had resulted in their being judged "prevailing parties," which entitled them to postjudgment fees related to the monitoring of prison officials' compliance with court decrees. The district court had established a system for awarding the fees semiannually and had set specific market rates for those fees. In this case, application of the cap would have reduced the rate payable to the prisoners' lead attorneys from $150 to $112.50 per hour.

The Sixth Circuit Court of Appeals held that applying the cap to cases that were pending on the effective date of the act would have an impermissible retroactive effect, regardless of whether the work for which the fees were sought was performed before or after that date. The Supreme Court reversed that decision and stated that the determinative time is not when the case was filed but when the work was performed. The cap on fees can therefore apply to pending cases, but only as related to services that were performed after the act's effective date of April 26, 1996.

Summary

This chapter has presented the highlights of Supreme Court cases decided in the 1998–99 term. The rulings discussed here touch on many aspects of local government management. While case summaries are presented to inform local government managers and other interested readers about the most significant aspects of these decisions, they do not constitute legal advice. Local government managers who find themselves in similar situations are urged to consult an attorney.

Editor's Note

The actions of the federal government's Supreme Court in fiscal Year 1998/99 were included in this volume in order to reflect the significant impact that this body has on our nation's fifty state and numerous local governments. This chapter shows the dramatic impact that this body has on our nation's lower-level governments as our nation enters the 21st century.

Chapter 30

The Politics of New Federalism

JOHN A. FEREJOHN AND BARRY R. WEINGAST

The renewed interest in federalism raises concerns about policy as well as constitutional law, as policymakers and researchers have begun to ask whether the devolution of some programs to the states might result in better policy. These inquiries are, necessarily, guided by the analysis of specific issues of the kind exhibited in this chapter. But such inquiries are also political, involving elected officials, parties, ideologies, and interest groups operating at all levels of American government. In brief, they involve the voters deciding the detailed character of the federal system.

This is as it should be. Federal authority expanded over the states and localities as a result of Democratic Congresses creating a wide variety of new programs over the past half century. With the sanction of a pliable Supreme Court, Congress either preempted state authority or enlisted state agencies in the service of federal programs. This expansion of federal authority over the states—most recently in the form of unfunded mandates—helped generate a political reaction against federal intrusion and a willingness to expand the powers of the states.

Indeed, many profound changes in the allocation of federal authority have already begun to flow from recent electoral outcomes at both the federal and the state level. These changes, which have taken place at all levels of government, involve judges as well as political officials. Moreover, they do not all point in the direction of the devolution of federal authority. Two cases revealing a more complex pattern of new federalist thinking are the continued expansion of federal criminal law, much of it with bipartisan support, and the recent Republican-led effort to regulate state tort law and limit punitive damage awards.

In recent years, judges and legal academics have begun to ask whether the constitutional jurisprudence that formed the basis of New Deal and Great Society legislation is constitutionally defensible. This inquiry is both broad, involving many policies simultaneously rather than one at a time, and deep, addressing the fundamental powers of the national government and, indirectly, that of the states.

Two events have greatly enlivened the debate about the appropriate powers and reach of the national government. The first involves the "new federalism" initiatives unveiled in the 104th Congress that attempted to turn a variety of regulatory and police powers back to the states. The second concerns the Supreme Court's decision in *Lopez* (1995), suggesting that it may reconsider limits on the national government under the commerce clause.

Although many of the new federalist initiatives originated in the 104th Republican Congress, some Democrats also believe that federalism can enhance public performance. Alice Rivlin, for example, argues that federalism provides a means of "reviving the American dream."[1] But although *Lopez* and the 1996 welfare reform legislation have attracted the most public attention, they are not isolated occurrences. Both Congress and the Supreme Court have evidenced an increasing willingness to rethink the relationship between federal and state authority and to revisit fundamental assumptions about the nature of American government.

For example, in a number of areas, Congress has begun to experiment with a kind of "statutory federalism" in which the states are permitted wider discretion within federal statutory schemes. The welfare reform legislation adopted in 1996 illustrates this effort. That legislation grants the states' vastly increased authority to craft their own welfare policies; further, Congress provides a substantial grant of funds for this purpose. This bloc grant is, in principle, supposed to permit each state to define its own welfare program free of federal interference. Nonetheless, Congress retains the power to regulate state plans. And Congress did restrict state plans in that legislation, attempting to ensure that states enforce welfare time limits and make progress toward moving welfare recipients into the workforce. Obviously, the success of statutory federalism depends greatly on Congress's willingness to abstain from micromanaging state policy processes. Yet it is by no means clear that either Democratic or Republican members of Congress will, or can, restrain themselves.

Since the *Garcia* decision, the Supreme Court has begun exploring ways to define a new constitutional federalism that curtails the domain of congressional authority. This effort has two prongs. The first, seen in *Lopez*, is aimed at limiting Congress's commerce clause powers. Although too soon to tell, this thrust may in time extend beyond the commerce clause to encompass the spending clause. The second prong of constitutional federalism is aimed at giving meaning to the Tenth Amendment. In a series of decisions, the Court has said that, although Congress may induce states and municipalities to participate in federal programs by dangling federal funds in front of them, it may not actually "commandeer" state policymakers to do its bidding. Commandeering the states, the Court has said, interferes with the relationship between state policymaking officials and their constituents by diminishing the states' capacity to be responsible and accountable to their electorates. Without this capacity, the independent authority of the states would wither and these governments would become administrative appendages of Congress. It is not yet clear how far this new theory of the Tenth Amendment extends. The Brady Bill, by requiring that sheriffs implement a congressional handgun control program, has been challenged on exactly these grounds.

Although the effectiveness of statutory federalism depends on congressional self-restraint, constitutional federalism is, in principle, policed by the Court and thus potentially provides a more secure basis for state autonomy — as it did before the New Deal. Whether this is so in practice depends on the willingness and capacity of the Court to enforce these new boundaries. For example, if the Court were to find that the Brady Bill's commandeering sheriffs is unconstitutional, Congress can use its spending powers to achieve the same purpose. A similar conclusion holds for *Lopez*; it is not clear whether the congressional authority to regulate guns near schools would be struck down if Congress could provide a plausible link to interstate commerce, which it failed to do in the Gun Free School Zones Act.

Although people on both ends of the political spectrum bemoaned or celebrated *Lopez*'s New Deal-shattering implications, whether it has such large implications depends on how it is elaborated both in subsequent decisions and in congressional explorations of the new constitutional terrain. A reinvigorated constitutional federalism might be attractive on the grounds that it would more securely reestablish the authority and responsibility of the states, but it is by no means clear how far the Court will go. Thus, statutory federalism, for all its political fragility, might be the only game in town, at least for now.

Several reasons suggest that redefining American federalism by statute is a good thing. For one, statutory federalism does not put the Supreme Court on a collision course with Congress. Historically, the Court has never been able to resist congressional assertions of authority for long, as the lessons of the New Deal demonstrate. Second, judicially imposed restraints are blunt tools in circumscribing congressional authority. As already suggested, the Brady Bill might have escaped constitutional scrutiny altogether had it relied on the spending clause instead of commandeering state officials. Its constitutionality has nothing to do with its substance or purposes, depending only on the specific legal forms through which these purposes were pursued. Third, refashioning commerce clause jurisprudence is a double-edged sword; narrowing the definition of commerce may limit congressional authority but at the price of limiting the authority of courts to restrain states from imposing interstate commercial barriers. Finally, statutory federalism places the policy question of which level of government is appropriate where it belongs: at the center of policy analysis and discussion and thus at the center of political debate. Statutory federalism does not presume that a particular program must be done at one level for constitutional reasons. Rather, the appropriate allocation of governmental tasks depends on the characteristics of the issues. Over time, because of technical or demographic changes, programs might properly be moved from one level to another without triggering constitutional questions.

Many leaders of both parties agree that, for many of our public problems, the states and localities should play a larger and more vigorous role than has been allowed to them in the past. The disagreements center on which problems to turn back to the states and how far the states may be trusted to address them. This chapter should help resolve some of these disagreements by focusing on the issue of the "race to the bottom" — the standard objection to enlarging the role of states and localities. Often such arguments are raised in journalistic or political settings, where careful analysis is scarce.

Researchers have taken seriously the possibility that interjurisdictional competition might have various adverse effects, but none finds much systematic evidence of a race to the bottom. Working in the welfare domain, an area where race-to-the-bottom arguments are common, the adverse effects of state competition are weak. In the area of environmental policy, the arguments for a race to the bottom are also weak, except when the specific policy concerns interjurisdictional spillovers. Moreover, the federal attempts to alleviate the negative effects of interjurisdictional spillovers can be counterproductive. State competition for corporate charters has had generally beneficial effects on the structure of corporate law. This competition has permitted the emergence of one state, Delaware, leading the way in innovative law governing charters. The result has been a legal regime favorable to corporate governance and economic efficiency. Taken together, these assessments undercut the idea that we ought, automatically, to be suspicious of programs in which states and localities play a substantial role.

A Look Ahead

Any analysis of federalism must resolve two political issues. First, as a matter of policy, the analysis must identify those problems best addressed at the state or local level and those best addressed at the national level. Second, the analysis must address the nature of states and localities as political units within the federal system. Although these political issues appear independent, they are not. If the states take on more responsibilities, they will become more vigorous and vital political units; they will therefore increasingly attract public attention and support, along with high-quality officials. In the early days of American federalism, politicians commonly left national offices to serve in their states. If states once again become "where the action is," their quality as political systems will improve.

Ironically, for the states to play an enhanced role the contributors envision for them successfully, they must also be limited in some ways. Some argue that, for state competition to be beneficial, states must operate with hard budget constraints and be restrained (by the courts) from interfering with interstate commerce or shifting the costs of their policies to others. They show that the success of American federalism, relative to federalism in other countries, is partly traceable to two features: American states operate in the bond market's unforgiving, tight financial environment, and courts have prevented them from restraining interstate commerce. Thus, the new federalism, whether statutory or constitutional, retains a substantial role for national institutions. Nonetheless, some caution that federal attempts to deal with financial problems that fall within the states' domain have usually made things worse.

For states and localities to address a wider range of policies effectively, they must be allowed to experiment with various approaches and to attract financial and other resources to meet their new responsibilities. The central issue of the new statutory federalism, therefore, is congressional restraint. But whether Congress can refrain from interfering in state domains is a difficult political issue. The movement toward new federalist solutions requires sustained popular support, which means that the people must stop expecting federal action on every problem. For the new federalism to be viable, congressional majorities must find the idea of restraint politically attractive. In the long run, this depends on the new federalism attracting sustained popular support in elections at all levels of the federal system.

Note

1. Alice Rivlin, *Reviving the American Dream: The Economy, the States, and the Federal Government* (Washington, D.C.: Brookings Institution, 1992).

• *Chapter 31* •

National Election Practices

CHARLES R. WISE

There is probably no other phase of public administration in the United States, which is so badly managed as the conduct of elections [Harris 1934, 1].

Sixty-six years later, following the 2000 presidential election, the above-quoted observation still seems apt. The breakdown led to a whirlwind of litigation in the federal courts, leaving much of the public wondering whether a country that has made a practice of assisting newer democracies with the administration of their elections might need help with its own.

Seldom has the relationship between courts and administration been the subject of such intense national focus, as it was with the judicial-administrative interplay during the 2000 election for the president of the United States. The unprecedented stakes riding on the outcome of the judicial-administrative decisions involved in election administration in Florida highlighted features of the judicial-administration interface and subjected it to public

scrutiny as perhaps no other area of public policy since the early desegregation decisions. Understandably, both the processes they observed and the outcome that resulted troubled many people. Charges of bias were directed toward judges, administrators, and legislators at state and national levels. Charges of judicial overreaching were plentiful on both sides: Gore partisans alleged judicial overreaching by the U.S. Supreme Court, while Bush partisans alleged overreaching by the Florida Supreme Court.

The purpose here is not to engage or evaluate charges of overreaching or partisanship; reams of legal and political commentary will be devoted to that enterprise for decades to come. Instead, the objective here is to examine the decisions for insight into what they might portend for improving election administration in the future and what they might tell us about the judicial-administration interface. I will attempt to draw out some initial lessons that

Originally published as "Election Administration in Crisis: An Early Look at Lessons from Bush versus Gore," *Public Administration Review*, Vol. 61, No. 2, March/April, 2001. Published by the American Society for Public Administration, Washington, D.C. Reprinted with permission of the publisher.

appear to derive from the events and decisions associated with the post-election controversy. Undoubtedly, there are numerous other lessons that will come out of these events. This is meant to serve as an early look.

Lesson I: Administrative Neglect in Critical Public Services Leads to the Courts

The first lesson is not a new one, but it seems to have received heightened public attention as a result of the post-election dispute. The lesson the nation seems to have to re-learn time and again is that when the requisites of administration in an important area of public service are neglected for a long period of time, breakdown inevitably results and the affected parties turn to the courts to resolve what has been allowed to develop into a crisis.

Time and again at the point of crisis, the courts have had to fashion solutions with little preparation and inadequate legislative guidance. This has occurred in many areas of public service such as mental health, prison conditions, and school desegregation (Cooper 1988). The courts are less like an advancing army charging in to dominate a territory and more like a fire brigade that has been summoned when half the building is already engulfed in flames. Nonetheless, the effect of judicial rulings in these areas was not only to force states and localities to address problems they had ignored for years, but also to put others on notice of minimum standards and that be enforced (Cooper 1997, 427).

In the area of mental health, for example, the federal court's entry into supervision and reform of mental health institutions came in the landmark case of *Wyatt v. Stickney* (325 F. Supp. 582 [M.D.Al. 1971]); the court's decision found the abysmal conditions to which Alabama had committed patients in state-operated mental health institutions violated the U.S. Constitution. The decision followed three decades of professional-association analyses and legislative reports that had clearly documented the unacceptable conditions, procedures, and policies to which patients in many states were being subjected. Because mental health patients are not a particularly powerful constituency, governors and state legislators rarely responded to the clearly demonstrated needs for additional appropriations and policy change to the point that many mental health institutions were violating patients' human rights. Congress also did not respond until the courts began to act. The federal courts responded in one state, Alabama, but it soon became evident the problem existed in many other states as well. A case such as *Wyatt v. Stickney* often picks up steam as interest groups and governments become aware of the impact of a judgment in the matter (Cooper 1997, 428).

So it is, too, with election administration. In the wake of election 2000, it is clear the inadequacies of the public infrastructure and policy framework for election administration that are employed in national election are not confined to the state of Florida. The per curium opinion in *Bush v. Gore* noted, "The closeness of this election, and the multitude of legal challenges which have followed in its wake, have brought into sharp focus a common, if heretofore unnoticed, phenomenon. Nationwide statistics reveal that an estimated 2 percent of ballots cast do not register a vote for President for whatever reason, including deliberately choosing no candidate at all or some voter error, such as voting for two candidates or insufficiently marking a ballot" (121 S.Ct. 529[2000]). After the election, the National Commission on Election Standards and Reform, consisting of 21 county officials, academics, and civil rights leaders, was formed by the National Association of Counties and the Association of County Recorders, Election Officials, and Clerks to address the national problem.

The commission's co-chair, Ernest Hawkins, who is also president of the Recorders Association, confirmed that the atomized electoral public has just not been considered an important enough constituency at the local level, where election appropriations are made. He observed, "When county budgets are determined, elections are simply not at the top of the priority list when compared to law enforcement, health care, and public works" (*New York Times* 2001).

As everyone now knows, in Florida 24 counties used the punch-card voting system, while 1 used a lever system, 1 used a paper system, and 41 used an optical-scan system. Now that the word "chad" has entered the national lexicon, the problems with punch-card systems are apparent. Nonetheless, the problems with such systems have been well known for some time. Judge Sauls found in *Gore v. Harris* that Dade and Palm Beach counties had been aware of balloting and counting problems for many years (*Gore v. Harris*, slip op., No. 00-2808 [Fla. 2d Cir. Ct. Dec. 3, 2000] Proceedings at 10). The decision makers in those counties had simply not appropriated funds for the more accurate optical-scan systems that 41 other counties had adopted. Even their awareness of the potential problems reportedly did not move election administrators to attempt to minimize them. Instructions to election boards using Votomatic voting machines recommend the devices be cleared of chads after every election to prevent errors, but Gore attorney Stephen Zack reported being told by Dade County officials that it had been eight years since their devices were last cleaned (CNN.com, 2000).

A longstanding debate exists in public administration about the extent to which the courts are the most appropriate forum for resolving breakdowns in the administration of public services (see Horowitz 1977; O'Leary and Wise 1991; Perales 1990; Wasby 1981; Wood and Vose 1990). There is plenty of room for debate, even if the courts must be involved, concerning which court is the appropriate forum to resolve the disputes. Nonetheless, it is difficult not to sympathize with the Supreme Court's per curiam statement at the conclusion of *Bush v. Gore*:

> None are more conscious of the vital limits on judicial authority than are the members of this Court, and none stand more in admiration of the Constitution's design to leave the selection of the President to the people, through their legislatures, and to the political sphere. When contending parties invoke the process of the courts, however, it becomes our unsought responsibility to resolve the federal and constitutional issues the judicial system has been forced to confront [*Bush v. Gore*, 121 S.Ct. 533 (2000)].

Although strong arguments were made by Vice President Gore's attorneys and justices Ginsberg and Stevens in dissent that the U.S. Supreme Court was not the appropriate body to resolve the dispute, a majority of the justices saw it as the Court's responsibility. According to the Gallup Poll, 61 percent of Americans agreed that they trusted the U.S. Supreme Court to make the final decision, as opposed to 9 percent for the Florida Supreme Court, 17 percent for the U.S. Congress, and 7 percent for the Florida Legislature (Gallup 2000). Nonetheless, the question remains whether the U.S. Supreme Court is an appropriate forum to resolve disputes over problems in the administration of elections.

In any event, as a result of events in the judicial sphere, a serious systemic problem is now on the national agenda and policy makers at local, state, and national levels must move to resolve it quickly, or we are sure to see more cases taken to the courts in close elections.

Lesson II: Equal Protection Applies to Election Administration

The second lesson is sure to provoke more court cases—the Equal Protection Clause of the Fourteenth Amendment has been found to clearly apply to election administration (at least in presidential elections), and thus violations may be heard in federal court. While the remedy offered by the five-justice Supreme Court majority in *Bush v. Gore* met with strong objections from the four dissenting justices, seven of the Court's members found equal protection problems with the remedy the Florida Supreme Court had ordered.

The Florida Supreme Court's majority opinion concluded, "because this is a statewide election, statewide remedies would be called for" (770 So. 2d 1292). The Court directed the circuit court "to order the Supervisor of Elections and the Canvassing Boards, as well as the necessary public officials, in all counties that have not conducted a manual recount or tabulation of the undervotes in this election to do so forthwith, said tabulation to take place in the individual counties where the ballots are located" (770 So. 2d 1293). The majority opinion specified that the standard for canvassing boards to use in the recount would be the "intent of the voter" as stated in the Florida statute.[1]

Specifically, the U.S. Supreme Court's per curiam opinion declared that equal protection does apply to the intrastate administration of elections.[2] What disturbed the justices was the kind of variability that had emerged in the process of recounting the votes, which was found to vary from county to county, and also within the same county.[3] As a result, the Court concluded, "The recount mechanisms implemented in response to the decisions of the Florida Supreme Court do not satisfy the minimum requirements for non-arbitrary treatment of voters necessary to secure the fundamental right" (*Bush v. Gore*, 121 S.Ct.

530 [2000]). The opinion stated that the "intent of the voter" standard was unobjectionable as an abstract principle, but it incurred a problem in ensuring equal application in the absence of specific standards. The Court stated, "The formulation of uniform rules to determine intent based on these recurring circumstances is practicable and, we conclude, necessary."[4]

Although this decision was pronounced in the context of a presidential election, and the majority took pains to emphasize the extraordinary circumstances, it is difficult to see why a similar analysis might not be applied to congressional elections as well as future presidential elections in close cases. Fourteen other states employ an "intent of the voter" standard (*Bush v. Gore*, Stevens dissenting, 121 S.Ct. 540, ftn.2). Regardless of whether successful cases are brought on equal protection grounds in future elections, the exposure of such variability would seem to counsel state legislatures to examine their states' voting procedures and to make affirmative decisions about how recounts are to be implemented in the future. Providing such guidance in legislation could go a long way toward avoiding confusion in future recounts and in ensuring more equal treatment for all voters.

Lesson III: Inadequate Legislation Leads to Judicially Fashioned Remedies

Another lesson that is being relearned is that, in the absence of clear constitutional or legislative direction, courts fall back on general grants of authority and accustomed methods to fashion remedies to resolve problems. The result may or may not be in accordance with what citizens would want if they were confronting the issue by means of deliberation in a democratic forum. Crafting a judicial remedy normally takes considerable time and is subject to significant fact finding: plan development, negotiation between the parties, and formal decision. The judge often plays a facilitative role as the plan for the remedy is developed, calling upon the parties to negotiate some kind of agreement as to how to resolve the problems that have been identified (Cooper 1988, 19). The election dispute the country witnessed after the presidential election seriously compressed the time frame for fashioning remedies, thus magnifying the potential problems in resolving the issues. This compressed time period sharply limited the extent to which the courts could gather information about the workability of the potential remedies.

Judges seldom possess extensive expertise in specific areas of administration; therefore, they must rely on the parties and outside experts (who often do not agree) to suggest methods to resolve the problems at issue. In cases involving mental health institutions and prisons, for instance, courts have taken many months to engage in fact finding, plan development, and negotiation to fashion an initial remedy; even after deciding on a remedy, they often revise the remedial order numerous times as implementation problems surface and are brought to the attention of the trial judge. In a normal case, the trial judge who is the original finder of fact is the primary actor in fashioning and supervising the remedy. It is a long-observed presumption among the appellate courts that the trial judge is most familiar with the dynamics of the situation and the parties who will be responsible for implementing the remedy. For this reason appellate courts typically defer to the trial judge on the particulars of the remedy. Even then, there is considerable analysis criticizing the legitimacy and effectiveness of judicial remedies in achieving administration reform (Melnick 1983; Nagel 1978; Rosenberg 1991). The compressed schedule of the presidential election dispute, which involved conducting a statewide recount in Florida, truncated the judicial process.

The Florida cases magnified the courts' difficulties in fashioning a remedy due to the compressed time schedule and the magnitude of the remedy invoked. Statutory ambiguities concerning the appropriate procedures for resolving problems at various stages of the process exacerbated the situation. One Florida statute provides for a "protest," in which requests for manual recounts are to be presented to county canvassing boards, which may order a limited sample manual recount (102.166 Fla. Stat.). Once the sample recount is completed and the canvassing board concludes there was an error in the vote tabulation that could affect the outcome of the election, another section (102.166[5] Fla. Stat.) sets out options for what is to be done, one of which is for the board to decide to manually recount all ballots.

Another statute, however, provides for a "contest" of the vote after the canvassing boards have certified the vote for their counties. The contest takes place before a circuit court judge and allows the circuit judge to fashion orders as he or she deems necessary to ensure that allegations are investigated, examined, or checked (102.168 [4] Fla. Stat). The relationship between the protest section of the statute and the contest section, which were passed by the legislature at different times, was a matter of dispute. One question was whether the judge presiding over the contest phase is to grant any deference to the canvassing boards' decisions regarding recounts, and another question was what standard the judge was to use in making the decision.

The trial judge concluded that, absent an abuse of discretion by the canvassing board, he could not order a manual recount (*Gore v. Harris*, Slip op. No. 00-2802 [Fla. 2d Cir. Ct. Dec. 4, 2000]). The majority opinion of the Florida Supreme Court disagreed, concluding that the trial judge had to conduct the proceeding as a new trial and that the abuse-of-discretion standard was wrong (772 So. 2d. 1261). Given the tight time schedule, it was very difficult to order the circuit court to conduct a new trial. Therefore, the majority further held there was sufficient evidence already presented at the trial to justify a recount; it ordered the recount, not just for the selected counties, but for the whole state (772 So. 2d. 1292). The dissenting opinion could find no basis for the majority casting aside the determination of the trial judge, based on the evidence he had received (772 So. 2d 1305). It is apparent that the difficulty was encountered because the Florida legislature had not coordinated the various sections of the law. The legislature needs to clarify at what point a recount (or recounts) must be ordered, who has the discretion to order them, whether there is any relationship between the decisions made in the protest phase and in the contest phase, and what standards are to be used in making the determination. This seems to be particularly important in resolving disputes in the administration of elections. Election-administration officials, judges, and candidates need to know and understand the rules in advance in order to resolve disputes fairly and effectively within a tight time schedule.

The Florida Supreme Court declared that the legislature's statutes were passed in recognition of the federal statute 3 U.S.C., sec. 5, which, in effect, indicated that the recount had to be completed by December 12 in order for the state to make its certification unchallengeable by Congress.[5] The Court ordered the statewide recount on its own, without benefit of the normal process of which courts avail themselves in crafting remedies. In the "normal" process, appellate courts have the benefit of seeing how lower courts have addressed similar problems and can provide adjustments to address disparities. In this case,

however, as Justice Breyer pointed out in his opinion, "time was, and is too short to permit the lower courts to iron out significant differences through ordinary judicial review" (121 S.Ct. 551).

Although the Florida Supreme Court acknowledged that time was very short to conduct a recount in every county, the majority expressed confidence that the counties could do it. Unfortunately, county canvassing boards encountered multiple problems in implementing the Court's order. In Duvall County, for example, the process had trouble getting started because the canvassing board members declared they did not have the computer software to cull an estimated 4,967 ballots with undervotes from the 291,000 ballots cast there. Similarly, in Polk County, elections clerks contemplated sifting through the county's 175,000-plus ballots by hand to get at the undervotes. In Orange County, 60 election workers sorted through 282,000 ballots to cull 966 undervotes (Canady and Filkins 2000).

Whether the Florida Supreme Court's remedy would ultimately have turned out to be workable in terms of resolving the issues was and is, of course, the subject of intense debate and disagreement among legal and political analysts, the public, and justices of the U.S. Supreme Court. There is not room here to review all of the positions in those debates.

The source, however, of the ambiguity surrounding the appropriate remedy is clear: conflicting statutes passed by the Florida legislature. When statutes are silent or unclear as to an appropriate remedy, courts rely on their own equitable powers and methods of interpretation to fashion a remedy. The Florida State Association of Supervisors of Elections voted at its winter meeting for a single set of standards to be formulated as to how to conduct a recount. This is not just Florida's problem, it is a national problem. In February, the

National Association of Secretaries of State adopted its "Election Reform Resolution," which, among other things, recommends that state and local governments: "adopt uniform state standards and procedures for both recounts and contested elections, in order to ensure that each vote is counted and to provide public confidence in election results" (NASS 2001).

Improvements can clearly be made, because examples of improvement exist. Michigan had a recount in a congressional district in fall 2000, and its law prevented the problems experienced in Florida. Punch card ballots were used there, too. In the eighth district, the Democratic candidate requested a recount after the Board of Canvassers certified the Republican candidate the winner by 160 votes. Under Michigan Law (Mich. Comp. Laws, ch. XXXIII, Sec. 168 [2000]), a vote is counted if a rectangular chad is completely punched through or is connected by one or two of the four corners. The recount revealed that the Republican remained the winner, and no legal challenge resulted.

Lesson IV: Coordinating the Resolution of Multiple Disputes Embedded in a Systemic Condition Is Problematic in the Courts

Another lesson derived from these cases is that conflict resolution by means of the courts is extremely difficult, if not impossible, to coordinate within the very tight time schedules involved in elections. By their very nature, courts focus on discrete cases involving individual contests of issues brought by particular people in specific venues. When the litigants in Florida filed suits in various selected counties, this meant that different trial courts would decide on the cases, making it more difficult to achieve a coordinated statewide resolution and provide equal protection for all voters.

The nation wondered, as multiple cases were initiated and proceeded through multiple courts in several counties, with the cases exhibiting many of the same systemic problems, whether over punch card ballots, absentee-ballot registration, or the counting of overseas ballots. These cases then could be subjected to appeals in state and federal courts.

The judicial system only "coordinates" its activities over time in deciding numerous cases through the appellate process. It is best suited for matters in which there is time to deliberate over the similarities and differences among various situations represented by the various cases. It is less well suited to treating systemic problems in compressed time frames.

Lesson V: Election Administration Is an Intergovernmental Responsibility

Issues involved in election administration, at least for presidential elections, are not solely a matter of state or federal responsibility — they are an intergovernmental responsibility. At the most basic level, this begins with Article 2 of the Constitution:

> Each state shall appoint, in such Manner as the Legislature thereof may direct, a Number of Electors, equal to the whole number of Senators and Representatives to which the State may be entitled in the Congress ...
>
> The Congress may determine the Time of choosing the Electors, and the Day on which they shall give their Votes: which Day shall be the same throughout the United States.

Federal statutes are also involved in setting the framework for state action. The controversies in *Bush v. Gore* may suggest that Congress revisit its statutes and assess how effective they are in setting a clear context within which the states are to act. To begin with, one federal statute affects the time frame within which the states operate to administer elections and resolve conflicts. How it is actually supposed to affect the time frame, however, proved to be a matter of dispute. Federal statute, 3 U.S.C. sec. 5, Determination of Controversy as to the Appointment of Electors, provides:

> If any State shall have provided, by laws enacted prior to the day fixed for the appointment of the electors, for its final determination of any controversy or contest concerning the appointment of all or any of the electors of such State, by judicial or other methods or procedures, and such determination shall have been made at least six days before the time fixed for the meeting of the electors, such determination made pursuant to such law so existing on said day, and made at least six days prior to said time of meeting of the electors, shall be conclusive, and shall govern in the counting of the electoral votes as provided in the Constitution, and as hereinafter regulated, so far as the ascertainment of the electors appointed by such State is concerned.

The meaning of this provision was, of course, disputed by the attorneys for Bush and Gore and by the justices of the Supreme Court. The per curiam opinion concluded that the Florida Supreme Court, having found that the legislature had intended Florida's electors to take advantage of process (specified by the statute) whereby any contest of votes had to be resolved by December 12, lacked sufficient time to accomplish that with a process that met minimal constitutional standards. The dissenters disagreed that the Supreme Court had the power to enforce the deadline pursuant to the statute, but it meant only that if the state missed the deadline for submitting a slate of electors, it would lose what has been called a "safe harbor." That is, if there were a dispute over that state's electors and they were submitted after the deadline according to the statute, the dispute would be resolved by Congress (Dissents by Justice Souter 121 S.Ct. 543;

Stevens 121 S.Ct. 540; and Breyer 121 S.Ct. 553).

To assist the states in making their own decisions about procedures for resolving contested elections, it would be useful for Congress to clarify the meaning of its statute. While it may be some time before we have a presidential election as close as the last one, there is little reason to allow the conflicting interpretations to remain as guidance for the states.

Clarifying legislation relating to the contesting of votes is just one area that could use some attention in the intergovernmental relationship of election administration. Attention should also be paid to standards for voting systems, research and development of voting systems, training of personnel involved in election administration, and funding.

With regard to voting-system standards, information surfaced during the litigation that demonstrated the widespread but extreme variation in voting errors among and within states, suggesting that the nation is some distance from equal treatment in "counting every vote." What the Florida cases revealed is that the problems are systemic and not idiosyncratic. The Florida Supreme Court observed,

> This Presidential election has demonstrated the vulnerability of what we believe to be a bedrock principle of democracy: that every vote counts. While there are areas in this state which implement systems (such as the optical scanner) where the margins of error, and the ability to demonstrably verify those margins of error, are consistent with accountability in our democratic process, in these election contests based upon allegations that functioning punch-card voting machines have failed to record legal votes, the demonstrated margins of error may be so great to suggest that it is necessary to reevaluate utilization of the mechanisms employed as a viable system [770 So.2nd 1290 ftn. 20].

While it is not possible to eliminate error, there can be little doubt that accuracy in election administration needs to be improved on a nationwide basis. There would seem to be little justification for permitting states to tolerate high error rates in presidential elections. While uniformity is not possible, narrowing the range of error is possible and desirable. The states and the federal government have collaborated in other public-policy arenas to address national problems. Numerous areas of intergovernmental policies administered by the states have involved setting minimum standards from protection of drinking water to building of highways. Given that the foundation of democracy is the act of voting, it would seem to be essential to arrive at minimum standards for the protection of the electoral process.

The issue is how to arrive at minimum standards. The National Association of Secretaries of State has called for federal funding to develop voluntary management practices standards for each voting system and to provide funding to the states to implement reforms (NASS 2001). Bills have already been introduced into Congress to accomplish this.[6] While it will be necessary to observe the Constitution's command that the states determine the time, place, and manner of elections, there seems to be no prohibition on Congress conditioning the receipt of money for system improvement on complying with minimum standards (see *South Dakota v. Dole*, 107 S.Ct. 22793 [1987]). Other than creating an environment in which federal officials direct states, the federal government has other methods of encouraging and influencing state action (see Conlan 1998; O'Toole 1993; Wright 1988).

There may also be an intergovernmental role in overseeing research and development of voting systems. While there has been an explosion of marketing of new voting systems already in the post-election

period, these systems must be evaluated according to multiple criteria, including their potential for error reduction and their capability to guarantee access for the elderly, minority, disabled, military, and overseas citizens. States need to develop mechanisms to collectively pursue research and development goals. It should be remembered that the now-infamous "butterfly ballot"— listing names of candidates on both sides— used in Palm Beach County was designed by that county's Democratic supervisor of elections because she thought it would allow names to appear in larger print for the county's large number of elderly voters. When asked after the election if she had market-tested the ballot, the supervisor had no answer (Tuchman 2001). Clearly, we want public officials to actively pursue administrative change to facilitate access for various types of individuals. Nonetheless, the Palm Beach experience illustrates that new mechanisms need to be thoroughly tested for their effects, expected or unexpected. The right intentions are not enough. The testing needed is probably beyond the capacity of any locality or even a single state — states will need to collaborate to achieve the needed level of effectiveness.

There may be a federal role here as well. As the United States has experienced in other areas of public policy such as environmental protection, federally sponsored research and development has assisted states' accomplishment of intergovernmental goals. There is no suggestion here that any federal role in research and development should be the dominant one. Private for-profit and nonprofit initiatives have been spurred on by the events surrounding the election. For example, the Massachusetts Institute of Technology and California Institute of Technology have initiated a collaborative research project to develop a new easy-to-use, reliable, affordable, and secure voting machine.

That effort is directed at one issue, but that is not the only one. Federal sponsorship of research, or at least federal collaboration with the states in such an endeavor, is worthy of discussion to address the agenda of research and evaluation issues.

With regard to the training of personnel, the states have the primary role. Nonetheless, there is little doubt that the training of election-administration personnel on a nationwide basis has been uneven at best. There is a demonstrated need to increase the quantity and quality of training in the election-administration system. There may be a federal role in this area as well, analogous to its role in assisting states in other areas of primary state and local responsibility. For example, the Federal Emergency Management Agency assists with training for state and local emergency-management personnel, and the FBI has long assisted state and local law enforcement personnel with training in various areas of law enforcement.

There can be little doubt that reform in election administration will require more funds. The bulk of it will need to be appropriated by state and local governments, and the expenditures will be sizable.[7] Increased funds will be required for capital expenditures, but also for improved human resource development. Capital expenditures will be necessary to replace outmoded equipment, such as the punch-card system, with more accurate systems. "Nonvotes" are one indicator of potential errors. As *Bush v. Gore* revealed, the percentage of nonvotes in counties using a punch-card system was more than twice that for counties using an optical-scan system.[8] In the capital-expenditure area alone, the secretary of state of Michigan has proposed a uniform, statewide election system that does away with punch cards, which she estimates will cost between $30 million and $60 million (Christoff 2000). Nonetheless, there could be some rationale for matching federal funds to encourage state investment and to assure improvements in poorer states and localities.

Lesson VI: Reform Must Focus on the Citizen-Administration Interface

The citizen-administration interface needs to be a consistent focus for election administrators as well as other public administrators, and improving it must be approached systematically. No other function of government directly involves so many citizens as the act of voting, and no other function is more central to the health of democracy. Yet understanding and improving the interface between the voting process and citizen participation has not received nearly the professional attention of many other government functions. The Palm Beach election supervisor had a legitimate motivation—to extend access to the elderly. Nonetheless, an understanding of all the elements that would achieve the intended goal without incurring undesirable side effects was missing. There is an understandable tendency to quickly make changes in the voting machines and eliminate the punch card ballot, for example. Officials and administrators need to ensure, however, that the newer technology really solves problems and facilitates a more positive citizen experience. Riverside County, California, for example, spent $14 million on 4,250 new touch-screen voting machines for its 714 precincts during the fall of 2000, in time for the presidential election. The process was very efficient, and results were reported one hour and 17 minutes after the polls closed (Seelye 2001). Nonetheless, a preliminary research report by the Caltech/MIT Voting Project, which is studying nationwide use of voting machines in presidential elections, concluded that electronic machines performed as badly as punch cards: compared to lever machines, the direct-recording devices produced a residual vote 1.23 percentage points higher. Although the researchers did not analyze why the difference in non-vote rates arose, they believe it reflects how people relate to the technologies rather than actual machine failures (Alvarez et al. 2001).

The issue of citizen-administration interface extends beyond ballot design. There are many persons in numerous categories who may be hindered rather than aided by various facets of the voting process. There have been allegations that minority voters were unlawfully discouraged from voting in some Florida counties, for example. Allegations have pointed to numerous precincts with a heavy concentration of minority voters containing the oldest voting equipment. Given the emphasis on equal protection by the Supreme Court's per curiam opinion, numerous jurisdictions could face increased legal challenges over disparate treatment of various groups of voters. A lawsuit filed in U.S. district court in Miami against several state and county election officials alleges that they failed to follow state and federal voting-rights laws to ensure that all voters were given an equal opportunity to vote. The suit also names a company that supplied the counties with a faulty list of convicted felons and dead voters to be removed from registration lists. Of course, there have been decades of efforts to ensure that discrimination against members of minority groups in voting is ended, and the federal government has continuing major responsibilities to ensure lawful treatment. A major challenge for voting administration is not only to ensure that no one is treated unfairly, but also to take proactive initiatives to increase access to those whose participation in voting has historically trailed that of the majority.

In recent years, public administration has engaged in an interesting debate as to whether the public should be treated as customers or citizens, and what is required of public administration with either approach (Fountain 1998; Frederickson 1992; King and Stivers 1998, 49–67; Rosenbloom and O'Leary 1997, 117–50). The voting context suggests that efforts to enhance its administration embrace both rubrics. That is, initiatives to improve the process need to take into consideration the characteristics of people in all their diversity to enhance the franchise for a larger proportion of the American public. Voting needs to be as "customer friendly" an experience as administrators and officials can make it. Aspects of the human-technology interface in voting, such as voters' habits, simplicity, and privacy, will need to be considered, and new technologies and methods will need to be validated against standards that embrace these factors. At the same time, citizens need to learn and understand their responsibilities in the voting process and demand that the mechanisms of voting receive at least the resources and attention that other public services have received, if not more so.

We should be under no illusions as administrators and officials pursue reform initiatives. There is and will be no such thing as an error-free voting system. There are technical, social, and sociotechnical risks that are common to all secure systems and pose threats to the security and integrity of the voting process. The newer electronic voting systems are not immune to these risks (Mercuri 1992; Mercuri and Nehman 2001). Public officials and administrators must recognize the potential errors in the new systems they develop, and they must construct and adopt procedures for resolving problems that will be effective within the time demands of the election cycle and will assure the voting public that the opportunity to ensure a fair and just result has been maximized.

Conclusion

The post-election events surrounding election administration in Florida were traumatic for the nation. There is no doubt that several of our institutions have been subjected to considerable, if not strident, criticism as a result. Election administration needs to move beyond the charges and criticism and take seriously the important lessons from the episodes that can point the way to reform for the future.

Public administration has not devoted attention to election administration with anything like the priority it has given to other areas of public policy. Neglect of election administration has characterized research, education, and technical assistance in the field. No area of the public's business is more critical to the success of American democracy than the election process. Public administration has much to contribute to ensuring that it is a fair, just, and effective one. The agenda is there to be engaged and, if furthering democratic governance is the hallmark of the field, it would behoove us to engage it.

There is much to do and, unless the agenda is engaged, there will be more episodes with attempts to resolve crises in the courts. Much deliberation needs to be devoted to better methods of administration and better ways to resolve conflicts. This is not to say that courts should be removed from the process of conflict resolution in the elections area. They have a role to play, but courts will be better enabled to play it in a context where the ground rules are clear and the activities of other institutions are better organized and coordinated. The needed reform agenda is both multifaceted and intergovernmental. If pursued systematically, public administration can prevent a repeat of the events during the fall of 2000.

Notes

1. "In tabulating the ballots and in making a determination of what is a 'legal' vote, the standard to be employed is that established by the Legislature in our Election Code which is that the vote shall be counted as a 'legal' vote if there is 'clear indication of the intent of the voter.'" See section 101.5614(5), Florida Statutes (2000) (*Gore v. Harris*, 772 So. 2d 1256).

2. "The right to vote is protected in more than the initial allocation of the franchise. Equal protection applies as well to the manner of its exercise. Having once granted the right to vote on equal terms, the State may not, by later arbitrary and disparate treatment, value one person's vote over that of another" (*Bush v. Gore*, 121 S.Ct. 530).

3. "[T]he standards for accepting or rejecting contested ballots might vary not only from county to county but indeed within a single county from one recount team to another. The record provides some examples. A monitor in Miami-Dade County testified at trial that he observed that three members of the county canvassing board applied different standards in defining a legal vote.... And testimony at trial also revealed that at least one county changed its evaluative standards during the counting process" (*Bush v. Gore*, 121 S.Ct. 531).

4. Justice Souter's dissent stated, "I can conceive of no legitimate state interest served by these differing treatments of the expressions of voters' fundamental rights. The differences appear wholly arbitrary" (*Bush v. Gore*, 121 S.Ct. 545). Justice Breyer's dissent, which Justice Souter joined, stated, "I agree that, in these very special circumstances, basic principles of fairness may well have counseled the adoption of a uniform standard to address the problem" (*Bush v. Gore*, 121 S.Ct. 551).

5. "These statutes established by the legislature govern our decision today. We consider these statutes cognizant of the federal grant of authority derived from the United States Constitution and derived from 3 U.S.C. sec. 5 (1994) entitled Determination of Controversy as to Appointment of Electors" (772 So. 2d 1251).

6. S. 218 Election Reform Act of 2001.

7. The National Association of Secretaries of State calls for state and local governments to "Provide election officials with increased

funding to implement recommendations of this resolution" (NASS 2001).

8. "The percentage of nonvotes in this election in counties using a punch-card system was 3.92 percent; in contrast, the rate of error under the more modern optical-scan systems was only 1.43 percent" (*Bush v. Gore*, Stevens dissenting, 121 S.Ct. 542, ftn.4).

References

Alvarez. R. Michael et al. 2001. *A Preliminary Assessment of the Reliability of Existing Voting Equipment: Version I.* February 1.

Canaday, Dana, and Dexter Filkins. 2000. Task Beginning with Confusion Across Florida. *New York Times.* December 10, 1.

Christoff, Chris. 2000. Michigan Law Spells out Rules for Tallying by Hand. *Detroit Free Press,* November 28, 1.

CNN. 2000. Voting-Device Designer Takes Stand for Bush, Gives Boost to Gore. Available at http://CNN.com. Accessed February 4, 2001.

Conlan, Timothy. 1998. *From New Federalism to Devolution: Twenty-five Years of Intergovernmental Reform.* Washington, DC: Brookings Institution.

Cooper, Phillip J. 1988. *Hard Judicial Choices.* New York: Oxford University Press.

_____. 1997. Court Involvement in Operations of State and Local Institutions. In *Handbook of Public Law and Administration,* edited by Phillip J. Cooper and Chester A. Newland, 424–39. San Francisco, CA: Jossey-Bass.

Fountain, Jane E. 1998. Customer Service: An Institutional Perspective. Paper presented at the American Political Science Association, Boston, MA. September 4.

Frederickson, H. George. 1992. Painting Bull's Eyes around Bullet Holes. *Governing* 6(1).

Gallup Organization. Dec. 22, 2000. Available at http://www.Gallup.com. Accessed February 12, 2001.

Harris, Joseph P. 1934. *Election Administration in the United States.* Washington, DC: Brookings Institution.

Horowitz, Donald. 1977. *The Courts and Social Policy.* Washington, DC: Brookings Institution.

King, Cheryl Simrell, and Camilla Stivers. 1998. *Government Is Us.* Thousands Oaks, CA: Sage Publications.

Melnick, R. Shep. 1983. *Regulation and the Courts.* Washington, DC: Brookings Institution.

Mercuri, Rebecca. 1992. Voting Machine Risks. *Communications of the ACM* 35(11): 138.

Mercuri, Rebecca, and Peter Nehman. 2001. System Integrity Revisited. *Communications of the ACM* 44(1): 160.

Nagel, Robert F. 1978. Separation of Powers and the Scope of Federal Equitable Remedies. *Stanford Law Review* 30 (April): 661–724.

National Association of Secretaries of State (NASS). 2001. *Election Reform Resolution.* February 6.

New York Times. 2001. Election Panel Calls for More Money for Equipment and Training. January 11, 4.

O'Leary, Rosemary, and Charles R. Wise. 1991. Public Managers, Judges, and Legislators: Redefining the New Partnership. *Public Administration Review* 51(4): 316–27.

O'Toole, Laurence J., ed. 1993. *American Intergovernmental Relations: Foundations, Perspectives, and Issues.* Washington, DC: CQ Press.

Perales, Cesar. 1990. The Fair Hearing Process. *Brooklyn Law Review* 56(3): 889–98.

Rosenberg, Gerald. 1991. *The Hollow Hope.* Chicago: University of Chicago Press.

Rosenbloom, David H., and Rosemary O'Leary. 1997. *Public Administration and Law.* 2nd ed. New York: Marcel Dekker.

Seeyle, Katharine. 2001. A California County Touches Future of Voting. *New York Times.* February 12, 1.

Tuchman, Gary. 2001. Ballot Nightmare Lingers for Palm Beach Elections Chief. Available at http://CNN.com. January 2.

Wasby, Stephen L. 1981. Arrogation of Power or Accountability: Judicial Imperialism Revisited. *Judicature* 65(4): 208–19.

Wood, Robert, and Clement Vose. 1990. *Remedial Law: When Courts Become Administrators.* Amherst, MA: University of Massachusetts Press.

Wright, Deil. 1988. *Understanding Intergovernmental Relations.* 3rd ed. Belmont, CA: Brooks Cole.

• Chapter 32 •

City Government

ROGER L. KEMP

Citizens throughout the world face the challenges of the 21st century, the dawn of our civilization's third millennium. Dynamic changes are taking place in society that will have a profound impact on our cities in the future. Evolving societal conditions and public perceptions have created trends that require communities to change in order to meet the public's expectation for effective and equitable governance. The milestone changes examined in this chapter are based upon established and predictable trends. They will have a measurable impact on municipalities across the nation during the coming years. Adapting to these changes will test the abilities of public officials as they strive to represent the citizens they serve.

Gone are the traditional and predictable days for local governments. When revenues were plentiful, public officials could merely adjust tax rates to balance budgets. The external environment was relatively tranquil, and did not pose many significant challenges, available opportunities, or impending threats. Public programs were merely increased in response to citizen demands for more services. In

the future, both the scale and mix of public services, as well as how they are financed, will be critically examined in response to changes taking place in our society. Our traditional election practices have long formed the basis of our local democracies. Minority and ethnic groups now demand greater representation in the governance processes of their communities.

The traditional municipal planning practices of the past were designed during periods of steady growth and routine change. They are now being questioned and replaced by more modern and relevant planning practices. The practice of strategic planning, the development of alternative scenarios, and the use of issues management techniques, long common in the private sector, have been at the forefront of this planning trend. The traditional planning practices of the past, characterized by merely projecting previous trends into the future, will increasingly be found to be lacking in their reliability and credibility. In the future, more sophisticated, technically accurate, and politically-acceptable planning practices will be developed to adapt municipal organizations to their changing environments.

The Forces of Change

The changes presently taking place in society will have a profound impact on our cities in the future, as well as how they are governed and managed. How public officials adapt to these evolving conditions will directly reflect on their ability to successfully adapt their municipal institutions in the future. Today's public officials are typically preoccupied with the present, and reactive to change. Most of the time government officials, at all levels, respond to change after the fact. Municipal officials are no exception to this common practice. Nowadays, external circumstances and public attitudes are changing so rapidly that the practices of the past are quickly becoming obsolete. The process of community governance and types of services provided to citizens are presently in a state of transition.

The magnitude and momentum of these changes will have a direct influence on public services during the coming years, as well as how they are financed, and the extent to which they meet the needs of citizens. By purposely adapting local democratic institutions to citizen expectations, and by productively planning for the future of municipal organizations, our public officials will be able to create a smooth transition for their local governments in future years. If this does not happen, city halls throughout America will increasingly become vocal forums for debating citizen demands for greater government accountability, citizen responsiveness, and organizational change.

To illustrate the extent of these changing societal trends, and to make them easier to understand, they are presented below using six categories. They include readily predictable demographic shifts, major economic factors, escalating environmental concerns, evolving political considerations, state-of-the-art technological trends, and changing urban patterns and shapes. The following paragraphs describe those changes presently taking place in our society, as well as how they are influencing the very fabric of life in our communities. The dramatic changes in these areas, and how they impact our local governments, are examined below.

Demographic Shifts

- Due to emigration from South and Central America, Hispanics will soon become the largest minority group in America. Their political impact will be felt in city halls in many communities, especially in those cities located in the southwest and southeast.
- A growing number of senior citizens will, because of their increasing lifespans and available leisure time, become more politically active, particularly at the local levels where access to local democratic institutions and processes are readily available to all.
- These senior citizens will demand more specialized public services, such as those provided by recreational, cultural, libraries, health, and social programs. Large-print books, health clinics, nutrition workshops, and exercises classes, are but a few examples of these types of services.
- A greater number of smaller households will require more high-density residential developments such as condominiums, townhouses, and apartments. These type of developments will place greater demands on existing public services in these residential areas.
- There will be a larger percentage of women in the workforce, and they will become more politically active in the workplace. Such issues as equal opportunity, comparable worth, sexual harassment, and family leave policies will increase in importance.

- A greater number of minority and immigrant groups will create new demands for more specialized public services such as the need to hire more bilingual employees, implement cultural diversity programs, and enhance equity in the delivery of existing public services to citizens.
- An increased number of minority and immigrant groups will become involved in the political process. This will create a greater demand for more equitable election practices, resulting in more minorities and immigrants in the political arena, and demands that a municipal workforce reflect a community's ethnicity.
- Due to the increasing number of families with female heads-of-households, community issues such as provisions for affordable healthcare, more after-school childcare centers, community policing programs, and specialized programs for young people, such as teen centers, will be high on the municipal agenda.
- Immigrant groups will continue to enter the United States through major port cities on the east and west coasts of the United States, expanding existing ethnic centers, as well as creating new ethnic neighborhoods in these highly-urbanized metropolitan areas.
- The second generation of American immigrants will increasingly relocate to other states surrounding the areas that contain these centers and, unlike their parents, they will move to the suburbs as they have families and assimilate into the mainstream of American society.

Economic Factors

- Because of limited discretionary money at the federal level, new grant-funded programs will be limited and earmarked for those local services that help achieve national goals, such as providing affordable housing, alleviating unemployment, the availability of shelters for the homeless, improved urban planning practices, and those programs that lower health-care costs.
- Public officials will increasingly focus on economic development as a vehicle to raise revenues without increasing property taxes. Cities in highly urbanized areas will have to resort to the intense redevelopment of "brownfields" areas for their very economic survival.
- Job retention programs that prevent employment opportunities from leaving to other cities will be high on the municipal agenda. The focus of economic development will shift, as land becomes more scarce, from incentives that favor job-creation to those that enhance job-retention programs.
- Since virtually every community finances and provides the essential "hard" services (such as police, fire and public works programs), a greater emphasis will be placed on how to pay for the quality-of-life or, so-called, "soft" services (such as recreation, museums, libraries, and cultural programs). User fees and charges will become more common.
- The public's aversion to escalating property taxes will continue, forcing local officials to look for other non-property tax related revenue sources such as new user charges, increases to existing fees, and improving the collection of taxes from already-approved revenue sources.
- A greater number of taxpayers will acknowledge that it is the legitimate role of government to provide "safety-net" services to their truly needy citizens. Taxpayers will not mind paying taxes for these necessary and important services on a temporary basis.
- Millions of Americans will continue to move to cities to chase their dreams. Sociologists call this the "bright-lights effect." Increased international trade, superior infrastructure, and greater access to technology, will make cities responsible for a growing proportion of the nation's economic production.
- The public will recognize the value of the social cohesion that only cities can provide. The vitality, excitement, and sense of community which cities can create and foster will increasingly be recognized and appreciated for its economic value. This trend, as well as the one listed above, will serve to limit suburbanization and urban sprawl in the future.
- Public officials will increasingly focus on economic development as a vehicle to raise revenues without increasing taxes.

Highly urbanized cities will have to resort to redevelopment for their financial survival. Municipal tax abatements will increase in popularity.

- Citizens do not mind paying for those services they use, but they will increasingly demand that other taxpayers pay their fair-share of taxes for the cost of providing those "other" services that "they" do not use. This will pose a political problem, since everyone uses selected services but no one uses every public service.

Environmental Concerns

- A greater emphasis will be placed on the need to create sustainable communities. Citizens will recognize the need to concentrate human populations in cities as essential to preserving America's agricultural and wilderness areas. Circular rather than linear urban systems will become necessary to recapture our nation's natural resources.
- Both planners and developers will become aware of the need for newly designed communities to provide a balanced quality-of-life within a traditional neighborhood setting. This trend will concentrate development, with commercial and high-density residential mixed land-uses in the center, while providing adjacent single-family residential areas surrounded by common open spaces.
- Greater urbanization, coupled with a renewed appreciation of our natural environment, will result in new planning models that provide for the multi-jurisdictional stewardship of those important natural amenities that transcend our traditional political boundaries.
- A new planning discipline will emerge called "horizon-line management," whereby communities and their public planners will take responsibility for managing scenic areas and corridors for such natural amenities as ridgetops, mountains, plateaus, as well as man-made urban skylines in densely-populated metropolitan areas.
- Quality-of-life issues such as air and water quality, the availability of parks and open spaces, and the preservation of natural amenities, will increase in importance as

citizens come to understand the positive relationship between the natural environment and the economic health of their community.

- Older and more politically sensitive land-uses, such as aging and outdated commercial buildings and industrial plants, will be upgraded and/or retrofitted with new improvements and amenities to make them more attractive to the public for both employment and shopping opportunities.
- The public will increasingly embrace comprehensive code enforcement as a vehicle to improve the condition of their aging residential neighborhoods. Department managers will be held accountable for enforcing these municipal codes to improve the housing stock within their communities.
- Citizens will acknowledge the need to properly plan for local natural amenities, such as coastlines, rivers, streams, lakes, wetlands, and other natural wonders designed for all citizens to enjoy. Once only the concern of individuals in high-income communities, citizens of all income groups will increasingly embrace these environmental issues.
- Citizens are starting to appreciate the main attributes of nature—the skies, the lands, and the waters—and will increasingly demand that their public officials, especially their elected officials and professional planners, properly plan for the stewardship of these natural resources to make them available for future generations to enjoy.
- More multi-city, city-county, multi-county, multi-state, and national-state agreements will emerge for the management of our unique natural amenities that "spill" over our artificial political boundaries. Public-private partnerships will also be developed to enhance the stewardship of these natural resources. Citizens will come to recognize the finite quality of our natural resources.

Political Considerations

- Increased demands will be made by minority and immigrant groups to change existing democratic institutions, such as traditional election methods and voting options. There will be greater pressure to move towards district elections and alternative voting practices.

- More federal and state laws, and court-decisions of all types, will greatly usurp the home-rule powers of locally-elected officials, central administrators, as well as functional managers, and serve to limit their municipal discretion in many ways as to how these services are provided to citizens in the future.
- While special interest groups typically pursue their own narrow goals, these groups will increasingly form broad coalitions around major issues of mutual interest at the local, state, and national levels. This will create a more turbulent political environment in public meeting halls throughout the country.
- Brought about by limited revenues, many political issues will have no simple clear-cut response, such as evolving debates concerning what services to reduce, options for holding down property taxes, what taxes to increase, and whether or not to increase program user fees and charges.
- Citizens will demand more public services but not want increased taxation, making it more difficult for public officials and administrators to set program priorities, determine appropriate service levels, as well as balance their annual municipal budgets.
- General responsibility for services will continue to shift from the federal and state governments to cities, forcing communities to solve their own problems. Because of the mismatch between available revenues and existing problems, those communities with a low tax base may have to resort to service reductions in order to balance their budgets.
- Minority group representatives, including women and immigrants, as they get more involved in the political arena, will place greater demands for more specialized and diversified public services. These individuals will advocate for more neighborhood services tailored to meet the needs of the minority and immigrant citizens they serve.
- The NIMBY (Not-In-My-Back-Yard) movement will continue to grow in size at the neighborhood and community

levels. Undesirable public facilities such as jails, wastewater treatment plants, and waste disposal facilities, will increasingly be difficult to locate or relocate within a community.

- More political coalitions and partnerships involving business, government, education, and the nonprofit sector will emerge to address a community's social and economic problems of mutual concern. A greater number of non-profit organizations will be formed to address these emerging problems in the coming years.
- Existing public officials, both elected and appointed, will feel the increasing political influence of these new special interest groups— seniors, women, immigrants, and minorities. When service reductions must be made in the future, it will be difficult to "cut" the services provided to these new constituent groups.

Technology Trends

- There will be an increased use of microcomputers in the workplace, brought about by more sophisticated hardware systems, advanced user-friendly software applications, and lower costs for both of these products. In the not-to-distant future, nearly every municipal workstation will have a microcomputer with state-of-the-art software.
- Microcomputer systems will increasingly incorporate and combine existing pieces of office-technology, such as facsimile machines, photographic copiers, document scanners, specialized printers and telecommunication devices.
- All municipal organizations will standardize their computer hardware systems and software applications in the not-to-distant future. This will create uniformity for these technological applications, facilitating the trend to conduct generic hardware and software training for all employees.
- Expensive organization-wide, stand-alone, computer systems will become a thing-of-the-past, primarily due to the development of improved and inexpensive mainframe computer systems and networking techniques, as well as the use of

a greater number of inexpensive and sophisticated microcomputers.

• Information management will become necessary as more advanced computer hardware systems and software applications facilitate the generation of all types of information. The emphasis will switch from merely receiving information to acquiring quality information in a timely manner.

• As utility costs escalate, computerized energy monitoring and management systems will gain in popularity and become less expensive, facilitating the widespread use of these systems to limit energy consumption in city halls and other public buildings in cities throughout the country.

• Because of more advanced videotaping equipment and more municipal-owned public-access cable television stations, a greater number of public meetings will be broadcast to citizens. This medium will be used to educate citizens about available public services, as well as those major issues facing their community.

• Greater energy costs will continue to shape our personal values, lifestyle preferences, and the future technological developments. Smaller automobiles, less spacious offices, new energy-saving devices, and more sophisticate building techniques are examples of this phenomenon.

• More advanced telecommunication systems with video capability will make conference-calling commonplace. This will limit the number of face-to-face business meetings and reduce travel expenses. More-and-more personal computers will have these devices as standard equipment in the future.

• Every municipal government will have an interactive website, which can be accessed by citizens and used to contact public officials in their local government 24-hours per day seven-days a week. Virtual city halls will emerge where citizens can make applications, receive permits, download public announcements, as well as view videos about their community, all on-line. Online voting will also become commonplace in the future.

Urban Patterns

• Urban sprawl will be on the increase, but will be primarily located along major vehicular transportation corridors, such as highways and freeways, and be contiguous to public mass-transit routes, those suburban transportation "rings" with "hubs" located outside of our nation's inner-city areas.

• Citizens will witness greater "in-fill" development in already high urbanized areas. Land areas that were once considered marginal for development will be purchased and improved to meet increasing community demands for more commercial and industrial development.

• In our country's central city areas, escalating land values will lead to increased gentrification of our inner-city neighborhoods, further exacerbating the need for more affordable housing for low-to-moderate income families in our nation's poorer metropolitan areas.

• New ethnic centers will emerge and evolve in major metropolitan areas. First-generation residents will stress maintaining their cultural traditions, personal values, as well as the unique customs brought to this country from their respective homelands.

• Higher energy costs and greater traffic congestion will create political pressure for public mass-transit systems. Emphasis will be placed on multi-modal systems that offer transportation options to citizens. Expensive construction costs will lead to more routes in densely-populated urban areas. Light-rail systems will become commonplace for longer routes connecting cities with their suburbs.

• Those inner-city public services provided by many urban cities will migrate to the suburbs. Since large numbers of individuals and families have moved to these areas during the past few decades, and public problems are more prevalent in densely populated areas, suburban communities will have to provide these types of services in the future.

• As the country's young people get older, and gain employment, they will increasingly use e-commerce to purchase many consumer goods. This will serve to limit the need for new regional shopping malls, and strip-commercial centers. Increased pressure will evolve for warehousing and distribution centers to meet the new demand created by e-commerce.

- Population shifts away from the northeast and midwestern United States will exacerbate the decline of the existing corporate tax base in these locations, possibly forcing public service reductions or property tax increases in the future. State-wide economic development incentives will be used to counteract this negative economic trend.
- Gentrification will continue as younger single people, childless couples, well-to-do empty-nesters, as well as active retirees, continue to move from the suburbs to inner-city metropolitan areas. This movement will occur because of less expensive housing, lower energy costs, and a desire to be closer to available commercial and cultural amenities.
- Our nation will witness a dramatic shift in the nature of the public's attitude toward our cities. These changing attitudes are being brought about by the realization that the social problems of our cities cannot be geographically contained. Wherever people move, and the population spreads, these problems will follow.

The Future

City halls in communities throughout America are undergoing a revolution in how their public services are financed and delivered to citizens. Significant numbers of public officials are striving to create more "user-friendly" municipal organizations. Many public managers are embracing more flexible and adaptive management styles to help achieve this goal. These contemporary management practices are creating more dynamic and citizen-responsive services. These new programs are dynamic because they are accommodating citizen-oriented change in a positive way. They are responsive because they are striving to improve the quality of services to taxpayers. Citizens are also being encouraged to coproduce public services, such as through recycling and neighborhood watch programs, in order to hold down taxes in their community.

The goal of today's local governments is citizen/customer satisfaction at a reasonable cost. Advanced citizen feedback instruments, process improvement techniques, more sophisticated planning practices, and the use of modern technologies, will help achieve this goal. Since organizations are merely legal entities, the employees in municipal government should be recognized for their willingness to embrace evolving customer service philosophies, adopt more positive work attitudes, utilize advanced operational practices, and implement the latest new technologies. To have effective government, roles must be clearly established and followed by all public officials as they strive to effectively and efficiently serve citizens during the coming years.

Employee productivity has been greatly enhanced through the use of contemporary computer hardware systems, state-of-the-art software applications, and other modern technological innovations. Local government services have always been labor-intensive. While the latest technologies may improve operations and services, they only assist employees as they strive to better serve the public. For this reason, the use of the latest technologies is merely an instrument to help employees improve customer satisfaction. This means improving service quality and/or reducing the cost of the public services to the public. Unlike the private sector, the demand for public services is always high. Each public service has its own constituency, and its users continually desire to enhance the quality of the specific service they use.

Since all of these changes are presently taking place, the future of our municipal governments has already been charted and is headed in these directions.

While the goal of delivering quality public services to citizens at a reasonable cost will not change, the many avenues available for public officials to achieve this goal are presently in a state of transition. While the interface between a municipal organization and its clients will primarily remain employee-to-citizen, a variety of processes will become available in the future to streamline and improve both the process of governance and the delivery of services to taxpayers and citizens.

These dynamic and profound, yet incremental, changes in our municipal governments encompass how public officials are elected, the duration of their terms-of-office, the scale and mix of services that they provide, as well as how they reflect the expectations of the citizens they serve. The state of our local democratic institutions will continue to be determined collectively by the will-of-the-people as expressed through their voting preferences. Therefore, one thing that will not change in the future is that America's local governments will continue to be *"of the people, by the people, and for the people."* This *essential essence* of American municipal government, which has been with us for over a century, will not change during the coming decades.

• *Chapter 33* •

County Government

Donald C. Menzel

Governing the American county in the 21st century will be more challenging than ever before in the nearly 400-year history of this often maligned unit of local government. Why? Consider the following. First, as federal and state governments shift, indeed mandate, duties and responsibilities to local governments, counties have taken on greater importance as service providers and participants in the American federal system. Second, the pace of change (often referred to as modernization) of the American county has increased significantly in recent decades and shows little sign of slowing. Many counties have been transformed in both form and function. A growing number have shed their "boss and patronage"-ridden images and have sought to place merit and performance high on their day-to-day work agenda. Others have changed from keepers of vital statistics to governments that compete, cooperate with, and, at times, resemble full-service American cities. Third,

although historically little more than "arms of the state," many counties are "new wave" governments in that they resemble neither municipalities, state agencies, nor regional governments. Instead, they are a unique, hybrid blend of each.

It is somewhat misleading to speak of the American county as if it were a monolithic social, political and governmental entity. Diversity rather than homogeneity characterizes America's 3,043 counties. Still, there are certain issues and challenges that are likely to face nearly all who govern these often "forgotten governments" as a new century approaches. This article outlines five issues and suggests what might be done to foster effective county governance in the 21st century.

Issues and Challenges Facing County Governments

A number of issues have surfaced or are likely to surface in the near future.

Originally published as "Governing the American County in the 21st Century," *Spectrum: The Journal of State Government*, Vol. 69, No. 3, Summer, 1996. Published by the Council of State Governments, Lexington, Kentucky. Reprinted with permission of the publisher.

These include the structure of county governments, their leadership capacity, fiscal conditions and management, intergovernmental roles and responsibilities, and their ability to affect local economic development.

Structure and Organization of County Government in the U.S.

The debate with regard to how the structure of county government makes a difference in the ability of counties to provide efficient, effective and economical services continues, especially in urban America where city-county-regional jurisdictional boundaries disappear when problems such as crime, homelessness, pollution and poverty are present. The traditional commission form of county government, where three to five elected commissioners exercise day-to-day hands-on administration, is often regarded as inadequate to deal with these problems. "The infirmities of the commission system," notes Frank J. Thompson (1993, 19) executive director of the National Commission on the State and Local Public Service, "and the growing awareness of the vital tasks that county governments perform have spurred movement to strengthen the hand of either an appointed or elected executive." Currently, more than one of every four counties appoints a chief executive or manager and or elects a chief executive.

Strengthening the power and authority of chief executives to get the job done — to integrate, coordinate and empower their workforce — is an important step toward making counties more viable governmental entities. Still, in many states, there remain many constraints, notably the fragmentation and sharing of administrative authority with constitutional officers, also known as "row" officers. These independently elected executives (and they are just that)—county sheriffs, clerks, tax collectors, property appraisers, coroners and others—are often powerful political figures who can frustrate the ability of chief executives and county legislative bodies to make their governments high-performing units. In its 1990 *Model County Charter*, the National Civic League asserts that the really big break with tradition will occur "when a reorganized county government brings under council control (and administration by the appointed manager) functions previously performed by independently elected officers or substantially independent boards and commissions."

County home rule is another structural development that has grown in popularity in the 20th century. Many counties, like their municipal counterparts, have sought to free themselves from state legislative dominance by seeking authority to rule or enact ordinances on their own, i.e., without a legislative grant of authority. Such "home rule" was first secured by California's counties in 1911. Since then, 37 additional states have passed legislation enabling counties to practice home rule. In principle, counties that enjoy home rule are able to exercise greater freedom and flexibility when confronting local issues.

Principle and practice, however, do not always go hand-in-hand. Indeed, home-rule powers and practices vary widely across and within states. In Florida, for example, 14 charter counties exercise home-rule powers but some are not always able to fend off unwanted advances by zealous legislative delegations who feel they know what is best for their county. County home rule does not necessarily "free" counties from their historic state master.

So, does the structure and organization of county governments matter or not? Does having an integrated executive make a difference? Are counties with home-rule powers more effective governments than those counties without home-rule powers?

These important questions are difficult to answer in a definitive manner. One might say that structure matters if it is defined in terms of the dynamics of authority, leadership, and decision making but does not seem to matter if defined only in terms of forms of government. While there is some evidence that the structure of county government — commission, commission-manager, elected executive — influences how much counties spend, there is little evidence that it makes much difference in the kinds of policies or programs enacted or the efficiencies produced. Park (1996), for example, reports that counties with an appointed chief administrator or elected executive spend more than those with a commission form of government but this finding is tempered by the fact that other variables such as state fiscal aid and region of the country have a greater influence on spending levels.

Leadership Capacity of Counties

The linkage between structure and performance will be debated well into the next century. It is an important debate. However, it may pale alongside the debate about the linkage between county leadership and performance. Indeed, it is even plausible to suggest that leadership can make the difference in how well or poorly a county performs across a wide spectrum of tasks and responsibilities. Unfortunately, knowledge of how leadership at the county level is exercised with greater or lesser effectiveness in rural and urban counties or traditional commission and appointed manager counties is sparse and impressionistic. One widespread impression is that "more than any other level of the federal system, counties have provided barren soil for the flowering of strong executives" (Thompson 1993, 19).

This "leaderless capacity" impression is reinforced even when one examines those counties with chief executives. There are approximately 1,200 appointed or elected county executives among America's 3,043 counties. Precious few executives, however, possess the formal powers often regarded as necessary to exercise strong executive leadership. Such powers as renewable terms of office, authority to appoint and remove subordinates, the ability to control budget submissions and outlays, power to veto proposed ordinances, and the authority to issue orders changing government organization are often absent.

The need to exercise more effective county leadership has spurred some movement toward putting greater power and authority in an elected county executive. Council-elected executive governments are in place in 373 counties, with 21 more elected executives or mayors occupying top posts in city-county consolidated governments. These numbers represent a three-fold increase since 1980 (*County News* May 1995). Whether this arrangement will result in more powerful county leadership is open to debate. Nonetheless, a growing number of counties are adopting this "reform" measure.

The leadership challenge will be made more difficult by the growing diversity of the county workforce and officialdom itself. Recent statistics suggest that the county workforce will be affected by the growing diversity of the U.S. labor force as a whole. Among other things, white males will be a minority in the U.S. workplace by the turn of the century, representing 39 percent of all workers. Racial and ethnic minorities are expected to constitute 26 percent of the U.S. workforce by the year 2000 (Kelly 1993).

Similar shifts are occurring in the composition of the state and local government workforce. Kelly's (1993) research shows that the proportion of public-service employees who are white males declined from 53.5 percent to 43.3 percent between 1974 and 1990. During the same period, the minority percentage increased from 19.5 percent to 27.1 percent.

Workforce diversity is expected to be accompanied by leadership diversity. In a survey of America's 100 largest counties, MacManus (1996) found that more women and racial minorities are gaining seats on county councils and occupying administrative posts. She notes, for example, that a 1988 International City/County Management Association survey found that women held 9 percent of all county board seats while her 1993 survey found that women held 27 percent of the board seats in large counties. While these figures are not entirely comparable, she concludes that "there does appear to be greater representation of women on county governing boards today than in the past" (Mac-Manus 1996, 66).

Diversity in the community and the county workforce does not necessarily bode ill for making America's counties more effective governmental entities. However, it does raise the issue of how such diversity might foster conflict or cooperation or both. The "good news," as Svara (1996) points out, is that county leaders may already have an edge in working through this challenge because many have found it necessary to become skillful negotiators, able bargaining agents, and effective conflict managers. One irony of American local government history may be that while counties were largely on the sidelines of change as the progressive reform movement swept across municipal America in the 20th century, county leaders have developed survival skills that have equipped them well for 21st century governance.

With regard to managerial leadership, the role of the county manager may have to be rethought, perhaps even reinvented.

More than "neutral competency" will be required of the local government manager. The effective manager, Streib (1996) contends, will have to embrace a wide range of values, including a commitment to openness, participation, intergenerational impacts of county decision making, and a genuine interest in what people think and do. "The pursuit of 'efficiency,' the hallmark of the effective public manager of the progressive era, is no longer a singularly sufficient value. Strengthening county management will require elected and appointed leaders who have a well-developed set of values that will serve as a roadmap for navigating through the frequently stormy environments that typify county rule by many masters" (Streib 1996, 136).

Fiscal Management Challenges

Creating a government that works better and costs less is an admirable goal of the federal government, states the *Report of the National Performance Review* (1993). Such a goal is no less admirable or desirable for America's counties. Nor is the challenge of accomplishing this goal any less daunting at the local level than at the national level. The search engine for this task is dollars—incoming and outgoing, revenues and expenditures.

Like the federal government, counties face growing citizen demands for services yet unrelenting opposition to increased taxes for such services, especially in the form of higher property taxes. Some counties have resorted to imaginative revenue diversification or enhancement programs while others have resorted to risky financial investment strategies. The Economic Development and Government Equity program in Montgomery County, Ohio, is an example of the former while the spectacular bankruptcy of Orange County, California, as an example of the latter.

The Montgomery County plan is a county-municipal tax sharing scheme that seeks to "insure that each community within Montgomery County has an equal opportunity to derive some benefit from development outside its boundaries" (Pammer 1996, 186). Key to the success of this effort was the willingness of Montgomery County to dedicate $50 million to an economic development fund that villages, townships and municipalities could draw upon to attract development which, in turn, commits them to sharing future tax revenues with neighboring communities (Pammer 1996). Although it cannot be determined at this time whether this "win-win" plan is just that, this initiative demonstrates that some counties recognize that continuing to do business in the same old way by raising property taxes will no longer suffice. They are undertaking new and imaginative efforts to keep their fiscal house in order.

Alas, not all counties have been so fortunate with perhaps the most well known being Orange County, California, which now occupies the record books for the largest municipal bankruptcy in United States history. On December 6, 1994, Orange County declared itself bankrupt, having lost nearly $2 billion in investments. The county's popular, independently elected county treasurer employed a high-risk investment strategy, one which included heavy borrowing to buy rate-sensitive derivative securities, that failed when interest rates went amok (Mydans, A14). Keeping taxes low without cutting services, which has been the preference in Orange County, apparently encouraged political and financial risk taking. Now, Orange County officials and residents face the reality of raising taxes, cutting services, and perhaps even selling county assets.

The fundamental fiscal challenge facing American counties is *how* to diversify their revenue base, not whether to diversify. Cigler (1996) offers helpful suggestions along these lines. She notes that counties continue to rely heavily on property taxes but that user charges are increasingly popular at county-owned or leased facilities such as airports, marinas, and recreation sites. Also growing in popularity are county-option sales taxes. More than 30 states have passed legislation allowing counties to use local sales taxes to enhance their revenue base. In states like Florida, heavy use is made of the local sales tax option as voters regularly decide whether to tax themselves and tourists for schools, prisons, health care and sports facilities. Local income taxes are another option, although less than a dozen states have adopted this practice (Cigler 1996).

Tax-increment financing (TIF) is also employed in some states and counties. This municipal financing tool calls for the designation of districts in which regularly assessed property taxes are earmarked for financing public improvements needed to attract new development which, in turn, is expected to generate new revenues. Tax-increment financing is dependent on potential development and uses millage rates for an entire jurisdiction (Cigler 1996). Practically speaking, this approach subsidizes new development by taxing only the value (increment) added on to the district when development occurs.

Mixing and matching these and other alternative sources of revenue to achieve the "best" arrangement for financing services in an equitable manner requires good judgment, common sense and financial know-how on the part of county leaders. It is no small challenge.

At the same time, as Cigler (1996) reminds us, revenue flexibility, as opposed to diversification, does not have to be achieved entirely through adding new revenues. Improved purchasing, contracting and financial forecasting can contribute to a county's fiscal health. Furthermore, other initiatives such as targeting state revolving funds to finance infrastructure, issuing bonds in a pool to influence credit ratings, and even establishing alternative dispute resolution centers, can yield significant financial savings.

Intergovernmental Roles and Responsibilities

The emergence of counties as significant service providers and political entities has catapulted them headlong into the intergovernmental arena. Unlike regional councils composed of representatives of local governments, counties may be more truly intergovernmental governments because they often have multiple identities and realities. A county can be a full-service local government, a quasi-state agency and a regional actor all at once. Indeed, Berman and Salant (1996) suggest that these multiple roles and identities sometimes cause counties to engage in contradictory, inconsistent, and even irrational behavior. As quasi-state agencies, for example, they are often "good soldiers" when carrying out their state duties. And as full service local governments attempting to meet the needs and demands of residents, they often resist state and federal authorities that seek to impose their will on them, especially when that will is reflected in unfunded and unsolicited state or federal mandates (Benton 1996).

The expansive role of counties in the vertical intergovernmental system is no less expansive in the horizontal intergovernmental system. Berman and Salant (1996) assert that counties "are major collaborators with other units through contracts and agreements, important participants in regional organizations such as councils of government, and direct providers of area-wide services such as solid waste, transit and health." And, as alluded to earlier, the increasingly important role of counties as initiators of programs such as city-county-township tax base sharing underscores their ability to broker win-win relationships among natural competitors.

Perhaps the central challenge facing counties as players in the American federal system is the somewhat amorphous nature of the game itself (Benton 1996). With budget deficit reduction high on the priority list of the 104th Congress and the Clinton administration, the remaining years of the 20th century may witness significant reductions in federal intergovernmental fiscal aid which, in turn, may motivate counties to be even more aggressive players in state and local arenas. One thing seems certain — counties will not be passive pawns on a federal chessboard. Rather, they are likely to assert themselves in an effort to obtain a fair hearing, if not a fair share, of rights, responsibilities and resources.

Fiscal aid cutbacks have already compelled many counties to be more inventive in finding ways to generate new dollars or shift existing dollars so as to "do more with less." Among other things, this has meant becoming more entrepreneurial and has resulted in initiatives to broaden user fees, establish development fees and privatize numerous services.

Economic Development

A number of counties are no longer waiting for economic development to happen in their jurisdictions. Rather, they are developing plans and strategies to make it happen. Some strategies are aimed at attracting, retaining, or expanding business firms. Among others, these include providing businesses with tax abatements, subsidies, loan guarantees, infrastructure investment and development, and fiscal commitments to build facilities such as a professional sports stadium. As a group, these measures can be described as supply-side incentives. One example can be found in Hillsborough County, Florida, where the Tampa Bay Buccaneers professional football ownership has vowed to relocate the team if the community does not build a new stadium. County officials once proposed to buy as many as 10,000 tickets per home game when the team attracted at least 45,000 fans. When such circumstances occurred, the county would be obligated to divert several million dollars from its revenue stream into the Buccaneers revenue stream. This particular plan faltered on the altar of public opinion and has since been replaced by a one-half cent sales tax referendum that the voters will decide on in early September 1996.

Across the Tampa Bay, similar efforts were taken by the city of St. Petersburg and Pinellas County to attract a professional baseball team when nearly two hundred million city/county tax dollars were invested in the construction of an enclosed arena. This "field of dreams" investment has netted the community a new baseball franchise. The Tampa Bay Devil Rays began play in 1998.

Strategies that employ market-like approaches or emphasize public-private partnerships are also employed by counties to help business firms develop markets or sell products abroad and at home. These strategies are often referred to as demand-side strategies and include measures such as trade missions and export-assistance programs. City-county-state initiated trade missions to Europe, Japan and other locations are increasingly commonplace. The siting of the Honda plant in Marysville, Ohio, for example, was promoted by a county-state trade mission to Japan.

County sponsored export-assistance programs are another means to foster local economic development in a global mar-ketplace. Such programs include county financing for market research studies for small-to-medium sized business firms, technical assistance and information, and organizing meetings for foreign firms to meet with local firms wishing to do business abroad. Montgomery County, Maryland, established an export-assistance program that assisted small businesses by (1) providing funds to conduct market research studies in the foreign country identified by a local business, (2) supplying free technical assistance through an arrangement with international trade experts retired from the U.S. Department of Commerce, (3) offering financial and staff support to firms to attend international trade shows, and (4) organizing meetings for foreign firms to meet with local firms wishing to do business overseas (Pammer 1996).

These initiatives point toward both a new attitude and a new role for counties in stimulating local public economies. Pammer (1996) astutely notes that the role of counties as agents of economic development will require county officials to adopt a different orientation than what has been accepted in the past. An orientation that embraces pro-active economic development strategies and regionalization will be necessary. Strategies that have been parochial and often resulted in fierce interjurisdictional competition for new businesses will have to be scrapped. Instead, the view that the "economic stability and prosperity of any single locality is critically linked to the fiscal health and attributes of its neighbors" must be adopted, concludes Pammer (1996, 185). Counties, if they choose to do so, can be catalysts for inter-local cooperation that promote local and regional economic growth and stability.

Moving Forward with an Eye on the Past?

Will America's counties transform themselves into more effective governments in the 21st century? Could they become *the* local governments of the future? Will counties be "reinvented," "re-engineered," "revitalized"— to use the "R" words of the 1990s? Or will the labels "ramshackle," "dark continent," "forgotten governments" and other unflattering phrases of the 20th century be tacked on to county governments in the decades ahead? Will counties be forced to move forward while looking backwards? The answers to these questions will depend on whether county leaders, state lawmakers, and the body politic are prepared to adopt new attitudes and strategies.

One proposed strategy advanced by the National Commission on the State and Local Public Service calls for "trust and lead" (1993, 9). High-performance government, according to the Commission, can rebuild public trust and confidence in government. Counties, as local governments that provide vital public services which touch the lives of thousands of people daily, are well-positioned to engage in this rebuilding task. The trust deficit which President Clinton noted early in his administration is real and must be dealt with by governments at all levels.

A "trust and lead" strategy will require county leaders, state officials, and the public to trust public employees to do the right things right. The demeaning of public service and the under-valuing of public employees must end. The county workforce must be treated as a valuable resource. Counties must invest in their human capital by providing education and by training and applying modern management techniques. Perhaps most importantly, county and state leaders must place confidence in and provide opportunity for the county workforce to become a high-performance workforce. Employee empowerment, the opportunity for rank-and-file employees to participate in a meaningful way in decisions affecting them and their community, is essential to the effective governance of the American county in the 21st century.

The movement to flatten organizational hierarchies should also be embraced by county boards and managers. Pushing responsibility out and to the lowest levels of the county workforce can succeed if there is a readiness and willingness on the part of all to accept that responsibility. Twentieth century management, which emphasized a culture of control, will not suffice in the century ahead.

The steady professionalization of the county workforce must also be sustained, perhaps even accelerated. In the past, counties frequently took the brunt of unflattering commentary about their lack of professionalization. This is changing rapidly but more change is needed. A more professionalized workforce will better position counties to shape policy and respond to the issues and challenges discussed in this chapter. Similarly, the movement toward electing or appointing professionally trained executives, especially if combined with reductions in the number of elected row officers, will yield greater political clout for counties and result in a more integrated executive.

Will counties meet the challenges of governance in the 21st century? This author believes they will. County leaders and state lawmakers cannot afford the luxury of weak county governments. The stakes are too high and too costly; the global challenge is real. America's communities and local governments are the bedrock on which the nation can erect a viable and prospering economy and democracy. The bumper sticker that proudly proclaims "think globally, act locally" goes to the heart of the need to insure that governing the American county in the 21st century will be a success story.

References

Benton, J. Edwin (1996). "Fiscal Aid and Mandates: The County Experience." In *The American County: Frontiers of Knowledge*, edited by Donald C. Menzel. Tuscaloosa, Ala.: The University of Alabama Press.

Berman, David R. and Tanis J. Salant (1996). "The Changing Role of Counties in the Inter-governmental System." In *The American County: Frontiers of Knowledge*, edited by Donald C. Menzel. Tuscaloosa, Ala.: The University of Alabama Press.

Cigler, Beverly A. (1996). "Revenue Diversification Among American Counties." In *The American County: Frontiers of Knowledge*, edited by Donald C. Menzel. Tuscaloosa, Ala.: The University of Alabama Press.

"NACO Surveys Elected County Executives." *County News* (May 8, 1995): 9.

Kelly, Rita Mae (1993). "Diversity in the Public Workforce: New Needs, New Approaches." In *Revitalizing State and Local Public Service*, edited by Frank J. Thompson. San Francisco: Jossey-Bass Publishers.

MacManus, Susan A. (1996). "County Boards, Partisanship, and Elections." In *The American County: Frontiers of Knowledge*, edited by Donald C. Menzel. Tuscaloosa, Ala.: The University of Alabama Press.

Mydans, Seth. "Taxes a Hard Sell in Orange County," *New York Times* (May 8, 1995): A-14.

National Civic League (1990). *Model County Charter*. Revised Edition. Denver, Colo.

National Commission on the State and Local Public Service (1993). *Hard Truths/Tough Choices: An Agenda for State and Local Reform*. Albany, NY: The Nelson A. Rockefeller Institute of Government.

Pammer, Jr., William A. (1996). "County Economic Development Strategies." In *The American County: Frontiers of Knowledge*, edited by Donald C. Menzel. Tuscaloosa, Ala.: The University of Alabama Press.

Park, Kee Ok (1996). "Determinants of County Government Growth." In *The American County: Frontiers of Knowledge*, edited by Donald C. Menzel. Tuscaloosa, Ala.: The University of Alabama Press.

Report of the National Performance Review, Vice President Al Gore (1993). *Creating a Government That Works Better & Costs Less*. U.S. Government Printing Office, Washington, D.C., September 7, 1993.

Streib, Gregory (1996). "Strengthening County Management." In *The American County: Frontiers of Knowledge*, edited by Donald C. Menzel. Tuscaloosa, Ala.: The University of Alabama Press.

Svara, James H. (1996). "Leadership and Professionalism in County Government." In *The American County: Frontiers of Knowledge*, edited by Donald C. Menzel. Tuscaloosa, Ala.: The University of Alabama Press.

Thompson, Frank J., ed. (1993). *Revitalizing State and Local Public Service*. San Francisco: Jossey-Bass Publishers.

• *Chapter 34* •

Regional Government

WILLIAM DODGE

A thousand years ago, in the late 900s, people literally feared the end of the world in some cataclysmic explosion.

Their fears caused them to consider reforms, especially of their spiritual behavior. Hoping that the end would coincide with the second coming, community leaders and citizens of the time, at least the Christian ones, dedicated themselves to a religious building campaign of colossal proportions. Their collaborative efforts resulted in constructing many of the monumental Romanesque cathedrals of Western Europe. Cluniac monk, Raoul Glaber, observed in 1003, "it was as if the whole earth, having cast off its age by shaking itself, were clothing itself everywhere in a white robe of churches."

Today, in the late 1900s, people fear the end of their local political worlds in some equally drastic change.

What used to be resolvable in their individual communities now defies resolution with neighbors across entire re-gions. What used to be clearly the responsibility of public, private, or nonprofit organizations now creates overlapping confusion. What used to be perceived as common — even American — values are increasingly contested by conflicted communities and interest groups.

Such fears have caused people to consider reforms, especially of their temporal behavior.

Not depending upon divine intervention for resolving their earthly challenges, community leaders and citizens are experimenting with new approaches to intercommunity and regional decision-making. These experiments have not yet reached colossal proportions, but they may preview a regional renaissance by the dawn of the 21st century.

Maybe, just maybe, our regions will be clothed with regional governance excellence in this change in millennia!

By regional governance, I do not mean metropolitan government, the one-big-

Originally published as "Regional Excellence," *National Civic Review*, Vol. 85, No. 2, Spring/Summer, 1996. Published by the National Civic League, Denver, Colorado. Reprinted with permission of the publisher.

government approach to regional challenges. Instead, I mean how we bring community leaders and citizens together to address challenges that cut across communities—from crime and drugs to economic competitiveness. This usually involves defining the challenge, assigning responsibility for addressing it to an existing or new regional mechanism, involving community leaders and citizens affected by it, designing a strategy for addressing it, negotiating responsibility and implementing the strategy, and monitoring and evaluating success in addressing the challenge. By excellence, I mean doing this in a more timely, flexible, and effective manner with each new challenge, so as to take advantage of regional opportunities before they are lost and prevent regional threats from exploding into crisis.

Regional Governance Has Risen in Importance

Regions are organic systems organized in ways surprisingly similar to flowers, fish, mammals, and humans. They have evolved out of less complex — but not necessarily lower — life forms, especially in urban areas that started with small settlements that grew into cities that, in turn, expanded into regions containing suburbs and exurbs. As a result, regions have one or more vital organs—central business districts and suburban employment centers and shopping malls—tied together with the sinews of transportation, the arteries of commerce, and the protoplasm of community.

Healthy regions nurture us, their individual cells, by concentrating the resources and providing the connections to pursue a desired quality of life, locally and globally. In turn, they need our care and feeding, since, like other living beings, their health and happiness is determined by whoever or whatever shapes and controls their growth.

States and nations do not usually stir the same biological thoughts. As critical as they are to providing military security, setting uniform standards, redistributing wealth, and even supporting local and regional initiatives, they appear more to be human contrivances than living organisms.

It is not surprising, therefore, that the region has emerged again as it has repeatedly over recorded history. This time, it has become more important as the cold war, which had required nations to develop competitive armies, cooled off, and the global common market, which now requires regions to develop competitive economies, heated up.

The era of the region is already being proclaimed worldwide. In Europe, the borders between nations are dissolving in the European community and a "Europe of Regions" is taking its place. In Asia, Hong Kong shows every sign of surviving its transfer from Great Britain to the Peoples Republic of China as a relatively independent region, one that now includes a considerable part of the Guangzhou province of China. I suspect that neither ideology nor nationalism will seriously restrict the behavior of this powerful living organism in the global ecosystem.

What might be surprising, however, is that this same Global Competitiveness, and four other major developments, or change drivers—Challenge Explosion, Citizen Withdrawal, Structure-Challenge Mismatch, and Rich-Poor Community Gap—have transformed regional governance from a nicety to a necessity.

Bottom line: Community leaders and citizens need to focus priority attention on the growth development—the governance—of their own living organisms, their regions.

Pursuing Regional Governance Excellence Requires a Guiding Star

We have a long history of being easy "creationists" and reluctant "evolutionists" concerning the region.

On one hand, as easy "creationists," we have all too readily bought into the idea that a metropolitan government, in the form of a single monolithic structure that directs all decision making, would eventually be created, almost overnight, and guide regional development. It, I suspect, is doomed to be the eternal will-o'-the-wisp of regional governance.

No matter how creative we become, we cannot anticipate the range of challenges or nail down the geographic scope of the region long enough to have it governed by a single structure. Even those places that have annexed extensively, such as Columbus, Ohio; consolidated city and county government, such as Unigov in the Indianapolis region; or created two-tier governments, such as Metro Toronto, continue to be confronted with irrepressible sprawl leapfrogging across their borders into the great beyond.

Unless we are willing to pursue the highly unlikely option of making each region a state, and to then redraw state boundaries every decade to conform with the changing spheres of regional influence, we will need to build a "network" of regional decision making mechanisms—processes and structures—to address emerging challenges in each region.

On the other hand, as reluctant "evolutionists," we have resisted the evolution of regional decision making mechanisms, condemning most of them to be ineffective "footballs without laces," giving all the appearances of addressing regional challenges but being genetically flawed in their powers, participants, practices, or perseverance. Or, even worse, we have flirted with the myth that the region was divisible—that the donut (the suburbs) is not connected to the hole (the central city). To borrow a metaphor from Peter Senge, author of *The Fifth Discipline*, dividing a region into parts has no greater chance of working than dividing any other living organism, such as an elephant, into parts; all one gets is a mess.

I believe that we now need to be strategic "pragmatists" and foster a regional renaissance. We need to pursue regional governance excellence in the closing years of the second millennium if we are to compete globally and thrive locally in the third. Achieving excellence, I further believe, requires launching initiatives to improve each of five components of regional governance; that is, we need to make it Prominent, Strategic, Equitable, Empowering, and Institutionalized.

Bottom line: The pursuit of regional governance excellence needs to be empowered by community leaders and citizens in each region and enjoy the involvement and support of state and national, governmental and non-governmental, organizations.

Achieving Regional Governance Excellence Will Strengthen, and Even Save, Our Federal System of Governance

Regional decision making complements local, state and national decision making by providing mechanisms for addressing cross-cutting challenges that cannot be sponsored by any one of those levels alone. It does not replace, but rather enriches and helps preserve our federal system of governance.

As regions continue to evolve, they will create a new political force in state capitals and Washington. At times, communities within regions will come together in a collective voice that has the clout to drive almost any agenda through the legislative process and shift funding streams to regional initiatives. Witness the success of regional lobbying efforts in many state capitals.

At times, these same communities will agree to differ and offer a divided voice but still probably make state capitals and Washington their battleground. In the Washington, D.C., region, for example, the political dividing line has shifted to the Beltway, with those inside who feel they are experiencing a declining quality of life — traffic congestion and resulting pollution, loss of contact with nature, increasing economic and racial segregation, and higher taxes to try to fix these issues — increasingly confronting those outside who still want to carve out a new place in the virgin hinterlands. Resolving regional challenges now consumes a considerable amount of the agendas of a city, two states and even the national government.

It might not be unreasonable to speculate that achieving regional governance excellence will someday result in strengthening the federal system. There is an excellent historical precedent for the impact of such challenges.

In 1785, representatives from the states of Virginia and Maryland met with George Washington at Mount Vernon to deal with the regional challenge of "jurisdiction and navigation" on the lower Potomac River. Finding that regional cooperation would not suffice and that part of the problem stemmed from the limitations of the Articles of Confederation that governed relations among the fairly autonomous states, the delegates decided to invite representatives from all of the states to a meeting in Annapolis the following year. The delegates at the Annapolis conference decided that the issues had such gravity that they decided to call a constitutional convention in Philadelphia the following year. The rest is history.

Will the challenge of "jurisdiction and navigation" on the growth "streams" sprawling out of our regions have a similar impact on national, state, and local government two centuries later? And this time, will it result in the ceding of critical authorities to regional governance mechanisms?

Bottom line: Resolving regional challenges could redefine our federal system of governance and breathe life into regional governance mechanisms.

Community Leaders and Citizens Need to Act Decisively Now to Achieve Regional Governance Excellence

Achieving Regional Governance Excellence Is More an Act of the Mind Than the Pocketbook

The real fears of addressing challenges regionally have to do with confronting unfamiliar communities and peoples, especially those that are richer or poorer or of a different ethnicity, and unpopular challenges, especially future growth, since whoever shapes it controls regional decision making.

Not that this lack of interaction has made life better or governance cheaper for any of us. When central cities decline, when crime and drugs escalate, when impoverished school districts cannot graduate productive workers, when segregated populations cannot find jobs, or when suburban communities are paved over with highways and parking lots, when the only way to get anywhere is by personal auto, when we squander resources on inefficient services, when we mourn the loss of community — then we all suffer and pay.

Achieving Regional Governance Excellence Needs to Begin Decisively, Now

We have attracted the attention of community leaders and citizens and are experimenting with regional governance initiatives. That's positive, but it raises questions: Are we handling each new regional challenge better than the last one? Are we developing individual regional decision-making mechanisms that efficiently guide community leaders and citizens through equitable and empowering processes that handle the most pressing challenges?

We have also attracted the attention of economic interests that are already jockeying for influence in each of the regional economies that constitute the global common market. That's also positive, but it raises a second set of questions: Are we shaping regional growth and development so as to compete globally and thrive locally? If we are, are we also overcoming intercommunity disparities and building regional citizenship and a sense of regional community? And are we developing a "network" of regional decision-making mechanisms that interact seamlessly to provide regional governance excellence?

Finally, we are witnessing radical changes in the responsibilities and relationships of state and national governments. It's difficult to say whether this is positive or negative for regional governance, but it helps reinforce the need for community leaders and citizens to act decisively, now.

Community leaders and citizens in some regions are already beginning to launch their regional renaissances. They have started to consider the communities of the region in the singular, as *us*, and not just in the plural, as *you and me*. Community leaders and citizens in other regions may join them. I have no doubt that those who pursue this journey will live in the most desirable regions at the dawn of the 21st century.

• *Chapter 35* •

State Government

Keon S. Chi

Governance

Legislative Branch

Legislative Reform

The legislative reform movement began in the wake of reapportionment in the 1960s. Since then, state legislatures have undergone a steady transformation to face new challenges. The organizational structures and institutional procedures of state legislatures as a whole remain as diverse and complex as ever. Some are highly professional legislative bodies with full-time legislators and year-round sessions, others are citizen legislatures made up of part-time lawmakers, and still others are hybrid legislatures with characteristics of both.

Compared to situations 30 to 40 years ago, lawmakers in most states now have more professional staff services. Most have several agencies to support both houses, and individual legislators employ staff members for constituent relations or committee work. Other improvements include higher legislative salaries, improved facilities, and furnished and equipped individual offices. Moreover, nearly every state now enforces ethics laws for legislators and lobbyists. All but seven states hold annual sessions, instead of biennial sessions. Special sessions frequently are held at the request of governors and legislators. The most obvious change in recent decades is that most legislatures now meet annually. Only 4 states held annual legislative sessions 50 years ago: that number increased to 34 in 1975 and 43 in 2000. Biennial sessions still are held in Arkansas, Kentucky, Montana, Nevada, North Dakota, Oregon and Texas. State legislatures now are more active during the interim periods between regular sessions, when standing committees often meet. As a result, the legislative workload has expanded. Legislators introduced more bills and enacted more laws in recent session than in earlier decades.

Originally published as "State Governance, Management and Policies: Trends and Issues," *The Book of the States*, Vol. 33, 2000-01 Edition, 2000. Published by The Council of State Governments, Lexington, Kentucky. Reprinted with permission of the publisher.

States also have increased the number of standing and joint committees. At the same time that the number of legislative leadership positions has increased, there has been a perceived decline in the authority of legislative leaders. This has been attributed to leadership selection methods, campaign finance reforms and, more recently, legislative term limits. In most states, the size of the legislature in most states is unchanged from 40 years ago. In the past four decades, Connecticut, Illinois, Massachusetts, Ohio and Vermont are among the few that have reduced the size of their legislative chambers. In 2000, the Minnesota Legislature at the request of the governor considered a constitutional amendment to switch to a unicameral legislature, patterned after Nebraska, but failed to pass it.

LOBBYING LAWS

An unprecedented movement has taken place in many states in the past several years to deal with government accountability and public integrity. Many states now have comprehensive ethics laws. Yet more needs to be done to meet public expectations. As national polls indicate, the widespread perception is that some state legislators are obligated to moneyed private interests. To many people, the power of special interest groups seems to drown out the voice of the average person. Lobbyists also have noted the negative perceptions of their trade.

Discussions on legislator-lobbyist interactions focus on: How can we change public misperceptions of legislative lobbying? How should legislators regulate their conduct and that of lobbyists? And, how can legislators and lobbyists improve the legislative environment without jeopardizing the flow of information and communication?

There are several actions state legislators might consider. To help the public better understand the complexity of legislative lobbying, legislators might want to initiate and/or participate in civic education programs. Legislators should disclose to the public their interactions with lobbyists. States should examine legislative standards of conduct to promote public integrity and to gain public trust. Further, states should revise legislative codes of ethics and revamp their lobbying enforcement agencies to address individual and institutional responsibility. Public integrity is ensured only when legislators realize a strong sense of accountability. Only by demonstrating and practicing accountability can legislators earn public trust.

LEGISLATIVE TERM LIMITS

In 1990, voters in California, Colorado and Oklahoma approved the first term-limit ballot initiatives. Term limits won voter approval in 11 states in 1992, 1 in 1993, 4 in 1994 and 1 in 1995. Only the Utah Legislature imposed term limits on itself by law in 1994. In 1998, a total of 217 legislators in seven states were ineligible for re-election due to term limits. In 2000, legislators in nine chambers in five states (Arizona, Florida, Montana, Ohio and South Dakota) were scheduled to be termed out.

Supporters of legislative term limits argue that such measures will prohibit career politicians from continuously enjoying the advantages of incumbency and will bring in new members to represent voter interests. Critics of term limits decry the loss of institutional memory and argue that term limits deprive voters of the right to re-elect veteran legislators. The irony is that in most states these reasons for or against term limits have not been seriously debated in legislative chambers. Instead, such pro and con arguments have taken place mostly in the media. Legislative term limits have faced court tests in more than a dozen states in recent years. In 1998, courts struck down term-limit laws in three states and upheld them in several others. As of mid–2000, legislative term limits remained intact in 18 states.

There are many questions to ask about the term-limits movement in states. Major concerns for state legislators center around the effects of term limits, especially in three areas: demographic characteristics of state legislators, institutionalized changes and legislative behavior. What effects will legislative term limits have on the workings of state legislatures? What do legislators, staff members and lobbyists say about the effects of term limits? Is it constitutional to limit the number of terms state legislators can serve? Why have some courts ruled term-limit laws unconstitutional? Who has jurisdiction over state legislative term limits, state or federal courts? What are the implications of previous court rulings for other states, with or without legislative term limits? Finally, what options do state legislators have in dealing with term limits? And what procedural recommendations should lawmakers consider in improving legislative procedures under term limits?

There are several policy options for consideration. For example, states may want to allow lawmakers an equal number of years of consecutive service in both chambers with no lifetime ban. They may want to limit the number of consecutive years of service in the legislature as an institution, not for each chamber. States may consider staggered term-limits dates for newly elected legislators so they can attain leadership positions. States also may consider sharing positions of influence by eliminating the seniority system as the criterion for electing leaders. They may consider new leadership roles and styles and a new way to set the legislative agenda. They may want to readdress legislators' roles, their learning curve, and their communications with fellow legislators and constituents.

Campaign Finance Reform

There exists a widespread perception among the public that money makes a significant difference in most, if not all, election outcomes. Unless the influence of big or improper money is reduced public confidence may continue to wane in government. In recent years, with a variety of innovative ideas, many states have tried to regulate the way candidates raise and spend money. Yet there is room for further reform. State policy-makers might want to consider several alternatives to campaign-finance practices. By requiring candidates and state agencies to report and disclose information on campaign finance in a more timely and comprehensive manner, for example, the public can be better informed of the candidates' financial status. Although the trend of limiting campaign contributions is likely to continue, state leaders are expected to be more mindful of constitutional issues, particularly in view of recent court decisions regarding contributors' First Amendment rights.

State leaders are likely to find room for improvement in the area of the independence, authority and capability of state agencies enforcing campaign finance laws. Reporting and disclosure is meaningless unless the state deals with campaign-finance law violations. Half the states have experimented with public financing with limited success. States are likely to try to find alternatives to the check-off and add-on systems and additional resources for campaign finance. Strengthening state political parties so they can play a larger role in campaign finance may help candidates wean themselves from wealthy individual and special-interest contributions.

Legislative Information Technology

The Internet has drastically changed state legislative operations and information systems. Every state legislature now has a colorful Web site with information about the workings of the lawmaking body. In most states, legislative information is available to legislators and staff, state officials in the other branches, lobbyists and the public. Moreover, legislators in many states use computers on the floor of the chamber, thus creating new dimensions in the legislative process. The scope of information available has expanded steadily over the years. In most states, digitized legislative information includes: administrative rules, bill status, bill text, resolution status, legislative analysis, committee meeting schedules and notices, committee reports, and legislative calendars, journals, rules and procedures, reports and voting records. In addition, many legislative Web sites now provide links to other states' Web sites, policy organizations, interest groups and federal agencies.

These developments open the door to questions about the effect of legislative information technology. Key questions include: Does information technology help or hinder legislative effectiveness and efficiency? What new politics or measures might be needed to strengthen the legislative branch in an era of rapidly changing information technology? These are some of the issues relevant to the use of technology in the state legislative process. The main question, however, is not whether more technology should or should not be used in the legislative process, but how best to use it, keeping in mind that we live in a new era of electronic government and electronic democracy. Therefore, state legislators might want to adopt new policies and regulations on the appropriate use of technology.

Executive Branch

RESTRUCTURING

Every year, government restructuring, ranging from comprehensive statewide organizational change to partial, targeted agency reorganization occurs in one-third of the states. In most cases, governors initiate restructuring efforts. For fiscal 2000, for example, more than 15 governors proposed major government restructuring. These restructuring proposals included creating new departments, changing the department-level status of agencies, reorganizing workforce development efforts and eliminating boards and commissions. Recent comprehensive restructuring has followed the traditional principles of executive reorganization, such as: grouping agencies into broad functional areas; establishing departments to enhance the span of control and make accountable the chief executive and legislature; delineating single lines of authority; administering departments by single heads; curtailing independent boards or commissions; reducing confusion in service delivery for the public, and producing cost savings and efficiency.

States routinely partially reorganize. Some states dealt with the proliferation and fragmentation of state agencies by creating an "umbrella agency" for functional areas such as human services, transportation, general services and administration. Proponents contend that comprehensive agencies would give top-level agency heads better administrative control without disturbing the authority of other cabinet-level agencies. Other advantages include more effective planning, better resource allocation and improved efficiency and accountability. On the other hand, critics contend problems of umbrella agencies include program complexity, inefficiency, poor coordination and uncoordinated services.

The two basic approaches used in executive reorganization are centralization and decentralization, whether called restructuring, reinventing or reengineering.

There seems to be no single direction for state reorganization efforts. One trend in executive restructuring has been toward creating more cabinet systems. The number of states using a cabinet model grew from 14 in 1965 to 40 in 2000. Authorization mechanisms for adopting a cabinet system include constitutional and statutory provisions, gubernatorial executive orders and tradition. Cabinets perform varied roles, and the nature and number of cabinet members also differ from state to state. Cabinets can help identify priority issues, serve as a policy-making body, allow the chief executive to maintain closer contact with the executive departments and give visibility to decisions.

In the area of elective executive officers, two trends are notable. The number of popularly elected executive offices in state government has remained the same over the past two decades, except for a slight decrease in the numbers of comptrollers, chief state education officers and public utility commissioners. Terms of office, however, have changed. Currently, governors in 48 states serve four-year terms, while governors in New Hampshire and Vermont serve two-year terms. While 18 states had no term limits on governors in 1980, only 9 did in 2000. Twenty-two of the 42 states with lieutenant governors place restrictions on the number of terms they can serve. Term limits apply to other constitutional officers in many states.

CIVIL SERVICE REFORM

As of 2000, states employed more than five million workers and most of those were covered by civil-service systems. A wide range of problems exists in many civil-service systems, however. Common complaints about the half-century old systems include time-consuming hiring processes, job classifications, lengthy dismissal processes, rigid reduction-in-force policies, job performance unrelated to rewards, and restrictions on agency managers. In response, many states have initiated reforms in recent years. A 1996 survey by the National Association of State Personnel Executives found revisions underway in 45 states in classification systems, in compensation in 27 states, and in merit testing in 26 states. Classification and compensation are frequently mentioned as ripe for reform. In 1993, the National Commission on the State and Local Public Service (Winter Commission) recommended reducing job classifications from thousands to no more than a dozen. The commission's report also advocated a simple pay structure to allow agency managers to use greater discretion in rewarding productive employees. Many governors also have called for radical reform of classification systems. Yet, the numbers of job classifications in many states have remained unchanged since 1993.

One recent development in the classification area is the use of broadbanding. Under broadbanding, a state pares away many salary grades and ranges, collapsing them into fewer job classes. The most common reason for adopting this practice is to complement the move to a flatter organization. Other reasons are to encourage a broadly skilled work force, support a new work culture or climate, support career-development opportunities and minimize job analysis and evaluation costs.

Another significant management development in state human resources is Georgia's unique approach to reforming its classification system. In that state, workers hired after July 1996 have been placed in an unclassified service not covered by the merit system and are employed at will. Although the state has reported positive outcomes of the reform, it is premature to evaluate the effectiveness of such a change. One challenge faced by state personnel executives, including those in Georgia, is the need to refine their strategic visions for human-resource management. States have many opportunities to revamp their civil service systems, and need innovative ideas from personnel executives, strong gubernatorial leadership and continued legislative commitment.

Judiciary Branch

COURT SYSTEMS

State court systems are evolving constantly. Like the other two branches of state government, the judicial branch also has been targeted by reformers over the years. Early critics pointed to the fragmentation and duplication of courts, overlapping jurisdictions, the absence of a central administrative organization and unqualified judges who were chosen more for party service than judicial merit. Since the 1970s, many states have responded to reformers' recommendations. Despite years of reforms, organizational patterns of state court systems remain diverse in their structures, jurisdictions, names, and methods of selecting and retaining judges.

JUDGES

The number of justices in the state courts of last resort has remained about the same, ranging from five to nine in most states, even though caseloads have increased in recent decades. In contrast, the number of the second tier of state courts—intermediate appellate courts—has increased sharply. Similarly, the number of intermediate appellate judges more than doubled in recent years to nearly 900. The number of such judges ranges from 3 in Alaska, Idaho and North Dakota to 63 in New York, 88 in California and 89 in Texas.

The organization of state trial courts is more diverse than that of appellate courts. As of 1995, 44 states had trial-court systems on two levels: general and limited jurisdictions. General jurisdiction courts tend to be partly state funded, while limited jurisdiction courts typically are supported by municipal or county funds. Perhaps reflecting growing caseloads, the total number of trial court judges was 8,791 in 1995, compared with 5,612 two decades earlier. In some states, including Arkansas, Illinois and Iowa, however, the number of trial court judges decreased in the past 20 years. But across the states, the average number of judges in trial courts increased.

State courts are faced with mounting pressures from increased workloads and complexity. At the same time, limited financial resources restrict their ability to respond to changing demands. More than a dozen states recently established futures commissions and others produced strategic planning documents to suggest ways to make court systems more effective and efficient.

Management and Administration

FEDERALISM

The most remarkable federalism issue for the states in recent years was the enactment of the Unfunded Mandate Reform Act of 1995. This act gives state and local elected officials the chance to seek a roll call vote on the floor of the House or Senate on any proposed unfunded mandate. Another major victory for the states was the new Executive Order No. 13132 signed by President Clinton on Aug. 4, 1999 after more than a year of negotiations between state and federal officials. The executive order, which became effective on Nov. 2, 1999, emphasizes consultation with state and local elected officials and sets forth fundamental principles of federalism, federalism policy-making criteria, and special requirements for pre-emption, legislative proposals, and intergovernmental consultation, and grants increased flexibility for state and local waivers.

The 106th Congress also considered bills designed to strengthen the standing of states in the federal system: the Federalism Accountability Act and the Federalism Act. The State Flexibility Clarification Act, a refinement of the Unfunded Mandate Reform Act, instructs the Congressional Budget Office to score a reduction in federal matching funds as a mandate. The other, the Financial Assistance Accountability Act, simplifies the grant application process for states. Perhaps the most noticeable victory for the states in 1999 was the tobacco settlement case. The Clinton Administration had claimed that states owed the federal government more than half of the money due them as part of the master settlement agreement with the tobacco industry. State legislators and governors mobilized behind anti-recoupment language inserted in the emergency appropriations bill that made its way through Congress.

Recently, governors made strong arguments in favor of a new federalism by calling for clarifying the roles and responsibilities of the levels of government. They said, "It is important to decide which level of government should create regulations and which level should enforce them and that it is critical to coordinate and rationalize federal, state and local tax systems."

Regarding the federal budget proposal for fiscal 2001, the nation's governors said that the federal government must first uphold its current funding commitments to states, including health and human services programs, transportation trust funds and senior prescription drugs. The governors also responded to the Congressional moratorium on Internet taxes. The governors said, "States will continue to work towards simplifying and streamlining their own state sales tax systems. The governors oppose efforts by the federal government to restrict or interfere with states' ability to collect existing tax liabilities."

State legislators also have urged the administration to protect state sovereignty by including in the fiscal 2001 federal budget measures such as maintaining the shared commitment to welfare reform and children's health through full funding of TANF (Temporary Assistance to Needy Families) and SCHIP (State Children's Health Insurance Program); maintaining state-federal entitlement and mandatory programs, such as Medicaid and child welfare; restoring full funding of $2.38 billion to the Social Services Block Grant; increasing funding for the Child Care and Development Block Grant; providing a comprehensive proposal for funding school construction; protecting the guaranteed funding levels set for highways; providing full funding for aviation programs; providing full funding for state revolving funds; and maintaining funding for child support programs.

QUALITY MANAGEMENT

Over the years, governors and other state policy-makers have experimented with improvements in public management and service delivery. In the 1960s and 1970s, for example, many states adopted the planning-programming-budgeting system. In the 1980s, states promoted management by objective and zero-based budgeting. Today, however, quality initiatives have replaced these management approaches in most states. Total quality management is a management approach that emphasizes meeting or exceeding public expectations for products or services. TQM emphasizes excellence in customer service and empowers workers to pursue a never-ending search for quality improvement. Quality management focuses on customers, teamwork and continuous improvement.

It is not easy to implement quality practices, however. The critical factors for successful quality initiatives in state government are leadership commitment, employee participation, flexible operational systems, result orientation and customer satisfaction.

For successful quality initiatives, governors and agency directors must "walk the talk" with organizational commitment and resources. Successful quality initiatives require a greater emphasis on employee participation in decision-making. Such initiatives should create a process that lets employees identify ways to continually improve the quality and productivity of their workplace.

State policy-makers need to streamline their work procedures by instituting a shorter chain of command. The overall management and service delivery system should be focused on results. The most important factor for a successful quality initiative is customer satisfaction. Finally, state managers and employees must be convinced that quality government is not a fad. They must overcome resistance from others who tend to favor the status quo.

PRIVATIZATION AND OUTSOURCING

In recent years, states have used the privatization approach to save money and provide better services. With support from governors, agency heads and legislative leaders, state agencies have privatized more functions and services—a trend state officials expect will continue in the next few years. Six out of 10 state officials who responded to a 1997 survey conducted by The Council of State Governments said privatization activity had expanded in their state or agency, while the rest said such activity had remained about the same in the past five years. State transportation agencies led executive departments in the number of privatized programs and services. Other departments with high numbers of privatized programs were general services and administration, corrections and social services. The CSG survey also showed that outsourcing is the most widely used method of privatizing functions and services, with 8 out of 10 activities using this method. Some agencies use a carefully crafted decision-making process. Overall, however, most state agencies have initiated privatization projects on an ad hoc basis without a standard decision-making, monitoring or evaluating process.

State officials consider cost the most important factor in determining whether to privatize a service, function or program. Before initiating major privatization projects, however, policy-makers should determine if constitutional, statutory, federal or internal regulatory barriers exist. Recently, many states have enacted privatization laws to revise civil service systems, which protect state workers and prohibit outsourcing functions or services. In most cases, the strongest resistance to privatization comes from employee organizations. Some states have addressed employee concerns by reassigning personnel within government, allowing employees to compete with private vendors and consulting with private organizations. The success or failure of privatized services depends on how the option is used. Agency managers have to plan, manage and monitor privatization activities carefully. They also should be aware that privatization does not mean the delegation of government authority or responsibility. Policy-makers are ultimately accountable to clients and taxpayers for privatized services.

Policies

A recent survey of governors and legislative leaders by The Council of State Governments indicated that education, economic development, health care and tax relief topped the policy issues states were considering in 2000.

Education Policy

Today, education remains the No. 1 public policy issue in most states as expressed in governors' state-of-state addresses. Governors mentioned early education, teacher quality, professional development, teacher salaries, school construction, school safety, standards-based reforms, literacy, technology, school choice, class size, postsecondary, access and technology. Governors mentioned less frequently math and science promotion, a longer school year, full-day kindergarten, exit exams and equity.

What can and should the states do to improve public education? Among reform proposals, state policy-makers might consider redefining educational goals, school finance, facilities, teacher training, data collection, alternatives to public school and accountability. State policy-makers might want to examine the education clause in their state constitution to ensure it is up-to-date and sets meaningful educational goals. Over the past two decades, many states have revised their constitutional provisions on educational goals. Educational goals should be realistic and measurable. In the past 10 years, more than 30 states have been sued for unequal educational spending. About half these states, under court orders, have implemented radical changes in funding public schools. Heavy reliance on local property taxes for education presents a major problem in achieving equal funding. In some states, courts declared educational systems unconstitutional because some districts had such poor school facilities. State policy-makers might consider alternative ways of raising revenues for education. States need to invest more in school facilities to boost student performance. More money is needed to reduce class sizes and to make educational technology available to every school, especially in poor districts.

States need to improve teacher recruiting and training programs. Today, four out of five teachers in public schools are ill prepared to teach the subject matter of their classes. Some states are setting new standards for classroom teachers to ensure they are experts in the subjects they teach. States need to devise new ways to compare student performance in their states with that of students in other states.

States might also consider alternative ways of providing public education, at least on an experimental basis. In the past decades, more states have implemented school choice, vouchers and charter schools. While it is premature to judge the effectiveness of such alternatives, state policy-makers might consider introducing competition to public education.

States also need to consider new systems to hold schools accountable to parents and taxpayers. Many states are considering school report cards, takeovers of low performance schools, and education and financial accountability for principals, administrators and teachers.

Educational reform is complicated by politics. As long as Congress and the president disagree, little change can be expected at the national level. Moreover, reform in public education is not likely without support from powerful teachers' unions. Yet several states, despite these obstacles, have successfully implemented educational reform.

Economic Development and Growth Management

Business Incentives

During the past few decades, states have offered tax and financial incentives to qualified companies to create, retain or expand jobs. The number of states offering employee-wage rebates almost tripled in the past 10 years. Many states also have customized company-specific incentive to lure large businesses. As a result, interstate competition has intensified. In response to a 1999 CSG survey, respondents from 32 states said their states increased the number of incentive programs in the past five years, while the number of such incentive programs remained unchanged in 14 states. Two states decreased the number. These figures can be compared with the 1994 CSG survey data: 38 states had an increase in business incentives; 10 states' activities remained the same and 2 states experienced a decrease during the previous five years. Over the next five years, a majority of the states expect to maintain incentive activities at current levels.

Recently, some state and local government officials and observers have questioned the effectiveness of incentives. State policy-makers might consider issues, such as business location, cost-benefit studies, legislative guidelines, interstate competition and emerging trends. Tax and financial incentives, albeit relevant, are not the primary factor in determining businesses' location. State policy-makers should rely on a formal cost-benefit model, not anecdotal examples, to gauge the effectiveness of tax and financial incentives. State legislators need to clearly define guidelines when debating business incentive packages and evaluating job-creation proposals. State policy-makers should refrain from engaging in bidding wars in which they offer large, customized incentive packages to large companies at the expense of existing companies, small or large.

The number of states creating tax and financial incentives is likely to stay the same or decline in the next few years according to the CSG survey. More states appear to be concerned about the return on their business-incentives investment. Regarding interstate competition, some policy consultants argue that when a state lures an existing company from another state, the "winning" state should pay the other state. An increasing number of states are reforming business regulations, including permits, environmental protection rules and workers' compensation laws. States also need to consider fairer competition in the global market, in line with international trade agreements.

GROWTH MANAGEMENT

Recently, various governors have expressed concern about the impact of economic growth. The chief executives in more than half the states addressed some aspects of the growth issue in their state-of-the-state addresses. Some used the phrase "smart growth" to describe their initiatives; others focused on specific policies, such as anti-sprawl efforts, open-space and farmland preservation, land-use planning, brownfields redevelopment, urban revitalization and transportation planning. Some governors also are trying to make their states more attractive to high tech companies. Many people are concerned about the negative impacts of urban sprawl.

Health and Human Services

MANAGED CARE

The debate over health-care problems continues, and cost and access for children and senior citizens tend to dominate reform activities. In particular, state policy-makers and administrators debate how to control spending for public health-care programs while expanding coverage of uninsured persons. Based on recent trends and forecasts, state policy-makers have options for health-care cost-control initiatives, ranging from managed care and purchasing alliances to preventive and primary health-care programs.

In implementing managed care, the challenges are how to cover the disabled and elderly, monitor cost shifting and obtain federal waivers. The emerging patterns in purchasing alliances include consolidating health-benefit plans of state employees with those of small businesses, Medicaid recipients and uninsured individuals. Key issues include utilization and payment levels, risk pools and anti-trust laws. The absence of reliable data makes it difficult to determine the quality of health services. Major issues are standardization, electronic transfer and barriers to data collection efforts. States need to reform health-insurance policies, especially those affecting purchasing alliances and small businesses, to control costs and expand coverage. Issues include guaranteed insurance, pre-existing conditions, portability and community rating.

Current trends in incremental Medicaid reform efforts are expansion of eligibility, emphasis on managed care and negotiated rates with providers. Major issues include federal waivers, block grants and the Employee Retirement Income Security Act. States need to emphasize preventive and primary health care and increase health awareness. States might take advantage of prevention programs such as early periodic screening. Key issues include lack of public awareness of preventive programs, preventable hospitalization and barriers to expanded primary care.

Health cost-control efforts should not be confined to programmatic reforms. Other issues include restructuring administrative agencies, changing organizational dynamics and defining new roles for the states in the health care field. Traditionally, states protected public health and safety, purchased health care, developed and trained health care resources and established rules governing health care

providers and health marketplace activities. Now, states are expected to perform several new roles, including directing overall policy development, controlling health care expenditures, and explaining health insurance coverage to the public.

Replacing Welfare

In 1996, Congress replaced the 60-year old Aid to Families with Dependent Children program with the new Temporary Assistance to Needy Families program. Under the TANF program, states were required to prepare and certify welfare-to-work plans by July 1, 1997, indicating how they intend to move welfare recipients to work. The total block grant was estimated to be $16.4 billion for each year from fiscal 1996 to 2003. Each state received a fixed amount — based on historical expenditures for AFDC benefits and administration, EA (Emergency Assistance) and JOBS (Job Opportunities and Basic Skills). The law has affected most of the 12.8 million people on welfare and almost all of the 25.6 million people receiving food stamps. It has changed benefits for more than one-fifth of the families with children.

To implement the TANF program, each state was encouraged to have clear goals and objectives for its welfare-to-work system to improve the process for determining eligibility and offer incentives and sanctions. States were to provide support services, such as child care, transportation and health services, to help families leave welfare within the federal time limits. In addition, states were encouraged to address preventive measures to enhance child support collections, reduce teen-pregnancy rates and promote recipients' responsibility. State policy-makers should mobilize community-based organizations and offer new incentives to businesses to create jobs for welfare recipients. To meet federal work requirements and implement effective welfare-to-work programs, state policy-makers should consider restructuring human service agencies and changing the culture of welfare administration for welfare workers and recipients.

It is encouraging that both the number of welfare recipients and welfare expenditures have declined in recent years. In some states, the number of welfare recipients dropped by more than half. As of March 1999, the nation's welfare rolls had dropped 47 percent from its 1994 peak, and in six states welfare rolls fell by more than 70 percent. Most states predict that the number of welfare recipients will decrease even more in the next few years. The reduced number of welfare recipients is attributed to several factors: a strong economy that created more jobs; tougher child-support enforcement measures that kept more children off the rolls; stringent work requirements in many demonstration projects that encouraged work instead of welfare; and improved administration and management using more sophisticated information systems.

Many critics of the 1996 law had forecast potential problems with states' welfare systems. Virtually no one predicted that states would receive more federal money under TANF. In 1999, for example, federal payments to the states were $6 billion higher than they would have been under the old law. The fact is that states' welfare rolls have dropped significantly while federal financing, by law, remains fixed at historic highs. On average, the federal government now awards states 64 percent more per family than it did before the welfare reform law took effect. In 12 states, the federal payment per welfare case more than doubled.

Fiscal Policy

TOBACCO SETTLEMENT

The 1999 tobacco settlement may be regarded as one of the biggest plums states received in recent history. Under a lawsuit settled between 46 states and the major tobacco companies, states are expected to receive $206 billion over the next 25 years. The suit sought to recover public-health costs of tobacco-related illnesses. However, the Clinton Administration had claimed that states owed the federal government more than half of the money due them as part of the master settlement agreement with the tobacco industry. State legislators and governors mobilized behind anti-recoupment language inserted in the emergency appropriations bill that Congress enacted.

According to "The Fiscal Survey of States," (June 1999), by the National Governors' Association and the National Association of State Budget Officers, most states planned to use tobacco settlement funds for health and smoking-cessation programs. In 1999, governors in 25 states proposed to use funds for health programs; 23 states, for children's health programs; 21 states, for smoking-cessation programs; and governors in 12 states proposed to use funds for education programs. Other proposals include creating budget stabilization funds and initiating capital spending. Most of the proposals for construction spending are health-related, such as constructing rural health centers and converting hospitals to other health uses. The NASBO report also said that in more than one-half of the states, governors were recommending that tobacco settlement funds be segregated in separate funds. Examples of separate funds include trust funds, nonprofit corporations, and funds earmarked for medical research. In about one-fifth of the states, the governor's budget does not include any proposed use of the tobacco settlement funds because of the uncertainty of the timing of the actual receipt of these funds.

LOTTERIES AND CASINOS

Recently, lotteries and casinos have become a major revenue source for many states. In 1999, lotteries operated in 37 states, the District of Columbia and Puerto Rico. According to a 1998 survey of lottery states by The Council of State Governments, about two-thirds of the states anticipated an increase in lottery players in the next few years. Survey respondents from more than 20 lottery states predicted their state will introduce additional types of games in the next few years. No states limit the number of lottery retailers by law. Several states have increased prize money to attract more players and reduced state revenues or administrative costs. Percentages of prize money awarded ranged from a low of 50 percent of revenues in Arizona to a high of 70 percent of revenues in Massachusetts. On average, states award 55 percent of gross revenues for prizes. The percent of revenues that goes to the state ranges from a low of 22 percent in Massachusetts to a high of 40 percent in Pennsylvania. The average is about 32 percent. More states now earmark lottery proceeds for specific programs rather than using them for general funds. Only 10 states currently transfer lottery profits to their general fund, compared with 22 states that did in 1994. Since 1994, the number of states using some or all lottery revenues for education has increased from 12 to 17. With these and other trends in mind, state officials are raising questions about their lottery's future: How should the state improve the way it regulates lottery games, retailers, procurement, conducts oversight, watches for fraud and abuse, and advertises? How should the state deal with compulsive gamblers and underage players? Perhaps, more importantly, how should the state measure true costs and benefits of lotteries?

Casino gambling was legal only in Nevada and Atlantic City 10 years ago. Today, however, more than 20 states allow casinos. Casinos are found in small towns and urban areas, riverboats, Indian reservations and racetracks. Casinos promote job creation, residential development, tourism and tax revenues. The most important contributing factor might be public and policy-makers' attitudes toward casinos. Ten years ago, less than half the U.S. public said casino gambling was acceptable. Today, a vast majority of adult Americans say that casinos are acceptable for themselves and others. Casinos largely attract players from the state where they are located. Most states expect more casino players in the next few years, and casino revenues are expected to grow as a result. Yet, most states have not conducted comprehensive studies on casino players' demographic backgrounds, whether casinos benefit the local economy or contribute to their revenue base. Most states have not assessed costs and benefits. State policy-makers are considering options for the number of licenses, regulations, tax rates, credit controls, underage players, treatment for problem gamblers, Indian gambling and Internet gambling. There are other issues relevant to interstate competition and federal-state-tribal relations. States need more facts so that they can determine whether casino operations are meeting the state's desired purposes and objectives.

E-COMMERCE TAXATION

In the past few years, the number of businesses and consumers shopping online has increased at an astonishing rate. Online retail sales of $20 billion in 1999 are expected to increase to $184 billion by 2004. Today's typical electronic customers are male, better educated and have higher incomes than Main Street shoppers, but the gap in buyers based on gender, age and Internet access—the so-called "digital divide"—is narrowing. More women, teenagers and people without household Internet access are expected to join the rising tide of e-commerce. To develop rational tax policies on e-commerce at all levels of government, Congress passed and President Clinton signed the Internet Tax Freedom Act of 1998. The act created the Advisory Commission on Electronic Commerce, and charged it to report to Congress on April 3, 2000. In the meantime, the federal government placed a three-year moratorium on state and local taxation on e-commerce.

Representatives of state and local government organizations argued before Congress that the moratorium unfairly preempted their authority. At the Commission meetings, state and local governments called for levying state sales and use taxes on e-commerce on several grounds. Internet remote sellers should not be given a tax advantage over local merchants. Imposition of sales and use taxes on e-commerce is necessary for a level playing field for all customers. If left untaxed, e-commerce as it grows would further erode the sales-tax base of many state and local governments. Although dealing with numerous taxing jurisdictions is challenging for multistate, remote sellers, software is available to do the job. If states and local governments cannot collect sales and use taxes on e-commerce, substantial revenue losses would affect public services. Opponents contend that sales and use taxes on e-commerce would reduce the volume of online retail sales, negatively affecting the economy. The strongest arguments against taxing e-commerce relate to the administrative burdens imposed on sellers by differing tax rates and tax collections for more than 7,000 state and local taxing jurisdictions.

Most states rely heavily on sales and use taxes, which provide more than one-third of all state revenues. The 45 states with such taxes collected more than $150 billion in 1998. Currently, 34 of the 45 states with state sales/user taxes allow local governments to levy additional sales taxes to provide public services such as education, police and fire protection, transportation and health services. So, the issue is: How can state and local governments reform their sales tax systems to deal more effectively with e-commerce?

Many reformers propose that states adopt uniform policies on tax rates, vendor registration, tax remittance and audit requirements, exemptions for business purchases and definitions of products and services. State and local sales and use tax systems could be simplified by eliminating tax compliance burdens for remote sellers, especially in tax returns, payments, tax audits, tax-rate monitoring and record-keeping requirements. They propose to shift e-commerce sales tax administration to third-party entities, such as software and credit card companies. They are asking states to adopt uniform legislation on e-commerce taxation either on a regional or national basis by states themselves before Congress makes the current moratorium on e-commerce taxation permanent.

In April 2000, the Advisory Commission on Electronic Commerce submitted its final report to Congress, recommending in part that the current moratorium of sales and use taxes be extended for a period of five years barring e-commerce taxation on sales of digitized goods and products, and that state and local governments work with the National Conference of Commissioners on Uniform State Laws in drafting a uniform sales and use tax act that would simplify state and local sales and use taxation policies. The U.S. House on May 10, 2000 approved a bill to extend the tax moratorium for five more years.

Prospects for States

State leaders and others at the start of the new millennium are asking, "What are the major forces that are likely to shape the future of state government?" While this is a loaded and difficult question, trends in the past two decades point to five such forces: federalism, public-private interactions, technology, public participation and state leaders.

First, federalism is a formidable force in shaping the role and responsibility of state governments. How the states will deal with public policy issues depends upon the changing nature of federal-state-local relations. To shape federalism, state leaders will need to continue their campaigns for more federal actions designed to strengthen the standing of the states in the federal system such as the Federalism Accountability Act and the Federalism Act of 1999. It is also important to continue the work of the "federalism summits" held in 1995 and 1997 by representatives of The Council of State Governments and other major state leadership organizations. These meetings were designed to improve the "partnership equilibrium" of federal and state governments. The principles adopted by the summits include requiring Congress to justify its constitutional authority to act on each given bill, limit and clarify federal pre-emption of state laws and federal regulations on states, streamline block-grant funding and simplify financial reporting requirements.

Second, relations with the private sector will have a considerable impact on the future of the states, especially in administration and management. Public-private interactions at the state level during the past 20 years have grown in three areas: government restructuring and cost control studies, planning and management, and alternative service delivery. Many states have included private-sector representatives on government reorganization task forces to identify cost-reduction measures patterned after private-sector practices. Most states also have established public-

private partnership projects aimed at strategic planning and benchmarking, economic development and management improvement. The most prominent and controversial area of public-private sector alliances in recent years has been and will remain to be privatization. The extent of outsourcing government services to private vendors is likely to shape the future of state government operations.

Third, technology already is shaping state government operations. State governments need information technology to operate effectively. Electronic democracy and electronic government are creating new dimensions in government and raising new questions and problems. The technology applications most widely available to state agencies are cellular phones, e-mail, the Internet, paging and voice mail. States have launched major initiatives in automation, emergency management, fleet management, procurement reform and telecommunications. Many states now use computers in their legislative chambers and courtrooms. Technology is a formidable force in all branches of state government.

Fourth, the future of the states depends on the extent and form of public participation in the workings of state government. In light of relatively lower levels of public confidence in state policy-makers, the public could either shun participation or seek to shape policy through statewide campaigns for voter initiatives where allowed. Recent campaigns have targeted taxation, education, lobbying, campaign finance and legislative term limits. The public also could help shape state legislative processes by directly accessing activity in legislative chambers through the Internet and other technology applications, bypassing traditional media coverage. The extent of citizen participation can be a determining factor in improving state government management.

Finally, elected and appointed state leaders have not only the authority and resources to shape the future of the states in many, if not all, policy and program areas. They are and should be the key movers and shakers of state government. While the national government has an impact on states, state leaders have a considerable amount of flexibility and discretion under the U.S. Constitution. States have a vast amount of reserved powers to exercise, ranging from the power to streamline government structures to reform state educational systems. Leadership and management styles can make a difference in the way states are run. State leaders and managers need to initiate or replicate innovations on a continuing basis to meet the challenges of the future.

References

Chi, Keon S. *Lobbying Reform*, Lexington, Ky.: The Council of State Governments, September 1996.

_____. *Replacing Welfare*, Lexington, Ky.: The Council of State Governments, April 1997.

_____. *State Health Care Cost Control*, Lexington, Ky.: The Council of State Governments, August 1995.

_____. *Total Quality Management*, Lexington, Ky.: The Council of State Governments, October 1994.

_____, and Daniel J. Hofmann. *State Business Incentives: Trends and Options for the Future*, Second Edition, Lexington, Ky.: The Council of State Governments, 2000.

_____, and Cindy Jasper. *Private Practices: A Review of Privatization in State Government*, Lexington, Ky.: The Council of State Governments, 1998.

_____, and Cindy Jasper. *Reforming School Finance*, Lexington, Ky.: The Council of State Governments, October 1997.

_____, and Drew Leatherby. *State Legislative Term Limits*, Lexington, Ky.: The Council of State Governments, February 1998.

_____, and Drew Leatherby. *States Ante Up: Regulating Lotteries and Casinos*, Lexington, Ky.: The Council of State Governments, October 1998.

The Book of the States: 1998–99, Lexington, Ky.: The Council of State Governments, 1998.

The Fiscal Survey of States. Washington, D.C.: National Governors' Association and National Association of State Budget Officers, June 1999.

Managing for Success: A Profile of State Government for the 21st Century, Lexington, Ky.: The Council of State Governments, 1997.

Restoring Balance to the American Federal System: A Report of the Proceedings of the 1995 States' Federalism Summit, Lexington, Ky.: The Council of State Governments, 1996.

State Government Organization Charts, Lexington, Ky.: The Council of State Governments, 1995.

• *Chapter 36* •

Federal Government

Robert J. Dilger

Those seeking political power, or seeking to influence those with power, routinely use and withhold information to achieve their ends. The most immediate confirmation of this is the rise in prominence in recent years of what the media have labeled the "Washington spin doctors," who attempt to mold public opinion by influencing the manner in which information is conveyed and perceived. An example of Washington spin doctoring is the rhetoric issued by recent presidential administrations of both political parties in response to bipartisan concerns about the budget deficit's possible negative impact on national economic growth and to the public's growing disenchantment with the national government's job performance (Public Attitudes on Governments and Taxes 1994; Pew Research Center 1998; Washington Post-ABC News Poll 1998).

Although it can be argued that President Reagan was more vehement in his calls to reduce governmental spending, Presidents Bush and Clinton also touted their efforts to bring national government spending under control, to reduce the size of the national government's annual budget deficit, and to improve governmental performance. In his 1996 State of the Union address, President Clinton went so far as to declare triumphantly that "the era of big government is over" (Clinton 1996). The political rhetoric concerning the end of "big government" in the United Sates apparently has had an impact. As one nationally prominent commentator wrote, "Few dispute anymore that the era of big government is over, as President Bill Clinton announced several years ago. It is ending not only in Washington but in state capitols where enthusiasm for new spending is hard to find" (Petersen 1999, 100).

Although recent presidents have seen political benefits in such declarations, the era of "big government" in the United States is not over. National government expenditures have increased (not decreased)

Originally published as "The Study of American Federalism at the Turn of the Century," *State and Local Government Review*, Vol. 32, No. 2, Spring 2000. Published by the Carl Vinson Institute of Government, The University of Georgia, Athens, Georgia. Reprinted with permission of the publisher.

every year—both in absolute and in real, inflation-adjusted dollars—since 1980 (OMB 1999). The same is true for national tax expenditures. Moreover, although the trend over the past decade is down slightly because of the nation's recent economic expansion, as a percent of gross domestic product, national government expenditures, state and local government expenditures, and all government expenditures combined have remained (with only mild variations) roughly the same since 1970 (OMB 1999). Also, despite the passage of the Unfunded Mandates Reform Act of 1995, the national government's use of full and partial preemptions, direct orders, crossover sanctions, and other forms of governmental mandates to influence state and local government behavior has continued relatively unabated and, by most accounts, is greater now than ever before (Posner 1997).

Politicians (and those who work for them) routinely use, withhold, and manipulate the flow of information to influence public opinion and the political behavior of others. Although the manipulation of information has been a part of politics for generations (Edelman 1967), technological advances in recent years (for example, the advent of global television broadcasts) may help to explain why the issue is receiving so much attention now. The escalation of spin-doctoring has made it increasingly difficult for both the public and the academic community to discern political fact from fiction. Of interest to practitioners and scholars of American federalism, intergovernmental relations, and state and local government is whether false or misleading political facts or assumptions exist and how they affect American federalism.

This chapter argues that the following three assumptions concerning the structure and/or operations of American federalism are *false* and that the presumption of their validity does matter:

1. national grant-in-aid funding is declining,
2. a "devolution revolution" is taking place or is about to take place, and
3. the national government typically does not make more than incremental changes in its budgetary allocations from year to year.

The first and third assumptions are widely accepted as true by scholars. The validity of the second assumption has been challenged by several scholars, but it has gained some measure of acceptance within the academic community and by the media and the public.

National Grant-in-Aid Funding Is Declining

In 1983 John Shannon, a noted economist and respected scholar of American federalism, published an article that correctly documented a decline in real, inflation-adjusted funding for national intergovernmental grants during the early 1980s. He called the phenomena *de facto* new federalism (Shannon 1983). He argued that the national government had started a slow retreat along the entire intergovernmental aid front, necessitated by the growing size of the national budget deficit. He predicted that the national government would be forced by its economic circumstances to focus its fiscal resources on four key areas that are the national government's sole responsibility: defense, social security, Medicare, and financing the debt. This, in turn, would leave little for intergovernmental grants that were, in his words, "the most dispensable segment of the federal budget" (Shannon 1983, 29). The end result, he predicted, would be a "fend-for-yourself" style of federalism, where state and local governments would be asked to take on more governmental responsibilities.

Shannon's prediction concerning the future of national grant-in-aid funding and the reasons why it would decline gained immediate and widespread acceptance within the academic community. For years, numerous scholars have written about the imminent decline of grant-in-aid funding (Wallin 1996; Schram and Weissert 1997). However, with only two exceptions (1982 and 1987), national grant-in-aid funding to state and local governments has increased in absolute dollars every year since 1960. Moreover, the U.S. Office of Management and Budget (OMB) predicts that national grant-in-aid expenditures will continue to increase well into the next century. Considering the recent increase in national funding for highways, the OMB's prediction may be too conservative (Jesdanun 1998; Welch 1998; OMB 2000).

The data confirms Shannon's observation that when expenditures are adjusted for inflation, there was a decline in grant-in-aid funding during the early 1980s. Based on 1992 dollars, national grant-in-aid funding fell from $155.7 billion in 1980 to $135.6 billion in 1985 and barely kept ahead of inflation for the remainder of the decade. Grant-in-aid funding also fell as a percentage of both total national outlays and state and local government expenditures from 1980 to 1990.

Shannon's prediction concerning "fend-for-yourself federalism," however, did not materialize — at least not in the way he anticipated. National grant-in-aid funding grew faster than the rate of inflation and as a percentage of total national government outlays throughout the 1990s and is expected to reach a new record high of 17 percent in 2001 (OMB 2000). As a percent of gross domestic product, na-

tional grant-in-aid expenditures are now at 1970s levels and would have exceeded record levels if not for the nation's recent economic growth.

National grant-in-aid funding is not declining. This, of course, does not mean that every nationally financed intergovernmental grant-in-aid program has seen its budget increase in recent years. Overall, national intergovernmental grant-in-aid expenditures increased by $131.8 billion from 1990 to 1999 (from $135.3 billion in 1990 to $267.1 billion in 1999). Fifty-one percent of that over-all increase ($66.9 billion) was due to expenditure growth in a single program: Medicaid expenditures increased from $41.1 billion in 1990 to $108 billion in 1999. Several scholars have argued that the dramatic increase in Medicaid expenditures denoted a fundamental shift in intergovernmental funding emphasis during the 1990s. In the past, most national grant-in-aid assistance was targeted to places and/or governments. Now most of that assistance is targeted to people (Kincaid 1992). This redistribution of aid has created a peculiar and unanticipated kind of "fend-for-yourself federalism," where state and local governments as organizational entities are less likely to receive assistance than in the past, but they still see increasing amounts of national assistance enter their communities. Thus, their control over who receives national assistance, how these funds are spent, and which neighborhoods receive assistance has diminished.

However, three out of every four national intergovernmental grant-in-aid programs (including many programs targeted to places and governments) had a larger budget in 1999 than in 1990 (OMB 2000). Moreover, between 1990 and 1999, national intergovernmental expenditures increased in almost every functional category of aid, including natural resources and environment ($3.7 billion to $4.1 billion);

transportation ($19.2 billion to $28.9 billion); community and regional development ($5 billion to $9.3 billion); education, training, and social services ($23.4 billion to $38.2 billion); health ($43.9 billion to $114 billion); income security ($35.2 billion to $64.2 billion); veteran's benefits ($134 million to $317 million); and administration of justice ($574 million to $4.8 billion). National intergovernmental expenditures fell during this period in energy (from $461 million to $158 million), agriculture (from $1.2 billion to $620 million), and general government ($2.3 billion to $2.1 billion) (OMB 2000). Overall, the national intergovernmental grant-in-aid expenditure trend is up — not down — and it is up in almost all categories of intergovernmental assistance.

The Devolution Revolution

For decades, political scientists, politicians, and journalists have used various terms to label the intergovernmental workings of American federalism. Morton Grodzins, for example, popularized the term "marble-cake federalism" during the late 1950s and early 1960s to describe the sharing of governmental functions inherent in American federalism. During the 1960s and 1970s, Daniel Elazar argued that "cooperative federalism" (a term introduced earlier by Edward Corwin and promoted by Grodzins) was a more appropriate description than "dual federalism" (Corwin 1950; Grodzins 1960; 1966; Elazar 1962). Since then, numerous adjectives have been used to label various eras in American federalism, including "creative federalism" (to describe President Lyndon Johnson's Great Society programs of the 1960s), "new federalism" (to describe President Richard Nixon's intergovernmental proposals of the 1970s and President Reagan's intergovernmental proposals of the

1980s), "pragmatic federalism" (to describe the behavior of intergovernmental participants during the 1980s), "fend-for-yourself federalism" (to describe intergovernmental fiscal trends during the early and mid–1980s), and "coercive federalism" (to describe the status of intergovernmental relationships in the late 1980s) (Glendening and Reeves 1984; Kincaid 1990; Shannon 1987; Walker 1995).

In 1996 Richard Nathan introduced the term "devolution revolution" to describe the apparent shift in power from the national government to the states that was taking place at that time (Nathan 1996). Since then, "devolution revolution" has appeared in the writings of the nation's leading authorities on intergovernmental relations and American federalism, in the testimony and speeches of state and local government officials, and, increasingly, in media reports (Weissert and Schram 1996; Weaver 1996; Schram and Weissert 1997; Downs 1996; NGA 1999; Petersen 1999). Although the term has not yet achieved the status of the leading descriptor of American federalism, its increased use warrants examination.

Decentralization and Devolution

During the 1990s, proposals to decentralize and devolve governmental authority from the national government to the states emanated both from members of Congress and the White House, but relatively few of these proposals actually were adopted (Kincaid 1998; Weissert and Schram 1998). The recent escalation in political rhetoric concerning the need for decentralization and devolution originated with the Reagan presidency. In his presidential nomination acceptance speech at the Republican National Convention on July 17, 1980, Candidate Ronald Reagan declared,

"Everything that can be run more efficiently by state and local governments we shall turn over to local governments, along with the funding sources to pay for it" (Reagan 1980). In his inaugural address on January 26, 1981, he proclaimed, "All of us need to be reminded that the Federal Government did not create the States; the States created the Federal Government" (Reagan 1981).

Reagan subsequently proposed the creation of block grants and a series of regulatory relief packages to devolve national government authority along a broad range of domestic policy areas to the states. In 1981 Congress did create nine new block grants and reduced funding for several nationally funded grant-in-aid programs. However, most of Reagan's efforts to decentralize or devolve governmental functions to the states failed to win support in the Democratic Congresses of the 1980s, and many of his proposals were abandoned even before they were formally introduced (Conlan and Walker 1983; Conlan 1986; 1988).

Concerns About State-Local Capacity

There are several reasons why Reagan's "new federalism" failed, including the Democratically controlled Congresses' ideological objection to the decentralization of governmental authority. The recession of the early 1980s, and its constraints on most states' fiscal capacity, also made it difficult at that time to justify a shift in programmatic authority to the states. Moreover, there was a widely held belief that some state and local governments lacked the political will to adequately finance and administer governmental programs targeted to meet the needs of the poor. Moreover, even if the states and localities did have the political will, it was widely believed (particularly among Democratic members of Congress) that many states and localities lacked the fiscal and/or administrative capacity to deal effectively with the nation's problems. Also, for many members of Congress and the American public, states' rights was a doctrine associated with racists (Riker 1964). Finally, the public interest groups (such as the National Governors' Association and the National League of Cities) lacked enthusiasm for and sometimes opposed many of the proposals, fearing that the proposals would ultimately result in less funding for their constituencies. These groups also could not always agree among themselves on which level of government should control the allocation of programmatic resources.

The concerns about the capacity of state and local governments to "govern well" began to change following the publication of Mavis Mann Reeves's *The Question of State Government Capacity* in 1985 and Ann O'M. Bowman and Richard C. Kearney's *The Resurgence of the States* in 1986 (ACIR 1985; Bowman and Kearney 1986; see also Sharkansky 1978). Both studies concluded that the states had improved their capacity to govern and were now capable of governing well. The states' uneven fiscal capacities and their competition for business investment continued to be seen as serious impediments to devolution, especially for the devolution of social welfare programs (Peterson and Rom 1990; Peterson 1995). However, following the release of these studies, the academic community began to accept the idea that states had improved their institutional capacity to govern and could be trusted with additional responsibilities (Dilger 1989).

By the late 1980s, two of the key barriers to decentralization and devolution had fallen by the wayside. States were no longer viewed as incapable of governing well, and the enforcement of national civil rights laws had rendered the race issue moot as part of the debate over the future of American federalism. At the same time, state fiscal systems were becoming more diversified and less regressive, with a growing reliance on state income taxes. Moreover, the national government's budgetary difficulties— as evidenced by the escalating size of its cumulative deficit ($380 million in 1970, $909 million in 1980, $3.2 trillion in 1990, and $5.6 trillion in 1999)— brought into question the long-held view that the national government's fiscal capacity was much stronger than that of the states. Then, in 1994, the Republican Party, which advocated smaller government, gained majority status in the U.S. Congress. The subsequent enactment of the Unfunded Mandates Reform Act of 1995 and the Personal Responsibility and Work Opportunity Reconciliation Act of 1996 (replacing the Aid to Families with Dependent Children program with the Temporary Assistance for Needy Families [TANF] block grant), coupled with the consideration of numerous block grant proposals, signaled for many the arrival of the devolution revolution.

A close examination of these two laws and the national government's actions since their enactment, however, suggests that the devolution revolution never fully materialized. Several studies, for example, conclude that the Unfunded Mandates Reform Act of 1995 has had relatively little impact on the status of existing unfunded mandates, and it has had only a minor effect on the enactment of new mandates (O'Leary and Weiland 1996; Posner 1997; Zimmerman 1997; Gullo and Kelly 1998). Moreover, a preliminary report by the U.S. Advisory Commission on Intergovernmental Relations (ACIR)— which recommended in 1996 that seven major unfunded mandates be removed and seven others modified — resulted in controversy, pitting advocates of state and local governments against advocates of various citizen organizations. In the end, the report was never officially released, and the ACIR, which had been struggling to retain its national funding, was disbanded (McDowell 1997).

The other act that signaled the arrival of the devolution revolution was the Personal Responsibility and Work Opportunity Reconciliation Act of 1996, which contains several provisions that further the decentralization of programmatic authority in welfare policy. Its 60-month benefit limitation is a milestone in the evolution of welfare policy in the United States. However, although "the states won new discretion and flexibility ... they also inherited onerous and prescriptive requirements" (Kincaid 1998, 23). TANF, for example, contains numerous mandates and requirements to assure that states behave in "appropriate" ways, including maintenance-of-effort spending requirements, eligibility limitations, and sanctions for failure to meet work-participation requirements.

Categorial Grants and Preemptions

Moreover — and most importantly — there is little evidence to suggest that the national government has significantly devolved its programmatic authority in other areas. In fact, the opposite may be true. Since 1990 only 5 new block-grant programs have been created and 2 have been eliminated, bringing the total in 1999 to 17. In contrast, 140 new categorical grants were created between 1989 and 1995 alone, bringing the total number of categorical grant programs in 1995 to 618. In terms of numbers, the national government's intergovernmental grant-in-aid system remains dominated by categorical grants. Moreover, the proportion of national intergovernmental funding going to categorical grants, even with TANF, is about the same as it was in 1981 (approximately 79 percent) (ACIR 1995; Posner 1996; Weaver 1996).

In addition, in recent years, the national government has preempted state and local government authority in several areas, including trade, telecommunications, financial services, and electronic commerce (Weisert and Schram 1998; NGA 1999). This does not mean, of course, that some decentralization and devolution of governmental responsibilities has not taken place. For example, Medicaid waivers provide states with more autonomy in designing their Medicaid programs; state and local government officials have more authority now than in the past in determining how national highway monies are spent; and, although there are restrictions, the "Ed-Flex" law adopted in 1999 does provide state and local government officials with additional flexibility in the design and implementation of nationally funded education programs (Schneider 1997; Dilger 1998; Koch 1999).

Outlays

It is also true that during the early 1990s, state and local government outlays from own sources increased at a faster rate than national government outlays from own sources. The spurt in state and local government outlays (increasing from $555.2 billion in 1990 to $735.3 billion in 1995) caused the ratio of national to state-local outlays to fall from approximately a 2.5:1 ratio during the 1970s and 1980s to just below a 2:1 ratio. Since then, state and local government outlays have increased at about the same rate as national government outlays.

Although the national government seemed poised to embark on a devolutionary path in the mid 1990s—and the increase in state and local government expenditures during the early 1990s fit the expectations of the devolutionary model—the changes that have taken place in nationally funded intergovernmental grants, in national regulatory policy, and in governmental outlays since the mid 1990s do not support the conclusion that a devolution revolution has occurred or is under way. Instead, the national government's actions during the late 1990s reinforced the national government's primacy in many areas of domestic policy. The increase in state and local government outlays, due at least in part to the nation's economic growth during the decade, reinforced the position of state and local governments as important partners in domestic policy. This latter development provides additional support for the argument that the era of "big government" in the United States is not over, especially since state and local government spending increased at a time when the Republican Party gained the majority of state governorships and increased its share of state legislative seats.

Incremental Budgetary Behavior

It is commonly assumed that the national government's budgetary actions typically are incremental in nature; that is, governments tend to make small rather than large adjustments in spending over time (Lindbloom 1959; Wildavsky 1964; 1980; 1992). "Incrementalists" argue that bureaucrats and others in the policy-making process are rational actors who view incremental change as a means to cope with the budget's complexity and to avoid political conflict. If incremental theory is correct, it could help to explain public dissatisfaction with governmental job performance at all levels of government. This dissatisfaction may in part reflect the public's frustration with the national government's inability to adjust its spending policies to respond to changing needs or desires.

Others have suggested that the public's dissatisfaction with governmental job performance is more structural in nature. During the 1980s, for example, the ACIR decried what it viewed as a dangerously overloaded intergovernmental system that threatened "American federalism's most trumpeted traditional traits—flexibility and workability" (ACIR 1980). President Reagan used that theme in his 1982 State of the Union address to support his proposal to sort out intergovernmental responsibilities (Reagan 1982).

More recently, President Clinton has repeatedly acknowledged that the national government needs to improve its performance as a service provider. A favorite theme in his presidential addresses is the need to reinvent the national government to make it work better and cost less (Clinton 1996). The administration's National Performance Review's recommendation to consolidate grant-in-aid programs corroborated the ACIR's view that structural impediments to the implementation of nationally funded grant-in-aid programs need to be addressed.

If the incrementalists are correct, the distribution of funding within the national government's budget would be expected to remain fairly constant over the years, with incremental changes (typically increases) to account for inflation and various other factors. The data indicates the distribution of funding among various national intergovernmental functional categories has varied significantly over the years, particularly from decade to decade.

During the 1960s, funding for transportation and income security dominated the intergovernmental grant-in-aid system. At that time, the national government focused its resources on the construction of the interstate highway and secondary road systems and on meeting the immediate needs of the poor through President Lyndon Johnson's "war on poverty." Later that decade, and during the 1970s, the national government accelerated its spending on education and on job-training programs to address the unemployment problems stemming from the recession of the mid–1970s. Also, aid to general governments skyrocketed during the 1970s and then plummeted during the 1980s, primarily due to the creation, expansion, and demise of general revenue sharing during that time period. During the 1980s and 1990s, the national government focused an increasingly greater proportion of its grant funding on health care. Thus, the national government's spending on intergovernmental programs does not fit the incremental model. There is a great deal of volatility in national intergovernmental grant-in-aid funding patterns, both within and among funding categories.

Conclusion

Politicians (and those who work for them) have a vested interest in manipulating information concerning the true nature of the political world. The idea that national government grant-in-aid funding is declining, for example, has been fueled by various interest groups in an attempt to achieve their respective political goals. In recent years, for example, various interests groups have routinely argued that proposed funding increases in many nationally financed intergovernmental programs (such as Medicaid) are actually funding decreases, because the funding levels are less than would have been spent if the program were renewed without any change.

The media routinely get caught up in this Washington spin-doctoring, proclaiming that Medicaid or some other nationally financed intergovernmental program is about to be slashed or cut dramatically, when in fact the program's funding is going to be — and subsequently is— increased, often even when taking into account inflation and/or changes in service-delivery costs. The media's well-documented influence in shaping public opinion and perpetuating a particular view of the political world has important ramifications for the future of American federalism, because the acceptance of that perception affects the policy-making process. Although it is difficult to determine the precise impact "spin-doctoring" has on the outcome of policy, the fact that numerous organizations spend so much time, energy, and money to shape political perceptions is proof that it has at least some impact on policy outcomes.

Not only is national grant-in-aid funding *not* declining, but two other assumptions— that the country currently is in a period of devolution and that national budgetary policy is incremental in nature — also affect the expectations and the behavior of interest groups, elected officials, and other participants in the policy-making process. Depending on one's political allegiances, acceptance or rejection of these views of the political world help or hinder the achievement of various political goals and, as a result, have an important (often overlooked) impact on the policy-making process and on the future of the American federal system. It is, therefore, in everyone's interest to challenge assumptions about the workings of American federalism and other facets of American governance.

References

ACIR. *See* U.S. Advisory Commission on Intergovernmental Relations.

Bowman, Ann O'M., and Richard C. Kearney. 1986. *The resurgence of the states*. Englewood Cliffs, N.J.: Prentice-Hall.

Clinton, President William Jefferson. 1996. 1996 state of the union address. January 23. http://www.whitehouse.gov/WH/New/other/sotu.html.

Conlan, Timothy. 1986. Federalism and competing values in the Reagan administration. *Publius* 16: 29–47.

_____. 1988. *New federalism: Intergovernmental reform from Nixon to Reagan*. Washington, D.C.: Brookings Institution.

Conlan, Timothy J., and David B. Walker. 1983. Reagan's new federalism: Design, debate, and discord. *Intergovernmental Perspective* 8, no. 4 (Winter): 6–22.

Corwin, Edward S. 1950. The passing of dual federalism. *Virginia Law Review* 36: 1–24.

Dilger, Robert Jay. 1989. *National intergovernmental programs*. Englewood Cliffs, N.J.: Prentice-Hall.

_____. 1998. TEA-21: Transportation policy, pork barrel politics, and American federalism. *Publius* 28, no. 1: 49–69.

Downs, Anthony. 1996. *The devolution revolution: Why Congress is shifting a lot of power to the wrong levels*. Brookings Policy Brief no. 3. Washington, D.C.: Brookings Institution.

Edelman, Murray. 1967. *The symbolic uses of politics*. Urbana: University of Illinois Press.

Elazar, Daniel J. 1962. *The American partnership: Intergovernmental co-operation in the nineteenth-century United States*. Chicago: University of Chicago Press.

Glendening, Parris N., and Mavis Mann Reeves. 1984. *Pragmatic federalism*. 2d ed. Pacific Palisades, Calif.: Palisades Publishers.

Grodzins, Morton. 1960. The federal system. In *Report of the President's Commission on National Goals, The American Assembly, Goals for America*. Englewood Cliffs, N.J.: Prentice-Hall.

_____. 1996. *The American system*. Chicago: Rand McNally.

Gullo, Theresa A., and Janet M. Kelly. 1998. Federal unfunded mandate reform: A first-year retrospective. *Public Administration Review* 58, no. 5 (September/October): 379–87.

Jesdanun, Anick. 1998. House OKs $217 billion transportation bill. http://allpolitics.com/1998/03/25/ap/transport.bill/.

Kincaid, John. 1990. From cooperative to coercive federalism. In *American federalism: The third century*, 139–52. Special issue of *Annals of the American Academy of Political and Social Science*. John Kincaid ed. Newbury Park, Calif.: Sage.

_____. 1992. Developments in federal-state relations, 1990–91. *Book of the states 1992–93*. Lexington, Ky.: Council of State Governments.

_____. 1998. The devolution tortoise and the centralization hare. *New England Economic Review* (May/June): 13–52.

Koch, Wendy. 1999. Bill would grant schools flexibility with federal aid. *USA Today* (March 1): 2A.

Lindblom, Charles E. 1959. The science of muddling through. *Public Administration Review* 19 (Spring): 79–88.

McDowell, Bruce D. 1997. Advisory Commission on Intergovernmental Relations in 1996: The end of an era. *Publius* 27 (Spring): 111–27.

Nathan, Richard P. 1996. The devolution revolution: An overview. *Rockefeller Institute Bulletin 1996*. Albany, N.Y.: Nelson A. Rockefeller Institute of Government.

National Governor's Association (NGA). 1999. Gov. Leavitt testimony before Senate Governmental Affairs Committee on Federalism. May 5. http://www.nga.org/RegReform/Testimony19990505Federalism.htm.

O'Leary, Rosemary, and Paul Weiland. 1996. Regulatory reform in the 104th Congress: Revolution or evolution? *Publius* 26 (Summer): 27–44.

OMB. *See* U.S. Office of Management and Budget.

Petersen, John E. 1999. The fiscal face of devolution. *Governing* (February): 100.

Peterson, Paul E. 1995. *The price of federalism*. Washington, D.C.: Brookings Institution.

Peterson, Paul E., and Mark C. Rom. 1990. *Welfare magnets: A new case for a national standard*. Washington, D.C.: Brookings Institution.

Pew Research Center. 1998. Deconstructing distrust: How Americans view government. National survey. March 10. http://www.people-press.org/trustrpt.htm.

Posner, Paul L. 1996. Block grants: A perennial, but unstable, tool of government. *Publius* 26 (Summer): 87–108.

_____. 1997. Unfunded Mandates Reform Act: 1996 and beyond. *Publius* 27 (Spring): 53–71.

Public Attitudes on Governments and Taxes. 1994. *Intergovernmental Perspective* 20, no. 3 (Summer/Fall): 29, 30.

Reagan, Ronald. 1980. Acceptance speech, Republican National Convention. Detroit, Mich., July 17.

_____. 1981. Inaugural address, January 20, 1981. *Weekly Compilation of Presidential Documents* 17, no. 4 (January 26): 2.

_____. 1982. 1982 state of the union address. http://www.project21.org/ReaganStateofUnion82.html.

Riker, William. 1964. *Federalism: Origin, operation, significance*. Boston: Little, Brown.

Schneider, Saundra K. 1997. Medicaid section 1115 waivers: Shifting health care reform to the states. *Publius* 27 (Spring): 89–109.

Schram, Sanford F., and Carol S. Weissert. 1997. The state of American federalism, 1996–1997. *Publius* 27 (Spring): 1–13.

Shannon, John. 1983. Federal and state-local spenders go their separate ways. *Intergovernmental Perspective* 8, no. 4 (Winter): 23–29.

_____. 1987. The return of fend-for-yourself federalism: The Reagan mark. *Intergovernmental Perspective* 13 (Summer/Fall): 34–37.

Sharkansky, Ira. 1978. *The maligned states*. 2d ed. New York: McGraw-Hill.

U.S. Advisory Commission on Intergovernmental Relations (ACIR). 1980. *The federal role in the federal system: The dynamics of growth; hearings on the federal role*. Washington, D.C.: ACIR.

_____. 1985. *The question of state government capacity*. Washington, D.C.: ACIR.

_____. 1995. *Characteristics of federal grant-in-aid programs to state and local governments: Grants funded FY 1995*. Washington, D.C.: ACIR.

U.S. Office of Management and Budget (OMB). 1999. *Budget of the United States government, fiscal year 2000*. Washington, D.C.: U.S. GPO.

_____. 2000. *Budget of the United States government, fiscal year 2001*. Washington, D.C.: U.S. GPO.

Walker, David. 1995. *The rebirth of federalism*. Chatham, N.J.: Chatham House Publishers.

Wallin, Bruce A. 1996. Federal cutbacks and the fiscal condition of the states. *Publius* 26 (Summer): 141–59.

Washington Post-ABC News Poll. 1998. http://www.washingtonpost.com/wp-srv/politics/polls/vault/stories/data012198.htm.

Weaver, R. Kent. 1996. Deficits and devolution in the 104th Congress. *Publius* 26 (Summer): 45–85.

Weissert, Carol S., and Sanford F. Schram. 1996. The state of American federalism, 1995–1996. *Publius* 26 (Summer): 5–9.

_____. 1998. The state of American federalism, 1997–1998. *Publius* 28 (Winter): 1–22.

Welch, William M. 1998. Senate OKs $214 billion transport bill. *USA Today* (March 15): 1A.

Wildavsky, Aaron. 1964. *The politics of the budgetary process*. Boston: Little, Brown.

_____. 1980. *The new politics of the budgetary process*. Glenview, Ill.: Scott, Foresman.

_____. 1992. *The new politics of the budgetary process*. 2d ed. New York: HarperCollins.

Zimmerman, Christopher. 1997. Unfunded mandates—The regulatory problem. *State Legislatures* (September): 32–33.

• *Chapter 37* •

Money and Democracy

MARK SCHMITT

Money alters and distorts American democracy. The ability to raise money is often the decisive factor in whether someone runs for public office. Although it does not determine the outcome of every election, money makes some candidates hopeless and others untouchable. Public officials and candidates are forced to spend much of every day on the phone asking for money. Money often determines who has access to elected officials and whose problems are heard. Seeking influence rather than ideology, money tends to protect incumbents and insulate the political system from healthy change. Money turns political parties into multilayered financing systems rather than groups of citizens brought together by shared beliefs. The effect of money on elections, on legislation, and on how representatives serve their constituents is elusive and uncertain; for that very reason, it corrodes the sense of trust that is essential to a working democracy.

At least as seen through the narrow lens of C-SPAN, the quest to change the way money affects politics looks as repetitive and hopeless as Wile E. Coyote's pursuit of the Road Runner. Every year since the mid–1980s has begun with the same great hope: this is the year, this time we'll pass something, anything. But by autumn, the result is always the same: the legislation dies quietly in a brief argument over procedures and technicalities, with the fundamental question (What is the proper place for money in democratic elections?) neither answered nor even asked.

Yet behind the public stage on which the latest performance of this well-rehearsed script played out in 1997, something very different has taken place. New perspectives and new possibilities are appearing, and it is suddenly possible to imagine a serious and constructive debate, not just about technical aspects of campaign finance legislation but about the role of money in a revitalized American demo-

Originally published as "The Challenge of Money in a New Vision for American Democracy," *National Civic Review*, Vol. 87, No. 1, Spring, 1998. Published by the National Civic League Press, Denver, Colorado. Reprinted with permission of the publisher.

cracy, before the next president takes office.

Three relatively new trends make this guarded optimism plausible. First, the Senate took up a very different bill this year, and as a result the options for dealing with the influence of money on elections at the federal level are fresh, and the solutions are finally connected to the perceived problems. Second, a genuine movement for campaign reform has begun to take hold in the states. Third, the Constitution no longer seems an insurmountable obstacle to a wide range of constructive changes.

New Federal Options

The Washington strategy on campaign reform over the years has been so twisted by endless inside negotiations in the effort to pass *anything* that it long ago lost sight of just what problem it was intended to solve. Behind such simplistic slogans as "there's too much money in politics," the centerpiece of every campaign reform bill has been a limit on total spending by House and Senate candidates. But the limit has been purely voluntary. (Mandatory spending limits were found unconstitutional in 1976.) Candidates were offered incentives—free or reduced-cost television time, free mailing privileges—to comply with the limit, but the incentives got stingier each year. And the spending limits weren't much lower than the average spent in all but a few races anyway. This approach created a dilemma for even the most earnest reformers: if these changes were posed as comprehensive reform, and were they to pass, Congress would be unlikely to revisit the topic for at least another twenty-three years; yet they would barely touch the basic practices by which campaigns are financed.

When in the fall of 1997 Senators John McCain and Russell Feingold put forward a revised version of their reform proposal, which is likely to at least frame the debate, they did drop a few valuable ideas (especially free television time for federal candidates), but they also finally freed campaign reform from the awkward grip of the voluntary spending limit. The new legislation, to be voted on in March 1998, makes no claim to be comprehensive reform of all the problems of money in politics. It simply seeks to close two loopholes that were blown wide open in the campaign of 1996: soft money (under which political parties can take unlimited contributions, even from corporations and labor unions, ostensibly for "party building") and issue advocacy (campaign ads loosely cloaked as nonpartisan discussion of issues to avoid regulations).

McCain and Feingold's new loophole-closing approach takes its place in the debate alongside two other strategies that similarly embody a clear vision of the problem to be solved. For the loophole-closers, the problem is what happened in the 1996 election cycle. The Federal Election Campaign Act of 1974 worked reasonably well until the mid–1990s, at least holding the line on the massive contributions from individuals and corporations that characterized Nixon-era politics. As parties gradually discovered what the Federal Election Commission would let them do with soft money, and then how soft money could pay for campaign ads disguised as issue advocacy, everything spun out of control; contributions in the hundreds of thousands of dollars flowed into both parties' campaigns from corporations, wealthy individuals, and, apparently, from shadowy figures representing foreign interests. Together, soft money and false issue-advocacy ads form a separate, unregulated, shadow system funding campaigns and amounting to several hundred million dollars. It would be an accomplishment, under this theory, just to close those two huge fissures in the existing law, to shut down this underground economy, and to return to the relative innocence of 1992.

Some have argued that in 1996 the campaign finance system went from the political equivalent of a low-grade fever to Code Blue. Yet it's hard to find anyone who believes that eliminating soft money and false issue-advocacy ads alone will solve all the problems of money in politics. Indeed, "low-grade fever" is probably the kindest description of the pre–1996 campaign finance system. But it is true that the practices mastered by political operatives in 1996 represent a sharp break from the recent past, and a thorough renunciation of the intent of the 1974 law. By contrast, the loopholes that were of greatest concern in the past — political action committees, or the practice of "bundling" contributions from like-minded individuals — seem trivial in the wake of the soft money scandal.

Loophole-closing has only a few critics speaking on substantive grounds. Some defend soft money on the original premise that, because strong parties are useful to democracy, they should still have special access to funds. (It seems more likely that parties need something other than money to regain their strength, as the fifteen-year soft money experiment has resulted in parties that are skilled at raising money but not much else.) More valid is the criticism of the restrictions on false issue-advocacy advertisements in the McCain-Feingold bill, which, in the effort to draw a simple distinction between true discussion of issues and disguised campaign advertisements, raise First Amendment questions, though those questions probably could be solved if reform advocates took them more seriously.

For another congressional faction, the problem is the 1974 law itself. Members of this group argue that the limits established by the post-Watergate law invite evasions and the resulting scandals. Under this theory, put forward largely by Republicans, there is not too much money in politics but *too little*, as House Speaker Newt Gingrich first suggested in 1995. All regulation is futile, under this theory, and particularly damaging is the $1,000 limit on individual contributions, which handicaps challengers. Over the past two years, this theory has gained credibility in Congress, along with its own counterintuitive academic literature, which argues for example that money spent on campaigns is (much as some see the right to bear arms) a way for citizens and small businesses to defend themselves against an expansive, confiscatory federal government.

The legislative embodiment of this theory had, as of October 1997, more cosponsors than any other proposal in the House. It would free contributions from all limits— the $1,000 limit on individuals, the $5,000 cap on PACs— and simply require that campaigns disclose all contributions immediately over the Internet. The assumption is that informed voters can protect themselves effectively without complex regulations.

Reformers tend to brush off the no-limits approach as "deform" but supporters of this approach raise issues that deserve to be taken seriously and may help us better understand the real workings of money in politics. The $17 spent on every American who votes in a typical election year is hardly too much to spend for useful political information. The question is whether or not the information is genuinely useful, or whether the money that pays for it comes with strings attached. The deregulators are also correct that the $1,000 limit creates all sorts of unintended consequences, forcing most candidates to spend even more time raising money and giving wealthy candidates willing to spend their own money an undue advantage.

The values of free expression, fair

elections, liberty, and equal opportunity are in such awkward conflict in campaign finance that it is tempting to wish them away, to hope that information and market-type forces could substitute for messy regulation. But in making their case, the deregulators put far too much burden on disclosure, which should be part of any campaign reform plan but cannot by itself protect voters from corruption. The average voter needs more information than just the name of the donor and the amount of the contribution. Without knowing what interest the contributor has in the outcome of an election, the information is of limited value. Similarly, the deregulators make a cult of the unintended consequences of contribution limits, overlooking the success of those limits (that is, until soft money emerged as an issue) at ridding politics of the $100,000 contributor to whom an elected official may owe his or her election. Even the Supreme Court in 1976 recognized the need to limit the potential for corruption that resides in large contributions, and it is an achievement that we should not dismiss lightly.

Whether the $1,000 limit is too low is another question, but an important one. Some common ground might be found between loophole-closers and the deregulators on a plan to eliminate soft money in exchange for an increase in the individual limit to $2,000, $5,000 or more; but this is likely to incite fierce opposition from some reformers, especially those who until recently were advocating $100 contribution limits.

A third faction, smaller in Congress than in the states, holds that the issue of money in politics is not a function of the 1974 law or the practices of 1996, but an eternal problem that can only be solved with a new approach: voluntary full public financing of campaigns. Whether money comes from PACs, party soft money accounts, bundling, or even small individual contributions, private money presents some of the same problems: it gives some candidates an advantage in being heard, and it comes with strings attached. However it is structured, public funding of campaigns would in theory solve just about all the problems of money in politics: it ensures that no candidate can drown out another's message and that all candidates (major-party candidates, at least) have the resources to communicate with voters. It eliminates the distorting influence and special access of big contributors. It allows politicians to concentrate on governing or regular campaigning rather than on dialing for dollars. There are plenty of occasions, however, when the best or purest policy is simply out of sync with the views of most Americans. In a time of rising distrust of government and elected officials, the slogan "welfare for politicians," which is certain to be used by opponents of reform, could prove a fatal retort.

Attitudes can change over time, and the victory of a public financing initiative in Maine in 1997, followed by legislative action on a similar plan in Vermont, may be a sign that public financing is viable. Recent opinion polls indicate that voters appreciate the merits of public financing — but only if it is voluntary (that is, candidates who choose to take public funds could not raise private money, and vice versa), and if it really changes the practice of politics. Members of Congress who had once supported public financing and later abandoned it as politically hopeless, like Senators John Kerry, Joe Biden, and Paul Wellstone, introduced federal legislation based on the Maine initiative. Massachusetts is likely to take up a similar ballot initiative in 1998. But more significantly as a test of the political viability of the idea beyond the good-government arcadia of New England, voters in Arizona, Idaho, and Washington may also have the opportunity to vote on "clean money campaign reform," as its supporters now call public financing, within the next few years.

It remains unlikely that Congress will enact public financing any time soon, given the effort required just to get a vote on incremental reforms. But there is a case to be made that the simplicity and clarity of the idea that public elections should be publicly financed will engage the public and build a true movement for campaign reform in a way that complex regulatory measures or loophole-closings never will. Although public financing was off the table for a few years, it is now certain to be part of the debate.

Incremental reform, a comprehensive deregulatory approach, and a comprehensive reform that is based on public financing: these three approaches represent a fairly complete range of possibilities. A weeklong, open, direct debate among advocates of these approaches, taking one another's ideas seriously, would be educational, constructive, and probably productive; it might even uncover some combination of ideas that can engage the public, bring Washington's factions together, and ultimately improve the quality of our elections and representation.

The Making of a Grassroots Movement

Underneath this policy debate is the unresolved question of whether the public can become engaged in the cause of campaign finance reform at all. It has been proven through hard experience that if campaign reform is purely an inside-the-Beltway drama, worked out in closed-door negotiations and prodded by good-government lobbyists, nothing happens. If the public doesn't demand reform — and hold members accountable for failing to act — Congress will not act.

Although various efforts to engage the public in the issue were undertaken this year (ranging from a major petition drive to million-dollar advertising campaigns), few were notably successful, in part because they had so little content. Citizens were encouraged to "demand action," but what action? A million signatures on petitions, each of which represents a few seconds of thought, are likely to have less impact than a few hundred thousand citizens who have learned something about how money affects politics, who have given some thought to solutions, and who are willing to put some time into the work of change. That is exactly what is happening at the state level. People who are not professional campaign finance activists but are instead primarily interested in the environment, civil rights, health care, state taxes, or education have come to believe that the influence of money in political decisions is not a secondary issue, but one central to their concern about the quality of their lives and their communities.

At the same time, the role of money in state politics has changed dramatically. Out-of-state money plays a larger and larger role, as national gambling corporations, private prison developers, for-profit health care firms, and contractors for welfare and child support services try to gain footholds in state legislatures, especially as more responsibility is passed down to states. It used to be possible for a community activist to run for a state legislative seat by raising as little as $30,000 from friends and neighbors. Such campaigns now routinely cost over $150,000 — close to what it cost to run for the U.S. Congress fifteen years ago — and are financed by out-of-state lobbyists. But because these developments are so recent, they also give cause for hope in the states. It's hard to get past public cynicism about Congress; campaigns have always been costly, and well-heeled lobbyists have always dominated.

But in states, it wasn't that long ago that things were different (not ideal, but different), and it is possible to imagine them being different again.

The emergence of an authentic movement for campaign finance reform in the states is the untold story of the past several years. It had some false starts in 1992 and 1994, notably a series of state initiatives attempting to impose contribution limits of $100 (which passed but were thrown out by courts). But the movement is now pulling together, even though the efforts are generally independent of one another and from national organizations. State initiatives for public financing of elections, discussed above, are only the tip of this iceberg. In many states, public financing is not yet a politically viable option, and the basic campaign laws (disclosure requirements, reasonable contribution limits) that we take for granted at the federal level are missing.

A New Legal Framework

A surprising feature of the approaches to campaign reform coming forward in Washington and being tested in the states is that they present few obvious constitutional problems. As recently as early 1997, many reformers were convinced that the 1976 Supreme Court decision of *Buckley v. Valeo* left so little room for action that there was no choice but to blatantly defy the Court or to amend the Constitution to clarify that election spending is not protected as free expression. A constitutional amendment (the first that would explicitly constrain First Amendment rights) seems an unlikely means of achieving election reform. Such a proposal failed to achieve even a bare majority in a 1997 Senate vote.

On the other hand, legal scholars at the Brennan Center for Justice at New York University Law School are finding new op-portunities for real reform within the existing bounds of the First Amendment, even under the Court's narrow reading in *Buckley*, which overturned the spending limits in the 1974 law and found that limiting specific political corruption was the only justification for campaign regulation. The Maine public financing initiative survived its first rounds of legal challenges. Limits on issue-advocacy ads will be tested in a Wisconsin case that will help draw a subtler legal line to protect true speech about issues while bringing ads that are really campaign ads into the regular system of limits and disclosure. A number of legal activists are testing other cases, such as a defense of a mandatory spending limit in mayoral elections in Albuquerque, which has been in place, unquestioned, since 1975. As these cases reach higher courts, they may lay the groundwork not for a complete rejection of *Buckley* but for a more subtle legal standard, one that might allow some justification for regulation other than corruption and that would more effectively balance the real concerns regarding freedom of expression with the values of open, fair, and free elections.

Purposes, Tactics, and Principles

For all the attention paid to the issue of money in politics; for all the hearings, referenda, conferences, and new organizations that are emerging; and for all the potential success in the states and the courts, some basic questions are still not being confronted. Questions about the fundamental purposes of reform and about the place of reform in a new vision of democracy are either taken for granted or avoided by both reformers and their opponents. To build a national movement, pass new laws, and hold elections under a fairer system, a deeper debate about the meaning of these ideas cannot be avoided.

The question of purpose becomes critical as the movement for reform expands beyond traditional good-government groups such as Common Cause. Many citizens who are motivated to get involved because of another issue — the environment, health, schools, economic circumstances— presumably expect that under a reformed campaign system the results will be different and tend to favor their causes. Traditional good-government groups are less concerned with changing the results of democratic processes than with making those processes inherently fairer; yet it's hard to motivate the majority of citizens around these procedural ideas. An aggressive public movement requires a promise of different results.

Still, elected officials will not support changing procedures unless they believe that they can be as competitive under a new system as under the old. And what about business leaders, who are just beginning to rethink their traditional participation in political campaigns and in some cases lend their names to reform efforts? Will they remain in coalition with community activists who want to shift their state's tax burden from individuals to companies? Most Americans would agree that the processes of democracy are broken, but how will we know when they are fixed? The dilemma of democracy is that you can't evaluate it by its results; you just have to have a fair process that citizens accept as legitimate, even if they don't always get what they want from it.

Another question of purpose that is rarely confronted directly is whether private money has any place in democratic politics at all. Some think of reform primarily as a way to increase the competitiveness of elections while reducing the disparate influence of large and wealthy interests; others (especially some supporters of public financing) seek a "clash of absolutes" between private money and public money, pointing out that all private money is potentially corrupting while public money is disinterested. This is true, but American politics doesn't handle the clash of absolutes very well; faced with a profound conflict of visions, the most likely action is to do nothing. It may be that in a time of mistrust of the public sphere, Americans will not be willing to give up the idea that it is a fundamental right to participate in elections with money as well as votes, even if they would be willing to accept some regulations along with public financing to make elections more competitive. This conflict manifests itself in arguments about tactics, such as whether incremental, loophole-closing reform is a step toward deeper reform or merely an incidental distraction; but these tactical conflicts reflect deeply different visions of purpose.

Finally, there are the basic questions of freedom and fairness, democracy and liberty that lie behind the legal questions. Overcoming the inflexibility of *Buckley v. Valeo* is one thing; working through the deeper conflicts between unrestrained expression and the rules that are necessary to ensure that democratic elections are fair and competitive is another. Money is not speech, but money and speech are often inseparable. Reformers talk about leveling the playing field, but doesn't that mean elevating the speech of some candidates while suppressing others? We talk about eliminating private money from politics, but isn't politics everywhere, and don't we risk suppressing intense, aggressive debate about issues— our most fundamental right?

Perhaps we should be clearer that when we talk about campaign finance reform, we're talking about a particular, special moment and place in a democracy: an election. A better metaphor is that an election is a kind of sanctuary, shielded from the market, shielded even from free speech. Democracy only works by having one secularly sacred place where the imbalances of power, money, and volume are not allowed to enter. You can't buy or sell votes (children, votes, and your own body are just about the only legal things you're not allowed to buy or sell in America), and you can't campaign within seventy-five feet of the voting booth. Beyond that line, anything goes. In the late 1990s, with the real election taking place on television, the challenge is to redefine the line that demarcates the sanctuary. The simplest way is to think about it as the sixty days before the election; this has been proposed as a standard for regulating issue ads. A balanced television forum might also be the sanctuary, providing free time for candidates but with requirements that the candidates speak for themselves. Spending limits and public financing both tightly define the lines around the election, without touching the chaotic, unregulated marketplace of ideas (and power) outside the lines.

There are many different views about what the appropriate height and circumference of the fence around the election should be, but the basic idea should be familiar because it is central to the practice of democracy. If Congress, the courts, state activists, incremental reformers, and comprehensive reformers begin to talk about the challenge of money in these terms; it is possible that they will find more common ground than they realize. With the idea of a sanctuary, fair elections and free speech are no longer incompatible but work together to build the kind of democracy in which we can all embrace the process, even when we disagree with the results.

• *Chapter 38* •

Public Opinion Polls and Democracy

CELINDA LAKE AND JENNIFER SOSIN

During the last thirty years, the use of public opinion polling in American politics has exploded. Practically every day, there is a press briefing in Washington on a new poll. In nearly every contested federal campaign, the candidates spend thousands of valuable campaign dollars on their own polls. Most of the country's biggest newspapers and television stations conduct polls regularly, as do the networks and newsmagazines.

What does all this mean for democracy? For one thing, it starkly reveals two fundamentally differing visions of how representative democracy should work. In one vision, representatives are elected to give direct voice to the people's preferences. In the other, representatives serve more as delegates than representatives; they are invested with the trust to exercise their own judgment.

Some say that, with the proliferation of polling, we are moving more and more toward the first vision of representative democracy. By this analysis, elected officials are functioning increasingly as instruments of a plebiscite, responding directly to what they perceive as public opinion, using the polls to decide what to believe, what to say, and how to say it. At the same time, we know that voters rarely choose their representatives simply on the basis of issue positions. Rather, most voters choose their candidates by combining an inclination toward one political party or the other with an assessment of the individual candidates' character and values. Issues may symbolize values, but few voters arrive at the polls with a checklist of litmus tests.

This raises a question: If voters treat their representatives as delegates, but if polls mean that representatives respond to the public as if they were instruments of a

Originally published as "Public Opinion Polling and the Future of Democracy," *National Civic Review*, Vol. 87, No. 1, Spring, 1998. Published by the National Civic League Press, Denver, Colorado. Reprinted with permission of the publisher.

plebiscite, what are the implications for the kinds of decisions that are made? This is the first question we explore in this chapter. The second is how this will change as polling and communications change in the twenty-first century.

Should Representatives Pay Attention to Public Preferences as Expressed in Public Opinion Polls?

There are plenty of arguments for a *no* answer to this first question, arguments that good public policy is somehow compromised or undermined when representatives pay slavish attention to polls. Indeed, we frequently hear at least four reasons why public opinion — as measured by public polls— should not guide public policy.

First, it is said that the public is misinformed. A classic example is the American public's belief that foreign aid is a significant drain on the federal budget, even though the true proportion is but a small fraction of federal spending. Moreover, this false impression is not without consequences, since it creates political pressure to reduce international spending.

Second, say others, the public is ill informed. It is not that the public has *wrong* information, they said; it is that people have too *little* information. Indeed, there is plenty of evidence that the public pays little attention to the details of public policy issues. For example, the Pew Research Center regularly runs polls on the attention paid to major news stories, and it consistently finds that the public pays far more attention to stories about celebrities than about public policy. In August 1997, for instance, 24 percent said they followed the Gianni Versace and Andrew Cunanan story very closely, compared to 14 percent

who followed the budget debate, and just 6 percent who followed the expansion of NATO.

Third, we hear that public opinion is easily manipulated. This critique emphasizes the popular media's ability to influence public opinion; indeed, the relationship between the news media and public opinion is complicated and circular. Clearly, because television is the dominant source of information in American life, public opinion is influenced by what the news media choose to cover, and how they cover it. For example, many argue that the high level of distrust toward government is fueled in part by the "gotcha" approach of the post-Watergate news media. At the same time, public opinion also influences programming, as television executives seek to maximize viewership.

Fourth, we hear that public opinion *polling* is easily manipulated. This is true. Sophisticated consumers of public opinion polls are well aware that sampling methodologies, question wording, and timing can have significant impacts on polling results. On top of this, even the same polling results can be interpreted in multiple ways by different observers. This leads some to argue that, whatever the truth of underlying public opinion, survey research is a poor and unreliable instrument for measuring it.

Given these critiques, can one see public opinion polling as anything but a distorting influence on policymaking and democratic decision making? We have two reasons for believing that one can see it otherwise:

1. Public opinion and the polling that captures it play a valuable role in setting direction and in checking political excess.
2. Public opinion polling keeps elected representatives, who are increasingly isolated, more in touch with their constituencies than they would be without it.

First, the public is much more sophisticated and thoughtful than many stereotypes suggest. Although it is true that the American electorate pays little attention to the details of legislative choices, most voters are clear in their minds about their priorities and their values. They then use these priorities and values to make choices about the elected officials they support and the issues they emphasize. Thus, public opinion, as expressed through polling, often provides a valuable check on political excess, and it often sets direction in a way that keeps pressure on elected representatives to accomplish larger goals.

The Republican "revolution" of 1994 provides a striking example of this. The Republican majority in Congress, elected in 1994, took office with an ambitious agenda, and a core of members who sought comparatively dramatic changes in the size and scope of government. Yet in the end, they were not able to implement very much of this agenda — and public opinion was one component of that failure.

As political consultants who work with a large number of Congressional campaigns, we witnessed this dynamic at work in the summer and fall of 1996, particularly on education issues. Public opinion polling consistently revealed that most voters wanted education to be a priority. Even when they disagreed on the specific role the federal government should play, most people opposed cutting spending on things like college loans and were uncomfortable with eliminating the federal Department of Education. How could education be a priority, they asked, if we were abolishing the department charged with responsibility for education?

The clarity of the polling on this issue prompted the Democratic party and most of its candidates to make education issues a centerpiece of their campaigns. The consequence is that the Republican candidates who were challenged on this issue lost ground, an outcome that was visible in our polling across many districts and almost certainly visible in the candidates' own polling. The result of their perceived vulnerability on this issue had a direct consequence for policy: in 1996, the Republican caucus restored every dollar of education funding they had earlier threatened to cut, and their candidates launched an onslaught of political advertisements defending their record on education.

Is this outcome dynamic evidence of a healthy interplay of public opinion and policy making, or is it proof that members of Congress are dangerously vulnerable to the prevailing winds of public opinion? The answer rests in part on how you feel about the funding that was restored. Those who support federal spending on education tend to believe that the pressure of public opinion saved the day; those on the other side decry the education debate as demagoguery.

We have been on both the winning and the losing sides of this kind of dynamic, and we have seen these dynamics at work on many issues, often with vastly differing outcomes. The dynamics of balancing the budget, welfare reform, and health care reform were all similar (although with quite divergent outcomes). In each case, public opinion polling reflected an electorate that was making these issues a priority, and political candidates and elected leaders responded by making these issues legislative priorities as well. Health care is a particularly interesting example. Public opinion pressure played a part in prompting the first Clinton administration to make health care reform a centerpiece, and public opinion also played a role in killing their plan. At the same time, despite this failure, public opinion continues to exert pressure on elected leaders to reform the system, with the consequence that legislative attempts at reform continue, at the federal and state levels. In the end, we believe that—agree or disagree with the specific legislative outcomes—public opinion, and the polling that captures it, plays a healthy role in setting direction and checking excesses.

Our second reason for seeing public opinion polling as making a valuable contribution to democratic decision making is its ability to keep elected officials in touch with the lives of the people they represent, particularly at the federal level. The average congressional district in the 1990s comprises roughly six hundred thousand people—far too many for the average member of Congress to meet individually. (Many new candidates begin campaigns wanting to knock on every door in their district. Assuming the typical district has 250,000 households, then at the rate of ten hours per day, seven days a week, and with no more than five minutes for each door, this would take more than four years.) This means that members often develop their sense of public opinion from the small circles in which they travel, primarily circles of organized interests, donors, and other political elites. These elites are hardly representative of popular opinion. For one thing, they pay much more attention to the details of politics and policy, Gallup polling has suggested that the average American voter spends no more than five minutes a week thinking about politics. No doubt this is considerably less than is spent by people whom members of Congress see often.

In addition, there is plenty of evidence that the opinions of the public at large and political elites differ. Last year, for example, we did a small public opinion poll among donors to federal candidates (an equal number of Democrats and Republicans), using identical questions to national random sample surveys. The opinions of the two populations—donors and voters—were considerably different. For example, although the majority of donors believe that "government regulations go too far now" (58 percent), most of the rest of America believes that "we need to make government regulations tougher" (53 percent). Similarly, by a margin of two to one donors believe that "government spends too much, taxes too much, and interferes in things better left to individuals and businesses" (55 percent to 29 percent). For the public, however, it is more true that "government is too concerned with what big corporations and wealthy special interests want, and does not do enough to help working families" (48 percent to 35 percent).

This divide between what the public thinks and what members hear from the people they come in contact with most often is quite visible to us every time we brief members of congress on national polling. Invariably, something in the polling surprises them and contradicts their own sense of public opinion. To their credit, however, this is one reason why members of Congress are so eager for polling data. Most work very hard to stay in touch, and they recognize that staying in touch requires effort; their constant quest for new and more thorough public opinion data reflects this.

What Does the Future of Polling Imply for the Future of Democratic Preferences?

Over the past fifty years, most technological changes have improved the accuracy of political polls. Once telephones became nearly universal among voters and computers made possible random-digit-dial sampling methodologies, sampling became more consistent and reliable. Computer assisted telephone interviewing (CATI) technologies have minimized error in questionnaire administration. Faster and more powerful computers allow more sophisticated data manipulation and analysis.

The next fifty years, however, are as likely to bring greater *inaccuracy* as greater accuracy. First, for example, although nearly universal telephone penetration among voters initially made telephone interviewing the best balance between cost and reliability, changes in telephone use may be introducing new sources of error. Greater use of answering machines to screen calls—as well as telemarketing burnout—may already be reducing incidence rates. Also, the explosion of area codes means there is less and less relationship between telephone exchanges and geography, making it more difficult to control sample distribution.

Addressing these kinds of inaccuracies is possible, but often costly, requiring more aggressive call-back methodologies and greater use of computer assistance in both sample and questionnaire administration. If the cost of accurate polling grows, this in turn suggests that *who* has access to polling is likely to change, with only wealthier organizations having the ability to commission independent polling.

Campaign finance reform also plays a role. If campaign spending by individual campaigns is capped, while the cost of communicating continues to grow (with the cost of communicating being the largest and most important expense), smaller amounts of money will be available for all the other things that political campaigns must do—which includes research and polling, as well as many other administrative and overhead costs. This means that ever less polling will be done by individual candidates, and that a higher proportion of the polling available to elected officials will be done by advocacy and lobby organizations. It may also mean that more polling is done by political parties, who

then share results across multiple candidacies.

This has two potential implications. If candidates must rely more on political parties for information about public opinion, it could enhance the strength of the political parties, giving them stronger tools for developing and enforcing a coordinated party message and platform. At the same time, if elected officials are also relying more on lobby groups for information about public opinion, it increases the influence of the wealthiest groups, while diminishing the voice of constituencies without organized representation to make their case. This is because, the value of polling notwithstanding, any *one* poll is likely to reflect the biases of its sponsor, while a plethora of polls from a variety of viewpoints paints the most accurate portrait of public opinion.

There is a third change brewing, which has less to do with public opinion polling but a great deal to do with how public opinion is translated into policy choices: the growth—particularly in the west—of both initiative voting and election-day reforms that expand turnout. In many western states, where the idea of direct democracy is most popular, ballots are growing in length each year as more referenda are put to a direct vote. At the same time, these states are among the most aggressive in implementing election-day reforms (including vote-by-mail elections and early voting) that are demonstrably expanding turnout. Thus, in many states, we are often closer to approaching the ultimate in rule by public opinion.

Together, what do these changes—consolidation of polling in the hands of wealthier organizations and political parties, combined with an increase in direct referenda on issues—mean for how public opinion is captured in polls, and how polling influences public policy? In our view, there are both perils and opportunities to these changes. The perils lie in the degree to which public opinion is defined by those who measure it. If fewer can afford independent public opinion research, do we risk muting those voices that are already weakest? On the other hand, an increased emphasis on issues and party positioning offers an exciting opportunity for more often engaging American voters in direct debates on policy priorities and direction. Such debates, we believe, are a sign of a vibrant democracy, and only to be welcomed.

• *Chapter 39* •

Technology and Democracy

Tracy Weston

American democracy is about to change. This change will involve deep, structural, even seismic shifts that will move this country away from its traditional reliance on representative democracy toward emerging forms of direct democracy. The current revolution in communications technologies will play a catalytic role. Two powerful trends will increasingly converge in the immediate future, possibly in an explosive manner, to transform our American system of electoral democracy into something very different from what we know today.

- *Rapid emergence of interactive communications technologies*— beginning with the Internet, but ultimately expanding to include seamless digital combinations of voice, data, audio, graphics, and video— all distributed instantly via optical fiber and wireless global networks.
- *Growing frustration with institutions of "representative government,"* coupled with emerging forms of direct democratic participation and driven by a mount-

ing desire to affect political systems directly and immediately.

The framework of this new form of *electronic democracy* is already beginning to emerge. There seems to be no stopping it. The challenge we all face now is how to control it, how to impose upon it electronic "checks and balances," and how to preserve the goals of democracy — fairness, truth, trust, deliberation, and balance in this electronic age.

The First Trend: Interactive Digital Communication

Each new communications technology has significantly altered the nature of the dialogue between citizens and their elected representatives. The hustings, or raised platform, created the political orator; radio sparked the fireside chats; and television introduced the Kennedy-Nixon

Originally published as "E-Democracy: Ready or Not, Here It Comes," *National Civic Review*, Vol. 89, No. 3, Fall, 2000. Published by the National Civic League Press, Denver, Colorado. Reprinted with permission of the publisher.

debates and negative advertising. But at no other point in history has a communications technology had such a rapid impact on society as has the Internet.

Voters now have twenty-four-hour access to information about candidates; they no longer have to wait for the morning paper or network news coverage, or depend on the judgment of editors and reporters to decide what is newsworthy. With a click of the mouse, voters can give direct feedback to candidates and elected officials, organize for or against them, volunteer, or make campaign contributions. As we move into the next century, interactive digital media have the potential to transform the architecture of American democracy.

The growth of new digital and wireless technologies is stunning. Take, for instance, the world's first major computer, ENIAC, built for the Pentagon in 1946. ENIAC contained eighteen thousand tubes and weighed eighty tons. The thousands of glowing tubes attracted so many insects that the wiring would be short-circuited and the insects would need to be removed by hand (hence the term "debugging").

By comparison, today's thumbnail-sized greeting card microchip that sings "Happy Birthday" when opened has more computing power than all of the Pentagon computers in the 1940s combined. A Ford Taurus has more computing power than the Apollo space program's lunar landing module. The average desktop computer has more processing power than whole corporations and governments did just a few decades ago. Ray Kurzweil, writing in *Scientific American*, predicts that by 2019 a $1,000 computer will at least match the processing power of the human brain. By 2029, the software for intelligence will have been largely mastered, and the average personal computer will be equivalent to 1,000 brains."[1]

In 1993, the World Wide Web barely existed. As of January 2000, over one billion Web pages were in existence. "Today, 160 million people worldwide are going online to shop, invest, trade, and email. This figure is expected to increase to 320 million" by the end of 2001, reports Larry Irving, former assistant secretary of commerce. According to AC Neilsen Corporation, the market research firm, almost two in three Americans over the age of twelve have access to the Internet and half of those go on-line every day.

America Online (AOL), the nation's largest on-line company, had one million subscribers in 1994, five million in 1996, ten million in 1997, eighteen million in 1999, and now has more than twenty-two million subscribers. More people now get their news from AOL than from the top five daily newspapers combined. In 1999 alone, Internet users generated nearly a billion instant messages a day — far more than the entire mail volume of the U.S. Postal Service. President Bill Clinton did not mention the Internet in this 1992 State of the Union address, but he mentioned it six times in his 1996 address. By the 1996 election year, more than one-third of voters had used the Internet.

The world is rapidly going digital. This new communications technology will not just affect democracy, it will transform it. Because democracy is an interactive form of government, the revolution in interactive communications will inevitably have its greatest effect on the most important "interactive institution" — the government itself.

The Second Trend: From Representative to Direct Democracy

The second trend is more subtle and less visible, yet more profound. It involves the slow movement from Western-style representative democracy to new hybrid forms of direct democracy.

Evolution of Representative Democracy. The oldest debate in Western philosophy, dating back to Plato and Aristotle, involved the very nature of democracy itself. How should citizens govern themselves—directly or through intermediaries?

Plato and Aristotle both believed that the universe was composed of matter and form. Plato thought that form, or the "ideal," could only be seen by a select few. Those few "philosopher kings" ("representatives") who could see the ideal polis should be given the power to rule. Aristotle, on the other hand, thought that form was inseparable from matter, and that every individual had the capacity to see the "just" or "good" society. The ideal political system should nurture this capacity in ordinary people, educating them to participate in politics directly.

If we fast-forward over two thousand years to the American Revolution, we see a similar debate over the architecture of democracy. Alexander Hamilton, distrusting human nature and seeing people as selfish and lacking in self-control, thought the reins of democracy should be placed in the hands of a select few. Thomas Jefferson, arguing that all men were created equal and that all people had wisdom and virtue, thought democratic government should place governmental control in the hands of individual citizens.

The Shays Rebellion tipped the scales in Hamilton's favor. In 1786, angry mobs of farmers protesting high property taxes drove the governor of Massachusetts from office and persuaded the state legislature to shift some of the property tax burden from farmers to the wealthy. Some drafters of the U.S. Constitution cited this evidence that "an excess of democracy leads to anarchy" and warned against creating a "mobocracy." James Madison's compromise created a U.S. system of representative government in which elected representatives would act as intermediaries between citizens and the powers of government.

Early Moves Toward Direct Democracy. During the past two hundred years, our system of representative government has evolved well beyond what the founders envisioned. Many of these changes have moved in the direction of "direct democracy."

- The president was originally elected indirectly by the electoral college—that independent body of "wise members" chosen by state legislators. Although the founding fathers sought to avoid the direct election of the president, their intent was reversed by the end of the nineteenth century. Today, citizens cast their ballots directly for the President.
- The vice president was originally elected indirectly as the second-largest vote recipient in the electoral college. Today, the President chooses the Vice President, and citizens also cast their ballots directly for the presidential "ticket."
- Senators were chosen in 1789 by state legislators, not by popular vote. Since August 17, 1939, voters have elected U.S. Senators directly.
- The voting franchise has been expanded considerably. Today, women and minorities have the right to vote, and the voting age has been lowered to eighteen.
- Term limits were not originally envisioned for the President or for Congress. Today, U.S. Presidents can only serve two terms, and attempts are pending to limit the terms of congressional office as well—a clear incursion into the powers of elected representatives.

Recent Symptoms of Distress. The institution of representative government itself has exhibited growing signs of distress over the last thirty years. One manifestation is a precipitous drop in public confidence.

In 1964, 62 percent of the people

polled trusted government to "do the right thing most of the time." In 1998 — thirty-six years later — only 13 percent agreed. That same year, when people were asked, "Do you believe the average senator will act to do the morally right thing?" only two percent said yes. Recall that our country's public representatives were initially viewed as gentlemen of the highest prestige, the nation's wisest men.

The last decade has witnessed an epic drop in trust toward government. For instance, a 1994 California poll reported that two-thirds of respondents thought it common for representatives to take bribes, 75 percent thought "the state was run by a few business interests rather than for the benefit of all people," 50 percent thought that "the government pretty much ignores citizens and pays little attention to what they think," and 89 percent thought that officials pay more attention to campaign contributors than to constituents.

A 1998 poll by the Pew Research Center for the People and the Press revealed that when respondents were asked to say in their own words why they did not like government, more than 40 percent of those with an unfavorable opinion offered complaints about political leaders or the political system. More than 40 percent said that politicians are

- Dishonest/crooks,
- Only out for themselves/for their own personal gain,
- Saying one thing and doing another, or
- Too partisan.

Television has unfortunately played an active role in intensifying this distrust of government. A May 1999 study of prime-time television[2] over the past twenty years has revealed that

- The image of elected officials on prime-time TV is worse than that of any other occupational group portrayed.

- Since 1975, three-fourths of all TV episodes involving the U.S. political system showed officials to be corrupt.
- Public officials on TV commit crimes twice as often as characters in other occupations.
- Not one episode on prime-time TV in the 1990s shows government serving the "public interest."
- Some 55 percent of viewers — and 66 percent of young Americans — believe that prime-time TV accurately depicts government officials and public servants.

And a 2000 poll revealed that 75 percent of all Americans still cite television, broadly defined, as their main source of political campaign news.

In 1996, a *Washington Post* poll contributed important insight toward understanding Americans' distrust in government. It found that public cynicism toward government was directly correlated with ignorance about government. The less one knew about government, the more distrustful one was. Ignorance had, quite literally, bred contempt. Television is directly implicated in encouraging the movement from representative to direct democracy.

Signs of Emerging Direct Democracy. Does the public lack confidence in its current leaders, or in representative government itself? Several factors, such as the following, suggest the latter.

Growth of Ballot Initiatives. The ballot initiative is a classic form of "direct democracy." The ballot initiative process allows citizens to draft proposed laws, circulate petitions for qualifying signatures, place those proposed laws on the ballot, and enact them directly by majority vote. Ballot initiatives circumvent the opinions and actions of elected representatives altogether. They quite literally allow the people to "take the law into their own hands."

Since 1900, twenty-four states and the District of Columbia have adopted the ballot initiative process. Four additional states — New Jersey, Pennsylvania, Rhode

Island, and Texas—are currently considering it.

The number of initiatives reaching the ballot has increased dramatically in recent years. Between 1900 and 1980, for example, the average number of initiatives qualifying for the ballot in all the states combined remained roughly constant. In the 1980s, however, initiatives reaching the ballot increased by 400 percent.

California, a leader in ballot initiatives, reveals similarly stark trends. California initiatives reaching the ballot have increased by 600 percent in the last thirty years. Since 1978—and, in every instance, over the opposition of elected representatives—California voters have used ballot initiatives to:

- Reduce property taxes
- Impose capital punishment
- Restrict gift and inheritance taxes
- Recommend a nuclear freeze
- Adopt a state lottery
- Limit tort damages
- Regulate toxic materials
- Restrict automobile insurance costs
- Raise tobacco taxes
- Support rapid transit
- Adopt campaign finance reform
- Impose term limits
- Abolish affirmative action
- Restrict immigration
- Partially decriminalize marijuana
- Adopt three-strikes sentencing
- End bilingual education
- Permit gaming on Indian reservations

Californians often spend more money to persuade the electorate to vote on ballot initiatives than they spend to persuade all of state government to vote on legislation. Clearly, in California, legislative power has shifted to a new branch of government—the electorate. Other states are moving rapidly to catch up.

Growth of Campaign Contributions. Campaign contributions also are a form of "direct democracy," particularly when they are made between elections to influence pending legislation. Campaign contributions reflect a desire on the part of the contributor to affect specific legislation without waiting to cast a ballot in the next election. Instead of just voting for candidates, the contributor casts a checkbook ballot for or against particular legislation.

In California, for example, campaign spending in general has jumped up by 5,000 percent in the past forty years—or 250 percent for every two-year election cycle. Comparable patterns are emerging at the national level as well. Presidential candidate George W. Bush, Jr., raised more than $78 million as of March 2000—thereby encouraging him to reject public financing and expenditure ceilings, and possibly encouraging other candidates to similarly reject existing spending restraints.

Growth of Public Opinion Polling. Elected officials today increasingly rely on public opinion polls to shape their votes, thereby giving citizens a new source of "indirect" control over policy and legislation. Polling has jumped up by 1,500 percent in the past fifteen years. Increasingly, political "leaders" have become public opinion "followers," waiting for the "overnight polls" before they take a position.

Growth of Term Limits. The term limits movement is widespread at the state level, and many citizens are actively working to bring it to the federal government. Term limits are an indirect attack on representative government. Despite an elected representative's accumulation of expertise and experience, voters are saying that the representative will inevitably become "corrupted" by the governmental process. Voters must therefore remove such legislators and elect new ones. Interestingly, the term limits movement itself has depended significantly on the existence of ballot initiatives at the state level. And term limits proponents are in the forefront of demanding that other states adopt ballot initiative procedures so that term limits can gain footholds nationwide.

Growth of Disintermediation. "Disintermediation," or the elimination of intermediaries, is occurring at an accelerating pace: on-line shopping is replacing department stores and catalogue shopping; financial Web sites are replacing bank tellers; on-line trading is replacing stockbrokers.

Disintermediation is also affecting our political system. Formerly, political parties would select candidates for office, raise their money, design their platforms, conduct their campaigns, get out the vote, and distribute patronage. Today, candidates bypass the political parties altogether and take charge of such activities themselves. In the process, the parties have become less relevant — even obsolete — and now they simply offer "voting cues" to the electorate, allowing voters to group candidates under broad, generic political banners.

Of course, elected representatives also are "middlemen"—intermediaries between the public and political power. Trend lines indicate that the public, in its frustration with the current political process, is seeking ways to circumvent or disintermediate elected representatives as well. The public is looking for ways to exercise political power directly. The Internet now offers that possibility.

Direct Democracy in Three Easy Steps (Or, Taking the Law into Our Own Hands)

These two trends— the explosive growth of interactive digital communications and citizen frustration with the lack of interactive government — are beginning to reinforce each other. The new, nationwide high-speed system of interactive dig-

ital communications— the Internet — will enable citizens to move their political activities on-line. The technology already exists for citizens to easily circulate, qualify, and vote for ballot initiatives on-line, without any intermediation by elected representatives. Whether we will choose to realize this technological potential, of course, is a question that still remains open. But in an environment where citizens are moving virtually all of their other activities to the Internet, it is logical to conclude that voting and political participation will move on-line as well. Recent surveys suggest that the public is certainly anticipating — and supportive of — such a move.

- A recent survey reported that almost a third of American households (32 percent) would be "much more likely" to vote in a local, state, or federal election if they could do it over the Internet, with the 18-to-24-year-old, 25-to-34-year-old, and 35-to-44-year-old demographics demonstrating most strongly (40 percent, 47 percent, and 41 percent, respectively) that this was the case.
- The same survey revealed that more than fourteen million American households have used the Internet to communicate with a government official by e-mail in the past twelve months. One out of every fourteen American households— or 8.4 million households— has signed an Internet petition asking the government to make a change.
- More and more citizens are turning to the Internet for news about the presidential election, especially as television gradually abdicates coverage of the story. The Pew Research Center for the People and the Press found that nearly a quarter of Americans are now getting at least some of their campaign news through the Internet.
- A January 2000 poll revealed that a majority of people surveyed (51 percent) felt that on-line voting would be an effective way to make local government work better. Most of the respondents (61 percent) said that the ability to do business with

government over the Internet would be an effective reform in local government.

An Emerging "Hybrid" of Representative and Direct Democracy.

Voters in the United States could in theory exercise the power of "electronic direct democracy" on many levels: city, county, state, and federal. If pure direct democracy were in place, however, voters would have before them thousands of legislative decisions per year — an overwhelming burden! It is unlikely, therefore, that pure forms of direct democracy will ever be used by voters to decide *every* legislative question currently pending before local, state, and federal legislatures. If California is any model, for instance, it is more likely that voters will vote directly on major public policy questions, leaving legislative bodies to act on smaller decisions or questions of implementation.

This pattern suggests that the democratic process of the future will consist of interactive, electronic dialogues between elected representatives and participating citizens. Voters might initiate, circulate, and vote on electronic ballot initiatives addressing the "hot ticket" issues of the day. Legislators will respond with modifications, corrections, and follow-up actions.

Getting There in Three Easy Steps.

How will all this happen? No state has yet formally adopted electronic voting, about half the states do not have the ballot initiative process, and existing legislative bodies are unlikely to create alternative direct democracy voting mechanisms that will subvert their own power. Isn't it therefore possible simply to "say no" — to refuse to implement "electronic direct democracy"?

One of the first experiments with Internet voting was tested in Arizona this past March, effectively tripling from twelve thousand to thirty-five thousand the votes cast in the 1996 Democratic presidential primary election. As evidenced by Arizona and the interest of several other states, popular support for electronic voting and forms of electronic participation is growing. In states where the initiative process already exists, electronic direct democracy could quickly emerge — for example, in the following three easy steps.

Step 1: Electronic Circulation and Qualification of Ballot Initiatives. Proponents of such a measure could easily draft a ballot initiative today, for example, which, if adopted, would permit the circulation and qualification of future ballot initiatives electronically on-line. Such an initiative, traditionally drafted and circulated on paper, would simply state that the secretary of state is directed to develop regulations by which voters could securely qualify ballot initiatives on-line. If the proponents of such a measure obtain the necessary signatures to qualify it, it would appear on a state ballot — perhaps as early as 2002. In light of the growing number of on-line users, as well as their higher inclination to vote, the chance that voters will ultimately adopt such a measure can only increase over time, and at some point it will become irresistible. Already, almost half of all Internet users visit government Web sites, according to a new study.

Step 2: Electronic Voting on Ballot Initiatives. Once an on-line ballot initiative qualification system is adopted, a second ballot initiative, using this new "e-ballot initiative procedure," could be drafted and circulated on-line. If qualified, this new measure would direct the secretary of state to develop a secure method for voting on ballot measures (and candidates) via the Internet by the year 2004.

Step 3: Accelerated Electronic Voting Shortly After Qualification. Assuming that citizens can now both qualify and vote upon ballot initiatives electronically, a third e-ballot initiative could then be circulated and qualified. This third initiative might simply propose the following: Since the problems facing the electorate are pressing, and since elected representatives are unresponsive, the secretary of state is directed to adopt regulations that would allow citizens to vote on electronically qualified ballot initiatives within, say, thirty days of qualification. Once citizens have the power electronically to qualify and vote measures into law, why would they delay exercising that power until a distant-seeming election? Why not act immediately?

Electronic Direct Democracy. Electronic direct democracy could thus be created — quickly, efficiently, and under existing laws — in three easy steps. California's secretary of state has already proposed electronic qualification of ballot initiatives. The *San Diego Union* (June 28, 1999) recently reported the following:

> Members of the task force on electronic voting convened by [California] Secretary of State Bill Jones — drawn from business, academia and government — are optimistic about delivering a report to the legislature this fall that will outline how California can move toward digital democracy.
>
> "I think you could have trials as early as next year," David Jefferson of Compaq Computers, chairman of the task force's subcommittee on technology, told the meeting last week.
>
> Just as the Internet has shaken up commerce and home entertainment, often taking the uninformed by surprise, members of the task force expect the revolution to move on to government almost as if driven by a kind of technological imperative: Because it can happen, it will happen.
>
> "I think Internet voting is inevitable," said Linda Valenty, a political scientist at San Jose State University.

Creating New Electronic Checks and Balances. The founding fathers were profoundly concerned about the power of the "mob" — an ignorant, impulsive, and angry group of citizens — to force ill-conceived measures onto the nation. To forestall such actions, they created a complicated system of "checks and balances" designed to slow democracy down, to create the time for deliberation and reflection. How can their highly desirable objectives be engrafted onto a process of "instant" electronic democracy? How can the impulsiveness of the "electronic mob" be dissipated in the new on-line environment? What electronic "checks and balances" can be put in place in the next century to preserve our democratic traditions?

Consider the following ideas:

- Signatures supporting electronically circulated ballot measures should only be valid if the voter signs the proposed measure twice — the two signatures being separated by at least one week (an electronic "cooling off period").
- Citizens wishing to sign an electronically circulated ballot initiative must first review the pros and cons of the measure and consult a list of proponents and opponents. These pages would appear before signers could reach a signature page.
- Citizens wishing to sign an electronically circulated ballot measure must first answer an on-line questionnaire, so that they are required to "educate" themselves about the issues first.
- An on-line path would be created linking the on-line initiative to the secretary of state's own Web page. This would require the on-line voter to be directed to a listing of all initiatives in circulation prior to reaching the initiative signature page. Each initiative would have a summary, a list of supporters and opponents, and a list of pros and cons. To qualify, initiatives must receive more supporting signatures than opposing signatures, and the number of both pro and con signatures must total at least 250,000 registered voters.
- Ballot measures that are voted upon electronically must receive a higher vote percentage (say, 60 percent) of the electorate to become effective, or they must be approved twice in two successive elections — or they will "sunset" automatically

in ten years and can continue only if they are again approved by the electorate.

Determining whether such "electronic checks and balances" and others like them would preserve the value of deliberation in an era of instant electronic democracy requires much thought. But our nation needs to begin this process. We need to anticipate the inevitable emergence of new forms of electronic direct democracy. We cannot complacently assume that they will never emerge, or that our elected representatives will never allow them, or that we can block them if we wish.

Conclusion

Over the past two hundred years, this country has invented a new form of governance — a remarkable departure from the monarchies and dictatorships of the past. This new system of government has enabled citizens to control their own destinies through the intermediacy of elected representatives. The success of this new form of representative democracy has depended, in turn, on fairness, equality, and trust — that is, fairness of the legislative process, the equality of the electoral process, and trust in both.

Today, the public increasingly distrusts representative government. In the next two decades, we will all have a chance to become founding fathers again. We will have the opportunity — perhaps the obligation — to create new hybrid forms of participatory democracy and to chart a new course between the "impulsiveness of the mob" and the "elitism of unresponsive representatives."

How and when this new hybrid will emerge, and what checks and balances we will create, is not yet known. What is known is that the debate will occur — and that it will be conducted electronically.

Notes

1. Kurzweil, R. "The Coming Merging of Mind and Machine." *Scientific American*, Fall 1999, p. 56.
2. "Images of Government in TV Entertainment." Center for Media and Public Affairs, May 4, 1999.

Chapter 40

The American Dream and Democracy

Marshall Kaplan

America is in deep trouble. We no longer find it in us to easily reach consensus on difficult public policy issues. Our leaders frequently advocate policies that reflect what they perceive as political, rather than policy, wisdom. No national leader appears willing to articulate hard economic and fiscal choices America must make to stay the course. Our leaders have become poor stewards of our nation's future.

Everything is made easy. According to both Republicans and Democrats, we, or at least the affluent among us, can have guns and butter simultaneously — the reflection of a national ethic or ideal of having our cake and eating it too. We can secure tax cuts, avoid reducing key entitlements (particularly those benefitting middle- and upper-income groups), increase military expenditures, and balance the federal budget. The tooth fairy lives.

Why have we lost the ability to reach public consensus on tough issues? Why do we allow our political leaders to pander to the lowest common denominator among us?

The questions are easy; the answers are difficult, but they may relate to the fact that Americans no longer subscribe to or believe in a unique set of ground rules that until recently governed our lives. The ground rules granted us hope that "the system," despite its flaws, could and would fairly balance individual and community interests. They merged myth and fact. They were inspirational as well as prescriptive. They lent substance to our personal and collective faith that we were all part owners of the American Dream. They permitted us to tap into the best in us and develop consensus concerning complex public policy issues. These ground rules include:

Originally published as "Whither or Whether the American Dream?," *National Civic Review*, Vol. 84, No. 1, Winter, 1995. Published by the National Civic League Press, Denver, Colorado. Reprinted with permission of the publisher.

- **The United States is "one nation indivisible."** Most Americans no longer hold to the view that we are Americans first, and blacks, Jews, Hispanics, lawyers, business persons, etc., second. Diversity is in; the American spirit and culture as a "tie that binds" is out. Perhaps we never were one community. However, the fact that we believed we were a single nation or community embarked on a common journey allowed us, at least at times, to consider trading off our self-interests for a purported, larger national interest.
- **Americans are part of a "melting pot."** While the pot never really melted, it was a useful Holy Grail. It was a font of optimism that we could bridge class and caste lines. It permitted us to remain optimistic concerning our ability to avoid the Balkanization that has caused bloodshed and strife in so many countries across the globe. We no longer believe in the melting pot. Those guys— a euphemism for both men and women — down the block are different from us; they always will be different from us. Their differences, rather than respected, often are converted into geographic and spatial bundling boards or Berlin Walls. If we do not see them, if they are separate from us, why care. Out of sight, out of public policy mind.
- **Higher expectations and equal opportunity are part of the American way of life.** Youngsters used to believe that they would have better, or more prosperous, lives than their parents. As a practical matter, the combination of expectations and opportunity never really worked for everyone. The "sort" concerning who gets what and how was never random. But the beliefs were important. It suggested we lived by the rules; that good work and patience would pay off, if not for us, then for our children and grandchildren. Sluggish income growth, combined with structural changes in the economy favoring lower-paying jobs, have helped make doubters of former believers. Now, for far too many individuals, the "quick fix" is in.
- **We are all born equal.** We do not need a rocket scientist to tell us that we are not all born equal. Environment, income, race, parents, culture, perhaps even genes, are only some of the variables that sepa-

rate us at birth and affect the odds of our success in life. But the belief, rarely defined in concrete terms, was critical to the stability of our civic life and our commitment to community. It granted individual empowerment; it established personal and civic responsibilities; it suggested normative standards of personal behavior and criteria regarding social justice.
- **Achievement determines success.** We once believed that hard work and study would improve our odds of moving up the ladder of success, whether defined by material wealth, or intellectual and professional achievement. Although the path was not always as easy as we were told and while some individuals— because of inheritance, innate intelligence, family contacts, or just dumb luck —could take short-cuts, that faith, again, was important. It helped foster dreams; it generated through sweat equity personal efforts to excel. Standards, ostensibly, were set by educational institutions and employers to reinforce the message that "you can't get something for nothing." If we met those standards we believed we would receive merit-based rewards, which often was the case.

Today, we have muted merit as a criterion for reward. Teachers receive promotions as long as they stay on the job. Symphonies can only practice so many hours or minutes before union stewards, based on negotiated contracts, say no longer. The rules of the work place often hide incompetence and discourage incentive to excel. Students pass through high school without meeting conventional, time-tested standards of achievement and competence. Those students who live long enough to graduate from high school — an increasingly challenging measure of life's progress in some cities— may be admitted to public colleges and universities demanding similarly modest levels of academic achievement. For too many institutions of higher education, securing head count for budget-allocation purposes and tuition dollars from parents is the core admissions policy. In some areas, comprehensive universities, state colleges and community colleges compete for the same students. In the process, they trivialize the meaning of higher education and minimize student choices.

- **Americans can determine right from wrong.** Life was simpler when we believed that there were rights and wrongs — when values were something that could be defined, accepted and used to govern our lives. We are now more sophisticated. Morality, values and ethics have become situational and relative. We now *explain* behavior harmful to the community rather than criticize and try immediately to abort it. We accept that one's personal life is off limits vis-à-vis one's professional (and political) life. Dysfunctional families, dysfunctional environments, dysfunctional people, dysfunctional politics, dysfunctional institutions — all are terms and phrases used to explain what is wrong with society and community. This grants us a convenient excuse to act as dispassionate observers, loath to pass judgments on errant behavior. We are not responsible; indeed *no one* is responsible. Regrettably, society pays the price.
- **American institutions and their officers are good and decent.** Remember the friendly cop on the beat? The helpful school teacher? The wonderful school principal? Remember, not long ago, that Jewish mothers wanted their daughters or sons to marry government officials because they were seen as honest and caring, and because their agenda was seen as good and useful? The Capitol Dome and the White House were not images to be trivialized in 30-second political commercials; the Presidency was seen as a "valued" institution, and the President was a "respected" leader.

Such positive perceptions of governmental institutions and public officers, of course, did not correspond entirely with reality. Police corruption, poor teachers and unethical governors, mayors, Members of Congress, and Presidents have always been with us. But somehow we overcame what we perceived to be negative idiosyncrasies. We believed, and the beliefs helped keep us together as a nation, state and community. We have found no adequate substitutes for our one-time faith in governing institutions. The difficulties are obvious. We no longer trust or have confidence in government. Deep cynicism has replaced healthy skepticism and made it difficult for our democracy to work well.

- **American democracy produces good leaders.** Americans have always been ambivalent about leadership. On the one hand we crave it, on the other, we fear it. Good old King George made us culturally afraid of the man — or woman — on the white horse, and for that matter any strong executive. But the belief that American democracy could and, when necessary, did produce good and wise leaders was yet another important article of faith for Americans. It permitted us, at the very least, to assign responsibility appropriately and hold our leaders responsible for their actions. In return, our leaders exercised responsibility with the confidence of a presumed mandate.

Patterns of citizen participation advocated by many groups — particularly when they extend to direct intervention in the policy-making process through the ballot initiative — suggest that we really want our leaders to be followers. Abraham Lincoln would never have moved forward with the Emancipation Proclamation under today's leadership ground rules; indeed, he would immediately have been targeted for recall. Tea leaves, public opinion polls and extensive participatory processes and hearings currently often substitute for a leader's vision, commitment, and will to seek reform through public policy. Thus, the leveling principle has set in: We all are leaders, and as a result, often no one can lead.

The point should be clear. The beliefs

that have guided our civic and personal behavior until relatively recently helped us believe that we could define the public interest — if only we were steadfast and searched hard enough. America, governed by its beliefs, may not have been perfect, but we were perfectible.

While we continue to talk about the public interest, it now is seen as the province of the naïve and the romantic. More and more, we feel comfortable articulating our individual or group self-interests as the public interest. Indeed, the search for the public interest no longer consumes much of our political leaders' time. Many important policies seem based more on a calculus concerning which special interests control which votes than an honest analysis of what is best for the nation. This fact mutes our nation's ability to make equitable and efficient, hard policy choices. It also may convert the American Dream into the American Tragedy.

About the Contributors

Affiliations are as of the time the articles were written.

Charles R. Adrian, Professor of Political Science, University of California, Riverside, California.

David R. Berman, Professor of Political Science, Department of Political Science, Arizona State University, Tempe, Arizona.

Lydia Bjornlund, President, Bjornlund Communications, and freelance writer, Oakton, Virginia.

Lee L. Blackman, Attorney and Partner, McDermott, Will & Emery, Los Angeles, California.

Keon S. Chi, Senior Fellow, The Council of State Governments, Lexington, Kentucky.

Olethia Davis, Assistant Professor of Political Science, Southern University, Baton Rouge, Louisiana.

Victor S. DeSantis, Associate Professor, Department of Political Science, Bridgewater State College, Bridgewater, Massachusetts

Robert Jay Dilger, Director, Institute for Public Affairs, and Professor of Political Science, West Virginia University, Morgantown, West Virginia.

William Dodge, Principal, Strategic Partnerships Consulting, Pittsburgh, Pennsylvania.

Julianne Duvall, Information Specialist, Municipal Reference Service, National League of Cities, Washington, D.C.

Richard L. Engstrom, Research Professor of Political Science, University of New Orleans, New Orleans, Louisiana

John A. Ferejohn, Senior Fellow, Hoover Institution, Stanford University, Stanford, California.

Michele Frisby, Public Information Officer and Deputy Director, Communications and Information, International City/County Management Association, Washington, D.C.

J. Eugene Grigsby III, Director, Advanced Public Service Institute, University of California, Los Angeles, California.

William H. Hansell, Jr., Executive Director, International City/County Management Association, Washington, D.C.

431

Theodore Hershberg, Professor of Public Policy and History, and Director of the Center for Greater Philadelphia, University of Pennsylvania, Philadelphia, Pennsylvania.

Herbert H. Hughes, Director, Finance and Administration Department, Bernalillo County, Albuquerque, New Mexico.

Marshall Kaplan, Dean, Graduate School of Public Affairs, University of Colorado, Denver, Colorado.

Roger L. Kemp, Author, Editor, Futurist, and City Manager, Meriden, Connecticut.

Celinda Lake, President, Lake, Sosin, Snell, Perry & Associates, Washington, D.C.

Charles Lee, Assistant to the Deputy Chief Administrative Officer, City of Albuquerque, New Mexico.

Erich R. Luschei, Attorney and Associate, McDermott, Will & Emery, Boston, Massachusetts.

Edwin Meese III, Attorney General (1985–1988), Department of Justice, U.S. Federal Government, Washington, D.C.

Donald C. Menzel, Director, Center for Public Affairs and Policy Management, University of South Florida, Tampa, Florida.

David Miller, Associate Dean and Professor, Graduate School of Public and International Affairs, University of Pittsburgh, Pittsburgh, Pennsylvania.

Richard P. Nathan, Director, The Nelson A. Rockefeller Institute of Government, and Distinguished Professor of Political Science and Public Policy, State University of New York, Albany, New York.

Tari Renner, Chair, Political Science Department, Illinois Wesleyan University, Bloomington, Illinois.

Robert Richie, Executive Director, Center for Voting and Democracy, Washington, D.C.

Dag Ryen, Communications and Development Manager, The Council of State Governments, Lexington, Kentucky.

Tanis J. Salant, Senior Research Specialist, Office of Community and Public Service, University of Arizona, Tucson, Arizona.

Mark Schmitt, Program Development Fellow, Open Society Institute, New York, New York.

Jennifer Sosin, Senior Vice President, Lake, Sosin, Snell, Perry & Associates, Washington, D.C.

Edward Still, Attorney-at-Law, Birmingham, Alabama.

Richard Sybert, Director and Chairman, Governor's Interagency Council on Growth Management, Office of the Governor, State of California, Sacramento, California.

Robert D. Thomas, Professor, Political Science Department, University of Houston, Houston, Texas.

Carl E. Van Horn, Professor of Public Policy and Political Science, Eagleton Institute of Politics, and Chair, Department of Public Policy, Rutgers University, New Brunswick, New Jersey.

Allan D. Wallis, Director of Research, National Civic League, Denver, Colorado, and Assistant Professor of Public Policy, Graduate School of Public Affairs, University of Colorado, Denver, Colorado.

Barry R. Weingast, Senior Fellow, Hoover Institution, and Ward C. Krebs Family Professor of Political Science, and Chair, Department of Political Science, Stanford University, Stanford, California.

Tracy Weston, Chairman, *grassroots.com*, and President, Center for Governmental Studies, Los Angeles, California.

Charles R. Wise, Professor, School of Public and Environmental Affairs, Indiana University, Bloomington, Indiana.

Joseph F. Zimmerman, Professor of Political Science, Graduate School of Public Affairs, State University of New York, Albany, New York.

Index